THE URBAN WEB

NELSON-HALL SERIES IN POLITICAL SCIENCE

Consulting Editor: Samuel C. Patterson
The Ohio State University

THE URBAN WEB

Politics, Policy, and Theory

Second Edition

Lawrence J.R. Herson
The Ohio State University

John M. Bolland
The University of Alabama

Nelson-Hall Publishers/Chicago

Project Editor: Dorothy Anderson
Text Designer: Tamra Campbell-Phelps
Illustrator: Corasue Nicholas
Text Compositor: Precision Typographers
Manufacturer: Capital City Press
Cover Painting: Christopher Buoscio, "Street to the City"

Library of Congress Cataloging-in-Publication Data

Herson, Lawrence J. R.
    The urban web : politics, policy and theory / Lawrence J. R.
Herson, John M. Bolland. — 2nd ed.
        p.   cm. — (Nelson-Hall series in political science)
    Includes bibliographical references and index.
    ISBN 0-8304-1458-4 (pbk : alk. paper)
    1. Cities and towns—United States.   2. Cities and towns—United
States—Growth.   3. Municipal government—United States.   4. Urban
policy—United States.   5. Sociology, Urban—United States.
I. Bolland, John M.   II. Title.   III. Series.
HT123.H47   1997
307.76'0973—DC21   97-27666
                                                                                          CIP

Manufactured in the United States of America

10 9 8 7 6 5 4 3 2

To our wives and children

Libby D. Herson
&
Eric, Viktoria, and John

and

Kathleen A. Bolland
&
Anneliese

May they always know the pleasure of travel to far-off cities

Contents

Contents

PART THREE   THE RULERS AND THE RULED

5   Political Rules and Political Realities in the City   69

6   Forms of Municipal Government and Formal Participants in the Urban Political Process   93

Contents

Contents

PART SIX   MUNICIPAL FINANCE AND SERVICE DELIVERY

13 Municipal Finance: A Prelude to the Urban Service Delivery Saga   305

Contents

Contents

EPILOGUE: LOOKING TO THE FUTURE

18 The Shape of Things to Come 477

Preface to the Second Edition

Much has happened to American cities since the Urban Web was first published. But even more has remained as it was. Thus, the idea of understanding cities through the concept of a web continues to be valid. So too is the idea that cities today are best understood by looking at their past. And what that past history suggests is that American cities are constantly changing, endlessly recreating themselves.

As Alexis de Tocqueville, perhaps our most perceptive foreign visitor, observed more than a century and a half ago, "An American . . . changes his residence ceaselessly." Today, as in the past, the character of city populations changes: New arrivals come to the city and old settlers leave for the safety and amenities of the suburbs. Surrounding suburbs grow. The central city is beset with problems that are in the city but not of its making. To adjust to a changing population and to compensate for revenues lost through population change, central cities must find new ways to perform essential services and, if possible, to staunch urban decay.

Ten, twenty, and thirty years ago, the engines of urban change were the economics of the private market joined to ambitious government programs. There was, in those days, an optimism about the capacity of government to improve the lives of its citizens and to alleviate social suffering. The results of that optimism were massive governmental enterprises—each with enormous impact on our cities.

Today, much of that optimism has disappeared. In its place is a wave of pessimism with respect to government's ability to accomplish major improvement in the quality of its citizens' lives. The era of big government is over, proclaim both the Congress and the president. If a better tomorrow is to be achieved, it will be through state and local programs, working in concert with a smaller, less ambitious national government. Thus, the national government is not soon likely to underwrite programs of massive aid to our cities. As a consequence (as it has been through much of our history) the economics of the private market have once again become the primary engine of urban change.

Two of the most recent consequences of that market are now everywhere on the urban scene: Common interest developments and edge cities. Common interest developments (condominiums, fenced and gated communities) are supported and controlled by "private governments," dedicated to keeping out those whom their governors tag as undesirables. Edge cities are urban enterprises built by private developers on the suburban fringe and at the city's edge, dedicated mostly to business and office spaces and shopping malls. What gives both places their contemporary quality lies in a threefold fact: Mostly they are newly settled and *unincorporated* urban places. As private enterprises, they perform for a fee many of the services ordinarily undertaken by urban governments. Reminiscent of the walled cities of the Middle Ages, they use private power to monitor and control access to their domain.

As we said in the first edition, suburbs tend to have revenues sufficient for their governments' needs. As home to a mostly middle-class population, their residents have both social skills and personal funds sufficient to sustain their suburban lives. In stark contrast, older central cities lack revenues sufficient for their governments' needs. And they are awash in a sea of problems that turn on matters of poverty and race. About those problems, little has changed in recent years, except that they receive more attention in magazines and newspapers (and in the pages of academic journals) than they did a decade ago. Nor has their web of connections changed: Poverty and race continue to connect to urban crime and urban decay, and both, in turn, connect to the outward flight of those sufficiently well-off to seek the comparative safety of suburban homes and streets. And all such problems and trends continue to connect to the awesome power of the automobile to determine where the urban dweller lives, works, and shops.

But, continuity is not *fixity*. What seems mostly to have changed in recent years is our society's diminished willingness to invest civic energy (and government programs) into saving and bettering our older cities, along with an increased willingness to invest civic energy in new towns and new developments on the urban edge. In doing so, and increasingly, we permit private developers to control the style and pace of urban change. Thus, an old problem remains: What can we do to preserve and improve our older central cities? And more important, what can we do to improve the lives of those who live there?

Our current thinking about cities continues to benefit from those people who encouraged and supported the collaboration that led to the first edition of *The Urban Web*. In addition, the second edition has benefited from discussion with Debra Moehle McCallum and Michael L. Berbaum, both of the Institute for Social Science Research at the University of Alabama. This, as well as the first edition, was edited by Dorothy J. Anderson and designed by Tamra Campbell-Phelps; both editions benefited from their careful attention, and we owe them a special debt. Finally, a second edition would not have been possible without the help of people, far too numerous to mention by name, who provided invaluable assistance in updating statistics about cities and urban services.

Preface to the First Edition

Books, like rivers, have many sources; but unlike rivers, a book may have more than one destination. Among the sources that feed our book are several excellent textbooks now in print on urban politics. We acknowledge our debt to the conceptual frameworks provided by Charles Adrian and Charles Press (1977), John Harrigan (1989), Bryan Jones (1983), Dennis Judd (1988), Robert Lineberry and Ira Sharkansky (1978), and Clarence Stone, Robert Whelan, and William Murin (1986).

Another source for this book is our own research on the politics of several small cities in Alabama, Kansas, Ohio, Colorado, Montana, and the state of Washington. In addition to instilling in us a good deal of respect for the political process in small-town America, our research also afforded insight into the manner in which policy and politics vary according to city size and geographic region. Thus, in writing this book, we have attempted not to slight small cities nor presume that only big cities have significant problems.

A third source for this book is our preoccupation over several years with the American value system and American political theory. This preoccupation has led us to attempt a stance of ideological neutrality in discussing matters of market economics, zoning, race, poverty, service delivery, and central-city decline. Our purpose is to enlighten and explain, not to convert the reader to an ideological point of view. But we are also mindful of the difficulties of keeping this stance. As a professor of literature recently reminded us: No student of human affairs can escape his or her own involvement with the subject being studied.

Both of us are city-travellers. We visit great cities as often as we can, taking pleasure in their architecture, their energy, their historic roles as creators and transmitters of culture. In writing this book, we have attempted to convey some sense of this pleasure, along with what Kevin Lynch (1960) calls "the image of the city."

A book may have several destinations. We have set our compass by the polestar of social science theory, hoping thereby to set our book apart from most others by its attention to theory. Our goal throughout has been to make explicit the theories that organize our knowledge about urban politics and that, accordingly, do most to explain those politics.

We have also attempted to steer toward the reader whose educational home is in the liberal arts. Our goal has been to work toward a triad of liberal arts traditions: To see how the past flows into the present, to see that all social processes are interconnected, and to understand that abstract ideas have real-world consequences.

In attempting to lay bare the real-world consequences of abstract ideas—especially those that nest inside ideologies—we are mindful that most of our readers will have had first-hand experiences with cities and city life. Our book is thus an attempt to put those experiences in perspective, to offer a theoretical framework within which our readers may better understand their own urban experiences, and to provide them with intellectual tools that will sharpen their judgment about present and future urban problems and policies.

But of all the goals that guide our book, none is more important than the one we take from the distinguished historian of art, Kenneth Clark (1956). Like him, we have done our best to "look with fresh eyes on a subject tarnished by familiarity."

We owe much to several persons for their encouragement and for their critical reading of our book in manuscript state.

Professor Emeritus Richard C. Snyder, the former Director of the Mershon Center of The Ohio State University, was first to encourage and support the collaboration that brought about the book. The present Director of the Center, Professor Charles F. Hermann, has generously assisted Lawrence Herson's several years' study of American political theory, and Professor Philip B. Coulter, Director of the Institute for Social Science Research of the University of Alabama, has given generous assistance to John Bolland's research into local politics and administration.

Several friends and colleagues read our manuscript in its entirety, offering precise and helpful criticism: Professor James Clingermayer (Texas A&M University); Professor Samuel C. Patterson (The Ohio State University; also, political science editor for Nelson-Hall Publishers); Professor Craig Rimmerman (Hobart and William Smith Colleges); Professor Clarence N. Stone (The University of Maryland); and with special concern for style, linguistic usage, and common sense, Kathleen A. Bolland (College of Education, The University of Alabama) and Viktoria Herson (Department of Slavic Languages and Literatures, The Ohio State University).

Several others have been generous in reading and criticizing portions of the manuscript: Professors Lawrence Baum, John Champlin, and Randall B. Ripley (all of The Ohio State University); Professor Joan E. Crowley (New Mexico State University); and John Selby (The University of Alabama). And still others assisted greatly in the research that underpins our book: Cheryl Wilson, Scott Clark, and Paul Mego (all of The University of Alabama).

To all these, we offer our sincere thanks. They have made our book far better than it might have been, but we remain fully responsible for the book's failings and omissions.

PART ONE

THE URBAN WEB

From the Shelton, chloride print, 1935, 24.1 x 29.2 cm
Alfred Stieglitz Collection, 1949.786.
Photograph © 1996, The Art Institute of Chicago. All Rights Reserved.

...experience has shown that a very populous city can rarely, if ever, be well governed. . . . For law is order and good law is good order, but a very great multitude cannot be orderly.

   Aristotle, *The Politics*

CHAPTER 1

The Urban Web:
An Introduction

Inquiries Old and New

This book is an inquiry into the politics of contemporary American cities, but it is inquiry built on foundations that are at least two thousand years old. As long ago as classical Greece, reflective minds attempted to unravel the puzzles of the city: How do cities get established and who comes to live there? Why do some cities grow large while others remain small? What kind of government is best for cities? Why is it that large cities are less easily governed than small cities? And why is it that some cities seem to bestow happiness on those who live there, while others seem forever bound in misery?

These are ancient questions, but they fit the present because the ancients understood the city to be more than a unit of government. A city is also an urban place—marked by a relatively dense population and by lifestyles that set city dwellers apart from country dwellers. A city is also a sociological entity, a collection of strangers who relate to each other by means of an elaborate network of formal roles. And a city is an economic enterprise, groups of people who make, sell, and exchange goods and services.

What the Greeks knew about cities and what we know about cities is a set of ideas that serves as the framework for this book. First, each city is a unit of government. Second, as a unit of government, a city is also a triad of related enterprises: an arena of politics, a creator of public policies, and a provider of public services. Third, what a city does as a unit of government is very much affected by its other attributes; it is an urban place, a sociological network, an economic activity. And fourth, what a city does as a unit of government can also have consequences for its sociology and its economics.

In essence, our framework of ideas means that each city is a *web* of interconnecting attributes; it is a government, an urban place, a sociological network, and an economic enterprise. The strands of the web connect, so that activity in any one part of the web affects every other part.[1]

It is the essence of a web that every strand connects with every other strand. Pull or twist even a single strand and all others are affected. At any point in the web, begin to trace any single strand and, sooner or later, the tracing travels across every other strand.

Those familiar with the literature of the social sciences will know that our definition of web has parallels to the concept of system. Quite deliberately, we do not use that concept so as to avoid its extensive (and for our purposes, limiting) terminology—for example, input, output, throughput, boundary-maintenance—and to avoid what may be its conceptual biases—for example, equilibrium as opposed to disequilibrium. We, of course, as students of political science, concentrate our attention on one part of the urban web, that which deals with government and the enterprises of government—politics, policy, and public services. But to concentrate our attention there does not mean that we ignore other strands of the web. Quite the contrary. We will, for example, examine the relationship between city politics and urban poverty, and, for another example, the relationship between city politics and city size. And we will also be mindful of the fact that the urban web does not stand alone. It is connected to other levels of American government and to their politics and policies. This is so because in the United States every city is a unit of government, but no city is an autonomous unit of government. Each city is affected and controlled by the activities of the national government, by the state in which the city is located, and by the presence of other, nearby cities. Thus, the urban web is anchored to the larger web of government in the United States. But if we are to keep the idea of an urban web fairly discrete, it will be useful to retrace some of our ideas, by better defining our terms, and by paying further attention to one of the oldest puzzles of urban life: How is it possible that a collection of strangers—and the city is

---

1. The dictionary offers several definitions of *web*. As a noun, a web is defined as any complicated arrangement; as an arrangement of interwoven or interconnected parts, for example, a woven cloth. As a verb, to web means to entangle or envelop, as in a spider's web.

mostly a collection of strangers—can live in close physical proximity in a reasonably cooperative manner, without doing each other violence and harm?[2]

Urban and City Defined: The City in History and Logic

The City is the People.
  Shakespeare, *Coriolanus*

Although the words *urban* and *city* are nowadays used almost interchangeably, there is more than a shade of difference between them, a difference that can be traced to their original meanings. The noun *city* incorporates the idea of government and administration, while the adjective *urban* carries the idea of a densely populated place and the lifestyles of those who live there. *Urban* comes from the Latin word *urbs*. The word derives from the palings or palisades that were once used to surround and protect a settled place from intruders. From the earliest of times, those who lived in settled, protected places developed a characteristic way of life associated with a nonagricultural, nonnomadic existence. Our English word *urbane* came into the language about 1500, and with it came a sense of the qualities of life and mind that are traditionally associated with lives lived in an urban setting.

The word *city* is also Latin in its derivation. *Civitas*, to the Romans, carried in its meaning the idea of citizenship and the rights and privileges of those who were citizens. The rise of cities as self-governing places began in Europe with the Greek city-states and continued until the end of the Roman Republic (about the last century B.C.). During the Roman Empire and through the successive stages of feudalism, European cities continued as walled enclaves, but not usually as self-governing entities. Then, sometime in the eleventh century, the city as a self-governing place came into being again. Feudal rulers bestowed certain degrees of self-government on their cities, largely as a result of the insistence of local craft guilds that they be free to conduct guild business, including the right to enforce contracts, conditions of work, and standards of craftsmanship. Cities as we now know them thus began with the granting of *charters* from their feudal overlords that bestowed on them a measure of self-government (Pirenne 1925). It was this tradition of the city as a group of citizens with a charter for self-rule that was carried into the New World when the first settlers came to build cities in the American wilderness.

Thus, the meanings that attach to the word *city* have mostly to do with its legal and governmental status, while the meanings that attach to the word

---

2. Finley (1966) and Kitto (1951) explore this puzzle as it applies to the lives of the ancient Greeks.

urban have to do with what is commonly called the culture of cities: their architecture, lifestyle, sociology, and economics. But the two sets of meanings meet and mingle. The reasons are not hard to find. Every city is an urban place and every urban place—if it has legally defined boundaries and a charter from its state—is a city.[3]

But despite this mingling, it will be useful to play out the differences between *city* and *urban* a little longer. Doing so will permit us to see more clearly how the activities of a city's government are a response to a city's urban qualities. We begin, then, with a sketch of urban places as settlement places, places that have meaning for their residents that goes beyond the conventional concept of commodity (i.e., a home is more than a house). But this fact—that the city represents the confluence of both objective factors (e.g., a house is a commodity) and subjective factors (e.g., a house is a home)—often creates considerable conflict and tension (Gottdiener 1993, Orum 1995). The implications of this confluence for urban governance are limned by historian Howard Chudacoff (1975).[4] The city as an urban place, says Chudacoff, is characterized by "communities of concentrated populations that coordinate and control large-scale activities."

> This phrase implies four major criteria: (1) that population density is a necessary characteristic; (2) that cities are focal points, or nodes that centralize and disperse goods, services, and communications; (3) that complex and specialized relationships characterize social life; and (4) that urban dwellers display particularly 'urbane' habits and shared interests. (P. vi)

Rural communities, in contrast, he says, are "less dense, contain lower proportions of wage earners, promote simpler, more close-knit social ties, and are less cosmopolitan in their outlook." These four characteristics (urban density, urban functions, urban society, and urban attitudes) set in motion those other qualities we associate with urban life and with the word *urbane*: cities as centers of human culture and creativity. What is more, by bringing "together people and resources, cities have encouraged the specialization that in turn has been responsible for economic and technological progress" (Chudacoff 1975, vi).

But if these are the urban qualities of the city, what is it that connects them to the government of the city? Broadly speaking, what do city governments do that reflects an "urban presence?" Our answer begins with the fact of urban density—the presence of large numbers of persons living in close physical proximity. By the logic of urban life, places of residence are divorced

---

3. This mingling of governmental functions and the culture of cities is examined historically in several books by Lewis Mumford (especially, 1938 and 1961).
4. Chudacoff and most others who examine the city in socioeconomic terms draw on the seminal work of Louis Wirth (1938, 1964).

from places of work. That is so because the urban dwellers do not farm surrounding land, nor cut timber, nor take minerals from the ground. Instead, the urban dweller trades things, makes things, transports things. And if he or she does not deal with material things directly, the urban dweller earns a livelihood by providing services for those who do. As a maker and dealer in goods and services, the urban person tends to earn a living as a member of a specialized group or organization whose logic of production requires that work be carried on in special buildings and specialized geographic areas.

This said, let us take the explanation one step further. The larger the urban population, the more it is likely that the urban place is a place of strangers, whose capacity for existing in a reasonably safe, comfortable, and healthy environment only partially can depend on the cooperation of friends and family and on the self-restraint imposed by a sense of shared existence.[5] To achieve a safe and comfortable life, the urban person relies on the services provided by the city's government, for it is government that (for example) uses a police force to keep the peace and restrain what society generally regards as harmful behaviors. It is city government that maintains the streets that carry the city dweller from place to place and from home to work. City government brings safe water to buildings where people live and work, and it builds and maintains the pipes and sewage plants that carry waste materials away. City government lays down standards for the safe construction of buildings and protects them from the hazards of fire. It supervises the sanitary conditions under which an urban population lives, and it performs a thousand other tasks that make life lived among strangers possible.

Politics and Public Policy

This, then, is what city government is all about, and this, then, is the connection between the city as government and the city as an urban place: rules that direct and constrain behavior on behalf of the collective good; services that make collective living possible; and money—raised through taxes—that pays the people who enforce the rules and provide city services.[6]

And here, too, is a working definition of *public policy*: the rules and services of government directed toward some specified end or purpose that is intended to serve the common good. And here, too, is the threshold of a def-

---

5. This quality of self-restraint that derives from a sense of shared existence is seen by many, and sorrowfully, as on the wane in contemporary American urban society (e.g., Bellah, et al. 1985). Some also attribute to this waning the now-pervasive presence of urban street crime and vandalism (e.g., Oldenquist 1986).

6. As disciplines, political science and economics are concerned with a common phenomenon: the allocation of scarce resources. This commonality can be extended by noting that government functions to bring order to otherwise random and dysfunctional social behaviors, while the market (and market exchanges) serves to bring order to otherwise random and dysfunctional economic behaviors.

7

inition of politics—for people quarrel over which rules are to be enforced, what services are to be provided, how much money is to be spent, and what (after all) is the common good?[7] These terms deserve further elaboration.

Public Policy

In simple terms, public policy is what government does or does not do. Public policy consists of the laws, judicial decisions, and administrative rules that determine the benefits and constraints that come from government. Thus, an inquiry into public policy not only looks at benefits and constraints, it also looks to see which persons and which groups are helped and hurt by those benefits and constraints. Of course, not every law, decision, or ruling is public policy. Common sense will suggest that while one police officer's decision to write a parking ticket is not public policy, the law under which the ticket is issued is public policy. Common sense will also suggest that the clerk who issues a building permit is not engaged in policy making, but that the ordinance that defines who may build what kind of building (and where) *is* public policy.

Public policy is thus understood to apply to a broad class of things, events, or persons. It is intended to be consistent over time and is generally said to be purposeful; that is, those who urge it and those who create it are expected to understand and anticipate its consequences. Every level of government creates public policy; but public policy in the city is a direct consequence of urban life. It is policy created by city government's need to make collective living possible within a densely populated environment.

Politics

In its oldest and most general sense, *politics* refers to the art and craft of governing. Used in this way, the word directs our attention to the broad purposes of government. In democratic societies, these broad purposes have to do with creating public policy in furtherance of the public good, and as determined by popular will and public demand. Used in this way, politics also directs our attention to competing definitions of the public good and to the values and arguments that underlie those competing definitions.

Another definition characterizes politics as the struggle to dominate government and determine its policies. This definition assumes that competing definitions of the public good, along with contending values and philosophic arguments, are all part of the struggle for dominance. And this same

---

7. As will be noted, any definition of the public good invites a quarrel (a cornerstone of the struggle that is politics). And as will be noted, quarrels over the definition of the public good are inescapably shaped by individual and collective values and beliefs (the essence of an ideology).

definition also includes the more ordinary, garden-variety politics—activities that turn on running for public office.

Harold Lasswell did much to bring this second definition into widespread use. Politics, as he defines it in a celebrated book title, is *Who Gets What, When, and How* (1936). Within this definition, politics can be found everywhere in human affairs, and recent years have seen a spate of books that describe church politics, family politics, even sexual politics. But the politics we are concerned with is the politics of city government. City politics thus deals with what city governments do and do not do—in short, with their policies. Politics in the city deals with the behaviors, strategies, resources, and ideas of those who seek to influence city policies. It deals with the timing of those policies—for today's decision is an accomplished fact, while next year's decision is at best a hope and at worst a promise unfulfilled. And politics also deals with long-term outcomes—the ultimate consequences of city policies.

Within this extended definition, city politics becomes inseparable from its urban anchorage. To understand city politics, it becomes important to pay attention to the sociology of the city, to see who among Chudacoff's "communities of concentrated populations" gets what, when, and how. Public policy affects nearly everyone in the city, but some groups are affected for the better, while others become worse off. Thus, to understand city politics, we need to ask which groups emerge better off from the struggle that is politics, and we also need to ask which groups emerge worse off. In short, to understand city politics, we need to see it as the knot that ties together the sociological, economic, and governmental strands of the urban web.

Choice, Change, and Constraints

If politics is part of governing, then governing is an exercise in choice. To govern is to choose among alternative courses of action. And unless the choice favors the status quo, choice results in change. But choices in government, as in private life, are neither free nor unlimited. Choices are almost always constrained by a clutch of considerations. As individuals, we choose among alternatives only in accordance with our ability to invent, imagine, or borrow those alternatives. We are further constrained in our choices by our values, those things and ideas and states of being that we prize and prefer (e.g., peace, liberty, low taxes, or an extension of the welfare state). The feasibility and practicality of a course of action is another constraint. So, too, are the costs and benefits we think will accompany any particular choice. And to these constraints, we need to add the constraint of resources (we are less likely to choose that which we cannot afford), along with constraints that come as we adjust what we choose to what we anticipate others will be choosing and doing.

These constraints upon private decisions are multiplied many times over for those who make decisions for city governments. Four sets of constraints

9

operate with special force on cities. First come constraints that result from the legal status of cities: cities are units of government, but not autonomous units. Any policy that a city may choose must conform to the policies of its state and also to the policies of the national government. Thus, no city may borrow money, nor hold elections, nor do anything else if what it does is not in accordance with the general policies of its state government or the national government. For example, no city may attempt to keep down the costs of providing services by forbidding the poor to settle there. No city may censor books or movies if they have been held by the courts to fall under the protection of the First Amendment. And no city may attempt to segregate persons by race. Cities are forever required to operate under the policy umbrellas of higher levels of government.

A second set of constraints involves money. Cities are among the governmental poor. They depend for income largely upon property taxes. Some also raise revenue by means of an income tax. But property taxes are slow to adjust to inflation. Upward adjustments are limited by state law to a fixed percentage of property values. And city income taxes are also limited by state laws which commonly require that city income taxes be approved by popular vote rather than by the city council.

Cities vary enormously in their taxable wealth. A few (mostly suburbs with expensive homes and high personal incomes) have revenues adequate to their policy desires. Most cities, particularly the largest cities, are revenue poor. These, as a rule, are also cities of slums, urban decay, and personal poverty. And these, also as a rule, are cities with the greatest revenue needs.

A third set of constraints is socioeconomic. Ancient and medieval cities were walled cities, whose walls served not only for defense, but to keep out those whom the urban governors did not approve of (Long 1972, Rybczynski 1995). Since at least the eighteenth century, people have moved freely in and out of American cities. In fact, the freedoms to choose one's form of livelihood and one's place of abode—with the troubling exception of blacks, American Indians, and other minorities—have been regarded traditionally as two of the freedoms implicit in our constitutional system (Herson 1990). What this means is that the size and composition of a city's population is very much a matter of individual and private choice: A city's population is the sum total of all those who choose to move in, move out, or stay in that city. Accordingly, those who make city policy must be constantly mindful that any policy that adversely affects a significant group in the city may cause members of that group to move elsewhere, "to vote with their feet."[8]

8. Albert Hirschman (1970) offers an elegant theory of political and market choices, neatly framed in his book's title, *Exit, Voice, and Loyalty: Responses to Decline in Firms, Organizations and States*, which says that critics and the dissatisfied can leave, voice dissent, or give their leaders loyalty. For an application to local politics, see Lowery et al. (1992).

Conversely, any policy that bestows significant benefits on any group may cause persons of similar social and economic circumstances to migrate to that city. Thus, policymakers are constrained to make policy that will keep in residence those who are regarded as desirable citizens, usually those whose affluence and education can contribute to civic leadership and the city treasury. And policymakers are also constrained by the prospect that some policies, however humane, may attract to their city a new group of urban poor, for the poor are those most likely to put the greatest burden on already-strained urban revenues and services (Clark and Ferguson 1983, Devine and Wright 1993, Rybczynski 1995).

A final set of urban policy constraints has to do with national economic conditions. The prosperity of every city is tied to the prosperity of the country as a whole. It is true, of course, that some cities (and regions) are less severely affected by economic downturns. And it is also true that some cities benefit less than others from periods of rising prosperity. But by and large, it is true that economic good times and economic bad times are in the city *but not of the city*. There is relatively little that cities can do to offset general economic conditions, and though many cities become desperate to invent policies that will bring them prosperity (for example, building a sports arena or a convention center), the hard truth is that only the national government has resources sufficient to grapple with widespread economic distress. Cities are constrained to operate on the margins of policies created by other levels of government. And they are also constrained by the knowledge that a policy intended to give any city an economic edge over neighboring cities—say, the building of a convention center or granting tax rebates to new industry— invites retaliation by those neighboring cities.

Thus, every city is part of an urban web. Its strands are many—economic, sociological, governmental. Political and policy choices and constraints are all part of the web. If we follow any single strand, sooner or later that strand will be seen to connect with every other strand.

City of Ambition, photogravure, 1910, 34 x 26.1 cm
The Alfred Stieglitz Collection, 1949.836.
Photograph © 1996, The Art Institute of Chicago. All Rights Reserved.

To most people, the vision of a great city is that of streets, parks, rivers, bridges, and endless and bustling crowds . . . but the idea which weighs on me . . . is that of a vast unexplored interior with a million forms of hidden life.

    J. A. Spender, *The Bagshot Papers*

CHAPTER 2

An Almanac
of Cities

Patterns and Variety

Thus far we have defined the American city in fairly simple terms: an urban place with a charter for self-government. But embedded in this definition is a set of rich and complex ideas. The word *urban* implies population density, a style of life, a network of social roles, and a variety of economic activities. And the term *self-government* implies an arena of politics and the institutions of government—both operating within the norms and values of democracy.

This definition helps identify patterns that are common to every American city. And it helps fix attention on the importance of cities to the American way of life, for the heavily urbanized areas[1] of the United States account for:

1. 87.7 percent of savings and loan deposits in the United States,
2. 82.4 percent of all bank deposits,
3. 82.8 percent of the value added to our economy through manufacturing,

1. A definition of metropolitan areas will be provided later in this chapter. Suffice it to say that metropolitan areas are the largest urbanized areas and that 81.7 percent of all people living in metropolitan areas also live in urban areas. Overall, 77.5 percent of the U.S. population live in metropolitan areas and 75.2 percent of the population live in urban areas.

4. 82.5 percent of the nation's personal income,
5. 83.6 percent of all retail sales, and
6. 75.6 percent of the value of all assessed property in the United States.

But in identifying these common patterns, this definition draws attention away from the great variety of urban places and the many varieties of urban politics. There are approximately twenty thousand cities in the United States, and each is unique. Every city occupies a singular territory. No two cities have precisely the same population demographics (age, gender, wealth, occupations, and so on). Each city is set within a distinctive geographic context. Every city has its own array of economic enterprises that provide jobs for its inhabitants and taxes for its government. And every city has its own history, a collective memory that helps mold and shape the conduct of its politics. Thus, endless variety forms the mosaic of American cities. How, then, shall we put them into classes and groups?

The Statistical City

Keeping track of American society is the job of the U.S. Bureau of the Census. It does so by gathering information and arranging data according to classes and categories. The United States was first described as an urban nation in the census enumeration of 1920. As of that date, more than half the population was reported to be living in urban (as distinguished from rural) places. Today, the proportion of urban dwellers stands at about 75 percent of the total population. We have thus become a nation of urban places and urban dwellers. The Bureau provides further details: An urban place is a geographic area with a population of at least twenty-five hundred. An urbanized area consists of a central city (or two central cities) with a population of at least fifty thousand—plus densely settled adjacent areas.

Of course, an urban place of twenty-five hundred is not what usually comes to mind when we use the term *city*. Closer to the popular image is an urban place with at least fifty thousand people. And closest of all is the metropolitan statistical area (MSA). The MSA is usually what is meant by a city: a large urban area dominated by a central city of at least fifty thousand people set inside a ring of smaller satellite cities.

At present, there are 342 MSAs in the United States,[2] the largest in population being New York (18,087,251 people) and the smallest Enid, Oklahoma

---

2. More accurately, there are 254 MSAs, 76 primary metropolitan statistical areas (PMSAs), and 12 New England county metropolitan areas (NECMAs). PMSAs are metropolitan statistical areas that are part of consolidated metropolitan statistical areas (CMSAs), the largest recognized population areas (they must have at least 1 million people). Currently there are 18 CMSAs; the largest is New York–Northern New Jersey–Long Island, which consists of 15 PMSAs (including New York, Newark, Trenton, and Waterbury).

(45,309 people). In area, the largest MSA is Anchorage, containing 1,698 square miles. The smallest is York, Pennsylvania, with only 5 square miles.

As was said earlier, the MSA fulfills the popular image of the city and is the most complete expression of what was earlier defined as an urban place: densely populated, marked by a great variety of social roles and an extensive specialization of labor—all linked by road, bus, and (often) rail networks.

The MSA's central city is generally home to what is often called the urban problem: slums, poverty, traffic snarls, a high crime rate, and racial tensions. And in many places the MSA's satellite cities are the suburbs of an affluent America—racially white, upwardly mobile, well-educated persons; the suburbs of expensive, single-family homes, large lawns, and backyard patios. But generalizations can mislead: The MSAs also contain pockets of suburban poverty as well as enclaves of dazzling central-city wealth.

Most MSAs are located in the Northeast quadrant of the United States. That is the area of our first urban settlements and hence our oldest cities. The newer MSAs are located in the southwest quadrant of the United States—"sunbelt cities"—and their newness reflects the recent shift of population southward and westward (see Perry and Watkins 1977, Sale 1975). Generally speaking, it is the older, central cities of the Northeast that evoke the image of cities in crisis while sunbelt cities are perceived, if not always correctly, as cities that are free from crises and therefore good cities to live in.

Central cities on the Bureau's list of MSAs are also the urban places that give us our sense of America as a nation of great cities. These are the creators and curators of the American urban lifestyle. But significantly, only about 30 percent of Americans live in MSA central cities and only about 40 percent of the population live in metropolitan areas defined by large central cities (those with over 300,000 people). Just as significantly, only about 45 percent of the population live in large urbanized areas (i.e., those with over 500,000 people) and over half of these live in suburban areas. Taken together, these two facts suggest that most Americans live in middle- to small-size cities.

The Sociological City

The essence of the city as an urban place is its variety of lifestyles: the larger the city, the more varied the lifestyles. Equally important, the larger the city, the greater the likelihood that among its lifestyles will be "problem lifestyles": lives that labor under poverty, limited education, substandard housing, high rates of unemployment and crime, racial and ethnic discrimination, and single-parent households.

Lifestyle is hardly a precise term, but a sense of lifestyle variety and lifestyle problems can be captured by comparing a number of logically derived "lifestyle indicators" for central cities, suburbs, and nonmetropolitan areas. Table 2.1 shows these comparisons.

15

Table 2.1 Lifestyle Indicators for Different Types of Cities

	Metropolitan Areas		Nonmetropolitan Areas
	Central Cities	Urban Fringe	
Median family income	$32,076	$42,550	$27,591
Percent of families living in single-family dwellings	46.7%	65.5%	84.0%
Percent of households headed by females	23.6%	13.7%	13.2%
Percent of families living in poverty	14.1%	5.7%	13.0%
Percent of families renting	51.0%	32.0%	27.6%
Percent of people (over 25) with high school degree	73.0%	80.8%	69.2%
Percent of employed residents with "managerial and technical" positions	34.5%	38.6%	25.7%
Percent of employed residents with production or laboring positions	17.9%	17.3%	26.5%
Percent of families living in subsidized housing	7.9%	2.8%	4.2%
Crimes per 1,000 residents			
assaults	38.3	27.2	22.0
robberies	87.9	70.0	45.3
burglaries	235.1	149.0	126.2

SOURCE: *Statistical Abstract of the United States* (1993); Bachman (1992).

Good Cities and Bad

The Census Bureau does not classify cities subjectively. But scholars and journalists do. One such ranking has been offered periodically during the past decade by Boyer and Savageau in *Places Rated Almanac*. They compiled these rankings by assigning variable weights (and personal judgments) to each of a number of qualities presumed to make for desirable urban living: good water, clean air, low crime rate, low level of joblessness, number of cultural events per thousand population, and so on. Using these and other categories to compile their most recent listing of livable cities in 1993, they judged Cincinnati to be the best of 343 American cities. By way of other rankings, Seattle, Philadelphia, Toronto, and Pittsburgh rounded out the top five cities; Sumter, South Carolina, Waterbury, Connecticut, Merced, California, and Yuba City, California, had the dubious honor of jostling for rankings number 340, 341, 342, and 343.

The Legal and Corporate City

The sociological city is defined by the character of its population, and good and bad cities by their quality of life; but legislatures and courts define the city differently. Legal definitions of the city begin with a curious historical fact: Both the modern business firm and the contemporary city descend from a common ancestor—the corporation. A *corporation*, says *Black's Law Dictionary*, is a group of persons united under a common name, the members of which succeed each other so that the corporation continues always the same, notwithstanding the change of individuals who compose it.

For certain purposes, a corporation is also considered a "natural person." As a "natural person," a corporation has the right to buy and sell property, sue and be sued, and to make rules governing its affairs. English corporations were created by a grant (a charter) from the Crown, and, prior to the eighteenth century, were used for three general purposes: for foreign trade and colonization, for charitable and educational enterprises, and for local government. The earliest English settlements in North America began their existence as corporations that combined all three corporate purposes, with governmental purposes only gradually coming to dominate (Scott 1910–1912; Lucas 1917). These first settlements took the form of villages (the better to achieve mutual assistance and common defense). However, the charter of incorporation was not to any single village, but to an entire territory or colony. Within a colony, as population increased, or as people grew unhappy with life in the settlement, new villages were founded, but they were still considered to be part of the original chartered colony.

At the time of the American Revolution, the laws of urban incorporation were only beginning to assume their present form (Frug 1984). Only about twenty cities possessed charters of incorporation. All the rest based their authority to exist and to govern on a patchwork of sources: on the authority for self-government given the original colony; on the rules of the craft guilds and merchant organizations in the former colony; and on a presumption of self-rule asserted by the pioneers who had come to build a city in the wilderness (Bridenbaugh 1938, 1955, Schlesinger 1933).

At the signing of the Declaration of Independence, all the powers of the colonial governments were presumed to have passed to their successive state governments. And the laws of urban incorporation began shifting toward their present form. Just as the king had once granted a charter of incorporation to a colony, the state governments now began granting charters of incorporation to cities and towns within their jurisdiction. And by about 1840, the laws and practice of urban incorporation were becoming everywhere the same.

17

Henceforth, every new city would receive a charter of incorporation from its state government (Frug 1984).[3]

The consequences of the laws of urban incorporation are considerable. They run like luminous threads through every aspect of city government and politics.

Cities as Agents

To understand this consequence of incorporation requires understanding a proposition grounded in both law and logic: those who bestow a charter are superior to those who receive it. Thus, every city is held to be subject to the government that grants its charter, the state. Every city (says a legal maxim) is both a creature and an agent of its state. No city (under the law of agency) may do anything contrary to the best interests or the expressed commands of its "principal," the state. Hence, every city is a unit of government, but not an autonomous government. Each city is subject to control by its principal—the state. And the history of American cities is a history marked by struggles for greater city autonomy from state government.

In the nineteenth and early twentieth centuries, cities were subject to continuous supervision by their state legislature, which often appointed and removed mayors, passed city laws, and granted street paving contracts. Sometimes this supervision (meddling, said city dwellers) was a result of rural legislators' distrust of city people and their urban lifestyle. More often, it was the result of legislators' attempts to use the city (its offices, its purchasing authority, its revenues) to aid political friends and punish political enemies. "Home rule" thus became a rallying cry for the cities as well as a reform movement that was to bring to the cities greater self-management and independence from legislative interference. Episodes of crisis (such as the near bankruptcy of New York City in 1975) tend to bring a reassertion of state control over problem-swamped cities. But overall, under terms of home rule, most states now permit their cities a good deal of leeway in managing their affairs—providing they conform to state laws and general state policies.

Cities and Courts

Still another consequence of urban incorporation is juridical. Because a city is required to conform to the terms of its charter as well as to state laws and the general tenor and purpose of state policy, cities are constantly subject to challenge in the courts. Cities, of course, enact their own laws (usually called

---

3. *Municipal* is the word most used in law to designate an urban place having a corporate charter. Thus, state statutes refer to "municipalities," "municipal law," and so forth (Latin, *municipalis*, of or pertaining to local self-government).

ordinances), but every city law is subject to courtroom challenges, whereby judges decide whether city laws conform to the principles of agency and the court's interpretation of the city's charter. Eternal litigation, it is often said, is the price cities must pay for their incorporation.[4]

The Metropolitan Patchwork

Another consequence of city incorporation connects to the long-standing American tradition that local populations are to be encouraged to undertake self-rule. Generally speaking, state legislatures have made urban incorporation fairly easy. And once accomplished, it is nearly impossible to undo. This tradition of easily accomplished incorporation is not only sustained by the American ideal of grassroots democracy, but is also nurtured by a tradition that looks with favor on the idea of America as a congeries of "republics in miniature" (Jefferson's felicitous phrase; see Wood 1959, Tocqueville 1945). But these republics in miniature, scattered across the landscape, and often crowded side-by-side (which is the essential definition of an MSA) make for the patchwork of jurisdictions that spring up all around large central cities. No city may intrude into the affairs of another city. More to the point, however much the central city may need to expand (to acquire new territory, to gain access to the taxable wealth of nearby communities), it may not do so if adjacent areas have previously been given separate charters of incorporation.[5]

The City as Proprietor

A last consequence of incorporation connects to the long-ago business and commercial aspects of city charters. All through the eighteenth, nineteenth, and early twentieth centuries, the activities of state and national governments were strictly limited. Government was very much in the style of what has been called "protective democracy" (Macpherson 1977), using its powers to protect life and property, but doing very little to provide services and amenities for its citizens. However, the cities were the notable exception to this style of protective democracy. The city was regarded as having proprietary powers—the powers of a corporation to do whatever its proprietors might decide would best serve the interests of the corporation. Accordingly, long before states and the national government were offering amenities and welfare services to the public, city governments were doing just that.

---

4. Technically, city laws are called municipal ordinances to convey three attributes: their limited, local jurisdiction, the fact that they are subordinate to state laws, and the fact that in giving cities power to pass ordinances, the state has not parted with its overall and superior law-making powers.
5. See the discussion of annexation in chapter 11 for exceptions to this general rule.

Today, we think of government services as proper and legitimate and quite ordinary. But in the nineteenth century, cities were the pioneers of service government. Cities built roads and streets to be used without charge. Cities provided water and sewage services and police and fire protection. Some cities even built gas works and electric generating plants. (Gas and water socialism, the critics cried.) And occasionally, cities carried their "business enterprises" to what must have seemed strange and wondrous domains: They built and operated zoos and art museums, established municipal colleges, funded symphony orchestras, and operated hospitals and food kitchens for the poor. (See Howe, 1905, for a reformer's plea for more urban proprietary enterprises.) In essence, the city's voters were seen by courts and state legislatures as possessing a business firm's powers, with city officials being the corporation's proprietors, able to do things ordinarily beyond the powers of other levels of government.[6]

Cities, Towns, and Villages

A final way of classifying cities is by size.

The Village

In every one of the fifty states, the village is the smallest incorporated place. The number of persons required for incorporation varies from state to state. In Arkansas and North Dakota, for example, no minimum population is set for incorporation, while Alabama requires seventy-five people to petition for and receive a charter of incorporation. In a number of other states (e.g., Colorado, Massachusetts), well over a thousand residents are required before incorporation will be considered. In most states when a village attains some specified population (determined by the state), it is required to accept a charter incorporating it as a town.

As befits its small size, charter provisions for village government are fairly simple. Most villages elect a fairly small legislature, the village council, of from five to seven persons. Villagers traditionally also elect an executive officer, the mayor, who is usually given authority to appoint a law-enforcement officer, the village constable. Some village charters provide for the appointment of a village clerk who often serves as treasurer also.

---

6. A generation ago, no textbook on municipal government (as the subject was then generally known) was considered complete without extensive discussion of the law of municipal torts: legal liabilities that followed from a city's use of its proprietary powers. (See, for example, Munro 1920, Herson 1957.) A city using its corporate (governmental) powers was generally held to be acting as an agent of state government, and therefore not to be sued. But a city using its proprietary powers was held to be acting in its "private, business" capacity, and thus open to lawsuits for wrongful and negligent actions.

The Town

Town government is likely to be more elaborate. Each state has its own population requirement for towns, and like villages, these requirements are highly variable from state to state. The town council is usually small (from five to seven members), but a town charter may require a larger and more complex administration. In many states, town voters may choose between a council-mayor charter or a council-manager charter. In the latter, the council appoints a nonelected administrator to head such town-government departments as police, fire, streets, and sanitation.

The City

The larger the urban population, the greater its need for the services that make urban living safe and convenient. And the more such services are needed, the more elaborate will be the city charter's provisions for elected and nonelected officials. City councils vary greatly in size. While most cities have councils consisting of five or seven members, Chicago's city council consists of half-a-hundred aldermen. Some city charters invest their mayor with considerable power, authorizing the mayor to hire and fire the heads of city agencies (police chiefs, fire chiefs, and the like), while other charters reduce the mayor's powers to the ceremonial: presiding over council meetings and serving as host to visiting dignitaries.

Later chapters will explore these types of organizational arrangements, but for now let us conclude our overview of the varieties and types of urban places by fixing attention on the diversity of cultural experiences that mark big cities, using New York as the yardstick against which all other cities tend to be measured.

The Big Apple

Within its population of more than 7 million, New York, in effect is many cities in one. For more than a quarter century, the South Bronx has stood as a symbol of America's urban tragedy: a moonscape of emptiness, a place of fearsome devastation, burned-out buildings, high crime, and grinding poverty. More recently, the South Bronx has begun to symbolize the city that refuses to die: Neighborhood action groups have restored and rebuilt several South Bronx streets, making them once again safe and pleasant places to live.[7]

Elsewhere in New York, there is another "city": Spanish Harlem, a racially mixed area that is home to immigrants from Puerto Rico and else-

---

7. As a symbol of the national urban tragedy, the South Bronx became an almost obligatory campaign stop and photo opportunity for presidential aspirants (Gratz 1989).

21

where in the Caribbean, redolent of the sights, sounds, and smells of a third-world country. In the Queens area, New York is a city of small, two-family homes, jealously guarded against racial and ethnic intruders by their white, working-class owners. And from Queens, the view is across the East River to the island of Manhattan, the city of affluence and elegance, high-rise apartments, powerful banks, Wall Street law firms, stockbrokers, museums of science and art, concert halls, and shops that cater to the tastes of a rich, consumer society. Here, too, is the New York that rightfully claims its place as America's center of culture. More art, music, dance, and drama are played and exhibited here in a single day than may appear in other cities in a year. Even an abbreviated list of a week's worth of entertainment and cultural events offers insight into one of the powerful dynamics of Western history: that cities—especially big cities—are the creators and repositories of much of humankind's artistic and cultural achievements.[8] By way of examples, there are about seven hundred galleries and museums in New York that display and sell visual works of art. For a recent fortnight, *New Yorker* magazine, in its "Goings on About Town," listed nineteen opera performances, forty-four symphony and recital performances, sixty-two plays and musicals, fifty-one dance and other performances, and (in addition to several dozen movie houses featuring Hollywood films) about two dozen movie houses dedicated to showing noncommercial and classic films.

But more than anything else, New York City is a place of people doing what people do (see Whyte, 1988, for a delightful discussion of street life in that city). Street vendors sell jewelry, books, luggage, umbrellas when it rains, sunglasses when it shines. They also sell a wide variety of food. Gone are the days when pedestrians' culinary choices were limited to hot dogs, soft pretzels, soda, ice cream, and chestnuts; today, they can buy souvlaki, falafel, Greek sausages, Italian sausages, bratwurst, omelets to order, Chinese beef, tacos, chili, quiche, stuffed Rock Cornish hens, and juice squeezed from fresh oranges. Street musicians are everywhere, many of professional caliber; so are jugglers, mimes, magicians, and hustlers trying to pull passersby into games of chess or three-card monte. And just when the seasoned New York resident thinks he has seen it all, he is treated to the most spectacular of street entertainments, a high-wire act. At 7:30 one morning, people walking or driving by were startled to see a figure walking back and forth with a balancing rod on a thin wire stretched between the two towers of the World Trade Center, 1,150 feet overhead. Traffic was stopped for a half hour. It was Philippe Petit, a street entertainer and mime, who once said, "When I see two oranges, I want to juggle. When I see two towers, I want to go across" (Whyte 1988, 32ff.).

8. Mumford (1938, 3) defines a city as a "point of maximum concentration for the power and culture of a community."

Cities as Opportunity for the Chance Encounter

Lewis Mumford, a distinguished student of cities, once remarked that the sense of excitement we experience in big cities springs from their ever-present opportunities for the chance encounter. We walk the streets of a city never quite knowing what or whom we will meet or see. The city's size is such that much of what happens seems unpredictable. And yet, beneath the happenstance are patterns that can be understood by those who study the city and take note of the theories that explain the patterns. Accordingly, and if we are to peer beneath and beyond the variety of twenty thousand cities, it is to theories of the city that we must now turn.

The Flatiron Building, photogravure, 1903, 32.9 x 16.7 cm
Alfred Stieglitz Collection, 1949.838.

Every why hath a wherefore.
    Shakespeare, *Comedy of Errors*

CHAPTER 3

Theories of Urban Politics

Behold! An Inner Logic

A book is usually built around two sets of ideas: an external outline and an inner logic. The external outline organizes the book's topics and sets out the order of their presentation in the table of contents. The inner logic gives the outline its coherence and makes the order of presentation cumulative. With a fair amount of effort, the inner logic can be deduced from a book's index, but it appears in nothing so handy as a table of contents.

A book's inner logic comes out of the authors' views on how the world works and why things happen. And it is no accident that an inner logic is part of the enterprise called theory, for the idea of theory has the same roots as the word *theatre*, from a Greek word that meant "to behold."

The inner logic of this book is built around theories of the city. And to better understand the idea of theory, it may be useful to examine an incident in the history of theater.

Theory as Compressed Knowledge

For more than three hundred years, playgoers have delighted in the antics of Monsieur Jourdain, who rollicks through a play by Molière and eventually announces in a voice overcome by astonishment that he has made an amazing discovery. Without even knowing it, he has been speaking prose all his life! The audience, of course, finds this funny. Imagine not knowing so obvious a fact of everyday life! Or funnier yet, imagine that anything has been changed merely by giving an everyday occurrence an elegant-sounding name. Yet, everyday occurrences do take on different meanings when given different names. (Think of the car dealer who calls his cars "previously owned" instead of used, or the member of Congress who avoids talking about new taxes by using the words "revenue enhancements.") All through the preceding pages, we have been using a special sort of language—the language of social science theory. Of course, theory is an everyday activity. Theoretical language is what we use when we try to explain the world around us. It is often the language we use when we want others to change their ways, or do as we say. Theory gives us an understanding of the whys and wherefores of behaviors and events. Theory connects and relates means to ends, antecedents to consequences, and causes to effects. Theory thus tells us how and why things happen; and in doing so, theory explains.[1]

A simple definition of theory is framed in terms of connections and relationships: Theory is a set of logically connected, experience-grounded observations. Sometimes these observations are of a prescriptive or normative variety (i.e., norms, standards, values). If you wish to achieve justice, we may say, then you should—you ought to—treat in like manner all persons accused of the same crime. Thus, prescriptive theory speaks to the world as we wish it to be and to the ideals and goals we wish to achieve.

At other times, these relational observations are of a descriptive variety. The larger the city, we may say, the more likely it is to contain a sizable number of economic enterprises. (In this theory, the number of economic enterprises connects to—is an outcome of—city size.) Descriptive theory is a statement about things as they are now or as they were in the past. Descriptive theory also has potential for dealing with things as they may become. It has predictive capacity when framed in an "if. . .then" manner: If Genoa City continues to grow (we may theorize), then it is likely to contain an increasing number of economic enterprises.

Descriptive theory deals with the world of our experience, and accordingly is also called *empirical* theory (from the Greek word for "experience"). More important, descriptive theory is an assertion of cause and effect.[2] Improve the schools, we may theorize, and new factories, attracted by the availability of an educated work force, will come to our city.

1. Given the importance of theory to all branches of knowledge, and as might be anticipated, the literature of theory is extensive. Works of importance in framing this chapter include Herson (1990), Popper (1963), and Hanson (1985).

2. In the social sciences as well as the natural and physical sciences, those who frame theories also seek to validate them. To assert that X is the cause of Y (and that Y is the consequence of X) may give us insight into the cause of things, but theory does not truly advance knowledge until we attempt to validate it, that is, subject the theory to various tests that increase our confidence that X is indeed the cause of Y.

Fulfilling a single prediction is a common form of validation. But for the social sciences, a more reliable form of validation involves a pattern of covariance: When a change in one factor is generally associated with a change in another factor, providing that coincidence can be ruled out, then the theorist is privileged to assert the cause that lies behind the change (e.g., Popper 1959, Cook and Campbell 1979).

Causation is an everyday term, but is philosophically elusive. Philosophers agree that causation is not some mechanical force that pushes and bumps things and behaviors in and out of place. Causation is better defined as patterned, rule-following behavior, expressed as covariance across time and differing conditions and/or as a consistent set of antecedent and subsequent conditions, behaviors, and events.

Prescriptive and descriptive theory can be separated in logic, but in everyday use they tend to blur at the edges. Take, for example, a much-used theory of crime: As poverty increases, an increase in crime is likely to follow. But those who hold this theory may, in fact, have more in mind than merely explaining the connection between poverty and crime. They may also have in mind a normative and prescriptive concern, subtly (or not so subtly) suggesting that since crime is undesirable, a useful and desirable way of combating it will be by reducing poverty.

Often, prescriptive theory (which is the bedrock of most political argument) is expressed as a simple set of means-to-desired-ends relationships: If we want our city to grow (we may theorize), then we must improve our schools. But to prescribe improving the schools may require that we use some component of descriptive theory. City growth (it has been previously observed) may take place under certain specified conditions—for example, as an outcome of having schools of sufficiently high quality to attract settlers with young children. Thus, when we say, "If we want our city to grow, we must improve the schools," we have built our prescriptive theory on foundations of descriptive theory.

Theory can be as short as a single sentence: For example, the older the urban neighborhood, the higher its insurance rates are likely to be. And theory can also consist of an elaborate arrangement of logically connected theories, as do those that connect poverty to such factors as racism, level of education, job opportunities, and general economic prosperity, and then further connect the resulting poverty to illness, loss of self-esteem, and families marked by domestic violence.

These more complex theories usually consist of a number of fairly short, concise theories that converge around a central idea or explanation. Accordingly, we shall call them *convergent* theories.[3] In the example of the pre-

3. Other terms for convergent theories are *organizing* and *concatenated* theories: "A network of relations . . .[framed] so as to constitute an identifiable configuration or pattern. Most typically, they converge on some central point. . . . The 'big bang' theory of

ceding paragraph, the convergence is on the many consequences of poverty. But whether short and direct, or complex and convergent, theory speaks to the how, why, wherefore, and whence of the world around us. In short, theory tells us how the world works or how it ought to work, and in so doing, theory not only explains, it organizes knowledge and compresses it, and thus makes knowledge comprehensible.

Convergent Theories as Organizing Theories

The two preceding chapters contain a number of convergent theories. For example, a theory of politics converges around the ideas of conflict and competing wants. A theory of governmental functions converges around the idea that strangers are not likely to provide the services necessary for collective living. And a theory of the urban place converges around the idea of the city as a spatial area in which places of residence are separated from places of work.

What is more, convergent theories are often strung together, like links in a long chain. Thus, a theory of the urban place converges on still another theory: The city is a place given to specialized economic activities that (as a consequence) attract a growing population that (as a further consequence) calls forth such specialized government activities as water, sewage, and sanitation services, and building inspection.

A considerable number of theories of the city are widely understood and easily grasped. Others are not so self-evident. They are, however, sufficiently important to require spelling out. As we do so, we will also lay bare the inner logic of this book and the way in which we see and explain the workings of the urban web. In the following paragraphs, we will outline a few of these theories. Later on, we will fill in the details.

Eleven Theories of Urban Politics

1. Grass Roots Democracy: A Prescriptive and Descriptive Theory

The American political culture places great emphasis on the importance of local self-government. We value that government and often make elaborate

---

cosmology, the theory of evolution, and the psychoanalytic theory of neuroses, may all be regarded as of this type" (Kaplan 1964, 298). Because they deal with a broad range of phenomena, organizing theories give us a broad understanding of the world around us. In contrast, *precision theories* deal with a fairly limited range of behaviors and events. Precision theories specify *determinate relationships* (for example, 1 percent increase in the consumer price index results in a specified decrease in the number of new houses built). Thus, well-framed precision theories lend themselves fairly readily to validation or falsification. Generally speaking, such validation helps give credence and validity to the broader organizing theory of which they are part.

claims for its supposed sensitivity to citizen wants and needs and for its use-fulness as a training school for citizenship. The average man or woman, the argument usually asserts, can know little of such matters as nuclear defense, monetary (as opposed to fiscal) policy, and so on, but he or she knows if garbage gets picked up and whether or not the fire department is on instant call. Hence, Mr. and Ms. Citizen are sufficiently knowledgeable to participate effectively in city affairs. And by participating in city affairs, they get educated to take part in the affairs of higher level, more complex government.[4]

It may be that our attachment to local government is also rooted in our experience as a frontier society when local government was the most mean-ingful and effective government. And it may also be that our attachment to local government is rooted even further back in our history, for the United States was first settled as a thinly stretched string of small villages. But what-ever the source of the attachment, our society is strongly imprinted with the idea that local government is virtuous government. As previously noted, the consequences for urban politics are significant.

States have traditionally made it easy for any settled place to obtain a charter of incorporation. And once incorporated, that place, without its vot-ers' express consent, may not be annexed to any neighboring city. Here, then, is explanation for the mosaic of towns, cities, and villages that make up the metropolitan area. And here, too, is explanation for many of the problems that beset the metropolitan area as a dozen (even a thousand) local governments struggle to co-exist in the same area. Where the problems of the area might be better solved by one single, overall government or by local government cooperation, the usual pattern is that of multiple local governments and sharp competition and rivalry among them. For example, much of the politics of affluent suburbs is dedicated to a strategy of exclusivity—devising ways (through zoning laws, building codes, and the like) to discourage the central city's poor from settling in the suburban ring. And central cities, though they may provide jobs and offer cultural enrichment for those who live in suburbs, as a general rule cannot require that the suburbs help pay the costs of central-city government.

2. The Unwalled City: A Theory of Permeable Boundaries

Suburbs may seek strategies for excluding those whom they view as undesir-able, but central cities have no such tradition of exclusivity. They accept who-

---

4. The perceptive reader will see here a blending of prescriptive and descriptive the-ory. A premise to the argument is the value of (preference for) citizen participation in gov-ernment and knowledge of its workings. How else is democracy's self-rule to be realized? The argument (in theoretical terms) then proceeds to connect local government to democracy's success, that is, to assert that participation in local government is one of the factors ("causes") of democracy's success.

ever chooses to settle there. They are cities without walls—either physical or legal (Long 1972). Their boundaries are permeable. Following the great immigration that began in the 1950s (as southern blacks and Puerto Rican poor people moved northward to seek a better life), central cities in the Northeast increasingly became home to a social and economic underclass (Lemann 1991). (In an earlier time those same cities were host to a social and economic underclass of newly arrived immigrants from Europe.) And with the arrival of this underclass (paralleled by the outward flight of an affluent middle class) came an increase in (and an increased awareness of) the problems we have come to regard as urban pathologies: crime, poverty, racial tensions, slums, drugs, disease, and the homeless.

Thus, a theory of permeable boundaries converges on the proposition that central cities are marked by stubborn social problems that are *in* the city but not *of* the city—which is to say, not of the city's making. Their sources and causes (whatever they may be) lie elsewhere in the larger society. This being so, the theory converges on still another proposition: City policies that try to grapple with urban pathologies usually will be outmatched and overcome by these urban ills. Central cities, it is often said, can attempt to cope with their poverty-rooted problems. But without state or federal assistance, they are not likely ever to solve them.

3. A Theory of Social Learning: How Not to Solve City Problems

Communities, like individuals, learn from experience. When new problems appear, the rationally minded may propose that we seek new solutions for those new problems. But a theory of social learning converges on the idea that societies, like individuals, generally try to apply old solutions to new problems (Lindblom and Cohen 1979, Brewer and deLeon 1983). Perhaps this preference for the tried and familiar springs from an all-too-human yearning for continuity; or perhaps this quality springs from the fact that new solutions are hard to come by. But whatever the source, this theory converges on the proposition that urban policymakers rarely attempt policies that redistribute wealth, or disturb the economic status quo, or attempt a full-scale assault on urban poverty (P. Peterson 1981). Past experience has taught them that the size of the problem is likely to outstrip a city's financial resources. Policymakers have also learned from past experience that redistributive policies may motivate affluent residents to seek the financial safety of nearby suburbs. And some policymakers also profess to have learned that solicitous concern for the poor will bring still more poor flooding into their city, shopping for a city with the most generous welfare benefits.

This theory of social learning links to a theory of permeable boundaries: Given the fact that the city is open to all who choose or can afford to settle there, practical considerations and past experience teach a city's policy-makers that an assault on the economic status quo is a perilous policy option.

4. The Commodification of Land and Buildings: A Theory of Market Externalities

Our society is deeply committed to an economic system that in ideal form would leave economic transactions solely to buyers and sellers. Our philosophic commitment to freedom of the marketplace has deep historical roots, and most Americans grow up convinced of the truth of the proposition (itself a theory) that liberties of everyday life find their greatest protection in a market economy: One's freedom to work, choose an occupation, pursue an education, settle on a place to live, and even select a spouse are all bound up with the freedom to buy and sell. Indeed, what is an intuitive truth for most Americans is, in fact, historical truth: Liberal, democratic societies grew up in and around—some would say, are inseparable from—the freedom of contract that is at the center of market economies. And what is more, most Americans are also convinced that a market economy (in contrast to what is sometimes called a command, or government-controlled, economy) is the most efficient and best arrangement for setting wages, prices, production, and distribution schedules (Friedman and Friedman 1981, Lindblom 1977).

A pure market economy has always been more an ideal than a reality, for market economies traditionally have been burdened by severe problems: over-production, cycles of boom and bust (good economic times followed by bad), monopolies that can drive prices skyward, harsh conditions of work, and for many workers, low or inadequate wages. As a consequence, most Americans accept the idea that a market economy must never exist without some form of government regulation. How much? and for whose benefit? are questions that help define contemporary liberals and conservatives. Thus, a fully operative market economy has been a lesser reality in the United States for the past half-century—ever since the rise of the welfare state in the 1930s, whose precepts and laws include government-set minimum wages, workplace health and safety regulations, unemployment insurance, old-age pensions, and a host of other market interventions (Lowi 1969a, Miles 1976, Herson 1990, Dahl and Lindblom 1953).

But whatever the gap between the ideal and the reality, the bedrock of a market economy is private ownership of property. Thus, the logical outcome of private ownership of property is that land and buildings are regarded as commodities to be freely bought and sold. With this fact of everyday life, the strands of our theory converge on a major explanation of urban politics: Policies that seek to curb the buying and selling of property are only carefully and cautiously attempted by American city governments. Much more important, a city's physical form is in very large measure the consequence of countless private-market (as distinguished from government) decisions—to buy and sell land, to build buildings, and to rent, exchange, and tear them down. Of course, decisions of government do affect the physical form of cities. Road location and freeway construction, for example, contribute to urban sprawl; and tax policies, for another example, may make it profitable to build highrise office spaces downtown or restore old buildings in the city's inner core. But however much government policies may animate and affect private market decisions, it is the private market that ultimately shapes the city's physical form (Garreau 1991, Rybczynski 1995). Thus it stretches the point only slightly to say that a city's physical form *is* market decisions cast in wood, steel, and concrete. Where the buildings go, people come, roads and streets get built, and specialized economic activities follow.

To carry the theory one step further requires that we define market externalities. In short, a market externality is nothing more than the consequences for others of a single market decision. To take just one obvious example: the high price that I may pay for land in the downtown business district has nothing to do with any intrinsic qualities of that land, but everything to do with the fact that people who do not own it gather nearby, in stores, offices, and traffic intersections. Land values downtown are thus a consequence of population densities and overall commercial use which, in turn, are the consequence of hundreds and hundreds of other market externalities.

In another example, I may decide that the expense of maintaining my apartment building, with taxes, repairs, and low rents, makes it unprofitable to keep it in good condition. I may even decide to let the building deteriorate to the point where it can never again be profitably restored to good condition. What takes place is a market decision between me and my accountant or between me and my tenants. But the social consequences are external to the decision. They fall on the entire community. And thus the market externality of what is essentially a private decision helps to create a slum.

Of course, one property owner's decision does not create a slum. But often, one decision feeds others until an entire neighborhood begins its downhill slide. In fact, much of urban politics has to do with responding to, heading off, or challenging the consequences of market decisions and market externalities. Land-use laws, zoning, slum clearance, building inspections, traffic routes, traffic and parking control, and street building are all issues that flow from market externalities, and they are at the center of much of urban politics and policy.

5. Looking for Mr. and Ms. Big: A Theory of Influence

Power in politics, as in everyday life, is sometimes defined as the capacity to influence the behavior of others—to get them to do what you want. The sources of political influence are numerous: wealth, status, organizational position, the gift of persuasion, and a commanding personality. In an ideally working democracy, power ought to be widely distributed and it ought to pass easily from person to person (a normative theory of power). Social scientists have worked diligently to discover the realities of power in America—to construct and validate a descriptive theory of power: Who has it? How widely is it distributed? Is it passed around? What do those who have power do with it? A fully descriptive theory of power in America has yet to be validated, but careful observers of the city are drawn to the conclusion that influence in urban politics is one of the spin-offs or consequences of the commodification of land and buildings.

This theory of influence is far from being an unvarnished Marxian postulate that political power is only economic power in disguise. But the theory does converge on the proposition that business leaders—especially those of importance in the downtown business district and in outlying shopping malls and apartment complexes—command the very respectful attention of political leaders and other governmental policymakers. "Business gets what business wants" is a common saying; and the suggested truth behind the aphorism is that large-scale property owners and developers, and managers of large-scale corporate enterprises not only have a disproportionate influence on what cities do—they are also able to assert a veto on programs that they think the city should not undertake.

6. A Theory of Lifestyle and Territory

Our theories of politics, power, permeable boundaries, and commodification all link to still another theory: lifestyle and territory. In a market society, most urban housing is privately owned. The house we buy and the rent we pay for space in somebody else's building represents more than cash payment for a domicile. It is cash payment for a style of life—a lifestyle that is maintained and protected as persons of like social status, like values, and comparable incomes establish themselves in neighborhoods and suburbs. A neighborhood is thus more than a fact of geography; it is lifestyle territory (Cox 1973, Smith 1993, Rybczynski 1995).

Urban politics is never far removed from lifestyle. Recall that politics is the struggle over outcomes; but outcomes are not limited to who wins an election or who gets what government job. Outcomes also include policy, and few outcomes in urban politics are as important as policy aimed at protecting a territory's lifestyle. In everyday language, this is the politics of turf.

Zoning struggles are one form of turf politics. So too are many of the debates over city services—such as the distribution of police and fire protection and the money that is to be spent on schools. And so too are the occasional outbursts of violence that flare forth in older, central-city neighborhoods where residents see themselves threatened by the incursion of persons of different race, ethnicity, or, most important of all, different social status. For example, for more than a decade (from 1974 to 1985) school integration was the explosive issue of Boston's politics, and for a good part of that time, the style of its politics was one of turmoil, anger, and resistance to court-ordered integration. And at least one mayoral election turned on the candidates' challenging each other as to which would do more to resist school busing.

7. A Theory of Urban Reform

A theory of urban reform turns on the pervasive corruption that marked big-city politics through the nineteenth to the mid-twentieth century. The theory connects with the social and economic conditions that helped produce that dishonest politics. And ultimately, a theory of urban reform converges on the lasting consequences of the reformers' attempts to clean up city politics.

One such consequence is to be found in the dispersal of governmental authority in many big cities. In an attempt to take power away from then-corrupt mayors and city councils, reformers in several cities established independent boards and commissions and gave them an independent authority to run selected units of city government. (Independently elected school boards are one example; police commissioners whose terms of office extend beyond that of the mayors who appoint them is another.) And while this dispersal of authority in some cities went a considerable distance in reducing the power of political bosses, this same dispersal has made it difficult for many present-day mayors to do the job they were elected to do: run their cities with a reasonable degree of authority and control.

Still another consequence of urban reform has been to bring to a number of cities an alternative to the usual pattern of American government. That usual pattern is the separation of powers (along with checks and balances) enshrined in the national Constitution and replicated in the constitutions of the fifty states. Under separation of powers, each branch of government is separate and independent of the others. Each elected official has an independent tenure, and each branch of government is expected to have a will of its own, checking and balancing the other branches (Herson 1986).

Reformed cities, however, are different. There, the inspiration for government organization is not the U.S. Constitution but the business firm. The city council (likened by reformers to a corporation's board of directors) makes general policy and, in addition, chooses a city manager to administer that policy. The manager is not elected; he or she is thus not independent of the council, but serves at its pleasure. Moreover, the manager is not expected to take part in the political process. Instead, he or she is expected to be a professional administrator, outside politics, whose job is to bring to city government the benefits of businesslike efficiency and economies.

8. A Theory of Urban Administration: Street-Level Bureaucrats

However much urban reformers long to bring efficiency and economy into city government, a city is not a business. Mayors and managers may strive to make delivery of city services efficient and economical, but it may be that city services can never be measured against what businesses do, if only because cities do things that business cannot be expected to do, such as provide police and fire protection in high-risk, dangerous situations. Equally important, cities are less likely to achieve the economies of private business because city services are distinctive. For the most part, they are labor intensive, which is another way of saying that their performance requires a high ratio of human labor to that performed by machines. And human labor, by its nature, is relatively expensive. City services are performed by people interacting with other people: the teacher in the classroom, the firefighter in the burning building, the police officer on the beat, the sanitation workers bringing trash from curbside to truck.

What is more, labor-intensive service involves a process that is loaded with opportunities for service deliverers to exercise a considerable degree of personal initiative and judgment. (Should the police officer give a ticket to a driver going through an amber light, or let the driver off with a warning? If the door to a restaurant storeroom is locked, should the health inspector come back another day? Or should he or she base inspection only on what can be observed directly?) In a word, cities are administered by what Michael Lipsky (1980; also see Judge et al. 1995) calls street-level bureaucrats: persons who are involved in the day-to-day delivery of urban services, and who must interpret policy guidelines in their day-to-day decisions.

Thus, a theory of urban administration not only takes account of the costs and the style of service delivery, it also converges on the proposition that services that require a high degree of in-the-street, on-the-site human interaction will never be managed easily from some central headquarters. Nor will such services ever be uniform all across the city. Nor will these services ever be without opportunity for bias, favoritism, and corruption (Yates 1977, Lipsky 1980).

9. A Theory of Ideology and Interpretations

The eight theories discussed above are the basic theories of urban politics, theories that help us to see and understand overall patterns. But another theory must be invoked, a theory drawn from the overlapping realms of psychology and politics; a theory of ideology and conflicting interpretations.

We can, for the present, postpone an extended definition of ideology and postpone as well an explanation of the two major ideologies of American political life, Liberalism and Conservatism. What we need to do, however, is take note of two ideas: First, ideologies consist of those important values and

35

beliefs we carry in our minds and hearts; and second, these values and beliefs serve as a lens (or screen) that blocks from our minds facts and ideas that contradict those basic values and beliefs. Said somewhat differently: An ideology is self-reinforcing. It is a pattern of values and beliefs so strong and persistent that each of us achieves a measure of psychological peace by blocking from our minds messages that challenge those values and beliefs.

Based on this provisionally sketched theory of ideology, we can expect that much of what we are likely to observe about cities is subject to being altered and interpreted by the ideology we hold. For example, what shall we make of an economically depressed, older city, with its high unemployment, its closed and obsolescent factories, its pervasive sense of social despair? For some, ideology leads to the belief that government has an obligation to intercede in the economy, to take care that none in our society are to suffer unduly, to set things gone wrong to right. These are the persons likely to "see" that the problems common to an old and failing city are society's problems (not the city's), and that the national government should pursue a vigorous program that will restore and reinvigorate cities in trouble.

But an opposing ideology leads others to resist government intervention in the economy, to believe that the national government is far too big and involves itself in too many tasks, or to believe that each of us is responsible for our own successes and failures. These are the persons likely to "see" an older city as a place whose problems are best solved locally—by those who live there. In this fashion, a theory of ideology helps us understand that what we "see" is often a consequence of the ideas (the values and beliefs) we carry to our field of vision, and this theory of ideology also helps us understand that policies aimed at solving urban problems are also molded and shaped by the ideologies of those who invent and propose such policies.

10. A Theory of Poverty and the Underclass

While the poor have always been with us, they inhabit American cities in greater numbers and with greater density than at any other point during the past forty years. This in itself is cause for concern, for it threatens to overwhelm municipal resources merely to provide services that those with little or no income require (e.g., emergency health care, public transportation, low-cost housing). But even more critical is the substantial increase in drug use (particularly crack cocaine), violence, teen sexual activity and childbearing, disconnection from the labor force, and welfare dependency among people living in poverty. William Julius Wilson (1987, 1996) argues persuasively that this is due not only to an increase in the absolute level of poverty in cities but also to an increase in the *concentration of poverty* in cities. Simply stated, his theory holds that members of any individual family are increasingly susceptible to drug and alcohol abuse, violent behavior, chronic unemployment, and early childbearing *as their income decreases*. When a large number of low-income families live in close proximity to one another, this susceptibility increases (as though through a contagion process); and as the number of nonpoverty families living in a neighborhood decreases, the risk increases even further for the low-income families that remain behind.

The growth of an urban *underclass* (low-income people living in increasingly poor neighborhoods and with a heightened risk of engaging in the destructive behaviors described above) has important implications for city governance, for it tends to change the entire character of the city. Those who are afraid of violence (or, more generally, of having their sensibilities offended by the sight of graffiti or by being panhandled) tend to stay away from areas where the underclass are concentrated—which increasingly are in or near downtown shopping and office districts. To accommodate these fears, cities have three options. First, municipal governments may take measures to keep "undesirable" people (e.g., the homeless, gangs of youths) away from the commercial, professional, and retail districts; these measures include passage and enforcement of ordinances against criminal trespass, panhandling, and loitering. Second, the city may seek funding for urban renewal and encourage private developers to revitalize the areas around the central business district that are most blighted (and therefore most threatening). Finally, businesses may decide to simply avoid the problem altogether by relocating to the suburbs. Each of these solutions comes with costs that substantially transform the character of the city.

11. A Theory of Multiple Realities

The city is by no means a single, homogeneous place suitable for simple characterization. As noted in the previous chapter, cities come in various sizes and shapes, populated with different types of people with different needs. The suburban city may list at the top of its agenda the need to control growth through appropriate zoning or the need to promote growth by attracting new businesses or industries. The small town may have the need to maintain its traditional lifestyle in the face of an ever-changing and increasingly complicated world, or it may desire to become part of that ever-changing world, entering the twenty-first century before its time. The central city is more complicated still. It may list at the top of its agenda the needs to provide safe neighborhoods for its low-income residents, maintain the property values of its more affluent neighborhoods, promote economic development through new downtown construction, and cut expenditures. Yet, all these cities are presumably governed by some common set of "urban" forces.

The neighborhood of small houses and grassy yards surrounded by white picket fences may be less than a mile away from high-rise public housing and tenement neighborhoods. The modern office building may be next to

37

a park and down the road from an old factory. New buildings are interspersed with boarded-up buildings. Yet, these are all part and parcel of the same city, governed by forces common to that city. In describing cities and their politics, we face the challenge of accommodating all of these multiple realities.

Next Steps

With these eleven theories of urban politics now in place, the next step as we thread our way through the urban web is to place these theories within their historical context, examining how the past has shaped the present.

PART TWO

A BACKWARD GLANCE

Two Towers, New York, photogravure, 1912, 33 x 25.4 cm
Alfred Stieglitz Collection, 1949.844.

Nothing which has entered into our experiences is ever lost.
William Ellery Channing, *Notebook*

CHAPTER 4

The Politics
of Urban Development:
The Development
of Urban Politics

Cities Moving West

In the popular imagination, abetted by novels and movies, the pioneers who settled the United States were a brave and heroic people who fought with Indians, moved westward in wagon trains, and built farmsteads in the wilderness. It is the story of men and women alone or in tiny bands living in remote isolation on the frontier.

The historian's truth is somewhat different. It is no less dramatic, no less heroic, but perhaps a touch less romantic. The historian's truth is this: America was settled as a long, thin line of urban places, scattering outward and westward from the Atlantic seaboard. The popular imagination has it that farmers came first and villages later. The historian's truth is that villages and towns came first, pulling farmers along to settle the land around and between urban settlements.

It is important to discard the image of expanding agricultural settlement bringing the towns along behind it.

In the first English settlement of the country, towns were the necessary bases from which farmers could move out and begin to subdue the new

> land to their purposes. . . . Indians and the problem of security alone would
> have dictated some kind of concentrated settlement before agricultural set-
> tlement could safely begin. (Glaab and Brown 1976, 24)

To offer this amended view of history is not to disparage the bravery or stead-
fastness of those who explored and farmed the western frontier. Rather, it is
to make an important point: Urban life, and hence urban politics, came with
the very first settlers, and present-day urban politics is part of a pattern that
extends backward from the present to the opening years of the seventeenth
century (Green 1957, Warner 1972, Bridges 1984, Bushman 1992).

Added to this is another important point, the point of paradox:
However much cities have been important to creating American society, the
overall pattern of our politics has been mistrustful of our cities (White and
White 1977). Thomas Jefferson gave voice to an early expression of this mistrust, saying that cities were a cancer on the body politic; and in our own
times, especially after the urban riots of the 1960s, cities came to be regarded
as the seeds and seats of our disorder (Shefter 1984). As we look to the sources
and consequences of this mistrust, we find in our past both a continuing concern for the impact on our society of those who have "huddled in cities" and
a recurring concern on the part of states and the national government to
impose varying forms of social and political controls over the cities.

But to make these ideas comprehensible, it will be useful to divide
America's urban development into historic epochs. We can start with the
period that runs from the first decades of the seventeenth century to the last
of the nineteenth, for that was the great time of city-founding in the United
States. St. Augustine, Florida, was founded in 1565; Jamestown, Virginia, was
founded in 1609; and the Massachusetts Bay Colony in 1620. And 1890 marks
the decade that closes the epoch of city-founding:

> With the exception of an occasional city such as Miami, Florida, which
> sprang up after a railroad was built along the east coast of Florida in 1896,
> or Tulsa, Oklahoma, located at the site of an oil discovery, most American
> cities destined to achieve even moderate size had been founded by 1890.
> (Glaab and Brown 1976, 100)

But to cut so wide a swath over three hundred years mows down too much.
To better understand the politics of urban development, still finer cuts are
needed. Thus, we look first at the Colonial period (1609–1776), then to the
period of the early republic (1776 to the Civil War), and then to several suc-
ceeding stages of city development. In each period, cities attempted to solve
the problems of their day, and in each period—consonant with the theory of
social learning advanced in the previous chapter—the problem solvers made
use of the past to solve the problems of the present.

The Colonial Town

English colonists, in what was to become the United States, moved outward and westward from two regions, Virginia and Massachusetts. Towns came first, hiving off one from the others, farmsteads spreading between the towns. Thus the beginnings of our country are to be found in its urban experience.

Immigrants came to the new world for a wide variety of reasons: trade, adventure, opportunities to live a better life, the quest for personal wealth, the search for religious freedom. The early colonists came mostly from the English "middling class" (Tocqueville's term), neither the richest nor the poorest of English society, but even so, they brought with them a well differentiated social structure (Warner 1972). What began as a few hundred settlers in the years around 1600, by 1700 had become a New World of 250,000 Europeans. And by 1775, the Thirteen Colonies had grown a thousand percent—to an astonishing 2.25 million. (The population doubled again in the following twenty-five years, so that by 1800 the European-descended population of the new United States was estimated to be something on the order of 5.3 million; see Kelley 1982.)[1]

The colonial period was thus a period of prodigious town founding and an even more prodigious time of town growth. By 1770, the territory that was to become the United States had become a nation of towns that included:

- in the New England Colonies—Falmouth, Portsmouth, Boston, Hartford, New Haven, and Newport;
- in the Middle Colonies—New York, Perth Amboy, Philadelphia, (and in the then far west) Pittsburgh;
- in the Southern Colonies—Baltimore, Alexandria, Stanton, Richmond, Williamsburg, Norfolk, Salem, Camden, Charleston, and Savannah.

As to population, Boston held 7,000 people in 1670 and 13,000 in 1730. New York had reached 7,000 by 1730 and Philadelphia's growth was startling: From 4,000 at the beginning of the century, it grew to 10,000 by 1720 and more than 30,000 by 1774. Next to London, it was the largest city in the English-speaking world (Kelley 1982, 70).

The circumstances of the founding and growth of American towns varied widely. Boston, New York, Baltimore, and Charleston came into being as trading centers and ports. Williamsburg was both trading center and capital of colonial Virginia. Philadelphia sprang from the vision of its Quaker founder,

---

1. Some sense of population scale can be gained by noting that in 1720 England had an estimated population of something over 5 million, increasing to about 6.5 million on the eve of the American Revolution.

William Penn, as the place where a religiously inspired social order might flourish—and even more to that purpose were the Pilgrim towns of New England. This is not the place to recount these early town histories, but from them can be distilled a number of patterns all pertinent to the politics of present-day American cities.

Economic Patterns

Even at a glance, three economic patterns make themselves visible. First, and almost without exception, colonial towns were founded for purposes of economic profit. Even where the search for religious freedom was dominant, the economic motive was never far behind. Towns came into being as centers of trade and commerce, places where their inhabitants were to make money. They were thus linked to a set of social forces as old as recorded history—urban settlements as places of economic enterprise (Jacobs 1970).

As places of economic enterprise, public and private goals were mixed and mingled. Settlers, as individuals, would come to the town for private and personal reasons, but in coming they became part of the town's collective purpose, that of creating a prosperous economic enterprise. What is more, as public and private purposes mingled, it was the general pattern that political and social leadership fell to those who exercised economic leadership (Warner 1972, Thernstrom 1964, Bridges 1984). All leadership, political, social, and economic, tended to collect in the same set of hands. Thus, the political role of "economic dominants" that so much characterizes present-day cities traces very directly to the earliest history of American urban settlements. (Perhaps it is the case that patterns once set become exceedingly hard to change.)

Self-Rule

A second pattern that marks the colonial town has been noted in previous pages: self-rule. From their beginnings (and especially because of their isolation from each other and from England), colonial towns enjoyed a considerable measure of self-rule. By present standards, this self-rule was far from democratic. Participation in public decisions was usually limited to persons owning property, and town-government itself was subordinated to the rules of the commercial corporation that had founded the town. (In the later colonial period, town government became subordinated to the rule of royal governors and the British parliament.) But however limited the scope of self-rule, it was there. Where the rest of the world was governed by autocrats and aristocrats, inhabitants of American colonial towns commanded a considerable degree of freedom in their own local affairs (Tocqueville 1945).

Property Rights as Civil Rights

A third, and perhaps most important, pattern that marks the colonial town has to do with property and property rights. In the New World, land was available for the taking. (At least, provided that it could be bought, traded, or forcefully taken from the Indians.) Conceivably, the towns could have entered into a collective way of life. They could have held their land, and the buildings on them, as common property, belonging to the town, dedicated to common purposes and benefits. They did not. Real estate was personal, privately owned, to be kept, to be bought and sold for profit. And with this commodification of land and buildings, there was set into place the pattern of property rights and the role of the property entrepreneur that have dominated American city politics for nearly four hundred years. As Howard Chudacoff (1975, 102) notes: "Americans have always considered the management and disposal of land and buildings as a sacred civil right."

Corporate and Political Patterns

With very few exceptions colonial settlements first came into being by means of a corporation charter. In the seventeenth and eighteenth centuries European statecraft was committed to founding colonies all around the world. Colonies for the English, Dutch, and French were begun by private persons (merchant adventurers, they were usually called) whose private intent was to turn a profit for those running the corporation and subscribing its capital. The public purpose behind such undertakings was to enrich the mother country by providing it with raw materials (gold, timber, furs, sugar cane, and the like).[2] Thus, those who dominated the economic life of the colony (merchants, traders, shipowners) were much favored by the mother country and encouraged (if, indeed, such encouragement was ever needed) to dominate the political life of the colony. Even more important, government in colonial towns was commonly put into the service of the town's economic enterprises.

> When, in 1644, three New Haven entrepreneurs proposed to deepen the channel of a creek, the authorities gave them four days of work from each male resident between the ages of sixteen and sixty. On another occasion, Newark offered three days of work from every able-bodied resident to assist anyone who undertook to set up a corn mill. (Glaab and Brown 1976, 4)

2. *Mercantilism* is the term used to describe this statecraft, using the "strength of the economy to defend the power of the state" (Lee and Passell 1979, 28).

Patterns of Social Control

In colonial towns, social and political controls took many forms and had many faces. And they were tied, one to the other. Some towns, for example, attempted to keep paupers and beggars out. Other towns tried to recruit workers with needed skills (shipwrights and millers, for example). And everywhere, in the interest of public morals and safety, colonial towns tried to control the behavior of their inhabitants. Then as now, crime against persons and property and offenses against the prevailing moral code were the special concerns of urban legislation (Glaab and Brown 1976, 14).

- In New Amsterdam, New York, in the seventeenth century, laws were promulgated to assure that the town authorities knew the name and whereabouts of everyone who came into the city.
- In Newport, Rhode Island, bond had to be posted for all newcomers before they could be admitted to the city.
- Beginning in 1705, Philadelphia adopted regulations (similar to those of New Amsterdam) requiring registration by name and domicile of all those entering the city.

The most pervasive and stringent social controls were asserted by the Puritan towns of New England. As Michael Walzer (1965, 209) observes,

> with the intense moral discomfort of the righteous and high minded, Puritans sought desperately to separate themselves from the chaotic sinfulness that they imagined to surround them. . . . [They wished] to create a society in which godly order would be the rule and sin not a possible activity.

These Puritan towns regulated matters of worship, work, dress, speech, and every conceivable aspect of social intercourse. And while the Puritans and their towns were never numerous, they helped create at least one legacy that is still very much part of the urban scene: the city as guardian of morals and promoter of citizen virtue. Present-day cities derive their powers to monitor morality from the *police powers* of their state. This term is not to be confused with administering a city police force (though the city's police force is legally based on the city's role as agent of the state). Judicially, police powers are the state's inheritance from English common law: the responsibility of the king as guardian of his subjects to regulate social life in the public interest, primarily in matters of health, welfare, morals, safety, and public convenience (Gunn 1969). Thus, cities attend to regulating manners and morals, and to "keeping the peace," and their vigor in doing so can be interpreted as a partial inheritance from Puritan towns.

Perhaps a second legacy of the Puritan town is our continued yearning for a sense of community. By present values, the Puritan town seems a costive and meddlesome place. But for all that, it was a town with a fierce sense of belonging, a sense of community. The essence of community is an urban place that is more than a place to live and work. It is a place of shared values that are to be nurtured and protected. It is a sense of "we fortunate few" against all outsiders (Stein 1960, Bellah et al. 1985). Today, of course, it is the small town that most embodies the sense of community. But it is the longing for community that continues to animate much of urban politics—the small town that tries to limit growth and development, the metropolitan-area suburb that tries to fend off apartment-house builders and industrial-plant developers, and the central-city neighborhood that draws its residents into fierce resistance against the intrusion of would-be settlers from the outside. This legacy of community thus appears in modern dress as the theory of lifestyle and territory.[3]

The Early Republic (1789 to the Civil War)

The early years of the republic were profoundly important to urban development. It was the period that saw the rise of cities as units of economic specialization. It was the period that ushered in the rise of the industrialized city—the place of tall smokestacks, soot and grime, and of "dark, satanic mills." It was a time that brought a politics of class conflict to the cities, and a time of spreading slums and urban congestion. It was also a period of growing resentment by white, native-born, "old Americans" against foreign immigrants, a resentment that brought the first waves of violence against the city's ethnic and religious minorities.

Urban Growth

At the center of these developments was the growth of older, established cities and the rapid founding of new towns. The older cities expanded their populations almost exponentially, so that by 1830 (to take an illustrative date) New York had grown to more than 202,000 and Philadelphia to more than 161,000. Equally important, this was the period in which the logic of a market economy moved cities toward economic specialization. The availability of nearby (and therefore cheap) water power created the thread-weaving, textile-spinning towns of New England. Boston, New York, and Philadelphia, as

---

3. Two portraits of small towns desperately trying to fend off the incursions of the outside world are provided by Vidich and Bensman (1958) and Baskin (1976). The longing for community remains strong in the American culture: As a money-making response to that longing, the Disney Corporation is building Celebration, Florida, a 49,000-acre town that will have all the technologies of modern life. But hidden behind timeless architecture will be traditional symbols and components of community: a town hall, a post office, a bookstore, and restaurants (*Economist*, Nov. 25, 1996).

47

major seaports, drew into their maritime trade shippers, brokers, wholesalers, and those important suppliers of money and credit, bankers and banks. New Orleans and Charleston prospered as trading centers that specialized in southern cotton. Thus the logic of the market (in its drive for efficiency that brings related enterprises into close proximity) set the stage for what in the late nineteenth and early twentieth centuries were to be cities of manufacturing specialization—Detroit as the center of automobile-making, Pittsburgh as the center of iron and steel, and the stockyards of Chicago and Kansas City as "butchers to the nation" (Green 1957, Chudacoff 1975, Warner 1972).

The City as a Symbol of Progress: The City and Land-Use Economics

Following the War for Independence (and later, with the Louisiana Purchase), the entire continent beckoned those who aspired to establish new towns and cities. New settlements sprang into being all across the receding frontier, and Americans took considerable pride in the rapidity with which new towns were established and even greater pride in the capacity of their new towns to bring civilization to the wilderness.

Here, for example, is what an early president of Yale had to say concerning his travels (in the early 1800s) through New England and upstate New York.

> The colonization of a wilderness by civilized man, where a regular government, mild manners, arts, learning, science, and Christianity have been intertwined in its progress . . . is a state of things of which the record of past ages has furnished neither an example nor a resemblance." (Quoted in Rifkind 1977, 3)

Thus, early on, Americans came to regard city building and urban development as the very essence of the American gift for progress and to see nothing but good in the city's intrusion on the countryside.

The new towns that sprang up on the frontier followed precedents laid down in colonial times. They came into existence as an enterprise in the private ownership of property, but with this difference: Most new towns were not developed by settlers coming to untitled and previously unowned land (unowned, that is, by Europeans). They came, instead, to land that was owned by land-development companies. These land-development companies were, in effect, wholesalers of land. That the western lands should be settled was national policy, and Congress sold these lands in great blocks to privately owned land companies with an understanding that the companies, in turn, would resell to small buyers.

In principle, Congress could have given the land free to settlers (as was done under the Homestead acts that followed the Civil War), or, alternatively, Congress could have sold unsettled land plot-by-plot to individual settlers. With few exceptions, neither course was followed. Instead, the land was sold in huge tracts to land wholesalers (land companies) that, in turn, resold it (at considerable profit) to individual buyers. Thus, land company employees surveyed the territory, laid out sites for new towns, and established land offices on the new sites (or in cities back East) from which lots and plots and blocks of land could be sold.

Settling new towns was big business and great fortunes were made in that business all through the nineteenth and early twentieth centuries. After the Civil War, companies dealing solely in land were superseded by railroad companies that repeated the wholesaling process: platting streets and selling lots in towns that would be built along the railroad's right of way (Swisher 1954). But whether new towns were organized by land companies or railroad companies, the economics of settlement was much the same: Land was a commodity to be sold at a profit. More important, the future value of any particular piece of urban land was contingent upon market externalities—upon future population density. Consequently, urban development, then as now, was tied to civic boosterism and the psychology of land speculation. Then, as now, the slogan "Come grow with us" was the key to the economics of urban development.

> Would you make money? [asked an advertisement luring settlers to Columbus, Nebraska]. . . . Find then the site of a city and buy the farm that it is to be built on. How many regret the non-purchase of that lot in New York, that block in Buffalo, that quarter section in Omaha? Once these properties could be bought for a song . . . fortunes [are to be made] that way. (Quoted in Glaab and Brown 1976, 108)

Social and Political Consequences of Industrialization

While new towns sprang to life, older cities expanded their commercial and industrial development. And profound political consequences followed. Cities grew in population and physical size, and they accelerated what had been the steady drift toward separation of places of work from places of residence. In colonial and post-colonial times, those who owned workshops and warehouses usually lived in or above their places of work. Businesses were small, and employees often lived with their employers or in lofts and odd rooms nearby. The sense of community was strong, and the interests of business owners were more often than not shared by their workers (Handlin and Handlin 1975). But with industrialization, the interests of owners and workers drifted far apart and a politics of social and economic class grew stronger. What is more, persons of wealth began shifting their places of residence outward and away from the commercial districts, and the first tracings were to be seen of what was to become in the twentieth century the city of concentric rings: a commercial and factory district in the oldest part of town, workers' housing in a ring around the old town, and homes for the middle class set in a wide circle outward and apart from the ring of working-class houses.[4]

As industry grew, the gap between rich and poor became wider and deeper. And housing for the poor became oppressive and unsanitary. The age of the slum had arrived. In 1843, a survey found 7,196 people living underground in New York.

> Within seven years as immigration expanded during the decade, the cellar-dwelling population had increased to 29,000. . . . A Cincinnati board of health report of 1865 told of a two-story tenement which housed 102 people for whom only one privy had been provided. (Glaab and Brown 1976, 69, 76)

Dust and mud and garbage in the streets marked the cities of the nineteenth century. Sanitary facilities and water supplies were provided mostly by backyard wells and earth-toilets, supplemented by privately owned water carriers and waste removers (often with the same contractor doing both jobs). Small wonder, then, that periodic epidemics swept the cities. Yellow fever, typhoid, and cholera were recurring urban diseases. Crime, too, was rampant, and as historians of urban violence frequently note, organized street gangs operated openly and with impunity, making life difficult and dangerous for rich and poor alike (Silberman 1978).

Housing laws and city-supervised housing standards were almost nonexistent. In 1867, New York pioneered the setting of standards for tenement construction. But municipal waterworks and city police came earlier. Philadelphia was the pioneer of the city-owned water supply. (It completed the Fairmont Water Works in 1822; New York began building its aqueduct water system in 1835.) Nine years later (in 1844), New York replaced the then-prevalent system of private watchmen with the nation's first city police force—eight hundred strong (Glaab and Brown 1976).

But even as the populous cities of the East were taking their first hesitant steps toward coping with problems of crime, public health, and sanitary housing, they were further beset with the problem of recurring crowd violence: All through the nineteenth and early twentieth centuries, the growth in urban populations came primarily from foreign immigrants, newly arrived to

4. This demographic pattern was given in classic formulation in 1925 by University of Chicago sociologists Robert E. Park and Ernest Burgess (reprinted in 1967). For a study of population mobility in a single city, Boston, between 1830 and 1860, see Knights (1971).

seek the promise of American life. But as immigrant ranks swelled, white, native-born Americans grew increasingly resentful of those with different cultures, customs, and languages. Resentment turned violent, and the 1830s were marked by what would become a recurring pattern of violence against racial, ethnic, and religious minorities.

> Anti-Catholicism first became a disturbing factor in American life in the 1830s when Protestant leaders began to declare that the Roman Catholic hierarchy was conspiring to win complete control of the United States. . . . The crusade resulted in several outbreaks of rioting; an Ursuline convent was burned by a mob in 1834, ten years later several Catholic churches were destroyed by a three-day riot in Philadelphia. (Parkes 1959, 263–64)

Thus, cities had become at one and the same time the focus of an anti-immigrant agitation and the places in which mob violence might be expected to flare forth. Those who lived in rural areas had their dislike of cities, with their foreign ways and foreign people, intensified; and those who lived in cities became part of a rapidly expanding population of foreign-born and newly arrived immigrants.

The Age of the Common Man

In the 1830s, a new spirit and style entered American political life—signaled by the election of Andrew Jackson (1832). The slogan of Jacksonian politics, "To the victor belongs the spoils," announced that henceforth the jobs and rewards of government would be handed to friends and supporters of those who won elections. In unmistakable terms it also announced that politics itself would belong to those who could organize with sufficient numbers and discipline to capture public office. Political participation would no longer be the restricted preserve of the literate and the wealthy; suffrage would continue to expand to include (in growing numbers) "the common man" (Schlesinger 1945).

Consonant with this style and spirit, a new form of political organization came to the cities. This new form frequently centered around volunteer fire departments. As organizations, they offered fellowship and social recognition to their members. Owing to the rapid growth of cities and the crowding of wooden buildings on narrow lots, the volunteer fire departments performed an increasingly important public service. Equally important (for political purposes) they were built around the efforts of the working classes. They thus provided the framework for a new type of political organization that would soon dominate big city politics. Mass-based and egalitarian in outlook—operating in hierarchical fashion, with leaders at the top and followers ready to take orders—this new type of political organization was called the *machine,*[5] and it carried into cities a politics of numbers, organizational discipline, egalitarianism—and corruption (Frug 1984, Bridges 1984, Bryce 1889). In the decades ahead (especially after the Civil War) it would come to dominate totally the politics of most big cities.

The Industrial Age

The decades after the Civil War were a period of unprecedented industrial, and therefore, urban expansion. Railroad building proceeded with astonishing speed. Before the war (in 1850) the United States had fewer than 9,000 miles of railroad, mostly in New England. Between 1860 and 1900, 163,000 miles of track were laid down. Big cities now had the ability to enter and then dominate the markets and economics of an entire region, and even smaller cities and towns were linked to regional, national, and even international markets. Capital invested in manufacturing rose from $1 billion in 1860 to $10 billion in 1890. During this same period, the number of industrial workers rose from something over 1 million to more than 5 million, and the "value of [their] annual product from less than $2 billion to more than $13 billion" (Parkes 1959, 395).

Immigration into the United States also shot skyward and cityward. From 1870 to 1900, it is estimated that nearly 12 million immigrants entered the country, some to take up rural life, but by far the greatest number to settle in the cities. There, those who arrived with limited work skills, little money, and scant command of the English language could hope to find jobs, housing, and the comfort and guidance of fellow countrymen who had arrived earlier.[6]

But none of this change and expansion was without social cost. The industrial city made it possible for an entrepreneurial few to make great fortunes and to display those fortunes in the imposing townhouses and mansions that stood in private parks and along avenues of urban opulence.[7] For the less fortunate many, life in the industrial city was considerably harder. Factory labor was monotonous. The workday was long, often ten, twelve, even fourteen hours. Wages were low, and loss of one's job because of an economic downturn was frequent. Industrial accidents were commonplace. (In 1900, for

5. The origin of the term is obscure. The great student of American slang and usage, H.L. Mencken (1963), thought that the term was first coined by Aaron Burr to describe Burr's own political organization in eighteenth-century New York. Whatever its origins, it nicely fits the American fascination with mechanical contrivances.
6. The classic study on the immigrant experience is Handlin (1973); for its significance for urban politics, see Harrigan (1985).
7. Some sense of the lives of the urban rich in the Industrial Age can be gotten from Thomas Beer (1961) and Edward Lucie-Smith and C. Dars (1976).

example, it is estimated that they caused twenty thousand deaths and 1 million injuries.) Under the legal doctrine of the time, neither victims nor their families were entitled to compensation. Little by way of public welfare existed, and aid to the poor, to orphans, and to the injured and the sick was almost completely a matter for private charity.

Some sense of life among the city poor can be gotten from Jacob Riis (1957, 36, 47, 124, *passim*), a pioneer photojournalist who took his camera to record lives of poverty in New York in the early 1900s.

> A Seventh Ward tenement was typical. . . . There were nine in the family; husband, wife, six children, and an aged grandmother. . . . All nine lived in two rooms, one about ten feet square that served as parlor, bedroom, and eating room, the other a small hall-room made into a kitchen. . . . Here, in this tenement, . . . fourteen persons died last year, and eleven of them were children. . . . With the first hot nights in June, police dispatches . . . record the killings of men and women rolling off roofs and window-sills while asleep . . . in hot weather, when life indoors is . . . unbearable.

This, then, is the social context of the industrial city. It is also the context for the politics of the machine.

The Political Machine

I want to say that I don't own a dishonest dollar. If my worst enemy was given the job of writin' my epitaph when I'm gone, he couldn't do no more than write, "George W. Plunkitt. He seen his opportunities, and he took 'em."

George Washington Plunkitt, quoted in William Riordan, *Plunkitt of Tammany Hall*

In 1889, when James, Viscount Bryce, sometime British ambassador to the United States, published his monumental study of American government (Bryce 1889), nothing dismayed or saddened him more than the governance of American cities.[8] His research and observations were extensive. He had traveled to cities all across the country, read their newspapers, corresponded with their leading citizens. Chicago, New York, Baltimore, New Orleans, San Francisco, Philadelphia, Cincinnati, Louisville, Minneapolis, Albany, Cleveland, and St. Louis were all part of his study. And everywhere, the story was the same: corruption, graft, dominance by a political boss or a small group of bosses ("the ring") who manipulated elections, sold city services, accepted

---

8. This two-volume work went through several editions, and for several generations was the standard "textbook" on American government and political life.

bribes, stole public money, and controlled a cadre of appointed city workers and elected public officials. What Bryce saw was a style of political organization everywhere called the machine, and whatever else might be said of American political life, Bryce concluded, "there is no denying that the government of cities is the one conspicuous failure of the United States" (Bryce 1889, vol. 1, 608).

In attempting to explain this failure, Bryce searched for its causes. He found no fewer than seven. Three of the causes were legacies of Jacksonian politics and an outlook that (since the 1830s) had equated successful democracy with the greatest possible participation in political life: frequent elections, universal suffrage, and numerous elective offices.[9] A fourth cause was an absence of stimulating issues, a consequence, said Bryce, of the fact that while national politics involves matters of war, peace, and prosperity, local issues are of the humdrum sort—street paving, housing inspection, and water-line locations. As a fifth cause, Bryce concluded, "the leading men are all intensely occupied with business," by which he meant that business leaders had little time for politics. They were too busy making money. Sixth, Bryce found "communities are so large that people know little of one another, and. . .the interests of each individual in good government is relatively small." Finally, he noted that the United States has

> a vast population of ignorant immigrants. . . . They know nothing of the institutions of the country, of its statesmen, of its political issues. . . . Incompetent to give an intelligent vote, but soon finding that their vote has a value, they fall into the hands of the party organizations, whose officers enroll them in their lists and undertake to fetch them to the polls.[10]

Even after a hundred years we can sense the moral indignation that Bryce poured into his assessment of cities. But how correct was that assessment? How close to the mark had he come? By every test, his reporting was accurate. The machine existed to enrich its members, and their concern for the public interest always ran a poor second to opportunities for members' personal enrichment. Legislation was exchanged for bribes, and contracts and city services were sold openly. City jobs went to those loyal to the machine, and those on the city's payroll used their jobs—and the promise of still more jobs—to turn out loyal voters at election time. Those who stood near the apex of the hierarchy often became exceedingly rich.

---

9. The Jacksonian ideal that politics was to be open to all meant, in effect, that popular control over government would be achieved by letting the people vote and vote often. It also meant that the more offices that were to be filled, the greater the opportunities for the ordinary citizen to fill them.

10. All quotations are from Bryce (1889, vol. 2, 95).

But what about Bryce's explanation (his theories) of the causes that lay behind the machine's power? With a century's hindsight, we can now see that many of Bryce's explanations were clouded by the bias of his own social class. (Like most others, he worked within the confines of an ideology and what we have previously discussed as a theory of ideological interpretation.) He felt strongly that persons of intellect and wealth were best suited to manage public affairs. He never quite saw that business leaders—the "better men" as he called them—were often the strongest supporters of the machine and the largest givers of the bribes that kept the machine rich. And he failed completely to understand that the loyalty of the immigrants to the machine was not a loyalty born of ignorance, but an act of considerable rationality and well-understood calculation.

Businessmen and the Machine

James Bryce's world is considerably removed from our own. His was a time in which the hard-fisted, scheming businessman was far closer to folk hero than villain. In Bryce's world the ultimate success story was the poor child who climbs from rags to riches up the rungs of the business ladder. Bryce's time was one of a pervasive public philosophy—loosely adapted from Darwin's theory of evolution—that saw success in business as tantamount to the survival of the fittest, and equally, saw poverty as the mark of personal defect and moral failings.[11]

Given the spirit of those times, and given the idea (as was often said) "that profits need no justification," it perhaps becomes understandable that bribery of public officials by business firms was an accepted and common activity. In fact, those who bribed city officials could and did take instruction from what went on in Congress and the state legislatures. The Industrial Age was the great age of railroad building; and railroad lobbyists were often the most influential nonelected actors in state politics and the national legislature. Scandals were frequent as railroad lobbyists exchanged money (and sometimes shares of stock) for free grants of land and for favorable rights-of-way.

The pattern in cities was similar. There it involved monopolies (franchises, they were usually called) for street railway lines. Again, the potential for profits was enormous. As cities grew in physical size, as their populations increased, and as workplace and residence grew farther apart, the commuting age arrived. Even before the electric streetcar, in the 1880s, steam trains were pulling passenger cars across the city; and before them, the horse trolley was commonplace. "In New York alone (the year was 1858) five principal [horse-

---

11. Among the best accounts of the influence of social Darwinism on American politics and social life is Richard Hofstadter (1955b).

drawn] street railways . . . were carrying 35 million passengers a year" (Glaab and Brown 1976, 141).

In addition to granting streetcar franchises, cities had other prizes that could tempt the business community into corrupt alliance with the machine: Franchises to build and operate gasworks, and gas-lines (for heating and lighting) were every bit as profitable as owning a streetcar company. The same held true for privately owned water and sewage systems. And it was no less true for contracts to pave streets, build city buildings, furnish coal, make policemen's and firemen's uniforms, and even haul bodies to a pauper's grave.

But to see the alliance of bosses and business as cemented only by the profits derived from franchises and city purchases is to see too little. To see still more, an important idea will need to be elaborated. One of the legacies of Jacksonianism was to overload the city with elected officials: a large city council, a mayor, perhaps an elected chief of police, and such other elected officials as a commissioner for streetcars, a commissioner for taxicabs, a commissioner (or board of commissioners) for water, gas, sewers, and so on.

Consider the ambitious business person who, for example, wishes to build a factory. Quite possibly, that factory will require a railway spur to ship its goods, a water line to run its steam boilers, an extension of the streetcar line to bring its workers, and dozens of building permits even before the first shovel of earth is turned.

Consider again, that in a government with a multitude of elected officials, each of whom might have to be persuaded—or even bribed—in order for construction to proceed on schedule, or even proceed at all, it may well be that our contemplated factory would never be built. But now, suppose that all these independently elected officials were not truly independent (each with an independent mind, purpose, and electoral mandate), but instead were all part of a common organization, taking instruction from one political leader (the boss) or a small group of political leaders (the ring). And suppose that the business person had only to persuade—or bribe—that one leader or that small group of leaders. The costs of bribery would be known in advance and could be figured into the overall construction costs. The boss or ring could be counted on to keep its word. There would be little or no construction delay. And the factory would be built. Small wonder, then, that in many cities the business community was an enthusiastic, self-interested, and rational supporter of the machine.[12]

---

12. Those who study politics in third-world countries suggest strong parallels between the nineteenth century American political machine and economic and political development in developing countries. There, one-party, strong-man government is often the primary instrument for suppressing ethnic and tribal loyalties, for bringing a degree of discipline to a dispirited and incompetent bureaucracy, for assuring the political stability necessary for capital investment. See, for example, Naipaul (1979).

The Business of Politics

But getting on with the business of business was not confined to the business community alone. The business person and the politician shared a common outlook that, since the age of Jackson, has been a cornerstone of all American politics at every level of government: Politics is a vocation, an income-producing job, and not a part-time activity to be indulged in by an affluent class moved by a sense of public service and civic obligation.[13]

Thus, the machine was run by "vocationalists," professionals for whom politics was a job and a business. And those who were in it had no reason to set their ethical standards on a higher or more moral plane than that which was everywhere common to business. If the business community could use money to buy what it wanted from government, then the machine's "businessmen" who were the government could surely take that money.

Listen, for example, to George Washington Plunkitt, boss of Tammany Hall (the machine that ran New York at the turn of the century):

> There's honest graft, and I'm an example of how it works. I might sum up the whole thing by sayin': I seen my opportunities and I took 'em. Just let me explain by examples. My party's in power in the city and it's goin' to undertake a lot of public improvements. Well, I'm tipped off, say, that they're goin' to lay out a new park at a certain place. I see my opportunity and I take it. I go to that place and buy up all the land I can in the neighborhood. Then the board of this or that makes the plan public, and there is a rush to get my land which nobody cared particular for before. Ain't it perfectly honest to charge a good price and make a profit on my investment and foresight? Of course it is. Well, that's honest graft. (Quoted in Conlin 1984, 234)

Immigrants and the Machine

What, then, of Bryce's views of the immigrants? In the main, he was correct in asserting that immigrant families provided the machine's voting strength. But every generalization has its exceptions. Milwaukee, for example, had a considerable concentration of German immigrants (it was often called Rhineland on Lake Michigan), and it was a model of good, clean innovative government (Buenker 1973). Kansas City, in contrast, had a mostly second and third generation, native-born population, but it was notorious as a stronghold of machine corruption (Zink 1930).

But was Bryce misinformed when he described the alliance between

---

13. See the comments by the early-twentieth-century German sociologist Max Weber (1946).

immigrants and the machine as an alliance of the corrupt leading the igno-rant? In fact, he was misinformed, for the immigrants were trading votes for social and economic assistance. Workers for the machine assisted the new-comers to America in countless ways. They often posted bond and pro-vided medical assistance for those who needed help in meeting immigra-tion rules. They assisted the newly arrived in finding housing and jobs. They served as interpreters for those who had yet to learn the English lan-guage. In an age when welfare was private charity, it was often the machine that ran the best-organized and most generous charity in the city (Merton 1957). It gave food and money to the poor, and coal to heat their stoves. It provided legal assistance to those who could not afford lawyers, and it soft-ened the harshness of the law for those who broke it. In short, the machine was an enterprise in social service, an activity best expressed by Martin Lomassy, the once political boss of Boston: "I think there's got to be in every ward somebody that any bloke can come up to—no matter what he's done—and get help. Help, you understand; none of your law and justice, but help."[14]

Beyond social service, perhaps the greatest contribution of the machine to the immigrants was to set them on the ladder of social and economic suc-cess and upward social mobility. The machine served as a kind of employment agency, letting the business community partially "pay" the machine by way of jobs in stores and factories. The machine also recruited into its own ranks ambitious young persons from immigrant families. And once on the ladder of politics, those with ambition moved up. Many (with help from political friends) started small businesses. For example, some whose jobs had begun as manual labor on construction sites (jobs originally found through the machine) ventured to begin their own construction companies. Their children went to school, and within a generation these children began to enter the professions. The details varied, but overall the pattern was the same: The machine offered opportunities and assistance in moving great numbers of immigrant families along "the tenement trail"—upward and outward to mid-dle class status and success.[15]

14. Quoted by Lincoln Steffens (1931, 618). Steffens was a tireless crusader against the machine.
15. The "details" would also stress the fact that all through the nineteenth century and well into the twentieth, immigrants and their descendants lived in compacted urban areas. Every city had its "Warsaw," its "Little Serbia," its "Bohemia," its "Little Italy," and so on, each served by its own foreign language newspaper, often its own foreign-language theater (and later, cinema), its ethnic restaurants. Churches and synagogues offered services in the language of the neighborhood, and in these and comparable ways, ethnic identities were reinforced. The term "tenement trail" is Lubell's (1956). For a recent assessment of the relationship between machine and immigrant and the role of the machine in better-ing the immigrants' lives, see Harrigan (1985); and for an early assessment, see Riordan (1963). A splendid account is also provided by Handlin (1973).

Urban Reform

Political reform is a periodic feature of American politics, like waves that come crashing across a swelling sea. One theory to account for waves of reform asserts that they arise from the clash of the "is and the ought"—the tension between our professed ideals and our everyday political practices—as, for example, in the civil rights revolution of the 1960s, between the lip service paid to "liberty and justice for all" and the treatment of blacks in our society (e.g., Herson 1990). Another theory explains periodic reform as part of a recurring clash between the professional politicians (the vocationalists) who run our government and the amateurs of politics—those who are moved by a sense of public duty, a call to ideology, and a moral desire to set wrongs to right (Wilson 1962). The amateurs of politics are often moved to action during times of crisis, when unsolved problems seem beyond the control of ordinary, everyday politicians. But for the amateurs, politics is an avocation, not a vocation. Their perseverance and persistence is usually limited. The professional politicians (the "pros") sometimes call the amateurs the "goo-goos" (short for good government), and the pros have long known that the energy and attention span of the goo-goos is usually short—resulting in quick bursts of reform followed by long periods of inattention.

Both theories of reform find easy harbor (and dozens of examples) in the period roughly from 1900 to 1920. During that time, urban reform was part of a larger, more widespread drive for changes on all levels of government (Hofstadter 1955a). Leadership of the reform movement was primarily middle and upper class, a loosely connected coalition of mostly amateur politicians who called themselves Progressives and marched under the banners of Progressivism.[16]

The agenda of the Progressives was piled high with proposals for reform. On the national level, they pushed for an income tax, for legislation to curb business monopolies, to outlaw child labor, and to improve conditions in shops and factories. On the state level, they proposed to give the electorate a more direct voice in government, using the initiative, referendum, recall, and direct primary.[17] And to give the electorate greater opportunity to hold their

---

16. Among the best studies of Progressivism are those conducted by Schlesinger (1957), Hofstadter (1955a, 1968), and Hays (1964). For the flavor of a Progressive writing in his own time, see Croly (1909).

17. Jay Shafritz (1988) provides definitions of these key terms:
Initiative: a procedure that allows citizens, as opposed to legislators, to propose the enactment of state and local laws.
Referendum: A procedure for submitting proposed laws or state constitutional amendments to the voters for ratification.
Recall: A procedure that allows citizens to vote officeholders out of office between regularly scheduled elections.
Direct primary: [An election] in which political party nominees are selected directly by the voters.

elected officials accountable, Progressives also tried to concentrate governmental authority by decreasing the number of elected officials.

Progressives and the City

Political reform is rarely, if ever, easy. Reform, after all, is an assault on power and privilege. The urban reformers could argue that they were seeking to act in the name of democracy to clean up government, to make it better, to give power back to the people. But in machine cities, the people already had significant power: With the help of the machine, they could get favors and services from their government. Thus, great numbers of those in the city did not want any change in the status quo.

As Hofstadter (1955a) and others persuasively argue, proposals for city reform often came down to nothing less than a clash of lifestyles, cultures, and ways of looking at the world (ideologies). On the one side were the reformers, mostly old-stock Americans who were animated on an ethical plane by democracy's abstract values but were often moved (if the truth be known) by resentment and downright dislike of foreign-born Americans. Many of the reformers were fearful of what was much talked of in academic and intellectual circles: the oncoming demise of traditional Protestant and west-European culture, soon to be swamped by tides of immigration from eastern and southern, Catholic and Jewish Europe (e.g., Grant 1916).

On the other side were the immigrants. Many had come from societies built around kinship systems and personal loyalties, societies in which personal dealings and personal favors were the norms. Coming from places in which feudalism was a living memory, immigrants from southern and eastern Europe had no difficulty in understanding the machine to be an American version of a society built around the patron and the personal protector. Most were untroubled by the idea of giving loyalty to their protectors. And most were equally untroubled that they preferred a machine system that delivered immediate and personal benefits instead of something as abstract and intangible as good government and the public interest.

The Reform Package

At heart, the Progressive reformers were prescriptive theorists, striving to bring better government to the cities. But as is often the case with prescriptive theorists, they were confronted by the dilemma of practicality, in this case, how to make the cities more democratic—which is to say, give power to the people—and, at the same time, keep the people from continuing to hand over that power to the machine.

Since "the people" were strong supporters of the machine, the reformers set their sights on changes designed to undercut the institutional foundations of the machine. The machine was to be brought down by means of no fewer than five reform measures that constituted the urban reform package.[18]

First, the reformers attempted to introduce the merit system and civil service appointments in city government. Under a merit system, appointment to city jobs would be based on written examinations, and thus (it was reasoned) the city would be served by better-educated employees, better able to resist the temptation of bribery, and more determined to resist being manipulated by political bosses. Under civil service, jobs once gained would be permanent, not subject to dismissal (except for incompetence), and thus removed from control by politicians.

Second, detailed accounting procedures were to be instituted so as to thwart theft of public funds. In a related move, legislation was to require that cities use competitive bidding in awarding contracts to buy and build.

Third, where it was decided that dispersed authority might better insulate an area or activity of government from boss control, provision was made for an independently elected board or commission. The independently elected school board continues as the most frequently used example of this third reform. Then, as now, its justification is that an independently elected school board "keeps the schools out of politics and politics out of the schools."

Fourth, and most significant, attempts were made to scale down the size of city councils and, even more to the point of reform, to do away with election by districts (usually called wards) and to substitute a city council elected at large—each council person chosen by all the city's voters. Much thought and planning went into this fourth reform. Its logic was as follows: for each district to have its own elected representative is to encourage a system of direct, visible personal leadership and fellowship. District-elected council persons know their constituents personally. To those they thus know and trust, they can offer favors, patronage, and a variety of social services. They can know who turns out to vote; and they can more or less know if that turned-out vote is a return for past favors.

What is more (the reformers reasoned) representation by districts favors ethnic representation. Everywhere (or so it was not so many years ago) immigrants lived in their own tight communities. Ethnic representation (the reasoning continued) feeds machine politics not only because the machine organizes the voters block by block and house by house, but also because the machine uses ethnic leaders as ward and community workers. Thus, to take machine politics out of the city council, take city council members out of districts.

18. To grasp the magnitude of their task, as well as their successive disappointments, see the autobiographies of urban reformers (e.g., Whitlock 1914; Childs 1952; Steffens 1931). On the program of the reformers, see Steward (1950). The term *reform package* is used by Davis and Weinbaum (1969).

Perhaps even more important for the better government envisioned by the reformers, an at-large council would be less involved in the affairs of immigrant ethnic groups. The ethnic immigrants might then lose interest in city affairs and perhaps stop voting. But not so the upper and middle classes. Control over cities' affairs would then pass to them, for they could be counted on to vote and, by their votes, to demand that the public good be more important than favors for friends or supporters.

Fifth, and perhaps most radical in its departure from the traditions of American government, the reformers proposed to do away with an elected chief executive, the mayor, and to substitute an appointed executive, the city manager, who, as a professional administrator, could be counted on to resist the tugs and pulls of politics.

In this fifth reform, the proponents of change had an important ally in many from the business community. For them, the city-manager plan had a real-world appeal. It reflected their own experiences and appealed to their deep-seated belief that if government was to be made better, it would need to be more like business—removed from popular whim and from the popularity contests of elections. In short, cities would do better by having a competent manager in command.[19]

The Demise of the Machine

Whether the urban reform package accomplished its purposes is difficult to say. What we know now, with more than seventy years' distance from the days of the Progressives, is that what we have previously called a theory of urban reform has taken hold in cities. First, the idea that cities are to be run with regard for efficient and honest use of their resources is now the norm for city government. Second, several parts of the reform package are everywhere in place today—civil service appointments, competitive bidding on city contracts, and careful keeping of public records, all open to public scrutiny. Third, a considerable number of cities make use of small city councils, elected at large. And fourth, well over two thousand cities have adopted the manager plan.

But whether any parts of the reform package or any of the reformers' agitation was directly responsible for driving out the machine is difficult to say. Machine politics continued to dominate large eastern and southern cities until well after the Second World War. The last of the great machines, no doubt, was in Chicago. Its machine did not go down until the death of its last boss, Mayor Richard J. Daley, who died in 1976.[20] Why and how the machines disappeared is not so much a mystery as a consequence of social

19. For critiques of this reasoning, see Waldo (1948) and Herson (1957, 1973).
20. On Boss Daley and his machine, see Rakove (1975) for a sympathetic account, and Royko (1971) for a scathing indictment.

forces that may have had nothing to do with the work of the urban reformers. Among these forces were:

- A rising tide of anti-immigrant sentiment that sharply reduced the flow of European immigration in the years that followed 1920;
- The Great Depression of the 1930s and the subsequent rise of the welfare state, which freed the urban poor from dependence on machine-sponsored charities;
- A general economic prosperity in the years following World War II and the rising affluence of once-immigrant families (combined with their geographic dispersal into the suburbs) deprived the machines of their former ethnic loyalists;
- The postwar, general economic prosperity may have brought a rising standard of living to the urban blue-collar class sufficient to make jobs on the city payroll less and less attractive.

But even if the old machines are gone as tightly disciplined organizations of bosses and followers, the style of machine politics continues to haunt many cities. To a considerable degree, the fact that in many places city employees are still open to being bribed (and city services bought and paid for) is a consequence of the on-the-site nature of city service delivery. *[Recall the theory of urban administration.[21]]* But in addition, machine-style politics in some cities may also be a cultural norm, a style of politics traditionally practiced in the Northeast, in the South, and in a scattering of cities along the Mississippi and Ohio rivers (Wolfinger 1972, Riedel 1964). In all these places, judges are commonly open to being bribed, probate courts award lucrative cases to lawyers who are part of a select ring of political "cronies," housing and health inspectors still accept "under the table" money, and city workers are still required to contribute a portion of their salaries to the election campaigns of party leaders. The machine as organization may be gone, but many of its practices remain. Though Viscount Bryce would no doubt be pleased by the enormous overall improvement in the honesty of city government, he would probably insist that many cities still have a long way to go.[22]

---

21. Here, and elsewhere, discussion is tied to the theories of urban politics outlined in chapter 3 by bracketed, italic references.

22. Three large cities, New York, Los Angeles, and Chicago, continue to provide ample instruction in machine-style corruption. Not long ago, one of Chicago's newspapers secretly established a retail business and kept records of the bribes and shakedowns demanded by city officials if the business was to escape being closed down. Fire inspectors, building inspectors, health inspectors, and police on the beat all came regularly to partake of the business' profits. In New York the administration of Mayor Edward Koch was buffeted by recurring scandals. For example, in November, 1985, four city officials (including the heads of the Democratic party in Queens and the Bronx) were found guilty of

The Great Depression and Beyond

The economic hard times that began with the stock market crash of 1929 were of a scale never before experienced in the United States. Millions were out of work, and for those lucky enough to have jobs, wages tumbled below living costs. By 1932, the Pennsylvania Department of Labor reported:

> Wages had fallen to five cents an hour in saw-mills, 6 cents in brick and tile manufacturing. . . . In Malvern, Arkansas, lumber workers received 10 cents an hour; women in Tennessee mills were paid as little as $2.39 for a 50 hour week. (Schlesinger 1957, 249)

Hunger was widespread, and yet farmers found no markets for their crops. "Some found it cheaper to burn their corn than sell it and buy coal. On every side, notices of mortgage and tax sales were going up" (Schlesinger 1957, 175). The urban poor suffered no less severely. "There is not a garbage dump in Chicago which is not diligently haunted by the hungry," wrote one reporter.

> Last summer, in the hot weather, when the smell was sickening and the flies were thick, there were a hundred people a day coming to one of the dumps, falling on the heap of refuse as soon as the truck pulled out and digging in it with sticks and hands. (Wilson 1958, 462)

The Great Depression, said that reporter, was an American earthquake. It knocked over the political party alignments that had governed the country since the Civil War and it leveled the American reluctance to create national welfare programs. It broke open the American style of federalism that had previously separated spheres of government responsibility—the national government attending almost exclusively to foreign trade, diplomacy, and national security; the states having charge of health, welfare, education, morals, and public safety (Herson 1990).

A new style of federalism emerged, one in which the national government dominates. Under this new federalism, the national government has come to assume responsibility for managing the nation's economy, supervising civil rights, regulating conditions of employment, protecting the environment,

---

"having turned a city agency into a racketeering enterprise for their own enrichment." The racketeering centered on a contract with the city, for $22.7 million, for "equipping the city's Parking Violations Bureau with hand-held computers for traffic agents to use in writing parking tickets" (Andy Logan, New Yorker, Jan. 5, 1987). And Los Angeles has thus far spent nearly $6 billion on its new subway system, making it the costliest public works project in the United States. Charges of corruption and mismanagement dog the project. With spending on so vast a scale, it is small wonder that there are more registered lobbyists at the project's headquarters than at the state capital (*Economist*, Aug. 5, 1995).

establishing safe standards for consumer products, and building a welfare society (Herson 1990, Miles 1976).

Under this new federalism, the national government has become increasingly involved with cities and with the people who live in them. Under the old federalism, cities were viewed by Congress and the courts as no more than creatures of the state, and the national government had almost no direct dealings with the cities. But since the 1930s and the new federalism, the national government has become an active participant in the government and politics of cities. Conversely, cities have become active participants in the workings of the national government.

This relatively new set of relationships between cities and the national government will be described in chapters that lie ahead. For now, it is useful to ask: What happened in the Great Depression to bring about these new relationships?

With the onset of economic hard times, the electorate followed its intuitions and acted out its traditional response to hard times. It voted the party in power out of office and swept a new party into power. From the Civil War onwards, the Republican party had been the dominant party in American political life. Now it was the Democrats' turn to govern. The election of 1932 brought a revitalized Democratic party to the center of the national political stage. That party drew its new strength from a new coalition. It was a fusion of traditional Southern, Protestant (and mostly rural) Democrats and the voters of the big cities—blacks, Jews, Catholics, blue-collar workers, and the children and grandchildren of former immigrants.

From now on, the key to winning the presidency would lie in the hands of voters in a dozen or so of the biggest cities and the largest metropolitan areas. Their voting strength would nearly dominate the Electoral College, and thus, those aspiring to be president would be forced to pay close attention to urban and suburban needs and demands. Henceforth, the problems of the city would make their way onto the agenda of the national government.

The Past Becomes the Present

Americans have always been ambivalent about their cities. The larger the city, the greater the ambivalence, the more divided the perception. We see the city as an instrument of progress and as creator of industrial and commercial wealth, a place of economic opportunity and a place that nurtures the arts. At the same time, we also see the city as a haven for crime, a place of congestion and physical decay, and a place whose scale and impersonal dealings are destructive of the human spirit.

These contradictory visions have a long history. To the Pilgrims and Puritans who came to the New World, all America was opportunity to build a New Jerusalem. "Come hither," preached Cotton Mather, "and I will show

you an admirable spectacle! 'Tis a Heavenly City . . . a city to be inhabited by
. . . Spirits of Just Men. . . . Oh! America, the Holy City!" And yet, negative
thoughts about the city have also been long with us. Some part of this wari-
ness may come from our religious traditions, for cities in the Old Testament
are depicted as places of depravity and sin. Another source of distrust may
come from our own history. Several of the founders of the American republic were mistrustful of the cities. Even as they framed the Constitution, they
could not forget that previous republics had been city-states and, as Hamilton
put it in *Federalist* 9, violence and political unrest in the city are always to be
feared:

> It is impossible to read the history of the petty republics of Greece and
> Italy without feeling sensations of horror and disgust at the distractions
> with which they were continually agitated, and at the rapid succession of
> revolutions by which they were kept in a state of perpetual vibration.
> (1961, 71)

Thomas Jefferson helped further this negative view of the city, for his
vision for a future America was one in which the farmer, working mostly
alone and always attuned to nature, would be calm and independent in his
political judgement, while city dwellers—too easily swayed by the opinions of
others and without property to give them a stake in the status quo—would
constitute a threat to the stability of our democracy (Griswold 1948, Ford
1914). Thus, as Lucia and Morton White (1977, 1) have said, we are nurtured
in an intellectual tradition that is notable for its anti-urban bias. "We have no
persistent or pervasive attachment to the city in our literature or in our philosophy."

No complex set of social and political forces ever has a single cause; yet,
it is difficult not to conclude that our ambivalence toward cities (what we
might call a "theory of ambivalent regard") contributes greatly to the dynamics of urban and suburban change: If our views and our emotions about cities
are mixed, then there is no consensus on what, if anything, we should do to
save them, and whether we should resist the constant tearing down of central
cities—sometimes in the name of progress, sometimes in the cause of economic profits—and the shift of business and people outward to the ever-
spreading suburbs. It is this same ambivalent regard that serves as backdrop for
the next chapter's exploration of urban politics. In that chapter, as in all the
chapters to follow, we shall see again how the past continues to shape the
future.

PART THREE

THE RULERS AND THE RULED

Old and New York, photogravure, 1910
Alfred Stieglitz Collection, 1949.854.

Politics in America is the binding secular religion.
   Theodore H. White, *Breach of Faith*

All politics is local politics.
   Thomas P. (Tip) O'Neill, *Man of the House*

CHAPTER 5

Political Rules
and Political Realities
in the City

An Extended Definition of Politics

As students of language know, the more important a word is in the lives of its users and the more frequently it is used, the more meanings it will acquire. *Politics* is a case in point. The term has acquired two long-standing meanings: the art and science of governing; and the struggle to dominate government and determine policy. These two meanings convey a variety of ideas, suggesting that politics is a process involving people, struggles, power, domination, and policies. Taken together, these terms convey an extended definition of politics as *a process or activity that has direct public consequences and that directly affects the public good*. The exact line dividing public and private good is difficult to pinpoint, and for guidance to its placement we turn to several contextual definitions of politics.

Webster's New Collegiate Dictionary (8th ed., 1979) defines *politics* in its first entry as "the art or science of government." Although this legalistic definition long dominated political science,[1] it has given way to a more anthro-

---

1. Even as late as 1957, Lawrence Herson's article arguing that the study of urban politics should entail something more than the study of municipal government (Herson 1957) met considerable resistance. About the same time, Charles Hyneman (1956, 26) stated that politics ". . . is that part of the affairs of state which centers in government, and that kind or part of government which speaks through law."

pomorphic view of politics (e.g., de Grazia 1965, Isaak 1984). More consistent with this changing view is another definition from *Webster's* which views politics as "the total complex of relations among men in a society." This definition, although too broad for our purposes, nonetheless has much to recommend it, for it implicitly recognizes that the process by which decisions are reached, whether by a family, a business firm, or a city council, is much the same. In each case, individuals interact, each attempting to persuade others to accept his or her position on an issue. And this process of interaction has four components that are central to an extended definition of politics: its human quality, its motivational basis, its ties to conflict, and its reliance on power.

Four Components of an Extended Definition of Politics

The human quality of politics. By emphasizing the importance of the individual in politics, definition moves beyond the conception that politics primarily reflects governmental institutions or laws. This emphasis does not suggest that individuals do not function politically as institutional representatives; as we will see, this is an important part of urban politics. Nor does it suggest that the institutional or legal resources used by individuals in their political activity are unimportant. Rather, it suggests that we may miss the essence of politics if we *simply* consider institutions without acknowledging the importance of the individuals who constitute them, or if we consider laws without acknowledging the importance of the individuals who pass and implement them (e.g., Van Dyke 1960).

Motives for political action. Emphasis on the individual leads to a consideration of the motives that underlie his or her political activity. Political activity never occurs in a vacuum. Rather, it is motivated by intertwined human needs and desires. A corollary of this proposition states that political activity is therefore purposive and usually rational. To understand its underlying rationality, however, we must understand the motives that drive an individual's political behavior. For example, the behavior of a mayor who denigrates his or her city may seem irrational if we assume a reelection motive; but it may be perfectly rational if he or she aspires to a higher political office (e.g., governor). And many seemingly irrational actions from an institution make perfectly good sense when examined in terms of the individuals who constitute that institution (e.g., Snyder et al. 1962).

Politics as conflict. A treatment of politics as conflictual (e.g., Wright 1950, Van Dyke 1960) implies that different individuals have different positions on any issue. This interpretation builds on the two previous components of politics, individuals and motives. Individuals, who are the essence of politics, come from different backgrounds and have different experiences, giving them different views of the world. *[The theory of ideology.]* Since their political behavior is purposive, that is, motivated by these different views, politics necessarily involves conflict.

Politics as the exercise of power. Our definition also treats politics as the exercise of power. Whenever conflict arises, power is necessarily involved in its resolution. This exercise of power may be subtle, as in the process of convincing others of the merit of one's own position. It may involve the legitimate ability to enforce compromise or call for a vote; or it may involve the invocation of formal authority (e.g., police, courts). It may be more blatant, involving coercive threats of physical or fiscal punishment or reward. But whatever its form, power is an inherent feature of human commerce. Since the Greeks, the concept of power has intrigued those who study politics, and it has found a place in many modern definitions of politics (e.g., Lasswell 1936, Easton 1953).

Public versus Private Action: The Zone of Demarcation

These definitions suggest that political activity does not differ from nonpolitical activity in form (i.e., individuals with various motives conflict and exercise power in both the public and the private sectors). However, political and nonpolitical activity differ in three *substantive* ways. First, political activity tends to be motivated by a desire to achieve a substantial reallocation of resources within some segment (or between segments) of society. Second, political activity tends to be systematic rather than random. And third, political activity affects (or at least has the potential to affect) the lives of the many rather than the few. Taken together, these three criteria form a *zone of demarcation* that separates private from public actions.

Resource allocation. The first criterion is the motivation underlying political activity: Politics is motivated by the desire to allocate or reallocate resources in society. The most obvious resource is money, and all activity involving public taxing and spending is clearly political. Other resources include knowledge, freedom, power, health, historical heritage, opportunity, and so forth. Based on this criterion, a number of activities typically associated with the private sector are political, including the following:

- The director of a community art center solicits contributions for art workshops.
- A neighborhood association protests the nearby location of a large factory.
- Concerned citizens protest the proposed demolition of an historic building.

71

• A private school board votes to fire a gay teacher.
• Black parents demand an Afrocentric curriculum in the schools.

Each of these cases represents the reallocation of an important public resource, and the action, no matter how private its intent, enters the public domain.

Systematic action. The second criterion holds that these actions must be systematic (i.e., part of a larger whole) rather than random. For example, we can imagine a number of actions that would seem to be guided by a logic of their own rather than by a systematic policy. A community garden club may decide to visit the gardens around Philadelphia rather than those around New York City, reflecting members' current preferences, based, for example, on a recent article about Longwood Garden in a national gardening magazine. By the same token, a local business firm may hire a white male instead of a black female for a particular job because he is better qualified. But if these decision rules become systematic policies, they *may* become political. For example, the Midwest Political Science Association's decision in the early 1980s to hold its annual meetings in Cincinnati and Milwaukee rather than Chicago may seem, on the face of it, to be no different from the garden club's decision to travel to Philadelphia. But the former was motivated by the systematic policy to boycott those states that had not ratified the Equal Rights Amendment (ERA), while the latter lacked any systematic rationale. By the same token, an employment policy giving preference to white males over females and minorities is systematic and therefore qualifies as political, whereas a single incident may be random and does not meet this criterion.

Size of impact. The third criterion for political activity is that it must directly affect the lives of a substantial segment of the population. This precludes a family's vacation decision, even if it is based on a systematic effort to distribute resources in society (e.g., "We will avoid Chicago because Illinois has not ratified the ERA"), or a builder's decision to construct a house of substandard material. But a builder's decision to construct an entire subdivision using substandard material may fall into the political realm because of its larger impact, its systematic character, and its impact on the distribution of public resources (e.g., safety). And the decision to locate a new retail shoe outlet in a community may not be political, but the decision to build a shopping mall is likely to be.

Rules of the political game: An introduction. Each of these criteria is somewhat fuzzy, and even when taken together, they provide only an approximate zone of demarcation between the political and the nonpolitical. But the distinction is important, for as activities or events, ostensibly private in nature, enter this zone, they are subject to a number of informal constraints, derived from democratic theory, that represent the "rules of the political game" (Truman 1951). Exactly how these norms were derived is unclear, although they appear to precede the founding of the republic (Tocqueville 1945, Dahl 1961, Dye and Zeigler 1975, Herson 1990). Their enforcement seems to be by "gentleman's agreement": Most people abide by the rules, and those who do not will likely incur the wrath of other participants (and occasionally, of the entire society). Most of us have accepted these norms, and our adherence to them has allowed democracy to flourish in the United States for over two hundred years.

The fact that these norms have guided politics in our society for more than two centuries does not, of course, mean that they have never been violated, for scandals are also a part of our political history. Cities are generally regarded as having violated our democratic norms the most. In the following sections, we will examine these informal norms in greater detail, exploring their role in urban politics.

Rules of the Political Game

Although a number of rules governing political behavior have been observed, we will concentrate on five, each with a long-standing tradition in American politics and each tied at least indirectly to democratic theory. These five norms are majority rule, protection of minority rights, participation, peaceful management of conflict, and the widespread distribution of political benefits.

Majority Rule

Majority rule is the best known and most sacred of our political norms. Democracy, by its nature, is rule by the people (from the Greek *demos*, meaning "people," and *cracy*, meaning "rule"). Democracy carries in its meaning the idea that all who participate in a decision shall participate on equal terms. Arguments must be settled and choices made by the one formula that provides for equal counting and the least contention concerning the terms and conditions of equal counting. That formula is majority rule.

Almost without exception, all voting and all public decision making in the United States are conducted through majority rule. Not only is the United States the oldest continuing democracy, it is also the one in which its citizens are asked to vote most often.[2] We elect public officials at every level of government—city, county, state, and national. Also, at the local level, we vote for bond issues and tax levies, and through the recall and referendum, the majority is able to dispose of unpopular legislators and legislation.

---

2. At the national level, the United States selects representatives to the lower house of Congress every 24 months, compared to an average of 28.8 months in Australia, 40.6 months in the United Kingdom, and 60 months in India. See Crewe (1981) for a discussion and other examples.

Minority Rights

Majority rule by itself cannot convey the full intent and meaning of democracy. Majorities can and do harm the minority that loses an election. The protection of minority rights is thus an equally important democratic norm. For example, the Declaration of Independence argues that humans are "endowed by their Creator with certain Unalienable Rights" that may not be infringed or curtailed by the majority.

Our political system attends to minority rights on every level of government. The U.S. Constitution, as well as those of the states, attempts to guarantee these rights. They provide for freedom of speech and press; they provide procedural safeguards for those accused of crimes; and they guarantee equal protection of all citizens under the law. If for no other reason, minority rights are important to a system of majority rule because a democracy does not consist of a single majority ruling for all time. It requires open and freely forming majorities, coming together and breaking apart on various issues. The only way to ensure that today's minority may become tomorrow's majority is to ensure that it has the opportunity to speak, argue, vote, and otherwise peacefully convince others to join it.

Peaceful Management of Conflict

The distinction between private violence and public violence has been maintained reasonably well in the United States for more than two centuries. On the private side, the violence of person against person is a common characteristic of American life, perhaps tolerated as an extension of our cultural commitment to individualism. Perhaps its roots lie in our history as a frontier society, in which western expansion was accomplished through conquest and war against the Indians, or perhaps these roots are located in the violence that was part of slaveholding and slavery. Whatever the reason, more murders per capita are committed in the United States than in any other Western industrialized society.[3] On the public side, however, the use of violence for political ends is generally unacceptable. Throughout our history, rebellions have been met with swift and decisive resistance, though the Civil War ground on through four terrible and bloody years.

---

3. The homicide rate for males in the United States is 12.7 per 100,000 people; other Western democracies with comparatively high rates include Northern Ireland (6.6), Israel (2.9), and Canada (2.7). Among all countries in the world, the United States ranks third in murders per capita among males, exceeded only by Puerto Rico and Paraguay (Rosenberg and Mercy 1991).

Participation

Participation in politics is essential to any democratic system: How else can new majorities form, the consent of the governed be realized, or representatives be informed about public wishes and desires? Participation in politics is celebrated as a civic virtue and an obligation of citizenship, and we are constantly reminded of that obligation.

In addition to overtly political participation (like voting), participation in civic activities is constantly solicited. Many urban residents are asked to volunteer time for a variety of community projects, including United Way campaigns, March of Dimes, and so forth. Significantly, many of those who enter local politics are attracted by their volunteer experiences in such community activities; more significant still, political candidates are often recruited from the ranks of those volunteers.

Widespread Distribution of Benefits

Unlike the legal and constitutional guarantees of majority rule and minority rights, this norm is an informal but nonetheless important component of our politics. It connects to the norms of minority rights (e.g., no loser ought to lose completely), and it probably derives from our traditions of a market society (business as an arrangement of freely negotiated contracts in which people are free to pursue their own interests to the best of their abilities).[4] In turn, this norm also connects to the norm of majority rule: Majorities form through coalitions and compromises, ensuring that all sides to a political issue emerge with some sense of benefit.

Of course, the norm of distributed benefits also connects to the peaceful management of public conflict, in that mollified participants do not usually engage in acts of violence. And it helps promote the expectation that politics involves fair play, which is achieved when all participants emerge from the political process better off for having participated.[5]

Rules of the Political Game Applied to Urban Politics

In several respects, the city is the place where democracy in America *ought to* flourish, and where these norms *ought* to receive greatest adherence. *[The theory of grass-roots democracy.]* After all, democracy had its earliest

4. In their defense of market economies, Friedman and Friedman (1981) argue that the liberty of economic contracts has been the historical source of democracy.
5. A variant of this logic has been formulated in economic and decision theory as Pareto optimality: A policy is Pareto optimal if it leaves no one worse off and at least one person better off.

American beginnings in the Pilgrim settlements of colonial New England, and subsequently in New England town meetings (Boorstin 1974, Tocqueville 1945, Mansbridge 1980). Moreover, urban government governs over a relatively small territory whose inhabitants often know through firsthand experience the issues of government and how those issues affect their daily lives. Democracy and democratic norms *ought* to flourish in the city if for no other reason than the fact that city voters have considerable opportunity to know both their officials and their fellow voters as neighbors.

But contrary to this expectation, the city is not the place where democracy has flourished in America. The style of city politics is different from the style of politics practiced at other levels of government; this difference springs largely from the fact that the rules of the political game are practiced differently in the city.

Most obviously, machine politics flourished for a very long time in our largest cities. Chapter 4 recounted the origins of that tradition—immigrant populations, their use of politics as a ladder to economic betterment, opportunities to use government spending for private advantage, and the ability of politicians to turn high population densities to their advantage through block-by-block and apartment-by-apartment control over voting.

And, historically, both large cities and small towns have violated what may be the most important democratic norm of all, that involving public violence. Riots, lynchings, and other forms of vigilantism—especially when intertwined with racial and ethnic repression—have been a recurring theme of urban and small-town history. Traditionally, these were treated as local problems and usually as acts of private violence. But in the 1960s, a rising public conscience combined with several long hot summers of urban violence to change the dominant view. Americans began to view such violence as public, bringing to bear not only condemnation but the full attention of the national government (National Advisory Commission on Civil Disorders 1968). More recently, the growing violence among young people, particularly African-American males living in inner cities, has reached epidemic proportions, and homicide now is the leading cause of death for young black males. This violence has, in some cases, spilled over from the inner city to surrounding areas to the point that the general urban population feels threatened. Like the riots of the 1960s, urban conflict and violence have crossed the threshold from private to public, and a political response has been mounted at all levels of government (Prothrow-Stith 1991).

Other, more contemporary factors also help explain the unique style of politics in the urban place. First, urban politics primarily addresses quality of life issues, about which most of us have strong opinions not readily subject to compromise. Partially because of the importance of these issues to our daily lives, urban conflicts are often emotional and bitter. Second, through voluntary, civic, and business associations, urban politics offers more avenues for political participation than those available at other levels of government. Third, the city is the level of government at which politics is usually practiced on a part-time basis. Fourth, and because of the part-time quality of urban politics, urban government has become government by administration. Fifth, power in the city tends to be concentrated in the private rather than the public sector. Sixth, private space and public space exist in close proximity, and appropriate uses for each tend to be confused and confusing. And finally, the city is comparatively less financially sound than are its state or national counterparts. We will now consider more closely these contemporary factors.

Quality-of-Life Issues

Even a cursory reading of the local section of most newspapers suggests the kinds of issues likely to concern most community residents. Typically, an article discusses the local school district. Another may concern the local police or fire department, or public parks. Particularly in smaller towns, a list of hospital admissions and discharges, as well as births and deaths, appears. Often these lists are accompanied by a story about newly acquired hospital equipment or new strategies in fighting disease. New businesses or industries that move to town always rate a story, often with a picture of the ribbon-cutting ceremony. Each week, a list of programs sponsored by the library, art center, or recreation department appears. And any contemplated zoning change or ordinance generates headlines.

The newspaper's repertoire of local articles is a reflection of residents' lives. While state, national, or international events are often of great interest and generate widespread debate, they seldom touch residents' lives *directly*. But local events are different, for they do affect the quality of residents' lives directly. Issues of local education directly affect their children's opportunity to get ahead in life, and many may feel the curriculum (e.g., evolutionary theories of biology, sex education) is contrary to religious beliefs or family values. The quality of local health care affects the life and death of urban residents, as may the quality of the local fire and police departments. Leisure time may be spent in a park, at local theaters or concert halls, at the public library, or shopping at a mall. Residents spend hours each week driving on roads they expect to be well maintained, negotiating traffic they expect to be well regulated. Their livelihoods depend on local jobs. And the biggest investment of their lives—their house—is protected by zoning regulations that prohibit apartment buildings, trailer parks, light industry, or shopping malls from being constructed next door.

In short, urban dwellers depend on the many things that urban life provides for them, and this very dependence tends to make them intolerant of change that might adversely affect the quality of their lives. *[The theory of lifestyle and territory.]* Given the importance of these issues, convictions are strongly held,

77

and compromise is difficult to achieve. Compromise may work well in homogeneous cities, where opinions about quality of life issues are shared. But politics becomes more difficult, and conflict more rancorous in heterogeneous cities where diverging views about what constitutes quality of life clash.[6]

Community Conflict

Students of urban politics note that a great deal of rancor often surrounds community conflicts. In one study, Robert Crain and his colleagues (1969) chronicled municipal decisions to fluoridate (or not fluoridate) water supplies. While this seems a tame issue today, it was anything but tame during the 1950s and 1960s, and it evoked hard-fought quality of life concerns. For the profluoridation forces, the concern was one of physical well-being: Parents wanted their children to have better teeth with fewer cavities. For the antifluoridation forces, concerns were more complex. One concern was philosophical, centering on the right of government to intrude into the daily lives of its citizens. Another concern was the potential risk of tampering with the city's water supply: Since a foreign substance was being introduced into the water, it would be easy for anyone who wanted to destroy the city (e.g., foreign agents or terrorists) to substitute some type of toxin for the fluoride, thus poisoning its inhabitants. A third concern was that fluoride is itself toxic, and that those drinking fluoridated water would suffer the physical and mental consequences of fluoride poisoning. Lewis Thomas (1983, 140), a noted medical critic and a member of the New York City Board of Health in the 1950s, views the fluoride debate from this perspective:

> The [public health] department viewed the prospect of fluoridation with zeal, for there was an opportunity to be professionally useful. The Board of Health passed the *pro forma* resolution mandating the installation of fluoridation, the mayor concurred, and then the roof began falling in. Public hearings were demanded by one after another civic group and their lawyers, protesting what was called an attempt to poison the public. . . . In its early stages and throughout the debates, the issue took on an ideological aspect which became increasingly bitter. At one long hearing, . . . the members of the Board of Health were accused by impassioned speaker after speaker of being Communists or tools of communism. In many parts of America, fluoridation was seen as a foreign plot to weaken the country, possibly by setting loose an epidemic of cancer.

It is easy to imagine how debate over the issue of fluoridation, which may have begun quite rationally, could have digressed into shouting and name

---

6. Note how this formulation contrasts with Bryce's view, discussed in chapter 4, that local politics is boring.

calling. For each side, the stakes were too high to acquiesce without a fight, and fights often followed.

An analysis of other major urban conflicts during the past four decades shows a similar pattern. Consider, for example, the stakes involved in controversies about suitable school textbooks or library books. On one side are parents (and other concerned citizens) who are offended that their children are subjected to what they view as pornographic or unpatriotic material, or material that runs contrary to their moral or religious values (e.g., biology texts that stress theories of evolution over those of creationism or novels, such as Steinbeck's *The Grapes of Wrath*, that use profanity). On the other side are those parents (or concerned citizens) offended by the intrusion of religious teachings into public education, or who desire to offer their children a wide range of literary experiences. The image of books being thrown into bonfires suggests the emotions that run rampant around this issue and of the unwillingness of either side to compromise.

Court-ordered school busing is another issue on which emotions have run high (adults in South Boston tossing stones at a school bus loaded with children suggests the intensity of the emotions; see Lukas 1985). So, too, is the construction of group homes for the mentally retarded or the mentally ill in neighborhoods, or the construction of low-cost housing for the poor in middle-class neighborhoods, or the use of parks by homeless people. Even seemingly noncontroversial issues, like the construction of a shopping mall, can create considerable and bitter conflict, with each side accusing the other of attempting to destroy the community as a viable shopping area.

Participation

A third area in which urban politics is qualitatively different from that of other levels of government is the opportunity for, and the level of, political participation. On the one hand, the city offers an abundance of opportunities for the individual to participate. In a study of participation in a twenty-square-block area of Manhattan's lower east side, for example, Yates (1977) found no fewer than two hundred different participatory organizations such as churches and social clubs. Even in less populous places, the typical citizen may participate in local politics through such organizations as Rotary or Kiwanis, political parties, neighborhood associations, various ad hoc citizen groups, formally constituted citizen advisory committees, and by voting. In light of these opportunities, individuals with very little political ambition may find themselves in positions of local leadership and be recruited to run for local political office (city council, school board). In contrast, participation in state and national politics is limited for most people to voting and to signing petitions.

In spite of these opportunities to participate, however, political participation in most cities falls far short of its potential. Voter turnout in local elections typically is far lower than in state and national elections. While something over 50 percent of registered voters turn out in presidential elections, probably no more than one-third of registered voters actually vote in non-concurrent local elections (Lineberry and Sharkansky 1978). Further, a number of nationwide trends and social forces reduce the proclivity for urban political participation (Bolland 1984). Consider the following changes in urban life.

Social trends affecting urban political participation. First, the average family has turned inward. Since the 1950s, television has become an important part of most people's lives, and the time the "typical American" spends in front of the TV has risen to nearly seven hours daily. For many people, television has become a substitute for interaction with neighbors as well as participation in community activities. This withdrawal is accentuated by the changing style of urban residential architecture. Houses built before World War II typically displayed large front porches that looked out onto the sidewalk and its pedestrian traffic. But since the Second World War, the privacy of the back patio has replaced the public accessibility of the front yard.

Second, the growing fear of crime has also caused people to turn inward. We are all familiar with the stories, whether apocryphal or not, about the "old days" when homeowners left their homes unlocked when they went away for the weekend. Today, those same people express concern about walking outside at night for fear of being mugged. Objective measures of crime tell only part of the story, although the story they tell is revealing: The crime rate has increased sixfold since 1960. More important, fear of crime is increasing at an even more rapid rate. This fear, which has become an obsession for many urban residents, breaks down trust among neighbors and turns residents inward rather than outward toward their community (Wilson 1975).

Third, more women participate in the labor force than ever before. In 1960, only one-third of married women participated in the labor force, compared with nearly one-half in 1980. This increase is most dramatic for women with children under six years of age, leading American families to change child-care patterns. Not only do more children need day care, but care is more frequently given outside the home (Lueck, et al. 1982). In 1958, more than half the children of mothers with full-time paying jobs were cared for in their own homes; by 1977, that figure had declined to 25 percent. In the past, mothers and children provided the social glue that held neighborhoods together, creating the opportunity for contact and social support. But today, fewer women are around the neighborhood by day, and working parents are often too preoccupied to venture away from home at night. The result is the deterioration of the neighborhood as a cohesive social unit in urban America.

Fourth, the out-migration from the inner city to the suburbs, a trend that actually began in the nineteenth century, continues unabated. The two-car garage is as much a cliché of suburbia as the split-level house, and with good reason: Virtually nothing is within walking distance, and most suburbs are poorly served by mass transit. As a result, suburbanites drive wherever they go, substantially reducing the opportunity for social contact among neighbors.

Fifth, the American family has undergone a great transition during the past two decades. A high divorce rate and the rise of alternative living arrangements have generated a sense of informality and transience in many households. In 1960, nonfamily households accounted for only 15 percent of all households; by 1980, this figure had risen to over 25 percent. This trend is accompanied by a substantial decline in the number of traditional (husband-wife) households, down from 74 percent in 1960 to 62 percent in 1978. The reduced stability of the typical household attenuates its attachment to the neighborhood and community and reduces participation in the community.

Sixth, the pattern of ownership of commercial retail businesses has changed dramatically since 1960. In the early 1960s, nationally franchised fast-food restaurants were built in virtually every American city, rapidly followed by nationally owned discount department stores. During this period, the sub-urban shopping mall also caught the fancy of the American shopper, and lit-erally thousands were built across the United States by 1975; typically only a third of the stores in these malls are locally owned, with the remainder being regionally or nationally owned chains.[7] This shift has resulted in a reduced commitment among a city's economic sector to the social well-being of the community, and a reduced tendency for that sector to become involved in local politics.

These trends toward nonparticipation are, no doubt, more pronounced in some areas of the country than in others. Their effect is likely to be great-est in suburban areas and middle-sized cities. Given the demographic trend toward suburbanization, nonparticipation is likely to become even more com-mon.

Part-Time Politics

Part-time politics is another distinguishing characteristic of urban political life. At the national and state levels, the chief executive and legislators hold full-time (or at least part-time) salaried positions. But with the exception of per-haps only several dozen cities, mayoral and city council positions carry only a nominal salary. Elected officials must also hold full-time jobs. In small and middle-sized cities, the mayor may be a lawyer, a banker, a physician, a hard-ware salesperson, or a land developer. Members of the city council typically have similar jobs. As a result, even the most civic-minded members of the

---

7. This rough estimate was derived with the assistance of the chambers of com-merce in several cities.

governing body cannot commit themselves completely to the task of governing. Instead, they rely on the city staff, and in reformed cities on the city manager, to provide them with information and implement their decisions.

In principle, the manager or administrator is subordinate to the governing body and serves at its pleasure. But seldom is the distinction between politics and administration as clear-cut as this principle presupposes. In reality, the city administrator typically has considerable influence in formulating policy, often more than that of the council he or she serves. Two factors account for this discrepancy between principle and practice. First, as a full-time employee, the administrator develops an expertise concerning the intricacies of city government that dwarfs that of council members; this leads them to defer to his or her judgment about the soundness and appropriateness of many policies. Second, in the implementation of policies handed down by the council, the administrator typically is given considerable discretion. This allows the administrator to interpret policies in accordance with his or her preferences. These factors are discussed in greater detail in the next chapter. In the interim, however, we will consider briefly the asymmetry of the relationship between the administrator (or city manager) and the council.

Administrative expertise and discretion. As head of the municipal bureaucracy, the city administrator is its most visible employee. Local newspaper articles often quote the administrator as a city spokesperson, and he or she is often visible at public events. Although this may prove time-consuming for the administrator, it also provides a window to the city that council members often lack. And citizens often contact the city administrator rather than council members about municipal problems, such as garbage collection. As a result, the administrator often develops a much better understanding of the community, its aspirations, and its concerns than does the council elected to serve it. In addition, many administrators have graduate degrees in public administration or management science, providing them with a foundation in budgeting, personnel management, and other management skills (e.g., cost-benefit analysis). This background, coupled with frequent discussion with department heads, allows the administrator to gain expertise about the city and its government rapidly.

This expertise provides the administrator with considerable influence in urban policy making, for council members typically defer to him or her for information, advice, and ideas. Although the council has the final say on policy issues (including whether or not to retain the administrator), the administrator typically sets the agenda by identifying the problems that need to be addressed by the council. And, in turn, the administrator typically provides the council with background information, possible solutions, and other advice concerning these issues. In short, all that is left to the council is action on the administrator's recommendations.

Even if the city council takes a more active role in formulating policy, the administrator retains considerable influence in the policy process, due largely to the discretion typically accorded him or her by the council in implementing its decisions. *[The theory of urban administration.]* Every municipal department uses discretion in implementing decisions enacted by the council: the police must decide when, where, and how to enforce the city's traffic code; building inspectors must decide if a minor violation of the city's building code is sufficient to scuttle a project; the tax collector must decide how hard to pursue delinquent taxes. In all cases, these departments fall under the purview of the city's chief administrative officer, who works with department heads to develop appropriate guidelines to flesh out—and ultimately to give meaning to—municipal ordinances.

Government by Administration

A change in the style of governance has accompanied the increasing power acquired by full-time urban administrators. The natural metier of the full-time politician is the provision of individualized services to those in need, often in implicit exchange for votes. (During the days of the machine, this involved provision of food, clothing, and shelter to new immigrants.) At the national and state levels, this provision of services involves finding ways to accomplish feats that are beyond the ability of the individual constituent. But this style of politics is time consuming, and the politician must either have time to spare or a staff able to perform these services. In today's city, most politicians have neither. As part-time politicians and full-time professionals (or salaried employees), they have little residual time to help needy constituents. And while the city government does hire a staff, staff members typically report to the full-time administrator (who has no need to garner votes through the delivery of personalized services) rather than to the elected officials.[8] As a result, the style of service delivery has changed in important but not altogether anticipated ways.

The first change has been in the direction of collective benefits. Cities have moved toward the provision of services designed to benefit the *typical* city resident rather than those that benefit specific, identifiable residents. For example, services such as recreation, education, public safety, and street maintenance provide benefits to all residents in roughly equal amounts. In contrast, the provision of food and shelter to the poor, political opportunity to the newly arrived, and jobs to the unemployed (all of which the city once delivered through the political machine) imparts benefits to selected individuals (or at least selected classes). In later chapters, these different approaches are discussed as *distributive* and *redistributive*, respectively.

8. In some larger cities, this seems to be changing somewhat, with staff assigned to council members. But in the vast majority of cities, this generalization remains true.

The second change has been in the direction of greater economic efficiency. This should not be surprising, given the academic backgrounds of many city administrators: They are taught to run the city as a business. Nor is it surprising, given the financial straits in which most cities find themselves (the urban fiscal crisis is discussed more fully in chapters 13 and 14). The dominant model governing economic efficiency is cost-benefit analysis, wherein a policy is deemed effective if its derived benefit outweighs its total cost. In the absence of a better unit of measurement, administrators often weigh costs and benefits in monetary terms. Thus, policies are designed to maximize the return on investment, or to use a popular political phrase, to provide the "biggest bang for the buck." For example, in deciding where to locate a new crosstown highway, decision-makers may attempt to maximize flow of traffic per dollar spent on construction. By considering monetary factors in assessing traffic flow and construction costs, decision makers are likely to discover that the most economical distance between two points is a straight line along which (a) the most people with the highest incomes can get to work most quickly and (b) the cost of condemning land is least expensive. As a result, new commuter highways are typically constructed through older, low-income neighborhoods, with a great social cost to these neighborhoods but a collective economic benefit to the city. Further, new highways are likely to be constructed so as to provide easy access to more affluent neighborhoods, since the salaries of residents in these neighborhoods (and their costs of commuting) are larger than those of residents in low-income neighborhoods. In short, politics by administration carries with it a middle- and upper-class bias that potentially threatens the protection of minority rights.

Private Power versus Public Power

Another distinction between urban politics and politics at the state and national levels involves the *locus* of political power. *[The theory of influence.]* In offering this distinction we enter a domain of considerable controversy. Put in its baldest form, the controversy involves a single question: Is power distributed equitably among the electorate, or is it concentrated in the hands of an elite few? An entire book could be devoted to this question, for it has generated a considerable literature, and its implications for democratic theory are profound. For now, we will merely touch on the issue of power; but we shall return to it in greater depth in chapter 8. Our conclusions can be summarized as follows: Whereas state and national power tends to be concentrated in the hands of those who hold public (and quasi-public) positions, local power tends to be concentrated in the hands of those in the private sector. This makes state and national politics more responsive than city politics to broad-based citizen input.

Admittedly, this conclusion contradicts several persuasive analyses of power in America. For example, C. Wright Mills asserts, in his provocative study, that, at every level of government, America is dominated by a power elite, a relatively small group of people "who are in position to make decisions having major consequences" (1956, 4). These people, continues Mills,

> are in command of the major hierarchies and organizations of modern society. They rule the big corporations. They run the machinery of the state and claim its prerogatives. They direct the military establishment. They occupy the strategic posts of the social structure in which are now . . . centered the power and the wealth.

It is true, of course, that a small portion of our society owns a disproportionate share of its wealth. And it is also true that the business community occupies a privileged position in this and every other market society, for it is the transactions of the market that drive the economy (Lindblom 1977). But to say that the business community has a position of privilege is not to say that it masters and dominates the larger society. The wealth of America may be generated by market transactions, but those transactions are both facilitated by governmental policies and subject to governmental regulation at both the national and the state levels.[9]

This regulation is largely lacking at the local level, however, giving individuals from the private sector substantial political power. The city, in effect, is an aggregate of small economic units, ranging from corporate headquarters and manufacturing plants, to small shops and businesses, to individual households. Taken by themselves, decisions made by any of these units may be of only marginal importance to the city's economy. In the aggregate, however, they may affect the city in profound ways.

The importance of individual economic decisions is easy to understand in the case of a corporate decision to move its headquarters or a manufacturing plant into or out of a city, upon which hundreds of jobs and millions of dollars of municipal tax revenues may ride. But how can a local clothier's decision to close his or her store affect the city in anything resembling a profound manner? And even more so, how can a family's decision to buy or sell a house affect the city's well-being?

---

9. At the national level, virtually all major industries are subject to considerable regulation and government control, even in an era of deregulation. As one example, the defense establishment is largely dependent on those who hold public positions (i.e., the president, Congress). The banking industry provides a second example. Although banks can influence the national economy through their investment decisions, the Federal Reserve Board largely controls these decisions through its regulation of monetary flows. And we find a third example in the construction industry, where tax deductions for homeowners are used as a tool to stimulate building and buying. In short, the private sector is just as dependent on government as government is on it, and a kind of equilibrium exists between the two sectors of society. This provides at least indirect accountability to the public in most political decisions (defined broadly) made at the national and state levels.

The answer lies partly in the psychological realm, but that makes its implications no less real. *[The theory of commodification of land and buildings.]* When a downtown merchant packs up his or her wares and moves to another location, two things happen. First, an unattractive (and psychologically troubling) void is left in the downtown: Dark, or even worse, boarded-up windows decorated with "for lease" signs provide a stark contrast to an otherwise bright and busy area. Second, shoppers who would have visited downtown to purchase goods from the now-vacant store take their business elsewhere. This can have an important spillover effect on nearby businesses, which counted on purchases by the now-absent shoppers. (Most downtown businesses count on a "spree" style of shopping, expecting shoppers who come into the shopping area for one purpose to also visit other stores and perhaps purchase something that catches the eye.) A strong downtown shopping area can survive a vacant building, and another business may soon locate there. But if other businesses are barely surviving financially, even a small decline in sales may force them to move also, leading to further decline. This "tipping point" is quite low, and the commercial viability of a downtown area may be in jeopardy when as few as 6 percent of the businesses have been abandoned (cf. Skogan 1990). It is no wonder business owners become nervous when one of their neighbors closes its doors and boards its windows, and that they feel relieved when a new business moves in.

Business and industry are not usually dependent on local government for their financial well-being; hence, they are free to pack up and move to another city, where they expect bigger sales, or lower taxes, or workers willing to work for lower wages. In fact, other cities are only too eager to invite new businesses to town, and they often offer tax and other incentives (e.g., Watson 1995). But rather than making the business or industry dependent on city government, these incentives merely demonstrate governmental dependence on the private sector. This dependence gives the business or industry substantial leverage in working with city government, and governmental officials are very attentive to the suggestions of business owners concerning such issues as parking areas, street maintenance, police or fire protection, and garbage collection. And this connection to city hall in turn gives the private business owner considerable political power.

This dependence is perhaps most pronounced in the case of the local land developer, an individual (or company) who develops property for residential or commercial use. This is the person who builds housing subdivisions and apartment complexes, shopping centers, and malls. He or she supports the local economy during construction by purchasing building materials and employing laborers. He or she also entices retailers to occupy the newly constructed stores. In short, the land developer invests capital into the community, and through this investment, he or she expects (and usually receives) access to city hall to discuss perceived problems in the city.

Even the individual household plays an important role in this local economic ecology. An empty house in a neighborhood reduces property values for other houses in the neighborhood ever so slightly; a number of vacant houses in a neighborhood reduces them dramatically. The individual home-owner's decision to buy or sell therefore has implications beyond his or her immediate pocketbook. While this impact is likely to be minimal in newer neighborhoods (someone is likely to buy and occupy the vacant house before *too* long), it is much more important in older and inner-city neighborhoods. An individual willing to move into and renovate an inner-city residence may literally be able to change the course of history in the neighborhood (after all, the herding instinct of humans is quite strong; after someone has demonstrated the economic viability of such a move, others may follow). These early inner-city homesteaders are likely to become well-known at city hall, and they often receive incentives for their bold actions. This, too, represents a kind of power that simply is not found at the national or state political levels.

One other factor affects the distribution of power within local politics: the "nonpolitical" form of many urban governmental units. Specifically, two characteristics of urban reform contribute to the concentration of power in the private sector. The first is the *nonpartisan* nature of reformed governments; the second is *at-large representation.*

At the national and state levels, considerable political power rests in the hands of the Democratic and Republican party organizations. While not for-mally within the public sector, these organizations can be viewed as "quasi-public," in that they are ultimately accountable to the same voters who elect and unseat public officials. At the local level, however, reformed governments tend to be divorced from the local political party organizations, leaving a power void. *[The theory of urban reform.]* This void often has been filled by pri-vate business interests.

At the national and state levels, every voter has his or her representative in Congress; and the voter is encouraged to believe that the representative has his or her interests in mind during each legislative vote. This system helps generate a sense of voter allegiance, and with it, a substantial amount of power in the legislative office. But in local reformed governments, city council mem-bers are often elected at-large, representing the city as a whole (and its inter-ests) rather than particular groups of people. Allegiances are much less tangi-ble in this situation, and the power of the at-large council is more ambiguous. This, in turn, gives considerable power to both the city administrator and to local business interests (which again fill the void).

Private Space versus Public Space

In addition to a distinction between public and private power, there is also in the city an important tension surrounding the private use of public space and the public use of private space. This same tension surfaces from time to time at other levels of government, for instance, when the federal government sells mineral rights or timber rights to national forests. But it has become an almost daily issue in cities. Private use of public land is perhaps best exemplified by restrictive ordinances passed in some cities governing access to sidewalks, parks, and streets for the purpose of sleeping, resting, or soliciting. For example, Seattle's antibegging laws make it illegal to interfere with pedestrian traffic. As another example, New York City laws make it illegal to sleep in subway stations, subway cars, or train stations, and at least four California cities have passed laws making it illegal to sleep in any public place (Stoner 1995). Finally, many cities have evicted homeless people from under bridges and overpasses where they had been staying, citing either ordinances against sleeping in public spaces or issues of safety and sanitation for their actions.

The tension surrounding appropriate private use of public space is not limited to concern about the homeless. It has also surfaced around issues of street vendors and street entertainers. For example, in New York City merchandise vendors are banned by municipal law from the business districts, from sidewalks less than 12 feet wide, from places within 20 feet of the entrance of a building, and from many other areas; in other words, they are banned from almost every public place. Street entertainers are also banned if (a) they are very loud, (b) the sidewalk is obstructed, or (c) they solicit money from their audience (Whyte 1988). Merchants have been the main force against street entertainers and street vendors, arguing that they hurt business. In short, the question comes down to the kinds of private use of public space a city is willing to tolerate and the kinds it feels will infringe on the rights of its citizens to enjoy the city's amenities and the rights of its merchants to make an appropriate profit. [The theory of lifestyle and territory.]

On the other side of the coin are questions about the public use of private space, also an issue unique to cities. Most notable here is the use of malls for political purposes, such as protests and rallies. During their early development, many suburban malls were initiated into political conflict when they were asked for space by activists to conduct rallies and demonstrations protesting the Vietnam War. Some of these erupted in violence, for example, in Detroit's Northland Mall during the Christmas season of 1969, severely disrupting retail sales. Many mall owners responded to this experience by banning political rallies and protests altogether, an action that was upheld by the United States Supreme Court in 1972; the Court ruled that the shopping center is not a public place, and property does not lose its private character just because the public is invited in. But the Court modified this view in 1980, ruling that state constitutions determine whether malls can be used to pass out leaflets and to get signatures on petitions. This lead to suits in a number of state courts, with some (e.g., Washington, California, and Massachusetts) ruling that these activities were constitutional but others (e.g., Connecticut, Michigan, and New York) ruling that they were not (Frieden and Sagalyn 1989).

Financial Security

A final comparison between politics at the urban level and politics at the state and national levels involves the relative financial standing of various governmental units. Government at the national level tends to be rather well-to-do, even in these times of fiscal cutback. This results at least partially from its ability to incur deficits to finance its day-to-day operations, a luxury from which its poorer cousins at the local level are legally prohibited. In addition, federal revenues represent the incomes of the wealthiest people across the country, from cities as well as rural areas, from businesses as well as individuals. State income suffers somewhat, but not much, in comparison. Some states are more wealthy than others; but even in the poorest states, a number of wealthy individuals and corporations reside. At the poorest end of the spectrum lie the big cities, whose inhabitants are typically among the poorest and whose financial responsibilities are typically the greatest.

In recent years, the federal government has made massive cuts in domestic expenditures, most of which previously had gone, in one form or other, to the cities. States have stepped in to fill some of the void, but much of it remains unfilled. As a result, competition for existing tax dollars has grown fierce, even more so than at the other levels of government. At least for the present, the politics of compromise in urban politics seems to be giving way to the game of political hardball, where "winner takes all." As the resource pie continues to shrink, its smaller and smaller pieces will become less and less acceptable, and urban interest groups will become more willing to risk receiving nothing in order to chance the possibility of receiving a sizable chunk of that pie. In short, rancorous politics is likely to increase at the expense of widely distributive politics, where everyone is a winner.

Urban Politics and Democratic Norms: A Theory of Political Style

We began this chapter with an extended definition of politics which, in turn, opened the door to two related topics: the connection between democratic norms and the practice of politics, and the connection between urban life and democratic norms. Both topics, in turn, converge on a third topic—the ways in which the style of urban politics differs from the style of politics at other levels of government.

Urban life alters the way in which democratic norms constrain the practice of politics. And this alteration helps account for the ways in which the style of urban politics differs from the style of politics at other levels of American government. It is a style marked by business domination and the

89

policy dominance of professional administrators, both of which constrict the norms of majority and minority rights. It is a style marked by low participation, both formal and informal. It is a style often marked by acrimonious conflict. And it is a style influenced by declining resources, which, in turn, may further constrict the norm of widespread benefit through participation. To explore still further the style of contemporary urban politics, we turn now to its institutional context: the forms of city government and the formal participants in the urban political process.

The Terminal, photogravure, 1892, 25.4 x 33.7 cm
Alfred Stieglitz Collection, 1949.848.
Photograph © 1996, The Art Institute of Chicago. All Rights Reserved.

The excitement of politics got into my veins . . . I knew I had to say "no," but seldom could bring myself to say it.

James Walker,[1] quoted in *Beau James,* by Gene Fowler

CHAPTER 6

Forms of Municipal Government and Formal Participants in the Urban Political Process

This chapter considers the formal participants in the urban political process. These include members of the city's elected governing body, the professional bureaucracy it employs, and the volunteer boards and commissions it appoints. These also include other elected officials, for instance the city clerk and municipal judge. We will attend carefully to several aspects of these positions: the personal characteristics of the individuals likely to hold them, their motives for seeking and maintaining the positions, their motives for actions taken in their positions, and the potential for conflict inherent in the positions. But before examining these features of formal political participation (and participants) in the city, we must distinguish among different municipal governmental structures, for these, too, impinge on the politics that is practiced in the city.

---

1. James Walker was known as the "whoopee mayor" of New York in the 1920s. His inability to say "no" seemingly extended to taking bribes.

An Inventory of Municipal Governmental Structures

As suggested in chapter 4, the history of the large city in America is marred by corruption. Corruption occurred primarily under the mayor-council format, particularly where the powers of the mayor were weak. The weak-mayor format left a power vacuum, with no single member of the governing body sufficiently strong to counteract the corrupting force of the political machine, where true power was concentrated. In an attempt to conquer corruption in municipal government, reformers proposed three structural modifications to municipal government. First, they proposed strengthening the power of the mayor within the mayor-council format. Second, they sometimes proposed combining the political and administrative functions of government into a commission. And most dramatically (and as their preferred solution), they proposed placing administrative responsibility in the hands of a city manager, leading to a council-manager structure. In what follows, we consider the features of the original weak-mayor format as well as those of each of the three modifications, their prevalence in American cities today, the functions they serve for various types of cities, and their strengths and weaknesses.

Weak-Mayor Plan

Under the weak-mayor plan, the electorate typically elects council members, who in turn select one among themselves to be mayor for (typically) a one-year term. In some cities, all council seats are up for election every two or four years. More commonly, members serve four-year terms, with terms staggered so that roughly half of the seats are up for election every two years. But as varied as the election procedures may be, all cities governed under this plan have one thing in common: The mayor has no formal powers beyond those of other members of the council. He or she is responsible for presiding over council meetings, is often quoted in the newspaper as a community spokesperson, and performs numerous civic duties (e.g., ribbon cuttings) spared other members of the council. But these ceremonial powers do not extend to city governance, where the mayor is merely first among equals. His or her vote counts the same as that of each other council member, and the mayor cannot veto legislation, set the agenda for council meetings, or hire and fire city staff.

In the weak-mayor plan, the council is responsible for formulating and passing legislation that guides the city. In addition, the council hires department heads (e.g., parks and recreation director, community development director, fire chief and so on), who serve at its pleasure. This plan also provides citizens the opportunity to elect a number of other administrative officials. But exactly which positions are elected and which are appointed by the council vary greatly from city to city. Adrian and Press (1977) reported that 29 percent of cities elect their treasurer, 24 percent elect their clerk, and 13 percent elect their tax assessor.

When administrators are elected rather than appointed by the council, the council's power is considerably weakened. Elected administrators are free to pursue their own agendas without fear of interference from the council, and the position of the council as the central (and technically, the only) policy-making body in the city is thus diluted. No one is clearly in charge. However, even in weak-mayor cities the percentage of administrative positions that are elected has been declining over time. In 1936, 70 percent of those cities with over 5,000 residents elected at least one administrative officer; by 1966, only 48 percent did so. During the same period, the number of cities electing police chiefs declined by over 50 percent (Adrian and Press 1977).

The weak-mayor plan is typically found in small cities, where it is consistent with a general skepticism of both politicians and of government itself. By spreading power, this arrangement keeps any one officeholder from becoming "too big for his or her britches." It is also consistent with the small-town ethos of civic responsibility, for the weak-mayor plan demands that public office be spread around the citizens of the community. Indeed, it is not uncommon for a small town to have had more than thirty different mayors, and more than one hundred and fifty total elected officials, during the past half century.

The weak-mayor plan has much to offer the small city. Politics becomes synonymous with civic responsibility, and the town is governed by friends and neighbors, each pitching in to do his or her share. The concept of the professional politician, or even the professional municipal administrator, is anathema to many small towns and their citizens, who would prefer to keep control of the city's administration in the hands of aldermanic committees. But as urban problems have become common to the small cities, amateur politics and amateur politicians may no longer be practical. For example, municipal liability for traffic accidents caused by malfunctioning traffic signals or alleged police brutality may demand a city attorney trained in municipal law rather than one who can appeal to the most voters. Increasing crime may require professionally trained police administrators. And the demands of economic development may require a politically minded mayor, one who is able to mobilize the community (or at least its economic sector), even if that means that he or she gains additional power in the process.

Even though the weak-mayor plan is most common in small cities, it can also be found in several middle-sized cities, particularly in the South. This may be cultural, for southerners are traditionally more conservative than their northern counterparts, a conservatism made manifest in suspicion of big (and powerful) government.

Strong-Mayor Plan

The increasing complexity of the city during the last quarter of the nine-teenth century, coupled with the municipal corruption that seemed to flour-ish under the weak-mayor plan, brought calls for reform in the structure of municipal government, particularly in the large cities. During this period, four inventions helped add physical miles to the diameter of large cities (e.g., Kingsbury 1895)[2]: the modern bicycle (1885), the trolley (1873), the tele-phone (1876), and the automobile (1885). With the advent of these conve-niences, people no longer needed to live within walking distance of employ-ment and friends; rather they could communicate and be transported over substantial distances with little effort. Many opted for the good life in the hin-terlands, not far from the center of town by today's standards, but away from the hustle and bustle and pollution of the central city by turn-of-the-century standards (Jackson 1985, Warner 1972). But with urban expansion came the need for better administrative coordination, something the weak-mayor form of government was unable to provide.

Other developments during this same period further demonstrated the complexity of the urban environment and brought demands for even more administrative coordination. For example, the steam fire engine received wide-spread use in the Chicago fire of 1871, and for the first time the municipal fire department served a functional rather than a symbolic purpose. Now cities could actually expect to win their battles with fires rather than just fight to limit damage. But with this advance also came a change from a volunteer fire department to a professional fire department in many cities and an attendant need for increased administrative coordination. The advent of the automobile and the police call box made possible a truly mobile police force, but it also brought the need for better administrative coordination.

In general, technological changes brought with them increased com-plexity, and increased complexity brought the need for stronger administrative offices capable of providing better coordination. The easiest (and least radical) way to achieve this end was to strengthen the position of mayor, providing him or her with control over the urban bureaucracy and a position of leader-ship on the city council. Unlike a weak mayor, a strong mayor is always elected separately from the rest of the council, providing an unambiguous delineation of power and authority. The strong mayor not only runs council meetings, he or she typically sets the agenda for these meetings and usually has the power to veto legislation passed by the council.[3] Also unlike the weak-mayor plan, administrative positions are almost never elective under the strong

2. Kingsbury's reference is reported in Banfield (1974).
3. Like the weak-mayor plan, there exist many variations on the strong-mayor for-mat; this discussion portrays a "typical" city, even though no existing city may have every one of these features.

mayor plan. Rather, the mayor has the authority to appoint department heads (who, in turn, are responsible for hiring staff); and he or she has the authority to fire them as well, often without even having to show cause. The strong mayor typically has a full-time position, even in smaller cities, and is paid a higher salary than other members of the council. (Council positions, in all but the largest of cities, are typically part-time or unpaid positions.)

Under the strong-mayor plan, the mayor emerges as the clear administrative and policy leader for the city. Although he or she is expected to perform a number of ceremonial duties, these are mixed with other responsibilities that carry with them a great deal of power. Since the mayor is able to appoint municipal department heads, he or she can build a team of administrators who share a common conception of municipal purpose and who are, therefore, able to work together. This results in a greater potential for coordinated services than is possible under the weak-mayor plan, where high-level administrators are either appointed by committee (i.e., the council) or elected by the voters. Under the strong-mayor plan, the mayor is the focal point of municipal government, and he or she can command credit for successful policies and is subject to blame for unsuccessful policies. The strong-mayor plan also places the mayor in a position of extreme pressure in dealing with various interests in the city. The mayor's veto power leads various citizen groups and economic interests to make constant demands on him or her. As a result, the strong mayor makes many friends as well as enemies, and it is only the astute mayor who can manage to hold office for several terms.

Although a number of cities are considered to have strong-mayor plans, almost none has adopted the model in toto. The plan is found most often in larger cities, including Baltimore, Boston, Cleveland, New York, Pittsburgh, and St. Louis. But some large cities with a strong-mayor plan have greatly restricted the power of the mayor. Perhaps the most interesting case is Chicago. Until his death, Richard J. Daley was arguably the most powerful mayor this half-century has witnessed. Yet, Daley's power derived not from the office of mayor but rather from his position as the head of the Cook County Democratic organization (the "Chicago Machine"). The actual limits to the power of the mayor in Chicago have become clear since Daley's death, with subsequent mayors having little success in pursuing their political agendas. The weakness of the mayor's office became particularly apparent in the administration of Harold Washington, Chicago's first black mayor. In the 1983 Democratic mayoral primary, Washington ran against the incumbent mayor, Jane Byrne,[4] and the machine candidate, Richard M. Daley, the former mayor's son, beating both; he subsequently defeated Republican Bernard Epton in the general election. But Washington was consistently outvoted in

4. In 1979, Byrne had run against and beaten machine candidate Michael Bilandic during the Democratic primary.

97

the city council by a coalition of machine and Republican aldermen during the first years of his term, and his policy initiatives were largely ineffective. Not until 1986, following court-ordered redistricting, did Washington's supporters achieve a majority on the Chicago City Council.[5] In 1989, Richard M. Daley was elected mayor. This marked the first time since his father's reign that a Chicago mayor has been in general agreement with the council (albeit the agreement is not as strong as it was under Richard J. Daley); and with the support of the council, the second Mayor Daley was able to enact fiscally conservative measures to combat declining municipal resources (Miranda 1992, Pinderhughes 1994).

No statistics differentiate between weak and strong mayors, and it is difficult to determine exactly how widespread each plan is. But whatever the breakdown, the mayor-council plan is clearly the most popular governmental structure for both small and very large cities, as shown in table 6.1. Nearly three-quarters of all cities in the twenty-five hundred to five thousand people range employ this format. And although its popularity drops substantially as city size increases, it again becomes popular with very large cities: Over three-quarters of those cities with over half a million people employ the mayor-council format, and each of the six largest cities in the United States has adopted it. In general, the weak-mayor plan is probably most popular in the smaller cities, and the strong-mayor format is most popular in the larger cities. But as noted previously, the weakness of the mayor's office in such large cities as Chicago demonstrate the inadequacy of this generalization.

The mayor-council plan is most common in the major industrial states of the Midwest and East. Fifty-six percent of all mayor-council cities with more than ten thousand people (these are the only cities for which *The Municipal Yearbook*, the primary source of such information, reports data) are located in just eight states: Illinois, Indiana, Michigan, New Jersey, New York, Ohio, Pennsylvania, and Wisconsin. Even granting that these states have more than their share of cities in this population range (they account for 37 percent of all cities in the United States with more than ten thousand people), we must conclude that industrialization leads to this governmental format. In part, this can be explained by the greater heterogeneity to be found in cities in these states. Industrialization leads naturally to a more pronounced class structure, and in turn to a greater potential for conflict in the city. The mayor-council plan, more than any other, recognizes the importance of this conflict and literally builds it into the system. This plan produces more elected officials than any of the others (even strong-mayor systems typically have larger councils than do council-manager or commission plans), and council members are

5. Actually, the 1986 election gave Mayor Washington a 25–25 tie on the council, which he could break with his vote.

Table 6.1   Form of Municipal Government as a Function of City Size

	Type of Government Structure							
	Mayor-Council		Council-Manager		Commission		Town Meeting	
Population	N	%	N	%	N	%	N	%
Under 2,500	131	32	220	54	3	1	50	12
2,501–5,000	1,532	70	466	21	39	2	164	7
5,001–10,000	1,000	57	579	33	33	2	136	8
10,001–25,000	735	46	673	42	54	3	125	8
25,001–50,000	236	36	365	56	30	5	21	3
50,001–100,000	106	35	179	60	9	3	5	2
100,001–250,000	40	34	72	61	6	5	0	
250,001–500,000	16	46	17	49	2	6	0	
Over 500,000	19	79	5	21	0		0	

SOURCE: Adapted from *The Municipal Yearbook* (1988).

more likely to be elected from geographically defined wards rather than at-large. These features tend to promote interest-group activity and encourage citizen participation. More important, citizens have a greater sense that they have a say in city government.

Council-Manager Plan

Installing a city manager, even more than strengthening the mayor's office, was viewed by reformers as the way to simultaneously root out municipal corruption and coordinate municipal administration. In 1899, for example, Haven Mason, editor of *California Municipalities*, noted that every city that receives or expends $50,000 annually should have a salaried business manager (Adrian and Press 1977). These municipal managers, he noted, should be versed in engineering, street construction, sewers, building construction, water and lighting systems, personnel, accounting, municipal law, fire protection, and library management. Other reformers made similar pleas, and in the first decade of the twentieth century, two cities—Staunton, Virginia and Sumter, South Carolina—each hired a general manager for their city. In 1911, Richard Childs, a reformer who was later to become president of the National Municipal League, drew up a model city charter for council-manager government (later adopted by a number of cities). The popularity of the council-manager plan grew rapidly, with forty-six other cities (the largest of which was Dayton, Ohio) adopting it by 1915. Today, nearly half of all cities between 10,000 and 500,000 people have adopted the plan (see table 6.1).

The fundamental assumption of the council-manager plan holds that there is no Democratic or Republican way to pave a road or fight a fire, and

99

that politics should therefore be removed from urban administration.[6] To this end, the city council hires a professional manager to oversee all the administrative responsibilities of the city, and the manager serves at the council's pleasure (i.e., the majority of the council can vote to fire the manager at any time, with or without cause). Although the manager serves at the pleasure of the council, the council typically refrains from meddling in the administrative affairs of the city, thus removing one source of politics from urban administration. In addition, since the manager is not required to seek electoral approval for his or her actions, a second source of politics is removed. Once appointed, the manager has complete authority to hire and fire department heads, who report only to him or her. This provides the manager with the opportunity to select a management team that reflects his or her philosophy of urban administration, thus increasing the opportunity for coordination. The manager is typically paid a professional salary, quite high by public-sector standards but considerably lower than that he or she might expect to receive for comparable responsibility in the private sector.[7]

Under the council-manager plan, the council is elected by the voters, usually in the same manner as that specified for the weak-mayor plan. Here, however, council members typically do not represent geographic wards but are elected at large, usually in nonpartisan elections; in fact, both government-by-management and at-large elections are outgrowths of the urban reform movement (see chapter 4). Mayors are typically selected by the council from among its members, usually for one-year terms. (In some cities, however, the mayor may be directly elected by the voters.) The office of mayor in the council-manager plan is, like the weak mayor, largely a ceremonial position, with no formal powers. Council members typically serve on a part-time basis and receive nominal salaries.

Under the council-manager plan, the responsibilities of the council and manager are clearly delineated, although as noted later, this delineation is clearer in principle than in practice. The council has responsibility for formulating general municipal policy. For example, council members develop taxing and spending policies, deciding where new revenue is to come from and priorities for spending it. They decide whether money for capital improvements will be spent to fix sidewalks and repair bridges, or whether to allocate money for new sewage treatment plants, fire engines, and additional police officers.

6. For a critical dissent, see Herson (1957).

7. A 1980 comparison of city managers and industrial managers with comparable responsibilities showed industrial managers to earn, on average, 29 percent higher salaries than city managers (Lubin 1981). Since then, city managers' salaries have increased by 156 percent. Although no exact figures are available for how much the salaries of industrial managers and chief executive officers have increased since 1980, the salaries of CEOs increased by 23 percent just between 1993 and 1995 (compared with a 6.8 percent increase during these two years for city managers).

And they decide how to generate funds to pay for these expenditures. Will neighborhood residents be charged, in the form of special assessments, for improving the sidewalks and roads in their neighborhoods, or will this cost be borne by all residents? Will the city seek to borrow money, through general obligation bonds? Will the sales tax be raised? Will fees be instituted for various services, for instance, using parks for organized softball leagues?

A second example involves zoning. The council typically decides where industries shall be allowed to locate, and whether duplexes (or apartments), grocery stores, and laundromats will be allowed in residential neighborhoods. A third example involves regulation and the development of ordinances. Council members often must decide what kinds of signs and billboards will be allowed within the city limits. They must determine speed limits for various roads in the city. And in some controversial decisions, city councils have banned the sale of drug-related paraphernalia and have attempted to outlaw abortions.

In contrast to these rather weighty responsibilities, the city manager's responsibilities seem light. He or she is responsible for preparing an annual budget and submitting it to the council, carrying out the policies that the council has formulated (e.g., ticketing speeders and building parks), and managing the urban bureaucracy, including making personnel decisions and resolving personnel conflicts. And the city manager may be asked to provide counsel and advice to members of the city council.

But herein lies the rub. Since council members typically serve on a part-time basis, they usually lack the expertise and the time to properly evaluate policy options. More often than not, they *do* turn to the city manager for counsel and advice, affording the manager many more responsibilities (and much more power) than his or her contract would suggest. Thus, the council may ask the manager to determine whether a new sewage treatment plant is warranted, the costs and benefits of constructing a new road, the viability of a new park, or the likely impact of an additional sales tax or a restrictive billboard ordinance. In short, the policy-administration distinction becomes blurred.

Table 6.1 shows the council-manager plan to be extremely popular among cities in the 10,000 to 500,000 population range and not particularly popular either in smaller cities or in the largest cities. This trend stems from the assumptions underlying the plan. The city manager plan is based, in essence, on the assumption that principles of scientific management can be applied to the problems of cities more efficiently than politics can. Take the paving of a road, for example. A city manager, who is able to divorce politics from administration, is able to choose a paving company based strictly on the merits of its bid, thus maximizing the quality of the job and minimizing its cost. A mayor, forced to make the same decision, has an additional set of factors to consider (i.e., those affecting his or her reelection), and efficiency must be tempered with the politics of not offending various bidders. Or take the decision to purchase new police cars. The manager again will consider cost and performance in choosing a local dealership from which to purchase the vehicles, whereas the mayor must also consider the political clout of the various dealerships. The conclusion seems inevitable: city government will be more cost efficient under a council-manager plan than under a mayor-council plan.

But is it really? Two factors cast doubt on this conclusion, or at least suggest that political costs are measured in more than money. First, politics is a way of life in small-town America. Constituents know their elected representatives on a first-name basis, and most interaction is very informal. By and large, elected officials know little about local government, and this keeps government from becoming too powerful (cf., Vidich and Bensman 1958). A professional manager potentially represents a threat to this ideal, making the municipal bureaucracy less accessible to the city's residents. The importance of this access for small-towners is suggested by Connery (1972, 140).

> [Small-town bureaucracy] is not a faceless bureaucracy, beyond the reach of the average man. The tax collector, visiting nurse, fire marshall, dog warden, probate judge, assessors, registrars of voters, park and recreation commissioners, justices of the peace . . . , members of the Board of Education, and others—they are all friends and neighbors. Like the teachers of our children, and the doctors and preachers and everyone else of importance, they are people we see on the street, meet in the stores, sit with in church.

Small-towners also tend to believe in the principle of accountability, that those in positions of trust are responsible for their actions, and any violation of the trust placed in them will be met with defeat in the next election (or, perhaps, with recall before the next election). A professional manager is not subject to this same accountability. Further, norms in small towns stress the importance of informal relationships, and successful politicians are "just one of the boys (or girls)." In contrast, city managers are often graduates of professional degree programs, and cities must typically hire outsiders to fill city management positions. Both of these factors militate against small-town residents accepting the city manager and against their using cost efficiency as a primary principle for evaluating their government.

In large cities, too, cost efficiency may not be the single most important factor in successful government (but for a different set of reasons). For example, the decision about which construction company to hire for paving roads may not be the most important one to make. A prior decision must take into account the relative merits of paving roads or providing other services, for example, day care for the children of working single mothers or shelter for the homeless. In cities with homogeneous populations, these policy issues are less important, for residents typically have similar priorities, and city management is the most effective way (because it is efficient) to implement priorities. But where urban residents are not homogeneous, stressing efficiency circumvents the need to examine priorities carefully, and, as suggested earlier, the middle class benefits to the detriment of the underclass. Large cities, particularly those in the industrialized states, therefore, tend to shun professional management in favor of a system that encourages politics, conflicts, and the sorting out of priorities.

But what of the findings, reported in table 6.1, that nearly 50 percent of American cities in the middle population ranges have turned to the council-manager plan? This seems to suggest its enormous popularity and its apparent success. But even these figures mislead. While forty-nine of the fifty states have at least one city in this population range using the council-manager plan, most of the cities employing this plan are concentrated in nine western and sunbelt states.[8] Outside these nine states, the popularity of the council-manager plan drops tremendously.

Commission Plan

The commission plan was another alternative to the strong-mayor format championed by municipal reformers. Its advent was more accidental than planned. In the wake of the hurricane in 1900 that destroyed large portions of Galveston, Texas, the state legislature suspended local government in the city, substituting a temporary government of five businessmen, the Galveston Commission. The commission's actions proved successful in the short run, and the city received a new charter in 1903 making the arrangement permanent (Adrian and Press 1977).

Under the commission charter, each commissioner is elected by the public but serves the dual role of legislator and administrator. Usually commissions consist of five members, although some small cities may elect only three commissioners. Each commission position carries with it administrative responsibilities for one sector of municipal government. For example, a commissioner of public safety is responsible for administration of the police and fire departments, and a commissioner of public works typically is responsible for administration of street construction and repair, water treatment, sewage disposal, and so forth. In spite of the clear differentiation among administrative responsibilities, the commission's legislative responsibilities are typically undifferentiated. While one of the commissioners is designated to chair commission

8. More than 80 percent of the cities over 10,000 in each of the following states use council-manager plans: Arizona, California, Colorado, Florida, North Carolina, Oklahoma, Oregon, Texas, and Virginia. Together, these states account for 52 percent of the cities over 10,000 using the council-manager plan (*Municipal Yearbook* 1988).

meetings, his or her formal powers are similar to those of a weak mayor. Thus, the entire commission formulates policy, but individual commissioners implement policy.

At first glance, this governmental structure should be among the most effective, for it provides a great deal of democratic accountability. In the weak-mayor plan, voters have direct control over a number of administrative positions. If an elected administrator betrays the public trust, the public is able to throw the rascal out of office in the next election. The strong-mayor plan makes accountability more difficult, for the mayor is in charge of all administration, and the public may be willing to overlook some areas of poor administration for other areas of good administration. For example, citizens may be willing to trade off poor park administration for well-maintained roads. Under the council-manager plan, the administrator is further removed from the public, and administrative accountability is all but lost to the voters. But under the commission plan, administrative responsibility is once again differentiated, and administrators are directly accountable to the public. The electorate can, for example, vote *nay* on the city's police department while giving the parks department a vote of confidence.

However, as Ralph Waldo Emerson said, every credit has its debit, and with the increased accountability of the commission plan comes increased difficulty in coordination. If the division between policy and administration were well-defined, the commission plan might work without a hitch. But as noted in the previous discussion of the council-manager plan, this division is not realistic. And under the commission plan, the breakdown of the division of labor sometimes has unfortunate consequences. The commission as a body develops policy, which is to be faithfully administered by the individual commissioners. But since administrators themselves have such a great impact on policy development, both through their expertise and through their discretionary implementation prerogatives, the commission format often finds individual commissioners pursuing policies that are at odds with the will of the commission as a whole. This situation sometimes leads to a great deal of political infighting among commissioners, who may develop very rancorous relationships with one another. More often, however, it leads to mutual accommodation, where the various commissioners acknowledge one another's administrative prerogatives and simply agree to maintain absolute power within each one's particular niche of municipal government. The result is a jealously guarded territoriality, with all pretense of overall administrative coordination abandoned.

Although initially championed by urban reformers, the commission plan fell from favor in a relatively short time. Following the Galveston experiment, Houston adopted the commission plan in 1905, Des Moines in 1907; by 1910 it had spread to 108 cities, and by 1917, to over 500 cities. At this point, however, a reversal began to take place, and today it is the least popular of the major municipal governance plans, with fewer than 5 percent of cities employing it.

Two factors may account for this decline. First, the initial success of the commission plan may well have been due more to the particular commissioners than to the nature of the plan. In Galveston, the commissioners were selected by the state legislature, reducing the impact of local politics on the plan's success. Further, those particular commissioners were apparently quite zealous in their efforts, and the situation itself was extraordinary. Other early converts to the commission plan may also have been attempting to respond to extraordinary circumstances. But after fifteen years of use, the commission plan began to show its defects, and it lost its appeal for many would-be converts. Perhaps more important, the decade between 1910 and 1920 witnessed the advent of the council-manager plan, which held even more appeal for municipal reformers.

Today, the commission plan is much more prevalent in middle-sized and larger cities than in smaller cities. Further, more than half the middle-sized and larger cities (i.e., over ten thousand people) with commission plans are located in just three states: Pennsylvania, New Jersey, and Illinois. All three are industrialized, with heterogeneous populations, suggesting that the commission plan may work best in cities with greater class conflict—by giving voice and substance to that conflict.

Town Meeting Plan

The most intriguing of the various municipal government arrangements is the town meeting. This format is the exclusive domain of villages, towns, and a handful of small and middle-sized cities in New England. Once a year (with as many additional meetings as may be necessary), the entire voting population of the town gathers to vote on whatever policy issues may be pressing. In addition, the town elects a board of selectmen to carry out the enacted policies. The meetings may be supplemented by various study groups and finance committees, whose task is to recommend policy actions in general and town budgets in particular. Given the small number of municipalities that actually use the town meeting, however, it remains mostly as a nostalgic reminder of the past.[9]

Norm versus Form: A Comparison of Adherence to Democratic Norms

At this point, a comparison of the major structural formats of municipal government is in order. Our point of reference is the previous chapter's discussion of democratic norms, and we will focus on the governing style of each of the

---

9. For more on the town meeting format, see Zimmerman (1984); a more extensive description of the strengths and weaknesses of the town meeting is also provided in the first edition of this book (Herson and Bolland 1990).

major forms of municipal government and the extent to which each is likely to fulfill democratic norms and expectations, especially with respect to citizen contribution to public policy and the extent to which majorities do rule and minority rights are protected.

Majority Rule

In discussing majority rule, we are concerned with the *distance* between the *citizen* and *public policy decisions*. In general, when this distance is small, as in the case of direct democracy, the *potential* for majority rule is maximized. On the other hand, when the citizen is separated from policy decisions by one or more buffers, which may or may not be accountable to the public, the potential for majority rule suffers. In this discussion, we consider the potential for majority rule rather than majority rule itself. Until cities achieve 100 percent voter registration and turnout, majority rule is merely an ideal rather than a reality. But with increasing citizen participation comes the opportunity for the majority of citizens to decide public policy issues.

The weak-mayor plan offers the greatest potential for citizen policy input and voter control. Under this plan, political power tends to be diffused among a number of elected officials, and in this situation, there exists a greater potential for the public, particularly an activist public, to contribute to the political agenda. Next in terms of fulfilling democratic norms is the commission plan: power is diffused among several elected officials, thus (in principle) increasing opportunities for citizen input; but in practice, this is usually offset by the resources of the commissioners (e.g., patronage, the ability to award contracts), which tend to insulate them from public demands.

Next comes the strong-mayor plan, where power is concentrated in the hands of the mayor. While this does not rule out the possibility of citizen input, it minimizes the impact of citizens because they have to work through individual council members. As the number of conduits for citizen inputs decreases, the impact of the citizenry on policy issues also decreases. Even so, the strong mayor is an elected official, which gives this format the nod over the council-manager format. Under the latter plan, power is not only concentrated, but concentrated in the hands of a nonelected official, and the public is twice removed from policy decisions.

But the distance between the public and policy decisions is not the only criterion by which we should evaluate majority rule. In addition the conflict between public and private sources of power differs under each of the formats, with somewhat different implications for the norm of majority rule. When public power is diffused—as in the case of the weak-mayor format—a power vacuum may invite private interest, including business owners, land developers, or neighborhood leaders, to take policy initiatives. While it provides the opportunity for citizens to become involved in the policy process, this kind of private power is typically less responsive to citizen input than is publicly held (i.e., elective) power, and the opportunity for majority rule is accordingly diminished. Power is somewhat more concentrated in the strong-mayor and commission formats, allowing less opportunity for private interests to gain power in the city. This linear trend breaks down in the case of the council-manager plan, however. Although power is concentrated in the hands of the city manager, the strong business orientation of the plan lends considerable power to various business interests in the community. They, in effect, typically have the ear of the manager, and thus they have considerable say in the resolution of public policy issues. So, in this case, public access to policy decisions is twice buffered, and the potential for majority rule is severely constrained.

Protection of Minority Rights

We might initially expect that the concentration of power would prove the greatest threat to the protection of minority rights, and in many cases this is so. As Lord Acton said, power corrupts, and absolute power corrupts absolutely. Yet, a number of studies in this country show that the exact opposite effect is likely to occur: When power is concentrated in the hands of a political leader (or a set of political leaders), minority rights are more likely to be protected than when power is diffused and lies in the hands of the masses. Thomas Dye and Harmon Zeigler (1975) note this *irony of democracy* in the following paradox. Political elites, as carriers of the political culture, tend to better represent the democratic norm of tolerance than do the masses. Thus, governance-by-the-elite is more likely to lead to tolerance in government and the protection of minority rights than government-by-the-masses; but in opting for the former over the latter, the norm of majority rule is, by definition, abridged. In contrast, majority rule is likely to sacrifice minority rights. By way of illustration, Lawrence Herson and Richard Hofstetter (1975) show that people with the greatest political tolerance tend to have higher incomes, to be better educated, professional, and politically active—exactly those who are most likely to hold municipal office.

This might lead us to expect, then, that minority rights may be least well protected in the weak-mayor format (since popular participation is more prevalent), and better protected in the strong-mayor and commission formats (since power is concentrated in the hands of the elite). But this is no simple (nor simply sketched) expectation. Much depends on the definition given to minority rights and on the specific minority being protected. If the minority in question is racial or ethnic, it will likely be best protected in strong mayor governments (especially when combined with council election by wards) and in commission governments. These offer minority voters direct electoral access to their urban governors. If the minority is defined as the economic

107

underclass, it may be served least well by the council-manager format, for the strong emphasis on efficiency leads to policies that tend to favor the upper and middle classes and discriminate against the underclass.

Participation

Studies suggest that reformed municipal governments, in their various incarnations (e.g., council-manager format, at-large elections, nonpartisan elections), have significantly lower voter turnout in municipal elections than their unreformed counterparts (Alford and Lee 1968). We should conclude, then, that mayor-council cities have the greater potential for participation, followed by cities with commission formats (which typically are nonpartisan and always at-large) and council-manager formats.

But, in addition to electoral participation, we must also consider other forms of political participation, including participation in neighborhood councils, local schools, protest groups, and so forth. And in considering this participation, we must also distinguish between *reactive* and *proactive* participation: The former involves participation in response to some perceived need or threat (e.g., a protest in response to a city council decision to locate a low-cost public housing unit in *my* neighborhood, or to zone *my* neighborhood for duplexes and apartment buildings), whereas the latter represents continuing participation intended to better living conditions in the community (e.g., a neighborhood association sponsoring neighborhood cleanups, or the League of Women Voters sponsoring a public forum about recycling). In general, reactive participation may be dysfunctional, leading to what Douglas Yates (1977) terms street-fighting pluralism and the popular press terms single-issue politics. Whatever its label, reactive participation leads to fragmented policies in which the context of issues is not sufficiently addressed. Issues are treated in isolation, without regard to how they impinge on other issues and with little concern for their long-term consequences.

In contrast, Bolland (1985b) shows that general political participation, particularly when it is accompanied by some sense of responsibility, leads to a better understanding of the interrelationships among various community issues. This sense of responsibility is typically associated with proactive participation, often born out of a sense of civic responsibility. Proactive participation is thus likely to lead to integrated and coordinated public policies and fewer contradictions in public programs.

But are the various governmental formats likely to differ in their degree of proactive versus reactive participation? Logic suggests that they are, although the evidence is only indirect. Strong political parties tend to take positions on most political issues (contrary to the views of the reformers, they believe that there *is* a Democratic and a Republican way to pave a street). Further, local parties provide both an ongoing organization and a number of offices—ranging from county chairman to precinct committee-man or committeewoman—to be filled by interested and loyal party members. Finally, parties have a political agenda that may supersede their reaction to specific events. These three factors, taken together, suggest that partisan governments provide a core of political participants who follow politics across issues, helping to ensure an appreciation for the contextual quality of urban politics. In a strong partisan system, this can militate against the tendency for special interests to form around specific issues. But in nonpartisan systems, this tendency toward single-issue politics is unchecked, and political activism tends to be overly responsive to events. We arrive, therefore, at a speculative conclusion that mirrors our conclusion about electoral participation: Proactive participation is most likely under the mayor-council format, while reactive participation is most likely under the commission and council-manager formats.

Peaceful Management of Conflict

As noted earlier, mayor-council formats are most common in heterogeneous, industrialized areas whereas council-manager formats are more common in the homogeneous suburbs. This provides an initial indication of the conflictual orientation of the various formats. The mayor-council format provides the greatest opportunity for input from diverse community groups and interests, and this diversity of demands creates the opportunity for open conflict about policy priorities. Particularly in cities with strong mayors, the mayor can often perform a cathartic function, drawing out concerns and policy demands from different groups within the city. In the council-manager format, in contrast, policy priorities are assumed *a priori* to be the efficient provision of municipal services (e.g., police and fire protection, garbage collection, street maintenance, traffic control).[10]

Thus, the conflictual orientation of the various municipal formats ties into the characteristics of the populations they serve: Heterogeneity leads to an overtly political format which in turn invites conflict, while homogeneity leads to a managerial format which in turn discourages conflict. But what happens when a mayor-council format is adopted in a homogeneous city, or when a council-manager format is adopted in a heterogeneous city? In the former case, conflict emerges around the edges of public policy issues (e.g., how many days to collect garbage each week, or priorities for snow

---

10. Even the buildings in which various cities conduct their business suggest their conflictual orientation. City hall in mayor-council cities is typically an older structure built in a Greek or Roman architectural style; it conjures memories of argument and conflict. In contrast, city hall in many reformed cities is a newer building, constructed in the style of a modern office building or public school; one gets the feeling that voices should be hushed, conflict should be muffled, and disagreement quietly negotiated.

removal routes), but by the very nature of the issues, the conflict is unlikely to become rancorous. In contrast, conflict over policy priorities in the latter case is suppressed, but not eliminated. Such conflict may fester until it reaches crisis proportions, at which time it may erupt as a breakdown in public confidence. In this situation, suppressed rancor may be unleashed, and it will take the city some time to recover. The conflictual orientation of the other municipal formats is less clear, although it seems likely that conflict may be encouraged by commission government. As suggested earlier, however, this may help defuse truly rancorous conflict that might otherwise fester in the community.

Widespread Distribution of Benefits

In their classic study, Robert Lineberry and Edmund Fowler (1967) report a higher correlation between a city's demographic characteristics and its expenditure patterns in unreformed cities than in reformed cities. They argue that this demonstrates a greater responsiveness to citizen inputs in unreformed cities, from which we should conclude that participants are more likely to be rewarded for their participation in unreformed cities. This may be due to the greater electoral accountability on the part of policy-makers in unreformed cities: By making sure that nobody goes home empty-handed, elected officials are investing in their own political future. It may be that the norms of efficiency and political evenhandedness stressed in reformed cities precludes politically motivated gifts to political participants. Or it may be that in big cities, which tend to favor unreformed governmental structures, the sheer number of interest groups may create a climate of compromise that facilitates the disbursement of benefits to all participants. The truth probably embodies some combination of all three explanations.

The commission format is more similar to the mayor-council format than to the council-manager format in its responsiveness to citizen input. Not only is the governing body highly political, but administration is also politicized (administrators, as commission members, are after all elected), and citizen demands are likely to be felt by both elected officials and administrators.

Formal Participants and Their Political Roles

We turn now to an examination of the formal political participants in the urban arena: members of the governing body, the mayor, the city manager, members of the municipal bureaucracy, municipal judges, and appointees to municipal boards and commissions.

The Governing Body

Who are the people who run for positions on a city council?[11] For the most part, the pay for council members is low: The typical salary for part-time council members across the United States in 1995 was under $3,600 (*Municipal Yearbook* 1996). Council members therefore are not people who are in politics to get rich. In fact, salaries are kept at a nominal level to discourage those interested primarily in gaining wealth from running for office. Rather, prestige and honor become the primary motivators for those seeking city council positions (e.g., Adrian and Press 1977), although other, less lofty motives are also present. For example, one successful candidate (of the authors' acquaintance) used his position as a way to meet people while drinking at local bars. Another ran for office to achieve a favorable zoning decision for his business interests. And still others use their positions to gain favors for their friends and neighbors in the community. In general, however, most people serve on a city council out of a sense of civic responsibility, and their primary reward comes in the form of honor and prestige.

The nature of this reward has important implications for the kind of person who is likely to seek municipal office. Because of the modest financial remuneration and the time required to do a good job (more about this later), only those in positions of some financial independence, or at least consider-able occupational flexibility, are able to seek public office at the local level. This includes, for example, attorneys, who have both sufficient income so that they can spend time away from the office and sufficient flexibility so that they are not penalized for doing so. Much the same can be said for a physician, a banker, a developer, or indeed, anyone who owns his or her own business. But note, however, that it may effectively preclude schoolteachers, nurses, secre-taries, many salespersons, and others who either cannot financially afford to take time off from their jobs or who do not have flexibility in their work schedules to take time off. This conclusion is consistent with several studies of city council members. Charles Adrian and Charles Press (1977) report that most council members are moderately successful businessmen who are finan-cially prosperous and relatively well educated. Particularly in smaller cities, these persons tend to be members of the community elite. A study of com-munities in Los Angeles County (Huckshorn and Young 1960) shows the typ-ical council member to be forty-nine years old and male (only 6.7 percent were females). By 1992, this had changed somewhat, but still only 26.1 per-cent of elected members of governing boards were females (U.S. Department of Commerce 1994).

11. Whereas seats on the city council are typically part-time positions that do not pay well, seats on the city commission are full-time, well-paid positions, and commission-ers resemble strong mayors more than they do city council members.

The nature of the city council position is further demonstrated by council members' attitudes about public service. A study of Kansas cities shows that two-thirds of city council members had never held other positions in government or in their political party and that they disliked campaigning (Stauber and Kline 1965). For them, apparently, the reward was in the public service itself rather than in the associated politics. In addition, a study of San Francisco Bay area communities shows that most (71 percent) council members had no further political aspirations, and that the majority (62 percent) would give up their seats if their regular jobs demanded that they do so. They view public service as a civic responsibility, not as a means to further (and grander) political position. And for them, civic responsibility takes a back seat to their primary career responsibilities (Prewitt and Nowlin 1969).

For the majority of council members who serve out of a sense of civic responsibility, the job can be very frustrating and tiring; perhaps this is why relatively few council members serve multiple terms. Consider the practical problems facing a city council member. Typically, he or she may be asked to run for the council position by members of a civic organization, a political party, a neighborhood association, or some other politically involved group (using the broad definition of *politics* developed in chapter 5). But after the initial flattery comes the hard work of campaigning, in which otherwise private people must bare their lives to the community. And with this inevitably come cheap shots taken by other candidates or interests, accusing the candidate of being unqualified, of representing special interests, of empire building. For the candidate who becomes politically involved at someone else's invitation and sees a council seat as a way of fulfilling civic responsibility, such accusations can be quite hurtful.

Now, assume that the candidate is lucky enough to be elected. What awaits him or her? Some cities have a half-day orientation for new council members, in which they are shown the ropes of public office. Others have a two-hour orientation, and some have no orientation at all. Yet, new council members are expected to attend their first council meeting and participate in a responsible manner. They are expected, for example, to understand the workings of the municipal bureaucracy, to know where to seek information, to understand community issues and their broad implications, to understand the community itself, and to know where public opinion falls on various issues. These would be Herculean tasks for even the most seasoned council members, and they are beyond the grasp of most newly elected members.

But city councils are in the business of making decisions, and members are required to vote on issues whether or not they understand the full complexity of the issues. And when these decisions turn out to be incorrect, or when a council decision runs contrary to some community interest, criticism results. Adrian and Press (1977) conclude that one of the most difficult aspects of service on a city council is adjusting to criticism. Again, imagine a small business owner who is encouraged to seek a council position and does so out of a sense of civic responsibility. When he or she is then openly criticized in the press for incompetence, or for naiveté, or even for voting incorrectly on an issue, he or she must begin to question whether election was worth the effort. That, coupled with the evening calls about barking dogs or garbage collection, and ten (or more) hours each week devoted to city business, leads many city council members to call it quits after their first term in office.

One of the most dramatic changes in the political landscape during the past two decades is the electoral success of minorities seeking city council positions. In 1970, 623 blacks held elective municipal offices. By 1992, this number had increased to 4,511; of these, 4,048 were elected to governing boards (U.S. Department of Commerce 1994). At least part of this increase is due to increased voter registration among blacks in the wake of the 1965 Voting Rights Act. But it is also due to intervention by the courts, pursuant to the Voting Rights Act, requiring that blacks be provided equal representation on city councils. In a number of cities, the courts found that blacks occupied far fewer council seats than their voting strength should command. To remedy this situation, they implemented two different solutions. First, in a number of cities where council members were elected by district, the courts ordered redistricting. Second, in other cities where council members were elected at large, the courts ordered a change to election-by-district (see Renner 1988).[12]

In their discussion of political equality, Rufus Browning, Dale Rogers Marshall, and David Tabb (1984) argue that minority election to council positions is an important component of *political incorporation* (i.e., becoming an effective part of the political process), which is, in turn, a necessary and sufficient condition for equality. According to the figures cited above, blacks (and other minorities) have come a long way toward the ideal of incorporation. Another component of incorporation is the election of minority mayors; it, too, is an area where much has been achieved over the past two decades. These changes are elaborated later. But first, we turn to a general discussion of the mayor's role in the urban system.

12. This represents one of the clearest challenges to the ideals of the reform movement, and it implicitly holds that by taking politics out of municipal government, the reformers may have infringed on the right of the minority. Or, put differently, the courts seem to have taken the position that politics may provide the best avenue for minorities to achieve equal status in our society. This position may be changing, however, with decisions handed down by the U.S. Supreme Court in 1995 (*Miller v. Johnson*) and 1996 (*Bush v. Vera* and *Shaw v. Hunt*) ruling that race alone could not be used as a criterion for establishing voting districts. Although these decisions pertained only to U.S. congressional districts, they may have implications for other levels of government (including municipalities) as well.

The Mayor

In weak-mayor and most council-manager cities, the mayor is just another council member who serves on a part-time basis with few extra powers or perquisites. But in strong-mayor cities, the mayor has considerable power. This section discusses the role of strong mayor.

Because the position of mayor is more powerful than that of council member, it tends to attract a different type of person. First, the strong-mayor position is typically full time, and with a full-time position goes a much higher salary. Even in small cities, mayors receive a quite respectable salary, and in large cities their salaries rival the pay found at most levels of political office. For instance, the mayor's annual salary in four American cities with over 1 million people averages about $110,000 (*Municipal Yearbook* 1996).

Second, a full-time mayoral position literally requires its holder to give up his or her regular employment, and it is very easy for the mayor to consider becoming a "professional" politician. The strong mayor may thus seek subsequent terms as mayor once his or her current term has expired. And some mayors will use their records and name recognition to seek higher office, for instance, a position in the state senate or house of representatives, the governorship, or even federal office. In two recent cases, incumbent mayors unsuccessfully tried to parlay their positions into governorships (Tom Bradley of Los Angeles and Ed Koch of New York). Other big-city mayors have been more successful in their quest for higher office (e.g., Hubert Humphrey of Minneapolis, Pete Wilson of San Diego, who became a U.S. senator from California and then governor of the state, and Richard Lugar of Indianapolis, who became a U.S. senator from Indiana). In this regard, Cleveland serves as a textbook example, with six mayors moving to positions of national political prominence during this century alone (Adrian and Press 1977). The actual success of mayors in seeking higher office is not the important point, however—in fact, *most mayors do not go on to higher office*.[13] But nonetheless, the perception remains that this is a possible launching point for a political career, and no doubt a number of people have sought the mayorship with exactly this in mind.

Third, the very fact that the strong-mayorship is a full-time position means that it attracts a different kind of person than does a part-time city council position. Because of its greater pay, its greater prestige, and its potential for political advancement, the competition for the mayorship is fiercer than that for council seats. As a result, mayors tend to be somewhat older than

13. The mayor's office was once a springboard to higher office, but for today's big-city mayors the office is mostly a dead-end political job. The reason? Reputations slide as the mayor finds himself or herself unable to satisfy all the demands made upon the office as the city finds itself overmatched and overcome by the problems that confront it. Another possible factor may be the popular movement against career politicians, reflected in efforts to establish term limits on elective offices.

their council counterparts, somewhat more successful professionally, and somewhat more visible in the community. They also tend to be self-employed, either as small business owners or as professionals with practices they can return to at some later time (e.g., lawyers, physicians). People in middle-level management positions would take a great risk were they to resign to become mayor, for their jobs may not be waiting for them when their term expires. In general, while civic responsibility is perhaps the primary motivation underlying the seeking of a part-time council position, it is not alone sufficient for seeking the mayorship.

Perhaps the biggest difference between the strong mayor and city council positions is the greater power incumbent in the former. The strong mayor, with power to appoint upper-level administrators, has greater access to information and bureaucratic support than do members of the governing body. By the same token, the mayor is the most visible person in the city. As Adrian and Press (1977) note, the mayor is expected to crown beauty queens, greet conventions, introduce presidents, dedicate parks, lay cornerstones, open baseball seasons, lead parades, launch charity drives, and cut ribbons. The mayor thus becomes the symbol for the entire city. And while these activities lack political substance (and often become tiresome for the mayor), they do afford the mayor with almost instant name recognition among the citizenry. In turn, this visibility provides him or her with easy access to the news media and, consequently, with a greater ability to publicize his or her own political agenda for the city than is afforded to council members. Just as important, strong mayors are able to lay claim to any positive things that happen within the city, whether or not they were responsible for them. For example, mayors who promoted downtown revitalization during the 1980s were able to reap the benefits of that growth, even though they may have been only peripherally responsible for it. These include Kevin White in Boston, George Latimer in St. Paul, and William Schaefer in Baltimore (Frieden and Sagalyn 1989). Further, in each case the mayor was able to use his accomplishments downtown to deflect criticism that he was ignoring other, deteriorating areas of the city.

Yet, the power of the office does not guarantee that individual mayors will be uniformly powerful in setting urban policy. Differences in mayoral power typically stem from two sources: the mayor's resources and his or her mayoral style.

Mayoral resources. Jeffrey Pressman (1972) identifies a number of resources necessary for mayoral effectiveness. He notes, for example, that the mayor's office must have sufficient financial and staff resources for the mayor to plan for rather than merely react to unexpected situations (recall the previous comparison between proactive and reactive participation). Along the same lines, the mayor's office must be a full-time position, freeing the mayor from other occupational responsibilities. Pressman also notes that the city, and particularly the mayor's office, must have jurisdiction over various social programs in the city (e.g., housing, job training). Even a mayor with considerable financial and staff resources will have little effective power if the city's low-cost housing program is under control of the court or if federal job-training money is available only with a variety of strings attached. In addition, an effective mayor must have access to a friendly local media willing to give front-page or prime-time coverage to his or her political agenda. Finally, Pressman notes that mayoral initiatives must be undertaken in an atmosphere of political support to be successful. Specifically, he observes that the mayor must be able to mobilize political organizations (e.g., his or her political party) if he or she expects policy initiatives to get off the ground.

This conclusion is perhaps Pressman's most important, and it has two significant implications. First, it suggests the importance of *political networks* through which ideas and information flow and ultimately through which power is transmitted. These networks are necessary to mobilize support around public policy proposals, and in accordance with Pressman's suggestion, the mayor must be at the center of the city's political network to mobilize sufficient support to ensure success. Second, Pressman implies that political parties are important in these networks and that a mayor who is also a party leader is more likely to be successful than one who is not. Mayors in nonpartisan cities are unlikely to hold important party positions, and by implication, they are less likely to be successful than their counterparts in partisan cities. And mayors who run as mavericks, without party support, are likely to enjoy a miserable tenure in office. Note, again, the difficulties of Mayor Washington in Chicago.

Mayoral style. John Kotter and Paul Lawrence (1974) expand this view of political networks in their discussion of mayoral style. They note that mayors set the political agenda in their cities, but that in order to call proposals off the agenda and turn them into public policies, they must mobilize their political resources by building, maintaining, and using political networks. Richard Lee, the former mayor of New Haven, was a master at mobilizing political networks. Robert Dahl (1961, 204) describes him in the following terms:

> The mayor was not at the peak of a pyramid but rather at the center of intersecting circles. He rarely commanded. He negotiated, cajoled, exhorted, beguiled, charmed, praised, appealed, reasoned, promised, insisted, demanded, even threatened, but he most needed support and acquiescence from other leaders who simply could not be commanded. Because the mayor could not command, he had to bargain.

A mayor's willingness to work within existing networks or attempt to expand these networks reflects his or her mayoral style. At one extreme, Kotter and

Lawrence identify the *ceremonial mayor*, who tends to focus on personal appeals to existing networks in the city. He or she feels comfortable in the role of ribbon cutter and parade leader and feels little need to initiate long-term policies or programs. When problems arise in the city, the ceremonial mayor reacts (or more frequently, instructs the municipal bureaucracy to react). Existing political networks are thus probably sufficient for the ceremonial mayor's purposes. To the extent that existing networks reflect the ideas and priorities of those who built them, the ceremonial mayor is likely to follow the agenda of his or her predecessors. At the other extreme lies the *entrepreneurial mayor*, who has a distinct set of policy goals for the city and attempts to expand existing networks in order to maximize the potential for bringing these goals to fruition. This mayor, like Mayor Lee of New Haven, brings people together in an attempt to get them to share ideas. If they initially seem unwilling to do so, he or she cajoles them, or charms them, or threatens them into cooperating. In the case of New Haven, Mayor Lee effectively operated through a network of interests, including members of the municipal bureaucracy, federal agencies, the city council, the business community, the Democratic party, and Yale University, to create support for one of the largest and most successful urban renewal projects during the 1950s (see chapter 10). By building political networks and paying constant attention to their maintenance, the entrepreneurial mayor is likely to be successful in his or her policy initiatives.

Some observers, however, have concluded that the days of the entrepreneurial mayor may have come and gone. Yates (1977) argues, for example, that declining resources have created greater fragmentation among urban interests, requiring the mayor more often to play the role of broker rather than entrepreneur. In such a role, he or she serves as a bridge between competing community interests that have no desire to communicate directly and work with one another. In addition, the dominant forces in city life today are economic and social rather than political. Economic forces largely determine the viability of downtown redevelopment, and social forces couple with economic forces to determine the size of and the threat posed by the urban underclass. These forces will be discussed at much greater length in later sections. Suffice it to say here that the mayor—even the activist mayor—is largely left to react to these forces rather than control them.

Declining municipal budgets also may contribute to changing mayoral style. When the mayor has control over discretionary funds, which he or she can dole out as rewards, network-building efforts are likely to be more effective than in the absence of such funds. Cajoling people with diverse interests to sit down together and exchange ideas is likely to be much more successful when they can be tangibly rewarded than when they can be only symbolically rewarded. A business owner, for example, is more likely to support the mayor when the reward is a new sidewalk or parking lot than when it is a plaque being installed in his or her honor.

In recent years blacks have achieved considerable electoral success at the local level, in both council and mayoral elections. In 1995, 367 black mayors held office (*Black Enterprise* May 1995), up sharply from the 48 black mayors who held office in 1970 (Williams 1987). Most black mayoral successes have come in small (usually southern) towns of under 5,000. However, blacks have also held the mayorship in twenty-seven cities with over 50,000 people, including five of the six largest cities: David Dinkins in New York City, Harold Washington (and his interim replacement, Eugene Sawyer) in Chicago, Thomas Bradley in Los Angeles, W. Wilson Goode in Philadelphia, and Coleman Young in Detroit.[14] Even though black mayors have been succeeded by white mayors in most of these cities, their electoral successes represent a component of political incorporation (Browning et al. 1984), one potentially capable of creating political equality among the races. We will explore the impact of incorporation more fully in the next chapter.

The City Manager

A tough row to hoe. As noted in table 6.1, well over two thousand cities in the United States employ city managers, making this a sizeable professional fraternity. Several universities (e.g., the University of Kansas) have graduate programs designed explicitly to train city managers. City managers have created a professional organization—the International City Management Association (ICMA)—and meet annually under its auspices. They also have adopted a code of ethics. City management has become institutionalized in the American urban system. And in contrast to mayors and council members, city managers are professionally organized, with goals and an agenda orchestrated largely through ICMA. Strong ties among managers are formed during school days, and some universities maintain an active alumni association of their city management trainees. The typical manager's career may take him or her to half-a-dozen (or more) cities, first as an intern, then as an analyst, then as an assistant city manager, and finally as a manager. During these experiences, more strong connections develop. So the annual meeting of ICMA represents an opportunity for old friends to get together. More than most professional organizations, ICMA serves as a strong support group for its members.

To understand city management, we must first understand the motives for embarking on a city manager career. The typical city manager has an

14. Blacks have been elected as mayor of a number of other major cities, including Carl Stokes in Cleveland, Marion Berry in Washington, D.C., Richard Hatcher in Gary, Kenneth Gibson in Newark, Andrew Young in Atlanta, Ernest Morial in New Orleans, Norm Rice in Seattle, Kurt Schmoke in Baltimore, and Richard Arrington in Birmingham. For discussions of black mayors, see Preston (1987), Nelson (1987), Perry and Stokes (1987), Rich (1987, 1996), Ransom (1987), Eisinger (1984), and Persons (1992).

undergraduate degree in the social sciences, and nearly half now have graduate degrees either in public or business administration (DeSantis and Newell 1996). This contrasts with a previous era, when most managers had an engineering background. Thus, most city managers are social scientists who believe that the best way to solve a problem is to work with the people involved, rather than engineers who approach problem solving from a more rigorous, technical perspective. Most city managers get their first taste of urban politics as undergraduates, perhaps as summer interns or through a course in urban politics or urban sociology. And this experience makes them aware of the challenges of municipal government, so that most of those entering graduate programs to receive formal training in municipal administration do so with a commitment to the importance of the public sector in contemporary urban America. For them, city management is not so much an occupation as a calling.

For most city managers, however, idealism is combined with a certain degree of naiveté, and they soon discover that their calling moves them along a rather bumpy road. DeSantis and Newell (1996) report that 32 percent of city managers held their previous city management position for fewer than three years and 79.7 percent held their previous city management position for fewer than seven years; the mean tenure of city managers in their current position is 5.6 years (Renner 1990). DeHoog and Whitaker (1990) report that while approximately half of the moves that city managers make are due to upward mobility (e.g., moving to a larger city), the other half are attributable to politics (e.g., being fired by the city council). Thus, over a thirty-year career, many city managers may be fired several times. It takes a special type of person to be willing to jump back into the saddle after falling off (or being booted off) the horse once, let alone repeatedly.[15] The ICMA provides emotional support for people who have been fired. It provides them with job leads. And it lobbies for severance pay for city manager positions, so that in the case of termination, the manager may be provided with up to six months of salary.

Sources of uncertainty. Why is the city manager's path so rough and fraught with uncertainty? Four major factors lead to job insecurity. First, the training and experience most managers receive are not commensurate with the demands of their positions. Second, the city manager serves at the pleasure of the governing body, and he or she is often forced to take the blame for its failures. Third, the city manager is often forced to take sides on policy issues, and he or she can get caught in the middle of policy conflicts. Finally, the city manager has a view of his or her responsibilities that differs from that of the governing body, often leading to friction and an eventual parting of the ways.

15. This uncertainty no doubt contributes to a considerable level of occupational stress among city managers. For a further discussion of the problem, see Green and Reed (1988).

First, consider the responsibilities of a city manager. The National Municipal League's *Model City Charter* (1964) specifies the following duties:

1. Oversee the enforcement of all municipal ordinances.
2. Appoint, supervise, evaluate, and fire municipal department heads.
3. Prepare and submit the municipal budget.
4. Keep the city council advised on financial matters.
5. Keep the city council and public informed about matters concerning the city's operation.
6. Prepare and submit reports and memoranda to the city council as requested.
7. Make recommendations to the city council on matters that are deemed desirable.
8. Perform such duties as the city council assigns.

When we consider that even small cities have sizeable operating budgets and a large number of employees, we can understand the types of demands placed on the city manager. Consider, for example, a city like Upper Arlington, Ohio, with 34,000 residents. The city manager is responsible for administering an annual budget of over $20 million and supervising (directly or indirectly) over three hundred employees. Obviously, as a city's population increases, its manager has increasingly greater responsibility. As city size moves beyond 200,000, the typical city manager oversees a budget in excess of $450 million and is responsible for several thousand municipal employees. And in the truly large cities—San Diego, Dallas, Phoenix—the city manager must oversee an annual budget in excess of a billion dollars, and he or she is responsible for over ten thousand employees.

The responsibilities of a city manager are no fewer or less important than those of a chief executive officer of one of America's second-level corporations. Yet, city managers tend to have less experience than most CEOs. The typical city manager is in his or her early forties, although some are still in their mid-twenties. In addition, most city managers are hired from outside, so they have no experience with the city, its problems, and its politics. Finally, their lack of experience is not compensated for by their professional education. Many graduate programs in public administration are, in effect, only one year long, and they frequently employ a curriculum lacking in analytic rigor. The typical graduate of these programs emerges well-steeped in professional orientation but has few of the analytic skills required to be a successful city manager. To make matters worse, the salaries of city managers are well below those of their counterparts in the business world. Even in the largest cities, managers' salaries average less than $150,000, and in the smaller cities they are substantially lower. The mean 1995 salary in cities between 50,000 and 100,000 was $95,500, and this dropped to only $41,000 in cities with fewer than 2,500 people. The disparity between managerial salaries in the private and public sector (see note 7) means that many of the more gifted city managers eventually will opt for the private sector. A case in point is Robert Kipp, the very successful city manager of Kansas City who resigned that position in 1983 to become president of the Crown Center Redevelopment Corporation. In short, then, people with fewer than fifteen years' experience in management and often with no experience in the local community are asked to administer sizeable annual budgets, supervise a small army of personnel, and offer sound counsel to the city council, all for comparatively little financial compensation. Our surprise should not be at a high rate of failure, but that so many city managers do so well.

A second factor that accounts for the high rate of turnover among city managers is their ready availability for blame in policy failures. This is not to suggest that the personalities of city managers are somehow aberrant, but rather that their governmental role itself invites criticism. A careful examination of the list of a city manager's responsibilities reveals that considerable formal power is invested in the office. He or she, after all, is responsible for implementing all of the council's decisions, for preparing the budget, for keeping the council abreast of community affairs, for advising the council on policy matters. With this responsibility, it is impossible for the manager to remain neutral on policy issues, and he or she is often asked to express preferences and policy recommendations to the council. Edward Banfield and James Q. Wilson (1963) observe that this expression of preference is very useful for the council. If a proposed policy is adopted and proves successful, the council can take the credit; after all, it had the ultimate responsibility for approving the measure. But what if the policy is controversial? Banfield and Wilson (quoting Kammerer 1961) suggest that if the boat must be rocked, council members want the public to think that the city manager's hand is at the tiller. And if the policy proves unsuccessful, council members can blame failure on bad advice and faulty information from the manager. In this situation, even if the manager is blameless, he or she may be sacrificed if the council is to maintain its public facade of innocence.

A third factor is the conflict that inevitably arises among proponents of the different sides of policy debate. Again, consider the responsibility of the city manager's position and how it forces him or her to take policy positions. No immediate problems arise so long as council members are in substantial agreement with one another. But when the council is divided, the manager's position becomes precarious. If the factions on the council are equally strong, an active—and according to Banfield and Wilson (1963), a smart—manager will play them off against each other. Such a strategy is not without perils, however, and sooner or later the manager likely will be accused of manipulation and come under fire. As an alternative strategy, the manager may remain inactive, simply performing his or her responsibilities without interjecting per-

121

sonal policy preferences into the process. But such a strategy is untenable in the long run, for each faction is likely to invoke the adage, "If you're not with me, you're against me."

When the council is divided but the balance of power lies with a stable majority, the smart manager obviously will side with the majority. As one city manager explained to the authors, he needs only to be able to count a majority of council votes supporting him to retain his job. In the short run, the manager who finds himself or herself in this position is likely to emerge as a strong leader in the community, able to pursue policy initiatives with the blessing of the council (or at least the blessing of its majority). But by openly playing to the majority faction, in terms both of policy preferences and willingness to dig out requested information, the manager alienates the minority faction. And given even a slight change in council composition, the manager may find his or her position in jeopardy. In other words, conflict is antithetical to happy management. This may help explain why most cities that have opted for the council-manager plan are homogeneous and have relatively few openly conflictual issues.

The fourth factor that accounts for the high turnover rate among city managers is the philosophical difference in orientation between the manager and council members. Despite the requirement that managers take policy positions in their reports and make recommendations to the council, most council members view city managers strictly as administrators. This view creates an obvious paradox in the demands the council places on the manager: It wants the manager to have a policy orientation—that is, play a political rather than strictly an administrative role—only when it asks him or her to, and it views any policy orientation outside those specific requests as inappropriate. But most managers understand that this shifting of roles at the whim of the council is impossible, and in 1952 ICMA dropped its repudiation of politics from the City Manager Code of Ethics. And as Robert Huntley and Robert Macdonald (1975) note, most managers claim a prerogative as policy leaders. In a survey of managers, they found that 90 percent claimed to set their local political agenda, 75 percent claimed to play a leading role in policy development, and 60 percent claimed to initiate new policies. This view is reinforced by a 1994 survey of city managers, which shows that 63 percent believe that the manager should work to address the needs and interests of a wide variety of groups in the city (Bressner 1995). In effect, this casts the city manager in the role of a policy entrepreneur. These figures seem amazingly high for a profession whose formal responsibilities are merely supportive of the council, and council members sometimes respond negatively when they see how powerful the manager has become. In another 1994 survey, for example, only 27 percent of mayors viewed the policy entrepreneurial role of the city manager as legitimate (Bressner 1995). The result, when this occurs, is usually less happy for the manager than it is for the council.

Race, gender, and municipal management. Even though minorities have made substantial gains toward electoral equality in local government, they have had little success in gaining equality in the managerial ranks of municipal government. For example, only 1.3 percent of city managers are black. Nor have minorities been successful in gaining top leadership positions in municipal departments: for example, 3 percent of police chiefs and 2.9 percent of planning directors are black. Hispanics are represented in the municipal management ranks at a comparable level. Women are somewhat better represented than minorities in municipal management, accounting for 12.1 percent of city managers, 15.9 percent of planning directors, 33.4 percent of assistant city managers, and 44.5 percent of personnel directors. Even so, they remain underrepresented in an absolute sense, and municipal management is dominated by white males.

The Municipal Bureaucracy

The municipal bureaucracy in the United States employs more than 4 million people, ranging from administrators to garbage collectors. Each year, members of the municipal bureaucracy make numerous decisions, ranging from the crucial to the mundane. For example, a city manager's decision not to fire striking firefighters, or the police chief s decision to crack down on speeding motorists, may have immediate and profound implications for the lives of community residents. At the other end of the spectrum, the decision by an individual police officer to cite a motorist for a faulty turn signal, or by a garbage collector not to empty a trash container that is marginally too heavy, may seem to be of little consequence in the larger urban picture. Yet, as Bryan Jones (1983) argues, it is the individually unimportant decisions that are collectively crucial to the urban lifestyle, exactly because of the discretion municipal bureaucrats exercise in making day-to-day decisions.

A bureaucracy, says Max Weber (1946), is any modern, rational form of organization possessing the traits of hierarchy, specialization, and impersonality. In the urban setting, bureaucracy's primary purpose is to provide services for the city's citizens, including police protection, fire protection, garbage pickup, street maintenance, animal control, clean drinking water and sewage disposal, public transportation, library services, and well-maintained parks.

Hierarchy. The first manifestation of Weber's bureaucratic principle is the hierarchy through which these services are provided. At the top of the hierarchy sits the city manager, the mayor, members of the city commission, or whoever serves as the city's chief administrative officer(s). He or she typically has the privilege of appointing department heads, each responsible for the provision of a different service, who serve at his or her pleasure. Seldom are these administrators protected by civil service guidelines: They typically can

123

be fired without cause, and often are as a new administration takes office. Under the department heads come those people who actually provide the services, described so aptly by Michael Lipsky (1980) as street-level bureaucrats. They, too, may be differentiated by rank; for example, a city's police department has an elaborate chain of command, from the precinct captain to the beat cop. But each of these positions is usually governed by civil-service law, with recruitment, selection, promotion, and salary based on objectively measured job qualifications. Further, once a street-level bureaucrat has served for a probationary period, he or she may not be fired except for cause. This protection gives substantial power to municipal bureaucrats, and they are well-represented by the American Federation of State, County, and Municipal Employees (AFSCME) to ensure that their civil service rights are not abrogated.

Specialization. The second manifestation of Weber's principle of bureaucracy is the specialization—and with it, the division of labor—found among municipal employees. As urban service delivery systems have expanded to provide more services, and as technological advances have provided more effective and efficient provision of services, the generalist has given way to the specialist. Take for instance the municipal firefighter. At one time, during the days of the bucket brigades and all-volunteer fire departments, literally anyone in the community with the willingness and the physical ability to be helpful could be a firefighter. But today, modern firefighting equipment is very expensive and sophisticated, and strategies for fighting fires have also become quite technical and sophisticated. Very few untrained people today could even drive a pumper, let alone figure out how to read the various gauges and engage the various pumps. Firefighters have become specialists, and in turn, experts in their field. Even garbage collection has become specialized, with several different types of trucks that may be used in different types of situations. Again, with specialization comes expertise.

The expertise that comes with specialization is important in the urban political process, for it makes the city council dependent on its administrative branch. Given the experience and expertise of the municipal bureaucracy, the city council often defers to the judgment of administrators, and it typically lends street-level bureaucrats a great deal of discretion in dealing with the day-to-day problems they encounter. *[The theory of urban administration.]*

Impersonality. The third manifestation of Weber's bureaucratic principle is impersonality, elaborated by Bryan Jones (1983) as the norm of neutral competence. This principle holds that a bureaucratic structure should not have its own agenda, or, put metaphorically, its own axe to grind; rather, it should grind the axe of the legislative body to which it is responsible. Thus, by taking politics out of administration, the bureaucracy becomes impersonal. In principle, any individual bureaucrat could be substituted for any other without changing the level of effectiveness or efficiency with which urban services are performed and without shifting the government's policy goals. This principle is Weber's undoing, however, for it does not hold true for the modern municipal bureaucracy.

In fact, most bureaucrats *do* have their own axes to grind. At the lower levels of the bureaucratic hierarchy, important goals are continuing employment, better pay, and improved benefits. The importance of these goals is clear from the work stoppages that have become prevalent, if not commonplace, among municipal employees. With few exceptions, public sector strikes are illegal, reflecting a belief among lawmakers that the common good of citizens (e.g., garbage collection, police and fire protection) outweighs the rights of city employees. And until the 1960s, this view was generally supported by professional organizations representing many public sector employees (e.g., the National Education Association and the American Nursing Association). But during the 1960s, these attitudes began to change, and public sector employees (and their unions) became more militant. For example, 1968 alone witnessed more public sector strikes than had occurred between 1958 and 1965 (White 1972). In one of the most publicized public-sector strikes during this period, the New York City Transit Workers Union, led by Mike Quill, went out on strike in 1966, literally bringing traffic flow in the nation's largest city to a standstill (see Yates, 1977, for a trenchant description of these events). Sixteen union officials were sent to jail for defying a court order to return to work, and the strike ended only after the city agreed to a 15 percent pay raise for its transit workers. Many other cities have also experienced public-sector strikes, which by 1980 were occurring at a rate of over four hundred per year.[16] They continue to result in jail sentences and fines, and in some cases, striking employees have been fired. Yet, at the local level, public-sector strikes continue and even increase in frequency.

At the upper levels of the hierarchy, important goals of bureaucrats are usually a larger budget and increased authority over programmatic decisions. Thus, bureaucrats are program advocates, and the continuation and expansion of their programs sometimes becomes as important as the effective or efficient provision of public services. This concern for *turf*, coupled with the power vested in the municipal bureaucracy (through civil service law and through expertise), has led Lowi (1969b, 87) to characterize it as the *new urban machine*:

> They [municipal bureaucrats] are relatively irresponsible structures of power. That is, each agency shapes important public policies, yet the leadership of each is relatively self-perpetuating and not readily subject to the controls of any higher authority.

16. Unfortunately, the Bureau of Labor Statistics discontinued its reports of work stoppage involving fewer than 1,000 workers in 1981, so current data are not available.

This, however, seems overly harsh, and a more benign view of the municipal bureaucracy is possible. While its motive for self-perpetuation and power is no doubt important, this represents a human motive as much as a bureaucratic motive. Indeed, our earlier definition of politics includes a power component, thus taking the municipal bureaucracy out of the purely administrative realm and placing it squarely in the political realm. We will defer discussion of the implications of this interconnection until later (chapter 16), when service delivery in the city is discussed more explicitly. But for now, it is sufficient to consider the municipal bureaucracy as a not-so-impersonal force of employees with human needs and motives, who are given (and as humans, take advantage of) the opportunity to interpret policies and make discretionary decisions as they see fit.

Other Formal Participants

Clerks. One of the least understood but most important positions in America's urban system is that of city clerk. Most cities have clerks (by formal responsibility if not by name), but their positions are particularly important in small, mayor-council cities. As noted earlier, nearly one-quarter of these cities elect a clerk. The clerk's formal responsibilities entail secretarial service to the city council. But in most small cities, the informal responsibilities (and power) of the clerk go well beyond those of office manager (Adrian and Press 1977). Particularly in cities without a full-time administrator, the clerk takes on the role of policy advisor to the governing body. The clerk typically has considerable longevity (in spite of the electoral status of the position in many communities, the job responsibilities are seemingly so innocuous that, once elected, the clerk tends to be reelected indefinitely), providing him or her with a great deal of experience (and expertise) in city affairs. As new council members are elected, they often learn the ropes of city government and municipal policy from the clerk, who often (either unwittingly or intentionally) provides the council member with his or her own interpretation of the municipal mission. *[The theory of ideology.]* Even experienced council members may treat the clerk as a trusted confidant, seeking advice on difficult policy decisions. But, as Adrian and Press (1977, 204) note,

> because the consequences of any action this advice may generate will be attributed to others—the council members, the mayor . . .—clerks go on their bland way toward retirement, calmly riding above the storms of controversy that confront their colleagues.

Judges. Another position that is important in the American urban system is that of judge. This position is sometimes elective, sometimes appointive, but almost always the selection process is noncontroversial, for municipal and county judges have relatively little judicial power. They are, in large part, bound by precedent at the higher levels of the judicial system, and their rulings are subject to reversal. On the other hand, they have no power of reversal themselves. On occasion, a local judge will come under fire for a decision, particularly in cases involving perceived insensitivity toward the victims of sexual offenses and domestic violence (e.g., *The Progressive*, Nov. 1985, p. 16). However, for the most part decisions are not controversial; but through these decisions, the judge may gain considerable power in the community.

Specifically, local judges become the center of what is often a fragmented and disorganized network of human service providers in the community. They have legal responsibility (and authority) to refer a guilty person to the community mental health center for counseling or to the local alcohol or drug abuse agency for treatment. They can refer abused spouses to a variety of social programs, and they have the power to do the same for abused children. They can assign those convicted of misdemeanors to perform community service, often through the auspices of social service agencies. In short, they have considerable contact with the human service sector of the community, and because of their authority, legitimacy, and high status, they often become de facto leaders and spokespersons for those services. Given the poverty, crime, and need for human services in most large and middle-sized cities, this provides judges with considerable power in the urban policy arena.

Board members. The final formal position we will discuss is membership on one of the city's many independent boards or commissions. Following the Civil War, many cities instituted a variety of independent boards and commissions to serve as the governing bodies for specific municipal departments. For example, many cities adopted a police commission, a library commission, a school board, a hospital board, and so forth. But as it became clear that coordination among various municipal agencies and departments was necessary to provide comprehensive services in a complex environment, the governing function of these boards and commissions gradually gave way to an advisory function (and in many cases, they were disbanded completely). Today, most cities have a host of advisory boards, many provided with the power to make recommendations to the city council or administration. But only the school board, and in some cases, the library board and the hospital board, generally retain the characteristics of a true governing body. Today, most other boards and commissions have little formal power to make binding policy decisions. For example, most cities have a planning commission, charged with the responsibility for developing the city's long-range plan. In principle, this plan has legal status, but it can be (and routinely is) ignored or reinterpreted by the city council. In addition, the council's power to appoint members to the planning commission for short terms means that an inconvenient plan can rewritten.[17] Cities also appoint citizens to a civil service board, a housing authority board, a parking board, an appeals board, and even a garbage and trash management board. In fact, some estimates hold that more than a million citizens participate on advisory boards, commissions, and councils *in education alone* (Davies 1980), and Adrian and Press (1977) hypothesize millions of hours spent each year by unpaid citizens serving as board members. Yet, the actual power of these citizens is doubtful. One evaluation of boards in Pennsylvania (reported by Adrian and Press 1977) found that although boards insulate the legislative body and the executive from political pressure and provide considerable amounts of staff time that would otherwise be very expensive, they are rarely able to take decisive action.

In short, advisory boards and commissions serve a number of useful functions, but not the one(s) which they were originally designed to serve. We have already observed the relative powerlessness of the city's governing body relative to its professional bureaucracy; a similar conclusion must be applied to most advisory boards. They simply do not have the experience or the expertise to compete with that of professional administrators, or even that of city council members. As a result, recommendations are often based on cues picked up from administrators or council members, or are tied to information that administrators provide for them. This difficulty is exacerbated by the charge of most advisory boards: they are asked to represent the entire community. And, in fact, many boards and commissions take great pride in their representativeness. But almost by definition, the greater the level of representativeness of the board, the more diverse its beliefs about the city, its problems, and its goals, and the greater the level of conflict and controversy on the board. If board members cannot even agree among themselves, they feel reluctant to push the administration to adopt their recommendations (Bolland and Redfield 1988).

But, as noted above, boards and commissions do serve several useful functions. They deflect political pressure from elected and appointed officials. They provide useful staff work in researching community problems. They are able to coordinate community resources, often serving as directors of fundraising or volunteer drives. They provide effective links between citizens and their government, often serving as useful conduits for information. And finally, they provide a mechanism for defusing potential controversy in the community. By appointing a vocal opponent to governmental policy to an advisory capacity on one of the city's boards or commissions, the mayor or council may co-opt the opponent onto the government team.

17. For a discussion of the controversy surrounding appointments of school board members in some cities, see Rich (1996).

But, if advisory boards and commissions are without power in most cities, why do millions of citizens continue to participate on them? And what are alternative outlets for citizen participation? We consider these questions in the next chapter.

The Hand of Man, photogravure, 24.1 x 31.8 cm
Alfred Stieglitz Collection, 1949.850.

The real illness of the American city today, and especially of the deprived groups within it, is voicelessness. . . . The Negro revolt is not aimed at winning friends but at winning freedom, not inter-personal warmth but institutional justice.

Harvey Cox, *The Secular City*

CHAPTER 7

Informal Citizen
Participation
in Local Politics

The previous chapter discussed two ways citizens can participate in local politics: by running for public office and by appointment to one of the city's boards or commissions. In each case, participation is largely an individual activity, reflecting the motives and interests of the individual officeholder or board member. This chapter considers two additional forms of individual participation: voting and citizen-initiated contacts (i.e., the behavior of individual citizens as they contact city government about problems or services). In addition, it looks at participation through groups, including political parties, civic organizations, business associations, neighborhood associations, and organized (and unorganized) protest movements. Finally, it considers how urban leaders emerge through a combination of individual and group activities. This, in turn, leads to a discussion of urban political power in the next chapter.

Who Participates and Why?

Before discussing outlets for citizen participation, we first explore, in a general way, the extent of this participation. Sidney Verba and Norman Nie (1972) define participation as any act aimed at influencing the government, either by influencing the choice of personnel or by affecting the choices made by those personnel. Using this definition, they found that approximately 78 percent of American citizens participate politically. The largest segment (21 percent) participates by voting only, while smaller segments combine voting with other, more active forms of participation. Only 11 percent can be classified as complete activists.[1] These data give both an optimistic and a pessimistic picture of political participation in America. From an optimistic perspective, it is comforting to note that democracy seems to be alive and well, with more than three-fourths of the adult population engaging in some form of political activity. But from a more pessimistic perspective, only slightly more than one in five adults devote more energy to the political process than an occasional pull on the lever of a voting machine. And only one in ten adults is anything like a well-rounded political participant.

Why do people participate in politics? At the national level, most political participation is of an expressive nature, reflecting largely philosophical or moral issues: gun control, the environment, defense spending, nuclear disarmament. At the local level, participation reflects more personal concerns that touch the lives of people on an everyday basis. For example, local issues involve dangerous intersections, zoning decisions, distasteful billboards, and baseball diamonds. People get involved in national politics largely to make statements expressing their values. But people get involved in local politics because they have problems they want to solve or complaints they wish to air.

Several studies of urban political participation shed light on who gets involved. Robert Lineberry and Ira Sharkansky (1978), for example, report that fewer than 15 percent of surveyed respondents claim to be active members of groups or organizations working to solve an urban problem. Even within this small set, a noticeable class bias exaggerates the process and outcomes of participation. At the upper end of the socioeconomic spectrum, over 25 percent claim activity in local groups or organizations, while at the lower end of the spectrum, this figure declines to approximately 6 percent. Accordingly the problems of the upper and middle classes may be addressed because of their participation, while the problems of the poor (and particularly the underclass[2])

---

1. These results have been replicated, with similar conclusions, by Verba et al. (1995).

2. The language of American politics often stumbles over words denoting social and economic class. Such words invariably carry emotional baggage. *Middle class* and *upper class* are acceptable terms, and descriptive symmetry might suggest the use of a threefold class division—with lower class as the bottom tier. But there is no escaping what Charles Stevenson (1963, 32) calls "persuasive definition." Lower class is easily associated with the idea of low class, and worse, it is regarded by many as a term with racist connotations and an ethnic slur. Thus, we use the term *underclass* and *poorer class*. The underclass are usually identified as the poorest of the poor, living in the midst of concentrated poverty (e.g., public housing neighborhoods) or with a tenuous attachment to American civic institutions (e.g., the homeless). While a behavioral component is often used in definitions of the

may be largely ignored. In another study, Elaine Sharp (1982) reports that only 11 percent of the poor in Wichita, Kansas, had ever contacted a municipal official, compared with 21 percent of middle-class citizens and 40 percent of upper-class citizens. Again, this trend suggests that officials are more aware of middle- and upper-class problems than of the needs of the poor.

These findings are strangely paradoxical, for we should expect those people with greatest need to be most active. Yet, we find exactly the opposite: Those with the least economic need are most likely to participate, while those with the greatest need are least likely to do so. This paradox is at least partially explained, however, when we take into account both the means for participation among the poor and the systemic bias of urban government against effective participation by those living in poverty. First consider means: Most middle- and upper-class urban residents have direct (or at least indirect) access to municipal government. They may have a friend or neighbor on the city council or who is a city engineer. This provides them with an immediate contact; and even if the contact is somewhat removed from the municipal leadership, the citizen can approach the mayor or the city manager with the introduction, "Carol Taylor [or whoever] suggested that I talk with you." Even without this direct contact, most middle- and upper-class residents may know a prominent business owner, lawyer, or other professional in town who can provide much the same introduction. In contrast, the poorer citizen (who is less well connected) must make his or her own introductions, a difficult task at best and particularly difficult for a person not used to moving among the powerful at city hall.

As an alternative, those living in poverty may go directly to the complaint bureau that many cities have established; but this is often bureaucracy at its worst, and the citizen seldom receives much immediate satisfaction from such visits. Imagine a municipal employee whose sole responsibility day after day is listening to the complaints of citizens about the way the city conducts its business. The first week might prove exciting as he or she hears about all of the city's "dirty laundry." But even for a person committed to improving the plight of the poor, the job soon becomes tedious and frustrating, and since the city employee is, in the complainant's eyes, at least partly responsible for the problems, he or she is likely to take the brunt of the complaints as personal attacks. Over time, the employee may begin acting defensively, asserting his or her authority when given the opportunity. (The employee sitting at the complaint desk is, after all, a street-level bureaucrat.) While this strategy may make the job more bearable for the employee, it makes the encounter with government singularly unsatisfactory for the citizen, and he or she is likely to think twice about complaining next time.

---

underclass (e.g., violence, use of drugs), we will not do so here; suffice it to say that people living in poverty, particularly concentrated poverty, are more susceptible to such destructive behaviors. *[The theory of poverty and the underclass.]*

Second, political information is more readily available to the middle and upper classes than to those living in poverty. Citizens often become informed about their municipal government through participation in such organizations as Rotary, Kiwanis, and the League of Women Voters. These organizations are typically bastions of the middle and upper classes, seldom frequented by the poor. The upper and middle classes also tend to read local newspapers more frequently, giving their members greater knowledge about the city and its government. While this is a subtle bias, its effects may be large; for as Francis Bacon noted nearly four hundred years ago, knowledge is power.

The paradox of participation breaks down, however, when we examine the relationship between need and participation, controlling for skill. Verba and Nie (1972) report, for example, that urban blacks participate in municipal affairs more frequently than whites with comparable social backgrounds. In a similar finding, Alex-Assensoh (1995) reports that residents of a predominantly black underclass neighborhood in Columbus, Ohio, are more politically active than residents of a predominantly white underclass neighborhood in the same city. Even more pertinent, Berry and his colleagues (1991) report that poor people living in low-income neighborhoods are more likely to be politically active than are poor people living in nonpoor neighborhoods. Finally, ethnic minorities participate more frequently than their nonethnic counterparts (e.g., Nelson 1979). In each case, participation is likely to reflect greater need. Or put more directly, people are more likely to complain when there is more to complain about. But just as important, people are more likely to participate when participation is easy, or at least when roadblocks to participation (cultural, social, or bureaucratic) are not encountered.

During the past three decades, the federal government has made great efforts to remove these roadblocks, often with indifferent success. President Johnson, as part of his Great Society program, set a goal of "maximum feasible participation" by the nation's poor. Since 1960, local citizen participation has become a condition for a number of grant-in-aid programs to cities. While only 5 of these programs required citizen participation mechanisms prior to 1960, 155 had such requirements by 1978 (ACIR 1980).[3] An instructive example of this type of mandated participation occurs in the Community Development Block Grant, enacted in 1974 to provide cities with funds for urban renewal, basic water and sewer facilities, and historical preservation. The act required applicants to provide satisfactory assurances that they (a) provide citizens with adequate information on the availability of funds and the range of activities that may be undertaken, (b) hold public hearings, and (c) afford

---

3. ACIR is an acronym for the Advisory Commission on Intergovernmental Relations, created by Congress in 1959 to monitor the operation of the American federal system and to recommend improvements.

citizens an adequate opportunity to participate in the development of the application. Even so, the early days of this program witnessed considerable dissatisfaction with the lack of involvement by lower-income groups (ACIR 1980). The 1977 reenactment strengthened the citizen participation requirements, mandating applicants to submit a written citizen participation plan. Many cities met this requirement by encouraging and facilitating the development of neighborhood organizations in low-income areas of the city. In many cases, they paid the operating expenses for these organizations, and residents of more than one urban neighborhood have enjoyed a picnic dinner at city expense. But for all this, it is still unclear whether participation by the poor can be successful, and systematic instances of successful participation are difficult to document. We will explore this phenomenon in greater depth later in this chapter.

Individual Modes of Participation

Beyond seeking municipal office or volunteering for service on a municipal advisory board, individuals can attempt to influence political outcomes in two ways—through voting and by initiating contacts with city hall.

Voting

As he signed the Voting Rights Act of 1965, President Lyndon Baines Johnson boldly proclaimed that the right to vote is "the most powerful instrument ever devised by man for breaking down injustice. . . ." Taken at face value, this suggests that voting serves a practical function, keeping politics and politicians honest and representative. More important, it suggests that the desire to achieve some desired outcome motivates the decision to vote. For instance, a citizen who is disenchanted with the way he or she is represented by an elected official can vote to replace the representative with someone who will better represent the voter's interests. And from the other side of the ballot box, the elected official who realizes that the citizen has this power is likely to modify his or her behavior accordingly.

This rational view of electoral behavior (and, in fact, of democratic theory) has been challenged in a number of quarters. One of the most trenchant criticisms holds that citizens may simply have insufficient knowledge, information, or understanding to vote their self-interest. A rational vote requires the voter to understand not only the differences between candidates, but also how those differences affect him or her. In many instances, party affiliation serves as a convenient heuristic for assessing candidates, but this has been effectively eliminated in many cities by the use of nonpartisan elections. Other criticisms of the rational model of democratic participation are equally important, and they are discussed below.

Ballot propositions. Particularly in the case of referenda and initiatives—which are often worded in language that is convoluted or otherwise difficult to understand—the voter may not know what he or she is voting for or against. David Magleby (1984) reports that the wording of ballot propositions in California and Oregon is readable at the eighteenth grade level (i.e., two years post-baccalaureate), well past the educational achievement of the vast majority of voters in those states.[4] As a case in point, consider the proposition listed in figure 7.1. Even after careful reading, the exact purpose of this amendment to the Alabama constitution, which *seems* to have important implications for municipal governance, is likely to be unclear.

The typical voter entering a voting booth (which for many people is itself intimidating) and encountering this proposition for the first time would likely be confused by such convoluted wording, leading him or her either to vote in an irrational (that is, uninformed) manner or simply to exercise his or her right not to vote on the issue.

Complicated wording of ballot propositions yields a middle- and upper-class bias to urban politics, particularly in cities without strong political parties. Low-income people, who are typically undereducated and poorly informed, may find the party label more helpful in voting their self-interest than do members of the middle and upper classes. By the same token, the poor may be influenced on ballot propositions by leaders of the local party. But in the absence of cues from trusted political leaders (e.g., the party), low-income voters must interpret ballot propositions by themselves, attempting to determine which choice is in their best interest. For many low-income voters, this may be an impossible task, given the grammatical complexity of most ballot propositions. The result may be either nonparticipation or irrational participation in the voting booth. The better educated upper and middle classes are better able to comprehend ballot propositions and make a rational determination of self-interest.

Nonparticipation among the urban poor clearly lends a middle- and upper-class bias to urban elections; but so, too, does irrational participation, since irrational participants, voting in an uninformed manner, are likely to cancel out one another's votes.[5]

Misplaced faith in the power of elected officials. Another criticism of the rational model of electoral behavior concerns the assumption that elected officials determine policies. Certainly, at all levels of government obstacles emerge

---

4. By way of comparison, Magleby finds that *Time* and *Newsweek* are readable at approximately the twelfth-grade level, and *Reader's Digest* at the tenth-grade level.

5. For these and similar reasons, many critics of our society view the election process as a significant instance of American class bias, and in the words of Sennett and Cobb (1972), another example of the "hidden injuries of class" in America.

FIGURE 7.1   A November 8, 1988, Ballot Proposition in Alabama

Proposed Statewide Amendment Number Four (4)

To propose and provide for the submission of an amendment to the Constitution of 1901, as amended; providing that no law whose purpose of effect is to provide for a new or increased expenditure of municipal funds held or disbursed by the municipal governing body shall become effective as to any municipality of this state until the first day of the fiscal year next following the passage of such law unless such law is approved by a resolution duly adopted by and spread upon the minutes of the municipal governing body of the municipality affected thereby, or such law (or other law) provides the municipal governing bodies with new or additional revenues sufficient to fund such new or increased expenditures; providing for an election thereon and prescribing an effective date for the proposed amendment.

Yes

No

to the faithful fulfillment of campaign promises. For example, a revenue shortfall may prevent a promised road from being constructed or a sidewalk from being repaired. Or a lawsuit may prevent an old building from being razed to make way for a new parking facility. Another impediment to the fulfillment of campaign promises is the relative impotence of the city council in cities that have adopted the council-manager form of government. As noted before, the power of the council is greatly diffused by its lack of information and expertise, and it relies on the city manager to set the agenda and make recommendations. Because of the council's relative impotence, the link between the voter and policy outcomes is weak, even though the link between the voter and the elected official may be strong. *[The theory of grass-roots democracy.]* (Again, there exists an upper- and middle-class bias, for upper- and middle-class interests are generally best served through government by administration—especially when the administration is dominated by white males.)

A major factor militating against the ability of elected officials to determine policies in the urban place is their inability to control private investment decisions. For example, a developer may choose to build a shopping mall just outside the city limits, where the city council is powerless. This decision will potentially draw businesses and shoppers from the downtown area. By the same token, a builder may decide to construct a new housing subdivision that will severely tax the city's existing water and sewer systems. So long as the builder meets local zoning requirements and building codes, the council is largely powerless to stop the construction project. Or a small manufacturing business may simply decide to move to a new city, enticed by attractive tax deferments and other incentives that are offered there. If the council lacks sufficient funds to match these incentives, it is powerless to stop the move and the loss of local jobs that will result.

137

A third factor intervening between the electorate and public policy is the growth of special-purpose governments (these will be explored in greater depth in chapter 11). Since 1952, the number of governments designated as special districts and public authorities has grown dramatically, from about 12,300 to almost 29,400; the largest number are for projects related to economic development (Kantor 1993). These special-purpose governments are often used to fund projects that have been turned down by popular vote. Notably, during the 1980s voters were quite wary of funding building projects (e.g., convention centers), which have typically received only about 40 percent popular support at the polls (G. Peterson 1991, quoted in Sanders 1992). Yet, a number of cities have built convention centers despite a negative public vote; their strategy has been to transfer authority for building the convention center from municipal government to a special-purpose government that requires lower levels of support (and, in some cases, no popular support at all) before committing funds and breaking ground. This approach has been used in Philadelphia, with the state's creation of the Pennsylvania Convention Center Authority; in Indianapolis, with the Marion County Convention and Recreational Facilities Authority; and in Atlanta, with the development of both a convention center and a domed stadium by the Georgia World Congress Center Authority. The capacity of these special-purpose governments to operate without a public vote on new taxes or debt has enabled cities to promote convention-center development and expansion despite the electorate's persistent concern. In the early 1970s, city governments accounted for over 60 percent of the dollar value of new convention centers and civic centers. But by 1990, city governments accounted for only 25.7 percent of these, with special-purpose governments accounting for more than 58 percent of the total (Sanders 1992).

In each case, policy is removed from the hands of the city council and twice removed from the hands of the voters. The impact on the upper and middle classes is softened, for capital investment decisions are typically in their best interests: new homes emerge, urban decay is excised, better roads are constructed, and so forth. But for the poor, the lack of effective representation is more critical. As a case in point, William Keech (1968) found that in Durham, North Carolina, the vote is more important for (and effective in) achieving legal justice than social justice. That is, the vote (or the threat of the vote) broke down governmental barriers to equal rights and services, but it did little to break down social discrimination. Keech (1968, 105) concludes that "the really striking gains of Durham's Negro minority have come through resources other than the vote."

Citizen-Initiated Contacts

During their adult lives, most Americans probably will have at least one run-in with city hall. It may take any of a number of forms. For example, a person may complain that trash is not picked up regularly. Or a road may be filled with potholes, or the sidewalk may be crumbling. He or she may be concerned about inadequate police protection or may object to a city ordinance requiring fire alarms to be placed in all rental property. The person may insist that heavy (and excessively fast) traffic flow on a nearby street demands a traffic control signal, feel disgruntled that there are not enough baseball diamonds, or that there are too many baseball diamonds and not enough jogging trails, or may complain that a neighbor's dog barks through the night, or that its master parties loudly through the night. The list of possible complaints is almost endless.

"You can't fight city hall" is one of the most common political adages, and if followed, would lead people with these concerns to (a) complain to their friends and neighbors (but not to their elected officials or to the municipal bureaucracy); (b) vote against incumbent council members in the next municipal election; or (c) move to another neighborhood or city. Yet, every year a large number of Americans defy the conventional political wisdom and take their complaints directly to city hall. These citizen-initiated contacts are a unique form of political participation, for they are typically carried out by individuals (as opposed to groups) and they are motivated strictly by self-interest. This form of participation has generated substantial interest within political science (e.g., Coulter 1992). But before we make too much of it, we should explore it further, paying particular attention to both its magnitude and its potential for class bias.

The fact that citizen-initiated contacts are individual expressions is important, for it makes them an unexpected form of participation. Another political adage (perhaps second in importance only to the supposed futility of fighting city hall) concerns strength in numbers and suggests that participation for most people is more palatable, less traumatic, and generally accomplished more easily when they act as part of a group rather than as individuals. Psychologists tell us, for example, that people become more bold in groups (Wallach et al. 1962). In contrast, citizen-initiated contacts are strictly the acts of individuals, and we may surmise that only special circumstances (i.e., a situation perceived as intolerable) would move a person to this kind of bold activity. For example, a citizen who yesterday ruined his muffler by driving through a pothole may today find his way to city hall to complain about the deplorable condition of the city streets. Or a business executive who botches an important presentation at work, brought on by a sleepless night of howling dogs and blaring music in her neighborhood, may take her case to city hall. But for most of us, the inconvenience of taking time to go downtown or even to find the right telephone number, and the intimidation of facing the vast municipal bureaucracy alone, leads us to a more pragmatic approach: We simply trust government to fix the problem itself (or perhaps we wait for someone else to complain).

139

Thus, it makes little sense to say that some neighborhoods with high levels of need will be the source of most complaints to the city. Inhabitants of these neighborhoods, who may be primarily poor, have fewer political skills than do their middle- and upper-class counterparts, and they are more likely to be intimidated by city hall. In addition, the expectations in many of these neighborhoods are likely to be lower. Uncollected garbage or barking dogs may be commonplace and therefore go largely unnoticed in underclass neighborhoods, whereas in middle- and upper-class neighborhoods, such events are unexpected and often draw immediate complaints.

A second conclusion holds that citizen-initiated contacts are motivated by self-interest. People contact city hall about potholes in the roads because it affects them directly, not because of a concern for the city's other motorists. People complain about the lack of softball diamonds in municipal parks because they want to play ball, not because of a commitment to increasing the cardiovascular capacity of the city's inhabitants. They complain about slovenly and haphazard garbage collection because they find garbage in *their* front yards, not because a passing motorist might find the situation aesthetically unpleasing.

And how does city hall respond to these complaints (if it responds at all)? Usually it does not reformulate its policies, but rather responds on a case-by-case basis. For example, the citizen who complains about potholes in front of her house may find a work crew filling those potholes the next morning, but ignoring similar ones a block away. Or a garbage truck, on a special run, may collect the missed garbage; but the city's garbage-collection policy remains intact. Given the motivations underlying citizen-initiated contacts and given the nonsystematic responses these contacts are likely to elicit, should we construe this activity as political?

In a word, *yes*. While the city is unlikely to modify its policies in response to a single complaint, it may, over time, modify policies in response to a series of related complaints. For example, the cost of sending out work crews to fix individual potholes in front of complainants' houses may be prohibitively high, and for only a little more money, the city may be able to systematically fill potholes all across town. Or the cost of sending a garbage truck on a special run to pick up spilled garbage, when aggregated over a number of complaints, may lead the city to reconsider its policy of leaving spilled garbage where it lies. In short, these private, self-interested complaints, taken together, may have important policy implications. But paradoxically, any complaint, considered alone, is likely to have little or no effect on policy, may or may not even ameliorate an immediate problem, and is accomplished at a psychological cost to the complainant.

Thus, we should expect that relatively few people take this route of political participation. Although a number of studies of citizen-initiated contacting behavior have been conducted, we are still somewhat unclear about the exact magnitude of the phenomenon. Estimates of contact with municipal government range from a low of 20 percent (Verba and Nie 1972) to a high of 58 percent (Katz et al. 1975; see Coulter, 1988, for a review). But in some of these studies, *all* forms of contact are recorded, including (a) reporting a crime; (b) obtaining a building permit; (c) receiving job training; and (d) visiting public health clinics. Such behaviors fall outside the purview of politics (as discussed in chapter 5), and they should not be confused with more overtly political activities, such as those described earlier in this chapter. Thus, when we examine actual *complaints* (as opposed to all forms of contact), we get a somewhat different picture. In Houston, for example, a central complaint agency set up to receive and address citizen concerns received only between thirty-five and fifty complaints a day (Mladenka 1977). This represents under 20,000 complaints a year in a city with over 1.5 million inhabitants, or a complaint rate of only 1 percent (or, put in terms of households, approximately 3 percent). The central complaint agency is not the only avenue for citizen complaints, however, and others may go to individual departments and agencies. But even assuming that complaints to the central agency represent only the tip of the iceberg, it would be hard to imagine a complaint rate of over 10 percent. Since a person who has contacted city hall once may do so a second time (and a third, fourth, or fifth time), this generous estimate drops considerably. Of course, data from one city does not allow us to generalize to citizen participation across the country. But even by the most generous estimates, citizen-initiated contacts with city hall, in which complaints are aired and solutions requested, must be far below those reported in many studies of citizen participation in America. In short, only a small fraction of urban dwellers take it upon themselves to participate as *individuals* in the political process.

Group Modes of Participation

Largely because of psychological, social, and political barriers to individual participation, groups have become the modus operandi of American politics. At the national level (and with the exception of political parties), these groups form largely around specific issues: the National Rifle Association, the National Organization of Women, the nuclear freeze movement, and so forth. At the local level, however, groups tend to have a multi-purpose orientation. For example, the local chamber of commerce gets involved in almost every economic issue (which, in the end, is virtually every issue), and neighborhood organizations often participate in a wide variety of social issues that affect them. One important distinction we can draw between individual participation and group participation at the local level is that the former tends to be motivated by self-interest (and to some extent by a sense of civic responsibility), whereas the latter often is motivated by concern for the group.

141

One of the most important elements of human nature is the need to affiliate with others. Humans (as Aristotle observed long ago) are social animals, which leads us to become involved in many different kinds of relationships. For example, marriage (and the family) has survived as a human institution in large measure because of our need for companionship. And each of us maintains a complex network of friendships that, when studied, meanders through the urban terrain (Wellman 1979, Fischer et al. 1977). We join bridge clubs, softball teams, bowling leagues, and sewing circles for exactly the same reason. And in the more political sphere, we join civic groups, neighborhood associations, and interest groups.

This is not to say that these political groups fill exactly the same human need as social groups. Participation in political groups actually serves two purposes: It is motivated by self-interest, and through it participants attempt to achieve those political and policy outcomes they believe to be important; and it is motivated by participants' needs to affiliate and to maintain contact with others. The mixture of these motives often leads political groups in directions different from those their individual members might take. For example, an emergent leader within a neighborhood association may have strong feelings about historic preservation within the community and get the association involved in efforts to save an historic train depot slated for demolition. Many members of the association may not care about the building; in fact, they may think it ugly and worthy of demolition. Yet, they go along with the association, for the value derived from membership in the group more than compensates for taking a political stance that mildly violates their self-interest. The same could be said for membership in such civic groups as the Rotary, Kiwanis, or the League of Women Voters. The various projects that these groups engage in probably reflects the interests of group leaders. Yet, members willingly go along, for the social benefits derived from membership in the group outweigh the costs of taking an insincere issue position. Note that in both of these cases, group leaders speak with the authority of the group, even though the group members, left to their own devices, may not individually participate in the issue at all.

With this as a precautionary note, we begin an inventory of political groups active at the local level. In each case, we will consider motives for joining the group, political strategies employed by the group, political and policy positions held by the group, and various impediments the group must overcome to be successful in its political mission.

Political Parties

Logic suggests that the power and the importance of the political party should be greatest at the local level of government. First, local party organizations are the building blocks of the national party. Congress, after all, represents local constituents (see O'Neill 1987), and even presidential candidates must put together coalitions of local leaders. Second, local parties are largely free from the ideological divisions of national parties. For example, Democrats in New York have a very different agenda from those in Alabama, who in turn differ from those in Nevada. Yet, they all go by the same name. In contrast, these differences are minimized within a region and particularly within an individual city. Thus, voters can give loyalty to the local party without the need to check the ideological credentials of individual candidates. Third, the party should be best able to reward its faithful supporters at the local level, for (a) it is closer to its members there than at any other level of government, and it should be better able to trade votes for services, and (b) most governmental jobs are filled at the municipal level.

However logical this may seem, parties are far from the center of political action at the local level. As noted earlier, much of this decline is due to urban reform, wherein politics (and hence the role of political parties) was removed from municipal government. For example, the advent of government-by-management concentrated great power in the hands of administrators who could act independently of elected officials. Thus, the symbiotic link between the party and its members, even if it still existed, could not guarantee desired policy outcomes. More important was the decline of patronage through the introduction of civil service requirements into municipal hiring decisions. More important still was the advent of the nonpartisan election, which is by far the most pervasive component of the reform package (e.g., city management, at-large elections). Among the largest cities in this country, only Pittsburgh, Jacksonville, Cleveland, Baltimore, New York, New Orleans, Philadelphia, St. Louis, and Indianapolis have fully partisan elections (Judd 1984). In contrast, Phoenix, Columbus, Dallas, Detroit, San Antonio, San Diego, Seattle, Los Angeles, Milwaukee, San Francisco, Memphis, Houston, Denver, and Boston have nonpartisan elections. In Chicago, the mayor is elected on a partisan ballot, while council members run without party labels. In small and middle-sized cities, partisan elections are quite rare.

In general, then, parties have been left with a much diminished role in local politics. As noted earlier, this results in a decline in electoral participation, particularly among the poor. And as Lineberry and Sharkansky (1978, 125–26; also see Welch and Bledsoe 1988) suggest, this probably increases the representation of middle class interests: "The voice of certain groups—e.g., business people, Republicans, upper-income voters, people who read newspapers regularly—is a bit louder." Thus, the urban reformers were more successful perhaps than even they had any reason to expect, not necessarily in their stated purpose (removing the political machine from the urban landscape), but in a largely unstated purpose (recreating urban politics as a middle- and upper-class enterprise).

143

Business and Economic Groups

Steven Elkin (1987, 31) states, "A reputation for being antibusiness, for not listening to local businessmen's schemes for making a greater city, is an invitation to fiscal trouble that even the hardiest progressive politicians are unlikely to be anxious to accept." For this reason, the most pervasive groups in urban politics are those based on economic interests; these include the local chamber of commerce, the local board of realtors, and ad hoc business groups formed to promote economic development. These often have overlapping memberships, although their aims are different and their leadership styles vary considerably.

Chamber of commerce. The most visible economic group is the local chamber of commerce. In most cities of over twenty-five thousand, the local chamber of commerce typically employs an executive officer and (particularly in larger cities) a variety of staff assistants. These persons assume responsibility for maintaining a healthy economic climate within the city, and they do so in a number of ways. First, the executive officer actively solicits new businesses and industries into the city. He or she accomplishes this task in a number of ways: writing brochures, making phone calls, providing guided tours for potential newcomers, and traveling extensively—knocking on doors and extolling the virtues of his or her community wherever anyone will listen. Second, and more important for our purposes, the executive director meets regularly with the city manager and/or the city council, lobbying for policies promoting local growth. For example, he or she may lobby for the expenditure of city funds to expand the local airport or to provide additional downtown parking, promote the aggressive use of tax incentives to attract new businesses and industries to the community, or argue for the development of a new industrial park with city-subsidized water and sewer lines. Third, the chamber of commerce staff serves as a kind of local support group for business and industry, providing advice, counseling, and just plain encouragement for those who need or want it.

But beyond its staff, what kind of organization is the local chamber of commerce? Membership is open to anyone in the community, both individuals and businesses (for a modest membership fee, typically between $100 and $300 per year). Members annually elect a president, usually from the community's business or industrial sector. The chamber of commerce also elects from its membership a board of directors designated to provide direction to its economic development efforts. It typically organizes several mixers each year, providing opportunities for members to see one another and exchange ideas in an informal atmosphere. In addition, it sponsors a variety of programs, ranging from "issue breakfasts" (known locally as "issues and eggs") and candidate forums to leadership development courses.

As is the case with many such organizations, the chamber of commerce is largely a staff organization, reflecting the efforts and concerns of its executive director. And as is the case with the city council, the board of directors usually has neither the expertise nor the information to challenge the judgments of the executive director, who becomes the de facto policymaker for the organization. (But unlike the city council, the membership of the chamber is quite homogeneous, and seldom is there ideological conflict between the executive director and the board of directors.) Further, most members have neither the time nor the inclination to attend meetings regularly or to serve on committees.

The membership roster of the local chamber of commerce is typically large, reflecting what appears to be an impressive level of participation, from virtually the entire business community. This kind of participation is what we may term "checkbook participation," however, reflecting members' willingness to pay their dues and let someone else get involved. They support the principles of the chamber; they like to show support for economic growth and development by proudly displaying a chamber of commerce decal in their window; and they are very pleased to have an established organization behind them should they have a run-in with city hall. They accomplish this through dues, however, rather than through active involvement.

In the end, the mission of the chamber of commerce may be too amorphous to generate active participation among more than a small percentage of its members. It has become established in most communities, and it is the very essence of respectability. But although this gives chamber members easy access to city hall to discuss economic development, it also leaves the chamber without many acute issues that mean the difference between success or failure for its members. It addresses the gamut of economic development issues (espousing pro-growth and low-tax policies) and thereby appeals to the widest possible membership. But, at the same time, it necessarily fails to concentrate on the individual issues about which individual members get excited (e.g., downtown development versus shopping centers). This void is filled by a number of other economic groups that often lack the broad base of support enjoyed by the chamber, but which may, as a consequence, enjoy greater short-term success.

Board of realtors. One such group is the board of realtors, a group of local business persons involved in the development and sale of local real estate. Members of this group have a single purpose, the promotion of their businesses, and they go about it by lobbying the city council and administration on policy issues that bear on real estate. Unlike the chamber of commerce, the board of realtors is a more narrowly focused group that does not spread itself too thin by pursuing a wide range of interests. In the same way, the very nature of the group encourages participation by its members. This, coupled with the importance of land development and promotion for the city's economic well-being, means that when the board of realtors speaks, people in positions of importance listen.

Downtown merchants' association. Another group that fills the void left by the chamber of commerce is the downtown merchants' association, a group of local business owners who organize to promote downtown economic development over that in outlying areas. Since the chamber of commerce represents all business interests in the entire community, it cannot take sides on the issue of downtown versus suburban development; but the downtown merchants' association can and does. It lobbies city hall for free downtown parking, for cleaner streets and sidewalks, for tax incentives to attract new retail businesses into the downtown area, and for renovation to make the downtown area more attractive. And in many cases, its efforts are successful. In an effort to revitalize downtown areas, many cities spend large amounts of money to plant flowers and trees in sidewalk planters and newly constructed medians, to install better street lighting, to build parking garages, and so forth.

Ad hoc economic groups. A third type of economically oriented group is that formed by local business leaders on an ad hoc basis. In San Antonio, for example, the Good Government League ran its own slate of candidates in each local election between 1954 and 1975. It was phenomenally successful during this period, electing seventy-nine of eighty-one candidates it nominated over a twenty-year period (Lineberry and Sharkansky 1978, Muñoz 1994). Similar groups have formed in other cities (e.g., Tucson, Dallas, San Jose). In each case, the group is composed of a coalition of business and other pro-growth interests whose purpose is to promote pro-growth policies in the city. Often, this is accomplished through local elections, where pro-growth candidates are supported and anti-growth candidates are opposed.

Another example of an ad hoc economic group occurred in Lawrence, Kansas, in 1982 (Schumaker 1990). At that time, the city manager in Lawrence had held his position for a decade and had demonstrated his friendship for local business and his support for aggressive growth policies in the community. But in 1981, two new anti-growth candidates were elected to the city council, giving anti-growth forces an absolute majority on the council. Most knowledgeable observers assumed it was only a matter of time before the city manager would be dismissed. Events reached a head one Friday in February, when one of the anti-growth council members wrote a letter to the city manager urging his resignation, with a council vote to dismiss him as the only possible alternative. Almost immediately (literally, over the weekend) a coalition of pro-growth individuals, primarily representing business interests, emerged under the name of the Lawrence Committee. It challenged the right of a council member to urge the resignation of the city manager, charged the member with malfeasance (among other things), and organized a strenuous recall campaign financed with contributions from a number of local businesses. In the end, the council member survived the recall election; but in a vote during the recall campaign, the city council opted not only to retain the city manager but also to give him a raise. In the next municipal election, anti-growth candidates were notable by their absence.

This example suggests that even when business interests are not formally allied in a community, clear lines of communication typically exist and can be activated at a moment's notice. These lines of communication are often activated, in fact, as various economic opportunities emerge and ad hoc economic development groups form, usually as an alternative to the local chamber of commerce. As was noted earlier, the local chamber is a multi-purpose and multi-audience group that serves a variety of interests, but it is often inadequate for the needs of individual businesses. It tends to be rather cautious in its initiatives, lest it offend any of its members; but this inertia may prove frustrating to those who want to quickly take advantage of new opportunities.

For example, a group may emerge around rumors that General Motors is considering the community as a site for a new automobile assembly plant. Or it may emerge to promote development of an industrial park on a parcel of land that has just become available. Or, as in San Jose, it may emerge to promote the community as a manufacturing center (Trounstine and Christensen 1982). In this case, David Packard, chairman of the board at Hewlitt Packard, Inc., and Robert Wilson, chairman of the board of Memorex, formed the Santa Clara County Manufacturing Group during the late 1970s. Its purpose was to bring together the county's largest manufacturing and banking firms into an umbrella organization that would become the voice for industry in the Silicon Valley. By 1980, the Manufacturing Group had largely accomplished this goal; it membership consisted of sixty-five companies, including Lockheed Missiles, General Electric, Owens-Corning Fiberglass, IBM, GTE-Sylvania, Bank of America, Ford Aerospace, American Microsystems, and National Semiconductor. The Manufacturing Group worked with both city and county government in an effort to promote efficiency and cut costs, and it became involved in a number of issues, including transportation, housing, employment, and taxation. Within a year of its formation, the Manufacturing Group had outstripped the San Jose Chamber of Commerce as a center of community power, and it showed promise of becoming the dominant source of influence in the area during the coming decades.

Another ad hoc economic group, an exemplar of what Clarence Stone (1989) terms an "urban regime," guided San Francisco's economic development strategy during the 1970s. At that time, a unified pro-growth coalition of downtown business elites, labor unions, and local government officials directed the city's economic development. With broad popular support, infusions of private capital, and large federal subsidies, the leaders of this coalition pursued a vision of remaking San Francisco into the Bay Area's commercial,

147

financial, and administrative headquarters and a link between the United States and the emerging Pacific Rim. Through these efforts, 34 million square feet of office space was added to the central business district between 1965 and 1985—a growth rate of more than 1.4 million square feet per year. By the mid 1980s, the pro-growth regime had largely collapsed, but its twenty-year run demonstrates the impact that an informal coalition dominated by business leaders can have on a city and its character (DeLeon 1992).

But just as ad hoc groups can spur economic development, they can also bring a halt to development. For instance, an anti-growth coalition emerged in San Francisco during the 1980s, largely in response to the aggressive development that had been overseen by the pro-growth regime during the previous twenty years[6]; it consisted of middle-class professionals, neighborhood activists, tenant union leaders, small business owners, and disillusioned ethnic minorities. In 1984, this coalition supported and won passage of Proposition K, which lowered allowable building heights around parks and playgrounds to preserve their access to sunshine. Encouraged by this success, the coalition supported and won passage of Proposition M in 1986, which imposed a permanent city-wide annual limit of 950,000 square feet on new office construction.[7] This was the most restrictive growth-control legislation in any major U.S. city (Whyte 1988, Collins et al. 1991, DeLeon 1992). Perhaps in response to what had happened in San Francisco, anti-growth coalitions have emerged in other cities. For example, in 1989 Seattle voters passed an initiative called the Citizens' Alternative Plan (CAP), which severely restricted the allowable bulk and height of buildings in the downtown area (Collins et al. 1991).

Civic and Social Groups

In almost every community, a number of civic groups and social clubs exists. Traditionally, these have been segregated by gender (although traditional gender barriers seem to be breaking down). On the male side, such organizations as the Kiwanis, Lions, and Rotary clubs and the Jaycees (a kind of junior chamber of commerce with a service orientation) are active. These groups

---

6. By the mid-1980s, San Francisco had twenty-one towers higher than 450 feet, most of them located along Market Street. Larry Ford (1994) notes that from Corona Peak, the Market Street skyline looks like a half-mile-long glass box. This is not only aesthetically unpleasant but also dysfunctional: Since the blocks on Market Street are extra long, access to anything south is psychologically as well as physically difficult.

7. Several unsuccessful attempts to stop growth were interspersed among the successes. In 1971, Proposition I, which would have limited new buildings to six stories, received only 37 percent of the vote; and in 1979, Proposition O, which would have imposed less-restrictive height limits, received 45.6 percent support. In 1983, the first Proposition M, which would have required developers to share financial profits from downtown high-rise construction with the city through contributions to public transit, affordable housing, and job training, lost by 1,919 votes (Collins et al. 1991).

have regular meetings during which members share lunch and listen to a speaker discuss an interesting political or social problem in the community. These organizations often take on civic projects, usually contributing money to some worthwhile cause (for instance buying eyeglasses for schoolchildren who could not otherwise afford them). While some of the money for these contributions comes from membership dues, most of it is raised through various projects, for instance selling Christmas trees during the holiday season.

On the female side, organizations such as the League of Women Voters, the Junior League, the Jaycee Janes, and the Soroptomists are active in many cities.[8] Like their male counterparts, members of these organizations break bread at regular meetings, listen to speakers discuss vital issues for the community, and target specific service functions. For example, the League of Women Voters sponsors debates among political candidates, and members of the Junior League do volunteer work in libraries, hospitals, and social service agencies. One difference between the two sets of organizations is that while the male organizations typically donate their money to community projects, women's organizations typically donate their time. A second difference is that while many male organizations (e.g., Rotary, Kiwanis, Lions) discourage female participation,[9] many women's organizations encourage male participation (e.g., the League of Women Voters).

People join these service organizations for a variety of reasons. One of the most important is social: They are able to dine with their friends on a regular basis and keep in touch in a way that busy schedules might not otherwise permit. When two businessmen meet by chance and agree to get together for lunch *sometime*, sometime rarely comes. But by joining Rotary, they regularly reserve lunchtime on Wednesdays to see each other (and other friends with whom they would like to keep in touch). A second reason for participation is to fulfill a sense of civic obligation. By joining the Junior League, a woman is returning to the community something of what it has given her, and it makes her feel good about both herself and about the community. A third reason for participation is political self-interest. By attending meetings, members have a chance to "network," to touch base with others who may be (or who may become) allies on policy issues. In one city the authors studied, managers from four industrial plants drove together to and from the Rotary meeting each Wednesday. During this time together (and whatever time they could manage

8. In Tuscaloosa, Alabama (a city of 78,000 people), sixty-four women's clubs are listed in the newspaper. Of these, at least thirteen are professional organizations, twenty promote individual development, and twenty support civic and philanthropic causes.

9. Until 1987, Rotary International stipulated in its bylaws that women were barred from membership. However, the U.S. Supreme Court (in *Board of Directors of Rotary International et al. v. Rotary Club of Duarte et al.*, 1987) overturned that stipulation, ruling that individual chapters could allow female membership. Even so, the organization remains overwhelmingly male.

together at the meeting itself), they discussed community issues relating to business and economic development. A fourth reason for joining is simply the visibility offered by membership in the organization. Administrators of a number of social and cultural service organizations (e.g., the Y.M.C.A., Boy Scouts, the Historic Preservation Society) attend because it gives them a chance to see and be seen by other important people in the community. By the same token, many banks, real estate firms, and other community businesses require senior-level employees to join at least one civic organization on the grounds that it simultaneously provides visibility for the business and demonstrates its civic commitment. A fifth reason for joining is the carryover that civic participation provides for more overt forms of political participation (e.g., campaign work, citizen-initiated contacting behavior). Brady and his associates (1995) argue that each form of participation increases the repertoire of civic skills that an individual possesses, making him or her more likely to engage in subsequent political and civic activities. In this sense, civic groups can be viewed as a testing ground for future political participation, where the stakes may be much higher.

Most people with the first two motives are likely to participate only sporadically. While collegiality and civic responsibility may draw many people to join an organization, they can be easily overwhelmed by more practical considerations.[10] For example, a bank vice president anticipating a lot of work during the next week may opt not to attend a League of Women Voters meeting; for her, work and professional advancement are more important than civic obligation. For another person, spending the weekend before Christmas with his family is more important than civic responsibility, and he will choose not to sell Christmas trees with fellow Rotarians. So although many civic organizations enjoy large memberships, relatively few of these members are regular and active participants in the organization. In addition, people who are most active are probably those who view their participation in self-interested terms: They use the organization for networking purposes, or they believe that the civic activities of the organization make an important policy contribution in the community.

Labor and Professional Organizations

In most American cities, a substantial proportion of working adults belong to some professional or vocational organization. For most blue-collar workers, this is a labor union, perhaps the United Auto Workers or the Teamsters' Union. For white-collar workers, it might be the American Medical Association, the American Bar Association, or the American Federation of

---

10. For a thoughtful inquiry into the meaning of civic obligation in American life, see Bellah et al. (1985).

Teachers. Yet as indicators of participation in local politics, high membership rates are deceiving for two reasons. First, most members of both labor unions and professional associations tend to be joiners but not participators. In the case of labor unions, membership is an occupational requirement in most states. In the case of professional organizations, membership is expected, and most people succumb to peer pressure and join. But in neither case is membership equivalent to participation in any but a nominal sense, and most members do little more than vote (for officers, to strike, and so forth).[11]

Second, most labor unions and professional organizations tend not to get involved in local issues. The American Medical Association has an active lobby in Washington, for instance, and a keen interest in a variety of health-related federal policies. It is also quite active in state capitals, lobbying for tort reform in the area of medical malpractice. But most health policy at the local level is merely a reflection of that developed at the federal or state level, and the AMA has had few local concerns.[12] While the American Bar Association does get involved in nominating candidates for local judicial positions, its major activity is also concentrated at the state and federal level. Finally, labor unions become involved in local politics through their decisions to strike or not strike. But while strikes by public employee unions (e.g., the American Federation of State, County, and Municipal Employees; the American Federation of Teachers) are designed to disrupt the flow of urban life, most private-sector strikes affect only the industry involved, the strikers, and their families.

Beyond job actions, however, most union political activity focuses at the state and national levels, where labor policy is decided. For example, minimum-wage legislation is passed or rejected by the U.S. Congress or state legislatures, as are occupational safety requirements. Labor unions, with an active interest in these and related matters, tend to lobby in Washington, D.C., and they maintain political action committees to support the campaigns of federal and state office seekers. But since little occupationally relevant legislation is passed at the local level, such effort would be largely wasted there. The one exception to this occurs for craft unions, whose members may have a great stake in local building codes and regulations.

Even when labor unions attempt to get involved in local politics, they are rarely successful. The membership of many unions is racially and ethnically

11. Often, membership in professional organizations provides economic and professional benefits for members, for example, group rates for professional liability insurance and access to law libraries.
12. This conclusion is changing, however, as various health providers are jockeying for position to control local managed health-care programs. Much of this involves large health-care corporations, but the local AMA is often caught in the middle of buy-outs, mergers, and take-overs, and by taking sides they can sometimes influence the ultimate configuration of health services in their city. With this notable exception, however, the generalization that the AMA tends to be uninvolved in local politics still holds.

diverse. And while this diversity has little impact on the union's support for national programs (minimum wage, occupational safety, comprehensive health insurance), it often creates disagreement about local policies. For example, many union members are critical of proposals to increase local taxes for such programs as subsidized day care, mass transit, or public health clinics, even though these programs may benefit the working class. As another example, middle-class housing in many cities remains, for the most part, racially segregated, and many white union members resent local ordinances designed to integrate neighborhoods. Yet, among the union's black membership, these ordinances are of great importance. Finally, most unions are quite divided on the use of ethnic, gender, or racial quotas. These cleavages, if allowed to surface, could tear apart the union; hence, most unions prefer simply not to get involved in local issues.

Neighborhood Organizations and Homeowner Associations

One of the favorite scenes of movie and television screenwriters shows an elderly man or woman, often the recent victim of a crime, looking out onto a dirty, rundown section of town and saying something like, "The old neighborhood just isn't the same anymore." This, no doubt, is an accurate observation. But, in fact, *American society is changing*, and it is merely taking its neighborhoods along for the ride.

Neighborhoods defined. Before considering exactly how neighborhoods are changing and the political ramifications of these changes, we must consider what constitutes a neighborhood. Schoenberg and Rosenbaum (1986) suggest five essential traits of viable neighborhoods: (a) neighborhood identity; (b) popular consensus over public order; (c) existence of formal organizations; (d) access to outside resources (e.g., organizational funding); and (e) a means of resolving internal conflict among neighbors. But this may be too stringent a requirement, beyond the reach of most areas we generally think of as neighborhoods (Bennett 1993). Anthony Downs (1981) elucidates several factors that may be used to define a neighborhood. At a broad level, he suggests that the *immediate neighborhood* is the small cluster of houses right around one's own. This is perhaps what most of us think of as a neighborhood, but it is too narrow for a discussion of urban politics. There are simply too many such neighborhoods, each with too little political clout. Downs suggests that the *homogeneous neighborhood* is the area up to where the market value of housing noticeably changes or where the mix of housing types or values changes. This, in fact, is the definition that many cities (most commonly suburban areas and small cities) invoke in identifying neighborhoods, particularly ones that are planned around future housing developments. A parcel of land is given some attractive name (Prairie Meadows, Ridgeland, Seminole Hills) and zoned for certain types of houses (e.g., a minimum of 2,000 square feet, a minimum of one-third acre, only single-family dwellings). Further, builders tend to construct houses in these new neighborhoods that conform roughly to a single architectural style (modern, split-level). And when a sufficient number of houses have been constructed and families have moved in, a neighborhood exists. These neighborhoods tend to be relatively small, seldom with over five hundred houses, and often with fewer than one hundred houses.

This style of neighborhood development is relatively new. Older neighborhoods tended to develop on some other basis. Downs suggests several possibilities. One is a common space as a focal point for personal interaction, perhaps a public park. A second is a common relationship with some nearby institution, perhaps an elementary school, a church, or a police station. A third is common membership in an ethnic group. In most large cities, Italian, Greek, Polish, Jewish, black, and Hispanic neighborhoods are common. A fourth is a common relationship to a physical barrier or a set of physical barriers. For instance, neighborhoods are often bounded by busy streets that children are not allowed to cross, thus encouraging intra-neighborhood rather than inter-neighborhood interaction.

Changing neighborhood character. As we consider different types of neighborhoods (for instance, those that are defined by social considerations versus those that are merely geographical), we begin to discern an important change in American society: the decline of social interaction as the basis of urban life. Several neighborhood-level trends suggest this shift. First, newer neighborhoods are constructed out of developers' plans and market considerations, whereas older neighborhoods emerged largely around social interaction. A second trend is demographic: The average person is older today (and even older tomorrow) than at any other time in recent memory. An elderly population is past its childbearing years; hence, there are (and will be) fewer children to play with one another, and in so doing, to help knit the bonds of neighborhood interaction. Moreover, an elderly population is less physically active than its younger counterpart. As a result, neighborhoods where the elderly are concentrated experience an absolute decline in the potential for social interaction. A third trend involves an increasing number of working mothers with little time to interact with neighbors. And with working mothers comes the need for child care, usually in a preschool outside the immediate neighborhood. Thus, children are more likely to develop friendships that take them outside the neighborhood to play. A fourth trend is increasing crime and fear of crime. The fear of crime may lead people to stay home and engage in indoor rather than outdoor recreation. A fifth trend is the aging process, in this instance not of people but of buildings. The infrastructure of most cities is simply getting older, and with age comes deterioration. In most inner cities, habitable apartment buildings are less habitable than they once

153

were, and in most large inner cities, habitable buildings are interspersed with burned-out structures. Sidewalks, too, are decaying. In general, the inner-city neighborhood as an inviting place for interaction has seen better days. Finally, Americans have become more mobile, and greater mobility leads to a greater sense of transience. Many neighborhood dwellers, particularly in newer neighborhoods, simply do not have a commitment to the neighborhood as a place where they expect to spend their lives. And even in older neighborhoods, many younger people discover that they can buy old, often run-down houses for bargain prices, live in them for a couple of years, renovate them, and sell their property for a handsome profit. This *gentrification* of older neighborhoods no doubt improves their physical appearance, but usually at a substantial cost to neighborhood stability.

Types of neighborhood participation. So the screenwriters are right: The old neighborhood just isn't the same. And the opportunities for social interaction—and as an outgrowth of social interaction, political participation—are fewer than they were twenty-five years ago. This general isolation makes neighboring, when it does occur, a very important activity. Neighboring can take a number of forms: watching after a neighbor's residence when he or she is away, lending a neighbor a cup of sugar or a loaf of bread, watching a neighbor's children, inviting a neighbor over for dinner (DeSena 1994). But this tends to occur most commonly in neighborhoods that are relatively free of social problems (e.g., graffiti, litter, crime) and, therefore, where social isolation is least likely (Perkins et al. 1990). Further, as an individual activity, neighboring tends to be spread unevenly within neighborhoods: whereas one block may have a number of residents engaging in neighboring activities, others may have no one doing so.

Many neighborhoods have responded by promoting various clubs, organizations, and institutions within their boundaries, most with dual (but related) purposes of promoting social interaction and neighborhood pride. In many situations, neighborhood associations have formed as umbrella organizations, designed to promote the overall interest of the neighborhood. These neighborhood associations, as well as a variety of the organizations that have emerged within neighborhoods, became an important vehicle for citizen participation during the 1970s and 1980s, and they seem to support the conclusion that American society has become more participatory over the years. But in considering neighborhood participation, the validity of this conclusion deserves careful inspection.

Several writers have discussed the kinds of organizations that are typically found within neighborhoods. Downs (1981) suggests that they include extended families, government service agencies (e.g., elementary schools), religious and social organizations (a Catholic Parish, a Salvation Army center), and political organizations (e.g., the Democratic precinct office). Douglas Yates

(1977) notes that many sections in the Lower East Side of Manhattan had two to three community organizations on the same block, and in a twenty-square-block area, he counted more than two hundred different community organizations. His list of these organizations includes:

church associations	community action agencies
neighborhood chambers of commerce	neighborhood health councils
service clubs (Rotary, Kiwanis, Lions)	tenant councils
parent-teacher associations	food co-ops
racial organizations (NAACP, CORE)	drug prevention groups
ethnic associations	street patrols
senior citizen centers	neighborhood associations

In addition, many neighborhood organizations distribute newsletters or flyers announcing events or activities, and some neighborhoods publish neighborhood newspapers. Some, for example the *Village Voice* from New York's Greenwich Village, have developed national reputations. Most, however, serve a local audience. In Minneapolis, for example, thirty-seven neighborhood newspapers were published in 1977, up from twenty-three only three years earlier (Boyte 1980); and in the 1980s, neighborhoods in New York City published forty-six weekly newspapers, with a combined circulation of over a million (Moss and Ludwig 1991). The largest single goal of these papers is to inform the neighborhood about itself and promote a sense of neighborhood identity and pride. Only of secondary concern are information about available social services and communication with outside interests.

These organizations no doubt facilitate social interaction within the neighborhood, but whether they have created an absolute increase in the level of social participation is open to question. In past decades, for example, many parents participated in local education through such activities as attendance at PTA meetings, and school newsletters served the function of today's neighborhood newspapers. Today, some observers feel that parental participation in the schools is lower than during past decades (e.g., Henderson 1988), due to a number of factors: the demographics of the aging process (fewer people have school-aged children); the logistics of two-income families (working parents have a hard time coming home from work at 5:30, cooking dinner, and finding the energy to attend a PTA meeting at 7:00); the breakdown of the family (participation is highest among families with both natural parents; Dornbush and Ritter 1988); and the demise of the neighborhood school in many cities (due to school busing). In many locations, an elected council of parents meets with educators in place of more general PTA participation. By the same token, the trends cited earlier have reduced the potential for social interaction in the neighborhood. In general, the proliferation of neighborhood groups and organizations has been useful in fighting the trend toward isolation that has occurred for many families, but it is unlikely that they have increased political participation beyond levels achieved during the middle years of this century.

Goals of neighborhood associations. At a higher level of aggregation, many neighborhoods have created neighborhood associations to promote the interests of the entire neighborhood. The viability of these associations ultimately rests on the assumption that the neighborhood is a homogeneous entity with a single interest. Or put differently, a neighborhood association is most likely to be successful in its mission if it represents a set of homogeneous neighbors. Downs (1981) describes the mission of a neighborhood association as follows:

1. enable children and adults to develop social and other skills through interaction with neighbors;
2. pressure government and private agencies to improve services to the neighborhood and neighborhood residents;
3. provide services to neighborhood residents;
4. create a local base for political support;
5. increase participation among local residents.

To these goals can be added:

6. increase neighborhood pride and identification;
7. increase (or at least maintain) the value of real estate within the neighborhood.

Obviously, many of these goals cannot be achieved if the neighborhood consists of heterogeneous groups. For example, one way in which real estate value is maintained is through the exclusion of (a) multifamily dwellings, and (b) houses that cost below the prevailing market value. But if a geographic neighborhood (but obviously not a social neighborhood) simultaneously consists of wealthy families living in expensive houses and poor families living in multiple-family units, a zoning decision that benefits one must necessarily hurt the other. So, too, a neighborhood that consists of both blacks and Hispanics may have difficulty creating a single base for political action. In any event, those seeking to create politically effective neighborhood associations must carefully attend to drawing geographic boundaries, with an eye to maximizing (where possible) homogeneity.

Once formed, how does a neighborhood association attempt to achieve its goals? First, many neighborhoods hold annual or semiannual picnics, during which they elect officers and hold their business meetings. In addition, the neighborhood may sponsor a Little League baseball team or an adult softball team. Both facilitate interaction among neighbors. Second, neighborhood associations pressure both public and private agencies for better services. For example, black neighborhoods may pressure retail or manufacturing firms in the city to hire more minorities or banks to provide more residential loans. In addition, many neighborhood associations work with local government to identify neighborhood problems and develop budget priorities for addressing these problems. For example, advisory councils from eighty-six Birmingham, Alabama, neighborhoods worked with city hall to develop service and program priorities (Coulter 1988); in Dayton, neighborhood priority boards ranked city problems for the purpose of fund allocation; and in Atlanta, the Division of Neighborhood Planning divided the city into neighborhood groups to set neighborhood priorities (Stone et al. 1979). Even where neighborhood participation has not been institutionalized into the city planning process, neighborhoods may become involved through less conventional protest activities. Poor neighborhoods, with the feeling of nothing left to lose, have been known to disrupt business at city hall until their concerns have been heard.

Third, neighborhood associations often sponsor or even provide services of their own. Perhaps the most common is Neighborhood Watch, a program sponsored by police departments in which neighbors (a) meet with a representative of the police department to learn how to deter crime and (b) commit themselves to actively watch for unusual occurrences that might signal a crime in their area. Some neighborhoods have also sponsored nonprofit daycare programs for the children of working parents (sometimes subsidized with federal, state, or local funds). And some neighborhood associations, for example the Woodlawn Organization in the South Side of Chicago, have contracted with cities to provide such services as managing a public housing project and conducting vocational education programs (Boyte 1980).

Fourth, neighborhood associations have often become bases for local political mobilization. This occurs most notably for minorities living in underclass neighborhoods, with the neighborhood association becoming a catalyst for black or Hispanic participation in local politics. Consider, for example, Chicago's Woodlawn Organization, created by Saul Alinsky and Father John Egan in the 1950s. It was largely responsible for mobilizing blacks during the early years of the Civil Rights Movement, and it served as a model for other black neighborhoods across the country (Boyte 1980). This type of neighborhood activity, organized around protest, will be considered again later in the chapter.

Even in middle-class neighborhoods, neighborhood associations often serve a political mobilization function. A case in point is the 1966 conflict in New York's Greenwich Village over New York University's decision to construct a new six-story library on a site adjoining Washington Square Park (Yates 1977). This library, the university argued, was necessary for continued academic excellence. Further, university administrators pointed out with

157

pride, it had contracted with a renowned architect to design a structure that would represent an important architectural contribution to the city. It would, they hinted, even provide the park with a symmetry and elegance of design comparable to the Place Vendome in Paris. But neighborhood residents were not convinced by the proposed architectural elegance. Instead, they were concerned about how the proposed building would impede the flow of sunlight to the park and the increase in pedestrian traffic that inevitably would follow. Neighborhood groups effectively mobilized and coordinated citizen participation. And although city hall finally overruled the neighborhood protest and allowed construction of the library, the neighborhood had become a potent political force in the dispute.

In fact, the neighborhood was able to use this newfound political clout to good effect only a few years later. By the late 1960s, New York City had selected an area at the edge of Greenwich Village for construction of middle-income housing, and in 1971 it asked the urban-renewal agency to apply for federal funds for the project. But the Villagers objected. Led by residents like Jane Jacobs, they spoke out at public meetings, visited city officials, and filed a lawsuit challenging the designation of the proposed site as blighted. Mayor Robert Wagner, in the midst of a tough reelection campaign, offered his support to Village residents on the eve of the primary election. After his reelection, the City Planning Commission dropped the "blight" designation, and the project died (Frieden and Sagalyn 1989).

Fifth, neighborhood associations often sponsor activities designed to promote neighborhood identification and pride. Many neighborhoods, for example, display luminaria (lighted candles) along their streets during Christmas season. Another favorite neighborhood activity is the annual cleanup, where residents volunteer to spend a Saturday picking up litter along the streets. In addition, most neighborhood associations put out a short newsletter to inform residents of neighborhood news (the date of the annual cleanup, recent births, available baby-sitters).

Sixth, many neighborhood associations, particularly in middle- and upper-class neighborhoods, view their primary purpose as the protection of property values. *[The theory of lifestyle and territory.]* In some areas, in fact, this emphasis is reflected in the name the association has taken, for example the Prairie Meadows Homeowners' Association or the East Lawrence Improvement Association. One way in which property values are protected is through zoning laws prohibiting multi-family dwellings, prohibiting nonstationary residences (i.e., trailers), or requiring minimum floor space in a house. Whenever a developer even suggests constructing duplexes (or even worse, apartments) in a neighborhood of single-family dwellings, neighborhood association representatives are in the front row at the next city council meeting arguing against any change in zoning. Or if the city proposes a subsidized low-income housing unit for a neighborhood, the association is sure to protest. In general, the neighborhood association looks out for the interests of its members; and for most members, their houses represent their largest single investment and therefore their primary interest.

One of the incursions that middle- and upper-class neighborhoods have most effectively fought is the development of highways within or near their boundaries. In 1970, Daniel Patrick Moynihan stated, "It is just about impossible to get a major highway program approved in most American cities" (p. 94). His conclusion came in the wake of successful neighborhood efforts to stop freeway construction (often in mid-project) in Philadelphia, Phoenix, Miami, Memphis, New Orleans, Chicago, San Francisco, and Seattle, and highway construction in Baltimore, Boston, Kansas City, Los Angeles, and St. Louis. The San Francisco case is instructive. Middle-class residents there protested proposed extensions of the Embarcadaro Freeway in 1959, largely because these would have obstructed their view of the historic Ferry Terminal. In response to these protests, the Board of Supervisors vetoed the extensions, turning down $60 million in federal highway funds in the process (Frieden and Sagalyn 1989). However, other neighborhoods have not been so successful at protecting their neighborhoods and property values from the disruptive effects of highway construction. Between 1957 and 1968, more than three hundred thousand urban housing units were destroyed as a direct result of the federal highway program, displacing 32,400 families each year. In large part, highways were built through low-income and black neighborhoods where property values were modest and neighborhoods were unorganized or lacked political clout; notable examples include Miami, Nashville, Richmond, St. Paul, St. Petersburg, Wilmington, Chicago, Boston, and New York (Frieden and Sagalyn 1989, Mohl 1993b).

The effectiveness of neighborhood associations: An assessment. Do neighborhood associations really increase political participation? Certainly, in the case of minority mobilization they have. Mayoral victories for such minority candidates as Tom Bradley in Los Angeles (1973) and Harold Washington in Chicago (1983) would not have been possible without substantial grass-roots mobilization in black neighborhoods. But on other levels, the answer is less clear. Annual membership dues for neighborhood associations are modest, typically a dollar, and seldom more than five dollars. This pays for duplicating the newsletter, providing supplies for luminaria, and preparing supporting materials for city council meetings. It also guarantees almost full membership. After all, who can't afford a buck a year? But while large membership lists are impressive to the city council as well as to those who study political participation, they may be misleading. In the final analysis, most neighborhood associations are staff organizations. They have a president, and when volunteers can be found, a vice-president, a secretary, and a treasurer. But in most cases, they have very few active members (often only these four officers). In one neighborhood association the authors studied, the president had held that position for four years. She was not power hungry; she just could not find anyone else willing to fill the position. She was faced with the situation of either continuing as its leader or dissolving the association. When she called meetings, she was able to hold them in her living room (and a small living room at that). People simply were not interested in participating, unless their self-interest was affected directly.[13] This type of limited participation may be more common than not. And those who argue, based on such evidence as the proliferation of neighborhood groups and associations, that political participation in American cities is increasing, are missing an important distinction between membership in organizations and active participation in the political arena.

Ad Hoc Groups

In the best tradition of American politics, a variety of groups spring up in urban areas to address many different kinds of social problems. An example is Mothers Against Drunk Driving (MADD), a national group founded by a mother whose child was killed by a drunk driver. Since its inception, local affiliates have formed in many cities throughout the country. Groups have also formed in many cities to protest a variety of other problems, including litter, racial or gender discrimination, poor traffic control, lack of low-cost housing, and so forth.

Some of the most active ad hoc groups to form in cities are those dedicated to historical preservation. In almost every city, people have come together in defense of a treasured landmark—perhaps an old school they all attended, a historic house, or an old train station. Often these groups have been unsuccessful, either because they are too small or because the forces they are up against are too powerful; the pages of architectural journals are full of laments about America's lost heritage that these groups were unable to save. But sometimes they have been successful, and since 1966, when Congress passed the National Historic Preservation Act, their success rate has increased. The number of properties and districts on the National Register of Historic Places increased from twelve hundred in 1968 to thirty-seven thousand in 1985 (Frieden and Sagalyn 1989).

Seattle is a city where historical preservation efforts have been particularly successful. Its Pike Place Market was historically a place where farmers sold their produce, but the number of farmers renting space declined around World War II, from more than five hundred in 1939 to about fifty in 1949,

---

13. Even in this neighborhood, self-interest was narrowly defined. During the time of our study, a neighborhood boy had been tragically struck and killed by a car on his way to school; yet, the president of the neighborhood association had difficulty mobilizing residents to demand that the city install a traffic signal.

and by the 1950s, the market itself had become structurally unsound and in danger of collapse. Spurred by downtown business leaders, the city of Seattle planned to level it and replace it with offices, apartment houses, and hotels. As the city government was developing a plan for federal approval, supporters of the market collected fifty thousand signatures for a "Save the Market" initiative. It was placed on the ballot in 1971 and received 60 percent support. As a result of the election, a seven-acre historical district was established (Frieden and Sagalyn 1989).

William H. Whyte (1988) argues that the public referendum on the Pike Place Market was a referendum on more than the preservation of an old food market. In supporting it, the public was declaring what kind of city it wanted Seattle to be. Actions by ad hoc groups in other cities have been no less noble in intent.

While these ad hoc groups may be fairly common in American cities, they do not represent large-scale participation. Much more important is the *number* of such groups that have emerged over the past decade, rather than the absolute level of participation they generate.

Participation Through Protest

A number of studies point to the importance of economic position in the community as a basis for effective group participation. Thomas Dye (1969, 249) notes that

> civic associations are the predominant style of organized interest group activity at the local level, that businessmen, reform groups, taxpayer associations, merchants, service clubs, developers all organize themselves into civic associations for action at the local level.

In a complementary finding, Betty Zisk (1973) reports the results of a survey of San Francisco Bay area city council members asking them to identify the most influential pressure groups. The results came out much as Dye indicates they might:

1. Economic groups, including the chamber of commerce, taxpayer groups, and neighborhood groups, were identified as influential by 43 percent of the respondents.
2. Civic groups, including Parent-Teacher Associations, the League of Women Voters, churches, and service clubs, were identified as influential by 31 percent of the respondents.
3. Special interest groups, including conservation associations, builders, and senior citizens groups, were identified as influential by 23 percent of the respondents.

4. Semi-official bodies, including the planning commission and other advisory boards, were identified as influential by only 2 percent of the respondents.

Others have concluded that power in such communities as Atlanta (Hunter 1953) and San Jose (Trounstine and Christensen 1982) resides in the hands of local business owners.

Taken together, these findings suggest that homeowners (through their neighborhood associations) and business owners (both through their chamber of commerce and ad hoc initiatives) are likely to benefit from their civic and community participation. By the same token, such traditionally middle-class organizations as service clubs and the League of Women Voters may also see their participatory efforts come to fruition as policy outcomes. But missing from the ranks of the influential are the poor and their advocates. For example, urban housing authorities, which oversee public housing and represent underclass interests, fall into the set of "semi-official bodies" that Zisk reports are largely powerless. The same can be said for most social service agencies, traditional spokespersons for the underclass (Bolland and Selby 1988). This leaves the poor with but two participatory options: electoral mobilization and protest.

Electoral Mobilization

Attempts to mobilize the low-income electorate are seldom successful for two reasons. First, the poor are not themselves homogeneous, and as a result they often experience severe cleavages in both strategy and tactics. In contrast to the upper class, which is racially (and, to some extent, ethnically) homogeneous, the poor comprise a number of racially, ethnically, and demographically distinct subgroups. Most cities for example, have a low-income black community, a low-income Hispanic community, and a low-income white community, each of which is mobilized by different kinds of issues; for instance, black voters tend to be mobilized by protest issues more than are white voters (Schuman et al. 1988). Further, each of these communities can be divided into elderly and nonelderly populations, which are poor for quite different reasons and vote according to different issues as well. The elderly, for example, may have belonged to the middle class at one time, but due to meager retirement benefits, they now find themselves in difficult economic straits. In contrast, younger people find themselves in difficult economic straits because of lack of jobs, poor education, racial barriers to advancement, and (often) mismanagement of their finances. The low-income white community can be further subdivided along ethnic lines, with different ethnic groups having different traditions and approaches to solving problems. In short, then, there is no single low-income community and no single low-income voting block within most cities.

These divisions make it very difficult for a candidate to mobilize the poor for an electoral victory. For example, Harold Washington won the mayoral election in Chicago in 1983 only because his Hispanic support increased from 13 percent in the primary to 75 percent in the general election (Muñoz and Henry 1986; also see Preston 1987). But such a "rainbow coalition" is more the exception than the rule, and it is difficult to maintain once established. Following Washington's death in 1987, no single African American was able to establish him- or herself as leader of the coalition, and in the 1989 mayoral election, Eugene Sawyer and Tim Evans split the black vote, virtually guaranteeing the election of Richard M. Daley (Pinderhughes 1994).

In New York City, as another example, an attempt to select a consensus minority challenger to Mayor Edward Koch in the 1985 mayoral election failed because when no strong black candidate agreed to run, blacks in Harlem refused to support the candidacy of Hispanic leader Herman Badillo (Mollenkopf 1986). Over the next four years, however, several racial incidents in the city (e.g., murders of blacks by white youths in Howard Beach and Bensonhurst; the "wilding" attack on a white female jogging in Central Park by a gang of black youths) convinced many New Yorkers that race relations were on a downward curve, and they helped solidify the black and Hispanic communities in New York (as did the 1988 presidential campaign of Jesse Jackson); in 1989, David Dinkins was able to outpoll Mayor Koch in the Democratic primary and defeat Republican candidate Rudolph Giuliani in the general election, receiving 51 percent of the vote (Mollenkopf 1991). During Dinkins' term as mayor, the city continued to experience racial violence (e.g., riots between blacks and Hasidic Jews in the Crown Heights section of Brooklyn), for which Dinkins came under considerable criticism. Although he was nominated handily in the 1993 Democratic primary, the coalition that had elected him had begun to decay; in the general election, Dinkins received only 62 percent of the Hispanic vote and 23 percent of the white vote (both less than he received in 1989), and Rudolph Giuliani received 51 percent of the total vote en route to his election.

Second, even if a rainbow coalition can be mobilized, it is not clear that election translates directly into policy outcomes. Many minority mayoral candidates find it expedient, either during their campaign or after their election, to invite business leaders into their coalition. This makes practical sense, for business leaders have the resources both to allow the candidate to wage a successful campaign and to run the government effectively. But including business leaders in the governing coalition dilutes the social agenda the candidate may have emphasized during the campaign. Thus, although the election of black mayors in the largest U.S. cities brought initial enthusiasm and expectation, the enthusiasm has waned considerably over time as urban residents have come to understand that electoral office is not sufficient to ameliorate the negative conditions of minority life in urban America.

163

Tom Bradley in Los Angeles. In Los Angeles, Tom Bradley courted the business community to fulfill his political agenda (Sonenshein 1986, Jackson and Preston 1994). This strategy is likely to pay impressive dividends in times of economic prosperity. For example, after his election in 1973, Mayor Bradley was able to use a mix of federal and private dollars to substantially redevelop the downtown area. At the same time, he was able to obtain federal money to begin a wide variety of new social service programs, most located in poor and minority communities. But while it is easy to put together a coalition of business owners and low-income residents in times of prosperity, it is considerably more difficult to do so in times of economic retrenchment.

Wilson Goode in Philadelphia. Wilson Goode made a considerable effort to be responsible to both sets of interests following his electoral victory in Philadelphia in 1983 (see Adams 1994 for a discussion of Goode's election and term in office). He was elected with overwhelming support from black voters, coupled with support from white liberals and some of the city's labor unions. During his first hundred days in office, he reaffirmed his commitment to a classic liberal agenda: His early initiatives included summer jobs for youth, housing and mental health programs for the homeless, and an adult literacy program (Muñoz and Henry 1986). But he went about his administration in a manner that most business people could relate to and appreciate. He appointed biracial boards to recommend people for his administration, for example, and almost invariably followed their suggestions. But before long, the bloom was off the rose. In a law-and-order gesture, Goode ordered police to assault the local headquarters of MOVE, a radical black protest group. As a result, an entire residential block in a poor, minority neighborhood burned to the ground, and eleven people (including five children) were killed (Wagner-Pacifici 1994). While this action may have displayed a symbolic insensitivity to the concerns of the poor, a more practical display occurred in the 1985 city council election. During the Democratic primary, Goode supported Angel Ortiz, an Hispanic, who finished seventh in a field of fifty-seven candidates seeking five seats. When one of the five Democratic nominees died during the general election campaign, Goode declined to fill the opening with Ortiz, choosing instead Francis Rafferty, a defeated incumbent (Muñoz and Henry 1986). And in 1986, Goode alienated organized labor in Philadelphia (which had supported him during his election) by breaking a strike by the city's sanitation workers. He also threatened to privatize garbage collection.

Kurt Schmoke in Baltimore. As he was running in 1987 to become Baltimore's first black mayor, Kurt Schmoke campaigned on issues such as lack of affordable housing, high unemployment among blacks, infant mortality, teacher pay, class size, and services for the elderly (*Jet*, Jan. 4, 1988). But once elected, Schmoke was forced to respond to a shrinking tax base and a declining middle class. In 1988, he ordered a general hiring freeze, exempting only teaching positions, critical public safety jobs, and judicial positions. As a result, the city abolished 1,442 municipal positions between 1989 and 1991. Along with downsizing, Schmoke has embraced privatization. For instance, a private firm has taken over management of the Baltimore arena, and a private company began running nine schools in 1992 (Imbroscio et al. 1995).

Coleman Young in Detroit. Like most other mayoral candidates, Coleman Young campaigned largely on social issues, but following his election in 1974, he inherited a deficit of $16.5 million and a growing exodus of middle-class whites to the suburbs. In 1975, he instituted a hiring freeze and laid off municipal workers, resulting in major cuts in services. Facing these stark realities, Young enlisted the support of the business community, which helped him obtain state resources for the city. He also worked with business leaders to seek and obtain voter support for an income tax increase. Young later used city funds to finance land acquisition for a new General Motors plant inside Detroit. Young's long tenure as mayor will be largely remembered for one accomplishment: He kept the auto industry in Detroit (Persons 1992).

Electoral mobilization and political incorporation. The previous chapter briefly discussed the concept of political incorporation, introduced by Rufus Browning, Dale Rogers Marshall, and David Tabb (1984). They argue that incorporation—which they suggest is both a necessary and sufficient condition for political equality—exists within a city when:

1. minorities obtain seats on the city council;
2. a minority candidate is elected to the office of mayor; and
3. minority officeholders become part of the city's dominant coalition.

On the evidence presented here and in the previous chapter, we should conclude that the first two components of political incorporation have been achieved in many cities. But the third is problematic, largely precluded by an intriguing paradox. As noted above, the dominant coalition within most American cities resides in the business community, stressing growth policies and economic development. This contrasts sharply with the needs of the poor (particularly those residing in underclass neighborhoods) within the community and the priorities of those representing the poor: social equality and social services (Browning et al. 1984, Bolland and Selby 1988). Minorities elected to municipal office are almost always faced with a dilemma. As elected officials, they require the support of the business community (and its resources) to govern effectively, and they are typically offered the opportunity to participate in its dominant coalition. But their participation carries with it a cost: minority officeholders participate only by accepting the pro-growth agenda of the busi-

165

ness community in place of that espoused by their natural constituents. Thus, virtually all black mayors in major cities have been accused of turning their backs on the needs of the poor in favor of the needs of local businesses. But if black elected officials turn down the invitation to participate in the dominant coalition, they run the substantial risk of an ineffectual administration at the hands of business opposition.

Just as important, the inability of black mayors to effectively implement the social agenda they promoted during their campaigns speaks to the intractability of many social problems. As candidates, they conducted campaigns of protest against intolerable social conditions. But with their election came a shift from protest to governance, and with it the realization that local government can play only a very limited role in social reform. The election of black mayors brought increases in the appointment of blacks to administrative positions in the municipal bureaucracy, some increases in social spending, and adoption of policies favoring minority vendors for municipal contracts. But, as Georgia Persons (1991, 96) concludes, "The construction of a new social and economic order is quite simply beyond the reach of local governments. Issues such as homelessness, teenage pregnancy, and chronic problems of low-income housing are poignant testimony to the general impotence of local government in the social sphere."

Violent Protest

In the absence of either electoral mobilization or group activity as an avenue to effective participation, many of the urban poor, particularly blacks, have taken a more violent route. When we think of urban political violence, we tend to think of the race riots of the 1960s, beginning in Watts on an August day in 1965.

> On August 11, 1965, a Los Angeles police officer named Lee Minikus, acting on a tip from a truck driver, pursued and stopped a young man named Marquette Frye for speeding, driving without a licence, and driving while intoxicated. By the time Minikus and his partner had arrested Marquette Frye an angry crowd had gathered, and before the night was over, the Watts district of Los Angeles was engulfed in a series of street riots. (Ross and Stedman 1985, 96)

In 1966, similar riots erupted in Cleveland and Chicago, and by the end of the decade, urban racial rioting had spread across the entire country, affecting over one hundred fifty cities, including Newark, Milwaukee, Detroit, Houston, Cincinnati, Phoenix, Atlanta, New Haven, Tampa, and Grand Rapids. During these riots, at least two hundred twenty people were killed, more than eight thousand were injured, and over fifty thousand were arrested (Downes 1970).

Yet, the 1960s were neither the beginning nor the end of violent protest in the city. Between 1917 and 1963, seventy-six major racial disorders occurred in urban America, beginning with riots in East St. Louis in 1917 and Chicago in 1919 (Fogelson 1971). During the 1980s, urban racial violence returned, with three different riots in Miami (in 1980, 1982, and 1989) and one in Baton Rouge (in 1988). And in the 1990s it returned again, this time in Los Angeles (1992) and in St. Petersburg (1996). The 1992 riot in Los Angeles (and, to a lesser degree, in other cities) occurred in the wake of acquittals for police officers accused of beating Rodney King. It was more destructive than any experienced previously, with over 16,000 people arrested, 2,383 injured, and 52 dead, and property damage approaching a billion dollars (Oliver et al. 1993). The 1996 St. Petersburg riot was also tied to police actions, this time the shooting of black motorist Tyron Lewis. Eleven people, including a police officer, were shot, and twenty-eight buildings in a twenty-five block area were burned. These recurrences suggest that this is a problem we may not yet have put behind us.

Violence as participation? But does violence constitute real political partic-ipation, or is it the action of hoodlums and hooligans who shoot, loot, and burn for strictly nonpolitical motives? Banfield (1974), taking a quizzical per-spective in a book chapter entitled "Rioting Mainly for Fun and Profit," views the riots as unrelated to race, attributing them instead largely to an underclass need for stimulation and excitement. Others also have taken a cynical view, attributing the riots to a relatively small (1-2 percent) "riff-raff" of unemployed, unattached youths, people with criminal records, and migrant rural Southerners who were disenchanted with life in the big city (see Fogelson and Hill, 1968, for a discussion of these theories).[14] Yet, neither explanation holds up to close scrutiny. First, the most common triggering event in the riots concerned the police, a symbol of oppression in most ghettos. For example, in Watts a black man was arrested; in Harlem in 1964, an off-duty white police officer shot and killed a fifteen-year-old black youth; in Miami in 1980, an all-white jury acquitted four white police officers accused of killing a black man; in Los Angeles in 1992, a jury acquitted white police officers of beating a black motorist despite graphic evidence of the beating provided by a bystander who videotaped the entire incident; and in St. Petersburg in 1996, a black motorist was shot and killed by a white police officer. In each case, the event demon-strated the impotence (both real and perceived) of the black community in using legitimate political channels and triggered a violent political response.

14. In an action reminiscent of these explanations from two decades earlier, the White House blamed the 1992 riots in South Central Los Angeles on Great Society pro-grams enacted during the 1960s and the 1970s to solve urban problems (*New York Times*, May 5, 1992).

Second, most of the participating rioters were politically aware of this impotence and resented it. When blacks were later asked to attribute cause to the riots, they almost universally identified societal causes, such as unemployment and racial discrimination. This is not to suggest that all rioters were politically motivated, however. No doubt, some were participating mainly for fun and profit. Yet, this seems to be a less important and less credible explanation for the bulk of participation than one that focuses on political motives.

Third, who actually did participate in the riots? Was it riff-raff or was it a broad cross-section of the ghetto population? Here, again, the cynics seem to be contradicted by the evidence. According to a study by Fogelson and Hill (1968), commissioned by the National Advisory Commission on Civil Disorders (Kerner Commission), the typical rioter

1. was slightly better educated than other ghetto dwellers;
2. was likely to have been born in the area where the riot occurred;
3. was employed, although at a job requiring little education;
4. had an income approximately equal to that of other ghetto dwellers; and
5. was no more likely than anyone else in the area to possess a police record.

Further, the Kerner Commission found that in Watts, 15 percent of ghetto residents were active participants in the riot and that between 34 percent and 50 percent of the residents were sympathetic. Similar figures emerged for other cities.

These findings raise a second important issue: Violence vents frustration, but does it result in long-term, positive outcomes? Few cities responded positively to the riots. Instead, cities that had experienced riots significantly increased police expenditures (Welch 1975). And a number of cities showed a tremendous white backlash; for example, in 1971 former police chief Frank Rizzo ran successfully for mayor in Philadelphia on a blatantly anti-black, law-and-order platform. With so much to lose and so little evidence of tangible gain, violent protest has understandably ebbed. In contrast to 1968, when nearly 20 percent of blacks believed that they should be ready to use violence to gain rights (Campbell and Schuman 1968), today relatively few believe that violence is an effective strategy. When it does occur, it appears to be spontaneous rather than part of an overarching political strategy.

Nonviolent Protest

Although violent protest makes newspaper headlines, nonviolent protest is much more common. In a study of 120 protest incidents in forty-three cities, Peter Eisinger (1973) found all but 6 percent to be peaceful. This is not to say, however, that nonviolent protest is not disruptive. In fact, Eisinger (p. 14) defines protest as "a device by which groups of people manipulate fear of disorder and violence while at the same time they protect themselves from paying the potentially extreme costs of acknowledging such a strategy." An example of such disruptive protest, but one that stands in sharp contrast to the riots of the past thirty years, occurred in the wake of the 1986 death of Michael Griffith, a black man whose car broke down in Howard Beach, a predominantly white area of Queens. As Griffith and two passengers were going for help, a group of twenty white youths attacked them, killing Griffith and injuring the two others. Following the trial, in which the youths were convicted of manslaughter, lawyers for the survivors of the attack, along with Reverends Al Sharpton and Herbert Daughtry, headed a "Day of Rage," in which protestors blocked bridges and subway links between Brooklyn and Manhattan and disrupted rush-hour traffic for hundreds of thousands of people. In a similar incident in 1989, Yusuf Hawkins and two other blacks were in the Bensonhurst section of Brooklyn to look at a used car they were thinking of buying; they, too, were attacked by white youths, and Hawkins was killed, setting off another round of peaceful but disruptive protest (Fainstein and Fainstein 1991, Pinderhughes 1993).

The very fact that a protest group has violence as an option but chooses to restrain itself potentially provides its members with leverage in dealing with municipal government. (Imagine the disruption that would have resulted had the New York City protests erupted into full-scale racial violence.) As we noted before, the public is not tolerant of violence as a political tool, and survey findings show that citizens believe more rather than less force should be used to squash violent protest (Converse et al. 1969).

This public pressure may cause governments to be unresponsive to protestors' demands. On the other hand, when protestors are more cautious in their strategies, they may avoid triggering widespread public reaction, and governments may be better able to fashion a positive response to protest demands (Schumaker 1978).

The restrained potential for violence has been the hallmark of the Civil Rights Movement in the United States, particularly under the leadership of the Reverend Martin Luther King, Jr. Again, it should be stressed, that movement was designed to be disruptive but nonviolent, for instance by conducting sit-ins and openly challenging statutes. And always underlying the movement was the idea of confrontation. Contention and disputation can be a useful way of forcing problems on the attention of those in positions to solve them. For it is nonviolent, direct action, said King (1964), that can create a crisis and foster so great a tension "that a community which has constantly refused to negotiate is forced to confront the issue."

Mobilizing the urban poor. A similar strategy, developed largely by Saul Alinsky, has been employed by those attempting to mobilize the urban poor.

According to Alinsky, the ghetto is a political structure, created and maintained by existing power arrangements between the haves and the have-nots in American society. It can be changed, he argued, only by mobilizing an effective counterforce to these arrangements. And since the ghetto poor do not have access to the traditional resources of power (wealth and interest group representation), they must rely on the resources they do possess—the ability to disrupt society through their protest. Alinsky's principles, set forth in his book *Reveille for Radicals* (1946), are worth noting briefly. First, advised Alinsky, people must be organized for power. They must be motivated by perceived self-interest around concrete issues; given this motivation, they can work together as a body, wielding more power than any individual might possess. Second, the organization must be built around indigenous leadership. In the Woodlawn neighborhood, for example, Alinsky worked toward organizing himself out of a leadership position by training local people to take over his functions. He worked toward developing and strengthening local networks of churches, clubs, small businesses, unions, and other institutions that could develop and act on self-interest. Third, Alinsky believed in organizing to win. He was the ultimate pragmatist, believing that for society's have-nots, the end justified any means that might be employed (Alinsky 1971).

Alinsky and his colleagues developed a number of tactics for advancing the cause of the poor, most of them disruptive and confrontational. For instance,

> He once proposed feeding a hundred kids a baked bean dinner before sending them off to a Rochester Symphony concert. Another time he threatened to use demonstrators in a literal sit-in to tie up the toilets at O'Hare Airport in Chicago. (Stone et al. 1979, 107–8)

Alinsky and his colleagues also organized a variety of rent strikes and secondary boycotts. But while these activities make good theater and produced some initial success, they had very little lasting impact. One reason has already been discussed. The urban poor are not a unified group, but rather a collection of very different people with different racial and ethnic allegiances and different problems and concerns. In most cities, once the initial enthusiasm of this loose coalition began to fade, the natural divisiveness of the groups in the coalition began to assert itself, and agreement on an agenda became increasingly difficult to obtain. In addition, the easy problems (like getting local merchants to hire minorities) were targeted early and solved, but much more resilient problems remained. Further, grassroots organizations, like the Woodlawn Organization in Chicago, became vested in the system after achieving initial success. As Alinsky implies, those with nothing have nothing to lose by trying to gain a foothold in the political system, and they risk nothing by using radical tactics. But once a foothold has been gained, the tactics must change for fear of losing the foothold. Thus, many once-radical organizations have begun to work within the system, and their threat of violence is greatly diminished. In fact, in the 1990s reference to Alinsky-style politics is more like a historical footnote than a description of current realities. Confrontational politics is out-of-date, replaced in many working-class neighborhoods by partnerships and coalitions *with* municipal government rather than *against* it.

Finally, the poor neighborhoods where Alinsky was most successful—those where poverty was rampant but where community institutions (e.g., churches, clubs, small businesses) were functional—have undergone substantial change. For example, Chicago's Woodlawn neighborhood claimed eight hundred commercial and industrial establishments in 1950. Today, only about one hundred remain, and those are primarily tiny catering places, barbershops, and thrift stores with only one or two employees. The population in Woodlawn has also declined substantially, from over 80,000 in 1960 to 24,473 in 1990 (Wilson 1996), and the major institution in many poor neighborhoods of the 1990s is the drug trade (Lott 1992, Staley 1992), which largely squelches any efforts to organize for political purposes. *[The theory of poverty and the underclass.]*

Political Participation in American Cities: An Assessment

Many scholars believe participation in America to be increasing. The previous discussion brings us to a somewhat different conclusion, however: Participation in urban politics is actually declining. This decline creates the opportunity for urban government and politics by administration (both governmental and ad hoc), but not for government according to the democratic precept of wide and effective political participation. *[The theory of grass-roots democracy.]*

We should, however, temper this conclusion by acknowledging the greater *opportunity* for participation, particularly in the urban arena, particularly over the past decade. Even as late as the mid 1970s, many cities still held their council meetings at 2:00 P.M. on a weekday, making it almost impossible for most citizens (other than business owners and professionals) to attend. Now things have changed, and meetings are held in the evenings, maximizing the opportunity for attendance. In many communities, city council meetings are also televised. In addition, the number of political groups active at the community level has proliferated during the past decade, with groups becoming more narrowly focused in their goals. We have seen this with the increase in neighborhood groups, support groups, ethnic and racial groups, and business groups. And with the proliferation of groups comes the opportunity for participation.

171

But, as noted previously, the opportunity for participation in no way guarantees participation. Granted, more people attend city council meetings; but still, the number of people who show up for any given meeting is limited, perhaps no greater than fifty or one hundred in most cities. So, too, the opportunities for participation in neighborhood politics has increased, but typically only a handful of people actually get involved. In contrast, the more general trends in American society create a countervailing force that is actually driving participation down in most cities.

Toward an Explanation of the Ungovernable City

A long but straightforward chain of logic leads us to the conclusion that decreased participation is contributing to the *ungovernable city*. It begins with the basic tenet of politics, forwarded by Madison two centuries ago in *Federalist 10*: Increased political participation serves to protect the rights of the minority.[15] For Madison, as well as other observers of the American political system, participation by a large number of people leads to self-interested competition, and through competition to compromise, wherein diverse attitudes and values are reduced to a common denominator. Thus, a person deciding alone can act quickly and decisively, having to consider only those consequences of the action that will affect him or her; two people acting together can act half as quickly and half as decisively; they must consider more consequences than a single individual; and a collective can only inch along, considering every possible angle of a decision and thus making few decisions that vary from the status quo. (This is one basis for what has been termed incremental decision making.) A group that cannot act decisively, that considers all possible consequences of a decision, and that tends to reaffirm the status quo is unlikely to engage a new policy that may intentionally or unintentionally abridge the rights of a segment of society.

But how does this affect the governability of a city? In fact, increased participation would seem to make a city more ungovernable by limiting its ability to act decisively. This is the argument made by Theodore Lowi (1969a) for national politics and by Yates (1977) for politics at the local level. But both authors note that it is not the individual participants in national or urban politics that make it ungovernable; rather, it is the proliferation of groups and group demands that causes government to react rather than lead. Yates went so far as to liken the urban political arena to a penny arcade where municipal officials are forced to play a political game similar to that found in a shooting gallery. Targets, in the form of group demands, constantly pop up unexpectedly

---

15. Madison says: ". . . take in a greater variety of . . . interests; you make it less probable that a majority . . . will have a common motive to invade the rights of other citizens . . . and to act in unison" (Madison 1961, 83).

and disappear from sight almost as unexpectedly as new demands emerge. But where do these group demands originate? Ultimately, with the group's active membership. And this takes us to the third link in the chain of reasoning.

A political group with a large, active membership is as indecisive as a political body in developing and articulating its demands, and once developed, the demands are likely to be relatively weak. In contrast, a group with few active members can act much more decisively, articulating much stronger demands. This is the difference between many local chambers of commerce and ad hoc economic development groups. As was pointed out in the discussion of San Jose, the larger, more diverse group must develop policy demands that satisfy all of its members, whereas the smaller group has fewer diverse members to satisfy. In Yates' terminology, the targets created by groups with large, active memberships will pop up more slowly and more predictably than will targets created by groups with a small active membership. But in the current era of proliferating groups and declining participation, city decision makers face the worst of both worlds: more targets that pop up faster and less predictably than ever. Thus, the number of targets is not the major problem; rather, the problem lies in the speed and decisiveness with which those targets emerge. This speed and decisiveness contribute greatly to reaction rather than proaction, and it leads, in large part, to what has been termed an ungovernable city.

One last link completes the logical chain. As a larger number of groups articulate their demands with increasing speed and decisiveness, they must necessarily compete with one another for governmental attention and resources. This competition leads to the potential for intergroup conflict that, if left unchecked, can threaten the social life of the city. Again, we can lay the cause for escalating conflict, when it does occur, directly at the feet of declining participation. A logical extension of Madison's argument holds that as political participation increases, people find themselves on both sides of cross-cutting cleavages. Edward Banfield and James Q. Wilson (1963, 46) summarize the logic of cross cutting cleavages as follows:

> If cleavages run across each other . . . , they may serve to moderate conflict and to prevent "irreconcilable differences," because those who are enemies with respect to cleavage *a* are close allies with respect to cleavage *b* and indifferent (and therefore in a position to moderate) with respect to cleavage *c*.

Members of two neighborhood associations may thus find themselves embattled with respect to the allocation of funds for sidewalk repair, but they may find themselves allied on historical preservation. Limited participation may mask this potential alliance, which may be discovered by residents in the two neighborhoods only with their regular attendance at historical preservation

173

meetings. And while it is perhaps easy to hate a "composite person" who lives ten blocks away and whom you never see, it is difficult to hate that person when you meet him or her in the flesh and actually work with him or her on a project of interest to you both. Thus, cross cutting cleavages repress the escalation of conflict (Coleman 1957). But cross cutting cleavages can occur only in a participatory society. If, as suggested, urban society is becoming less participatory, then it is also becoming potentially more conflictual and hence less governable.

Perhaps the ultimate but heretofore unstated question posed by this discussion concerns the distribution of power in American cities. After all, people are drawn to political participation when they expect to achieve desired outcomes. How does participation affect power, and how does power affect participation? These are questions we consider in the next chapter.

The Mauretania, chloride print, 1910, 11.3 x 9.1 cm
Alfred Stieglitz Collection, 1949.786.
Photograph © 1996, The Art Institute of Chicago. All Rights Reserved.

Power is always gradually stealing away from the many to the few, because the few are more vigilant and consistent.

    Samuel Johnson, *The Adventurer*

CHAPTER 8

Power in the City

The search for power—who has it, how they got it, and how they use it—is an enduring theme that haunts the literatures of biography, fiction, drama, history, psychology, sociology, and, of course, politics. Politics, some would say, is nothing more than power struggling to find a home. Thus, a discussion of power in the city can bring to temporary closure the ideas discussed in the previous chapters.

The Early Studies of Community Power

One of the earliest systematic studies of political power in America was conducted by Robert and Helen Lynd (1929) in Middletown, a pseudonym for Muncie, Indiana. Since then, researchers have studied political power in numerous cities. In these studies, the focus on power at the urban level is synecdochic, for most of the conclusions are directed at American society in general rather than the city itself. This larger purpose is typically justified on several counts. First, since most Americans live in cities, what better location to study the use of power in the political process? Second, researchers make the simplifying (although not necessarily accurate; see chapter 5) assumption that city politics provides a microcosm for American politics, and that findings from cities provide an adequate depiction of the overall American society. Third, cities provide a convenient laboratory in which studies of power can be conducted. The emphasis here is somewhat different, however. We do not wish to explore the distribution of power in American society; rather, we will explore the literature on power to further consider the effectiveness of participation in America's cities.

A Theory of Stratification

The earliest studies found power to be concentrated in the hands of a small number of economically advantaged individuals and families. These findings provide the basis for an emergent *stratification theory* of power, which holds that society is marked by distinct and separate social "layers": upper, middle, and lower. Each layer (or stratum) is united by common interests and beliefs. In some variants of the theory, these beliefs are determined by social standing, but in most variants (e.g., Weber 1947) wealth (or lack of wealth) determines social class and political behavior. The theory holds, moreover, that each stratum works to promote its own interests, often at the expense of the other strata. Thus, stratification theory contains more than a hint of the Marxian postulate that politics is the struggle among economic classes. Polsby (1980) summarizes the conclusions of stratification theory as follows:

1. The upper class rules in community life.
2. Political and civic leaders are subordinate to the upper class.
3. A single "power elite" rules in the community.
4. The upper-class power elite rules in its own interests.
5. Social conflict takes place between the upper and under classes.

A number of studies have found support for these postulates (Lynd and Lynd 1929, Hunter 1953). The most famous of these, Floyd Hunter's study of power in Atlanta, was published in the midst of Joseph McCarthy's Senate hearings on communism and an America much obsessed with anticommunism. Yet, here in the very midst of academia were scholars (mostly sociologists) who argued openly that democracy in America was a sham (see Wildavsky, 1979a, for a discussion that places these studies within a broader political context). Thus, it is understandable that another group of scholars whose field was political science would examine the state of American democracy from a different perspective and that they perhaps would come to a different conclusion.

A Theory of Pluralism

The most notable of these latter studies was Robert Dahl's (1961) research in New Haven. Dahl found support for one of the basic principles of *pluralist democracy*: power is diffused, not concentrated in the hands of a few. It is fluid and mobile, dependent largely on a person's interest and motivation for participating in the resolution of an issue coupled with the resources (expertise, experience, and perhaps money) he or she can bring to bear on that issue. Further, Dahl argued that democratic processes were practiced in New Haven: most adult residents were legally entitled to vote, and elections were free from violence and fraud, contested by two political parties that offered rival slates of candidates. Dahl was not willing to argue that this guaranteed equal power to all citizens. He did argue, however, that "New Haven is a republic of unequal citizens—but for all that a republic" (Dahl 1961, 220). A number of other researchers using a similar research method have reached the same conclusion.

So, What's the Real Story?

How is it that researchers studying the same question could reach such different conclusions? John Walton (1966) provides a partial answer. In a telling study comparing the findings of community power studies conducted by political scientists and by sociologists, he found that sociologists tend to uncover concentrated power, while political scientists more often than not find dispersed power. This, says Walton, may be due to a difference in the research methods that sociologists and political scientists typically used in studying power: Sociologists tended to study reputations of power among community informants, while political scientists tended to study individuals' successes and failures in supporting or opposing specific community issues.

Neither of these research methods is beyond criticism; in fact, some have argued that the conclusion reached may largely be an artifact of the research method used to derive it. While this may be easy to understand in retrospect, it was clouded at the time by each side's certainty that it was right. The debate that ensued was one of the most rancorous in the halls of academe during the twentieth century.[1]

Unfortunately, the name-calling detracted from a much more interesting conclusion that began to materialize in both political science and sociology: American cities are neither uniformly stratified nor uniformly pluralistic. Rather, cities may differ in their distribution of power (see Herson, 1961, for an early discussion), and even the same city may experience changes over time in its distribution of power. This may be due, at least partially, to differences in the participatory style found in different cities. James Madison, writing two hundred years ago in *The Federalist Papers*, concluded that power tends to be

---

1. This debate and the issues that separated the two sides seem dated today. Yet, they form an important part of the developmental heritage of the social sciences. In the previous edition, we devoted considerable discussion to them; here, we opt for a somewhat shorter treatment. For a more complete discussion, see Herson and Bolland (1990).

diffused through participation. Thus, in communities with an activist population, concentrated power tends to be difficult to achieve.

Political Participation and Political Power in Two Cities

Lawrence, Kansas, is an activist city. In a study of power there, Schumaker (1990) found more than six hundred people (out of a permanent population of only thirty-five thousand) active in various community issues, and Bolland (1984) found the concentration of power to be significantly lower than in other comparably sized cities. Whenever an issue was contested, a coalition was able to emerge to either block or delay action. For example, the merits of a downtown shopping mall have been debated in Lawrence for over a decade, and three different developers of record have been named; but each was ultimately denied the opportunity to construct a commercial shopping mall. In the same way, at least one residential development has been blocked by citizen protest. As one influential figure noted, "every time I try to take a shortcut in getting something done, someone is there to stop me, and I have to backtrack." In Lawrence, community activism prevents decisive action, and influentials have largely stopped trying to assert their power. The message is clear: Citizens there value the ethos of political participation and shared power much more than the potential economic benefit to be gained through quick and decisive decisions, and they refuse to muzzle the activist minority that emerges on individual issues.

By way of comparison, consider Olathe, Kansas, a suburb of Kansas City with forty thousand people, located only thirty miles from Lawrence. A study (Bolland 1984) showed power in Olathe to be concentrated in the hands of four people, two with considerable wealth and two with important administrative positions in public agencies. Political participation in Olathe is notable by its absence: In contrast to the more than six hundred participants found in Lawrence, only about two hundred active participants were identified in Olathe (Bolland 1984). Also notable in Olathe is the speed with which changes are accomplished. In less than the time that it took to *contemplate* a mall in Lawrence, the housing stock in Olathe doubled, with little protest. Further, this construction was spearheaded largely by the two economic elites identified in the study, and they made considerable profit from their investments. In addition, a new high school and hospital were planned and built with speed that would have been impossible in Lawrence.[2]

2. In almost every city, residents can band together to prevent change from happening more effectively than they can initiate change. The previous chapter chronicles the successful efforts of neighborhood groups to prevent (or stop) highway construction that threatened their neighborhoods. As another example, Seattle businessman Frank Ruano was able to delay construction of the Seattle Kingdome for four years by mounting two successful referenda on its location (Sears 1976).

Determinants of Participation Reconsidered

What makes a community politically active? Several partial explanations are considered here. As we explore each of these factors, we will pay specific attention to how they differ in the two Kansas cities, Lawrence and Olathe.

Zoning policies and architectural style. For the most part, newer areas of a town are subject to Euclidean zoning norms (named after the city in Ohio, not the Greek mathematician), wherein residential areas are strictly residential and commercial areas are strictly commercial. This zoning pattern creates more homogeneous neighborhoods with higher property values, but it precludes the potential for neighborhood businesses (e.g., grocery stores, laundries). Thus, the mom-and-pop store, which in days gone by provided neighborhoods with convenient shopping and the opportunity for social encounters, has disappeared from the new urban landscape. In newer neighborhoods, residents now drive instead of walk to the store to buy their groceries, and the possibility of the social encounter (or for that matter, any encounter other than a fender bender) is largely reduced. In addition, recent architectural styles favor the back patio rather than the front porch, so that now even if people were to walk through their neighborhood, they would meet few others with whom to converse.

One of the most important bases of grass-roots political activism is neighborhood contact, already reduced by social trends such as crime and increased television viewing. When social contact is further reduced by zoning and architectural constraints, an almost insurmountable burden is placed on community activists, and community activism is restricted still further.

As an example, consider Lawrence and Olathe. Zoning regulations in Lawrence are relatively inclusive, with 34 percent of all housing units located in areas zoned for multiple (including commercial) uses. In contrast, Olathe has relatively exclusive zoning, with less than 1 percent of its housing units located in areas zoned for multiple uses. Also by way of comparison, Lawrence has nearly three times more houses with front porches than Olathe. Both of these factors may help explain why Lawrence has higher levels of political participation than Olathe.

Nonpolitical participation. Opportunities for nonpolitical participation may, in turn, enhance the likelihood of political activism (see Brady et al. 1995). A college town like Lawrence provides a large number of activities and events that residents can participate in or attend. Virtually every day the university offers sports events, concerts, recitals, films, forums, and/or debates that are open to the public, and a surprisingly large segment of the population takes advantage of those opportunities. In contrast, most small towns offer little by way of such cultural opportunities.

Participation in these sports and cultural events accustoms people to the idea of going out during the evening rather than staying home. Thus participation in evening meetings of neighborhood associations or activist groups may seem routine. Further, participation in cultural activities provides an opportunity for additional social contacts with others likely to be one's allies (or even one's opponents) on political issues, increasing the strength of interpersonal ties (in an insightful turn of phrase, Edward Laumann (1973) referred to these ties as the *bonds of pluralism*).

Community commitment. Commitment to the community encourages political participation. As noted earlier, we are becoming a more transient society, with more and more people expecting to live in their current house (or their current city) only until they become wealthy enough to move to a better location. Given this outlook, people are unlikely to form strong attachments with their neighbors or to their neighborhood, for they realize that these bonds will be temporary. By the same token, they are unlikely to participate politically, for they expect to be gone by the time that desired change is implemented. Another type of community commitment comes from business and industry. Capital investment decisions are more likely to benefit the community when businesses and industries are locally owned than when they are owned in absentia. After all, decisionmakers in the former situation are part of the city, and civic responsibility is an important motive potentially underlying their decisions. In contrast, the decisions of absentee owners are motivated by profit considerations, and they are potentially less beneficial to the community. Local owners of business and industry may be powerful political participants in the community; again in contrast, managers or franchisers of absentee-owned industries or businesses are less likely to participate in community affairs, for their loyalty moves in corporate rather than community directions. With the advent of the grocery chain, the fast-food franchise, and the shopping mall (where virtually all stores are absentee-owned and locally franchised), it is difficult to find a community where local ownership is the norm rather than the exception.

A new manifestation of this phenomenon is the advent of corporate buyouts and takeovers during the past decade. A case in point is evident in San Francisco, where the strong progrowth coalition that promoted the city's economic development in the 1960s and 1970s fell apart after corporate takeovers during the 1980s. New corporate owners replaced an entrepreneurial core of community-oriented local business leaders with new management-oriented executives who lacked strong ties to the city, and the coalition fell apart at least partly due to a lack of progrowth local leadership (DeLeon 1992). Such corporate takeovers have become commonplace during the past decade, particularly in such businesses as banking, and they have an important impact on the distribution of power in the cities where they occur. Further, recent trends toward corporate downsizing have removed millions of people from middle-management positions, people who had used their corporate affiliation as a resource to legitimize and enhance their political participation; this, too, has reduced the number of active participants in cities across the country.

City size and heterogeneity. Participation is likely to be higher in smaller cities than in larger cities or in suburbs, due to what may be termed an energy factor. In today's labor force, where nearly as many women work as men, couples run out of energy by the time they get home from work, cook dinner, and do the dishes. In a small city, where the time to commute home from work is minutes, there is still time to recover before an evening meeting or concert. But in a large city or a suburb, where the time to commute home from work may exceed an hour, the logistics of political activity in the evening become difficult.

Heterogeneity also facilitates participation. In a perfectly homogeneous city (if one could be found) political participation would be nonrational. Since all residents should have similar concerns and goals, one spokesperson could speak for everyone, alleviating the need for political participation by others. But as a city becomes more heterogeneous, political concerns tend to diverge, and political participation becomes a necessary ingredient of survival.

Form of government. Finally, certain kinds of political structures are more likely to facilitate political participation than others. Nonpartisan and at-large elections reduce the likelihood of citizen participation. And council-manager governments reduce the role of the city council in policy development, which in turn may limit the attractiveness of (and the competition for) those positions. Further, the elected mayor is an important political force who can potentially generate political activity around a community issue. But in cities with council-manager governments, the mayorship is a ceremonial position largely without this kind of influence.[3]

Some Conclusions about Power in American Communities

The foregoing comparisons lead to several conclusions about the distribution of power in American communities. In communities with exclusive

---

3. These various factors help explain the differential participation rates and concentration of power in Lawrence and Olathe. For example, Lawrence is an ethnically and racially heterogeneous college town, while Olathe's population is technically and racially homogeneous. Lawrence's nonstudent population is more stable, while Olathe's is more transient. Business in Lawrence tends to be locally owned, while that in Olathe tends to be absentee-owned. Only in form of government are Lawrence and Olathe similar. Both use the council-manager plan. See Bolland (1984) for a more detailed comparison of these cities.

zoning policies and modern-style, porchless homes, power is likely to be more concentrated than in cities with inclusive zoning and older-style homes. We might further note an obvious relationship between these factors and the city's age. Euclidean zoning is a fairly recent development (dating back no earlier than 1926; see chapter 12 for a further discussion of zoning), and 1950 is an approximate turning point for residential architecture, away from the front porch and toward the back patio. Not surprisingly, studies have shown that older cities have higher levels of participation (e.g., Alford and Lee 1968) and less concentrated power (e.g., Gilbert 1968) than their newer counterparts.

Beyond these, four other conclusions emerge. First, increased opportunities for social contact may lead to increased political participation, and in turn, to more diffused power. Second, absentee ownership of businesses and industries leads to more concentrated power. Third, power is more concentrated in reformed cities than in unreformed cities. And fourth, central cities may have generally less-concentrated power than suburbs.

This last observation is more ambiguous than the others, and several factors may account for it. Given their size and cultural diversity, central cities tend to have more *types* of politically relevant organizations than suburbs, including more industries, unions, and state and federal agencies. The social problems of central cities are typically greater than those of suburbs, leading to a wider participation in the former than the latter. In addition, suburban workers typically commute further to work than their urban counterparts, and they have less time and energy for political participation.

Community Power: Toward an Alternative Theory

Previously discussed theories viewed power in *systemic* terms as the ability to affect the *political system* in some manner and achieve some desired political outcome. For example, stratification theorists hold that power resides in the hands of an economic elite because urban policies are generally biased in their favor (see Stone, 1980, for a discussion). And pluralists hold that power resides in the hands of diverse groups and individuals within the city, with specific decisions reflecting diverse preferences of political participants. But neither formulation acknowledges that power is a multifaceted concept consisting of several distinct components. First, some people (e.g., city council members, school board members, the mayor) have power because they are able to vote directly on policy proposals. Second, some people (e.g., the city manager, individual police officers, the school district superintendent) have power because they exercise discretion in the implementation of policies once they are enacted. Third, some people (e.g., lawyers, protestors) have power because they are able to stall policies once they have been enacted, either through litigation or through disruptive protest. Fourth, some people (e.g., business owners, homeowners) have power because of their private or corporate investment decisions. And fifth, some people have power because they are able to influence others and mobilize support around policy proposals. The dynamics of these different components of power are quite different. If they are lumped together into a single phenomenon called *power*, the results are bound to be misleading. As an alternative, we will develop a multifaceted definition of power that breaks the concept into three different components.

The first component, which might be described as *direct power*,[4] is the ability to affect policy outcomes *directly* through one's actions. This is the easiest type of power to conceptualize and describe, and it is what most of us imagine when we think of power. Direct power in urban politics lies in the hands of formally designated policymakers and their agents (members of the urban bureaucracy).

A second component of power, which we might term *indirect power*, is the ability of private citizens to affect outcomes through their decisions and actions. For example, citizens, through their vote, elect policymakers. For another example, the land developer who decides to place a large housing development on the city's west side may affect the city's growth patterns for years to come, which in turn affects the city's decisions concerning the location of new schools and zoning policies. By the same token, the chief executive officer of a major manufacturing corporation who decides to renovate a local plant rather than move it to another location affects the city's employment patterns (and through them, its tax base and service delivery policies). And for a third example, the attorney who files suit to stop construction of a highway, or a protest group that threatens to stage sit-ins at city hall, may delay the implementation of an enacted policy indefinitely. While these people are unable to affect the city's policies directly (after all, they have no formal authority over the enactment or implementation of those policies), they are able to affect policy outcomes indirectly.

A third component of power, which we might term *interpersonal power*, is the ability of any citizen (either private or holding a governmental position) or group to affect urban outcomes by mobilizing support around one or another policy proposal. This may take place during the enactment of municipal ordinances; for instance, a local business owner may be able to lobby a council member to support her position on a specific piece of legislation. Or it may occur during the agenda-setting phase of the policy process, as local problems are identified and possible solutions are discussed and debated within the community. This type of power is least studied (and least understood), and in the following section we will consider it in some detail.

---

4. While these components of power inevitably blur around the edges, each is sufficiently recognizable that we can proceed as if they were truly distinct.

Interpersonal Power

When people talk politics, they seldom attempt to coerce one another.[5] Rather, they attempt to convince each other of the relative merits of their ideas, suggesting that if a political problem is viewed from their perspective, the solution will become clear. Thus, *ideas* are the coin of the political realm, and the exchange of ideas is the essence of interpersonal power.[6] (Herson, 1990, recognizes the importance of this formulation with the title of his book on the history of American political thought: *The Politics of Ideas*.) Thus, the power to lobby a council member reflects the ability to exchange ideas about a particular issue. And in these same terms, the power to set the agenda[7]—that is, to mobilize support for and generate consensus around policy priorities and long-range policy goals—is *the ability to spread ideas*.[8]

Hence, interpersonal power is based on interpersonal relationships: An individual, *A,* has power over another person, *B*, to the extent that *B* solicits and listens to *A*'s ideas. But in order for this power relationship between *A* and *B* to materialize, *B* must have some motive for listening to *A*. *B* may believe that *A* has good ideas, because his or her ideas have been good in the past. *B* may believe that *A* has access to important information or that he or she possesses expertise on a particular subject. *B* may find *A* to be charismatic or may be impressed by his or her willingness to commit substantial time to community projects.

To the extent that ideas are transmitted from person to person and permeate the community's political agenda, they become ideas "whose time has

---

5. While it is true that politicians have been known to take bribes in exchange for legislative votes, and that voters have also been known to take bribes for their support of political candidates at the polls, we should view this type of coercion as an anomaly, not often likely to affect the process of urban politics. By the same token, some politicians may be coerced through blackmail, but again this occurs infrequently enough that we should ignore it in our discussion of interpersonal power.

6. Victor Hugo seemingly took much the same approach to understanding politics when he observed, "Greater than the tread of mighty armies is an idea whose time has come." But the present argument diverges from Hugo by taking a more anthropocentric approach. It holds that great ideas do not just emerge, they are generated and spread by people. The great idea that no one hears is not great. But on the other hand, even the mediocre idea that spreads effectively through the body politic will have important consequences.

7. As chapters 11 and 12 suggest, the ability to set the urban agenda lies to a large extent outside the city's boundaries, in county, state, and national governments. But, for now, discussion concentrates on forces indigenous to the city.

8. "I have a dream," exclaimed the Reverend Martin Luther King, Jr., in his 1963 speech commemorating the centennial of the Emancipation Proclamation. Rev. King's dream is an example of our *idea*, and much of King's power lay in his ability to communicate that idea to others. His and others' ability to mobilize support around the dream of an equal society was, in large part, the impetus of the modern Civil Rights Movement in America. But while the dream no doubt had been dreamt by many others before, it had failed to trigger anything approaching the activity it generated during the late 1950s and the 1960s. This suggests the importance of great people over great ideas.

Power in the City

come," likely to affect political thinking and policy development in the community. In considering the ability of political participants to influence one another—and thus to influence the agenda—we must take stock of the resources they possess and see how these resources work to facilitate the flow of their ideas through the community. In the following section, we consider various types of political participants, exploring the ways their resources enhance their interpersonal power.

Who's Powerful and Who's Not: An Inventory of Urban Political Participants and Their Resources

Formal Political Participants

The governing body. The most obvious participants in the urban political process are members of the governing body (either commissioners or council members). These individuals exercise *direct* power, for their votes are the ultimate determinants of many urban policies, ranging from taxing and spending to land use and zoning. But, as was suggested earlier, most council members have neither a firm grasp of nor a strong desire to learn the complexities of urban economics or service delivery. They are therefore largely dependent on those people who possess this expertise, mostly administrators and bureaucrats inside government and successful business managers outside government. So, although members of the governing body may make formal and binding decisions (and thus exert direct power), they must often rely on the advice of others when it comes to setting the agenda and enacting policy legislation. In other words, they are subject to the interpersonal power of others. Some council members are able, in turn, to exert interpersonal power as they lobby one another during policy enactment and mobilize support during the agenda-setting phase of the policy process. After all, they run for office with varying political orientations. *[The theory of ideology.]* And once in office, they may be expected to act on those orientations. But in many cities, the long-term consequences of the urban reform movement, in its attempt to remove politics from government, have reduced the probability that persons with platforms and agendas for change will be elected to the city council. The mathematics and logic are straightforward: In an at-large election, those elected tend to be candidates whose political preferences (and political orientations) are acceptable to the greatest possible cross-section of the electorate, which is to say, candidates without strident views or extreme preferences.[9] Thus, lobbying

9. Unlike partisan primary elections, where party activists (whose views tend toward extremes of liberalism or conservatism) influence the slate of candidates considered in the general election, nonpartisan elections are characterized by a moderating influence, and extremist candidates tend to be weeded out early.

and agenda-setting activities of council members in reformed cities will be largely in support of the status quo.

For those council members who seek to set the community's agenda, one resource is very much theirs to use: They have the legitimacy of office. They are, after all, elected by the citizenry, and thus they are the legitimate spokespersons for that citizenry. As elected spokespersons, they are in an advantaged position to spread their ideas through the community. But even so, anecdotal evidence from a number of community studies (e.g., Lynd and Lynd 1929, Hunter 1953) suggests that other, high-status people in the community (business leaders) view municipal elections as mere popularity contests and, accordingly, have little interest in listening to what elected officials have to say. Bolland's (1984) findings from Olathe and from Lawrence suggest that each council member had a small but loyal following who listened attentively every time he or she spoke; but beyond these small audiences, few people were motivated to attend to their ideas.

Further detracting from legitimacy as a resource of council members is an often present public cynicism concerning the honesty of public officials, "The finest city council that money can buy," is one of the hoary jokes of urban politics. To the extent that the public thinks it true, this perceived truth further limits the ability of council members to spread ideas and build consensus for those ideas.[10]

What about more personal resources, for instance, charisma, creativity, and the contribution of time to community projects? In many instances, individuals who possess these resources have little interest in running for council seats. Others will listen to their ideas whether they hold public office or not, and most often they are more effective working outside the public limelight. By running for office, much of their power may actually be diluted by the excess publicity to which politicians are subjected.

The mayor. In contrast to members of the city council, the occupant of the mayor's office may possess many of the resources necessary to exercise both direct power and interpersonal power. In strong-mayor governments, the mayor usually presides over council meetings and usually casts the deciding vote in cases of a tie. The strong mayor is also the city's chief administrator, a position that gives him or her access to bureaucracy's information and (as a result) considerable expertise in day-to-day governmental operations. These resources give the mayor considerable direct power.

Just as important, as chief executive of the city, the mayor usually has free access to the media and to various groups and committees within the city.

10. Ironically, urban reform seems to have had little affect on this cynicism. Even today, most citizens believe that corruption occurs in municipal government, and there is some evidence that municipal corruption may be widespread. For discussions of this problem, see Gardiner and Lyman (1978) and Gardiner and Olson (1974).

This access (enhanced by the fact that he or she is the elect of all the people) is a resource providing the mayor with considerable interpersonal power, for it means that when the mayor talks, people (including council members) listen. And as they listen, the mayor is able to spread his or her ideas and policy priorities through the community.[11]

Administrators. Another set of persons with both direct power and interpersonal power is the city's chief administrators: the city manager in council-manager cities, the school district superintendent, the administrator of the city's public hospital, and others who oversee a large public budget. Like the mayor in mayor-council governments, local administrators have access to—in fact, are responsible for collecting—information in urban bureaucracies. They are in a position to tell the city council, the school board, or the hospital board which issues demand action and which do not, and how those demanding action should be addressed. In one telling set of studies of urban school boards, Harmon Zeigler and his colleagues (Zeigler and Jennings 1974, Tucker and Zeigler 1980) found that board members deferred to the superintendent's recommendations in the vast majority of all decisions. We should expect similar findings for hospital board members and city council members. Thus, administrators have considerable interpersonal power in dealing with their governing bodies.

Also like strong mayors, administrators develop considerable expertise in a short period of time, and others in the community are interested in hearing ideas developed through this expertise. Further, they usually have advanced professional degrees, giving them the benefit of a theoretical as well as a practical understanding of the city and its problems. Finally, the mere fact that they exercise so much administrative authority provides them with a wide audience for their ideas. Given that their preferences are likely to influence policy decisions, others in the community are anxious to understand these preferences, so as to anticipate their consequences. The studies of both Lawrence and Olathe support these conclusions: In both cities, the city manager was at the center of the policy network[12]; and in Olathe, the school district superintendent also maintained a central position. Philip Trounstine and Terry Christensen (1982) found similar results in their study of power in San Jose.

11. Even in weak-mayor systems, the mayor is likely to have greater interpersonal power than other council members. Research in Olathe and Lawrence shows, for example, that the mayor (although operating in a weak-mayor system) was more central in the policy network than any other member of the council.

12. A policy network consists of the web of interpersonal relationships through which political participants share ideas and information relevant to the city's policies. In this way, we add a layer of meaning to the concept of interpersonal power: Those who are located at the center of the community's policy network have the greater interpersonal power. For further discussion of the concept of networks in urban politics, see the work of Laumann and his colleagues (e.g., Laumann and Pappi 1976, Laumann et al. 1977, Galaskiewicz 1979).

In addition to interpersonal power, urban administrators are able to exercise considerable direct power. As was previously noted, city managers have the power to hire and fire municipal staff, and hospital and school district members have the power to hire personnel in their organizations. Thus, the behavior of individual police officers, school teachers, nurse supervisors, and other employees will at least partially reflect the orientations and preferences of these administrators. Urban administrators, in addition, frequently provide policy directives to their staff, to be implemented by the various street-level bureaucrats within the community. Again, these policy directives reflect the preferences and orientations of the administrators issuing them. Finally, administrators implement the policies developed by their elected superiors. But since these policies are often ambiguous, the administrator is afforded great latitude to instill his or her own preferences into policy decisions.

Street-level bureaucrats. Another set of urban political participants with direct power consists of employees within the city's governmental bureaucracies (e.g., police officers, street maintenance personnel, schoolteachers, nurses, physicians). As has been noted throughout, these individuals have considerable direct power, reflected in their ability to use discretion in implementing policies handed down from above. For example, the police officer exercises considerable discretion in deciding when to stop speeding motorists and when to issue traffic citations.

Just as important, street-level bureaucrats become experts in a narrow range of urban policy, providing them with a basis for interpersonal power. For example, a patrol officer may be the city's greatest expert on crime, and perhaps even life, in the area he or she patrols. And a first-grade teacher is one of the city's great experts on the behavior problems of first graders. This expertise provides street-level bureaucrats with an ability to influence others, at least within the narrow area of their expertise. However, since this area of expertise tends to be narrow, their overall impact on the urban agenda, and the range of their lobbying efforts, is likely to be small.

Members of community advisory boards and commissions. Still another set of formal political participants with the potential for interpersonal power consists of members of the community's advisory boards and commissions. This power is, however, in most cases, quite limited. In some cities, advisory boards may be elected to office. Much more frequently, they are appointed. Overall, advisory board members are hampered by the same constraints that keep members of the city council from exercising interpersonal power, but even more so. They work without compensation, so the effort they put into their positions is strictly dependent on their sense of civic responsibility. But unlike members of the city council, they have little opportunity to parlay that effort into interpersonal power. As was noted earlier, members of the city council have public recognition: They are quoted in the newspaper, they are seen at public events, and so forth. A member of the parks and recreation board, in comparison, enjoys relative anonymity, with his or her efforts known only to friends and relatives.[13]

Members of advisory boards are also without much direct power. Like the city council, they are dependent on municipal administrators to provide them with information and to set the agendas for their meetings. Advisory committees typically vote to *recommend* policy decisions, whereas the city council and the school board actually vote to *enact* various policies. Thus, advisory board members are once removed from positions of direct power.[14]

Informal Participants

As we move from formal urban participants to informal participants, we leave direct power behind, for the ability to enact and implement legislation is the exclusive domain of formally designated policymakers and their agents. But at the same time, a discussion of informal participants yields new applications of indirect power and interpersonal power. Among informal participants in the city's governance, two groups—voters and protestors—play important roles, although they are relatively powerless in setting the urban agenda. In contrast, neighborhood groups and business associations are notable for their indirect and interpersonal power—and through that power for their overall influence on urban politics.

13. Of course, members of advisory committees are often important in setting the urban agenda or in lobbying council members before important votes, but not because of their positions on the advisory committees. For example, an important developer may be appointed to the parks and recreation board, or the president of the chamber of commerce may be appointed to the mental health board. But in these cases, the appointment derives from his or her power rather than vice versa.

14. Another set of formal political participants consists of municipal judges, who have a paradoxical potential for interpersonal power. They, along with the chief of police and the county sheriff, are the community's greatest experts on crime and punishment. Further, many of their cases directly or indirectly involve social services. For example, claims of mental illness, as well as of alcohol or drug dependency, must be considered in sentencing decisions; as another example, the court must decide whether minors are to be remanded to a social service agency in the case of domestic disputes. This provides judges with great expertise in the link between crime and social services in the community. Judges hold high-status positions in the community, and their presumed impartiality gives them great credibility. No one expects them to have an axe to grind. In short, people are willing to listen to what judges have to say. Paradoxically, however, most judges do not have much to say on community issues, for they view political activity as counter to their judicial roles; for them, involvement in community issues would destroy the impartiality that allows them to be effective judges. In other words, judges have interpersonal power only until they attempt to use it, at which point it may disappear.

Voters. In principle, voters are the ultimate holders of indirect power in the city, for it is they who elect the officials who enact public policy. Voting, however, is not an ongoing political act. In most cities, municipal elections occur only once every two years. Except in instances where policy is created through referenda and bond elections, voters do not exercise direct power. Between elections, city officials may attend to what the electorate thinks (e.g., by answering telephone calls from concerned citizens; stopping for offhand advice during social meetings), but there is little evidence that officials actively seek out voters' advice or that they attend to that advice once given. For one thing, most elected officials devote most of their time and energy attending to specific complaints (trash collection, police response, and so forth). For another, typical voters simply do not possess the resources (beyond the vote) that would give them interpersonal power, and few people beyond friends and relatives seek their advice or ideas on political matters.[15]

Within the electorate, of course, individual voters are not as powerful as voting blocks. But even voting blocks often find themselves without much interpersonal power once the election has been decided. For example, Hispanics and Jews provided the crucial votes in Tom Bradley's victory in the 1973 Los Angeles mayoral election, yet these groups often felt slighted by the actions and policy decisions of his administration (Sonenshein 1986). And as was noted earlier, the policy actions of Mayor Wilson Goode in Philadelphia were often aimed more at local white business owners than at the predominantly black coalition that elected him.[16]

Protestors. In principle, protestors have indirect power. On the one hand, stubborn and rancorous protest, not to mention violence, can potentially be used to delay the implementation (perhaps indefinitely) of policy legislation. But just as often, it hardens the resolve of council members or administrators

---

15. That the electorate generally plays a passive role in the policy process gives rise to a good deal of discussion among democratic theorists. Of course, the principle of representative government begins with the proposition that elected officials are surrogates for the electorate. But as surrogates, are they to give the people what they want or what the representatives believe will best serve the public interest? Each answer has its philosophic defenders. For John Stuart Mill (1926) and others, full citizen participation in all aspects of government helps promote citizen virtue, intelligence, and morality. But given low voter turnout, coupled with citizens' limited grasp of complex issues (Converse 1964), it may not be surprising that another group of democratic theorists argues that a healthy democracy does not require direct voter involvement in policy formation. It is enough (say these theorists) for voters to choose those who do make policy (Lipset 1960, Schumpeter 1947). But in rebuttal, see Bachrach (1967).

16. In some cases, events rather than personalities conspire to limit the success of voting blocks in translating preferences into policies. For example, in 1973 Janet Gray Hays ran for (and was elected) mayor of San Jose. She ran an essentially no-growth campaign, employing the slogan "Let's make San Jose better before we make it bigger." Yet, during her tenure in office, San Jose was the fastest growing city in the United States (Trounstine and Christensen 1982).

already committed to a policy.[17] Most often, rancorous or violent protest results in symbolic gains for the protesting group. For example, the race riots of the 1960s netted the establishment of the Kerner Commission to study the racial situation in American cities, but they resulted in very few policy changes. Just as important, rancorous or violent protest alienates those to whom it is directed, and protestors often relinquish any interpersonal power they might otherwise have claimed.

On the other hand, nonviolent protestors may have considerable indirect power through their ability to bring issues to the top of the political agenda, particularly if the public believes their grievance to be genuine and their demands legitimate. The nonviolent civil rights protests of the 1950s and the early 1960s are a case in point. By bringing intolerable conditions to the attention of the nation, Martin Luther King, Jr. (along with others) was able to create a climate for changing civil rights policy within the United States (Branch 1988). In addition, nonviolent protestors do not burn bridges behind them. Their actions, while forceful, do not disrupt avenues of interpersonal communication and power.[18]

Neighborhood groups and economic interests. Although we could consider a large number of other informal participants in the urban political process, we will concentrate on two more: neighborhood groups and economic interests. In the final analysis, these may be the most important sources of indirect and interpersonal power in the city.

In order to understand this power, let us reconsider one of the themes of this book, that the city is at heart an economic entity. Although the city has many functions in today's society, its primary functions center around the creation of jobs and the provision of services. Both, in the end, are economic functions. Jobs obviously provide a livelihood for the city's inhabitants, and they provide the capital necessary for the city to collect taxes. Services are the

17. Examples of rancorous protests that successfully halted policy actions are difficult to identify. On the other hand, numerous examples of unsuccessful protests come to mind, including the Clamshell Alliance's attempt to stop EPA approval of the Seabrook Nuclear Reactor in New Hampshire and the American Agricultural Movement's tractorcade in Washington, D.C., not to mention the race riots of the 1960s. This is consistent with Schumaker's (1975, 521) conclusion that "the effect of militancy may be overestimated by some scholars."

18. Perhaps one of the best examples of this principle is the rise and fall of the homeless movement. As a result of nonviolent protest and persuasive argument, the nation came to view people as "the homeless" rather than as winos and bums; even more important, advocates for the homeless etched into the public consciousness the belief that the typical American family is only two paychecks away from homelessness. By the late 1980s, eradicating homelessness had achieved a place on the national agenda, and many cities sought ways to do their part to solve this American tragedy. But by the mid 1990s, the homeless were once again being viewed as bums and winos, due in part to their aggressive panhandling of urban residents and visitors and their sometimes blatantly antisocial behavior and disregard for the sensibilities of those they came into contact with.

primary source of urban expenditures (both through capital outlays, such as police cars and playground equipment, and through the salaries of those who provide the services). Thus, except for the exclusively "dormitory suburb," the city is necessarily an economic enterprise, with the success of municipal government coupled to the local business climate. This gives the business community considerable indirect power. When the climate is healthy, new businesses and industries move to town, providing more jobs and more taxes to provide better services. And in turn, businesses and industries are more likely to move to cities that provide good services and good neighborhoods for their employees. Thus, we observe a three-way relationship between business, neighborhoods, and municipal services that serves to define the city's economic climate and its growth potential.

The three-way relationship in action. With this in mind, then, let us consider how local business and industrial leaders affect policy decisions, and in doing so, offer a final canvass of both indirect and interpersonal power. Through their capital investment decisions (in the case of owners) and recommendations (in the case of managers), business owners and managers directly affect the lives of a number of urban residents (i.e., their employees) and the city's coffers (i.e., the recipient of their tax dollars). It therefore behooves the city's decision-makers to listen when business leaders talk about the needs and goals of the community. This dialogue may focus on specific issues, for example the construction of a downtown parking garage or a convention center, or it may be more amorphous, relating to broader issues such as crime, education, and the quality of urban services. But whatever the issue, business leaders generally have open access to the mayor, city council members, and/or the city manager. This, in turn, provides them with considerable interpersonal power.

But it should be noted that this access is not strictly, or even at all, coercive. In other words, it is not necessarily the threat of closing down manufacturing plants or retail businesses that makes decision-makers want to listen to the ideas of economic leaders. Just as important is the fact that these individuals are economically successful and, over the years, have built up credibility as community boosters. Recall that the city management movement grew out of a desire to run cities as businesses and that many city managers are trained in a business tradition. Further, note that most city council members are themselves part of the business community, as bankers or lawyers or insurance salespersons. They respect people with demonstrated success in financial management. Finally, most successful business owners have put considerable time and money into their businesses. For them, what's good for the community is good for business, and vice versa. Over the years they have developed into local boosters, often serving as chair of the United Way campaign or chair of the local delegation to the community's sister city in Japan. They are well known. And perhaps most important, they are trusted. All of these factors make them among the most valued political friends and advisors of many formal decisionmakers, who frequently turn to them for ideas and advice.

With homeowners, we face a somewhat different explanation for power. Individual homeowners have very little power, either indirect or interpersonal, but as a group they are able to exercise considerable indirect power over a rather narrow range of issues. For example, a group of homeowners is often able to block the placement of a low-income housing unit, a group home for mentally retarded adults, or a new fire station in their neighborhood. In principle, they have no more direct access to council members, who make the final decision on these issues, than do any other groups of voters. But in reality, theirs is an implicit threat to move if an intolerable situation arises—to "vote with their feet" (Hirschman 1970). And if even as few as 6 percent of a neighborhood's residents put their houses up for sale at the same time, neighborhood instability may result (Skogan 1990).

Do all neighborhoods have equal power? As a rule, no. Low-income and particularly underclass neighborhoods typically consist of rental units, often characterized by high transience (as much as 40 percent turnover each year; see Whyte 1988). They are also often seen as problem areas, requiring more than their share of the city's services (e.g., fire and police protection, emergency medical services, and so forth). The city council is not easily swayed by the threat to move from these neighborhoods. But in middle- and upper-class neighborhoods, two factors make the council take note. First, residents of these neighborhoods are professionally (and therefore residentially) mobile, and moving to a new job in an adjacent city would present them with little hardship. In other words, their threats to move are not to be taken lightly. Second, the neighborhoods themselves are more stable, so an outflux of residents would be quite noticeable and potentially quite disruptive to the community's economic climate.

Idiosyncratic Factors Affecting the Distribution of Power

Finally, we should note that every city is different, and the distribution of power (of whatever type) in each city has its own idiosyncrasies. *[The theory of multiple realities.]* In university towns, for example, the university president and members of his or her staff inevitably exercise indirect power by contributing university resources to solving local problems. In Lawrence, Kansas, for example, the University of Kansas joined the city in designing and developing a high-tech industrial park; in Tuscaloosa, Alabama, the University of Alabama contributed its technical expertise to improve efficiency in the local Rochester Products (a subsidiary of General Motors) plant, and it was instrumental in attracting a JVC plant to Tuscaloosa during the late 1980s. But in turn, this commitment allows university administrators access to other, impor-

195

tant people in the community, providing them with interpersonal power. In addition, most cities have at least one dominant church, and the pastor of that church may be a vocal participant in social and moral issues within the community. Pastors in predominantly black neighborhoods command considerable respect among their parishioners, and they are usually quite important in mobilizing the black community around political and social issues.[19] And many cities have at least one charismatic leader who may hold no formal political or economic position in the community, but nonetheless is able to command the attention of people due to his or her "presence."

Implications for Public Policy

Based on this discussion of power, several general conclusions can be suggested about the role of power and the powerful in the development of urban policy. First, there exists an *economic bias* in this process, with policies generally favoring economic interests within the city. City officials in Detroit are, no doubt, convinced that what is good for General Motors (and Ford and Chrysler) is good for Detroit, and, where possible, public policies are supportive of (or at least not detrimental to) the auto industry. Other cities share a similar orientation toward their dominant industries. If we introduce a somewhat artificial distinction between economic and social issues within a community, this distinction will suggest that economic issues take highest priority, with social issues finishing a poor second.

Second, a *class bias* exists in the development of public policy, even though it is often subtle and may even go unrecognized by those in positions of authority. Successful people, people of accomplishment, are the ones who command the attention of others. By definition (and popular perception), those living in poverty are not successful, and they therefore fail to command attention. Once people attain positions of importance in the community, they also tend to listen to the ideas of others with similar experiences and backgrounds, further reducing the voice of the poor.

Third, urban public policy reflects technical considerations more than social considerations. Considerable power resides in the hands of municipal bureaucrats, who gain expertise in the day-to-day management and operation of their agencies. This experience often may lead to choices based on factual and technical considerations rather than on social considerations. For example, the city manager, in projecting the path of a new street, may be likely to consider the cost of condemning property, the terrain through which it must pass,

19. In promoting the development of Harborplace in Baltimore (see chapter 10), developer James Rouse met with fifty leading black ministers to convince them of the importance of the project for minority jobs and business opportunities in the inner city. Prior to the public vote on Harborplace, the black churches distributed 50,000 handbills supporting it; the referendum won approval (Frieden and Sagalyn 1989).

and its capacity to move vehicles efficiently rather than the social disruption that it may cause for a neighborhood. The former is easily quantifiable in dollars and cents, while the latter is not.

Fourth, the more people involved in the policy development process, the slower and less definitive it is. Like the camel in the old joke (a camel is a horse designed by a committee), public policies designed by a large collective tend to be lumpy and ungainly, while those designed by a small group of like-minded people tend to be sleek and decisive. Both types of policy carry costs as well as benefits. In general, however, the more participants, the more diffused power is in the community. And without someone (or a small set of people) to serve as an issue entrepreneur, few dramatic changes will occur.

Fifth, when policymakers listen to the ideas of a large number of people, policies are more likely to address public problems successfully than when policymakers limit the number of people to whom they listen. If a decisionmaker consults only those in his or her inner circle, he or she will seldom be exposed to alternative views of the world. This is self-limiting and leads to a type of insularity that Irving Janis (1982) described as *groupthink*, wherein advisors tell a decisionmaker only what they believe he or she wants to hear. Many of the foreign policy catastrophes of this century can be blamed on groupthink, and, arguably, many urban policy failures have similar origins.

Finally, poor public policy results when competing interests in the community distrust the motives of one another. This, essentially, is the situation characterized by Yates (1977) as street-fighting pluralism, and he blames it for what he sees as our ungovernable cities. But an alternative formulation suggests that the ungovernable city derives from the breakdown of democratic norms in the urban political style. Adherence to these norms creates an atmosphere of trust and fair play, while deviance from them engenders suspicion and uncertainty. Mistrust engenders rancor, and rancor breaks down communication. In turn, uncertainty grows for political participants. Their ability to anticipate the course of community issues deteriorates, and their style of participation becomes defensive and reactive. With defensive reaction, groups become internally more cohesive (i.e., members become more supportive of one another) but more externally combative (Bolland 1985a). And the agenda-setting process fragments still further as competing groups refuse to cooperate with one another.

But despite these difficulties, cities continue to make policy and provide services to their residents. The following chapters consider more thoroughly the urban policy process and the policies it generates.

PART FOUR

URBAN POLITICS AND POLICY: CONTEXT AND CONSTRAINTS

The Steerage, chloride print, 1907, 11 x 9.2 cm
Alfred Stieglitz Collection, 1949.705.
Photograph © 1996, The Art Institute of Chicago. All Rights Reserved.

Nothing is harder than to make people think about what they're going to *do*.
  André Malraux, *Man's Fate*

CHAPTER 9

The Styles and Stages of Urban Policy

Dreams and Reality: "World Enough and Time"

In the prescriptive-democratic theory of philosophers' musings, public policy is a completely rational enterprise. Goals are plainly stated. Means to ends are carefully considered. And goals are always achieved effectively and efficiently—which is to say, actions produce their intended effect with the least expenditure of time, money, and other things of value. What is more, those who construct this rational policy always keep in the forefront of their minds a well-considered vision of the public interest. Consider, for example, the following fanciful dialogue among rational policymakers.

First Policymaker: What is the problem? Exactly what are we trying to achieve?

Second Policymaker: What has been tried in other places? And how has it worked?

Third Policymaker: Which among these many possible solutions is most likely to solve the problem that confronts us? Would an alternative solution work just as well—but cost us less in terms of money, time, and effort?

Fourth Policymaker: Well then, are we all agreed? We try our preferred solution for a limited time? And if it doesn't do what we
hope it will do, we try something else?

In the real world, this scenario is rarely, if ever, enacted. Anyone who
attends a meeting of a city council (or county commission, or state legislature, or Congress) quickly learns that the give and take of policy discussion
bears little resemblance to the rational style and courtly utterances of a
Platonic dialogue. In the real world, policymakers operate within constraints
that limit rational problem solving. First, they are constrained by resources—
time, knowledge, and money. Second, they are constrained by selective perceptions and the screening out of information that contradicts the policymakers' dominant ideologies. *[The theory of ideology.]* And third, they are
constrained by the piecemeal responsibilities and scattered jurisdictions of
local government (e.g., Ripley and Franklin 1987, Herson 1986). *[The theory
of grass-roots democracy.]*

Constraints Imposed by Limited Knowledge

In creating rational policy, no resource is more important than knowledge.
Those who aspire to rational policy need to be able to choose from alternative courses of action. Moreover, they need to know how and why things happen—which is to say, they need well-validated descriptive theories. They need
to know the likely costs and benefits of an intended course of action. And, to
the best of their abilities, they must anticipate the unintended consequences of
any proposed policy (Rivlin 1971, Rein 1976).

Unanticipated and Other Consequences

Who could have foreseen the unintended consequences of the great highway building projects of recent decades? Highways were built primarily to
link distant cities and to ease traffic congestion within cities, but their unanticipated consequences have been awesome—and some would say, devastating. The new freeways contributed to the flight to the suburbs of an affluent and mostly white middle class, leaving the central cities with an
increasingly poor, black, and Hispanic population. Freeways cut through old
established neighborhoods, dislocating the mostly poor and elderly who
lived there. And in cutting through old neighborhoods and tearing down
houses that were in the way, freeways also depleted the stock of low-rent
housing available to the poor. In all, 330,000 housing units were destroyed
between 1957 and 1968, displacing more than a million people (Mohl
1993b). Freeways also destroyed many small, family-run businesses. They frequently isolated what was left of older neighborhoods. In these and other

ways they broke the social and economic bonds that had once served to create a sense of community.[1]

Equally important for what might be called the economic good-health of the cities, freeways also helped close down the central city's business area as a lively shopping place. They accomplished an unanticipated deterioration of downtown by making commercial property on the city's rim easily accessible by car. Shopping malls sprang up on what had once been farmland. Compared to downtown land prices, mall developers got cheap land and often put cheaply constructed store spaces on them. Merchants were attracted by rents lower than those downtown, and customers were lured by unlimited free parking and the visual pleasure of modern shops built in a consistent architectural style. Shopping malls became urban gathering places. To go there was more than a shopping trip; it was to see and be seen, an important social occasion. (For the young, a Saturday at the shopping mall has become a replacement for yesteryear's Saturday movie matinee.) Meanwhile, in many cities, downtown shopping went into steep decline. Stores and cinemas were boarded up and abandoned by their owners to avoid high property taxes. In many cities, the once-bustling downtown has been transformed into a parking-lot desert, its sidewalks menacingly empty, its stores gone away.

Thus, freeway building may have begun as an enterprise in improved transportation. Whether intended or not, it solved one problem, but created a host of others.[2]

Urban Policies: A Problematic Context

As will be said several times in this book, most of society's important problems are located in the city, but not created by the city. They are visible in the city, but like icebergs, their mass lies elsewhere, in the larger society. Urban policy-

1. In Miami, I-95 largely destroyed eighty-seven acres of housing and commercial property in the center of Overtown, a black ghetto in the city. In St. Paul, I-94 displaced half of the city's black population. In Richmond, an expressway was built through a stable black community north of the central city. And in Nashville, the Tennessee Highway Department routed I-40 through the center of the black business district (Mohl 1993b). Just as disruptive as the destruction of black neighborhoods, however, was the way highways isolated them from the rest of the city. In Tampa and Orlando, I-4 created a physical barrier separating black and white areas of the city. In Gary, the Tri-State expressway separated blacks on the north side of the city from whites on the south side. Highways created similar barriers in Los Angeles, Memphis, Hamtramck, Charlotte, Charleston, El Paso, Flint, Indianapolis, Kansas City, and Ossining, New York (Mohl 1993b, Rabin 1987). In at least some of these cases, the isolation of black neighborhoods seems to have been the determining factor in selecting the highway's route. For example, in Atlanta, highways were designed as racial barriers built "to sustain racial ghettos and control black migration" (Bayor 1988, 3).

2. Studies detailing the impact of the automobile on cities are numerous. See, for example, Caro (1974), Garreau (1991), and Frieden and Sagalyn (1989). Yergin (1991, 13–15) notes, "It is oil . . . [and the car] that makes possible where we live, how we live, how we commute to work, how we travel—even where we conduct our courtships."

makers can and do attempt to pound at the iceberg's tips, but they realize that if the larger mass is to be moved or made smaller, only the national government may be equal to the task (Ripley and Franklin 1987). Urban policy-makers may try to solve the city's social problems, but their efforts are marked by a gnawing sense that as far as effectiveness goes, most city policy can do no more than touch the iceberg's tip.

Even in touching the iceberg's tip, however, urban policies often suffer a fatal flaw: In all too many cases, our stock of empirical theories is deficient. We are far from certain that we know the causes of a problem we are attempting to solve. Moreover, what we see as a cause of the problem may not be *the* cause at all, but the consequence of the viewers' beliefs and values. *[The theory of ideology.]* Take, for example, poverty (or for that matter, homelessness, crime, urban gangs, or the widespread use of illegal drugs). Is poverty (or homelessness, or crime, or gang warfare, or drug use) the result of a personal failing? Or is poverty (or any other social problem) a consequence of our economic system, or perhaps a failure of our society to wipe out racism, or perhaps of our society's failure to take proper care of its poor and its maladjusted?[3] (See the aptly titled *The Dilemmas of Social Reform*, by Marris and Rein, 1973.[4])

Our stock of empirical theories is deficient in a second important sense. Careful observation may help us to see what changes, if any, came after a new policy was put in place; but given the tangled skein of all that constitutes human nature and human motives, we are far from certain that any specific policy resulted in (caused) the changes that followed. For example, if student performance on college entry tests improves over time, shall we assume that the improvement was caused by different teaching methods or by such other factors as a change in the motivation or social class of those seeking college admission (see Rivlin 1971)?[5]

---

3. As an example, three causal interpretations of alcoholism abound in our society: the moral interpretation (i.e., alcoholism as a character flaw), the medical interpretation (i.e., alcoholism as a disease), and the social interpretation (i.e., alcoholism as a result of the demands placed on an individual by a drinking society). For a discussion of these perspectives, see Watts (1982).

4. James Q. Wilson (1975) offers a spirited critique of policymakers who attempt to fight urban crime on the basis of the search for its root causes. The search for root causes, he argues, is perforce an exercise in futility. Better, he says, to concentrate policy energies on dealing with criminal behavior and on lessening opportunities for such behavior.

5. It is not surprising that the problem of discovering and tracing social causation has vexed social scientists for a very long time (e.g., MacIver 1942). In fact, as Thomas Haskell (1977) so brilliantly demonstrates, the establishment of modern social science disciplines came about because the academic community had grown impatient and mistrustful of amateur scholars asserting that they had discovered the "true" causes of social change and the links between social behaviors and root causes. Most contemporary social scientists are (as are lawyers) content to work at discovering "proximate" rather than root causes. For a joining of the physicist's and social scientist's concerns over causality, see Norwood Hanson (1958).

If we are unsure about what it was in past policies that "really worked"; if we are unsure about the "real" causes of a problem; and if we are also prone to ideological quarrels over the "best" steps we can take to meet the problem—most likely, our policy steps will be halting, reluctant, and small. (There is an old saying in politics: The bigger the problem, the smaller will be the steps to resolve it.)

Given our society's success at solving technical problems ("We put a man on the moon, didn't we?"), it is understandable that we are reluctant to concede that our most important social problems may be unsolvable. ("Well, then, why can't we stop drug addiction? Why can't we solve the problems of the homeless?)[6] But social problems contain too many imponderables to admit any easy solution—or perhaps any solution at all! And that being the case, those who make social policies labor under few illusions that they are going to solve those problems. They know that they will do well if only they can cope with (and perhaps, alleviate) social problems by tackling them one small step at a time.

Incremental versus Reconstructive Public Policy

To create public policy in small steps is, of course, an attempt to make social and political change also in small steps. This style of small-step policy and change is not confined to cities. It is a style in general use at all levels of American government. *[The theory of social learning.]*

Incremental policy. This incremental style of policy making (to give it its social-scientific label) is, in fact, common to all democratic societies. The reasons for its widespread use are several. First, incremental policy is relatively nonthreatening to the status quo (proposed changes are small). Second, the monetary costs of incremental changes are also relatively small. Third, incremental changes are less likely to unroll a long chain of unanticipated consequences—or, if they do (and if they are unwelcome), policymakers can then attempt corrective action.

Incremental policies abound on the local level, the most obvious example being the city's annual budget. Policymakers invariably decide on what is to be spent (and where the money is to come from) by building on the city's present budget—adding a program here and there, putting additional money into selected programs, taking funds from others (Wildavsky 1979b).

Of course, it would be an almost impossible task for the city council to start afresh every budget year, with no established plans or commitments. Every city has standing programs and obligations (fire protection, police, parks, and so forth). To begin at the beginning every year, with every expenditure

6. For an insightful exploration of the moon-ghetto metaphor, see Nelson (1974).

205

and every program to be (potentially) terminated would be unthinkable—a time-consuming and wearying process. It would lead budget makers into a swamp of indecision and delay (not to mention interest group anxiety over threatened programs). Thus, budget makers tinker with last year's budget and then proceed by means of incremental changes.

Reconstructive policy. Reconstructive policy stands in sharp contrast to incremental policy. As its name is intended to suggest, reconstructive policy seeks to alter and reconstruct the status quo. Reconstructive policy usually tries to alter and remedy a fairly wide range of social, political, or economic affairs. It is often the goal (or consequence) of reformers and reform movements, and though urban policymakers do not attempt to reconstruct the economics of city life, other types of reconstructing policies do get tried. *[The theory of social learning.]* As the earlier discussion of the Progressive era (chapter 4) indicates, what is presently in place as the urban reform package is a noteworthy example of reconstructive urban policy.[7]

Symbolic versus Substantive Policy

Both incremental and reconstructive policies attempt genuine change. Their intent is substantial and thus *substantive*; they are intended to deal effectively with a problem or an issue. *Symbolic policy*, in contrast, deals only with the surface of an issue (Edelman 1964). Symbolic policies are cosmetic in that they seek to cover or disguise the problem; they do not assault, obliterate, or remedy the problem. It is often the case that urban policymakers, when puzzled about what to do, or hesitant about incurring the costs of substantive policy, will escape into symbolic policies. Thus, as a familiar form of symbolic decision (and symbolic policy), city councils often appoint a committee of inquiry to study and make recommendations for future council consideration of an important problem or issue (e.g., violence in the schools, a rising rate of building abandonment, the decline of downtown shopping). Or, as another form of symbolic policy, urban administrators may make a visible display of what the public is intended to see as "action." Thus, if the crime rate is perceived as rising, or if murders go unsolved, those making law-enforcement policy may

---

7. In general, reconstructive policy is the province of the national government. Such policy usually occurs in a time of crisis (war, economic depression, and the like). As will be noted in chapter 12, many of the national government's policies of the 1960s were reconstructive in intent (the War on Poverty, the Civil Rights acts) and directly affected the cities. Another explanation for the fact that cities do not attempt reconstructive policy intended to alter the economic status quo is consistent with the theory of influence and is persuasively advanced by Bachrach and Baratz (1962). The city's economic elites, they argue, usually have sufficient influence to prevent such policies from rising high on the urban political agenda.

conduct street-sweeps of suspicious persons or increase the frequency of police patrols in a high-crime area.

Symbolic policy offers the symbols of change. It affords the policymakers (and sometimes a clamoring public) the sense that something is being done. By its nature, symbolic policy is low in cost.[8] It is therefore a form of coping with difficult and perhaps unsolvable problems without great expenditure. Moreover, it buys time. And meanwhile, perhaps, public attention will flag. The heat will be off the policymakers. And perhaps—just perhaps—the problem will go away all by itself.

Limitations of Time

Though symbolic policy will sometimes buy time for policymakers, it must also be recognized that time itself is an important constraint on policymakers' ability to achieve effective and rational policy. In most cities, the council's agenda is crammed to overflowing. There are taxes to be levied, a budget to be passed, complaints and petitions to be heard, contracts to be approved, and ordinances to be considered. The bigger the city, the fuller the agenda. And with only rare exceptions, councils do not employ an administrative or a research staff to help with their work. Thus, to be a council member is usually to have too much to do and too little time to do it.

But to conclude that the constraints of time do nothing more than limit the amount of information (or careful canvass of alternatives) available to council members is only to state the obvious. Other, more subtle constraints are also at work. First, as was noted in chapter 6, council members in most cities serve on a part-time basis, deriving their principal incomes elsewhere. They tend to hold jobs that permit (or are enhanced by) council service. In most cities, council members are lawyers, real-estate brokers, insurance agents, employees of banks and public utility companies. Occasionally, they are union officials. Thus, they carry into the council a view of the public interest that is biased by their occupation and social standing. *[The theory of ideology.]*

A second consequence for policy follows from the first. With too much to do and too little time to do it, city councils tend to get information (concerning costs, the experience of other cities, and so forth) either from the city administrators or from data furnished by persons and groups interested in a particular policy or an item of legislation. Thus, councils may often frame policy around the testimony and viewpoints of organized groups: the chamber of commerce, real-estate developers and the like—all of whom have a direct and

---

8. It may have high opportunity costs, however. That is, the opportunity to develop a substantive policy that may prove useful in ameliorating a problem is lost when a symbolic policy is implemented.

obvious interest in policy formation and policy outcomes. *[The theory of power and influence.]*

A third consequence that follows from time constraints has to do with the style of urban public policy. Again, our reference point is prescriptive democratic theory. In an ideal democracy, public policy ought to be far seeing and carefully arranged with respect to thoughtfully considered priorities. Policy ought not be a hasty response to a single, immediate problem, but a considered response to a host of connected problems. In short, policy ought to be *proactive* rather than *reactive*.

But in the real world, most urban policy is reactive—a specific reaction to a specific problem. Douglas Yates (1977) calls this style of policy "crisis hopping," putting out fires already lit and burning, using resources of government to take care of present problems, but paying little attention to those that may lie ahead. And while this may not always and in every case make for nonrational policy, it surely leads (through the connection between time and reactivity) in a direction away from policy at its most rational best.

The Politics of Policy Making: Four Types of Policy

The previous classification of urban policies has led us to distinguish between substantive and symbolic policies, and between incremental and reconstructive policies. But however informative these distinctions, it must be confessed that in real-world practice, they are not always sharp and clear. For example, symbolic policies, however cosmetic their intent, sometimes have substantive outcomes. Thus, beefed-up police patrols and periodic street-sweeps may bring new ideas about how best to use police personnel—which, in turn, may bring a reassessment of the most efficient use of motorized equipment.

Nevertheless, distinctions and classifications provide useful details. They help convey the realities of city government-in-action. And they also introduce us to the politics of policy making: what the stakes may be, who wins and who loses, who the players are, and what strategies are most likely to be used by those seeking to influence policy outcomes.

To introduce the politics of policy making, four other types of policy will be sketched; but once again, it is easier to assert a set of policy types in the abstract than to find them neatly separated in real-world use.

Regulatory Policy

Regulatory policy involves the direct and open attempt to control citizens' and business firms' behavior. Most typically, regulatory policy deals with matters of health, safety, and morals. Familiar forms of regulatory policy are ordinances that deal with crime, prostitution, the quarantine of those with communicable disease, the regulation of barbershops, taxicabs, restaurants, and automobile traffic. Regulatory policy also establishes standards for building construction and maintenance and extends to zoning—restricting certain kinds of businesses and buildings to designated areas of the city.

As might be expected, every regulatory policy falls more heavily on some persons (and groups) than on others. Regulatory policy makes a difference in the way persons or groups are treated—some being restricted in what they do, others being let alone. Thus, as it is being framed and as it is being enforced, regulatory policy almost always produces conflict and bargaining: protests, arguments, petitions from those who stand to win most and from those who stand to lose most. Such actions, of course, are the essence of ordinary, everyday politics; it is for this reason that regulatory policy is usually perceived by policymakers (and the general public) as being part of the ordinary process of government and a necessary activity on behalf of the public good. As a consequence, quarrels over regulatory policy are fairly subdued, often being resolved in the courts. They usually entail argument over the wisdom or usefulness of the policy, not die-hard, acrimonious protest from those who will be adversely affected. (However, for exceptions to this general rule, see the discussion of zoning in chapter 12.)

Distributive Policy

As the term may suggest, distributive policies are those that parcel out the services and resources of government among and between the citizenry. Garbage collecting, street paving, police and fire protection are among the commonest forms of distributive policy. Distributive policies can be broken down into two sub-types: those (e.g., street paving, police and fire protection) intended to be evenhanded and to distribute benefits equally among the citizenry; and those that single out groups and geographic areas for benefits and assistance (e.g., neighborhood parks, shelters for the homeless, high intensity street lights, public swimming pools).

Distributive policies sometimes invite more intense political conflict than regulatory policies; the reason lies in the fact that no matter what the intent, distributive policies can never operate according to a principle that everyone agrees is fully just and fair and equal. For example, in the abstract, most would agree that benefits for the poor are morally and politically justified, but disagreement often follows when questions are raised as to whether benefits to the poor should take priority over, say, installing needed street lights or beautifying downtown to attract new business and thus provide more jobs for the city's poor.

More difficult still is deciding how to weigh the special needs of areas and neighborhoods against equal treatment for all areas and neighborhoods. Consider, for example, street paving, fire and police protection, and garbage pickup. No matter how policymakers may attempt an even-handed distribu-

209

tion of services, the distribution will be open to challenge. Again, consider fire protection: City policy may call for one fire station for every three square miles. Under this standard, fire protection could be said to be equally distributed. But by another standard, it is not. Neighborhoods with newer housing and fewer persons per living unit will have fewer fires than areas of older housing, higher population density, and lower per capita income. Perhaps, then, the decision rule ought to be one that allocates personnel and equipment according to the number of fires likely to occur in an area. If that is the decision rule (and in many cities it is), those with property in less-protected areas are likely to complain that, as a consequence of the rule, their fire insurance rates are too high.

In essence, distributive policies are arranged according to decision rules built around ideas concerning equality and equity (of which more later), and it is argument over what constitutes equal benefits that fuels the politics of distributive policy. Argument over equality and equity also helps blur the distinction between distributive and redistributive policies.

Redistributive Policy

These are the most conflict-laden policies. They seek to redistribute the resources of government (and in the long run, of society) from one social and economic class to another. Usually, this redistribution runs from those better off to those least well off. The income tax is the basic vehicle of redistributive policy. Under its terms, those whose incomes are highest usually contribute most to government. This arrangement comports with what has become a basic precept of our society: Equity and social justice—"a fair share for everyone"—require that each member of society be brought up to some minimum standard with respect to those things necessary to maintain a reasonably decent and healthy life.

This precept is at the center of ideological dispute (and thus, of politics) in America today. Some would ask, What is fair about fair shares? Is it fair to take money from those who have earned it to help those who have not? Others would ask, Is it not the case that those who have earned money have been able to do so because the government (which after all, represents *all* the people) has maintained and protected the economic system that makes possible the accumulation of wealth? But even if such points and counterpoints are not readily resolved, most in our society accept the concepts of equity and social justice but continue to disagree on their real-world application—just how much by way of government benefits and services does it take to achieve fair shares?

In our political system, most redistributive policies lie with the national government (Ripley and Franklin 1987). But while wealthy towns and suburbs engage in virtually no redistribution at all, central cities with sizeable numbers of poor do what their politics and resources permit: city funding in support of hospital emergency care, shelters for the homeless, counseling for drug users and the mentally disturbed, the rehabilitation of run-down, low-income housing. (For details concerning redistributive policy in New York, see Morris 1980.) Most such redistributive benefits are undertaken as part of larger federal- and state-supported welfare programs, with city funds being used to supplement those programs. Even so, the politics of city redistributive policies assume a familiar ring. How much is our city's fair share? Should our money be used for other purposes?

Development Policy

Development policies aim to ensure the economic growth and prosperity of the city (P. Peterson 1981). Familiar examples of development policies are proposals to build a sports arena or convention center, to bring new industry to the city, and to revive the central business district (Pelissero et al. 1992, Baim 1994, Rosentraub et al. 1994). *[The theory of commodification of land and buildings.]*

Development policies often require levying additional taxes (or issuing bonds to be repaid with tax revenues over the next decade) to build the proposed sports arena and convention center and to rebuild downtown. Bringing new business to the city often requires the lure of tax abatements (relinquishing a tax ordinarily collected). Development policies are advanced as being good for the entire city. ("It will bring new jobs to our town. It will be something we can all be proud of.") But oftentimes, as is the case with most policy proposals, argument erupts over who will derive most benefit, who will pay a disproportionate share of new taxes, and who will lose most in city services if the arena is built or the tax abatement is used to bring new industrial development.[9]

Development policies have a considerable allure, but they also entail social costs. In 1980, for example, the city of Detroit, suffering from high unemployment, attempted to keep General Motors from locating a proposed new plant elsewhere. To make it possible to build the new factory inside the city, Detroit used its powers of eminent domain[10] to clear a large tract of land and turn it over to General Motors.

---

9. These tax abatement programs and other inducements to private developers have been widespread and massive. For example, the New York State Commerce Department's Job Incentive Board granted hundreds of millions of dollars in ten-year tax credits between 1975 and 1980, with beneficiaries including the Long Island newspaper Newsday ($16.2 million), Lehman Brothers ($3.4 million), Morgan Stanley ($5.6 million), Proctor & Gamble ($14 million), Hooker Chemical Company ($40 million), Alien & Company ($1.3 million), and WKBW-TV ($1.7 million). For a discussion of the New York (and other) tax abatement program and for a critical assessment of the use of tax abatements, see Tabb (1984).

10. Eminent domain is "a government's right to take private property for the public's use," on payments of fair compensation (Shafritz 1988).

211

Under the terms of the clearance, eleven hundred homes (along with 146 schools, businesses, and churches) were razed in an old neighborhood called Poletown (a sobriquet connoting the area's ethnic inhabitants). The new factory built on the Poletown site was designed to provide six thousand new jobs for auto workers. But choosing Poletown was an excruciating policy decision. Should the city destroy an old neighborhood with its distinctive way of life, its shops, its parish church, its houses that represented a lifetime of pride and ownership, in order to bring new jobs to the city? Or should it risk the almost certain outcome that an industry that had been a mainstay of Detroit's employment for three-fourths of a century would relocate elsewhere?

In the end, despite mass demonstrations by the people of Poletown and their angry and emotional appeals to save their way of life *[The theory of lifestyle and territory]*, the argument of the greatest good for the greatest number prevailed. Poletown was torn down. But for those who once lived there, the psychological scars remain. (For more details of the Poletown saga, see Kantor and Savitch, 1993; for news reports of the event, see the *New York Times*, March 15, 1981 and April 30, 1981.)

As the story of Poletown suggests, development policy aims at the common good, but achieving the common good may have its price. To explore this tension more fully, it will be useful to look at other examples of development policy. Doing so will further sketch the politics of making policy and lead to an outline of the several stages of policy making.

From the Window of 291, platinum print, 1915, 25.2 x 20.2 cm
Alfred Stieglitz Collection, 1949.710.
Photograph © 1996, The Art Institute of Chicago. All Rights Reserved.

Let the great world spin forever down the ringing Grooves of Change.
   Alfred Lord Tennyson, *Locksley Hall*

CHAPTER 10

Policy Entrepreneurs and Agendas

Policy Entrepreneurs

Most policy, but especially development policy, springs from the energy and commitment of policy entrepreneurs—the handful of persons who become fixed on a proposal and dedicate themselves to pushing it, step by step, stage by stage, to its final accomplishment. Policy entrepreneurs are found everywhere in city government: on the council, in the administrative bureaucracy (fire chiefs, for example), and in the office of the city's chief executive. Most policy entrepreneurs concern themselves with small-scale matters, dealing with such things as the arrest powers of the police, enforcing building codes, scattering miniparks around the city, and so forth.[1] But when it comes to

---

1. New York City, with its more than 38,500 police officers, affords its police commissioner ample opportunity for policy entrepreneurship. In 1995, Commissioner William Bratton directed that crime reports be compiled and computerized daily. Using that information, police assignments concentrated on high-crime areas, and officers on the beat began making arrests for minor as well as major offenses. The net result is that residents of high-crime areas reported an improvement in their quality of life, and the overall city homicide rate tallied 17 percent fewer murders in the first half of 1995 than in the first half of 1994.

development policies, persons outside the government in what is usually called the private—meaning business—sector often play a crucial role. Inside the government, it is usually the mayor or the city manager who plays the role of development-policy entrepreneur.

Mayors and Managers

Mayors and managers are newsworthy. They command public attention. They draw on the knowledge and expert advice of the city's bureaucracy. Mayors make use of the political influence that derives from their role in party politics (in partisan cities) and their expertise (in all cities with strong mayors). What is more, mayors can also claim a special sort of policy legitimacy. As the sole occupant of one branch of government (unlike the multiple members of the city council) and as the elect of all the voters, mayors can claim to know best what the voters want, and they can further claim to speak on behalf of all the people of the city.

In big cities especially, mayors have been successful in creating what are called executive-centered coalitions. During the 1950s, coalitions of mayors and business leaders were responsible for a number of large-scale projects: freeways, housing complexes, and revitalization of the downtown business district (Banfield 1974, Salisbury 1964). Nearly all of these projects turned on a massive infusion of federal funds. In recent decades, as federal funds for large-scale urban construction have declined, executive-centered coalitions have shifted their energies to projects such as locally-funded convention centers, downtown shopping malls, and sports arenas. Mayors who work at downtown development tend to be rewarded with reelection and widespread voter approval (Frieden and Sagalyn 1989).

Land Developers and Business Leaders

But policy entrepreneurs do not come exclusively from the ranks of public officials. In most cities—and particularly when it comes to development policy—the most effective entrepreneurs are often business leaders. As has been the case for more than two centuries, real estate developers continue to change the face of cities. *[The theory of commodification of land and buildings.]* Office construction and downtown shopping malls are the present forms of this change, with tall buildings rising against the sky all across the country and new retail shopping areas emerging in their shadows. And in many places, developers are building "urban complexes"—office and apartment buildings, shops, and theatres, all sited together—in an attempt to bring back

216

shoppers, residents, and visitors, and in so doing to give vitality to the old downtown.[2]

Pittsburgh's Golden Triangle, Boston's Faneuil Hall shopping area and tourist attraction, and Detroit's Renaissance Center are all examples of the accomplishments of the business (private sector) entrepreneur. Working with elected officials, these private sector policy entrepreneurs provide money and leadership for massive urban development.

Policy Entrepreneurs and Development Policy: A Tale of Several Cities

Richard C. Lee and New Haven

Richard C. Lee is the archetype of the entrepreneurial mayor who builds and then leads an executive-centered coalition.[3] First elected mayor of New Haven in 1953, he was reelected for eight consecutive terms, choosing not to run again in 1969. During his sixteen years in office, Lee became one of the best-known, most written about mayors in the United States.

Under Lee's entrepreneurship, New Haven accomplished massive slum clearance and large-scale urban renewal. One project (the Oak Street project) cleared and then rebuilt forty-four acres of dilapidated, run-down housing. Other projects followed. Most of the money for what was accomplished came from the federal government. Lee was one of the first mayors to realize the potential for massive change that lay in federal urban-renewal funds. More important, his was one of the first cities to prepare a comprehensive plan to support an application for federal money. (As is often the case, federal agencies, when they are charged by Congress with distributing money, work willingly with those who are first in line for that money.)

The federal government responded to New Haven with massive support, and toward the end of the 1960s, it was estimated that federal urban-renewal allocations to New Haven "were equivalent to $790 for each man, woman, and child. By contrast, Newark, New Jersey . . . was getting $286 per capita; Boston had $268 and New York had $42" (Powledge 1970, 19). A large

---

2. For a critical view of the role of business persons in city development, as well as a critical view of the entire principle of the commodification of land and buildings, see Molotch (1976, 1993) and Ambrose and Colenutt (1975). And for a discussion of successful downtown redevelopment projects, see, for example, Black et al. (1983) and Frieden and Sagalyn (1989).

3. The executive-centered coalition described by those studying New Haven is similar in nature to the growth machine described by Molotch (1976, 1993) and the urban regime described by Stone (1989); the latter is described by Stone as "the informal arrangements by which public bodies and private interests function together in order to be able to make and carry out governing decisions" (p. 6).

part of New Haven's success in getting federal funds was due to Mayor Lee's creation of a Citizen's Action Committee (CAC), which satisfied Congress's requirement that urban renewal involve broad citizen representation (Wolfinger 1974). The CAC not only served to legitimate Lee's program but also constituted a powerful coalition, nearly one hundred strong, that included businesspersons concerned with retail sales and traffic congestion downtown, union leaders who foresaw job opportunities in new construction, and political liberals concerned about New Haven's slums and the plight of the poor who lived there.

The CAC was the pivot of Lee's highly successful urban coalition. At the height of its effectiveness, the CAC had become what one writer called "the parallel government" of New Haven (Powledge 1970, 34). It was outside the formal government but inside every important development decision, and it was completely part of the business community.

Mayor Lee's successes are impressive. New Haven was physically transformed. A shabby downtown became new and architecturally distinguished. A road leads from the interstate highway directly downtown, and acres of slums were replaced by modern housing.

But success in reshaping a city physically does not readily translate into solutions for its social and economic problems. Policy achievement often has unanticipated consequences. The poor in New Haven stayed mostly poor. White flight to the suburbs continued, and New Haven's unemployment rate rose and fell with national trends. When urban rioting flashed across the country in the 1960s, New Haven was not spared (its major riot took place in 1967). And the New Haven riot produced considerable discomfort for those in Mayor Lee's coalition. New Haven, after all, was supposed to be a model city. What had gone wrong?

With the wisdom of hindsight, it is now argued that the CAC could not have represented the community (or given outreach to pluralistic participation) as had once been touted. The CAC included no blacks. Perhaps, then, what had been accomplished was done over the objections and resentment of an important segment of the city. Almost seven thousand families and individuals had been dislocated because of urban renewal. Nearly all were poor, and very large numbers of them were black. Sizeable numbers had not been relocated in equally good or equally affordable housing. And as to the much-vaunted beautiful new New Haven, said not a few critics, perhaps those shining symbols of urban affluence served only to remind the poor of their powerlessness and their alienation from the progress that Mayor Lee had once proclaimed.

Henry Ford and Detroit's Renaissance

When Henry Ford created the first mass-produced automobile, he changed America forever—and most of the rest of the world as well. What had once been a plaything for the rich soon became a social and economic necessity for everyone else. Henry Ford (it is often said) put America on wheels, and the social, political, and economic consequences have never stopped spinning.

Henry Ford's masterpieces of mass production were made first in Detroit. Other car makers also set up in Detroit, and for half a century (from about 1905 to the 1950s) Detroit prided itself on being the motor capital of the world. But after World War II, "Motown" fell on hard times. Car makers shifted production elsewhere, and the American car industry was devastated by foreign competition. By the 1960s, Detroit was a city in trouble. Its downtown had nearly as many vacant lots as stores. Its middle class had gone suburban. Urban blight was spreading. Poverty and unemployment were widespread. Large patches of the city had been burned down in the urban riots of the 1960s. Racial strife was marked by sporadic violence—in police shootouts such as the Algiers Motel incident (Hersey 1968)—and in the resistance of white enclaves to black incursion. What is more, Detroit had achieved the dubious distinction of murder capital of the world—its population being reduced by more than one homicide a day.

Added to a pervasive sense of Detroit as a city in deep trouble was the undeniable fact that the office-building boom, going on in other cities, had thus far failed to take hold in Detroit. Headquarters for the automobile industry had long ago moved out of downtown, and (said one observer) "the city's skyline is remarkably unchanged from the 1930s" (*New York Times*, July 3, 1983).

In the 1960s, Henry Ford II (grandson of the first Henry),

> then confident about the future of the auto industry, decided that only a gargantuan building project could revive the urban core. So he set out in 1971 to build what became a $357 million office and retail complex named, hopefully, the Renaissance Center. Ford's . . . [company's] $300 million total outlay . . . may represent the largest civic investment ever made by a private corporation. (*New York Times*, July 3, 1983).

The RenCen (as it is called) is handsome urban architecture: four glass-sheathed, octagonal thirty-story office towers standing on elevated ground, facing the lake, surmounted by a seventy-three-story hotel. But, sad to say, the RenCen has not fulfilled the hopes of Henry Ford and those who planned with him. Urban decay has continued in downtown Detroit (see Chafets, 1990, for a gripping portrayal of Detroit's decline; see also Vergara, 1995, whose photoessay chronicles the deterioration of Detroit's downtown). And the RenCen's finances have been perilous: It went into default in 1983, and its sponsors lost $143 million (Frieden and Sagalyn 1989). But financial difficulties aside, the RenCen took on a special life and purpose: that of an isolated bastion of beauty and plenty that caters to visitors and

219

businessmen who enter the RenCen's protected parking garages, and who, once inside, remain safely insulated from the urban life outside. In 1996, the fortunes of the RenCen took an ironic turn: General Motors bought the Center and announced that it would give its present seventy-four-year-old landmark headquarters in downtown Detroit to the city to serve as a new city hall. After GM executives moved into the RenCen, displaced Ford Motor tenants would be invited to move into the former city hall (*New York Times*, Sept. 23, 1996).

It may be that a single, grandiose project discourages rather than encourages other projects. Or it may be that too much industry has moved from Detroit to sustain a large-scale office complex that houses those who provide services to local commerce and industry. It may also be that the fault of the RenCen is in its design. It sits, fortresslike, on high ground; best approached by cars that enter its interior garage, it does not beckon the downtown walker or contribute to foot traffic in the downtown core. Or it may simply be that Henry Ford chose to promote the wrong kind of project. Policy entrepreneurs, when they work on a grand scale, always envision an alternative future. Sometimes, though, the vision may be faulty.

James Rouse and the City as Festival

The late James Rouse was a different type of urban visionary. Like Henry Ford, Rouse sought to revitalize cities through private investment. The managers of his corporations expect city officials to work within the outlines of a master plan—shifting streets, passing special ordinances, and making way for new construction by exercising the city's power of eminent domain. But unlike Ford's RenCen, the Rouse projects encompass very large urban areas. More important, Rouse projects are marked by a number of singular goals and features: Their usual aim is to upgrade and restore old buildings that have fallen into disrepair and disuse.[4] Their usual goal is that of preserving and restoring a historical section of the city. And for commercial success, the Rouse projects rely on shoppers and tourists seeking the pleasure and excitement of the urban experience.

In size, money, and accomplishment, the Rouse corporations are massive. To date, they have financed and developed half a hundred retail shopping complexes in the United States and Canada (and operate twenty-five others),

---

4. Rouse is credited with inventing the term "urban renewal," which was applied to the government program implemented during the middle decades of this century. Certainly, Rouse's projects embody the best use of renewal, upgrading and restoring old buildings and supplementing them with newer, architecturally consistent buildings; this contrasts mightily with the wholesale destruction of old buildings that cities used federal urban-renewal funds to accomplish. It is intriguing to wonder what cities would look like today had the Rousian vision of renewal been implemented forty years ago.

with assets of nearly $5 billion. The company's properties include retail, office, and industrial spaces; in addition, it is the developer of the planned city of Columbia, Maryland, which will house eighty-three thousand residents and twenty-five hundred businesses.

Outside the business community, Rouse's considerable fame came from his distinctive—and distinctively successful—projects in city redevelopment. Wherever possible, he renovated old buildings rather than tearing them down. He gave old buildings new life by giving them new use, retaining their distinctive eighteenth- and nineteenth-century styles. And he took advantage of each redevelopment site's historical resonances by revitalizing waterfronts, warehouse districts, and old-towns.

Jane Jacobs (an eminent architectural critic and urban historian) argues that cities derive their vitality from thronging people—strolling, shopping, and watching each other (Jacobs 1961)—and Rouse made human dynamics the mainspring of his restorations: Baltimore's Harborplace, Santa Monica's Santa Monica Place, Philadelphia's Market Street East, New York's South Street Market, Boston's Quincy Market, and Atlanta's Underground (see Nelson 1995).

Baltimore's Inner Harbor development exemplifies Rouse's projects. Some forty years ago, the 3.2 acre site was part of the Inner Harbor area, a "250-acre wasteland of rotting wharves, warehouses, and railroad yards, the worst of Baltimore's then decrepit downtown" (*Time*, Aug. 24, 1981). Today, Inner Harbor is a vibrant shopping area and tourist attraction, vying with Disneyland in the number of visitors it attracts each year. A tall, angular, modern building houses one of Inner Harbor's major attractions, an aquarium. But mostly, people come to Harborplace to move in and out of its two retail pavilions "to eat, drink, shop, stroll, play and just lounge around in the evocative maritime atmosphere" (*New York Times*, May 26, 1985). The jobs and projects for retailers, hotels, and restaurants have brought a new prosperity to Baltimore (not to mention the value added to its tax rolls). In the years since its opening in 1980, Harborplace has become the anchor "of a genuine waterfront renaissance that Baltimoreans believe has transformed the look and the life of their once tired city" (*New York Times*, May 26, 1985).

But major change is rarely accomplished without critical sallies or without unanticipated consequences. *[The theory of commodification of land and buildings.]* Critics argue that places like Harborplace take money and attention away from a city's other problems—slums, for example—in less picturesque parts of the city. Others complain that building an economy based on frivolity is a sorry substitute for attending to such pressing problems as a rising crime rate or the quality of city schools. But success always has many friends, and all across the country, cities send delegations to Rouse's corporate planners, hoping that their city may be next on his entrepreneurial agenda (*New York Times*, Aug. 29, 1977; Frieden and Sagalyn 1989).

221

Stages of the Policy Process

Public policy is not created all at once and in final form. It is built in stages, and there is a pattern to these stages. Generally speaking, there are three stages: first, an initiating or *agenda-setting* stage; second, a *policy-formulation* stage; and third, an *implementation* stage. Each of these stages flows one into the other; but often the process comes to a halt at one or another stage, leaving the process unfinished, the policy never carried through.

Of the three stages, implementation is perhaps the most complicated, for implementation in the city is characterized by a considerable dispersion of policy authority. In implementation, policy authority rests in many hands. It is dispersed and highly pluralistic, so much so that cities are sometimes described as governments that do not govern—they merely administrate.[5] But, to understand this assertion, a closer look at the stages of policy making is now in order.

Agenda Setting

An agenda is a statement of priorities, a list of things to be accomplished.[6] In the agenda-setting stage, the critical act is an obvious one: getting policymakers to pay attention to one of the many matters that vie for attention—getting them to put the problem on their agenda. How that happens is sometimes a matter of chance, but a number of factors contribute to a common pattern. For one, the problem must be (or must be thought to be) one that can be dealt with by government action. (Nothing that cannot be dealt with is likely to make its way onto the policymakers' agenda.) For another, policymakers must be able to perceive that the problem does, in fact, exist and that it is important enough to deserve government's attention. Third, problems that make their way onto the policymakers' agenda are those that can be transformed into an issue—a proposal around which contending groups or persons

5. Theodore Lowi (1969b) uses the phrase, "functional feudalities" to describe the administration of large cities; each department (and sometimes divisions within it) resisting control by elected officials and maintaining its independence from all other administrative units—insulated and protected by employees' civil service status and the support of the interest groups that it serves. For a more recent treatment, see Miranda (1994).

6. Every government agency has its own long-standing agenda, shaped by its history and its overall mission. Within cities, for example, the public works department is almost always committed to improving traffic flow, and to that purpose, the department will have on file (and in the plans and dreams of its administrators) an overall, general agenda—widening the major arteries, building ring roads around the city, limiting the number of on-street parking places, and so forth. And, as a rule, every city agency's standing agenda is in competition (for funds and authorization) with the standing agenda of every other agency. Thus, the standing agenda does not become an effective agenda until (a) its several components are arranged according to a set of priorities, and (b) one or more of its priorities can capture the attention of policymakers and policy entrepreneurs outside the agency.

can rally and take sides. (In other words, the problem must generate politics, animating policymakers and an attentive public to think and worry about who gets what, when, and how.) And last, but hardly least, the problem that does make its way onto the policy agenda is more often than not a problem that is of special concern to a person or group of persons who assume the role of policy entrepreneur (C. Jones 1983, Cobb and Elder 1983, Crenson 1971). This last point is particularly important, for it ties back to the previous discussion of agenda-setting as the exercise of interpersonal power in the city. And it suggests that the policy entrepreneur must have access to at least some of the resources associated with interpersonal power (e.g., charisma, information, standing in the business community, public office, and so forth).

Policy Formulation

Many issues get on the policymakers' agenda, but most are not of sufficient importance to go to the very top of that agenda. If an issue *does* get to the top, sooner or later it is likely to receive further attention. When it does, the critical and necessary act is twofold: identifying the goals to be reached and deciding which course of action is most likely to achieve those goals. Here, of course, policymakers encounter their fullest opportunity for policy rationality. And here is where all the impediments to rationality have opportunity to flourish.

Vague or imprecise goals must now be made narrower and more precise. Alternative courses of action can now be considered. Information must be assembled so that costs and benefits can be weighed. Interest groups must be given opportunity to be heard, and opposing demands must be reconciled. Eventually, a course of action is decided on, and policy can now be "actualized" and legitimated by means of an ordinance or an administrative ruling.

Agenda Setting and Policy Formulation as Interacting Processes

The agenda-setting and policy formulation stages often take place almost at the same time, each interacting with the other. In this interaction, both policy entrepreneurs and interest groups play important roles. Newspaper reporting also plays a part—particularly the newspaper exposé that makes for lurid reading. (Consider the attention commanded by the headline: "Crime, Drugs, Prostitution in Our City!") Sometimes a disastrous or lamentable event will define the problem and move it high on the policymakers' agenda—a devastating flood, the murder of a prominent citizen, a nursing-home fire, or the collapse of a building under construction.

"The idea whose time has come": The War on Poverty as a case in point. Large-scale projects, of the sort that deserve the label reconstructive policy, are moved through the policy stages by forces and factors that defy easy analysis.

Philosophers have long puzzled over such forces, wondering why, at certain times and in certain places—great social and political changes burst forth. *Zeitgeist*, the spirit of the times, is the term sometimes affixed to these elusive forces.

It is sometimes the gift of the policy entrepreneur to catch the spirit of the times. And occasionally it will be the work of scholars that serves as catalyst to agenda setting and policy formulation. To illustrate these forces, consider the arrival, in the 1960s, of the national government's War on Poverty.

Widespread poverty is among the oldest of social problems. But from the period that ran roughly from the end of World War II to the 1960s, poverty in the United States lay largely outside public attention. Then, in the 1960 presidential primary campaign in West Virginia, John F. Kennedy made poverty a campaign issue, influenced largely by what he saw around him in the coal fields. Then in January 1963, President Kennedy read a review of Michael Harrington's much talked about new book *The Other America*, in *The New Yorker*, and his views on poverty were profoundly reinforced by what he read (Devine and Wright 1993).

Harrington and the presidential candidacy of Kennedy helped make poverty a matter of public concern, but the road from public concern to an item on the policy agenda is never straight. A matter of public concern must first be made actionable before it can move high on the policy agenda. Someone must have an idea regarding what to do. A proposal for action must come forward, and the proposal must be such that it can take on the qualities of a political issue, with interest groups and opinion leaders taking sides on that issue. Thus, in the case of poverty moving from public concern to political issue, the work of another scholar was to play a critical role.

Oscar Lewis (1959, 1965), an anthropologist, had studied poor families in Mexico, Puerto Rico, and the Hispanic settlements of New York City. From his studies of families in poverty, Lewis derived the idea of a *culture of poverty*: Families in poverty have characteristic ways of thinking about the world and of their lives in that world. *[The theory of ideology.]* What Lewis saw in families living in a culture of poverty was their sense of being ruled by fate, of being unable to take charge of their own lives, and of being unable to change their lives for the better.

From Lewis' work, other scholars (with assistance from the Ford Foundation) took the short but logical step of calling attention to the *cycle* of poverty—the process by which poverty enters the lives and thoughtways of a family and gets carried down through subsequent generations. It was only a short step further for the ideas of the culture and cycle of poverty to make their way onto the joint agendas of Congress and President Lyndon Johnson by means of an actionable program: The War on Poverty.

The War on Poverty was an umbrella term for a series of policies all united by the idea that government could break the culture and cycle of poverty by providing poor families with job training, with nutritional and educational programs for their children (school lunches, Operation Head Start), and with opportunity to develop self-esteem and a sense of personal efficacy—this last to be accomplished by giving the poor a voice in urban agencies established to administer War on Poverty funds.

Recounting the further history of the War on Poverty will wait for chapter 12. For the present, perhaps all that needs to be said is that in its agenda-setting and formulation stages, the War on Poverty brought the national government full tilt into urban politics, and, in its search for new and experimental policy, seemed to embody the "spirit of the '60s."

Policy Implementation

The policy implementation stage generally has two components. The first is fairly obvious: a policy has been enacted, but provision must be made to carry it into effect. Money must be appropriated, and often new personnel will have to be hired.

The second component is less obvious, but more important. It involves the procedures and arrangements under which the policy is put into effect. As a general rule, it usually falls to administrators to decide on the specific details of such procedures and arrangements. Funds must be acquired, legislation must be interpreted, staff must be trained, and services must be delivered "in order to put flesh on the [policy] bones" (Ripley and Franklin 1987, 2). In these and complementary ways, administrators create a supplementary (implementing) set of policies. And they do so largely removed from public view. It is here, in the implementation stage, that policy becomes fleshed out, and it is here that policy making becomes dispersed and pluralistic.

Administrators as policymakers. Few, if any, policy decisions are self-enforcing. For example, the city council may decide to invoke a teen curfew. The resulting ordinance might specify the age of those subject to the curfew, the hours of the curfew, and punishment for its violation. But it is usually the chief of police, in consultation with division heads, who decides how many police are to be assigned to enforce the curfew, what kinds of patrols are to be mounted, whether warnings or arrests are to be emphasized, whether undercover officers are to be used, and, most important, for how long a time curfew enforcement is to receive special attention. (Is curfew enforcement to be symbolic or substantive?)

Obviously, if the police chief decides merely to include curfew enforcement in the long list of laws the police are presently enforcing, the results will be very different from those that would follow a decision to give special attention to the curfew. Supposing that the chief of police (or head of the juvenile crime unit) decides to enforce the curfew to the fullest possible extent, in which areas of the city does he or she concentrate police effort? If drive-ins and pizza-parlors are singled out for special attention, owners of those businesses will complain of police harassment. Alternatively, if the chief decides that areas of high juvenile crime get special attention, then other parts of the city may complain of neglect. And if enforcement is even-handed across the city, middle- and upper-class parents are likely to complain (and even go to court) over what they perceive as police harassment. In the end, the chief will use his or her best judgment and make what seems a useful and practical decision. And the "real" policy will be the policy made in the implementation stage.

Street-level bureaucrats as policymakers. Policy implementation in cities has a special quality that is captured by the previous reference to a theory of urban administration and street level bureaucracy (Lipsky 1980). The term *street-level bureaucracy* refers to the fact that much of city policy is carried into the lives of city residents by officials who interact with city dwellers directly, personally, and often on a one-to-one basis.

Federal and state policies, in contrast, are enforced more impersonally. Taxes are paid by mail, and it falls to those who owe taxes to take the initiative in paying them. Violators of the law are usually not arrested in handcuffs, but summoned to appear in court or before an administrative agency. Enforcement of city policies is different. The city's police are on the street. Firefighters, sanitation workers, and health inspectors appear at houses and places of work.

In such circumstances, implementation is dispersed and pluralistic, often a matter of personal judgment and personality. True, street-level bureaucrats must operate within the policy framework established at central headquarters. But central headquarters cannot follow street-level bureaucrats on their daily rounds, supervising their moment-by-moment activities.

Thus, sanitation department rules may require that trash be set curbside, in containers or securely tied in bundles. But it is the trash collector who decides whether or not to haul away a curbside stack of discarded auto tires and whether or not the container left on the lawn is more or less equivalent to being at curbside. Department policy usually instructs the police "to keep the peace," meaning maintain order and prevent violence and crime. But it falls to the officer on the beat to decide whether keeping the peace requires dispersing a group of streetside idlers (the "corner gang"), whether a suspicious looking person is to be confronted, and whether a sidewalk poet declaiming his lines is a breach of the peace (Wilson 1972, 1975, Muir 1977). Far more important, every police department in the country has rules concerning the permissible use of deadly force, but as every watcher of television drama knows, written rules do not always decide whether a situation is truly life-threatening, or what the police should do if it is.

Thus, street-level bureaucrats implement policy in a personal and personally judgmental way. Street-level bureaucrats bring government directly to the people, and the consequences are important. By its nature, street-level bureaucracy is labor intensive. It is therefore costly, consuming a significant portion of the city's budget. By being labor intensive, street-level bureaucracy is also labor extensive, requiring a high ratio of public employees to city population. As the number of city employees increases with city size, they become an important interest group. They try to influence budget allocations and legislation. And in cities where they are unionized (in most cities of any size), the wage and work demands of employees' unions become part of city politics and a factor in the constantly rising costs of city government.

Street-level bureaucrats are a recurring source of government corruption. In former machine cities, where traditions of plunder are well established, street-level bureaucrats help maintain that tradition. It is, after all, relatively easy for the police to look the other way when prostitutes solicit, gamblers gamble, and drug dealers deal. And it is just as easy for the health inspector, fire inspector, and building inspector to demand a bribe—or else!— threatening to close down a business or force the owner to suffer the costs of constant reinspection.

Street-level bureaucrats have stirred the cauldron of racial and ethnic unrest and the disaffection of minorities and the poor who perceive (often correctly, but sometimes wrongly) that they are being treated harshly or are being singled out for close surveillance by those who are supposed to protect and serve them. Where such grievances are long standing, a triggering incident (what sociologists call an *occasioning factor*) has several times resulted in race rioting and mob violence. Such was the case in the urban riots of the 1960s—and the rioting in Los Angeles following the *not guilty* verdict that was returned against police officers caught on film savagely beating Rodney King.[7]

Thus, the implementation stage—as do all the stages of policy making— brings to mind two often-quoted adages:

Multitudes, Multitudes
In the Valley of Decision
(*Book of Joel*, 3: 11)

For forms of Government, let fools contest
Whate'r is best administered is best.
(Alexander Pope, *Essay on Man*)

It will be useful to keep these adages in mind as we turn to politics and policy in the metropolitan area in the next chapter.

7. That beating serves as a reminder of the ability of street-level bureaucrats (in this instance, Los Angeles police officers) to bend general policy to their own purposes. Like every big city, Los Angeles has a well-defined policy requiring minimum force in making arrests and an even more fully-defined policy prohibiting acts of racial discrimination (Walker et al. 1996).

PART FIVE

AN EVEN LARGER WEB: CITIES, STATES, AND THE NATION

From Room 3003—The Sheldon, New York, chloride print, 1927, 9.2 x 11.9 cm
Alfred Stieglitz Collection, 1949.786.
Photograph © 1996, The Art Institute of Chicago. All Rights Reserved.

Extend the sphere and you take in a greater variety of parties and interests; you will make it less probable that a majority of the whole will have a common motive to invade the rights of other citizens.

James Madison, *Federalist 10*

CHAPTER 11

Beyond the Central City: Cities, Their Suburbs, and Their States

Most Americans are imprinted on the idea that local government is preferred government. *[The theory of grass-roots democracy.]* Dividing the country into small units of government (says conventional wisdom) will enable each unit to protect its own definition of the public interest. Not to permit the citizens of an entire state (or the entire nation) to constitute a sole and single voting majority will thus safeguard the interests of those who, though a majority in their own unit, might be a threatened minority in a vastly enlarged unit of government.

This line of reasoning helped give rise to our federal system and the Constitution's provisions for separation of powers and checks and balances. And it is this reasoning that helps give rise to the multiple units of government that constitute the metropolitan area. However rational it might be to consolidate these units into one, overall government, the idea of localism stands as a first line of defense against metropolitan consolidation. And lacking this consolidation, the metropolitan area stands sharply stratified and divided— racially, socially, economically. Blacks, Hispanics, and other minorities are concentrated as an economic underclass in central cities, while whites of the middle and working classes dominate the suburbs, generally segmented there by income and, occasionally, by religious and ethnic allegiances.

Politics and Policy in the Metropolitan Region

Seen from an airplane, a metropolitan area is all of a piece: a sprawling spread of buildings, a network of roads, a swarm of motor vehicles, and (it may be presumed) a mass of people. Seen through the windows of an automobile, the metropolitan area appears in greater detail: a central business district, areas of industry close to the business district, sectors of older houses and apartment buildings, often mingled with factories and warehouses, and then, gradually, as the car moves across town, more affluent neighborhoods. On one side of a street may be houses inside the territory of the central city; across the street may be houses that lie in an adjacent suburb. The demarcation is not always clear. Further on, green spaces and countryside will appear, then another cluster of houses or a shopping mall, or perhaps a small town, complete with its own business district.

The distance between the central city's business district and that "last" cluster of houses may be considerable. For example, in the Columbus, Ohio, metropolitan area, the motorist would have to travel as much as fifteen miles from the city's center before coming to open country. In other, larger metropolitan areas, this distance is considerably greater. And even then, another town may be just ahead—all part of the urban-suburban sprawl.

In crossing the metropolitan area the traveler is hard put to discover where one town or city ends and another begins. If it were not for signs and notices, the jurisdictions of the separate governments would be invisible to the eye. Even more invisible, for often there are no marking signs, are the other governments that crisscross the metropolitan area—townships, counties, and special purpose governments. Each has its own officials, its own authority to make policy, to tax, and to spend. Thus, for the resident of the metropolitan area (and for the student), obvious questions arise: How did this patchwork of governments come about? What do the governments do? Do they coordinate their efforts? If so, how? And, perhaps most important, which social classes and which groups are most helped and which are most hurt by this configuration? We begin with some fairly obvious observations.

Cities and Their Suburbs

As a rule, the central city came first. Suburbs came later as the railroad (and later the automobile) made it possible for upper- and middle-income wage earners to commute to work. Hence, it was usually the affluent who went first to the suburbs. Generally speaking, the impulse behind the move was *status differentiation*—homes on large lots and a countrified lifestyle were emblems of superior social status. Philadelphia's Main Line suburbs came into being this way (on the main line of the Pennsylvania Railroad). So did the North Shore suburbs of Chicago (set along the North Shore Line).[1]

As the automobile became more affordable, the impulse to achieve suburban status was no longer limited by the proximity of railroad lines. New suburbs filled in the land between railroad lines; and, at the same time, what had once been small towns outside the commuting reach of the central city became (in the 1920s) dormitory suburbs for a commuting middle class.

In the decades after World War II, the great out-migration from central cities was in flood tide. It was a time of the exploding metropolis. New technologies (interurban trucking and heavy, motorized material handling) made possible the building of suburban factories and the settling nearby of industrial employees (Banfield 1974). For an increasingly affluent working class, the motive of status differentiation was now overlaid with the values and aspirations that are part of owning a single-family home. Whereas, in Europe, the affluent have traditionally remained as apartment dwellers inside the central city (the closer in, the greater one's status), affluent Americans seek to escape the city and apartment living. We share with the British a tradition that countryside living in single-family houses is the rightful badge of the socially and economically successful.

During the 1940s and the 1950s, another great migration had begun—the migration of over 3 million poor southern blacks to northern cities (Lemann 1991). Small-scale (and sharecropping) farming was on the decline; labor-intensive agriculture was being superseded by cotton-picking machinery and other capital-intensive equipment. Thus, the motives of status differentiation and single-family home ownership were layered onto a rising desire of urban whites (regardless of social and economic status) to flee the increasingly black central city.

By the 1960s, suburbia was no longer the province of the upper and middle classes. Suburbs were now of many kinds: upper class, middle class, working class, and here and there, a predominantly black suburb. Some suburbs are home to the truly affluent, while others are home to those who live in poverty. Some suburbs cluster around a nearby factory; some are completely dormitory suburbs—wage earners drive elsewhere for employment. And some suburbs carry on the tradition of the small towns they once were—cities in miniature, with neighborhoods and small-town business districts.

Thus far, we have explained the metropolitan patchwork by invoking a number of converging theories: grass-roots democracy, status differentiation, land development through a market economy, and a cultural tradition that dri-

---

1. This discussion draws chiefly from works by Warner (1972), Glaab and Brown (1976), Jackson (1985), Kantor (1988), Halberstam (1993), Lemann (1991), and Garreau (1991).

ves Americans to prefer home ownership to apartment living.[2] To round out this explanation, one more factor must be noted. Suburban sprawl has also been propelled by two policies of the national government: tax policy and transportation policy. Federal income tax policy permits a tax write-off for interest paid on a home loan; by 1990, this tax write-off totaled $37 billion a year for home owners living in the suburbs (Rusk 1993). In effect, this policy has amounted to a governmental subsidy for the middle class, permitting it to offset (with lower taxes) a significant portion of the costs of home ownership. Without this subsidy-through-taxes, far fewer Americans would now be living in single-family houses. Just as important, suburbanization could not have occurred without increasing the access of suburban residents to downtown areas, where many of them work. This was accomplished through the construction of highways and freeways during the 1950s and the 1960s, funded primarily by the federal government. By 1990, the federal government had spent $260 billion on its highway program, about half of it in suburban areas (Rusk 1993).

Industrial Parks and Edge Cities

Two of the most important suburban developments of recent years have been industrial parks and (to use journalist Joel Garreau's telling phrase) edge cities (Garreau 1991). Both are created by private enterprise seeking market advantage. Unlike the slow, step-by-step growth of the older, traditional cities, both are very much the consequence of what has come to be called "land developer's drive." In fairly quick sequence, site selection, financing, land acquisition, and then bulldozers and construction crews change the suburban landscape dramatically.

In general, industrial parks and edge cities are unincorporated places, located at the edge of cities and towns. One example of a thriving industrial park is the City of Industry, located adjacent to Los Angeles. (In this instance, however, it is a legislatively chartered, incorporated city with a council-manager government.) Its primary purpose, says an official brochure, is to provide "a well-organized center for industry and commerce of all types" (*City of Industry Fact Book* 1995, 2). As of 1993, the City of Industry had a resident population of 631, 1,650 industrial firms, and a commuting work force of 68,000! Municipal services are contracted out to Los Angeles County and private providers. Given its sizeable tax base and small resident population, the city's politics and policies are very much in keeping with its public promise: providing a "stable city government" that offers a "probusiness environment."

Whether full-fledged incorporated towns or simply unincorporated

2. For a comparative perspective on land development and the market economy, see Cox (1978), Ambrose and Colenutt (1975), Castells (1977), and Orum (1995).

places, industrial parks are just that: places that produce tangible goods. Their buildings are mostly factories, horizontal, and fairly low to the ground. Because shipping and transport facilities are essential to their purpose, industrial parks also provide shipping, loading, and parking facilities for the giant trucks that carry manufactured goods across the country.

In contrast, edge cities produce mostly intangible goods essential to the computer and information age—software, advertising, legal opinions, and the like. In contrast to industrial parks, edge cities (as Garreau so neatly puts it) are "office cities," built vertically, high above the ground. Their location (and this applies equally to industrial parks) is determined by the availability of relatively inexpensive acreage and an automobile-friendly site, adjacent to fast, multilane highways. Equally important is the availability of land for parking. The two primary laws of land developers, says Garreau, are that an American will not walk more than 600 feet before getting into his or her car, and that each car will require 400 square feet of parking space (plus a reasonable share of driveways and lanes). Given the often remarked-on love affair between Americans and their cars and given, too, the scarcity of free (or even available) parking spaces in the downtown business district, it becomes understandable that edge cities are now the fastest growing urban places in America. One estimate has it that more than two-thirds of American offices are now located in edge cities.[3]

Closed and Gated Communities

Still another development on the urban scene is the closed and gated community. Sometimes set inside the central city and sometimes in a suburb, the gated community (like most shopping centers and malls) operates under private government, formed of landlords and tenants. Owners, and sometimes residents, are formed into a governing body that sets rules and regulations for visitors and occupants, often enforced by a private police force. These are often termed "common interest developments"; the common interest being protected usually involves safety and security (e.g., guards placed at the entrance gates), architectural harmony (e.g., rules governing building construction and lot sizes), and behavioral norms of residents and visitors (e.g., rules governing parking, signage, and noise). In contrast to shopping malls, which are also common-interest developments, closed communities seek to keep the general public and the casual visitor away. However much their owners and tenants may like their community and the lifestyle it represents, they are often

3. In chapter 13, we will explore the outmigration of corporate headquarters from the large cities (like New York). One obvious place where they are heading is to the suburbs, particularly to edge cities. Between 1965 and 1975, for example, thirty-eight Fortune 500 corporations moved out of New York City, thirteen to other parts of the county and twenty-five to the suburbs (Drennan 1991).

criticized for being elitist and (sharpest barb of all) a throwback to the Middle Ages and their armed and walled cities! But for those who live there, no amount of criticism offsets the sense of security that the gated community provides.

As we will reiterate later, all through our history American urban places have been constantly changing, constantly reinventing themselves. Industrial parks, edge cities, and gated communities are only three of the most recent changes to make their way across the urban landscape.

Counties

Counties share with cities, towns, and villages a common legal status. They are all *general purpose* governments, empowered to enforce and implement the overall policies and laws of state government. Thus, they are empowered to deal with matters within the state's police powers: health, safety, welfare, morals, and public convenience.[4] Both counties and cities are responsible for enforcing state laws within their jurisdiction, but cities are also empowered to implement state laws through legislation (ordinances) that deal with problems that are primarily urban—problems that arise when people live in close physical proximity.

Typically, county government is in the hands of an elected, multiple-member, policy making board called the county commission. It is also the usual case that heads of county offices (sheriff, recorder, tax collector, real estate assessor, prosecuting attorney, judges, engineer) are directly elected (and thus, independent) officials, creating what is, in effect, a dispersed and pluralistic style of county governance (Bollens 1969).

The county covers a relatively large territory. Cities sit inside a county (sometimes within two counties), and the metropolitan areas spread across one or more counties. County government is only peripheral to our concerns, except to note that every city must accommodate itself to the authority of the county or counties that contain it. Often, state statutes spell out the details of this accommodation. But state laws are implemented through legal contracts, memoranda of agreement between county and city officials. Thus, the sheriff's department (and county engineer) usually does not operate within city limits. The city, however, will depend on the county treasurer to collect and disburse the city's share of county taxes. City and county health officials cooperate in enforcing quarantines, while the city's health department usually will take responsibility for testing the purity of city water and inspecting restaurants and food stores within the city limits. And it is often the case that small villages,

---

4. Two states, Connecticut and Rhode Island, have no counties. Alaska and Louisiana have administrative units comparable to the county, called boroughs and parishes, respectively.

instead of operating a village police force, will contract to pay the county sheriff for police protection.

But the line of demarcation between city and county responsibilities is constantly shifting. As cities grow in size, they lessen their dependence on the county. And more important, as counties become urbanized, the unincorporated areas of the county are given county services of the kind that once belonged exclusively to city government. Many counties, for example, now operate fire departments, libraries, and refuse-collection services.

Special-Purpose Government

Special-purpose governments are the fastest growing units of American government. Their number today stands at over forty-five thousand (including school districts), and it continues to increase.[5] Sometimes called ad hoc government, special purpose governments are created to accomplish special rather than general-government purposes. Table 11.1 provides a guide to the functions of different types of special-purpose governments operating in the United States today. School districts are the most common variety of special-purpose governments. Their jurisdiction has mostly to do with building and maintaining school buildings, hiring teachers, and planning and implementing instruction.[6]

What special-purpose governments lack in scope, they make up for in sheer numbers. They are everywhere on the governmental map. Several may exist inside the boundaries of a single city (e.g., park districts, transportation authorities, and water districts). Some cross city and county boundaries, bringing central cities and distant suburbs into their special domain (water districts, sewage disposal districts, and mosquito control districts are the commonest form of boundary-crossing ad hoc government). And some even cross state lines, bringing their special authority to bear on otherwise separate jurisdictions.

5. By way of comparison, there were only about nine thousand special-purpose governments during the decade of the 1940s. See McFeeley (1978) and MacManus (1981).

6. This discussion of school districts formalizes what has been treated informally to this point: the relationship between cities and school districts. In some cities, education is the responsibility of the municipal government. But most often, primary and secondary education are under the auspices of a special-purpose government, the local school district, which is totally autonomous from the general-purpose municipal government. Yet, the style of politics that is practiced within a school district is much like that practiced within the municipality. Municipal issues impinge on school district issues, and vice versa. For instance, the school district, in attempting to control drugs in the schools, may seek the assistance of the municipal police force. And the same people involved in local municipal issues (e.g., crime, streets, and recreation) are also likely to be involved in school issues. Much the same can be said for the host of other special-purpose governments that reside within the urban area. See Rich (1996) for a discussion of the relationship between school districts and municipal governments.

Table 11.1 A Catalogue of Special-Purpose Governments

Content	Purpose	Examples	Jurisdiction
Natural Resources	Conserve and develop parks, wildlife areas, nature preserves Control animals and insects	Park board Forest preserve Water conservancy district Mosquito control authority	Usually extends across metro area but can operate as special district inside one city
Public Utilities	Administer water supply: impound, transport, purify Administer sewage system: purify and dispose Administer electric system: generate and sell	Water reservoir authority Sanitary district Public power authority	Metro wide Some may be of primary service to single city Most operate plants and facilities outside city limits
Transportation	Build and maintain toll roads, airports, bus depots	Turnpike commission Airport board Transportation authority	Metro wide
Building	Build and maintain sports arena, convention center, low-rent housing	Housing authority Local building authority Civic improvement board	Usually within a single city
Amenities	Administer zoos, recreation centers, libraries, racetracks Regulate betting, racetrack operations	Zoo board Library board Racing commission	City specific, but sometimes county wide Often operates outside city that funds and controls it
Education	Operate primary, secondary, and special schools Operate state and city universities	Board of education Board of trustees	Usually city specific, but can be county wide or state wide

As a rule, special-purpose governments are created (some would say imposed) by the state legislature. The reasoning behind their creation is three-fold. First, and most obvious, ad hoc governments are created to overcome the problems that follow from multiple jurisdictions existing side by side in the same geographic area. After all, most problems do not stop at government boundaries. And many are too complex to be managed by one local government. For example, if control of mosquitoes is to be accomplished, insecticide must be sprayed area-wide. And if water resources are to be conserved, water management must extend across an entire watershed. There is, of course, an irony (and more than a little counterlogic) in this reasoning: The legislature creates more governments to deal with the problem of too many governments!

Special districts are also created as a residue of what was earlier described as the urban reform package, an attempt to "take politics out of government." Of course, no such thing is possible, nor in a democracy would we want it so. But school districts as special-purpose governments, for example, were often created in an attempt to free the schools from the depredations of political machines. Education, it was usually said, is too important to be a plaything of politicians. For another example, forest and park districts have been established in hopes that their managing boards would consist of conservationist-minded citizens and horticultural specialists instead of the usual run-of-the-mill politicians.

A third reason behind creating special governments has to do with money. Cities and counties are limited by their state constitutions (as well as statutes) in the amount of money that can be raised through taxes or borrowed by issuing bonds to be paid back later with tax revenue. But special governments can tax and borrow independently, often without putting their proposals to a public vote. Think now of the problems that can be solved and the temptations that arise in special purpose governments. City and county governments can be cut free of the costs of maintaining parks and schools and the like. Cities and counties may have reached the limits of their indebtedness. (State constitutions and statutes usually limit local bonds to a percentage of property values in each local government.) But a special district can issue its own bonds and thus make available to the local area an additional source of government money. Equally important, interest groups can gain the opportunity to promote new and controversial projects such as a sports arena, a convention center, and even publicly financed housing projects for the poor.

The Port Authority of New York and New Jersey, or What's Wrong with Special-Purpose Government

Some special-purpose governments have so much power that they dominate the social and economic life of an entire region. The Port Authority of New

York and New Jersey exemplifies this domination. Created in 1921 through a compact between the two states, its governing board (a "businessman's board," appointed mostly from the ranks of corporation executives) is appointed jointly by the two state governors. Once appointed, its members are almost beyond removal and are thoroughly insulated from popular control.

The Authority's purpose is to develop commercial and transportation resources in the two-state area. It was given no taxing powers, but quickly developed its own highly lucrative revenue sources, initially by issuing bonds, later by charging for its services.

> By 1931 it was operating four toll bridges and the Holland Tunnel. The next year it opened a freight terminal. In 1944 it opened a grain terminal, and in 1948 it took over its first airport. During the 1950s, it acquired the rest of New York's major airports. During the 1960s it entered the real estate business and constructed the 110-story twin towers of the New York World Trade Center. By the start of the 1980s, the Port Authority's assets had grown to nearly $5 billion, and its various enterprises brought in about $3/4 billion in annual revenue. Port Authority facilities include six interstate bridges and tunnels, two bus terminals, the World Trade Center, and one railroad system. (Harrigan 1985, 267)

But however successful as a profit making enterprise, the Port Authority has long had its bitter critics. For half a century it has promoted automobile transportation instead of mass transit, leading, critics charge, to a worsening of New York's traffic congestion as the Authority's bridges and tunnels became giant conduits through which commuter traffic pours into the city. (In Manhattan, many times each day, congestion is so bad that it is quicker to walk a mile than to ride.)

Worse still, say the critics, these same bridges and tunnels also serve as "population pumps," with devastating consequences not only for New York but for every place within fifty (and even a hundred) miles of the city. Easy road access to the suburbs has quickened outward migration from the city, leaving the city's population increasingly poor, black, and Hispanic. In the process, outward migration has also destroyed the open countryside, leaving in its wake an ugly urban sprawl. And the spaghetti-like strands of freeways in and around New York have sliced open and destroyed once lively and liveable neighborhoods.

The Port Authority has also been accused of working with and perpetuating local political machines, mainly by way of the jobs, influence, and money that are part of its construction projects, land purchases, bond-issues, and bank loans. But the most trenchant criticism turns on familiar questions: Whose definition of the public interest prevails here? A definition arrived at by the Authority's nonelected governing board? Or that which might have been arrived at if the Authority were run by elected officials? Would the Authority's sprawl-creating projects have been carried through by elected officials? And would elected officials have been more sparing when it came to tearing down houses and razing neighborhoods to serve the needs of the automobile commuter?

Appraising the Metropolitan Patchwork

Metropolitan areas have great variety and also a common pattern: The larger the central city, the greater the number of separate governments within its metropolitan area. Metropolitan New York City, for example, contains more than fifteen hundred separate governments. Metropolitan Chicago has over twelve hundred governments, Pittsburgh has over seven hundred, and Philadelphia over nine hundred. And even though New York City has only thirty-six special governments, their capital funds exceed those of the municipal government (Kantor 1993).

What, then, are the consequences of numerous governments layered over each other and stacked side by side? Frankly, much depends on the values that the appraiser brings to the subject. *[The theory of ideology.]*

Simplicity versus Organized Complexity

For those who prize symmetry and simplicity, the metro area is an affront. It follows no simple organization. It is not easily charted in schema or diagram (e.g., Wood 1964, Bollens and Schmandt 1982). And its everywhere-present, multiple-member governing boards and commissions contradict our tradition of separation of powers. Critics find even greater fault in the complex layering of governments in the metropolitan area that (when combined with multiple officials to be elected) confounds several cherished notions concerning democratic responsibility.

A Theory of Democratic Responsibility

In framing a government which is to be administered by men over men, the great difficulty is this: you must first enable the government to control the governed; and in the next place, oblige it to control itself.

James Madison, *Federalist 51*

Democratic theory has no objection to policy authority resting in many hands. For an important group of theorists (*pluralists*, as they are usually styled), shared and distributed power better assures majority preferences than too narrow a concentration of policy authority. In parallel fashion democratic theory also makes room for the argument that local government is better able to protect the local interests of local residents than a large, centralized government. *[The theory of grass-roots democracy.]* On these grounds, a strong case can be made for the multiplicity of governing units that make up the metropolitan area.

But in prescriptive theory, almost every argument has its counterargument. When governing authority lies in many hands, it may also be obscured from public eyes. It is difficult for the electorate to know which official has responsibility for doing what. And hence, the electorate may be diminished in its ability to control its rulers.

By obscuring the locus of power and responsibility, the metropolitan patchwork may invite and encourage political corruption. (If we don't know who is responsible for doing what, how can we vote against the wrongdoers?) As a matter of historical record, county governments—with their multitude of elected officials and multiple-member governing boards—have had a long tradition of political corruption. And, so too, have special-purpose governments. To exemplify, we turn to another of the numerous ad hoc governments that honeycomb the New York metropolitan area and scrutinize one of its most influential officials.

Robert Moses of New York. Robert Caro (1974) presents a massive indictment of New York's Triborough Bridge and Tunnel Authority. Its long history of corruption, he concludes, springs from three sources. First, it has been run by nonelected officials, not therefore subject to the public scrutiny that ordinarily takes place at election time. Its massive building projects and the revenues generated by those projects enabled its long-time head, the late Robert Moses, to build a personal political machine out of the willing cooperation of labor unions, revenue-bond brokers, lending banks, and elected officials. And in building and using his political power, Moses was further assisted by the Triborough Authority's public relations office, which constantly touted the engineering accomplishments of the Authority.

Robert Moses held no elected office, but as Caro puts it, he was "a political boss with a difference."

> He was not the stereotype with which Americans were familiar. His constituency was not the public but some of the most powerful men in the city and state, and he kept these men in line by doling out to them . . . the sugar plums of public relations retainers, insurance commissions and legal fees. . . . Robert Moses was America's greatest builder. He was the shaper of the greatest city in the New World. . . . To build his highways, Moses threw out of their homes 250,000 persons. He tore the heart out of a score of neighborhoods. . . . By building his highways, Moses flooded the city with cars. By systematically starving the subways and the suburban commuter railroads, he swelled that flood to city-destroying dimensions. By making sure that the vast suburbs, rural and empty when he came to power, were filled on a sprawling, low-density development pattern relying primarily on roads instead of mass transportation, he insured that the flood would continue for generations. . . . For highways, Moses dispossessed 250,000 persons. For his other

projects . . . he . . . dispossessed close to half a million. . . . He evicted tens of thousands of poor, nonwhite persons for urban renewal projects, and the housing he built to replace the housing he tore down was . . . not housing for the poor, but for the rich. The dispossessed had no place to go but into the already overcrowded slums. (Caro 1974, 17ff)

This portrait of the power of a single official may be overdrawn; but it is an accurate portrayal of the power that can lie with a single, special-purpose government. And as portrait, it sharpens our appreciation of democratic theory's insistence that one of the surest safeguards against arrogant or unwise government is to insist upon popular election of its officials.

Prescriptive Theories of Social Justice and Social Equity

Nothing more easily invites argument than an attempt to define social justice and social equity. Both terms are grounded in prescriptive theories of equality, ethics, and fair dealing. Social justice carries in its definition the idea of equal treatment, and social equity carries in its definition the idea of fair shares. Both terms are thus grounded in ideas about social and ethical responsibility: Should the individual person assume primary responsibility for what happens in his or her life, or does some large part of that responsibility rest with society?

As our earlier discussion may suggest, theories of social justice and equity link to redistributive policy: What do the rich owe the poor, and what are society's obligations to its least well-off and least autonomous members (infants, the elderly, the ill)?

Around such questions liberals and conservatives draw the battle lines of argument.[7] As conservatives see it, social justice and equity are to be judged

---

7. It would mislead to suggest that liberal and conservative ideologies are limited only to questions of social justice and equity. Other questions include:

a. government's use of its power to promote and protect citizen morality and virtuous conduct and to preserve society's traditional values. Conservatives generally favor vigorous government action, while Liberals seek to give the individual as much life-space freedom as possible.

b. the extent to which government should steer the economy (and intervene in market transactions) in order to alleviate economic distress and prevent underemployment, inflation, and falling industrial productivity. Conservatives tend to be wary of such interventions in the market; Liberals tend to favor them, most fully when they work to assist the least well-off.

c. the proper locus of policy-making authority: Should such authority be given back to the states or kept at the national level? Here, the arguments conflate with (a) and (b) above. Conservatives often speak of getting government (especially the national government) "off our backs and out of our pockets," and they generally argue for handing power back to the states. Liberals argue that only the national government has the resources, authority, and compassion sufficient to effect redistributive policies—and thus assure, for everyone, a degree of equal outcomes.

The literature that explains, defends, and argues the liberal and conservative positions noted here is vast. References and further discussion may be found in Herson (1990).

primarily in terms of equality of opportunity. Each person shall be free to make of life what he or she is able to—without undue government interference. Each person shall be permitted to compete for life's rewards as he or she defines those rewards—again, without undue government interference.

As liberals see it, the moral quality of any society is in direct proportion to its concern for its least well-off and least autonomous members. Poverty and other social problems, they reason, are as much a consequence of our society's social and economic arrangements as of personal failings. Accordingly, responsibility for social outcomes must lie with society as well as with the individual. Thus, social justice and equity are to be judged in terms of equality of outcomes. Government shall take responsibility for ensuring that every person receives something that approaches an equal—or at least minimum—share of life's needs and rewards (including income, housing, education, and health care).[8] Equally important, government shall do all it can to spare minorities and the poor the burdens of segregation—whether it be in jobs, education, or place of residence—for segregation not only leaves psychological scars, it also hinders equality of outcome by denying those who are segregated full access to jobs, housing, and social services.

Social Justice and Social Equity in the Metropolitan Area

These seemingly abstract considerations operate with great vigor in any appraisal of metropolitan governance.[9] Consider the following facts. Metropolitan regions tend to be highly segregated. Their central cities contain a disproportionate share of the metropolitan area's poor and minorities. Central cities are home to most of the region's major social problems: violent crime, drug abuse, school dropouts, not to mention the homeless. But central cities are revenue poor and have great difficulty in responding to their social problems. Per capita, they are less able than most suburbs to spend for such basic services as fire and police protection, and they are even less able to spend for such urban amenities as parks and recreation.

In contrast, many suburbs are revenue rich. They are able to provide a high quality of education for their children as well as a high standard of urban services and amenities. And even where not revenue rich, most suburbs are white and given over to the several strata of the middle class—"white collar" and "blue collar." Thus, all through suburbia, housing as well as urban services

8. On these matters, two of the most influential liberal spokespersons of our generation are John Rawls (1971) and Michael Walzer (1983); conservative views are represented by the journal *The Public Interest* and in the writings of its editors (e.g., Kristol 1978).

9. See, for example, Smith (1979, vii), who examines American cities from the point of view of writers who see the cities as a "repressive social institution" and urban problems as consequence of our society's "economic and social inequality."

reflect the socioeconomic status of their residents. What is more, suburbs use their governmental powers to keep their social, economic, and racial distance from the central city—and from all would-be settlers of a different social or economic class. They use that power to maintain zones of exclusivity, often passing ordinances that limit house construction to single-family homes, often to be set on large lots. Some suburbs require that builders, not the city, pay the costs of installing gas, water, and sewer lines, and that developers pave the streets in new housing developments. All such requirements drive up housing costs and serve to price out of the market those families with incomes below the suburb's norm. And many suburbs also forbid the location of businesses and industries of a type that might be expected to employ low-skill, low-wage earners. *[The theory of lifestyle and territory.]*

It is not the suburbs alone that contribute to the social, economic, and racial separation within the metropolitan region. By concentrating welfare assistance facilities such as medical services in central cities—especially in the inner core of central cities—state and county governments also serve to anchor the poor there.

Consider now how life in the metropolitan area might change if all territorial boundaries were swept away and suburbs merged with the central city.[10] Central cities would have their tax and revenue bases enhanced and might then attempt redistributive policies aimed at improving the lives of the poor. The quality of urban services—including education—would be equal all through the metropolitan area. Low-rent apartment buildings could be sited all through the area, and minorities and the poor would no longer be confined to the central city. The location of factories and shopping malls might be made a matter for area-wide planning, and urban sprawl might be better controlled through more orderly land development. And with a single government operating throughout the area, there might be less need for constantly multiplying special purpose governments.

Of course, the changes we sketch are not likely to happen anywhere soon. Our society's preference for localized government probably has too strong a hold on our culture to permit this sort of reconstructing policy. What is more, obliterating suburbia would also challenge the values that are part of our society's commitment to a market economy. Not only do many of us believe that lifestyle and territory ought to go together, many of us also believe firmly in the idea of market equity: Each of us ought to be free to buy whatever lifestyle we can afford—providing, of course, that it is not illegal or immoral. Thus, suburbia tends to pit market equity against social equity, with market equity thus far the winner. In fact, the metropolitan area has been likened to an arrangement of lifestyle markets. Those who offer this analog

---

10. This scenario is suggested by the analysis in Lowi (1969a). On "opening up the suburbs," see Downs (1973).

suggest that each separate governmental jurisdiction functions as a market-place, with those living there likened to consumers who have purchased the lifestyle that goes with that territory. To merge jurisdictions, it is argued, would deprive lifestyle consumers of their freedom of choice. The argument is strengthened by the further assertion that the metropolitan area is a series of competitive market economies, with each governmental unit attempting to improve its position relative to all other units in the area. In this view, each unit is seen as the producer of a package of values that is purchased by those who live there. Each unit, therefore, if it is to retain its residents (and attract new settlers), has an incentive to produce its values competitively, offering services, amenities, and tax rates in such fashion as to generate the optimal degree of consumer satisfaction. In this view, the metropolitan area ought not be viewed as a patchwork at all. Rather, it is to be judged as a governmental arrangement that maximizes opportunities for satisfying the preferences that go hand in glove with freedom of choice, lifestyle, and territory (Tiebout 1956, Ostrom et al. 1988).

The Metropolitan Area as a System

Whether the metropolitan area is seen favorably as a competitive market or unfavorably as a patchwork that thwarts the spread of social equity—and preserves the racial, social, and economic status quo—very much depends on the observer's point of view and (of course) the observer's angle of ideological vision. But not to be overlooked is the fact that from still another point of view, the area works well as an integrated economic system, with goods, services, shoppers, and commuters moving freely across the area. It also works well as an integrated communications system, with electric lines, telephone lines, and roadways also moving freely throughout the area (Williams 1971). Seen in this way, the present organization of the metropolitan area has its many defenders who often invoke the practical adage "If it ain't broke, don't fix it."

The Metropolitan Area as a Bargaining Arena

Because the dozens and even hundreds of governments in the metropolitan area are each independent policymakers, each is more or less free to create its own policies more or less independently of all the other governments. Sometimes, however, cooperation is preferred. One or more governments may think it useful and economical to buy services (e.g., police and fire protection, sanitation service) from another government. And governments may also choose to share the costs of providing a needed service (a water purification plant, for another example).

In such arrangements, and even though each unit of government is a more or less free agent and free bargainer, many find cooperation to their mutual advantage. Matthew Holden (1964), in fact, likens the intergovernmental arrangements in the metropolitan area to intergovernmental relations in international politics. Independent bargainers pursue their own definitions of self-interest through diplomacy, alliances, and occasionally harmful conflict (also see Dye 1962). Of course, the analogy is imperfect. Real wars do not break out—although some have likened the competition among cities for business, and with it economic viability, to war (Watson 1995); and unlike national behavior in the international arena, cities are answerable to a higher authority, their state and the national government. But even as an imperfect analogy, it points, as we now shall see, to the possibility of cooperative steps toward greater degrees of metropolitan integration.

Steps toward Metropolitan Integration

The great and chief end of men . . . putting themselves under government, is the preservation of their property.
John Locke, *Treatises*

Whatever arguments may have arisen in the past over the existence of a . . . privileged aristocracy, it is clear to me that today no argument can stand that supports unequal opportunity or any intrinsic disqualification for sharing in the whole of life.
Margaret Mead, *Blackberry Winter*

For more than a half century, metropolitan integration has been the goal of many policy entrepreneurs. To date, five fairly distinct reform arrangements have been used to advance metropolitan-area integration: annexation, service delivery contracts, city-county consolidation, two-tier government, and planning coordination. In attempting—or even suggesting—these arrangements, policymakers are strongly influenced by economics and lifestyle differences (Keating 1995).

Annexation

With annexation, a city takes over an area that lies on its border. This is a strategy cities use almost universally for expanding their area (and their tax base); 80 percent of all central cities stretched their geographical boundaries between 1950 and 1990 (Rusk 1993). In most states, annexation requires the approval of a majority of voters in the area to be annexed. Where voters perceive few lifestyle differences between themselves and those living in the annexing city,

247

annexation is easiest. Conversely, it is most difficult to accomplish where there are obvious lifestyle differences between the annexing city and the place to be annexed. *[The theory of lifestyle and territory.]* Occasionally, two towns have merged; but because a town's charter of incorporation is protected by legal safeguards, the most common type of annexation involves an area on the city's rim that is unincorporated and relatively unpeopled.

A number of annexing cities have adopted carrot and stick strategies: inducements to come under the annexing city's umbrella and disincentives for staying out. One such strategy is to withhold city water and sewage services to any area that refuses annexation. And where the refusal crimps pending plans for real estate development, the strategy is sometimes effective. (A partially rural, partially urbanized area can make do with wells and cesspools; but state health laws usually require a centralized water and sewage system for any urbanized area reaching a prescribed population density.)

Carrot and stick strategies are not always effective, however. Those living in the area proposed for annexation may like things as they are: a rural or near-rural environment without city taxes and without city laws, especially zoning and building codes, constricting their cherished lifestyle.[11] Of considerable importance in recent years has been the preference of those outside the central city to stay outside and thus escape incorporation in the central city's school district and whatever school busing (to achieve racial integration) the federal courts may have imposed on it.

Thomas Dye (1964) enlightens us on these matters. He studied annexation and population growth in 212 Standard Metropolitan Statistical Areas (SMSAs)[12] for the years 1950 to 1960. Thirty-five cities in this study had populations that surpassed fifty thousand for the first time in the 1960 census. On average, these cities had annexed 22.3 percent of their population during the 1950s. In contrast, the forty-nine cities that had achieved fifty thousand people by 1890 had annexed only 4.2 percent of their populations during the 1950s. In other words, the older the central city, the less its reliance on annexation as a tool of metropolitan growth.

We can infer from these data that the older the central city, the more it is likely that its suburbs will also be old, and an old suburb is likely to be venerated by those who live there. More important, lifestyles in those suburbs have been fixed over time. So too have the social relationships and social adjustments that are part of that lifestyle. As Dye (1964, 305) says,

11. Donald Connery (1972, 155), quoting an anonymous New Englander, nicely sums up the frustration of many small-towners forced to deal with increasing regulations "Every time you want to do something in this town there's some damned ordinance that says you can't."

12. In June 1983, the Bureau of the Census gave up its SMSA designation in favor of the MSA—Metropolitan Statistical Area.

The longer these adjustments have been in existence, the greater the discomfiture, expense, and fear of unanticipated consequences associated with change.

Other explanations are also embedded in Dye's data. In the older central cities of the Northeast, status differential between central cities and suburbs is greater than between central cities and suburbs in the newer metropolitan areas of the Southwest and West. And the greater the status differential, the greater the resistance of those of higher social status to being annexed to the central city. Equally, where race and ethnic differences are most clearly marked, these differences also become motives to resist annexation.

Service Delivery Contracts

Everywhere in the metropolitan area, governments sell services to other governments. But the one arrangement that commands greatest attention has as its prototype the arrangement between Los Angeles County and the nearly one hundred incorporated places within the county. The county maintains an inventory of about sixty services for sale, and any town, village, or city in the county can buy these services. The inventory includes: administration of local elections, health inspection, jail facilities, prosecution for violations of local ordinances, tax assessment and collection, ambulance service, fire protection, and helicopter police patrols. This arrangement is known as the Lakewood Plan (named after the first city to use the services of Los Angeles County; see Kuyper 1970).

Counties elsewhere offer parallels to the Lakewood Plan. And their experience helps policymakers to understand a question that has long puzzled those who propose metropolitan integration: Will further steps toward integration promote *economies of scale?*

In everyday language, economies of scale are the savings that result from activities comparable to mass production in industry (Thompson 1968, Bish 1971, Hirsch 1976, Reich 1983). Whether it is making automobiles or collecting garbage, the unit costs of production tend to go down as output increases and as the same product is continuously produced in a long production run. After the factory is built or the garbage truck paid for (these are sometimes called "sunk costs"), the expenses of building the factory or truck can be charged off against each subsequent unit of production—the greater the number of units, the less the cost of investment for each unit. But at some point, economies of scale stop. This occurs in part because the costs of labor and other materials remain relatively fixed and in part because no piece of equipment can go on forever without wearing out or needing repair.

Thus, cities can save money by contracting for services that involve a substantial investment in equipment to be used in long production runs; but it is not clear that contracting for services that are primarily labor intensive will result in economies of scale. For example, police protection and health and building inspection require that they be carried out by people more than by machinery, and the people who perform these services make small-scale individual (often on-the-spot) decisions, not long production runs. *[The theory of urban administration.]*

There are also many urban services for which economies of scale are less important to policymakers than citizen satisfaction. And citizen satisfaction is often tied to local control, for it is local control that can bring urban services into conformity with local lifestyles (e.g., the respectful behavior of small-city police, the fire department ready to rescue cats from trees). In this vein, Elinor Ostrom (1973) reports that citizen satisfaction with the work of police departments is inversely correlated with the size of the department. Thus, a small and relatively costly to operate police department may be preferred to a larger department whose contracted services might result in an economy of scale (also see Wilson 1972). *[The theories of grass-roots democracy and lifestyle and territory.]*

City-County Consolidation

As the term implies, city-county consolidation involves merging these two levels of government. A single government merges all chartered local governments in the county (central city and suburbs) with the government of the county. Thus, the county commission is replaced by a county council; all city councils are abolished; city police departments merge with the sheriff's department to become the county police; and mayors are abolished countywide and replaced with a county manager or administrator.

As a reform proposal, city-county consolidation has been around for nearly two hundred years. In the nineteenth century, it was carried through in New Orleans (1805), Boston (1822), Philadelphia (1822), New York (1898), and Honolulu (1907). Then the consolidation movement came to a halt. As is often the case, reformers' energies moved to a different cause: In the Progressive period the cause became the urban reform package.

But following the Second World War, proposals for city-county consolidation again caught the attention of policy entrepreneurs. This was the time of the exploding metropolis, the time of the great out-migration from the central cities, and thus the time of spreading suburbia. Although most proposals for city-county consolidations were defeated by the voters during the middle years of this century, by 1993 forty-eight metropolitan areas representing twenty-one states were served by metropolitan-wide governments. (For discussions of city-county consolidations, see Rusk 1993, Jackson 1985, and Bollens and Schmandt 1982.)

Three cases are instructive. In Indianapolis local reformers, long frustrated in their attempts to strengthen the mayor's office, persuaded the state legislature to pass a consolidation statute that required no approval from metropolitan-area voters. The state legislature (traditionally dominated by rural Republicans) saw in metropolitan consolidation an opportunity to dilute the voting strength of Democrats concentrated in Indianapolis. *Unigov* (as the consolidation proposal was named) was thus partially an attempt to improve government in metropolitan Indianapolis and partially an attempt to settle old political scores. Unigov was imposed by the legislature, and the imposition thus avoided Unigov's almost certain rejection by suburban voters—had they been permitted to vote. As was said by suburbanites, they had not migrated into the suburbs to be thrown back into association with the government and politics, lifestyles and ethnicity of Indianapolis (Wilburn 1973, Rusk 1993).

Nashville, Tennessee, has had a long history of political corruption and machine politics (Key 1950). By the 1950s, partly as a result of desire to escape the machine, most of Nashville's population growth was in its suburbs. But the suburbs were revenue poor, and an estimated hundred thousand suburbanites were using backyard wells for drinking water and septic tanks for waste disposal, at least 25 percent of which were faulty. Contaminated drinking water from septic tank leakage was a threat to public health. Police and fire departments were understaffed and underequipped. More and more, suburban residents were turning to private police and fire protection. For suburbanites there, the incentives for city-county consolidation outweighed the disincentives. The vote for consolidation was carried in 1962 (Hawkins 1966).

In Jacksonville, Florida, the consolidation proposal was propelled by a series of crises and exposés. The city's school system was far enough below standard to have been threatened with loss of accreditation. Sewage was polluting the river. And indictments had been recently returned against eight city officials for offenses that ranged from grand larceny to bribery and perjury. (In short, machine-style politics was alive and well in Jacksonville.) Thus, for Jacksonville voters, the proposal for consolidation was moved by a strong incentive: the opportunity to sweep away an unsatisfactory city government and begin again under a new, consolidated government (Carver 1973, Rabinowitz 1969).

Two-Tier Government

To understand the logic of two-tier government, two previously stated ideas must be kept in mind. First, integration in the metropolitan area is resisted where lifestyle differences are marked. Second, the metro area works well as an integrated economic and communication system. Well, then, why not take advantage of what is easiest to accomplish and avoid debate and argument over what is resisted? Such is the logic behind the two-tier government established in Dade County, Florida, in 1957.

At the time, twenty-six municipalities were anchored across the county, and traffic between them was snarled and slow. Each city insisted on its own speed limits and its own traffic pattern. Urban services in the unincorporated areas were often minimal, if not primitive. And the quality of services in each city was a direct function of that city's wealth. The biggest city, Miami, provided water and sewer services to nearby cities, but lifestyle differences underscored by race, ethnicity, and per-capita income made other forms of intercity cooperation almost nonexistent.[13]

As a way of addressing Dade County's metropolitan problems, the Florida state legislature asked the county's voters to approve a new county charter. Under terms of the charter (approved by the voters in 1957), both county and all city governments in the county were reorganized. The reorganized county government was given responsibility for county-wide (mostly service) functions and problems, including mass transit, water pollution, public health, and some police and fire services. All other functions—particularly those wrapped around lifestyle maintenance—remained with the cities: education, police, local zoning, and land use. The elected county commission retained its traditional legislative powers, but provision was made for an appointed county manager whose authority included power to appoint a number of county officials who previously had been elected. And each city retained its own form of government mostly intact (Sofen 1963, Lotz 1973).

The new governmental organization did not, of course, eliminate friction between Dade County cities, nor did it solve the problems of problem cities. Miami, in particular, is a city with problems. It has a history of police corruption and, more recently, of police violence against blacks. Miami, in addition, has become celebrated as the "Cuban capital" of the United States, with refugees from Castro's Cuba now prospering and assuming roles of leadership in the city—and, unusual for urban politics, making anticommunist foreign policy an important concern of local politics. In addition (as watchers of a recently popular television series know), Miami is notorious as a major drug distributing center in the United States. Understandably, nearby cities have resisted being drawn into too close cooperation with Miami, but overall (most observers conclude) the quality of county-wide services has improved under two-tier government.

13. The lifestyle differences between Miami and its exclusive and wealthy neighbor, Palm Beach, produce almost daily friction. Until a 1985 court decision enjoined Palm Beach, its ordinances required all those coming into the city for employment to carry identification cards. In that case, lawyers for Palm Beach argued that registration of outsiders was a means of protecting the lives and property of the city's residents, Palm Beach being an island of affluence in an ocean of surrounding poverty.

Councils of Government

If we cast our thoughts back to the analogy of the metropolitan area as a group of free bargainers akin to nation states, one logical device for achieving mutual cooperation and assistance lies in creating an agency (something on the order of a "United Nations") to promote that cooperation and assistance: a *council of governments* (COG) that plans solutions to metro-area problems. The first such council was probably created in the Detroit area in 1954, but their numbers did not greatly increase until the 1960s. By early 1970, three hundred COGs were in existence, brought into being by a push from the national government.

The national government did not so much impose COGs as offer incentives for their creation. What happened was this: As the number of federal grants to cities began to multiply in the 1960s, congressional concern also grew that cities were about to engage in intense competition for those grants (with losers demanding remedial action from their congressional delegations). Moreover, concern also grew over the prospect that federal grant money would produce duplication of effort. (After all, how many airports might a metropolitan area need?) Thus, the Housing and Urban Development Act of 1965 made councils of government eligible to receive planning and research money for a broad range of activities, including data collection, land-use planning, and economic and resource development. In other words, it would cost metro-area cities nothing to cooperate in setting up COGs, and the result promised to be beneficial to all who cooperated in doing so. Then, in 1966, Congress stipulated that all new grants to cities in a metropolitan area must be approved by a metro-wide authority (Wikstrom 1985, Scarborough 1982). And in 1969, the Office of Management and Budget (OMB) further extended the review process (now termed A-95, after the OMB memorandum detailing its use).

How successful have COGs been in coordinating metro planning? One view has it that they serve as a forum for the exchange of ideas that in the long run leads to intergovernmental planning and cooperation. Another view has it that since COG members are appointed by their cities, they function mostly as places for intercity argument and trading favors (logrolling, to use a familiar political term). As complaints about COG bickering mounted, the Reagan administration abolished the federal requirement for A-95 reviews, and shortly thereafter about a third of the six hundred COGs shut down.

"To Thine Own Self Be True": Counterlogic and Countertrends

As this discussion thus far has indicated, steps and arrangements to promote metro-area integration are accomplished most easily where "system access" (e.g., road-building, and waste disposal) is the issue, whereas no arrangements are easy where lifestyle access is the issue. Where lifestyle is visibly and directly threatened, countertrends are sometimes set in motion. In some instances, they move the metropolitan area toward smaller, more localized governance. Other times they involve a desperate determination to keep lifestyle from being altered by newcomers' incursions.

Old Settlers versus New

One manner in which suburbs differ is in the degree to which their populations split between old settlers and new. The old settlers are often more than merely long-time residents. Frequently, they are children and grandchildren of those who settled the city when it was a nonsuburb, a town far outside the ambit of the central city. As old settlers, they watch with growing unease the rising tide of new arrivals. Characteristically, the old settlers resist attempts by more recently arrived settlers to change the town's package of urban services in the direction of added amenities (parks, social centers, counseling centers, and the like), and they also resist services that result in higher taxes.

Resistance may well turn rancorous as newcomers attempt to introduce into the schools what old settlers see as big-city values. Where the town historically has served as a commercial center for nearby farms (with a grain elevator, feed and hardware store, tractor sales, and so forth), the old settlers carry traditions of a rural life. They are thus understandably resentful of proposals to change the schools—for example, by emphasizing a college-preparatory curriculum at the expense of vocational training, or by altering the schools' dress code. And nerves may be rubbed raw as new settlers attempt to bring what old settlers regard as big-city values to books in the school libraries.[14] Overall, such issues, like tax issues, may be no more than emblematic: a rallying point for those who seek to stem the tide of metropolitan-area integration. (The larger social context for this rallying point is conveyed by the title of Vidich and Bensman's 1958 book, *Small Town in Mass Society*.)

Another Dimension of Equity: Race and Ethnicity in Central Cities

Previous discussions highlighted the distinction between social justice and market equity and the implications of this distinction for separate govern-

---

14. For example, Clarence Stone and his coauthors (Stone et al. 1979, 91) report that when the old settlers of the Long Island suburb of Island Trees, New York, asked the school board to ban such books as Vonnegut's *Slaughterhouse Five*, Morris' *The Naked Ape*, and Cleaver's *Soul on Ice*, the new settlers responded with an attempt to take over the school board by means of a hard-fought election, and some went to court to seek an injunction against book banning.

ments in the central cities and suburbs. There, we noted that the ideal of social justice might have to be achieved at the expense of market equity and that metropolitan integration might be demanded as the suitable instrument for achieving area-wide equity.

But in politics, as in life generally, few arguments stand without exceptions or without taking into account changing times and conditions. As central cities have become increasingly black and Hispanic (and as the Voting Rights Act of 1965 changed voting patterns across the country), more and more black and Hispanic mayors have come to office, and increasing numbers of minorities have taken seats on city councils and become heads of central-city administrative departments. There is a new emergence of black (and Hispanic) political power in central cities, and those who hold that power (as well as whites who approve of this new arrangement) are now reluctant to see the dominance of black and Hispanic voters in the central city diluted by proposals to wipe out or expand the central cities' boundaries. They fear that an expanded (metropolitan-wide) voting unit would return the city's blacks (and Hispanics and other ethnic groups) to a voting minority in a government that extends over the entire metropolitan region (DeHoog et al. 1991).[15] Some also fear that dispersion into the suburbs of blacks, Hispanics, and the poor might also subject them to patterns of non-protection and general indifference at the hands of the police and other suburban service providers. For it is generally the pattern in urban America that in everyday dealings with the public, service providers reflect the outlook of the community's dominant social and political classes. Thus, with a logic that mirrors that used by the early urban reformers, many who now resist metropolitan integration argue that election by small constituencies best assures that elected officials will be sensitive to the concerns and demands of those who live in those constituencies. *[The theory of grass-roots democracy.]*

If there is a lesson to be learned from these examples of counter logic and counter trends, it is an obvious one. While metropolitan integration that promotes system access (roads, communication, and the like) will no doubt continue, lifestyle integration will remain a difficult and emotion-fired enterprise. But to gain some further purchase on these lessons, it will be useful now to turn to the legal and political relationships between cities and their states, the units of government which in very large measure control what cities may and may not do.

15. Section 5 of the federal Voting Rights Act requires municipalities in twenty-nine states with substantial minority populations to clear proposed annexations with the U.S. Justice Department for exactly this reason. Since 1971, the Justice Department has objected to 518 proposed annexations out of 35,081 submitted for review (Rusk 1993).

Cities and Their States

The complex relationship between cities and their states is framed by three broad principles of American political life. First is the principle that operates everywhere and at all levels of American government, that policy-making authority must be scattered and dispersed. Behind this dispersal lies a political tradition grounded in fear of concentrating power too narrowly. As Madison said in *Federalist* 47,

> The accumulation of all powers, legislative, executive, and judiciary, in the same hands . . . may justly be pronounced the very definition of tyranny. (1961, 301)

In previous chapters, we surveyed this dispersal of policy authority in cities, noting the use there of separation of powers; the role of administrators in agenda setting, policy framing, and policy implementation; and the important role played by persons in the private sector in framing and implementing policies—especially development policies.

The second broad principle that frames city-state relationships has also been previously noted. Cities are creatures and agents of their state government. As such, they are required to enforce and implement state laws and policies; and all that cities do must be justified legally as stemming from a grant of authority from the state.

The third broad principle is that cities do not have exclusive jurisdiction over their own territory. Each city shares and competes for governing authority with its county and with numerous special-purpose governments.

The upshot of all this is that city governments do not govern merely by carrying out or implementing state policy. Instead, they govern through a complex process that involves pressure-group politics, rural-urban rivalries, and the often difficult business of negotiating, bargaining, and adjudicating with their state government and with the counties and special-purpose governments that surround them. To explicate this process, we look again at the legal principles that bind cities to their states.

Legal Principles of City-State Relationships

When the American Revolution turned colonies into states, the evolving American legal system carried forward the logic and law of the colony. States were deemed to be the effective units of government, and every city within a state was held to be subordinate to that state. As creatures and agents of the state, cities were required by state courts to enforce state laws within the city's domain, and to do nothing to contravene state laws.

As general legal principles, these requirements might seem obvious and straightforward. But few things in law are either obvious or straightforward. Does a city need specific authorization from the state legislature for its every ordinance? Or may a city enact ordinances so long as they do not expressly contravene state law? For example, if state law does not expressly forbid a certain practice (say, a tax on business), can the city enact that tax? For another example, if the state has in place a tax on business, can a city levy an additional tax—or does the state tax preempt all city business taxes?

Alexis de Tocqueville, the great commentator on American democracy, remarked that, in the United States, sooner or later all questions of policy end up before the courts. The courts settle policy cases by applying such general rules as *principal* (the state) and *agent* (the city). But as Supreme Court Justice Oliver Wendell Holmes once noted, general rules do not decide concrete cases. Thus, over the decades, case by case, and state by state, courts have built up an enormous body of case law that decides what cities may and may not do—all within the abstract principle of agency and the related principle that cities are creatures (and agents) of the state.

Dillon's Rule

Something approaching a nationwide doctrine was achieved in the post-Civil War period when a state judge, John Dillon of Iowa, published his treatise, *Commentaries on the Law of Municipal Corporations* (1872). In that treatise, Dillon enunciated his now famous rule[16]:

> It is a general undisputed proposition of law that a municipal corporation can exercise the following powers, and not others: first, those granted in express words; second, those necessarily or fairly implied in or incident to the powers expressly granted; third, those essential to the . . . purposes of the [municipal] corporation—not simply convenient, but indispensable. Any fair, reasonable, substantial doubt concerning the existence of power is [to be] resolved against the corporation and the power denied. (Dillon 1911, 448)

In 1923, the U.S. Supreme Court gave approval (and standing in Federal Law) to Dillon's Rule:

> The city is a political subdivision of the state, created as a convenient agency . . . for the state. . . . The state, therefore, may at its pleasure, modify or withdraw all such powers [as it gave to the city] . . . and [even] destroy [the city]. . . . In these respects, the state is supreme. (*Trenton v. New Jersey*, 262 US 182)

16. See Buckwalter (1982) for a further discussion of Dillon's Rule.

257

Dillon's Rule still stands, more or less, as the law in every state, but legal doctrine is also bound up in practical considerations. States have rarely abolished cities, and rarely have they attempted to take over the day-to-day administration of cities. State legislatures, however, have frequently interposed in financial matters, in granting franchises, and in creating special-purpose governments. Over the years since Dillon, however, the rigidity of his rule has been softened (Grumm and Murphy 1974). A brief historical sketch will outline this softening and note its connection to the changing nature of urban-rural conflict.

A Bold and Meddlesome Hand

The New York legislature . . . passed more laws for New York [City] . . . in the three years from 1867 to 1870 than Parliament passed for all of the cities in the United Kingdom from 1835 to 1885; in the year 1870, thirty-nine state laws were passed for the city of Brooklyn alone. Jersey City's charter was amended by state action ninety-one times between 1837 and 1875.

Charles Glabb and Theodore Brown, *A History of Urban America*, p. 163

In the nineteenth and early twentieth centuries, it was the practice of state legislatures to play a bold hand with their cities. Sometimes that hand was played in helpful and benign ways—helping cities to solve problems that lay beyond their territorial limits. For example, in 1905, the New York Legislature created a special district, the City of New York Board of Water Supply, which enabled the board to acquire a chain of water reservoirs and an aqueduct system reaching to the Catskill mountains and the Delaware River, thus ensuring a water supply for New York. And following the devastating hurricane of 1900 in Galveston, Texas (one-sixth of its population drowned; one-third of the city's property destroyed), the Texas legislature abolished Galveston's government and set in its place a commission of five businessmen to manage the city's government and take charge of its physical reconstruction. At other times, state legislatures have intervened in city government out of concern for the corruption of big-city politics. For example, the legislature of Missouri long ago gave the governor power to appoint the commissioner of police for St. Louis.

At still other times, it was corruption in the state legislature itself that produced state intervention in city governance. Such was especially the case where fortunes were to be made in granting franchises to operate streetcar lines. For example, in Illinois (in 1895) Charles Yerkes, the streetcar baron of Chicago, bribed members of the legislature to grant him a ninety-nine-year monopoly over Chicago's streetcars, and offered the governor a half-million dollars to sign the "eternal monopoly" into law. When the governor rejected the bribe and vetoed the bill, Yerkes returned to the legislature, this time bribing members to enact a new law that returned franchise-granting powers to the Chicago City Council—whose members Yerkes had correctly surmised were not beyond his powers of cash persuasion (Andrews 1946).

Rural-Urban Conflict

But over the years, the cultural rivalry between rural and urban America has played a larger role than either money or helpfulness in legislative interference with cities. All through the nineteenth and the first half of the twentieth century, state legislatures everywhere were dominated by representatives from rural areas. And almost until the present, those from rural areas tended to see cities (especially big cities) as the vortex of foreign and evil ways. Thus, there was present in the legislature—sometimes as undertone and sometimes overt—a rural-urban lifestyle conflict. And even in those states where city populations had become a majority in the state (New York, Illinois, Pennsylvania), rural representatives held power in the legislature by refusing to reapportion and redistrict their state according to population.[17]

Lifestyle conflict between rural and urban America has had many dimensions. In recent decades, the conflict has taken on overtones of race: blacks, black-Hispanics, and Asians in central cities versus rural and suburban whites elsewhere. A half-century ago, the conflict turned on modes of livelihood (agriculture versus commerce and industry), on religion, on the recency of immigrant status, and on the ethnic identity of that immigrant status. As earlier chapters point out, all four dimensions of the conflict were interwoven in the nineteenth century, when cities were home to vast numbers of European immigrants. It was then that livelihood differences were exacerbated by religious and ethnic differences (native-born Protestants residing predominantly in the countryside, more recently arrived Catholics and Jews residing predominantly in the city).

But religious differences between rural and urban America have been more subtle and more profound than can be indicated by distinguishing merely among Protestants, Catholics and Jews. John Buenker (1973, 167) sees the religious dimension of rural-urban conflict as a cultural struggle sometimes involving "almost incompatible world views." Cities have been home to what is sometimes called the *ritualistic tradition* in religion. For Roman Catholics,

---

17. A celebrated case, *Colegrove v. Green* (328 US 549, 1946) had the U.S. Supreme Court upholding the Illinois legislature's refusal to redistrict, saying that redistricting was a political matter, in which (given the principle of separation of powers) the courts ought not intervene. At the time of the suit, the Illinois legislature had not reapportioned its house of representatives for fifty years. The Chicago area had a preponderant majority of the state's population but only a minority of seats in the Illinois House. But in 1962, this practice of malapportionment came to an end. The Supreme Court reversed the Colegrove case and mandated that the Fourteenth Amendment required that state legislatures adhere to the principles of equal representation and one person, one vote (*Baker v. Carr*, 369 US 186).

> the commandments of God and the Church serve . . . as guides to moral
> conduct. . . . The key . . . in the use of all fleshy pleasure . . . [is] modera-
> tion, and defect . . . condemned . . . [as much] as excess . . . [Q]uestions of
> morality . . . [are thus] left to the individual conscience, with the Church
> as the only guide.

Jews, notes Buenker, closely resemble "the ritualists in their attitudes and practices." Man had it within him to descend to great evil, "but he was not inherently bad" (Buenker 1973, 169).

Contrast, then, these views with an outlook prevalent in rural America.
Traditionally, the countryside has been home to pietistic religions. Rejecting a
prescribed ritual, pietists tend to stress the requirement of personal conversion
(as opposed to membership at birth) and the individual is

> much more on his own against evil in the world and hence much more
> anxious to eradicate all potential barriers to his own and his neighbor's sal-
> vation. . . . [T]he only way he . . . [can] do that is to purge the world of
> evil. (Buenker 1973, 167)

With these ideas in mind, it becomes perhaps easier to understand the
preoccupation of earlier, rurally-dominated state legislatures with perceived
misconduct and sinfulness in big cities and to understand one aspect of the
origins of legislative interference in city government.

Home Rule

Politics (as the old saying goes) breeds strange bedfellows. Consider, in the
early decades of this century, the alliance between urban Progressives and rural
state legislators. Both wanted to clean up the mess of city politics. And both
perceived the immigrants to have a hand in that mess. Progressives wanted to
bring worthwhile citizens into city politics—a goal generally approved by legislative moralists. But to make the efforts of what Lord Bryce had called "the
better class" effective and rewarding, Progressives also proposed that cities be
given a greater measure of control over their own affairs.

As Frank Goodnow, one of the early leaders of the Home Rule
Movement, put it,

> the fact that a city is an organization for the satisfaction of local needs
> makes it necessary that its actions be determined by local considerations. To
> this end, it must have large local powers. (Quoted in Glaab and Brown
> 1976, 175; also see Goodnow 1895.)

The home rule proponents had an early success in a revision of the Missouri
constitution in 1875 and still more success during the high tide of

Progressivism. Since then, about half the states have given home rule to their cities. Today about two-thirds of all cities with a population of 200,000 or more are beneficiaries of some form of home rule. Each state, of course, has its own version of home rule. The National Municipal League (in an effort to standardize these fifty versions) offers a model and definition for home rule that is proposed for incorporation in every state constitution:

> A . . . city may exercise any legislative power or perform any function which is not denied to it by its charter, is not denied to . . . cities generally, or to . . . cities of its class, and is within such limitations as the legislature may establish by general law.[18]

But despite its name, home rule is not *complete* home rule. Cities are never to be free from state control. (Otherwise, they would be separate state governments—for example, "The State of the City of New York.") No city may pass laws that contravene state law or general state policy. Essentially, what home rule accomplishes is a softening of Dillon's Rule in some or all the following ways.

1. When they achieve some specified population size, cities may vote to choose among alternate forms of city government (for example, a council-manager form instead of mayor-council form).
2. In choosing an alternate form of government, cities are to receive from the state a prepackaged charter (a home rule charter) whose provisions usually include concentration rather than dispersal of executive authority (the mayor or manager being given power to appoint and remove heads of major service-delivery departments). The package charter also usually provides for a small rather than a large city council—usually elected at large.
3. By declaring itself to be a home rule state, the state constitution (and legislative statutes) serves notice to courts and judges that doubtful cases concerning the extent of a city's authority are to be resolved in the city's favor (in effect stating that the severity of Dillon's Rule is no longer to be in force).

But when all home rule reforms are said and done, doubtful situations will continue to arise and to find their way to the courts. Home rule charters are an attempt to distinguish the general powers of the state from matters that are of purely local concern, but such distinctions are never fast and firm. Sooner or later, they will require the intervention of the courts.

18. The National Municipal League, *The Model State Constitution*, Sec. 8.02. See also Bender (1983).

What does a court do when it faces a dispute about local control of traffic on a state highway which runs through the middle of a city? Is that a local matter because the street is in the city, or a state matter because it concerns a state highway? Are the working hours and conditions of local employees a matter of 'municipal affairs' or does the state's power over labor and public employment supersede the powers of the city? (Lockard 1963, 124)

And so, home rule or no, cities remain in the state and of the state. How then is their relationship with the state carried forward? How do cities deal with their states?

Cities and States: Mandates, Politics, and Bargaining

Cities deal with their states—and states with their cities—through complex arrangements that move along multiple pathways, including cooperation, bargaining, mandates, incentives, and disincentives. The circumstances under which these activities take place are considerably different than they were thirty or forty years ago. Some degree of rural–urban conflict continues in the state legislature, but it has been moderated considerably by at least three sets of social forces. First, television, the two-car family, and fast roads have made urban life much more accessible to those living in rural areas. The city is no longer a place to be experienced vicariously, through books and sermons from the pulpit. Second, urban dwellers today are less concentrated in big cities than they were fifty or seventy-five years ago. Most urban dwellers today live in the suburbs, and suburbs are perceived by rural legislators as having lifestyles congenial to their own and, accordingly, deserving of respectful legislative treatment. And third, state legislatures are no longer as dominated by rural representatives as they once were. (The U.S. Supreme Court has mandated periodic redistricting of state legislatures to conform to the one person, one vote principles.[19]) Accordingly, cities and states now deal with each other along the lines described below.

Mandates

As state governments attempt to wrestle with the issues and problems of contemporary life, they often resort to mandates (orders to cities that they carry out designated tasks and perform specified functions). For example, a state legislature may require all cities of a certain population (say 100,000 or

19. *Baker v. Carr* (see note 17). Periodic redistricting to reflect population shifts means that sparsely populated rural areas will have fewer legislators than densely populated urban and suburban areas.

more) to add emergency medical services to fire department duties—along with equipment for such services. Or, for another example, the legislature may require all cities to carry personal injury insurance to cover accidents on city playgrounds. Or, for still another example, the legislature (responding to what it perceives to be a decline in patriotism) may mandate that all schools offer instruction in the American system of government. Sometimes, the legislature will appropriate funds to assist cities in meeting the mandate. Frequently, it does not—leaving it to each city to provide the necessary funding.[20]

Court decisions are another form of mandate. And given the blurred boundaries between state and local matters, every city (it is often said) is either preparing to defend some ordinance in court, or is in the process of doing so, or has just finished doing so.

The City as Lobbyist: Legislative Policy Formation

Urban representatives elected to the state legislature are constantly at work lobbying for—or lobbying to defeat—proposed state laws. This is especially true when one or more cities are considering a local policy that is new or that departs from established precedent. For example, many cities now levy some form of tax on income, on theater admissions, and/or on restaurant dining. But will a proposed tax on hotel rooms stand up in court when challenged by hotel owners?[21] One way of assuring the legality of the new tax is to get the legislature to add hotel-bed taxes to the list of taxes it permits cities to levy.

Given the fact that city administrative personnel usually have ties to professional associations and to their counterpart administrators in other cities, it is quite usual for them to join in statewide organizations: the state's mayors' association, the state association of city health workers, the state police chiefs' association, the state association of city police, the state association of city treasurers and accountants, and so on. Thus, as bills affecting their areas of administrative and professional competence move through the legislature, it is also quite usual for spokespersons for a relevant professional association to appear before the legislature seeking to mold and shape the proposed legislation (in other words, to work as lobbyists on the cities' behalf.)

20. Some states have attempted to restrict the legislature's ability to pass legislation that requires municipal expenditures. The Alabama state constitution, for example, was amended in 1988 to require that municipalities be given at least one year to plan for these added expenditures. Unfunded federal mandates are discussed in chapter 12.

21. Although not a tax per se, during the 1980s Seattle developed a zoning policy requiring developers who demolished downtown housing stock to replace it elsewhere. But in *San Telmo Associates v. City of Seattle*, the Washington Supreme Court ruled that this amounted to a tax that the city had no authority to levy (Collins et al. 1991).

The City as Lobbyist: Policy Implementation

More and more, state legislatures pass laws that set forth general policy goals, leaving it to city administrators to implement the laws through the development of local standards and procedures. Thus, city officials engage in constant interaction with state administrators charged with the task of transforming policy goals into policy action. In doing so, city officials work to bring state policy into accord with city goals. For example, city street engineers negotiate with state highway officials in establishing routes for new roads. City water officials work with state environmental protection agents to establish water purification procedures. Quite often city officials negotiate and bargain with state officials over the standards that will be used to establish the quality of city water. City health officials confer with state officials on the vaccines to be used in school inoculation programs. And city officials frequently lobby state officials to get them to change implementation rules and procedures.

Variations on this theme of city-state relations are extensive. But the main point is this: Cities are creatures of their state, but not passive or supine creatures. They follow state laws and policy directives, but they do so only after they have had full play in attempting to shape those laws and directives. City administrators and elected officials constitute an informal interest group (or groups) that works at influencing the state legislature. City administrators bargain and negotiate with state officials in the implementation of state laws. Urban representatives are in the legislature. They form coalitions there, and they lobby their fellow representatives to pass legislation that will benefit the cities. City officials are charged with enforcing state laws. They do so, and in the process often bend and interpret those laws to suit city purposes. And city voters have an important voice in the outcome of state elections. Their votes help decide who will be elected to state offices—governor, treasurer, judges of the state supreme court, and so on. Thus, the web of urban politics is not confined merely to politics in the city. It is politics that extends into the operation of state government as well.

An Even Larger Web

City voters also have a powerful say in the outcome of national elections. As we turn next to consider the relationship between cities and the national government, it will be useful to keep in mind the fact that cities are well represented in Congress. Some 269 members of the House of Representatives (62 percent) come from predominantly (i.e., two-thirds) urban districts, and 90 senators come from states where the urban population is in the majority. As the nation has grown more urbanized, the president has come to depend more and more for his election on voters from the cities. From the 1930s until about 1960, it was the big, central cities that were critical to his election. In 1950, the suburbs contained about 25 percent of the U.S. population, and in 1960, 33 percent. Today, however, approximately half of the American population lives in suburbs. Accordingly, it is now the suburbs that have become critical to presidential elections.

We turn now to exploring the extended web: city-national government interactions.

From the Shelton, chloride print, 1935, 24.1 x 29.2 cm
Alfred Stieglitz Collection, 1949.786.
Photograph © 1996, The Art Institute of Chicago. All Rights Reserved.

Nationwide thinking, nationwide planning, and nationwide action are the three great essentials to prevent nationwide crises for future generations to struggle through.

Franklin D. Roosevelt, Speech, New York, April 25, 1936

We will neglect our cities to our peril, for in neglecting them we neglect the nation.

John F. Kennedy, Message to Congress, January 30, 1962

CHAPTER **12**

Cities and the
National Government

Cities and the Nation

For the student of politics, few subjects are more intriguing than the ways in which a political system changes or the ways in which political practice diverges from formal constitutional pronouncements.

The United States Constitution is the organizing framework of our system of government. It sets forth and defines the authority of the national government. By reference and implication, it also defines the authority of the states. This division of authority between central government and constituent states is the essence of federalism—an arrangement whereby two independent governments occupy the same territory. Better said, federalism is an arrangement whereby the central government and constituent states are each assigned a specified set of powers and authority (Riker 1964, Leach 1970, Beer 1993).

In the American federal system, the states came first. Their union was provided for in the Constitution ("We the People of the United States . . ."). In the Constitution, the national government is given powers that have mainly to do with commerce, trade, and national defense. By implication (and the words of the Tenth Amendment) the states retain the power to do everything else—to regulate matters pertaining to health, welfare, morals, public safety, and public convenience. In short, the states retain the power to regulate matters pertaining to the affairs of everyday life: marriage, the family, crime and criminality, business transactions and employment, ownership of property, public education, and proper moral conduct.

In the Constitution, no mention is made of cities. The Constitution ignores them. Presumably, as subdivisions and agents of their states, they are part of their state's constitutionally assigned governmental authority. Strictly and formally speaking, they are not connected to the national government. And from the adoption of the Constitution in 1789 to about half a century ago, the national government had almost no direct dealings with cities. Then, in the 1930s, an explosion of relationships took place. Without formal amendments to the Constitution, the old pattern of federalism was shunted aside to make way for a new federalism that blurred the distinction between national powers and states' powers. Under this new federalism, the national government would henceforth take responsibility for solving all the major problems confronting our society—including the problems of American cities.

Most great governmental changes are powered by the engine of crisis, both real and perceived. And the crisis that hoisted the new federalism into place was the Great Depression which had begun in October 1929. The faltering economy, with its strangled productivity, widespread poverty, and millions of unemployed could not be dealt with by state governments. Their resources were not adequate. More important, the United States was an integrated economic system—only the national government would have the resources and the geographic jurisdiction to deal with the entirety of the nation's economic system. By congressional action and Supreme Court consent, a new style of federalism displaced the old dual federalism.

Under this new federalism, the national government would take responsibility for managing the economy. It would use its taxing and spending powers to stimulate industrial productivity, regulate conditions of employment, and give welfare and other aid to the poor (Herson 1990, Beer 1993). The upshot of the new federalism was that, henceforth, the national government and its policies would be a visible presence in the policies and politics of American cities.

The New and Newer Federalism

The new federalism has been a constantly changing concept. The idea of the *new* has a powerful hold on the American political imagination, and every president since Franklin Roosevelt has proclaimed his version of a new federalism. As a rule, Democratic presidents have urged an increased measure of national government policy initiatives, while Republican presidents have urged that the national government give power and policy-making responsibility back to the states. And true to what was begun under Roosevelt, whichever version of a new federalism has been enacted in the intervening years, it is the national government that has been the initiating center of major policy programs, including, of course, urban programs. From Roosevelt to Lyndon Johnson, the powers of the national government almost always expanded, drawing the cities more and more into the federal web. Under the Republican presidencies of Nixon, Ford, Reagan, and Bush, attempts were made (especially through federal block grant programs) to return urban policy initiatives to the states. But as the 1990s spin to a close, it has been Democrat Bill Clinton proposing that the states be given increasing policy initiative. (For a delineation of the new federalism under President Nixon, see Reagan 1972; for its meaning under President Reagan, see Benton 1985; and for Carter and Bush, see Ames et al. 1992.)

Under the new federalism, none of the national government's programs has been self-accomplishing or self-enforcing. All require administrative implementation. They thus bring a large corps of federal administrators into direct contact with state and local officials; for instance, the Department of Housing and Urban Development (HUD) employs over thirteen thousand people, and the Department of Education employs twenty thousand. As a consequence, the new federalism is marked by a high degree of interaction among administrative personnel at all levels of government: national, state, county, and city. The pattern of their interaction is comparable to that between city and state administrators—cooperating, bargaining, compromising, and ultimately deciding on the rules and procedures that transform policy into the specifics of governmental action. To understand this interaction we note some of its components.

Fiscal interdependence. None of the new federalism's programs is self-supporting. Each requires a considerable outlay of money. One consequence is the rise of government spending at every level of government. Another consequence is the very great dependence of cities and states on federal money. Cities and states continue to raise their own revenues, but a large percentage of the (total) money they spend comes from the national government.

The two principal vehicles by which federal funds have been given to cities and states are the grant-in-aid (also called the categorical grant) and the block grant. The usual arrangement for a grant-in-aid is that the national government contributes the greater portion of funds, with states and/or cities contributing some matching percentage of the money—say, 80 percent to 90 percent coming from the federal government, with cities or states contributing the rest. The usual arrangements for a block grant are as follows: Existing categorical grants are bundled together rather than funded separately, and the bundle is apportioned to the states (accordant to some legislative formula) to be implemented, usually in keeping with each state's priorities (but subject to such guidelines as Congress and the president may lay upon the grant).

Policy interdependence. In grant-in-aid programs, Congress not only specifies the purpose for which receiving governments are to spend the money ("a grant in aid of . . ."), but it often specifies the conditions that are to be part of the grant. (In politics, as in country dances, he who pays the fiddler gets to call the tune.) In this way, the national government not only promotes a specific policy, but it can also implement vast and sweeping social programs. To illustrate, Congress has used grants-in-aid to enable cities to build low-income housing. In accepting such grants, cities are required to enforce a federal regulation that stipulates that all building construction using federal money shall pay prevailing union wages; that no person or corporation or governmental agency receiving federal money may discriminate in its hiring practices; that every federally supported housing project must use a specified tenant-income formula in admitting occupants; and that it must be located in such fashion as to contribute to citywide racial integration.[1]

The grant-in-aid thus works to draw cities and states into the federal web in both a direct and indirect way—direct in the sense of enlisting city and state into serving designated categories of federal programs (road construction, welfare assistance, low-income housing, airport improvements, and hundreds of others) and indirect in the sense that still other and broader social programs (e.g., affirmative action) can be wrapped around the categorical grant (Sundquist 1969, Berkeley and Fox 1978, Hale and Palley 1981; for liberal and conservative perspective of these grants, see Wright 1968 and Kantor 1988).

In contrast, a block grant would likely gather a number of related grants together under a single umbrella, for instance, a program to improve public safety equipment used by municipal police departments. Once the funds were distributed to the states and passed on to the cities, municipal officials would decide whether to use the money to buy new police cars, communication equipment, or perhaps computers. But even under block grant dispensation, the city would still be required to stand in conformity with all applicable federal rules and regulations.

Policy spillovers. Just as cities are drawn into the federal web by grants, they are pulled there even more forcefully by national programs that deal with national defense and the management of the nation's economy. In its attempts to maintain a sound economy, the national government makes use of two techniques and strategies: fiscal and monetary controls. Fiscal controls involve taxing and spending for what are sometimes called countercyclical purposes: taxing and spending to counter (and reverse) economic cycles. In times of declining productivity and underemployment, the national government has

---

1. Some cities have found these requirements so restrictive that they have opted to do without federally funded housing developments. Other cities have spent considerable time and effort—usually to no avail—attempting to contravene these requirements.

increased its purchases of goods and services, for example, those connected with national defense,[2] and it has appropriated money for major construction projects, including highways, airports, river and flood control, and public housing. Every city has been affected by countercyclical spending projects. The greatest of these has been the interstate highway system, (launched in the 1950s, it is often said to be the greatest public works project since the Egyptian pyramids), whose urban throughways and ring roads have completely changed land-use and development patterns in every metropolitan area in the nation.

The national government (through its Federal Reserve Board) exercises monetary controls by expanding and contracting the nation's money supply and raising and lowering the interest rates banks charge for lending money. The prevailing interest rate affects the ability of cities to borrow money by issuing bonds, and it also has a decisive effect on the home and commercial building industry—building new homes, refurbishing old houses, and building factories and office towers. In this way, the national government's control over the money supply and interest rates powerfully affects the physical structure of cities. The growth and decline of a city's central business district (CBD), its network of factories, the spread of its suburban ring, and its overall physical form are all directly and intimately affected by the national government's changes in monetary policy.

But for overall effect on cities, nothing compares with a single provision of the national tax code: permitting homeowners and real estate financiers a tax deduction for interest paid on borrowed money. This tax provision is of enormous importance to the middle class. (Some would say it creates and defines the American middle class.) With it, the middle class has been assisted in buying single-family homes, and in so doing, has spread residential neighborhoods to the borders of the city and, leapfrogging the city, has created the urbanized metropolitan area. Needless to say, this same tax provision has also fueled the engines of shopping mall construction, the building of suburban business parks, and the building of office towers in the CBD. It is only a slight exaggeration to say that in the past half century, every building in the city and around the city has been the beneficiary of federal tax policy.[3]

---

2. Cities such as Houston, Seattle, Huntsville, and St. Louis that are heavily dependent on the space, defense, and aircraft industries have been very directly affected by federal spending: A cutback in defense orders brings a local but acute economic depression. Houston and Dallas are also very much affected by federal policy with respect to oil (e.g., search and depletion allowances, gas taxes, and above all, the price and availability of oil on the international market).

3. In addition to tax benefits for money as interest on loans, federal tax policy affects urban development in other important ways. For example, most interest paid on money borrowed by cities and states (i.e., interest on state and municipal general revenue bonds) is free of federal income tax. As another example, commercial real estate is permitted a tax write-down (i.e., for tax purposes and federal tax payment, the value of the property can be depreciated over a considerable number of years). As may be anticipated, the financial benefits extended by U.S. tax policies to homeowners, real estate developers, and bond buyers is part of the larger argument concerning fair shares and social equity. Is the mid-

The New Deal and the New Urban Politics

In the economic turmoil of the 1930s, voters behaved as they have always behaved in bad times. They voted the party in power out of office. From the Civil War onward (with an occasional interregnum) the Republican party dominated both Congress and the presidency. But in the election of 1932, Franklin Roosevelt and a Democratic Congress were swept into office by an electoral landslide. And ever since that election, all candidates for the presidency have campaigned as did Roosevelt on promises to guard the national economy and set to rights all the major problems that beset the country. High on the list are the problems of urban America.

The election of 1932 thus signaled the importance to national elections of the urban vote. Given the workings of the Electoral College (with a majority of each state's voters awarding that state's entire Electoral College vote to the majority candidate—winner take all), the urban voter is crucial to a presidential candidate's capturing a majority in the Electoral College. Accordingly, every presidential candidate in the past half century has been mindful of the need to court the urban voter and address the nation's urban problems. Those who become presidents thus stand ready to put urban problems fairly high on their policy agenda. In doing so, they set in motion the wheels of urban policymaking in Congress. And equally important, they animate the hundreds of interest groups and thousands of lobbyists who seek to advance their own definitions of urban needs and their own visions of urban public interest.

National Policy and Interest Groups

As federal programs have grown and developed, one consequence has been the attending growth of interest groups seeking to benefit from these programs. These interest groups are the city-based lobbies seeking tax benefits for their members, trying to head off legislation harmful to their members, working to get those who implement federal policy to shape that policy so as to benefit their members.

Many interest groups that are vigorously active today were founded long before the 1930s ushered in an explosion of federal programs. But as that decade got underway, every interest group with hopes of influencing national legislation in any significant way expanded its Washington staff and considered moving its headquarters there to be near the source of money and power.

---

dle class deserving of what is, in effect, financial assistance, while those who cannot afford to buy a house receive nothing? Are municipal bonds a tax haven for the rich, while money in the bank accounts of the less well-off remains a source for taxation? Does tax depreciation for commercial property encourage needless office-tower building and the proliferation of endless suburban shopping malls—all the while leaving central cities to cope with their consequences?

Several interest groups deserve special mention for their roles in influencing the course of national urban programs over the past half century: the National Municipal League, the International City Management Association, the United States Chamber of Commerce, the National Association of Real Estate Boards, the Outdoor Contractors Association, the American Federation of Labor-Congress of Industrial Organizations, the Mortgage Bankers Association, the United States Savings and Loan League.

These groups—and hundreds like them—also deserve special mention for their roles as spokespersons for the ideologies that dominate our political system and our political thinking. For instance, interest groups that represent realtors, bankers, builders, and business persons are powerful voices in support of the free market and an unregulated economy. Traditionally, they have resisted public housing for low-income families. On the other side of the policy coin, such housing projects are usually supported by central-city officials and economic liberals (union spokespersons, for example, and leaders of associations for welfare rights).

But to better understand present-day federalism and the connection between cities and the national government as well as the connection between federal programs and interest groups, another backward glance is in order, a brief canvass of a half century of federal urban programs. In the more than half century since Franklin Roosevelt first took office, the national government has enacted several hundred programs that affect the nation's cities. Among those with greatest impact are programs (and policies) dealing with jobs, home mortgages, low-rent housing, slum clearance, highway construction, the amelioration of poverty, and grants for the support of city services. Because important federal programs are extensive in scope and costs, they may begin under one president but not reach their apogee until the administration of another. Nevertheless, some sense of chronology is useful, and for this reason federal urban programs will be outlined by presidential tenure.

Roosevelt and the New Deal[4]

Jobs and Mortgages

In 1932, with the country battered by business failures, President Roosevelt and a cooperative Congress inaugurated the programs that were to constitute the New Deal. Their purpose was to get the economy moving upward and to lessen joblessness and its resulting poverty. The programs that had the greatest

---

4. Histories of Roosevelt and his New Deal are extensive. Of general importance to the present discussion are Schlesinger (1959), Leuchtenburg (1963), and Goldman (1956). Of more specific relevance are Mollenkopf (1983), Jackson (1985), Warner (1972), and Gelfand (1975).

effect on cities were not city programs as such, but programs to help those who lived in cities. Officials of two newly created government agencies, the Works Progress Administration (WPA) and the Public Works Administration (PWA),[5] worked hand-in-glove with city and state officials to plan and build streets, bridges, sewers, and parks, along with such urban amenities as bus-stop shelters, public drinking fountains, and recreational facilities. Their primary purpose was to give jobs to the unemployed; but the consequences were to leave in policymakers' memory the idea that the government can serve as employer of last resort and that the employed poor—who are given "workfare not welfare"—can be put to work improving the quality of urban life. (This memory was to come to life again in the Comprehensive Employment and Training Act of 1973—CETA; and the idea of "workfare not welfare" has moved in waves through periodic considerations of welfare reform, including the 1996 Welfare Reform Act.)

A second of the national government's indirect aids to cities was the National Housing Act of 1934. The act created the Federal Housing Administration (FHA) and the Federal Savings and Loan Insurance Corporation (FSLIC). Both were designed to bring life to the then-moribund house building industry and to stop the tide of bank foreclosures on family homes. Neither act was intended to bring government into competition with the mortgage banking industry. Instead, private mortgage banking was to be assisted by the government, and through that assistance, the homeowner and buyer were to benefit. Then, as now, the issue of government intrusion into the marketplace was the occasion for heated ideological debate. And then, as now, the usual resolution was to have government assist the private sector, not supplant it.

The FSLIC offered government insurance for savings accounts, and was thus intended to coax private savings out from under the mattress and into savings and loan associations; those corporations would then use this money to make home mortgages. In addition, the FHA served as insurer for mortgage lenders. The rationale for the FHA was simple. With government insurance against loss, lenders would have incentive to make loans available, would require a smaller down payment, and would charge less interest. Borrowers would thus have an incentive to buy new homes, refinance existing mortgages, and restore and repair old homes. And jobs in the building industry would expand, more persons would be able to afford homes, older homes would be renovated, and cities would be spared the strain of spreading slums.

Much of the FHA program worked as planned, and the FHA and FSLIC programs remain today the backbone of the mortgage and home-

5. It was the New Deal that popularized the practice of naming government agencies using initials and acronyms.

building industries.[6] But as with most government programs, the law of unanticipated consequences also took its toll. FHA mortgages have done relatively little to improve inner-city housing, and the net effect of FHA has been to support and intensify the segregation of urban blacks and the poor. The poor, after all, do not buy homes. They are apartment dwellers, and FHA lenders have consistently shown preference for single-family homes over apartment buildings. What is more, FHA administrators have tended to share the ideological orientations of those with whom they work most closely, the banking and real estate industries. Until quite recently, that orientation was not one to champion racial integration. Thus, FHA mortgage money was an important factor in the racially white suburban explosion of the 1950s, as upwardly mobile white families used that money to make house dreams come true (Warner 1972).

Housing for the Poor

If there is a dominant American view on housing for the poor it is probably captured by the phrase "filter down." In this view, housing for the poor is best provided by the private sector of the economy. The poor take the housing they can afford, and as persons rise on the economic scale, they move from less desirable to more desirable housing—making available what they have vacated to those on lower rungs of the economic ladder (in short, allowing better housing to filter down to the poor).

Filter-down housing has been the traditional arrangement in American cities; and the principle underlying filter-down housing has been largely responsible for the historic movement of new-home construction outward from the city center. For economic Liberals, filter-down is not a satisfactory policy position. *[The theory of ideology.]* Dilapidated housing (Liberals argue) should not be all that is available for the poor. A concern for equality of outcomes requires that the government help provide good housing for the poor.

Economic Conservatives take a different view. Government works best (they argue) when it does not compete with private industry. If the poor are to be assisted to better housing, government ought to stimulate the overall economy so that more jobs become available to the poor. Over time, Conservatives continue, the poor will move up the economic ladder and buy housing suitable to their improved economic status.

---

6. Today, several federal agencies insure home loans, accounting for $317 billion in mortgages on 8 million homes in 1993. Many families who in pre-FHA days might never have been able to afford home ownership have acquired homes of their own. FHA's mortgage practices have also created industry-wide standards. Thus, today's mortgages often run thirty and thirty-five years (compared with the ten-year mortgage common in the 1920s).

275

The New Deal helped turn liberal sentiments into policy, and a Housing Division was established within the Public Works Administration to build low-cost, low-rent housing for the poor. As might be anticipated, spokespersons for the building, banking, and real estate industries objected strenuously,[7] and though the PWA built relatively few low-income apartment buildings, precedent was established for later housing programs (Jackson 1985). Equally important, the PWA housing ventures set into place many of the implementation practices now common in state-city-federal programs. For example, state governments created local housing authorities (special-purpose governments that could accept federal grants for purposes of building low-rent housing), and these local housing authorities were authorized to operate under principles of state sovereignty for purposes of acquiring building sites. (Thus clothed with state sovereignty, the local housing authority could use the state's power of eminent domain to condemn existing buildings and force their sale to the housing authority so as to provide building sites for new construction.)

The 1937 Public Housing Act established the United States Housing Authority (USHA). The USHA was empowered to make long-term loans (as it turned out, sixty-year, low-interest loans totaling upwards of $800 million) to local authorities for the construction of low-rent housing. States and localities, in turn, were to become partners in the projects by contributing operating and maintenance costs (over time, the federal government used its own funds for these costs), with local officials—operating under federal guidelines—setting rents and standards for tenancy.

All in all, the USHA and its successor agencies have constructed nearly 4.5 million low-rent housing units. How shall this effort be judged? Much depends on one's angle of vision, and on the ideology which focuses that vision. Judged by their numbers, national housing ventures, with state and local cooperation, would be pronounced a considerable success. But low-rent housing projects are not judged by numbers alone. They are also judged according to one's vision of the good society and government's responsibility for that good society.

With lofty rhetoric, the 1949 Housing Act spoke of "a decent home and a suitable living environment for every American family." No government program has ever even remotely approached that goal. And a significant portion of the low-rent housing that has been built has been plagued by serious problems: tenant destructiveness, inept and incompetent management, general disrepair, and tenant crime—gang wars and shootings, drug-dealing, burglary,

7. In its original formulation, public housing was designed for the working poor. But in sharp contrast to this conception of housing for the working class, real estate interests wanted public housing to be used only for the poorest families; they were concerned about the effects of government competition within the private home buyer and rental markets, and they used their considerable influence to steer public housing in this direction (Atlas and Dreier 1992).

and personal assaults, with the poor victimizing the poor. For liberal critics of public housing, such problems are understandable and foretold. Listen, for example, to Sam Bass Warner, Jr. (1972, 239):

> Since the goal of . . . a "decent home and a suitable living environment for every American family" has never been popularly accepted as a right of citizenship either by the victimized poor or the fearful affluent, a terrible incubus of philanthropy has plagued public housing and steadily brings on its cycles of sickness. With public housing perceived as a burden and an expression of charity rather than a right of citizenship . . . both local and federal governments have consistently scrimped, saved, and limited the program.

The costs of site acquisition, when combined with the resistance of middle-class neighborhoods to the "intrusion" of public housing, almost always means that public housing has been set inside former slum territory. And at least in its early days, low-rent housing was massive—high-rise apartment buildings, squarely set on "concrete lawns."

These, of course, are serious issues and *problems*, and they became dramatically visible in 1972 when one of the largest public housing projects, Pruitt-Igoe in St. Louis, was dynamited by housing authority order. Thirty-three eleven-story buildings (containing twenty-seven hundred apartments) crumbled into smoke and dust—as television cameras whirred—what had been built only twenty years earlier as the showcase of American public housing and was pronounced by a conservative commentator as a "graveyard of good intentions" (Glazer 1967).

Overall, the slash of conservative criticism of public housing has a familiar ideological edge. As many conservatives would put it:

> Buildings don't make slums. People do. To take slum dwellers and put them in new buildings is only to set in motion—all over again—the process that starts slums. Instead of building public housing for the poor, let the filter-down process work. The poor will be better assisted by rent subsidies. And they can use those subsidies in the private market. Landlords will have incentive to keep their buildings in repair. Destructive tenants can be removed. And the poor—instead of suffering the stigma of living in public housing—might take better care of where they live.[8]

---

8. Milton Friedman, one of our most distinguished (and conservative) economists, argues for a system of rent vouchers to replace public housing. Qualified poor are to be given publicly-paid-for rent vouchers which they may then use as rent payment (full or partial, depending on their needs, desires, and abilities) in privately owned housing. With rent vouchers, the poor will escape the stigma and isolation of public housing, landlords will make a profit and thus be encouraged to maintain their buildings, and in the long run (it is asserted), the costs to taxpayers will be far less than is the case with public housing (Friedman and Friedman 1981). This approach has been adopted by the Department of Housing and Urban Development as part of its long-range plan during the 1990s.

Liberals are far from persuaded.

> The best kept secret about public housing is that most of it actually pro-
> vides decent, affordable housing to many people. Properly run, it remains
> one of the best options for housing the poor. There are about 1.3 mil-
> lion public housing apartments and about 800,000 families on the wait-
> ing lists of the nation's 3,060 local housing authorities. (Atlas and Dreier
> 1992, 75)

The Truman Presidency

New government programs are rarely new. They usually depend for inspiration and legitimacy on programs previously established. New programs build
on the old by layering new purposes on old programs and by altering their
scope. And if the old program is one that engendered fierce ideological
debate, the new program will usually carry the scars of those old debates. Such
was the case with urban renewal (Greer 1965).

The 1949 Housing Act was an amalgam of three purposes: low-rent
housing for low-income families; slum clearance; and support for the private
real estate market. The first two purposes were more or less compatible. The
third was not. Taken together, the three were to produce a highly volatile
politics.

Under the 1949 Housing Act, the Housing and Home Finance Agency
(HHFA) was empowered to offer grants-in-aid to local public agencies; these
agencies would purchase blighted, inner-city property and sell it to private
developers, who in turn would raze decaying buildings and construct in their
place low- and medium-cost housing. To induce private developers to take
part in the program, local agencies were empowered to use federal money to
"write down" acquisition costs by buying sites at fair market value and selling
them below cost to private developers. A 1954 amendment to the Housing
Act shifted the emphasis from destruction and reconstruction to renovation,
giving rise to the term *urban renewal*. This amendment also allowed 10 percent
of funds to be used for nonresidential construction; by 1961, the allowance
had been raised to 30 percent. And while urban renewal money was not given
merely for the asking, it was reasonably available to those cities with trained
grant writers: Between its enactment and 1974, the Housing Act of 1949 provided $7 billion to over two thousand projects.

Under these arrangements, urban renewal stirred up strenuous and often
acrimonious politics. In city after city, old neighborhoods resented and resisted
being designated as slums. Neighborhood groups pressured the city council to
look elsewhere for slum clearance. Chicago's experience was typical. All
through the 1950s, its politics was dominated by issues of urban renewal
(Meyerson and Banfield 1955). In the abstract, urban renewal might be splen-

did, but in practice it was an election death knell for any city council member who failed to resist efforts to put it in his or her ward.

Even more daunting for elected officials than the prospect of razing a neighborhood was the certainty that a slum-cleared area would be a devastated area for years to come. New construction would not (could not) begin anytime soon. Ten years from start to finish was a realistic timetable. Daunting, too, was the fact that those moved out of areas slated for renewal were the city's poorest residents. And for the most part, they were black as well. In Detroit, 8,000 housing units were demolished; New Haven lost 6,500 units; and Newark lost 12,000. In Cincinnati, 20,000 housing units were demolished, many of them in Kenyon-Barr, Cincinnati's oldest black neighborhood. In addition 300 commercial establishments and 500 shops, churches, and other nonresidential facilities in the neighborhood were razed (Halpern 1995). Nationwide, 63 percent of the families that were displaced through urban renewal were nonwhite (Frieden and Sagalyn 1989). Those displaced were not going to be welcome in white neighborhoods. And threats were in the air that force would be used to keep displaced blacks away (Kaplan 1963, Henig 1985).

Still another issue roiled the waters of a proposed urban renewal project: What would replace the old slum area? In most cities (and Chicago was typical), run-down areas border the CBD. To the business groups that dominated the CBD (department stores, hotels, restaurants, office buildings, theaters) and to business-oriented interest groups (e.g., the chamber of commerce, the board of realtors, and newspapers), the answer was obvious: rebuild and revitalize the CBD.

Their arguments were difficult to assail. Chicago depended on the CBD—the famed Loop—for its economic good health and for its sense of civic identity. Moreover, if the city was to stop losing its middle class to the suburbs, it would need to upgrade close-in neighborhoods and attract the middle class back toward the CBD (Sanders 1980, Mayer 1978).[9]

The issues and arguments of urban renewal in Chicago were typical of what went on in other cities. However, their resolution in Chicago was much more decisive—thanks to the power of Chicago's political machine. Urban renewal would concentrate first on downtown renewal, and if it extended into residential neighborhoods, it would be mostly confined to black neighborhoods. (That, of course, is what we encountered in the earlier discussion of New Haven's urban renewal.)

Nationwide, and in about a decade (from 1950 to 1960), urban renewal tore down about 126,000 housing units, most of which were substandard.

9. In the process of slum clearance, some cities (e.g., Kansas City, Nashville, Charlotte) were also able to use urban renewal to direct expansion of minority residential areas away from the CBD; in many of these cities, decisions implemented four decades ago continue to influence residential patterns (Rabin 1987).

Using this measure, supporters give high marks to urban renewal. But fewer than 30,000 housing units replaced those torn down, and of these, relatively few were low-income units. As is often the case with government policy that combines antithetical purposes, urban renewal has had paradoxical outcomes. Initiated with liberal intentions to further social equity, urban renewal ended by becoming what Martin Anderson (1964) called "the federal bulldozer." It decreased the stock of housing available to the nation's poor; it sent black families from poor housing into poorer and even more overcrowded housing; it expanded the nation's reliance on filter-down housing; it rebuilt the CBD; and—paradox on paradox—it enriched the private real estate industry.

Although the best known federal program, urban renewal was not the only program to provide cities with grants. During the Truman presidency, between 1946 and 1952, 71 federal grant programs were authorized; and during the Eisenhower presidency, 61 new authorizations were added, for a total of 132 grant programs in 1960 (Walker 1981). One major, albeit indirect, program, the Hospital Survey and Construction (Hill-Burton) Act of 1946, funded states to inventory their hospital facilities and needs, and where necessary, to construct public and private hospitals. Most of this money was channeled through cities, and by 1960, forty-four hundred construction projects had been approved at a cost approaching $1.2 billion (Bingham et al. 1978).

The Johnson Presidency

Lyndon Johnson's presidency coincided with a time of turbulent, mass-action politics: student takeovers of college campuses; demonstrations against the Vietnam War; protests and marches against hunger in America; and marches, sit-ins, sit-downs, and lie-ins to overturn racial segregation in the South and racial insults in the North. Against this backdrop, the Johnson presidency provided leadership for two far-reaching packages of legislation—the civil rights acts of 1964 and 1965 and a variety of legislative actions widely known as the Great Society Program.

Cause and effect in policy-making can be traced only with uncertainty. Policy proposals do not rise high on the legislative agenda until public attention turns them into issues. And issues do not get translated into policy until they can command a significant measure of public support. Thus, the marches and protests of the early 1960s no doubt helped set the stage for the civil rights acts of 1964 and 1965 and the Great Society Program.

Especially important for the civil rights acts was the role played by television in arousing the conscience of the nation against racial discrimination. Beginning with television coverage of the bus boycott by blacks in Montgomery, Alabama, in 1955–56, viewers nationwide came into visual contact with racial segregation in the South. And what began as more or less detached curiosity turned into public dismay and mounting anger as the camera eye caught scenes of peaceful civil rights marchers knocked to the ground by fire hoses and attacked by police using clubs, cattle prods, and dogs.

What was being protested was an iron-bound discrimination in the South: laws that required blacks to ride at the back of trains and buses, use separate toilets and drinking fountains and confine themselves to separate waiting rooms in public places, stay out of all-white restaurants, marry only blacks, and enroll only at all-black schools and colleges. Equally important was a network of laws and customs (backed by threats of violence) that excluded blacks from voting. In the North, as an aroused national conscience was becoming increasingly aware, segregation was based primarily on social practice, not law. But custom was almost as effective as law in creating all-black neighborhoods, and all-black primary and secondary schools.

The Civil Rights Acts of 1964 and 1965

The vote is the most powerful instrument ever devised by man for breaking down injustice and destroying the terrible walls which imprison men because they are different from other men.

Lyndon Johnson, Address on voting rights, August 6, 1965

The Civil Rights Act of 1964 and the Voting Rights Act of 1965 were the most comprehensive attempts by the national government in a hundred years (since the post Civil War's Reconstruction era) to make good on the promises of the Fourteenth and Fifteenth Amendments to the Constitution. Among their many provisions, they guaranteed blacks equal access to public accommodations and equality of employment opportunities. They required all state officials to administer registration and voting laws in a nondiscriminatory manner (banning discriminatory literacy laws as a condition of voting), and they authorized the U.S. district courts to suspend, where necessary, local registrars from office and to appoint federal examiners to supervise the election process.

Old practices and reigning social outlooks die hard, and the transition from a color-biased society to a color-blind society is far from complete. Nor have the great changes of the past twenty-five years come easily. (Constant litigation has been part of this transition.) Among the important consequences of the civil rights acts of 1964 and 1965 has been the coming to political office of black city officials all across the country and the belief of black and other minorities that in city politics, as elsewhere, participation is a key to social and political change. But electoral equality does not necessarily translate into social equality. Or put differently, the dominant market emphasis of our political tradition couples with the power of the business entrepreneur to make it likely that, left to their own initiatives, cities will develop agendas and policies promoting economic development in the private sector over social

281

development for the poor (Bolland and Selby 1988). Aware of these realities, the federal government pushed forward the programs of the Great Society.

The Great Society

Ever since Franklin Roosevelt, presidential speechwriters have strained to create the *magic phrase* that captures popular imagination, commands voter support, and remains fixed in public memory. Lyndon Johnson's speechwriters hoped that they had discovered the magic phrase when the president declaimed in a New York speech on May 28, 1964:

> So I ask you tonight to join me and march along the road to the future, the road that leads to the Great Society.

As Johnson and his advisors saw it, the Great Society would go the New Deal one deal better. It would be guided by the polestar of liberal aspiration, equality of outcomes. And guided by that aspiration, from 1963 to 1967, Congress legislated 209 new grant programs, 70 of which provided direct disbursement of funds to cities (Walker 1981). These included the Economic Opportunity Act of 1964, which created the Office of Economic Opportunity (OEO) and provided funding for such programs as Head Start and Community Action Programs; the Elementary and Secondary Education Act of 1965, which provided grants to public schools to assist in the education of economically disadvantaged children; public housing legislation, passed in 1968, to provide housing subsidies; a 1965 amendment to the Social Security Act establishing the Medicaid Program, which was administered through state agencies to provide medical assistance to the indigent; and the Demonstration Cities and Metropolitan Development Act of 1966, which funded the Model Cities Program. Arguably the most important of these for America's cities were the Economic Opportunity Act, which initiated the Johnson administration's War on Poverty and the Model Cities Program. For the first time in the long development of national policy, city problems were proclaimed a matter of national public policy. (Previous programs had addressed city problems, but only indirectly. They aimed at helping those who lived in cities, not cities per se.) And even more of a departure from the past, the War on Poverty and the Model Cities Program did what no national legislation had ever done before. They gave the poor a direct vote in government programs intended to afford them a better life.

The War on Poverty. Floated with appropriate rhetoric ("For the first time in our history it is possible to conquer poverty. . . .") the Economic Opportunity Act (EOA) was committed to a theory of social causation that saw poverty as *structural* rather than personal. This theory holds that the causes of poverty do not lie with the person (as a result of such factors as lack of ambition or bad luck); rather, it asserts, the poor are victims of the society that has created the circumstances of poverty—bad housing, poor education, prejudicial hiring practices, poor health care, and so on. Structural conditions help foster a culture of poverty wherein poverty gets passed from one family generation to the next (e.g., Ryan 1976, Piven and Cloward 1971).

Thus, the War on Poverty was fought not only by giving material benefits to the poor (e.g., food stamps, school lunches), it was also fought by attempting to pull the poor out of their culture of poverty. The Head Start Program provided pre-kindergarten schooling for poor children so they would be better prepared for first grade. The Upward Bound Program encouraged poor children to set their sights on college by means of special counseling and by visits to and study on college campuses. The Adult Workshops Program taught job applicants the importance of good work habits, and similar programs created job workshops to teach employable skills. Volunteers in the Vista Program (a domestic counterpart of the Peace Corps) went to the inner cities to assist the poor toward managing their daily lives better; and lawyers in the Legal Services Program set up storefront offices to help the poor thread their way through government bureaucracies, claim legitimate welfare benefits, and (in many instances) protect themselves from predatory landlords and police harassment.

In what turned out to be two of the most controversial aspects of the War on Poverty, state and city governments were bypassed in favor of direct links between federal agencies and the urban poor, and the poor were given a direct voice in managing poverty programs through the Community Action Program (CAP).

The Community Action Program required the establishment of Local Community Action Agencies (LCAAs) that would make decisions dealing with coordination of

> the delivery of services in their [local] neighborhoods, make decisions regarding the specific mix and style of programs undertaken, and provide the poor with a greater sense of involvement and commitment. (Henig 1985, 103)

Providing the poor with a sense of involvement and commitment was in keeping with a theory of structural poverty and its concern to break the poor free of their culture of poverty. (To take charge of one's own life, to acquire a sense of one's own efficacy is, after all, the embodiment of the self-reliant person, able to rise above structural constraints.) And to this purpose, the law creating CAP had mandated "maximum feasible participation" by all those benefiting from the program—which was translated into a requirement that representatives of the poor serve as voting members of LCAAs (Moynihan 1969).

Just who found their way onto the governing boards of LCAAs is still a matter of controversy. The method used for putting "people's representatives" onto the LCAAs varied widely. Elections were a common method, but even more common was low voter turnout. Most observers conclude that those who served on the LCAAs were not typical of the urban poor, but were "poverty entrepreneurs" who used entry into the LCAA as foothold for entry into other enterprises (e.g., the permanent bureaucracy, politics, and business—especially the business of operating job workshops paid for by the War on Poverty). On these terms, CAP may not have given most of the urban poor a sense of control over their lives, but it did provide opportunity for many to rise up the social and economic ladder.

As to bypassing state and local governments, Dennis Judd (1988, 316) reckons that

> of all community action funds spent by OEO by 1968 only 25 percent were given to public agencies at all, the remainder going to private organizations, including universities, churches, civil rights groups, settlement houses, family service agencies, United Funds, or newly established nonprofit groups.

Understandably, city officials and city politicians were upset by the presence of and funding for LCAAs. Not only did they bypass the city's fiscal structure, they were creating a new group of politically important persons, operating outside the ordinary arrangements of city politics.

Congress responded by passing legislation to rein in OEO's poverty warriors and blunt their lances. Henceforth, all OEO agencies would be required to work with elected city officials and their administrative departments.

Model Cities. Mindful of the whirl of uncoordinated activities that marked the work of LCAAs, a President's Task Force on Urban Problems (appointed in 1965) recommended a concerted effort in selected areas within a few selected cities. The objectives were:

> to completely eliminate blight in the designated area, and to replace it with attractive, economical shelter . . . [thus changing] the total environment of the area affected, with ample provision of public facilities, schools, hospitals, parks, playgrounds, and community centers. (Haar 1975, 296)

In this way, the selected areas would serve as path-breaking experiments, demonstrations for future urban programs.

These were ambitious goals, and the Demonstration (Model) Cities Act of 1966 contained the following words:

> The Congress hereby finds and declares that improving the quality of urban life is the most critical domestic problem facing the United States. (Public Law 89–754)

But between the ambitions of the president's task force and the realities of congressional politics, several important changes were made in the Model Cities Program. First, and as might be anticipated, few members of Congress were willing to support a program that omitted important cities in their districts. Thus, the legislation was extended to invite the participation of every city in the United States. (By late 1966, sixty-three cities had been awarded Model Cities planning grants, and during 1968, another eighty-seven were approved.) Second, and mindful of the tension between city officials and LCAAs, Model Cities implementers, located in the recently created Department of Housing and Urban Development (HUD), made it a point to require that every city's demonstration agency be closely connected to the decision-making power of elected city officials.

The funding for the Model Cities program was generous but not exorbitant. Congress had appropriated $1 billion for the first three years of Model Cities, but this was to be spread over sixty-three cities. (By way of comparison, it is estimated that in a single year, 1967, $20 billion was spent on a single "federal program," the Vietnam War.) The federal government would contribute 80 percent of each city's matching contribution to all other federal grants being used in the demonstration area. And cities would have considerable discretion in using federal "demonstration dollars." Thus, a city might use federal money in place of its required contribution to a grant-in-aid, or it might underwrite projects not federally funded, but needed by the city—such as improving refuse collection or playground equipment.

Given this funding arrangement, and given, too, Model Cities' provision for control by elected officials, two results were likely—if not inevitable. First, participation by residents of targeted areas was far less than under the Poverty War's Community Action Program. And second, city officials were understandably given to spending Model Cities money less on services for the poor and more for such established city services as schools, police, sewage, and sanitation.

Model Cities as exemplar: What's wrong with grants-in-aid. Overall, Model Cities had promised much but delivered relatively little. Urban services were assisted, and targeted areas were improved. But slums remained slums, and the quality of life in the inner cities was not much altered. Four factors account for the failure of the Model Cities Program to deliver what it promised. First, although applications were to be evaluated on their merits, the final decisions were largely political (Harrigan 1985). Most of the sixty-three cities chosen to participate in the program in 1966 were large urban centers with representative urban problems, but several were conspicuously different. For example, Smithfield, Tennessee, home of the chairman of the House Appropriations subcommittee that oversaw the HUD budget, was chosen. Montana, home of Senate Majority Leader Mike Mansfield, saw two of its cities selected; and

Maine, home of Edmund Muskie, the bill's floor leader, contributed three more. These instances reflected a general pattern in which the most needy cities did not necessarily get the most money in federal grants. Rather, the funding of project-based, categorical grants is largely driven by a "pork-barrel" mentality, where a representative or a senator can parlay funded projects back home into votes in the next election.

A second deficiency demonstrated by the Model Cities Program was lack of federal coordination. One of the purposes of the program was to coordinate a number of federal programs channeling funds into urban neighborhood redevelopment; it attempted to accomplish this through its stipulation that model cities were to receive priority in getting related grants from other government agencies. But, for the most part, this intended cooperation never occurred, and various agencies continued to set their own priorities. It became clear that urban problems were not unidimensional but rather multidimensional. Urban neighborhood decay, for example, was not simply a function of deteriorating buildings but also of crime, poverty, lack of education, and a host of other social maladies that combined in complex ways to create the problem. And it became equally clear that the vast federal bureaucracy, with its various autonomous agencies and fiefdoms of power, was not capable of mounting a comprehensive and coordinated effort to address simultaneously the multiple components of the problem.

A third difficulty of categorical grants-in-aid, relevant to the Model Cities Program and also to most other programs, was their matching requirement. Urban Renewal, for example, provided cities with vast amounts of money to tear down or renovate their slum areas (although, in some cases, cities were allowed to count improvements for schools and parks as part of their match), and with such a carrot few cities could refuse the opportunity to apply for funds. But for each million it received in federal dollars, a city was required to put up between $250,000 and $333,000 of its own money. Thus, municipal priorities were often shifted away from the development of parks or the construction of roads or libraries to the construction of office buildings and department stores.

Finally, the Model Cities Program, as well as other categorical grant programs, demonstrated the difficulties of excessive *conditionality* on intergovernmental funding. The federal bureaucracy tends to be insulated from local politics, and many of the conditions attached to categorical grants assumed that the application for federal dollars (a political activity) could be divorced from the administration of those funds (a bureaucratic activity). Yet, this politics-administration dichotomy is not functional at the local level, and politics tinges virtually all administrative decisions. Thus, the ability to spend grant money in a way that simultaneously addresses local problems and conforms to local political norms may be constrained by federal requirements, often leading to political squabbles and roadblocks that prevent funds from reaching targeted populations and areas at all. For example, in 1951 Toledo received federal urban renewal funds earmarked for the Chase Park project. Eleven years later, the *Toledo Blade* (June 27, 1962, 20) wrote,

> The Chase Park project may look simple on paper, but it's hard to recall a single undertaking in recent years that got bogged down in such a mass of confusions, frustrations, blunders, and boo-boos as has struck activities in Chase Park.[10]

Stinchcombe (1968) argues that the project failed largely because of political squabbles it raised.

The Nixon Presidency: A Change in Approach

All in all, the Great Society period was a time of rising federal aid to cities. The change in public mood signaled by the election of Richard Nixon ushered in a new approach to federal spending on cities. Ever since Franklin Roosevelt, a mainstay of the major conservative tradition has been mistrust of national power and a yearning for the old federalism, in which power and policy initiatives lie with the states. Some of this yearning is rooted in fears of an overly powerful national government. Some is rooted in a conservative tradition that dislikes social experiments. (State governments, historically, have not been much given to social experiments.) And still another source of this yearning is rooted in economic self-interest, tied to the historical fact that states have been less willing than the national government to interfere with private-sector economics.

But whichever tradition of conservatism most animated them, Presidents Nixon, Ford, Reagan, and Bush (as did President Eisenhower before them) spoke of turning back the rising tide of government, "getting the national government off our backs and out of our pocketbooks." The Nixon version of federalism was built on the idea of "sorting out" the functions of government. The national government, said the president, ought to do what it does best: raise money and distribute it to state and local governments to do what they do best—solve state and local problems. But even so, Nixon was sensitive to the special needs of cities, and during the Nixon and Ford administrations federal aid to cities achieved its highest levels ever (Ames et al. 1992). It is in this context that we can understand the Nixon program for an altered federalism to be accomplished not by cutting funds but rather through the increased use of block grants and a program of revenue sharing.

10. Quoted in Stinchcombe (1968).

Block Grants

President Nixon inherited two block grants from the Johnson administration. The Partnership for Health Act of 1966 consolidated seventeen separate categorical grant programs into the Partnership for Health block grant, whose purpose was to help localities develop comprehensive health plans. And the Omnibus Crime Control and Safe Streets Act, passed in 1968 in the wake of the urban riots, established the Safe Streets block grant to assist state and local governments in the development of innovative crime control programs. In addition, at Nixon's urging Congress passed the Comprehensive Employment and Training Act (CETA) in 1973 and the Housing and Community Development Act in 1974. The latter consolidated into the Community Development block grant seven on-going grant-in-aid programs, including Urban Renewal, Model Cities, water and sewer facilities, open spaces, rehabilitation loans, and public facilities loans; it represented "a watershed in the development of federal grant programs directly aiding the cites" (Brown et al. 1984, 27). The Comprehensive Employment and Training Act ran parallel administratively to the Housing and Community Development Act, replacing the Great Society programs that provided job counseling and training and on-the-job work experience.

A blurring of purpose: The problem with block grants. With the advent of block grants, several of the problems associated with categorical grants-in-aid were circumvented. But an analysis of the Safe Streets, Community Development, and Comprehensive Employment block grants suggests that they were not without their own problems. Chief among these was the latitude that localities were given in using the funds and the extent to which congressional purpose was ignored. For example, the Safe Streets Act established the Law Enforcement Assistance Administration (LEAA), which was charged with three major responsibilities: (a) to encourage states and localities to prepare and adopt comprehensive plans based on an evaluation of state and local needs; (b) to authorize action grants to states and localities to implement these plans; and (c) to encourage research on innovative approaches to the prevention and reduction of crime.

However, although eligibility requirements were established, LEAA was lax in providing guidelines for program development. As a result, action grants were often applied to marginally relevant programs. For example, California spent $75,000 to study learning problems of kindergarten children, and New York approved $216,000 to fund a youth employment service project; such actions led the General Accounting Office to conclude that as much as 30 percent of the funds allocated to California and New York had been spent on inappropriate projects. In addition, planning requirements were often overlooked in the allocation of funds under the block grant, and state and local plans tended to be insufficiently thought out, poorly developed, and only loosely followed. As a result, much of the allocation to localities was spent on hardware (e.g., helicopters, automobiles, firearms and ammunition, computer information systems, communication control systems, police radio equipment, and electronic surveillance equipment) without concern for either need or interagency coordination (Palley and Palley 1981).

The Community Development and CETA block grants suffered from a similar distortion of purpose. With funds from these grants firmly in the hands of elected city officials, traditional city politics came to the fore. Federal funds were spent more on traditional city services than on services for the poor (not because elected officials were indifferent to the needs of the poor but usually because every city is constantly short of money for basic city services). And in many cities, the CETA program was turned from job training into public-works employment. For instance, cities used the better educated CETA trainees as substitute help in city departments, and they used younger, less educated trainees for general maintenance and clean-up work (Aronson and Hilley 1986). Several studies of the Community Development block grant (Brown et al. 1984, Goldfield 1993, Miranda and Tunyavong 1994) found similar abuses, with political considerations guiding the choice of projects far more than level of neighborhood need.[11] While turning over the grants to local control remedied one of the objections to categorical grants-in-aid (they ignored the reality of local politics), it also violated congressional intent.

In all four of the block grants, Congress eventually intervened to tighten requirements on the use of funds. Consider the Safe Streets block grant: Following the publicity that surrounded its abuses, Congress passed the Crime Control Act of 1973, which revised the grant substantially. First, the legislation strengthened the planning requirements by mandating that localities with more than a quarter million people submit comprehensive plans with their applications for pass-through funds (i.e., funds received by the states but designated for cities). This requirement was designed specifically to curb the uncoordinated purchase of police equipment. Second, a number of specific project grants were incorporated into the block grant; for example, the federal government would provide 90 percent of the funding needed to implement

---

11. In its first-year evaluation of the block-grant program, HUD reported that 71 percent of funds were allocated to priority areas. In the second year, however, evaluation procedures focused on actual recipients rather than geographic areas, and the figures were much more disturbing: Only 44 percent of funds had been allocated to directly benefit low- and moderate-income groups. This abuse was particularly notable in Southern states, where the Southern Regional Council concluded that "local diversions from national purpose are not just occasional abuses, but rather form a pattern inherent in the implementation of the Act" (quoted in Judd 1984, 350). One reason for these diversions was local pressure to produce results, leading local politicians to target funds from the Community Development block grant to marginal areas where improvements could be quickly demonstrated rather than to the poorest neighborhoods where quick results are more difficult to achieve (Goldfield 1993).

programs to strengthen public protection, recruit and train personnel, provide public education for crime prevention and police-community relations, and develop neighborhood crime prevention councils. In addition, it would provide 50 percent of the funding necessary to construct correctional facilities, centers for drug addicts, and temporary courtroom facilities. Finally, increased reporting and review requirements were instituted. For example, applicants were required to certify compliance with twenty-seven federal statutes addressing such issues as animal welfare, historic preservation, clean air, safe drinking water, solid waste disposal, and discrimination (Walker 1981). With these changes, the Safe Streets block grant largely reverted back to a series of categorical grants over which the federal government retained substantial control. The Partnership in Health block grant underwent almost identical modifications, with Congress adding eighteen separate categorical grant programs as supplements and extensions between 1970 and 1976 (Bingham et al. 1978). So, too, increased regulation was added to both the Comprehensive Employment block grant and the Community Development block grant over the next few years.

Revenue Sharing

In spite of the apparent popularity of block grants, or perhaps because of the local abuses to which they were subjected, block grants never really replaced categorical grants as a mechanism for intergovernmental funding. In 1966, before the Partnership in Health block grant, categorical grants accounted for 98 percent of all federal assistance to states and cities.[12] This figure had declined to 72 percent by 1977 (Bingham et al. 1978), but by 1980 it was back up to 80 percent (Walker 1981). Further, not all of this erosion was due to the introduction of block grants. In 1972, Congress passed the State and Local Assistance Act, which provided $30.2 billion over a five-year period in unconditional, general purpose grants to states (33 percent) and localities (66 percent). In 1976, the allocation was extended for an additional five years at the same level. These *revenue sharing funds* were allocated according to a formula based on population, per capita income, and tax effort. And because of their unconditionality, they were vigorously embraced by the Nixon administration. The act gave mayors and councils a good deal of discretion in spending the money they received. And for the first time, "all subnational general-purpose governments were made part of the federal aid system" (Brown et al. 1984, 27).

Cities benefited greatly from the flexibility provided by general revenue sharing funds. These unconditional grants provided 43 percent of all direct

12. Since these figures represent grants to both cities and states, they do not give an accurate picture of the relative importance of categorical grants and block grants to municipal finance. These estimates are not easily obtained, since a proportion of many federal grants awarded to states are passed through to cities.

federal aid to cities in 1974, although this figure declined to under 30 percent by 1975 and stabilized at approximately 23 percent by 1980. Over its first decade, general revenue sharing funds accounted for between 3 percent and 4 percent of total municipal revenues. Most cities used this income for capital improvements, for example, the construction of a new city hall or a new water treatment plant. Some, however, used the additional funds to reduce property taxes or delay tax increases.

Even in this least restrictive of federal aid programs, the federal government imposed a number of restrictions on the expenditure of revenue sharing funds. For example, they could not be used to match federal categorical or block grants or to retire municipal debts. Further, localities were required to establish mechanisms for citizen participation, provide audits of expended funds, comply with prevailing wage scales for construction workers, and protect against discrimination in the recruitment of various population groups (Walker 1981).

Revenue sharing continued in conjunction with block grants and categorical grants through the Ford and Carter presidencies, and the first years of the Reagan presidency, with few substantive changes. However, since revenue-sharing funds remained fixed at 1972 levels, their importance to cities declined with the ravages of inflation (each revenue-sharing dollar allocated in 1983 purchased only 43 percent of what it would have bought a decade earlier).

Presidential Policies after Nixon

The Presidencies of Gerald Ford and Jimmy Carter

Gerald Ford, in filling out Richard Nixon's remaining term in office, modified little of his predecessor's philosophy. His one important contribution to federalism occurred when he refused to bail out New York City from its near bankruptcy in 1975, reaffirming the Republican belief that local matters are best handled at the local level.

In 1977, Jimmy Carter made a well-publicized visit to a devastated, abandoned, and burnt-out neighborhood in South Bronx. There he promised a national urban policy that would turn around the nation's inner cities through public-private initiatives. The centerpiece of this policy was the Urban Development Action Grant (UDAG) program. These grants were intended to create new jobs in distressed cities through public-private partnerships; local governments were required to negotiate "deals" with private firms to locate or expand in their cities in exchange for low-interest loans, grants, and/or construction of needed infrastructure using UDAG funds. In addition, many cities were able to establish revolving loan funds, with money paid back by one borrower used to make loans to another. Although the UDAG program was terminated in 1989, revolving loan funds started with

291

UDAG money continue in existence; by the mid 1990s, cities have received more than \$1 billion in loan repayments, and another \$1.5 billion is due (Watson 1995). UDAG funds could be used for a variety of purposes, but most went toward commercial development. For instance, New York City used 80 percent of its eighty-five UDAGs to underwrite commercial development and 20 percent to underwrite housing development; and one-third of the first fifty UDAGs awarded in 1978 were earmarked for hotels and convention centers (Frieden and Sagalyn 1989, Rogowsky and Berkman 1995).

Perhaps more than anything else, however, the Carter presidency was marked by growing inflation and general fiscal strain, which was felt keenly in America's cities; in this climate, few urban success stories were likely, and few occurred. Partly as a result, the Carter White House became increasingly ambivalent toward urban areas, and by 1979 it had moved away from a specific urban policy in favor of a national economic policy under which presumably all cities would benefit (Ames et al. 1992).

The Reagan and Bush Presidencies

President Reagan's policy priorities were not with urban affairs. And true to Reagan's belief that grants-in-aid were not to be encouraged (or perhaps even countenanced), during his presidency seventy-seven urban grants-in-aid were consolidated into nine block grants, and federal spending was reduced by 25 percent. During this period, increased spending for national defense, combined with tax cuts and a rising government deficit, required that cities learn to make do with less federal money. To make matters worse, remaining federal aid to cities followed the population to the suburbs, with suburban governments receiving a larger portion of grant money in 1992 than in 1980 (Parker 1995). This state of affairs has marked federal-city relationships ever since.

The Clinton Presidency: Advancing toward the Year 2000

Bill Clinton's presidency has been marked by an eclectic approach to implementing the new federalism, one resulting from a unique combination of circumstance and ideological orientation. As a Democrat, Clinton has attempted to bring cities (and the urban constituency) back into the national government's agenda, and he has championed a set of city-oriented proposals that passed through Congress early in his presidency. These include the AmeriCorps Program, designed to provide young people with an opportunity to serve their communities in exchange for college tuition, and a tough crime bill intended to restrict the availability of handguns and assault weapons, and to add 100,000 officers to the ranks of city police departments. Clinton's agenda also included a promise to end welfare as we know it, reflecting a growing frustration (both within the Democratic party and the nation) with the inability of the existing welfare program to ameliorate poverty in the United States. Two years into the Clinton presidency, the Republican party captured both houses of Congress, and it pushed its own agenda for change (extending further the priorities of the Reagan and Bush presidencies to create a smaller, less intrusive national government). Faced with pressure to balance the budget and with legislation that would have largely dismantled the federal role in the welfare state, Clinton signed a welfare reform bill in 1996 that would give to the fifty states (in the form of block grants) funds to develop their own unique welfare programs. Thus, the Clinton presidency has been marked by both expansions and contractions in the federal role in urban affairs.

One of the battles yet to be decided, however, concerns unfunded mandates. In recent years, Congress has taken to cutting federal spending and setting urban policy through these mandates: On pain of losing existing and future grants, cities are ordered—mandated—to take specified actions but without using federal funds to pay for them. There is considerable disagreement about exactly how big a burden this is, with different studies estimating that between 20 percent and 90 percent of municipal budgets are in response to federal and state mandates (Berman 1996). One example of an unfunded mandate is the Americans with Disabilities Act of 1990, which requires states and local governments (under threat of forfeiting federal grants) to guarantee that handicapped persons are not impeded by stairs too high to climb, by toilets too difficult to use, or by alarm buttons too far to reach. And however laudable these mandates,

> state and local governments no longer have the right to decide how much compassion for the disabled they can afford in the light of competing supplications for compassion by other groups. (Lorch 1995, 36)

In recent years, mayors and governors have protested vigorously against unfunded mandates, and Congress passed the Unfunded Mandate Reform Act of 1995. Although this legislation makes it more difficult for Congress to impose unfunded mandates on cities and states in the future, it does nothing to provide relief from existing mandates, and the issue is likely to be revisited as fiscal pressures at all levels of government continue.

The Supreme Court's Urban Policies

The United States Supreme Court has also been a major actor in creating policies that directly affect the cities. Most such policies are those involving racial and ethnic discrimination, and they come mainly from the Court's interpretation of the Fourteenth Amendment, which reads in part:

No State shall make or enforce any law which shall abridge the privileges and immunities of Citizens of the United States; nor shall any State deprive any Person of life, liberty, or property without due process of law; nor deny to any Person within its jurisdiction the equal protection of the laws.

Cities, as agents of their states, thus come under the provisions of the Fourteenth Amendment.

Supreme Court rulings have affected cities directly and indirectly in a number of different areas: law enforcement protocols and the rights of the accused, zoning and residential segregation, protocols for the targeting and delivery of municipal services, school desegregation, and affirmative action. We will consider three of these areas in the following discussion.

School Segregation

Although the Fourteenth Amendment was ratified in 1868, for three-quarters of a century the Supreme Court gave it only the most timid reading, preferring to let social practice and state discriminatory laws stand.[13] Then, after World War II (fought, after all, in democracy's cause), the Court began interpreting the amendment more vigorously. Several decisions struck down blatantly discriminatory housing practices (these will be considered in the next section). But no plain reading has had greater impact on cities than the Court's new approach to state-mandated school segregation. The bombshell case was the now-famous *Brown v. The Board of Education of Topeka*.[14] In that case, the Supreme Court overturned what had been an undemocratic and unhappy fixture of American life—the legality of state laws that provided for separate education for blacks and whites. Such separation, said the Court in its *Brown* ruling, "had hung the badge of inferiority on Negro children."

> To separate them from others of similar age and qualification solely because of their race generates a feeling of inferiority that may affect their hearts and minds in a way unlikely ever to be undone.

Public anger in the South, where segregated schools were almost everywhere the law, went quickly beyond mere indignation and denunciation of the Court. The language of the *Brown* decision was vague, calling only for a prompt and deliberate start to desegregation. This encouraged some school districts, particularly in the South, to resist integration through a number of different ploys. Most blatant was Arkansas Governor Orville Faubus's decision to close the schools in Little Rock rather than integrate them; this was overturned by the

---

13. The controlling case was *Plessy v. Ferguson* (163 US 537, 1896), which announced *separate but equal* as a constitutional principle.
14. 347 US 483 (1954).

Supreme Court in 1959.[15] Other states employed more subtle, although ultimately no more effective, means to delay or circumvent the integration order (Lord 1977, quoted in Johnston 1984): Mississippi, for instance, passed legislation claiming that *Brown* did not apply there. Virginia disbanded its public education system, replacing it with grants to whites attending private schools. Georgia's legislature declared the Court's decision to be null and void and of no effect in the state; and Louisiana made desegregation by school officials

> a crime, placed control of New Orleans' schools in a special legislative committee, and denied accreditation, free textbooks, and financial aid to desegregated schools. (Kelly and Harbison 1955, 952)

All of these efforts to maintain segregated school districts were overturned in the courts (see Johnston, 1984, for citations). In short, the courts had ruled that students have the right to attend the school nearest their residence.

By 1969, the Supreme Court had replaced its "all deliberate speed" criterion (*Brown*) with one requiring "immediate operation of unitary school systems."[16] While that decision seemingly laid to rest the question of *de jure* segregation, it left the question of *de facto* segregation unanswered (and unaddressed).[17] From that point forward, however, the focus of the courts changed to *de facto* segregation: What should be done when segregated housing patterns create segregated school districts? In two 1971 decisions, the Supreme Court concluded that busing was the answer, specifying that students in all-black or all-white catchment areas should be bused to other schools to achieve racial balance.[18] With these decisions, the Supreme Court turned over to federal district courts the responsibility for implementing *Brown*, instructing them to get on with the job of desegregating the schools "with all deliberate speed."

One by one, and case by case—sometimes school district by school district—the federal courts had forced integration on the South. But until the

15. *Faubus v. Aaron* (361 US 197, 1959).

16. *Alexander v. Holmes Board of Education* (369 US 19).

17. *De jure* segregation is segregation by law, for example, when blacks and whites are statutorily required to attend different schools. At the time of the *Brown* decision, cities in twenty-one states (plus the District of Columbia) were allowed (or required) to maintain separate schools for whites and blacks. Just as important, but more subtle, is *de facto* segregation, where blacks and whites attend different schools due to segregated housing patterns.

18. Due to residential segregation, nine elementary schools in Mobile County were all black. In *Davis v. Board of School Commissioners of Mobile County* (402 US 33, 1971) the U.S. Supreme Court ruled unanimously that in such situations busing must be used to break down segregation. In the Charlotte-Mecklenburg School District (which provided educational services for residents of the city of Charlotte and Mecklenburg County), the situation was more complicated, since most blacks resided in the city rather than the county. Nonetheless, the U.S. Supreme Court ruled in *Swann v. Charlotte-Mecklenburg Board of Education* (402 US 1, 1971) that the district must provide free transportation to any student who voluntarily moved away from an all-black or all-white school, and that noncontiguous catchment areas should be grouped as a means for creating racial balance.

1970s, judicial interventions had been confined largely to the South. There, federal courts had intervened against state statutes and city ordinances used to maintain segregated schools. Then the issue of segregated schools moved north. In the 1970s, the Supreme Court began hearing school cases in northern cities, and it affirmed its earlier decisions[19] by ordering district-wide busing in cities (e.g., Denver,[20] Dayton,[21] and Columbus, Ohio[22]) where it found a pattern of segregation that had been aided by past or present school board actions. "Desegregation plans," said the Court, "cannot be limited to the walk-in school."[23]

However, the Supreme Court has been unwilling to take a next step, requiring metropolitan-wide busing to rectify racial disparity *among* metropolitan school districts. In a test case, the U.S. Supreme Court overruled lower court decisions requiring busing among the Detroit School District and fifty-three suburban school districts serving the Detroit metropolitan area.[24]

Housing Patterns and Residential Segregation

Restrictive Covenants. Until the middle years of this century, cities employed heavy-handed approaches to keeping minorities and the poor out of established white neighborhoods. In the late-nineteenth and early-twentieth centuries, for example, a number of municipalities (e.g., San Francisco, Baltimore, Atlanta, and Louisville) enacted ordinances mandating racial or ethnic segregation. These were uniformly overturned by the courts by 1920 (Rice 1968, Johnston 1984). As an alternative, cities, neighborhoods, and land developers fashioned a number of strategies for maintaining residential segregation. The most effective of these was the *restrictive covenant*, a formal and binding component of the deed of sale prohibiting the owner of land from certain specified activities or behaviors associated with the property. Some covenants prohibited the owner from selling property to members of specific racial or ethnic groups, for example blacks and Jews. Such restrictions were widespread in many major cities (Vose 1959). This practice was allowed to stand until 1948, when the United States Supreme Court, in *Shelley v.*

19. However, in refusing to hear an appeal of *Bell v. School, City of Gary, Indiana* (342 F2d 209, 1963), the Supreme Court established that if school boundaries are established without consideration of race, desegregation is not required. The district court noted that the Constitution does not require integration, it forbids segregation.

20. *Keys v. School District No. 1* (413 US 89, 1973).

21. *Dayton Board of Education v. Brinkman* (443 US 526, 1979).

22. *Columbus Board of Education v. Penick* (443 US 449, 1979).

23. *Swann v. Charlotte-Mecklenburg Board of Education*, 1971.

24. *Milliken v. Bradley* (418 US 717, 1974). However, the Supreme Court did allow a metropolitan-wide solution to segregation in Wilmington, Delaware, by refusing to overturn a lower court decision (*Evans v. Buchanany*, 379 F Supp 1218, 1974). For a discussion of desegregation in Wilmington, and why the courts allowed a metropolitan-wide solution to be adopted there, see Stave (1995).

Kraemer,[25] ruled it unconstitutional. By that time, however, housing patterns had largely been established in American cities, and once established they were difficult to break down.[26]

Zoning. One result of the *Shelley* ruling was that cities—particularly sub-urbs—invoked other, more subtle practices and ordinances to achieve comparable restrictive purposes, resulting in *de facto* segregation. Beginning in 1926, when it ruled in *Village of Euclid v. Ambler Realty Co.*,[27] the U.S. Supreme Court has consistently upheld the right of municipalities to regulate the use of their land as a means of ensuring the public welfare.

In the years following *Euclid*, most urban governments have taken advantage of this right, for example, by enacting ordinances to designate certain areas as "industrial," others as "commercial," and still others as "residential." Within these broad divisions, cities have been able to designate subdivisions, for example, "light-industrial" versus "heavy-industrial" and "single-family residential" versus "multifamily residential." Even within these subdivisions, cities may set further restrictions on land use; for instance, many zoning ordinances specify minimum lot sizes, setbacks, side yards, and floor areas for specified single-family residential neighborhoods; others restrict trailer parks.[28] The result maximizes the preservation of housing values; but it also leads to class (and often racial) segregation. *[The theory of lifestyle and territory.]* In some cases, in fact, zoning ordinances have been little more than thinly veiled racism. Even so, they have been justified by the courts in three ways.

1. zoning protects neighborhoods from unwanted externalities (e.g., noise, litter)[29]

25. 334 US 1.

26. Other types of covenants were invented in an effort to keep blacks and ethnics out of neighborhoods. One provides neighbors (and in some cases the land developer) with first right of purchase if a lot in the neighborhood is placed on the market. Another ties residence to membership in a particular social group or club (for example, membership in a country club may be required of all residents in a neighborhood bordering a golf course). In the first case, blacks and ethnics may be effectively prohibited from purchasing land through neighbors' right of first refusal. In the second, they may be prohibited residence through exclusionary membership policies of the social group or club.

27. 272 US 365.

28. The courts have generally upheld these ordinances (e.g., *Village of Belle Terre v. Boraas*, 416 US 1, 1974; *Vickers v. Township Committee of Gloucester Township*, 371 US 233, 1962; *James v. Valtierra and Shaffer v. Valtierra*, 402 US 137, 1971; *Warth v. Seldin*, 442 US 490, 1975). See Johnston (1984) for a discussion.

29. In the *Belle Terre* case (see note 28), residents kept students attending a nearby college from locating in their community through a single-family zoning ordinance. In upholding this ordinance, the court wrote:

The regimes of boarding houses, fraternity houses, and the like present urban problems. More people occupy a given space; more cars rather continuously pass by; more cars are parked; noise travels with crowds. . . . [The right to zone] is not confined to

2. the poor can equally well live elsewhere[30]
3. a law that disadvantages a particular group (e.g., the poor) does not necessarily deny equal protection[31]

The latter argument was used again by the Supreme Court in *Arlington
Heights v. Metropolitan Housing Development Corp.*[32] Residents in Arlington
Heights, a Chicago suburb, objected to the construction of a federally funded,
high-density housing development on land designated for single-family residences. The city denied the Metropolitan Housing Development Corporation's request for a zoning variance, citing the availability of land already
zoned for apartments. The Court upheld the city's decision, ruling that
although it precluded predominantly black public housing recipients from
locating in the area designated for single-family residence, this differential
impact is insufficient evidence of intent. Rather, the Court argued, "proof of
a racially discriminatory motive, purpose, or intent is required to find a violation of the Fourteenth Amendment" (Mandelker 1977, 1236).

One case where this burden of proof was met occurred in Black Jack,
Missouri. In 1970, the Federal Housing Administration (FHA) approved a federally subsidized housing development to be located in Black Jack, an unincorporated area of three thousand people (93 percent of whom were white)
located near St. Louis. Sponsored by the Inter-Religious Center for Urban
Development, the project was to contain 108 two-story racially integrated
townhouses in an area that had been previously zoned for multifamily units.

Residents of Black Jack were angered by the proposal. Some spoke
openly of their fears of bringing another Pruitt-Igoe to their neighborhood;
others confessed even more openly of their fear of black intrusion. The residents petitioned the county commissioners for legal incorporation of Black
Jack. The incorporation was granted and (as might be anticipated) the newly
formed city council of the new town of Black Jack enacted a zoning ordinance that would keep new multiunit dwellings out of the city. As might be
further anticipated, the zoning ordinance was challenged in the courts by the
Inter-Religious Center and a number of outside groups pledged to the principle of racial integration. Thus, the *Black Jack* case was transformed from an
issue of local politics to one of national importance.

In 1974 the U.S. Court of Appeals ruled against the city in favor of the

---

elimination of filth, stench, and unhealthy places. It is ample to lay out zones where
family values, youth values, and the blessings of quiet seclusion and clean air make
the area a sanctuary for people. (P. 804)

30. *Ybarra v. City of Los Altos* (503 F2d 250, 1974).
31. In the *Valtierra* case (see note 28), the court explicitly noted that discrimination
on the basis of wealth is not a constitutional violation since, it concluded, discrimination
by wealth does not necessarily mean discrimination by race.
32. 429 US 252, 1977.

plaintiffs,[33] and the Supreme Court denied petitions for appeals.[34] But meanwhile, the time allotted for funding the proposed project had run out. Thus, Black Jack had its victory after all.[35] (On the *Black Jack* case, see Danielson 1976, and Kirby et al. 1982.)

The *Black Jack* case notwithstanding, the Court has consistently maintained that municipalities may zone as a way of ensuring economic homogeneity without violating the equal protection clause of the Fourteenth Amendment, even though race and income are highly correlated.[36] But a 1975 decision by the New Jersey Supreme Court raises questions about the long-term acceptability of zoning to keep out the poor. In 1975, the Court had ruled in *Southern Burlington NAACP v. Township of Mt. Laurel*[37] that the New Jersey Constitution, in providing its citizens the right to acquire, possess, and protect property, precluded municipalities from excluding the poor to keep property taxes low. The decision established:

> every developing municipality has an obligation to provide the opportunity for the satisfaction of its fair share of the regional need for housing of persons of low and moderate income. This "opportunity" must be provided through non-exclusionary (or "inclusionary") land-use controls and other "necessary and advisable" actions. (Bisgaier 1977, 140; quoted in Johnston 1984)

In other words, it established a precedent for protecting the poor as well as minorities from unequal treatment (at least in New Jersey). By the 1980s, the Court was dismayed to discover that municipalities were doing little to change their exclusionary zoning policies. However, the enforcement mechanism it provided—litigation—was unlikely to be effective for three reasons (Bisgaier 1983):

33. *United States v. City of Black Jack, Missouri* (508 F2d 1179).

34. 442 US 1042, 1975; 443 US 884, 1975. In a related decision, the court awarded the developers $450,000 in damages (*Park View Heights Corp. v.. City of Black Jack*, 467 F2d 1208, 1972).

35. Winners and losers in this case had an old principle of politics reaffirmed: Take every case to court. Sometimes the court will be on your side; sometimes not. If you lose, appeal to a higher court. And if enough times goes by, your opponents may run out of energy, or money, or both.

36. However, the courts have taken a less permissive view of boundary decisions, often overruling decisions that they viewed as capricious or that otherwise violated due process. For example, in the mid 1950s, 80 percent of the residents of Tuskeegee, Alabama, population 6,700, were black and unregistered to vote. The predominantly white electorate voted to change the boundaries of the town from a square to a twenty-eight-sided figure, thus placing 80 percent of the black population outside the city limits. The U.S. Supreme Court overturned this boundary change (*Gomillion v. Lightfoot*, 364 US 339, 1960) as an abridgment of black residents' Fourteenth and Fifteenth Amendment rights. See R.J. Johnston (1984) for an excellent review of this and other decisions.

37. 67 NJ 151.

1. there were few private litigants and no public litigants willing to undertake litigation;
2. litigation was costly and tended to drag on endlessly, and there was no guarantee of success in the lower courts;
3. recalcitrant municipalities had little fear of the consequences of losing suits, since they were in existence before the *Mt. Laurel* decision.

To remedy this situation, the New Jersey Supreme Court issued a second decision on Mt. Laurel *(Southern Burlington NAACP v. Township of Mt. Laurel)*[38] In *Mt. Laurel II* (as it was called), the court changed the enforcement mechanism to a so-called builder's remedy: Builders who successfully litigate cases are granted approval, within certain limitations, of their proposed developments. This created an enormous incentive for builders to challenge vulnerable municipalities, creating overnight a large class of potential plaintiffs (Bisgaier 1983). The prospect of massive litigation prompted the state legislature to pass the New Jersey Fair Housing Act of 1985, which created the Council of Affordable Housing (COAH) to help increase the production of low- and moderate-income housing in the suburbs. By 1994, COAH had certified applications from 270 municipalities, with a potential for the construction of between fifty-four thousand and eighty-four thousand low- and moderate-income housing units (Haar 1996). The Council on Affordable Housing has reduced the need for litigation, and the time spent in litigation has dropped from an average of 9.0 years to an average of 1.4 years (Anglin 1994). Although the final implications are not yet clear, it seems likely that this ruling will create an incentive for municipalities to modify their reliance on exclusionary zoning.[39] And just as important, the courts in other states (e.g., New York; see Bellman 1983) have considered similar actions. Yet, given the conflicting standards set down by the U.S. Supreme Court in its *Arlington Heights* decision and the New Jersey Supreme Court in its *Mt. Laurel* decisions, nationwide change in exclusionary zoning laws seem unlikely in the near future.

Affirmative Action

The intellectual roots of affirmative action lie ideologically in the idea of equality of outcomes. Blacks, Hispanics, Native Americans, and women are to

38. 92 NJ 158, 1983. Since the Court based its *Mt. Laurel* decision on the New Jersey Constitution rather than the Fourteenth Amendment of the U.S. Constitution, it is unlikely to be overturned in federal courts.

39. The *Mt. Laurel* decisions have been challenged in the New Jersey courts on several occasions (*Hills Development Company v. Township of Bernards*, 1986; *Holmdel Builders Association v. Township of Holmdel*, 1989; and *In re Township of Warren*, 1991); these have become known as *Mt. Laurel* III, IV, and V, respectively. But so far, the principles established in the original decisions have stood up to these challenges. See Haar (1996) for citations and a general description of how these decisions have changed the housing debate in New Jersey.

have educational, career, and job opportunities in proportion to their numbers in the population, and they are to achieve those opportunities through affirmative government action. Affirmative action thus links to the idea of fair shares and additionally to the concept of intergenerational equity (i.e., government must take action to compensate the present generation of minorities and women from the discriminatory behavior of the white, male society of generations past). But affirmative action also raises questions of equity and equality: Should one group (usually white males) be denied equal opportunity in order to redress another group's access to equality?

Affirmative action cases are of great importance to cities, particularly as they relate to municipal hiring practices and to the use of minority contractors. In the first instance, minorities argue that their underrepresentation in selected municipal departments (usually fire and police departments) is evidence of discrimination, and lower courts have often sided with the plaintiffs. In a typical case, the courts prohibited a city from hiring any new white police officers until its police department achieved a specified racial mix (e.g., 25 percent minority officers). This approach has been challenged in the U.S. Supreme Court,[40] where it was upheld. But the use of affirmative action guidelines in hiring decisions is far from settled, and Congress has debated legislation that would abolish its practice. As an ethical issue, it will continue to command attention in municipal personnel practices, and it is guaranteed to spark vigorous and contentious debate wherever it is considered.

The second area where affirmative action has import for cities is in the use of minority contractors. As black mayors and city council members have been elected in cities across the country, they have passed municipal ordinances that reserve ("set aside") a specified percentage of minority contracts for minority-owned businesses. In Richmond, for example, Mayor Roy West and the city council initiated an aggressive affirmative action policy that required public contractors to set aside 30 percent of subcontracts for minority-owned firms. Between 1983 and 1986, the percentage of contracts going to minority-owned businesses increased from 0.67 percent to 40 percent (Goldfield 1993). Other cities experienced similar expansion in their use of minority contractors under the leadership of black municipal administrations (see Rice 1993). But early in 1989, the Supreme Court ruled that Richmond's ordinance,

> similar to measures in effect in 36 states and nearly 200 local governments, violated the constitutional rights of white contractors to equal protection of the law. (*City of Richmond v. J.A. Crosson Co.*)[41]

40. *International Association of Firefighters v. City of Cleveland* (478 U.S. 501, 1986).
41. 102 L.Ed. 2nd 854, 1989.

The Court decreed that such set-asides were not in accordance with the Constitution unless it could be proved that they were a remedy for specific (and specifically proven) acts of prior discrimination. Though the population of Richmond is 50 percent black, and though only two-thirds of 1 percent of the city's contracts had been previously awarded to minority firms, these statistics (said the Court) did not prove that specific acts of discrimination had occurred. Further, said the Court,

> an amorphous claim that there has been past discrimination in a particular industry cannot justify the use of an unyielding racial quota. (*New York Times*, Jan. 24, 1989, 12)

However, the Court also stated that its ruling does not preclude municipal actions to rectify specified effects of identified and documented discrimination.

By the end of 1990, over fifty cases had been filed in the courts involving challenges to minority set-aside programs, and forty-six municipalities had abandoned their programs. The impact on minority contracts was substantial: Atlanta's contracts with minority-owned businesses fell from 37 percent in 1989 to 24 percent by mid 1990, Richmond's fell to 11 percent, and Philadelphia's fell from 15 percent to 3.5 percent (Rice 1993).

In response to the Court's language in *Crosson*, cities began to document specific instances of racial disparity that could be rectified by set-aside policies. For example, the Atlanta disparity study produced an eight-part, eleven hundred page report finding a substantial income disparity among Atlanta's black population as well as discrimination in several business areas, including construction, real estate, law, architecture, accounting, engineering, commodity sales, security, consulting, and energy. Other cities found similar evidence of racial disparity, and they have used these studies to justify the enactment and implementation of new set-aside policies. However, these studies are subject to methodological flaws that raise questions about their conclusions (Rice 1993), and no doubt we have not heard the final word on the use of minority set-asides to achieve affirmative action goals.

Next Steps

In these past several chapters we have traversed a considerable intellectual distance, moving from ideal public policy, to types and stages of urban policy, and finally to the interlocking of city, state, and national policies. To learn more of the ways that policies are carried into effect, we turn next to the delivery of urban services and the means for financing them.

PART SIX

MUNICIPAL FINANCE AND SERVICE DELIVERY

Icy Night, New York, platinum print, 1898, 26 x 34 cm
Alfred Stieglitz Collection, 1949.689.
Photograph © 1996, The Art Institute of Chicago. All Rights Reserved.

Taxes are what we pay for civilized society.
    Oliver Wendell Holmes, *Compania v. Collector*, 275 US 87 (1904)

CHAPTER 13

Municipal Finance: A Prelude to the Urban Service Delivery Saga

Wars and economic depressions are powerful levers of social and political change. The Great Depression of the 1930s brought the national government full tilt into the welfare state and altered forever federalism's relationships among states, cities, and the national government. The Second World War was no less important as a fulcrum of social and political change. As a crusade against fascist dictatorships, it helped arouse the American conscience against the racism then endemic to our society. Almost immediately following war's end, President Truman ordered racial integration of the armed services. And that same year, 1948, the Supreme Court ended restrictive housing covenants. Two years later, the Court forbade racial discrimination in admission to law schools and graduate schools (*Sweatt v. Painter, McLaurin v. Oklahoma State Regents*), and in 1954 it handed down its dramatic decision on school desegregation (*Brown v. Board of Education of Topeka*).

Each of these events had profound consequences for our cities, and the great chain of cause and effect continues to unroll. The war production effort, which provided job opportunities hitherto closed to blacks, combined with agricultural mechanization to create a great migration from the South to northern cities by the 1950s. At war's end, with cheap mortgage money now available to veterans, the great out-migration from central cities to suburbs also began. By the 1960s, northern cities had been transformed into enclaves of blacks and the poor, so that by decade's end the urban riots could be understood—at least retrospectively—as violence waiting to happen. (Or as the Spanish philosopher Ortega y Gasset once said of violence: It is reason exasperated.)

These events and their attendant social forces have brought profound changes to our cities, not merely in terms of their racial and social composition, nor only in terms of blacks' accession to council and mayoral positions, but also in terms of the city's role as *provider of urban services*. City government, as we have observed before, exists to make life liveable for city dwellers. And particularly since the Second World War, quality of life has become conflated with the provision of city services.[1]

We will examine this increased demand for urban services in the next chapter. But first, we must consider the fiscal foundations of urban services.

Growth and Retrenchment

Over the past four decades, the growing demand for city services has carried a substantial price tag. Municipal general expenditures, most of which go toward the provision of public services, grew by 307 percent (in constant dollars)[2] in the twenty-five years between 1950 and 1975, and by over 500 per-

---

1. Douglas Yates (1974) argues that the "save the cities" agenda that was prominent during the 1960s (and was reflected in such programs as Model Cities and the War on Poverty) has been replaced by an agenda that emphasizes service delivery as the central issue and problem of urban policy making.

2. Because of inflation, the purchasing power of the dollar is not the same today as it was in 1945, or even what it was last year. In times of low inflation (e.g., 1950–1960), only a minor adjustment is necessary to compare dollars. But during periods of high inflation (e.g., 1970–1980) dollar figures are incomparable without a substantial adjustment. In all analyses in this chapter, dollars are converted to a 1967 base, when the consumer price index was arbitrarily set to 1.00, i.e., $1.00 would purchase exactly a dollar's worth of goods and services). The price index for other years are listed below.

1950	.721	(i.e., 72.1 cents would purchase a dollar's worth of goods and services)
1955	.802	
1960	.887	
1965	.945	
1967	1.000	
1970	1.163	
1975	1.612	
1980	2.468	
1985	3.222	
1990	3.913	
1994	4.437	

cent between 1945 and 1975.[3] While this is a large expansion of the public sector by any standards, its true enormity can be gauged best by comparison with the federal budget. We tend to think of the 1960s and the early 1970s as a time of enormous growth in the federal government.[4] During this decade, a number of new programs greatly expanded the role of the federal government. Yet, the federal budget increased by only 240 percent between 1950 and 1975.

Common sense suggests that municipal budgets could not continue to expand indefinitely at this rate of growth. Expansion ground to a halt between 1975 and 1980, with municipal budgets (and the services they fund) in the 1980s actually retreating from their 1975 levels.

Before considering the factors contributing to the dramatic growth and then retrenchment in the provision of municipal services, we must first understand the sources of municipal revenue and how these have changed since 1945. Municipalities have several sources of revenue, and like persons selecting food in a cafeteria, they tend to mix and match these sources to meet their preferences and needs. The first, and most common, source of revenue is taxes. Another common source of revenue is fees charged for the use of urban services. A third source of revenue is intergovernmental aid handed down from both federal and state governments. A fourth source of revenue is municipally owned water, electric, or gas utilities and municipally owned transit systems. Finally, cities have a number of other minor sources of revenue, including fines and interest on municipal accounts. The following sections of this chapter discuss each of these sources of municipal revenue, suggesting how they have changed in response to social, economic, and political pressure since World War II.

Taxes

Municipal finance is greatly complicated by the place of the city in the intergovernmental system. While the city is home to most social problems, it faces the greatest restrictions in generating revenue to address these problems. These restrictions result from state laws and constitutional provisions limiting the taxing power of municipalities.

As noted in previous chapters, the U.S. Constitution specifically acknowledges the needs of the nation, the states, and the people. But notice-

---

3. Unattributed statistics in this chapter were obtained from the *Statistical Almanac of the United States and City Government Finances*, both published by the U.S. Department of Commerce.

4. In fact, the growth in the federal budget between 1950 and 1975 nearly rivals that encountered during any twenty-five year period in the nation's long history. Only those twenty-five year periods ending during a war (e.g., 1839–1864, 1892–1917, 1919–1944) and those encompassing the New Deal (e.g., 1925–1950) showed greater federal growth.

ably lacking is any mention of cities. In the minds of the Founding Fathers, municipalities fell under the aegis of the states. Municipal needs were to be met through state resources, and municipal prerogatives were to be limited to those allowed by state constitutional and statutory law. Most states allow cities to levy taxes on property, and cities traditionally have used the property tax as their major source of revenue. Only two states—Ohio and Pennsylvania—universally allow cities to levy income taxes, although other states allow income taxes on a city-by-city basis. And most of the forty-seven states that levy a sales tax also allow cities to levy a tax on sales. But in each case, the amount of tax that can be collected by municipalities is strictly limited by state law.

Property Tax

Rationale. The property tax has traditionally been the most important source of municipal revenue. In principle, this tax can be levied against either real property (e.g., land, buildings) or personal property (e.g., furniture, automobiles, stereo equipment). Logistical considerations make the latter very difficult, however, and most personal property (with the exception of automobiles) is exempt from taxation. The rationale underlying the property tax is straightforward: real property is *real* (i.e., true) wealth. Moreover, the ownership of real property is related to (a) ability to pay a fair share of the costs of government and (b) need for governmental services (e.g., the costs of maintaining courts and records for ensuring the safe acquisition and sale of real property, the cost to government of protecting that property). And for city government, a tax on land and buildings has an additional element of legitimacy. Since the value of urban real estate is influenced much more by population density (and the market factors that accompany density) than by improvements the owner may make, the community may legitimately tax that property in order to address the negative externalities of population density (e.g., crime, traffic congestion). For further discussion of the rationale underlying the property tax, see Hale (1985).

To this day, the property tax continues to be an important source of municipal income; but its original rationale has diminished. In an age of "paper wealth" (stocks, bonds, and bank accounts), real property is no longer a measure of either personal wealth or of ability to pay a fair share of the costs of government, and the property tax is generally viewed as *regressive.*[5]

5. A tax is progressive to the extent that people with greater assets (i.e., the rich) pay a larger *percentage* of their assets in taxes than those with fewer assets, and regressive to the extent that this does not occur. Property tax may be viewed as doubly regressive. First, it taxes expensive and inexpensive real property at the same rate (although Feiock, 1986, suggests that inexpensive property may be taxed at a higher rate than expensive property, exacerbating regressiveness). Second, a larger portion of the disposable income available to the poor is tied up in real property than that available to the rich (although

Assessment procedures. For all the mystery that surrounds property tax, it is rather straightforward. A tax assessor gauges the value of real property, based on its fair market value, and multiplies it by the *assessment rate* (typically between 25 percent and 100 percent), to determine the assessed value of the property. The owner is billed the assessed value multiplied by the *nominal tax rate* (which is set by the city and its voters, but must fall within state limitations).[6] Thus, the owner of a house whose assessed value is $50,000, living in an area where the nominal property tax rate is 6 percent, would have an annual property tax bill of ($50,000 × .06) = $1,200. The assessment rate, multiplied by the nominal tax rate, yields an *effective tax rate*.

State law may limit the effective tax rate in any of three ways. First, it may set a maximum assessment level; for example, municipalities may be prohibited from assessing property at more than 60 percent of its fair-market value. Second, it may limit the nominal rate at which property may be taxed.[7] For example, Pennsylvania limits the nominal tax rate for *some* types of taxing jurisdictions (e.g., nominal tax rates for third-class cities are limited to 2.5 percent). Or third, states may limit the effective tax rate. For example, Washington limits effective property tax rates to 1 percent of the property's fair market value (although residents can exceed this limit through a vote), and Alabama sets the effective tax rate to no more than 1.25 percent. Ironically, voters in these two states have created very different effective property tax levels from those allowed constitutionally. In Washington, local voters have approved effective tax rates that average 1.34 percent; whereas, in Alabama, local voters have kept the effective tax rate to an average of less than 0.4 percent. Table 13.1 shows assessment rates, nominal tax rates, and effective tax rates for several large cities. Clearly, both assessment rates and property tax rates vary widely across cities, with the highest effective tax rates generally occurring in the Northeast and Midwest, and the lowest in the South and the Southwest. As is also clear, effective property tax rates have generally declined since 1975.

---

this trend may have begun to reverse during recent years; see note 15 in chapter 14). Much of contemporary debate over tax policy turns on considerations related to "fair shares." However, the rationality of the debate is muddied by the fact that the underlying concepts—regressive and progressive—are veneered with additional emotive meaning, with progressive conveying the sense of progress, and regressive conveying an opposite meaning.

6. The logistics of assessing personal property are considerably more difficult. In the case of real property, what you see is what you get, and the assessor's task is straightforward. But to adequately assess personal property, the assessor would be required to actually inventory all the owner's belongings and assign a value to them. In the case of automobiles, this is relatively easy. But in the case of artwork, stereo and camera equipment, and jewelry, much of which could be conveniently "hidden" when the assessor comes calling, the task would be enormous.

7. The nominal tax rate is the rate at which a property's assessed value is taxed. Sometimes it is called *milleage*.

Table 13.1 1992 Assessment Rates and Property Tax Rates for Selected Cities

	1992			1975
	Assessment Rate	Nominal Tax Rate	Effective Tax Rate	Effective Tax Rate
Detroit, MI	0.494	0.0917	0.0453	0.0371
Milwaukee, WI	0.999	0.0384	0.0383	0.0359
Philadelphia, PA	0.320	0.0826	0.0264	0.0309
Baltimore, MD	0.400	0.0611	0.0244	0.0276
Jacksonville, FL	1.000	0.0215	0.0215	0.0167
Houston, TX	1.000	0.0200	0.0200	0.0244
Indianapolis, IN	0.150	0.1165	0.0175	0.0423
Atlanta, GA	0.300	0.0581	0.0174	0.0239
New Orleans, LA	0.100	0.1606	0.0161	0.0096
Phoenix, AZ	0.100	0.1528	0.0153	0.0173
Chicago, IL	0.160	0.0931	0.0149	0.0171
Boston, MA	1.000	0.1120	0.0112	0.0784
Seattle, WA	0.955	0.0105	0.0110	0.0176
Denver, CO	0.143	0.0673	0.0097	0.0116
Washington, DC	0.947	0.0096	0.0091	0.0180
New York, NY	0.080	0.1089	0.0087	0.0193
Memphis, TN	0.250	0.0268	0.0067	0.0194
Los Angeles, CA	0.612	0.0103	0.0063	0.0294
Honolulu, HA	0.843	0.0035	0.0030	0.0082

SOURCE: U.S. Department of Commerce, *Statistical Abstract of the United States* (1975, 1993); Government of the District of Columbia (1979, 1988).

Problems with the property tax. The property tax has had an uneven history, and municipal reliance on it has been declining over the past fifty years. At the turn of the century, nearly 75 percent of all municipal general revenue was generated through the property tax, and this heavy reliance continued for the next forty years. But in the 1940s, the need for alternative revenue-producing strategies became apparent, and by 1960 property taxes accounted for only 50 percent of all municipal general revenue. By 1980, this figure had further declined to less than 30 percent. Several factors have accounted for this increasing disaffection with the property tax. One was the taxpayer revolt of the late 1970s, which reduced caps (i.e., ceilings) on property assessments and tax rates. Another was the increased availability of state and federal funds during the 1960s and 1970s. But also of importance, other forms of taxation began to replace the property tax in municipal revenue generation schemes. Figure 13.1 shows the decline of the property tax and the growth of the sales tax in the years following World War II. For the most part, this shift reflects inherent weaknesses in the property tax, which we will consider now.

The first weakness is a built-in bias in assessment rates that favor older property. Property values are not assessed every year, or even every five years, and as a result most assessed property values lag a number of years behind

FIGURE 13.1: Percentage of Total Municipal Tax Revenue Produced by Property, Sales, and Income Taxes, 1942–1992

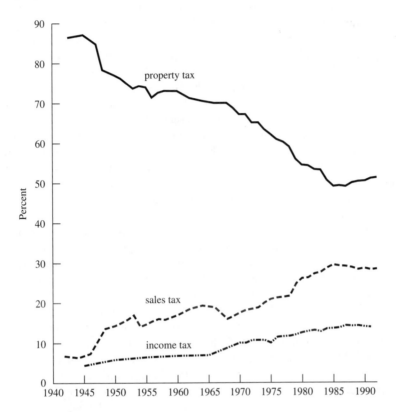

their true market values. In uninflationary times, this makes little difference. But runaway inflation during the 1970s resulted in substantial underassessment in older neighborhoods. In contrast, the value of new houses is assessed at the time of their construction, resulting in a higher assessed value in newer neighborhoods.

Second, a considerable amount of property, including that used by non-profit, charitable, and religious organizations, and by government units, is exempt from property taxes in most cities.[8] While the value of this property

8. The U.S. Supreme Court established this principle of exemption for governmental property in *McCulloch v. Maryland* (2 Wheaton 316, 1819). "The power to tax is the power to destroy," said Chief Justice John Marshall, meaning that if states and the national government were to be independent of one another, neither should be permitted to tax the property of the other.

initially may seem inconsequential, it can be quite high. In 1986, $520 billion in assessed property was excluded or exempted from the tax base; were these properties added to the tax base, it would increase by 12.7 percent. Exclusions and exemptions tend to be highest in heavily urbanized areas; for example, New York's real property tax base would expand by 44 percent if exemptions and exclusions were eliminated (U.S. Department of Commerce 1987).[9]

Third, it is unclear how property should be assessed, or more precisely, exactly what constitutes fair-market value. Is this the value that the property would bring if it were sold for its current use, for instance farming? Or is it the value that the land could bring if it were sold for a more lucrative purpose, for example a shopping mall? The discrepancies in these two valuation procedures can be enormous, and the standard chosen generally reflects the power of various lobbying groups. Realtors and land developers are powerful lobbies, and most undeveloped land thus tends to be underassessed.

Finally, the property tax is difficult to collect. Unlike the sales tax, which is collected at the point of retail payment, and the income tax, which is automatically deducted from paychecks, most people pay their property taxes only when they receive tax due (or tax overdue) notices in the mail.[10] Delinquency rates for property tax payment in major cities range between 2 percent and 15 percent (Lake 1979).[11] Most often, delinquent taxpayers are those owning unprofitable commercial property such as slum apartment buildings, and they often find it more profitable to abandon the property than to pay taxes on it. In such cases, the city usually takes possession of the property, but like the former owner, seldom finds it profitable (in fact, the cost of remodeling or razing the building is often greater than the sale value it will command).

Delinquent taxes also have a habit of backing up on residential developers, particularly in times of economic stagnation. Developers construct houses and housing subdivisions with the expectation of quick sales; when this happens, all tax liability transfers to the new property owners. But in a slow economy, when new houses often remain unsold for months at a time, developers are responsible for the taxes assessed on the unsold property (and as we observed above, these assessments on new houses are disproportionately high). When this unexpected expense is added to an already precarious cashflow situation, many developers are unable to meet their tax obligations. Cities are left with two options: they can either seize the delinquent property, or they can defer tax payments on these properties until the economy improves. Cities

9. According to some estimates, excluded and exempted property accounts for 41 percent of total urban property, with 54 percent of the property in Boston, 35 percent of the property in New York City, and 50 percent of the property in Washington, D.C., tax exempt (Meyer and Quigley 1977).

10. This applies to owners of commercial property more than to owners of residential property, whose property tax payments are most often collected by the bank as part of their mortgage payments.

11. Quoted in B. Jones (1983).

tend to view developers' contributions to the community very favorably, believing that capital investments in the community are essential to its economic viability. City officials therefore are usually unwilling to alienate developers by seizing their property. Scrupulous developers will pay their tax bills as soon as they are able; but a sizeable number of developers *always* seem to be living on the edge of bankruptcy, and they may carry a tax bill with the city for a number of years and never pay what is owed.

Sales Tax

Rationale. A second tax used by municipalities is the sales tax, collected as a percentage of goods (and in some locations, for instance New York City, services) sold within the city limits. As with the property tax, the tax on sales is assumed to tap one's ability to pay for services provided by the city; but it has the added benefit of tapping the resources of out-of-towners who come to the city to benefit from its retail, business, or cultural opportunities. Most states allow cities to supplement state sales tax with a municipal sales tax, although again they limit the rate of supplemental taxation. As indicated in figure 13.1, reliance on sales tax has increased since World War II, perhaps in response to growing discontent with the property tax and its faults. But the sales tax raises a different, although no less important, set of problems.

Problems with the sales tax. The first problem with the sales tax is its marked regressiveness. The philosophy underlying the sales tax assumes that purchasing power is commensurate with wealth. A wealthy family can afford more expensive clothes, meals, cars, and other goods and services than a poor family. But a family living at the edge of poverty must spend nearly 100 percent of its income on essential commodities, and therefore most of its income is subject to sales tax (except, of course, that spent on rent). In contrast, middle- and upper-income families often are able to put a substantial portion of their income into savings accounts, the stock market, or other investments, thus protecting much of their income from sales tax. Further, many of the services on which middle- and upper-income families spend their money (e.g., babysitting, gardening, legal advice, accounting services) are often not subject to sales tax. Some states attempt to reduce the regressiveness of the sales tax by excluding certain commodities from taxation, such as food and prescription drugs. But this has created considerable confusion. For example, Ohio taxes food purchased for consumption in a restaurant, but does not tax that same food if it is eaten off the premises. Thus, the consumer pays sales tax on his Big Mac if he eats it at McDonalds, but not if he eats it on the road.

Several states, in contrast, appear to have formulated their sales tax to make it starkly regressive. For example, the state sales tax in Alabama is 4 percent, and many municipalities supplement this with an additional 2 percent to

FIGURE 13.2: Total Retail Sales of Durable and Nondurable Goods

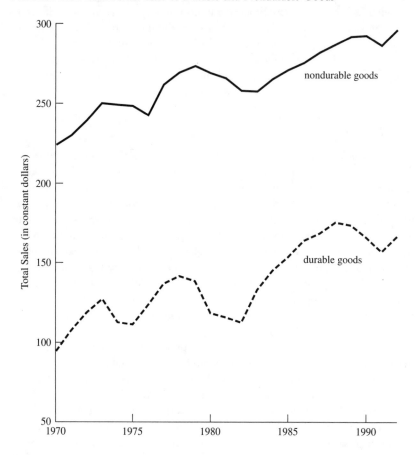

4 percent. But the state sales tax on new automobiles is only 2 percent, and new automobiles are exempt from local sales tax (used automobiles receive a lesser reduction on sales tax). This gives a substantial tax break to people who can afford to buy expensive new cars (and today, all new cars are expensive).

A second problem with the sales tax as a source of municipal revenue is its susceptibility to economic trends. Figure 13.2 indicates the variability of retail sales for durable and nondurable goods since 1970, measured in constant dollars. Since everyone must eat, even in economic recessions, the trend for nondurable items is relatively stable, and cities are guaranteed at least some revenue from the sales tax in good times and bad. But particularly in cities that do not tax food and prescription drugs (which account for nearly one-third of all nondurable goods purchased in the United States), sales-tax revenue depends largely on purchases of durable goods, prompted by extra cash on hand. A sizeable chunk of this revenue comes from "big-ticket" items, such as a new refrigerator, a home computer, a videocassette recorder, or an automobile. In good economic times, this type of purchase is common, and the city's coffers may swell with sales tax revenues. But in bad economic times, such as 1974 and 1980 (see figure 13.2), these purchases are less common, and sales-tax revenues are insufficient to finance urban services. Any city counting on stable sales-tax receipts to finance services will inevitably feel the pinch in recession years.

Herein lies the paradox of the sales tax. If the city requires a stable source of revenue, then the sale of disposable goods must be taxed, and the sales tax becomes quite regressive. But if the city desires to reduce regressiveness by exempting the sale of certain disposable goods from taxation, it then runs the risk of unstable and unpredictable tax revenues.

Income Tax

Rationale. The third major source of tax revenue for municipalities is the income tax. In comparison with the sales tax and particularly the property tax, the municipal income tax is a little-used method of revenue generation (see figure 13.1). Even so, a number of large cities rely on the income tax as a means of financing municipal services; these include Washington, D.C., Baltimore, Detroit, Philadelphia, Pittsburgh, Kansas City, St. Louis, New York, Cincinnati, Cleveland, and Columbus. Large cities rely more on income tax than small cities do for two reasons. First, it provides a way of taxing people who work in the central city but live in the suburbs (small cities do not have suburbs). Second, the tax base for property tax is relatively lower in the central cities than in other areas, while the income-tax base may be higher. Table 13.2 indicates the strength of the relationship between city size and income tax. Cities that assess an income tax are not uniformly distributed across the country; rather, they tend to be concentrated in the Northeast and Midwest (particularly in Pennsylvania and Ohio).

Table 13.2 Municipal Income Tax Assessments by City Size, 1992

City Size	Percent of Tax Revenue Generated by Income Tax in 1992
1,000,000 or more	25.8%
500,000–999,999	16.6
300,000–499,999	9.0
200,000–299,999	9.6
100,000–199,999	2.8
50,000–99,999	2.3
49,999 or fewer	6.0

SOURCE: Adapted from U.S. Department of Commerce, Bureau of the Census, *City Government Finances in 1991–92.*

Problems with the income tax. Like the property tax and the sales tax, the municipal income tax is a flawed source of revenue. In principle, the income tax *can* be progressive, as it is at the federal level; that is, the tax rate can be scaled to income. But in practice, municipal income tax is typically assessed at a flat rate (e.g., 5 percent) across all income categories, thus making it regressive. Even so, however, it is not as regressive as the sales tax, which is assessed at a flat rate *and* applied disproportionately to wealthy versus poor individuals and families.

Second, like the sales tax, the income tax is sensitive to changes in the economic climate in general and to unemployment in particular. When urban unemployment rates hit 10 percent (and inner-city unemployment rates hit 20 percent), annual revenues from income tax are bound to suffer. In general, the impact of fluctuating urban unemployment is not great, since those most prone to unemployment are unskilled or semiskilled workers with low earning power. (Seldom are bank presidents or other high-salaried professionals the victims of unemployment, although midlevel managers have become an endangered species as corporations have downsized during the 1990s.) Much more problematic, however, is the long-term industrial and corporate decline of many northeastern and midwestern cities that rely on the income tax. For example, when steel plants shut down in Pittsburgh and Cleveland, or when automobile plants cut back production in Detroit, those cities lose the income of many skilled, well-paid employees, as well as the tax on their income. And when New York City loses the corporate headquarters of American Airlines to Dallas, or Cleveland loses the corporate headquarters of Diamond Shamrock and Harris (both members of the Fortune 500) to Dallas and Melbourne, Florida, respectively, they also lose the income of a number of high-paid corporate executives. New York has been the hardest hit of such cities: Whereas 128 Fortune 500 companies maintained their headquarters in New York City in 1965, only 48 remained by 1988 (Rogowsky and Berkman 1995). The most dramatic of these moves were toward the South and Southwest; but as table 13.3 demonstrates New York also lost a number of corporate headquarters to the suburbs. The corporate shifts from New York City are only manifestations of a larger national trend, however. Between 1969 and 1989, for example, the proportion of corporate headquarters located in the South doubled, as did the proportion located in suburbs (Ward 1994). Regardless of the circumstances of the migration, it is costly to cities that rely on an income tax.

Other Taxes

In addition to the three types of tax discussed above, cities collect a number of miscellaneous taxes. New York, for example, assesses a *corporate tax* for the privilege of doing business in the city. The present rate (approximately 9 percent)

Table 13.3   Selected Corporate Outmigration from New York City, 1969–1985

To Sunbelt Cities		To Frostbelt Cities	
Shell Oil	Houston	Continental Oil	Stamford, CT
Atlantic Richfield	Los Angeles	General Electric	Fairfield, CT
American Petrofina	Dallas	American Can	Greenwich, CT
Harcourt Brace		AVCO	Greenwich, CT
Jovanovich	Orlando	Standard Brands	Stamford, CT
American Airlines	Dallas	Hooker Chemical	Stamford, CT
M.K. Kellogg	Houston	Ingersoll-Rand	Woodcliff Lk., NJ
Oxford Paper	Richmond	Bangor-Punta	Greenwich, CT
Warner Bros.	Los Angeles	Pepsico	Harrison, NY
MGM	Los Angeles	Uniroyal	Oxford, CT
		Union Camp	Wayne, NY

SOURCE *Fortune*, 1968–1986; Quante (1976).

is levied on the entire net corporate income or the portion thereof allocated to New York City. But many corporate activities, including those involving major financial transactions, are nontaxable. Further, since both New York City and New York State corporate taxes are high, national companies try to keep their New York transactions (and hence their tax assessments) as low as possible. As a result, corporate taxes in New York City account for a relatively small proportion (approximately 6 percent) of the municipal tax revenue. New York City also charges a *commercial rental tax* (4.5 percent on all annual rent over $21,000), but this, too, accounts for relatively little (3.6 percent) municipal tax revenue. And like many other cities, New York City charges a tax on motor vehicle licenses, on the sale of alcoholic beverages, gasoline, tobacco products, and other selected items, and on the use of public utilities. But altogether, these selected sales taxes and other taxes total less than 10 percent of New York City's tax revenue (New York City Department of Finance 1996). Across the country, the same trend holds, with miscellaneous taxes seldom totaling more than 15 percent to 20 percent of a city's total tax revenue. Figure 13.3 shows the breakdown of New York City's tax revenues for 1995.

User Fees

Rationale and Level of Use

In addition to taxes, which are assessed more or less according to an individual's, family's, or company's ability to pay, fees are assessed for a number of services provided by the city more or less according to the amount an individual, family, or company uses them. Across all cities, fees and charges account for approximately 18 percent of general revenue. Table 13.4 provides a general breakdown and specific examples of the revenues generated by various types of services in large cities.

FIGURE 13.3: Sources of New York City's 1995 Tax Revenue

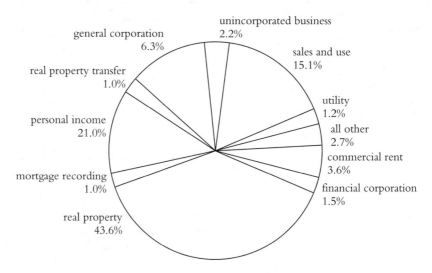

general corporation
6.3%

unincorporated business
2.2%

real property transfer
1.0%

sales and use
15.1%

personal income
21.0%

utility
1.2%

all other
2.7%

commercial rent
3.6%

mortgage recording
1.0%

financial corporation
1.5%

real property
43.6%

Cities differ in the services and commodities they offer and for which they charge. Relatively few cities, for example, have municipal colleges, art galleries, stadiums, zoos, or municipal golf courses. Most do have parks and recreation departments, however, which may or may not charge for participation in softball leagues or for tennis instruction. Greens fees for municipal golf courses vary widely from city to city, as do transit fares (in some cities, bus passengers ride free in downtown zones). By the same token, some cities allow free parking, while others charge for virtually every available parking space. Finally, some cities establish "benefit districts" in which residents pay special assessments for street, sidewalk, and sewer improvements in their district, while other cities distribute the costs of such improvements across the entire tax-paying populace.[12]

Ironically, even though large cities have considerably more opportunities to collect revenue for services rendered, they take less advantage of that opportunity than do smaller cities (more about that later). And even large cities vary considerably in their reliance on user fees as sources of revenue. One useful point of comparison is the ratio of revenue generated from specific fees and charges to that generated by general taxes, shown for large cities in table 13.5.

12. Some consider benefit districts to be different from user fees (e.g., ACIR, 1985). They are combined here for the sake of parsimony.

Table 13.4   Revenue from Municipal Charges and Fees in Cities over 300,000

General Area Specific fees and charges	Percent of Municipal revenue
Education	0.3%
School lunches	
Adult education tuition	
Municipal college tuition	
Charges for books	
Charges for gymnasium uniforms or equipment	
Highways	0.9
Road tolls	
Bridge tolls	
Health and Hospital	1.9
Hospital charges, including per diem rates and service charges	
Ambulance charges	
Inoculation charges	
Sewerage	4.2
Sewer system fees	
Other Sanitation	0.9
Trash collection fees	
Industrial waste charges	
Parks and Recreation	0.6
Parking charges	
Concession rental	
Golf course greens fees	
Softball league enrollment fees	
Tennis class charges	
Day camp charges	
Admission charges to municipal swimming pools	
Admission charges to zoos, museums, etc.	
Housing/Community Development	1.0
Rent from public housing	
Street-lighting installation charges	
Convention center charges	
Airport	2.5
Terminal rental	
Landing and departure fees	
Hangar rental fees	
Water Transport Terminal	0.5
Parking Facilities	0.4
Miscellaneous Commercial Activities	0.1
Other	1.0
Charges for false burglar alarms	
Fees for fingerprinting	
Leases on municipal stadiums	
Building inspections	
Licenses (e.g., liquor, taxicab, etc.)	
Emergency 911 service	
Special Assessments	0.2
TOTAL	14.5%

SOURCE: Adapted from U.S. Department of Commerce, *City Government Finances in 1991–92;* Mushkin and Vehorn (1980).

Table 13.5 Ratio of Service-Generated Revenue to Tax-Generated
Revenue for Cities Over 300,000 in 1977 and 1992

	Ratio				Ratio		
City	1992	1977	Form[a]	City	1992	1977	Form[a]
Austin	1.327	.894	Mg	Baton Rouge	.451	.194	M
Long Beach	1.092	.648	Mg	Indianapolis	.450	.418	M
Atlanta	.942	.598	M	Portland	.449	.386	CO
Denver	.861	.501	M	Columbus	.432	.423	M
Albuquerque	.802	.544	M	Milwaukee	.428	.219	M
Dallas	.766	.210	Mg	Honolulu	.419	.233	M
Phoenix	.704	.302	Mg	Detroit	.400	.317	M
Tulsa	.702	.354	M	Buffalo	.399	.209	M
Oakland	.669	.456	Mg	Toledo	.382	.593	CO
Charlotte	.631	.289	Mg	Miami	.367	.115	CO/Mg[a]
San Diego	.628	.524	Mg	Fort Worth	.362	.408	Mg
Memphis	.625	.481	M	Tucson	.356	.288	Mg
Minneapolis	.532	.336	M	St Louis	.338	.219	M
Houston	.521	.289	M	Chicago	.329	.152	M
Jacksonville	.515	.836	M	Boston	.312	.165	M
Oklahoma City	.501	.309	Mg	Nashville	.284	.292	M
Cincinnati	.499	1.139	Mg	Omaha	.283	.231	M
New Orleans	.491	.454	M	Kansas City	.260	.311	Mg
Newark	.489	.034	M	Cleveland	.252	.556	M
Los Angeles	.483	.285	M	Philadelphia	.226	.148	M
San Jose	.482	.387	Mg	New York	.209	.166	M
Seattle	.482	.482	M	Baltimore	.152	.229	M
San Francisco	.479	.244	M	Washington	.112	.089	M
El Paso	.469	.498	M	Pittsburgh	.052	.050	M
San Antonio	.460	.396	Mg				

SOURCE: U.S. Department of Commerce, *City Government Finances in 1991–92; City Government Finances in 1976-77.*

a. Form of government: Mg = Council-Manager; M = Mayor-Council; CO = Commission; Miami has a Commission government with a strong mayor, but it also has a city manager.

Problems with User Fees[13]

Some user fees are little more than highly regressive taxes in that they are assessed to all residents regardless of their ability to pay; these include fees for trash pickup, sewer hookup and monthly charges, and emergency 911 service. In other cases, user fees represent a means for regulating use of selective services, in that the city provides them on a pay-as-you-use basis; these include services provided by the parks and recreation department, admission to municipal facilities (e.g., zoos, museums), and parking in municipal parking lots. But by regulating services through user fees, many of the city's poor are effectively precluded from using important services.

13. A more complete discussion of both the benefits and problems of user fees is provided by ACIR (1985).

Some cities would not be able to offer services if they did not charge for them. But other cities have found a way to avoid these fees, particularly in the area of recreational services. For example, Chicago and Newark charge no user fees for park and recreation activities, allowing all residents to participate in these activities regardless of their ability to pay. Ten other cities use fees to fund less than 15 percent of their total Parks and Recreation budget. On the other hand, twelve cities use fees to fund more than 30 percent of their Parks and Recreation budget. Overall, big cities are relying on user fees to fund larger portions of their Parks and Recreation budgets than occurred in 1986, when we first did this analysis (Herson and Bolland 1990).

Many city services are provided for the public good, reflecting a philosophy that what benefits the city as a whole should be financed by the city as a whole, through general taxes. Such services as crime and fire protection, street and park maintenance, and trash collection obviously fall under this classification. But many argue that this conception of the public good should be expanded to include a number of other services, such as public transit, recreation programs, social service programs (e.g., day care), public health, and public housing. Even if these services are used disproportionately by the economically disadvantaged, they benefit the community in important ways. For example, recreation programs keep juveniles out of trouble. Public housing keeps families out of tenements. And public transit not only provides opportunities for people without cars to find jobs and commute to work, it also reduces traffic congestion. In other words, each of these services directly benefits its clientele. But it also provides indirect benefits to virtually all other segments of the community.

Most cities accept (although perhaps grudgingly) this view of the public good, and as noted previously, municipal funding for public services has increased steadily and dramatically since World War II. As table 13.5 shows, however, the large "frostbelt" cities, particularly those located in the Northeast, tend to embrace this philosophy more readily than their counterparts in the South and West. These northern cities tend to fund programs mostly through tax dollars rather than through user fees, with a mean fee-to-tax ratio of .327; in contrast, large cities in the South and the West embrace the pay-as-you-use philosophy much more fully, with a mean fee-to-tax ratio of .597. Table 13.5 also shows that reformed cities have higher fee-to-tax ratios (.624) than unreformed cities (.438). This finding is similar to that reported in table 14.3, which shows that unreformed cities have achieved a much higher rate of public transit ridership than reformed cities. Both the reliance on user fees and encouragement of private means of transportation suggest that reformed cities treat municipal services as private goods, to be paid for by people who use them. In contrast, unreformed cities seem more willing to treat municipal services as public goods, to be paid for through general municipal revenue. This is consistent with the overriding philosophy of the reform movement, that cities are to be managed efficiently, like businesses. *[The theory of urban reform.]*

Table 13.5 also suggests that many cities have turned to user fees to replace revenue lost to the municipal tax revolt of the late 1970s. Overall, the ratio of user fees to taxes increased between 1977 and 1992. This increase is particularly noticeable in California. Between 1977 and 1992, per capita tax revenues in large and middle sized California cities increased by only 7.4 percent while per capita user fees in these cities increased by 84.6 percent. This disparity pushed the mean fee-to-tax ratio in these cities from .273 to .473 during this period, and user fees increased from 7 percent of total revenue in 1978 to 38 percent of total revenue in 1990 (O'Sullivan et al. 1995). While the ratio of fees-to-taxes has been increasing nationally, the large jump in California is attributable to Proposition 13, a ballot issue that capped the property tax that municipalities in California could assess.

Intergovernmental Revenue

Federal Aid

Another major source of municipal revenue is provided by other governmental units, particularly the federal government. Expenditures for municipal services grew at a much faster rate than municipal tax receipts in the years between 1945 and 1975, suggesting alternative sources of municipal revenue. Part of this additional revenue was generated by user fees and by several other revenue-producing strategies to be discussed later. But *most of the increase was provided by federal funds*. In general, since World War II—but particularly with the advent of the Great Society programs during the 1960s—the federal government began to recognize that cities are unable to solve their problems without financial help, and as table 13.6 shows, that help increased at a substantial rate during the 1960s and the 1970s. However, table 13.6 also shows that the federal commitment to cities declined precipitously during the Reagan and Bush presidencies, decreasing by 56 percent between 1980 and 1992; the largest cuts occurred in community development, education, social services, employment, and job training programs (Kantor 1993).

State Aid

In comparison with cities, states tend to be revenue rich, for most levy both a sales tax and an income tax; and by the late 1970s many states were accumulating budget surpluses (Pfiffner 1983). Thus, it is not surprising that as direct federal aid to cities began to decline, states felt pressure to fill the void. Overall, state aid to cities dwarfs federal aid, as suggested by table 13.6. Although state aid is very important for the city's survival, accounting for between 15 percent and 20 percent of all municipal revenue (and between 35

Table 13.6 Federal and State Aid to Cities, 1950–1992 (In millions of constant 1967 dollars)

| | Federal Aid to Cities | | |
	Total	Revenue Sharing	State Aid to Cities
1950	$ 128.9		$1,181.7
1955	251.9		1,541.1
1960	544.5		2,106.0
1965	635.8		2,904.8
1970	1,149.6		5,307.8
1971	1,534.2		6,101.4
1972	1,997.6		6,653.6
1973	3,283.2	$1,206.6	7,283.2
1974	3,695.3	1,590.4	7,084.6
1975	3,625.3	1,369.7	8,097.4
1976	4,364.8	1,281.5	8,077.4
1977	4,912.9	1,311.3	7,843.5
1978	5,237.5	1,272.7	7,411.5
1979	4,984.8	1,150.4	7,116.8
1980	4,405.2	996.8	6,458.3
1981	4,142.1	907.9	6,240.1
1982	3,804.2	856.7	6,553.8
1983	3,574.4	827.1	6,611.6
1984	3,305.0	791.7	6,599.8
1985	3,194.3	760.4	7,170.4
1986	2,988.1	726.2	7,498.8
1987	2,466.9		7,768.3
1988	2,058.4		7,927.4
1989	1,979.0		7,957.7
1990	1,928.2		8,751.1
1991	1,867.3		8,558.4
1992	1,912.2		8,622.2

SOURCE: U.S. Department of Commerce, *Statistical Abstract of the United States*

percent and 50 percent of local school district revenue) during the past two decades, it is qualitatively quite different from federal aid. One major source of state aid to municipalities is federal funds that are passed through states to the cities. This, in effect, is not really state money but rather federal money that the states happen to receive as an intermediary. They often, however, have discretion in deciding to which municipalities federal funds will be allocated. A second major source of state aid is tax-sharing funds, the majority of which go to fund public education (62 percent in 1984, down from 86 percent in 1982). By restricting the taxes municipalities may collect, and by exempting different types of income and property from taxation, the state in effect becomes the tax collector and controller for the city. Tax sharing is simply a way of returning some of this "controlled" revenue, although again the state can exercise discretion in the allocation of tax-sharing funds to municipalities.

A third and relatively recent source of state aid has occurred as cities and their states combine resources to attract new businesses and keep old ones.

Cities have always attempted to put their best foot forward in an effort to show prospective new businesses how much they would benefit from locating or staying there. But during the past decade, the stakes have increased as cities struggle to counteract the flight of good paying jobs to the suburbs and the population exodus that accompanies them; knowing this, businesses have demanded more and bigger incentives to locate in a city (or to keep from relocating elsewhere), and cities often lack the resources that they would need to compete in this marketplace. Hence, they have moved into partnership with their states. The high cost of competing for business and industry and the nature of state-local partnerships that have developed is demonstrated in two examples.

In April 1993, Daimler-Benz announced that it was planning to open its first manufacturing facility in the United States and that it would be searching for a site over the next several months to build its new Mercedes-Benz sports utility vehicle. More than thirty states proposed sites and put together incentive packages that they believed would attract the auto manufacturer. The package that the state of Alabama, in conjunction with several municipalities, offered to Daimler-Benz was valued at over $253 million plus additional tax abatements and deferments. This includes $183 million from the state for plant construction, a training center, and highway improvements; $29 million from the City of Tuscaloosa; $12 million from Tuscaloosa County for site preparation, a railroad spur to the plant, and extension of water and sewer lines; $5 million each from the City of Birmingham and from Jefferson County; and $1 million from the City of Northport. In addition, the state offered to purchase twenty-five hundred sports utility vehicles produced at the site at a cost of $75 million (Watson 1995, *Tuscaloosa News*, Oct. 1, 1995). In September 1993, Daimler-Benz announced its decision to build the Mercedes-Benz plant in Tuscaloosa County, with a promise of fifteen hundred new jobs for the area.

In the summer of 1989, United Airlines announced it was planning a new maintenance hub that would bring nearly a billion dollars in investment and generate seven thousand jobs. Within a few months, over ninety-one localities and/or states had offered incentive packages that were being considered, including $115 million from Denver and $120 million from Oklahoma City. United Airlines delayed its decision, hoping that cities and states would enhance their offers. In 1991, nine finalist cities were selected and invited to put together final incentive packages—which by then had gotten very expensive. Kentucky pulled out of the bidding at $341 million in cash, land, and tax abatements; so too, did Colorado. Indianapolis was ultimately selected after putting together a $300 million package of incentives (Kantor and Savitch 1993, Watson 1995).

In each of these examples and hundreds more like them, businesses were able to extract a price that cities are unable to afford on their own. States have stepped in to assist cities, largely filling the void that has been created by declining federal revenues. Ironically, the "newest federalism" is hardly federalism at all but, rather, a revitalization of relationships between states and cities.

This relationship is not without its own problems, however. Whereas federal transfers tend to be progressive, with the majority of aid targeted toward low-income and minority populations, state aid tends to be more regressive, reflecting political considerations more than need. For example, cities with strong mayors tend to get more assistance from their states than do reformed cities. Thus, mayors may benefit from links with state officials in ways that nonpolitical city managers cannot (Clark and Walter 1994).

Other Sources of Municipal Revenue

Utility Charges

Municipalities have at their disposal a number of other sources of revenue, most of which provide them with little flexibility in their provision of services. The most important of these is revenue generated from municipally owned utilities. In 1992, for example, municipalities took in over $33 billion (15.1 percent of all municipal revenue) from the sale of water, gas, and electricity to municipal residents, and an additional $1.9 billion (0.9 percent of all revenue) from transit fares. While this may seem to be an important source of revenue, it is illusory: Cities expended $34.9 billion to provide water, gas, and electricity, and an additional $5.6 billion to provide public transportation for their residents. In other words, every penny of revenue generated by municipal utilities (and considerably more) was tied up in production costs.

Minor Sources of Municipal Revenue

One minor source of revenue is the sale of municipally owned property (e.g., undeveloped land, office buildings, housing stock, municipal utilities). Overall, this accounts for only a small percentage of a city's total revenue, with a national average ranging between .13 percent and .51 percent since 1973. Yet, during any given year, it can become an important source of a city's revenue. For instance, in 1986 both Denver and Tucson received 2.5 percent of their total revenue from property sales; in 1984 Oakland received 13 percent of its total revenue from property sales; and in one of the largest sell-offs ever, Honolulu received 18.7 percent of its total revenue from property sales during 1990 and 1991. In general, revenues generated from property sales are decreasing over time, representing the reality that property can be sold only once. In most cases, the sale of municipal property does not make headlines. But in some cases, it has been politically contentious, as when San Diego sold some of its attractive park land (Clark 1994).

A second minor source of revenue is the collection of fines and forfeitures, which accounted for 1 percent of total 1992 revenue in large cities. Although the most easily recognized type of fine, the traffic ticket is a relatively unimportant source of this type of revenue; much more important are fines imposed on businesses and homeowners for violations of municipal codes and ordinances. A third minor source of revenue for most cities is interest payments from banks and other financial institutions. Municipal expenditures tend to be spread over the course of a year, while much of its revenue (e.g., property tax, income tax) is received in lump sums. A smart city administrator will place these funds in interest-bearing accounts until they are needed. Because of annual fluctuations in sales tax and income tax revenues, some cities will show surpluses at year's end, which will also generate interest if properly invested. For the nation's largest cities, interest earnings in 1992 accounted for 3.9 percent of total revenues, with southern and western cities showing the largest percentage (e.g., 20.3 percent for Tulsa, 14.9 percent for Albuquerque, 12.5 percent for San Diego) and frostbelt cities the smallest percentage (e.g., 0.9 percent for Newark, 1.1 percent for Boston, 1.2 percent for Buffalo, 1.5 percent for New York City).

In general, large reformed cities differ from large unreformed cities in their reliance on these types of revenues; in no case are these differences large, however. For example, unreformed cities raise more revenue through fines than do reformed cities; this perhaps reflects a greater hesitancy on the part of reformed cities to offend local businesses by imposing fines on them. On the other hand, reformed cities raise a somewhat greater proportion of their revenue through interest earnings and property sales than do unreformed cities. The greater reliance on interest earnings may reflect a tendency on the part of reformed cities to conduct government as a business, investing surpluses rather than spending them in response to political demands; the greater reliance on property sales may reflect a view in reformed cities that property is a commodity to be bought and sold as an investment rather than hung onto as an integral part of the public interest.

Bonded Indebtedness

The federal government is the only government permitted to borrow money to pay general operating expenses. Thus, municipalities are forced to pay personnel costs, equipment costs, energy costs, and so forth out of their general revenue, or with surpluses from previous years.[14] In a lean year, they may be forced to lay off personnel and curtail services as money runs out. In fact, many school districts have been forced to close their doors early in the face of

---

14. Municipalities are allowed to obtain short-term loans to improve their cash flow, so long as these loans are backed by expected revenue (e.g., property tax receipts).

budget crises, for they are not permitted to borrow money to fund their normal operational expenses.

Were this principle applied to all municipal expenditures, the city would never have developed as a service delivery system, for the costs of capital construction and improvements are simply too large to be accommodated within a single year's budget. For example, school construction costs are now measured in the millions of dollars, and the cost of a municipal park, complete with playground equipment and baseball diamonds, may exceed $3 million. The cost of a new waste-water treatment plant may exceed $60 million. And a new urban hospital may cost $150 million to construct. Clearly, the cost of any of these projects would be well beyond the capacity of most cities (*total* general expenditures in cities with between 75,000 and 100,000 people averaged $58 million in 1992, and general expenditures of cities with fewer than 75,000 people averaged only $3.9 million).

However, cities *are* allowed to issue bonds, typically to finance large, capital construction and improvement projects. During the late 1970s and early 1980s, cities used their long-term borrowing capacity to issue industrial revenue bonds (IRBs), designed to provide incentives (e.g., tax abatements, low-interest loans) for new businesses and industries to move to (and existing businesses and industries to remain in) the city. IRBs accounted for only 4 perecnt of total long-term municipal bonds issued in 1975; by 1980, this had grown to 15 percent, as cities competed for business and industry during a period of economic uncertainty. The Tax Reform Act of 1986 dramatically reduced the extent to which many capital projects could qualify for tax exempt bond status, however, and added more complexity to the process by which state and local governments can issue such debt (Bowman et al. 1992). Alberta Sbragia (1983) provides a useful discussion of long-term municipal bonds, particularly the debate over their benefits to the public and private sectors.

In 1992, municipalities issued $35.8 billion in bonds, a 32 percent reduction from 1986 levels (when Congress passed the Tax Reform Act). Municipal bonded indebtedness totaled over $241 billion in 1992, with thirty-three individual cities having each accrued a debt of $1 billion or more. These include Houston ($3.4 billion), Dallas ($3.5 billion), Philadelphia ($3.7 billion), Washington, D.C. ($3.9 billion), San Antonio ($4.1 billion), Jacksonville ($4.7 billion), Chicago ($6.0 billion), Los Angeles ($7.9 billion), and New York ($33.3 billion). Even some relatively small cities had acquired considerable debt by 1992; for example, Kansas City, Kansas, with a population of 150,000, owed nearly $1.7 billion in bonds. In 1992, the bond issues of cities, school districts, and other special purpose governments totaled over $134.7 billion. And when municipal debt is combined with school district debt, total local indebtedness exceeds $599 billion (compared with a 1992 national debt of $3 trillion).

When bonds are issued, interest rates are determined largely by the city's bond rating, assessed by one of two financial services (Moody's Investor Service, Standard and Poor's Corporation) to establish the city's credit risk. These ratings, conducted for an annual fee of between $500 and $2,500, are based on a confidential formula that employs several factors related to growth and tax base. This proves beneficial to cities located in the South and West, where bond ratings have improved relative to those in the North and Midwest (J. Peterson 1981).

In recent years, municipal bonds have been attractive investments for the middle and upper classes, for the interest they yield is tax free[15] and they are for the most part a safe investment. This former point means that municipalities can pay interest somewhat below the prevailing market rate, resulting in a de-facto federal and state subsidy to municipalities. The latter point, concerning risk, is more problematic. Between 1838 and 1969 there were six thousand recorded government defaults on bonds. But fewer than 33 percent of these involved municipalities, and most occurred during the Depression years of 1930–1939. Since 1945, 431 governmental units have defaulted on bond obligations. But the largest defaults are by four special-purpose governments: the West Virginia Turnpike Authority, the Calumet Skyway Toll Bridge, the Chesapeake Bay Bridge (ACIR 1973), and the Washington Public Power Supply System (Leigland and Lamb 1986).[16] During this period, municipalities teetered on the edge of bankruptcy (e.g., New York City), and some managed to fall over the abyss; but even Cleveland's default based on a $14 million payment that it failed to make on December 15, 1978, was technical in nature, for the city had already arranged to repay the loan later, which it did on February 27, 1979.[17]

During the 1990s, however, municipal bonds seemed less safe and secure. In 1991, Philadelphia flirted with bankruptcy; its deficits had increased from $32 million in 1987 to $284 million in 1992, and city leaders showed lit-

15. The 1986 tax reform law limited tax exemptions for IRBs; but it maintained the tax exempt status for general obligation municipal bonds to fund other projects (e.g., wastewater treatment plants, school construction, parks).

16. The West Virginia Turnpike Commission, Calumet Skyway Toll Bridge, and Chesapeake Bay Bridge and Tunnel Commission defaults accounted for approximately $333 million. In contrast, the Washington Public Power Supply System default accounted for $2.25 billion.

17. Sbragia (1983) convincingly argues that Cleveland's was a "political default," brought about by antagonism between then–Mayor Dennis Kucinich and Cleveland's business community, including local bankers who held Cleveland's short-term notes (see note 14). Members of the business community (including the bankers) had earlier spearheaded a recall campaign against the mayor, who in turn referred to them as "blood-sucking vampires." It is not surprising, therefore, that the banks refused to extend Cleveland's short-term credit until its cash flow stabilized. Sbragia (1983, 83) notes "the refusal by banks to extend further credit may thus reflect not only a judgment on the city's finances but also the state of relations between the city government and the business community."

tle ability to either cut spending or to raise taxes. In 1991, the Pennsylvania Intergovernmental Cooperation Authority was created by the state to oversee the sale of bonds to raise needed money for the city and to impose discipline on its budgeting process (Adams 1994). Philadelphia was not the only large city to experience fiscal stress, however. During 1990, Standard and Poor downgraded its ratings of 474 municipal bond issues (Bowman et al. 1992; also see Dearborn et al., 1992, for an in-depth discussion of the finances of the nation's largest cities during the early 1990s). This uncertainty was capped by an unexpected event that brought home the realization that even seemingly stable municipalities can falter in a risky and uncertain stock market. During the early 1990s, the treasurer of Orange County, California, the nation's fifth most populous county, engaged in an aggressive strategy of investing the county's governmental resources in the stock market. Until early 1994, this strategy seemed to be working, and the county's stock portfolio had more than doubled, reaching $20 billion. But the risky strategy began to unravel early in 1994 when interest rates began to rise, and by the autumn of that year the value of the stock had declined precipitously. In an effort to recover from this loss, the county treasurer shifted the portfolio to a relatively new but poorly understood and largely unregulated type of investment called derivatives and lost $1.7 billion of the county's funds in the process.[18] On December 6, 1996, Orange County filed for bankruptcy and was faced with the prospect of cutting as many as one thousand jobs. By 1996, the county had worked its way back to fiscal solvency, but the impact of the default will be with it for some time to come. (See Flickinger and McManus, 1996, for a discussion of the Orange County bankruptcy and its implications.)

In most cases, the urban fiscal crisis has been brought on by a declining tax base coupled with growing demand for municipally provided services. But it has been exacerbated by a tax revolt promulgated by voters during the 1970s. The next chapter explores the factors that led to the growth in urban services between 1945 and 1975, and the factors that have led to their subsequent decline.

18. By the 1990s, risk-taking has become one of the municipal strategies for dealing with fiscal strain. Clark (1994) described these high-risk strategies as "innovative" approaches to borrowing and investing money, and he concluded that one of the riskiest—derivatives—could allow city governments to synthetically create a wide variety of bond structures and potentially cut the cost of borrowing money in half. Thus, Orange County was not alone in its recklessness; the extent to which other government units will be devastated by the volatility of the stock market remains to be seen.

From an American Place, Looking North, chloride print, 1931, 23.8 x 18.9 cm
Alfred Stieglitz Collection, 1949.788.
Photograph © 1996, The Art Institute of Chicago. All Rights Reserved.

". . .it takes all the running you can do to stay in the same place. If you want to
get somewhere else, you must run at least twice as fast. . . ."
    Lewis Carroll, *Through the Looking Glass*

CHAPTER 14

Growth, Decline, and Resurgence of Urban Service Delivery: 1945 to the Present

Service Delivery as the *Raison d'Etre* of the American City: 1945–1978

Since World War II, municipal governments have increasingly taken responsibility for delivering services to their citizens. We can see exactly how important the city's service delivery function has become by comparing the post-World War II increase in municipal general expenditures (most of which are consumed by the delivery of services) with the increase in population during this period. Taking population as a roughly objective indicator of the need for given service levels, figure 14.1 shows that these levels (measured in uninflated dollars) far outpace what would be required by population growth alone. (In figure 14.1 and all subsequent figures, the vertical axis describes the increase or decrease in expenditures and other trends from 1945 levels.[1])

Of course, the changing role of municipal governments has not occurred in a vacuum; rather, it is a response to a number of changes that have occurred in urban society. Perhaps the most important of these changes,

1. As in the previous chapter, all fiscal statistics in this chapter are calculated in constant dollars.

FIGURE 14.1: Increase in Population and Municipal General Expenditures, 1945–1992 (expenditures in constant dollars)

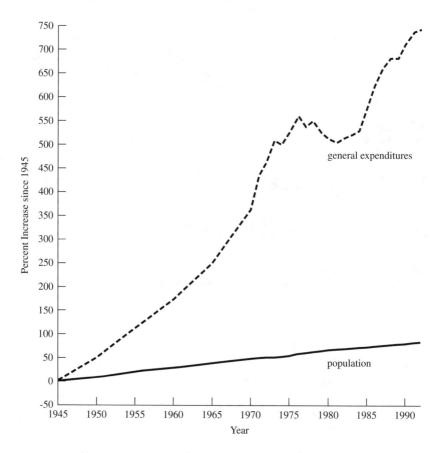

and the one that has triggered many of the others, is the greater affluence of the average American household. As shown in table 14.1, the standard of living in the United States improved dramatically during the middle years of this century. However, this growing affluence has had a number of important side effects for most Americans, which has led to their increasing dependence on the delivery of urban services.

Garbage and Garbage Collection

By way of a simple example, the consumption of nondurable goods increased by over 140 percent between 1945 and 1980, and in turn American families

Table 14.1 Median Family Income 1945–1992 (in constant 1967 dollars)

1945	$3,949	1979	$9,010
1950	4,603	1980	8,518
1955	5,509	1981	8,219
1960	6,336	1982	8,105
1965	7,362	1983	8,273
1970	8,484	1984	8,969
1971	8,479	1985	8,773
1972	8,872	1986	8,970
1973	9,054	1987	9,106
1974	8,735	1988	9,088
1975	8,751	1989	9,214
1976	8,773	1990	9,035
1977	8,820	1991	8,812
1978	9,028	1992	8,706

SOURCE: U. S. Department of Commerce, *Statistical Abstract of the United States.*

had need to dispose of ever-increasing amounts of rubbish and garbage; by 1975, the average family of four was generating 14 pounds of garbage *each day* (by 1993, this had risen to 17.6 pounds per day). It is not surprising, then, that most cities had instituted biweekly garbage pickup by this time, and many cities supplemented this schedule with an additional pickup day for special types of trash (e.g., tree branches, washing machines, and other bulky items). In short, opportunity (affluence) increased demand, and demand increased service. But in addition to increased demand, two other factors have increased costs associated with garbage collection. First, with growing ecological awareness has come a mandate for recycling, with federal requirements (established in 1993) that cities recycle 25 percent of their solid waste. But while early efforts at recycling were able to tap into a hot recycling market, the market has since cooled, and cities are actually losing money in their efforts to keep the environment clean. Second, technological advancement has also made garbage collection more costly. In contrast to the modified dumptrucks that were used to collect trash immediately following World War II, all garbage trucks today have hydraulic trash compactors to increase their load. And garbage trucks come in different sizes and styles: hydraulic front-loaders, rear-loaders, and side-loaders, all designed to mechanically hoist dumpsters of various sizes and shapes. This technology makes garbage more convenient to store for the consumer, easier to load for the trash collector, but more costly for the taxpayer. In the years between 1945 and 1978, municipal budgets for trash collection (and other forms of sanitation) increased by 765 percent (see figure 14.2).

Paradoxically, the more trash a city collects, the more difficulty it has disposing of it. In an effort to euphemize *trash*, cities have turned garbage dumps into "landfills." But a garbage dump by any other name is still a garbage dump: It is unsightly, it stinks, it attracts rodents and insects, and it reduces property

FIGURE 14.2: Increase in Expenditures for Selected Urban Services, 1945–1992 (expenditures in constant dollars)

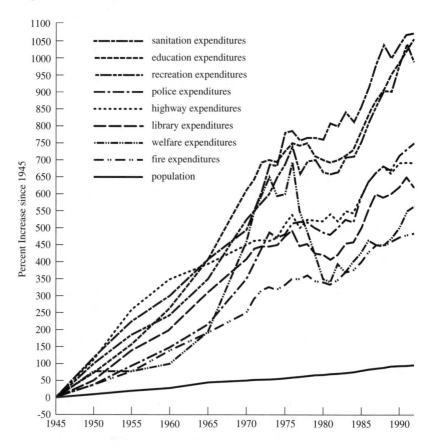

value in the area. Several innovations have been used to solve the garbage problem, some with more success than others. One of the more creative is the use of incinerators to burn garbage.[2] These incinerators in turn produce energy, which can be sold to commercial customers. Today at least one hundred cities and counties have built trash incinerators, but at a considerable construction

2. Another, much less successful innovation is the attempt to ship garbage away from the area where it is collected. A case in point is the freighter *Pelicano*, which set sail from Philadelphia in September, 1986, filled with 14,000 tons of incinerator ash. It spent more than two years at sea, looking in vain for a port to unload its cargo. Between 1986 and 1988, some three million tons of hazardous waste have been transported from the United States and Western Europe on ships like the *Pelicano* to countries in Africa and Eastern Europe (*Time*, Jan. 2, 1989). Others, far less scrupulous, simply dumped their garbage at sea, creating a crisis along the Eastern Seaboard during the summer of 1988 as trash washed up on public beaches.

cost: For example, Batesville, Arkansas (with a population of seven thousand) spent $1.2 billion; Broward County, Florida (with a population of over a million) spent $570 million; and New York City's Department of Sanitation has estimated a cost of $3 billion. While these plants may be profitable (Peekskill, New York, receives a $1 million annual credit from Con Edison, which purchases the electricity produced by the plant), operating expenses eat up much of this profit (Hershkowitz 1987). And many are concerned that the pollution produced by the incineration may be worse than the original garbage.[3]

Crime and Law Enforcement

A second (but not necessarily direct) consequence of the growing American affluence has been the growth of crime. With increasing disposable income, Americans have been able to purchase new luxuries that had never been available or affordable before.[4] For example, by 1960 nearly 90 percent of American homes had at least one television set. By the 1970s, many households had blenders, stereo record and tape players, and stereo cassette players in their cars. And since the 1980s, a growing number of homes have acquired food processors, microwave ovens, expensive camera equipment, videocassette recorders, and microcomputers. Each of these items makes our lives a bit easier or a bit more fun. But each is also easily stolen and easily "fenced" at a tidy profit for the burglar. As figure 14.3 shows, crime has increased since 1945, reaching its period of fastest acceleration between 1960 and 1975; during these years, reported burglaries (per capita) increased at an annual rate of 8 percent (although during the following decade, they actually decreased by a small amount). This rise, coupled with rapidly growing violent crime (8 percent per capita annual increase between 1960 and 1975, with a levelling effect following 1975), has led many Americans to fear crime as the most important domestic problem facing this country.[5]

3. One of the inevitable emissions of garbage incinerators is dioxin, which is suspected of causing a wide range of illnesses, including cancer and birth defects. To date, no standards for dioxin emissions have been established in the United States. In addition to emissions, the ash produced by incineration is also toxic, containing dioxin and heavy metals, and its safe disposal continues to be an unresolved issue. See Allen Hershkowitz (1987) for a discussion of these and other issues related to garbage incineration.

4. James Burke (1978) argues that new technologies are often due more to social forces than to scientific advancement. Thus, the increase in leisure time following World War II, coupled with the increasing profitability to be found in new "gadgets" for modern living, may have contributed to the myriad new inventions of the post-war period.

5. The fear of crime in cities has played a role in presidential politics. No one who observed the 1988 presidential campaign can forget the Willie Horton commercials and how they helped solidify public concern about crime. In another instance, President Clinton sponsored legislation in 1995 that would put 100,000 additional police officers onto the streets of America's cities, largely in response to the same set of concerns. By 1996, all categories of crime were showing significant decreases, although this is not necessarily due to this intervention.

FIGURE 14.3: Increase in Crimes and Municipal Police Expenditures, 1945–1992 (expenditures in constant dollars)

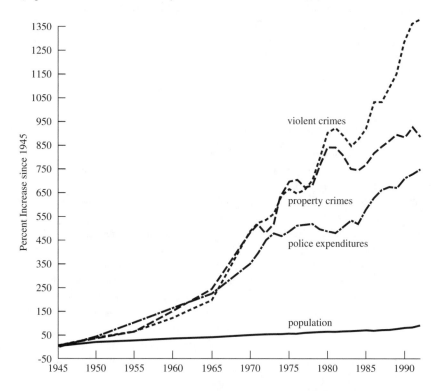

Cities responded quickly during the years immediately following World War II by hiring more police officers (an annual increase of over 1 percent) and purchasing more sophisticated law enforcement equipment; the result was a steady increase amounting to a 527 percent rise in municipal expenditures for police protection between 1945 and 1978. Figure 14.3 shows that this increase keeps rough pace with the increase in crime during the same period, and it greatly outdistances the population increase during the same period. Between 1975 and 1980, however, municipal expenditures for police protection remained nearly constant (an increase of less than 2 percent in constant dollars), only to rise again during the 1980s.

Fires and Fire Protection

A third consequence of growing affluence is escalating property value. Between 1955 and 1994, the median size of a new house grew from 1,140 square feet to 1,940 square feet; this, plus more elegant interiors and other amenities, drove the median price of a new house up by 72 percent during this same period. Escalating property values have driven insurance companies to lobby for stricter municipal fire codes; and to keep insurance ratings low, many cities have invested in new and better fire-fighting equipment. Although the number of residential fires in the United States has decreased over time, the economic losses associated with each fire have increased (in constant dollars), reflecting the increasing value of the residences that are destroyed or damaged (see figure 14.4). Figure 14.2 shows that between 1945 and 1978, municipal expenditures for fire protection increased by 365 percent.

The increase in municipal expenditures for fire protection can be attributed to two factors. First, fire-fighting technology has expanded, and equipment today is more effective in controlling fires. As one example, some departments now use helicopters for rescue work. As another, modern equipment has greater pumping capacity than older equipment; it carries with it a

FIGURE 14.4: Median Size and Median Selling Price of Houses, 1955–1993 (selling prices in constant dollars)

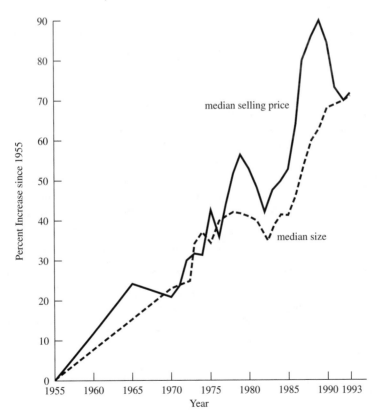

greater variety of ancillary gear (e.g., self-contained breathing apparatus, foam, smoke ejectors, high-volume hoses); it carries more water; and it is designed to be more reliable. In 1945, most residential fires were fought with a head-on assault, which had the effect of washing most household furnishings out the back door, and water damage was often greater than that caused by the fire. With modern equipment, today's firefighters are able to find the heart of the fire and combat it effectively with a minimum of water damage. In addition, modern equipment is safer to drive, with more visible flashing lights to alert traffic. Finally, dispatching procedures have become more sophisticated over the past three decades. In the 1950s, these were rudimentary, relying on telephone or radio communication to alert firefighters to the location of a fire. Today, these procedures are computerized in many larger cities and are often tied into the city's emergency 911 network. Further, cities that have gone to computerized systems typically have the special needs of virtually every residence, office, or other structure in their jurisdiction cataloged in the computer; and firefighters know immediately about any hazardous material (or other potentially complicating factors) that they must contend with.

Improved equipment is costly, however. For example, a state-of-the-art pumper cost approximately $25,000 in the early 1950s ($30,000 in 1967 dollars). Today, a state-of-the-art pumper costs as much as $300,000 ($67,500 in 1967 dollars). Additionally, as fire-fighting procedures have become more effective, more municipalities have turned away from an all-volunteer fire department to one that uses career firefighters (or a mixed career-volunteer department; see Jacobs 1976).[6] By 1994, almost all cities with more than twenty-five thousand people relied on career fire fighters working together with volunteers; and although 75 percent of municipalities continue to use all-volunteer fire departments, these tend to be smaller cities (i.e., under five thousand people). Overall, 75.3 percent of the U.S. population is covered by departments that employ at least some career firefighters (Karter 1995).[7] While the shift toward professional fire departments is at least partly responsi-

---

6. Two major differences between volunteer and professional fire departments involve training and response time. Professional firefighters receive considerably more training than volunteer firefighters, allowing them to respond to a wider variety of situations. Professional firefighters can also respond to fires more quickly than volunteer firefighters, since they are located at the fire station. And since the speed of response is critical in controlling damage, this makes professional departments more effective. In 1979, for example, volunteer fire departments averaged $2.85 loss per $1,000 of valuation, compared to a loss of $1.05 for professional departments. Interestingly, those departments that used both paid and volunteer firefighters fared best, with a loss of $.78 per $1,000 of valuation (Bryan and Picard 1979).

7. Data showing how the composition of fire departments has changed over time is sketchy. However, since 1983, the total number of career firefighters has increased by 17 percent, while the number of volunteer firefighters has declined by 9 percent (Karter 1995).

ble for the reduction in fire damage, it also entails an obvious increase in operating expenses.[8]

Leisure Time and Recreational Activities

A fourth area where increasing affluence yields benefits for the typical American family is leisure time. With greater income (generated largely from two wage earners), fewer people find it necessary to work overtime or at a second job, and the average number of hours spent at work each week declined substantially between 1945 (43.4 hours) and 1994 (39.2 hours). Many people spend their newfound leisure time in front of the television set. But others spend the time playing softball, golfing, jogging, or reading. As figure 14.5 shows, the number of golfers increased by over 750 percent between 1945 and 1992, and the number of adult softball teams increased by nearly a factor of twenty during the same period. But with this leisure activity comes a substantial price tag. For example, the number of municipal softball diamonds increased by 42 percent between 1950 and 1965, and the number of municipally owned golf courses increased by over 300 percent between 1950 and 1992. Overall, municipal budgets for parks and recreation increased by 691 percent between 1945 and 1978; and municipal budgets for libraries increased by 451 percent during the same period. As with the increase in police expenditures, the increase in expenditures for parks and recreation is clearly in response to demand (e.g., golfers, tennis players, softball teams) rather than to the increase in population (see figure 14.5).

Transportation and Streets

A fifth consequence of growing affluence is the love affair between Americans and their cars. In 1950, only 59 percent of American families owned a car; by 1974, 84 percent of families owned at least one car (with nearly half owning more than one car), and by the 1990s this figure had reached nearly 90 percent. Since the end of World War II, the number of miles logged by passenger cars in urban areas has increased dramatically, from 111 billion in 1945 to 1.6 trillion in 1993 (see figure 14.6); during this same period, the number of passengers riding buses in urban areas actually decreased, from 9.89 billion in 1945 to 5.5 billion in 1993 (see figure 14.7). By 1974, 78 percent of all peo-

---

8. A third factor in the growth of municipal expenditures for fire protection is the advent of the emergency medical services (EMS) component of many fire departments. EMS crews are trained in the provision of emergency health care, and they respond to local calls entailing all types of medical need, including heart attacks, burns, and trauma. Again, the human resources training, and equipment required to provide EMS for the community is expensive, and it accounts for an important part of the real growth in fire department budgets since World War II.

FIGURE 14.5: Increase in Municipal Recreational Expenditures and Demand, 1945–1992 (expenditures in constant dollars)

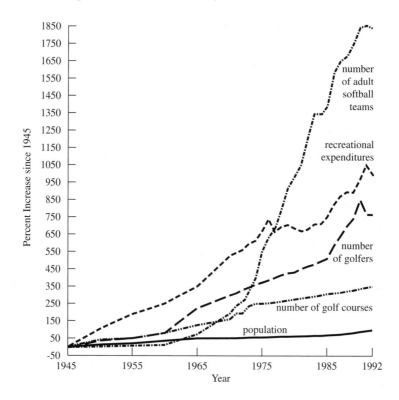

ple commuting to work in urban areas drove (or rode as passengers in) private cars. The figures for 1980 and 1990, broken down by individual MSAs with over a million inhabitants in table 14.2, show that only one city (New York) achieved a sizeable public transit ridership. They also show that transit ridership in large northeastern and midwestern cities seems to be increasing from its already high levels, whereas transit ridership in most southern and western cities is showing only small increases.

As a result, public funds increasingly have been allocated to the construction and maintenance of urban streets and highways during the middle years of the century.[9] As figure 14.6 indicates, the amount of urban highway mileage under local control has nearly tripled since 1945, and municipal

9. Robert Moses, testifying before Congress in the mid 1950s, stated, "I still have not found anybody who can tell me how you are going to keep turning out all these cars without decent, first class modern highways for them to run on" (quoted in Feagin and Parker 1990, 161).

FIGURE 14.6: Increase in Local Roads, Passenger Miles, and Municipal Highway Expenditures, 1945–1992 (expenditures in constant dollars)

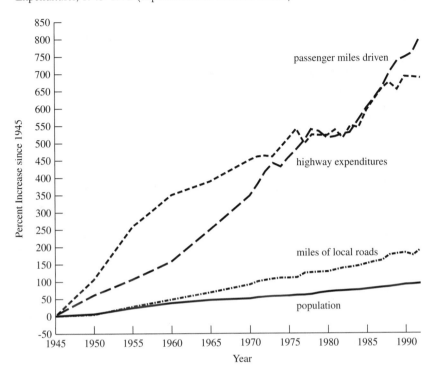

expenditures for maintenance of these streets increased by 40 percent between 1950 and 1960 alone. Municipal expenditures for highways increased by 522 percent between 1945 and 1978.

One of the inevitable byproducts of this expansion in the use of the private automobile is the demand for more and better transit arteries in America's larger cities. As more people drive their cars to work, the task of negotiating rush-hour traffic becomes more difficult and time consuming. Nobody knows the exact rush-hour capacity of urban arterials, but anyone who has driven in rush-hour traffic in New York, Chicago, Los Angeles, or any other major city knows that we are approaching that capacity. And in New York, during public transit strikes, capacity was surpassed as automobile traffic ground to a virtual halt. Observers have even coined a name for the situation—*gridlock.*

Most major cities have developed public transit systems as a means of relieving some of the rush-hour pressure on their arterial system. Some cities,

FIGURE 14.7: Change in Mass Transit Ridership and Expenditures, 1945–1992 (expenditures in constant dollars)

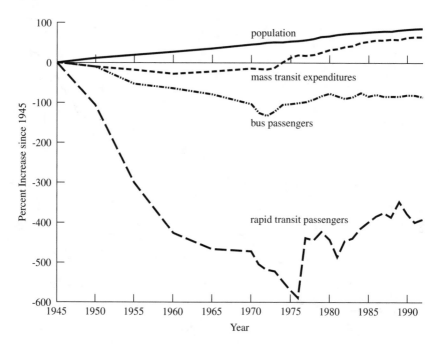

such as New York, Chicago, Boston, Washington, Cleveland, Philadelphia, San Francisco-Oakland, and Atlanta have invested billions of dollars in rapid rail systems. When the Bay Area Rapid Transit System (BART) opened in the early 1970s, it represented the first major mass transit system to be constructed in the United States in many years, and it was quite expensive: The original 1962 referendum allocated $800 million, but costs totalled over $1.5 billion by the time it was completed. The mass transit systems in Atlanta and Washington, constructed after BART, carried with them price tags of over $2 billion and $6 billion respectively. The efforts of other cities have been much more modest, mostly in the form of bus systems and trolley cars. Since 1952, municipal expenditures for public transit have totaled over $60 billion, with only about half of that recovered in the form of fares (in recent years, fares have accounted for only a third of municipal expenditures). And between 1945 and 1992, expenditures increased by 62 percent, while at the same time ridership showed a decline; for example, although BART was designed to accommodate 200,000 riders each day, actual ridership tended toward only 125,000 during its first decade (although it is somewhat higher today). And Washington, D.C.'s METRO system ran at approximately one-third capacity

Table 14.2 Principal Means of Transportation to Work, 1980–1990

| Metropolitan Area | 1980 | | | | 1990 |
| | Private Vehicle | | | Public Transportation | Public Transportation |
	Drive Alone	Car Pool	Other		
New York, NY	30.7%	11.6%	12.6%	45.1%	53.4%
Chicago, IL	57.6	16.7	7.7	18.0	29.7
San Francisco, CA★	57.9	15.7	9.9	16.4	33.5
Oakland, CA★					17.9
Boston, MA	56.0	17.0	11.3	15.7	31.5
Washington, DC	53.7	22.9	7.9	15.5	36.6
Philadelphia, PA	59.1	17.6	9.2	14.0	28.7
Pittsburgh, PA	60.7	19.4	8.4	11.5	22.2
New Orleans, LA	61.7	20.6	6.8	10.9	16.9
Newark, NJ	64.0	17.9	7.4	10.7	24.6
Cleveland, OH	67.9	16.0	5.5	10.6	14.1
Baltimore, MD	59.8	22.3	7.7	10.3	22.0
Seattle/Everett, WA★	63.9	18.2	8.3	9.6	15.9
Minneapolis, MN★	63.1	19.9	8.3	8.7	16.0
St. Paul, MN★					10.5
Portland, OR	65.3	18.0	8.2	8.4	11.0
Milwaukee, WI	65.0	19.0	8.3	7.7	11.0
Atlanta, GA	68.7	19.6	4.1	7.6	20.0
Los Angeles, CA★	68.7	16.8	7.5	7.0	10.5
Long Beach, CA★					6.0
Miami, FL	67.4	19.6	6.4	6.6	12.9
Buffalo, NY	66.6	18.6	8.2	6.6	13.4
Cincinnati, OH	68.8	18.8	5.8	6.5	11.2
Denver, CO★	65.4	20.2	8.3	6.1	8.0
Boulder, CO★					
St. Louis, MO	67.3	21.4	5.6	5.7	12.2
San Antonio, TX	66.9	19.9	8.6	4.6	4.9
Columbus, OH	70.3	18.2	6.8	4.6	4.7
Kansas City, MO	69.3	21.5	5.1	4.1	5.8
Detroit, MI	75.1	16.9	4.3	3.7	10.7
Sacramento, CA	69.0	17.6	9.9	3.5	4.0
Dallas, TX★	71.2	20.6	4.8	3.4	6.7
Ft. Worth, TX★					1.7
San Diego, CA	63.8	17.4	15.5	3.3	4.2
Indianapolis, IN	70.3	21.0	5.5	3.2	3.3
San Jose, CA	72.5	16.6	7.9	3.1	3.5
Houston, TX	69.5	22.4	5.0	3.0	6.5
Anaheim, CA★	74.8	16.1	7.0	2.1	3.8
Santa Ana, CA★					8.4
Phoenix, AZ	70.2	19.0	8.9	2.0	3.3
Tampa, FL★	72.0	18.4	7.8	1.8	3.4
St. Petersburg, FL★					3.0
Riverside, CA★	71.9	18.3	8.9	0.9	1.6
San Bernadino, CA					

SOURCE: U.S. Department of Commerce, *Statistical Abstract of the United States*; U.S. Department of Commerce, *County and City Data Book*.

★1980 statistics combine data from the two listed cities; 1990 statistics describe them separately.

during its early years. But it costs just as much to operate a subway system with a few as opposed to a lot of passengers, and cities seem to have concluded that public transit represents a "public good" for which they are willing to expend considerable money.

Education and Public Schools

In addition to affluence, other factors contribute to the city's increasing role as a deliverer of services to its residents. First, and perhaps most important, a pair of events occurred in the 1950s that, jointly, contributed greatly to the increasing budgets of most school districts. One of these events (or perhaps trends would be more accurate) was the coming of school age of the post–World War II "baby boomers." Between 1950 and 1960, the number of school-age children in the United States increased by over 40 percent (figure 14.8) requiring

FIGURE 14.8: Increase in School-Aged Children, Educational Expenditures, Teachers, and Special Needs Students 1945–1992 (expenditures in constant dollars)

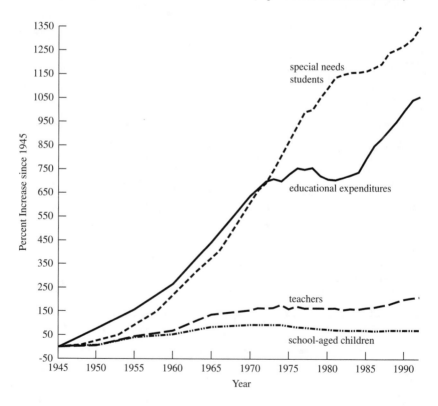

a substantial increase in capital outlay for school maintenance, repair, and construction (95 percent), number of teachers (52 percent), and local taxes for education (88 percent). This expanding cohort of youngsters (in the years between 1945 and 1960) and young adults (in the years between 1960 and 1970) also had an inevitable impact on crime. Crime statistics show that over half of all arrests involved youths in the fourteen to twenty-four age range, even though they accounted for only about 15 percent (in 1945) and 20 percent (in 1975) of the population. It should be clear that this growth in the pool of young adults substantially increased the number of people engaged in criminal activity, and coupled with the increasingly attractive targets of crime, led to the large increase in crime and police services between 1945 and 1978.

Not all increases in educational expenditures can be attributed to demographics, however; a second event occurred in 1957, one that shook the foundations of American education for a decade or more. In October of that year, the Soviet Union launched Sputnik I, the world's first man-made Earth satellite; a month later, the Soviets proved that this was not a technological fluke by launching Sputnik II, a satellite that carried a live dog. The United States clearly had been beaten, and beaten badly, in the space race, and our national pride was severely wounded. As a response, the federal government encouraged an expanded math and science curriculum in the public schools, and it encouraged special enrichment programs for gifted students. Local school districts enthusiastically jumped on both bandwagons; between 1958 and 1963, for example, the number of schoolchildren participating in "gifted" programs rose from 52,000 to 215,000, increased steadily over the next decade (to 481,000 in 1971), and grew at an even faster pace during the 1970s and 1980s (reaching 2 million by 1990).[10] But the bandwagon turned out to be expensive. Although the federal government footed some of the bill (e.g., through the National Defense Act in 1958, Public Law 91–230 in 1969, and Public Law 93–380 in 1974), cities and states were responsible for the rest,[11] and this expansion of the curriculum accounted for at least some of the increase in local educational expenditures during the decade.

Services for the Needy

Another factor in the growth of urban services has been growing public sensitivity to the plight of the needy. For example, following World War II, the

10. The number of students participating in gifted programs is inexact, since definitions of these programs have changed somewhat over time. Even so, the increase is difficult to mistake.

11. In 1982, the federal government phased out its Office of Gifted and Talented and virtually the entire cost of providing gifted education fell on states and localities (see Sisk 1987 for a review of the history of funding for gifted education). However, in 1988 Congress passed the Javits Gifted and Talented Students Education Act, providing $8 million in seed money to school districts and universities for programmatic development.

public became increasingly aware of and sensitive to the needs of exceptional children (e.g., those who are visually, aurally, or speech disabled, socially or emotionally maladjusted, learning disabled, mentally retarded). As these children were deemed educable, special education programs were developed and implemented in the public schools, with enrollments growing dramatically through the 1960s (figure 14.8): 1947 enrollments totalled only 378,000, whereas 1970 enrollments totalled over 3 million. This trend has continued gradually to the present, but with one important difference. In 1975, Congress passed the Education for All Handicapped Children Act (Public Law 94–142), mandating that all children are entitled to a free and appropriate public education in the least restrictive environment (Levine and Wexler 1981). The intent of this law was to "mainstream" exceptional students out of special education classrooms and into regular education classrooms whenever appropriate, and it largely succeeded in this intent. The special education movement and the mainstreaming movement successfully expanded the scope of public education to 3 million new students, but at a considerable financial cost. In the case of special education, this included new teachers, new equipment, and new facilities, while in the case of mainstreaming, it included additional teacher training and more new facilities.

The plight of the mentally ill is another area where increased awareness has led to increased services. The needs of the mentally ill have been dramatized in recent years by a number of events, beginning with the development of psychotropic drugs in the 1950s. As a result of this breakthrough, state psychiatric hospitals gradually began a process of deinstitutionalization, through which patients were released into the community to receive therapy on an outpatient basis. In 1963, President Kennedy urged Congress to pass legislation funding community mental health centers, arguing that this would enable the mentally ill to be treated in their own communities. However, following passage of the Community Mental Health Centers Act in 1963, community mental health centers were slow to provide services to deinstitutionalized mental patients, focusing instead on new populations in need of acute services. By 1980 these centers were servicing over 3 million clients each year, only a portion of whom had previously been institutionalized (Goldman and Morrissey 1985). This trend was complicated, however, by several court decisions in 1973 that found the circumstances and the conditions of psychiatric institutionalization to be wanting. In the wake of these decisions, state psychiatric hospitals opened their doors for a mass exodus of mental patients into the community, with community mental health centers serving as their only source of clinical support (see Badger et al., 1981, for a further discussion of the impact of these decisions).

Yet, at exactly the time of this mass institutional exodus and the burgeoning demand for community mental health services, federal support for community mental health centers began to decline. In many locations, state tax dollars have picked up the slack; but in other cases, it has been the localities (through both public and private funding) that have paid for mental health services. In 1990, 17 percent of the total support came from local governments, 14 percent from the federal government, 53 percent from state governments, and 16 percent from private insurance and other sources (Redick et al. 1994). In many communities, the municipal government also provides support for other social services, including homes for battered spouses, drug and alcohol counselling services, public health clinics, shelters for the homeless, and meals for the hungry. Even when these facilities and programs are not funded directly by the city, they often receive public contributions through local agencies such as the United Way. For example, in 1995, United Way contributions in the United States exceeded $3 billion. However, since 1960 total United Way contributions have increased by only 34 percent (in constant dollars) while demand has increased considerably more than that. In the end, the survival of these programs depends largely on the willingness and the ability of municipal government to support them, and as we have seen, municipal government has often risen to the challenge. As figure 14.9 shows, between 1960 and 1978, public welfare expenditures by cities, for a number of social programs including those discussed above, rose by 446 percent.

The Theme Restated

Let us return now to the original argument and examine more closely its implications. We began by noting that the delivery of services has become the most important function of the city during the last half of this century. And we have seen that economic, demographic, social, and technological factors have all contributed to its growth. But as the demand for services has increased, so has their cost. First, cities are simply providing more services than ever before, to more people than ever before. Second, technological developments are pushing the price of services upward. But a third, and perhaps most important factor in the rising cost of urban service delivery is the increasing labor costs of providing services. The greater the demand that is placed on a commodity or a service, the more it typically costs. When demand was low for garbage collection, sanitation workers could be paid a low wage, and nobody was much affected if they walked out on strike. But as urban residents have come to depend on twice-weekly trash pickup, the social costs of uncollected garbage escalate, and cities are willing to pay sanitation workers more money to ensure that garbage is picked up efficiently. Much the same can be said of education and law enforcement. In periods of low crime, police could be underpaid with little consequence. But in periods of high crime, law enforcement officers can command higher salaries; between 1965 and 1975, for example, police salaries increased at an annual rate of approximately 7.5 percent, exceeding annual salary increases in the private sector (approximately

FIGURE 14.9: Increase in Population and Municipal Welfare Expenditures, 1945–1992 (expenditures in constant dollars)

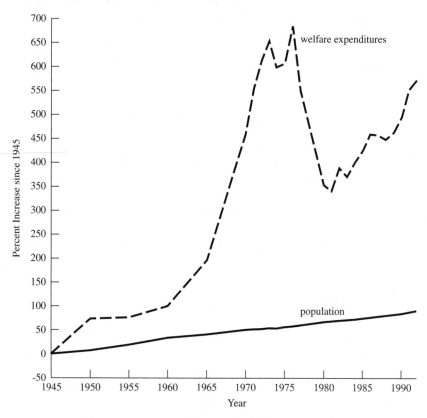

6 percent). Since urban services tend to be labor intensive, even small wage increases magnify the overall costs of services.

With increasing demand and increasing cost, municipal expenditures for services accelerated between 1945 and 1978, as indicated by figure 14.1. But after 1978, expenditures actually began to decline, as did the number and scope of services funded by the municipal budget. In the next section, we will explore this trend, seeing specific causes and considering specific responses.

The Decline of Urban Services: 1979–1982

New York on the Verge of Bankruptcy

In 1975, the expansion of municipal services came to a dramatic halt in New York City as the Big Apple teetered on the brink of bankruptcy.

Although municipal bankruptcy had been commonplace during the Depression, it has been rare in the years since; this, coupled with the pre-eminent place of New York City in our urban hierarchy, demands that we pay New York's fiscal crisis more than passing attention, for it served notice to the rest of the nation that the era of unbridled expansion in the growth of urban services was at an end.

Following Levine, Rubin, and Wolohojian (1981), we will examine New York's fiscal crisis in its component stages.[12] Its earliest roots are found in the years between 1965 and 1970, when the city responded to growing racial unrest and rioting. During this period, expenditures for social programs for blacks increased greatly.[13] Also during this period, the city made a commitment to higher education, greatly increasing funding to municipal universities and hospitals. These budgetary increases had little adverse effect, since the economy was expanding. But an expanding economy led to inflation during the last years of the decade, and New York's union leaders sought substantial pay increases. After the embarrassment of the Transit Workers' strike in 1966, Mayor John Lindsay saw union support as necessary both to his reelection and to his ability to govern effectively, and the city acceded to union demands for higher wages.

Had economic growth continued, New York City's fiscal crisis likely would never have occurred. But the economic slump of the early 1970s brought with it an erosion of private-sector jobs in the city, particularly high-paying manufacturing jobs. Further, federal grants to the city declined in the early 1970s. The city administration made some effort to respond by cutting eight thousand fire, sanitation, and education jobs; but increasing funding for higher education and hospitals more than compensated for these cutbacks. As a final resort, Mayor Lindsay took the politically expedient route of covering budgetary shortfalls with short-term loans (which carry higher interest rates than long-term loans); by 1974, 20 percent of New York City's total debt was in the form of high-interest, short-term bonds. This situation could perhaps have continued indefinitely, except that in 1974 the New York State Urban Development Corporation—created by the New York Assembly to sell bonds, and with the proceeds of the bond sales to make loans to New York cities—defaulted on payment of its debt, and creditors became concerned about New York City's ability to pay *its* debt. Several banks sold their New York City bonds, setting off a panic that effectively ended the city's ability to issue any further short-term bonds.

12. For other perspectives on New York's fiscal crisis, see Morris (1980), Shefter (1980), and Sbragia (1983).

13. New York and Chicago experienced roughly comparable economic hardship during this period; yet, Chicago had fewer fiscal problems—due largely to its political style. In any city, the mayor's capacity to centralize and control the budgetary process and to a limited degree to deflect the demands of interests within the city affect its fiscal stability. While Chicago's strong political machine allowed Mayor Daley to ignore demands from blacks and the poor in Chicago, mayors in New York lacked the strong party apparatus to allow them to turn down such demands (Fuchs 1992, Miranda 1994).

Thus, by the beginning of 1975, default seemed imminent, and the only way that it could be forestalled was to borrow money outside the bond market. The federal government in general, and particularly President Ford, seemed uninterested in bailing out New York. The *New York Daily News* summarized Washington's sentiment with its large-type headline on October 30, 1975: FORD TO CITY: DROP DEAD. As a last resort, New York State created the Municipal Assistance Corporation (MAC) to lend New York the money it needed to service its debt. But over time, even MAC had difficulty selling bonds, and it was forced to negotiate austerity measures with the city and its unions. These included:

1. a wage freeze, and deferral of a 6 percent cost of living increase for municipal employees;
2. a rollback to 1973 wages for management-level employees;
3. a promise from the city to avoid frills in future union negotiations;
4. increased user fees for municipal services;
5. a $22-million cut in the city's budget allocation to New York University;
6. consolidation or elimination of several municipal departments; and
7. appointment of a management team to oversee the city's fiscal practices.

When the city's deficit was discovered to be four times larger than projected, however, another state agency—the Emergency Financial Control Board (EFCB)—was created to act as a receiver for the city. EFCB consisted of the mayor, the governor, the city and state comptrollers, and three additional gubernatorial appointees, so that effective control was placed in the hands of the state rather than the city. All municipal revenues were deposited directly into an EFCB account and disbursed according to a three-year plan developed by the city. Between 1975 and 1978, New York City cut sixty thousand municipal jobs and established severe guidelines for labor negotiations. Although no one was happy with the arrangement, an uneasy peace had been established by 1978 among the city, the state, the federal government (which, in the end, did provide some short-term loans), the unions, and the banks. Today, New York City is on firmer financial footing, and its officials would prefer to forget how close to financial catastrophe it had come during the mid-1970s.

The factors that led to New York City's financial crisis are faced by all large cities, to a greater or lesser degree. By the same token, the austerity measures employed by New York are also used by other cities in combating fiscal stress. In the remainder of this section, we will take a closer look at the factors creating fiscal stress in American cities. And in the following section, we will consider in greater depth the steps cities have taken to regain fiscal solvency.

Taxpayer Revolt

Previously, this chapter outlined a trend of growing affluence in the United States, beginning immediately after World War II. The steepest part of this growth curve occurred between 1960 and 1973, when median family income increased by 43 percent. By 1973, the typical family had annually $2,700 (indexed to 1967 consumer prices) more at its disposal than it had in 1960. But beginning in 1974, another trend began to emerge in the United States. The growth in affluence ground to a halt, and it actually began to reverse itself. Between 1973 and 1977, for instance, median family income fell by 3 percent, while municipal expenditures increased by 5 percent, and per-capita local taxes to pay for these municipal expenditures remained stable. Figure 14.10 shows median family income, local taxes, and municipal general expen-

FIGURE 14.10: Increase in Municipal General Expenditures, Per Capita Municipal Taxes, and Median Family Income, 1945–1992 (expenditures, income, and taxes in constant dollars)

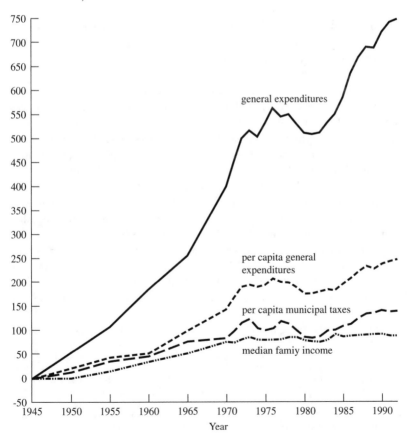

ditures. It is clear from the nearly coincident plot of income and taxes that the growing affluence of American families fueled the growth of municipal budgets. It is also clear that these budgets—and the taxes to pay for them—took on a life of their own, and particularly in the period between 1960 and 1973, deviated from trends in income. But by 1980, both municipal budgets and taxes had come into line with the stark reality of the American economy.

Several factors converged during the early and mid-1970s to bring taxes and expenditures back into line with income. First, taxpayers staged a revolt during this period, protesting any new or increased taxes and in some cases rolling back taxes to previous, lower levels. Although Proposition 13 in California and Proposition 2½ in Massachusetts are the best-known instances of this tax revolt, it has its origins in the early 1970s in cities and school districts across the country. In most states, school districts must regularly go to the voters for approval of such projects as new construction and the development of new programs. During the 1960s, the voters of most cities regularly said yes to such requests; approximately 70 percent of the school bond issues passed during that period and 70 percent of the requested funds were approved. By the early 1970s, however, fewer than 50 percent of the school bond issues put to the voters passed, with only about 40 percent of the requested funds approved. Although both passage rate and allocations improved slightly during the late 1970s, neither approaches the level it achieved during the 1960s. These trends are reported in table 14.3.

Municipal bond elections followed a similar pattern. Cities must seek voter approval to sell bonds necessary for most capital improvement projects, including the construction of municipal pools, parks, water treatment plants, and so forth.[14] Long-term bonded indebtedness of American municipalities, also reported in table 14.3, increased substantially from 1950 through 1970, then slowed and gradually declined through the 1970s and the early 1980s. The implication is clear: Whereas the voters in urban America were willing to finance new municipal projects while their earning power was increasing, they became wary of such projects once their earning power leveled off.

These indications of taxpayer concern were, of course, formalized with the 1978 passage of Proposition 13 in California, which cut property taxes in the state by 60 percent (and strictly limited future property assessments). California voters overwhelmingly supported Proposition 13, concluding that

14. During the 1980s, the public continued to vote for bond issues for construction of water and sewer systems, with typical levels of support for these projects ranging between 69 percent and 77 percent during the late 1980s. However, the public also showed its disdain for using public funds to construct buildings (e.g., convention centers, civic centers) during these years, with levels of support ranging between 38 percent and 44 percent (G. Peterson 1991). Many cities, eager to stimulate their economies through such ventures, found other ways to finance the construction of buildings, including use of special districts (Sanders 1992). As a result, as little as 15 percent of municipal bonded indebtedness in recent years has been approved by voters (Frieden and Sagalyn 1989).

Table 14.3   School District Bond Issue Success and Long-Term Municipal Bonded Indebtedness

	School Districts		Municipalities
	Percent of Bond Issues Approved	Percent of Value Approved	Long-term Bonded Indebtedness★
1950			$12,514
1951			12,375
1952			15,236
1953			16,121
1954			17,257
1955			19,080
1956			20,609
1957			21,569
1958		72.8	22,371
1959		79.6	23,999
1960		67.1	24,694
1961		75.9	26,001
1962	72.2	68.8	27,703
1963	72.4	69.6	28,176
1964	72.5	71.1	29,896
1965	74.7	79.4	30,984
1966	72.5	74.5	31,782
1967	66.6	69.2	32,185
1968	67.6	62.5	32,942
1969	56.8	43.6	33,036
1970	53.2	49.5	33,422
1971	46.7	41.4	34,740
1972	47.0	44.0	36,579
1973	56.6	50.6	37,029
1974	56.2	53.0	36,148
1975	46.3	46.0	34,609
1976	50.8	46.1	36,433
1977	55.5	54.0	36,875
1978			38,374
1979			34,477
1980			33,365
1981			32,254
1982			33,051
1983			36,757
1984			38,468
1985			42,145
1986			48,460
1987			53,390
1988			53,472
1989			53,572
1990			54,399
1991			55,555
1992			57,498

SOURCE: U.S. Department of Commerce, *Statistical Abstract of the United States*.

★millions of constant (1967) dollars

NOTE: The National Center for Educational Statistics compiled school district data only for the years shown.

government spending could be cut by as much as 25 percent without any deterioration in services (Sears and Citrin 1982). But several other factors also contributed to the success of those who sponsored Proposition 13 (most notably the organizational efforts of Howard Jarvis, a California businessman). First, they were able to enlist the support of conservative voters who resented the growth of governmental subsidies for the poor, with two-thirds of those who voted *yea* believing that welfare payments should be cut. In contrast, citizens generally opposed cutbacks in police, fire, education, public transportation, recreation, or mental health expenditures (Sears and Citrin 1982). Thus, supporters did not necessarily resent paying taxes, just those taxes earmarked for welfare and related programs.

Second, voters seldom have the opportunity to directly indicate their opposition to taxes, and when given that opportunity they are likely to take it. Opponents were not necessarily protesting local taxes; in fact, by 1978 resentment toward federal taxes equaled that toward local property taxes (Rose 1980). But since federal taxes cannot be directly challenged, many voters apparently took out their frustrations on the only available target: local property taxes.

Third, property taxes had really become quite a burden in the late 1970s, particularly in California. The value of residential property across the state grew at an annual rate of over 12 percent between 1973 and 1976, with annual growth rates in large cities (e.g., San Francisco, Los Angeles) approaching 20 percent during this period. With this increase came higher property tax assessments, which increased by as much as 30 percent a year in San Bernadino and Orange Counties during the same period.[15] Again, this occurred during a period when earning power was not increasing, and the additional taxes became unbearable for many people.

It is unclear (and perhaps unimportant) exactly how much each of these factors contributed to the passage of Proposition 13 in California. What is important is that the measure gave notice to governmental units across the country that unorganized instances of taxpayer revolt were becoming organized, and that municipalities and states must moderate their spending before the voters forced them to do so.[16] Post-Proposition 13 sentiment across the

15. During this period the middle and upper classes were purchasing ever larger and more expensive homes, which helped boost the housing market so dramatically. Homes simultaneously became a status symbol and an investment. As the middle and upper classes invested a larger percentage of their savings and earnings into houses, the regressivity of the property tax largely disappeared, and it became among the more progressive of local taxes. Ironically, the taxpayer revolt occurred not among those paying an unfair and regressive tax (as we might expect) but rather among those who were subjected to a fair and progressive tax.

16. Even before Proposition 13 passed in 1978, several states had placed a cap on tax rates (Arizona, Indiana, Nevada, Ohio, Oklahoma, Washington, and West Virginia) or limited growth in property tax revenues (Alaska, Arizona, Colorado, Indiana, Kansas, Minnesota, Washington, and Wisconsin). For a useful treatment of the tax revolt, see O'Sullivan et al. (1995).

country favored restrictions on property taxes, with two-thirds of those surveyed expressing sentiment for tax reform (Sears and Citrin 1982). About the
same time as Proposition 13, voters in many other states considered similar
propositions, which either strictly limited (or rolled back) property tax or limited municipal spending levels. In 1978, residents of Idaho (with an already
low property tax burden) and Nevada passed Proposition 13-type measures,
limiting increases in assessments to 2 percent per year. In the same year, voters
in Arizona, Hawaii, Michigan, and Texas approved bills limiting spending
(Lucier 1980). But in contrast, 1978 witnessed the defeat of tax relief propositions in Oregon and Colorado, and voters in Michigan defeated a compan-
ion bill to the one they approved. In 1979, property tax relief measures were
passed in twenty-two states, income tax reductions in eighteen states, sales tax
reductions in fifteen states, and spending limits in eight states (Poole 1980;
O'Sullivan et al. 1995). And in 1980, residents of Massachusetts passed
Proposition 2½, which limited property tax to 2.5 percent of assessed real
estate value. As a result, by 1980 per capita taxes on urban residents across the
country had dropped to 75 percent of their 1973 levels; by the 1990s, however, per capita local taxes had regained their 1973 levels, and more (see figure
14.10).

Although the most publicized cause of decreasing municipal revenues
and expenditures, the tax revolt was not the only (or even the most important)
cause. Indeed, it simply came at a time when other trends were severely limiting the ability of municipal governments, particularly in large cities, to provide services, exacerbating the impact of those trends. The first of these trends
was the economic slumps that intermittently plagued the United States during the 1970s and 1980s. The second is the movement to the suburbs, initiated after World War II but particularly important during the 1970s. And the
third is the changing policy of the federal government toward sharing revenue
with the cities, begun in 1981 with the inauguration of President Reagan.

Economic Stagnation

During the 1970s and the early 1980s, the economy performed in a generally
sluggish manner, moving between recession and mild recovery but never
toward full recovery. In this poor economic climate, unemployment ranged
between 6 percent and 10 percent nationally, and considerably higher than
that in the nation's inner cities. Thus, income tax receipts that might help the
city directly (in those cities that assess an income tax) or indirectly (through
state or federal grants) were significantly down. By the same token, unemployed people do not spend as much money on nondisposable goods, and
municipal sales tax receipts also lagged. In such a sluggish economy, new business starts were down and business failures were up, again reducing the tax
base. Finally, the 1970s witnessed an important industrial trend in the United

States, with many manufacturers moving their base of operation overseas (where labor is cheaper); a complementary trend saw an increase in overseas imports of manufactured items (e.g,, steel). For example, a 1984 survey showed that in the previous five years, 11.5 million workers had lost jobs because of plant closings or other economic cutbacks (Wicker 1987). The two trends converged to create a sharp reduction in high-paying manufacturing jobs in American cities (of those people who were victims of manufacturing displacement, most eventually found work, although at levels of pay considerably less than that they previously received; see Newby, 1989, and Jaret, 1991.)

Economic stagnation and unemployment also lead to increased need for city services. People without jobs still need to eat, and the burden of providing food often falls on municipal agencies. Continuing unemployment leads to psychological depression and anxiety, and demands on the community mental health center are likely to increase. In addition, high rates of unemployment, particularly among youths, may contribute to greater crime within a city, and demands on municipal police departments may increase. But in each of these cases, fewer resources are available to meet greater demands.

Population Shifts

Also during the 1970s, a long-term population shift toward the suburbs continued, with twice as many people moving from central cities to suburbs as from suburbs to central cities. In the early years, this shift largely reflected changing life-style preferences: Americans, tired of the bustle, crime, and poverty of city life, opted for a place in the country (or at least in the suburbs). The freeway construction program of the 1950s and the 1960s made this movement possible by substantially reducing the commuting time for people who opted to work in the city but live away from its problems. Thus, the continuing outmigration from the central city reflects another type of taxpayer revolt, with both citizens and corporations voting down higher taxes with their feet rather than at the ballot box. Like Howard Jarvis' coalition in California, these citizens and corporate heads are not opposed to services and taxes: They typically support strong fire and police departments, street repair, libraries, parks, and schools. They are, however, unwilling to pay the taxes required for services aimed at ameliorating (or at least controlling) the problems of the inner cities, for example, mass transit, subsidized health care, and public housing. Ironically, however, they are the very people who can best afford to pay for these services. By moving away from the central city, they escape both the problem and the need to pay for it. But they leave in their wake a much smaller tax base for the city.

Another important demographic shift has been away from the northeastern and midwestern frostbelt states and to the western and southern sunbelt states. As table 14.4 indicates, the population in the West has been grow-

Table 14.4 Regional Growth Patterns, 1930–2000
(percent change)

	1930–1940	1940–1950	1950–1960	1960–1970	1970–1980	1980–1990	1990–2000 (proj.)
Northeast	4.5	9.7	13.2	9.8	0.2	3.4	2.1
Midwest	4.0	10.8	16.1	9.6	4.0	0.8	7.0
South	10.1	13.3	16.5	14.3	20.0	13.4	13.8
West	16.7	40.4	38.9	24.2	23.9	12.3	19.9

SOURCE: U.S. Department of Commerce, *Statistical Abstract of the United States.*

ing at a faster rate than that in other parts of the country for the past half century. But while growth rates in the Northeast and the Midwest declined precipitously since the 1970s and 1980s, those in the West remained high and those in the South accelerated. The impact of this migration is even more clear if we examine population shifts in major cities in each region, as reported in table 14.5. Most of this migration is *not* a movement of unemployed people looking for work: Only about 10 percent of inter-regional migration involves people living in poverty. Rather, it represents a shift in the location of professional and service jobs, with over one-third of all inter-regional migration involving people in the professional or managerial classes (U.S. Department of Commerce 1984). And as tables 14.4 and 14.5 suggest, most of this movement has been out of the Northeast and into the South and West—although by 1990, several large cities in the Northeast and the Midwest (e.g., New York City, Philadelphia, Boston, and St. Louis) had stemmed their outmigration and were actually growing. The growth in telecommunications may be at least partially responsible for this. For example, when large corporations like Coca-Cola moved their corporate offices from New York City during the 1960s and the 1970s, they took their professional employees with them. But this was just the tip of the iceberg, for corporate relocation also triggered movement in banking and financial institutions, law firms, and a host of other business support organizations (cf., Mollenkopf 1983). But with the expansion of telecommunication during the 1980s, support organizations in New York City can meet the needs of corporations in Los Angeles, Atlanta, Dallas, and any other city in the United States (or abroad). In fact, the business and professional services sector was one of the biggest growth areas for New York City during the 1980s (Drennan 1991).

Federal Cutbacks

The previous chapters chronicled a shifting pattern of federal aid to American cities, beginning with categorical grants and moving through block grants and revenue sharing into the Reagan presidency. But the story was left largely

Table 14.5   Growth Patterns of Selected Metropolitan Areas, 1960–1990 (percent change)

	1960–1970	**1970–1980**	**1980–1990**
Northeast			
New York	4.5	-3.6	3.1
Philadelphia	11.1	-1.2	3.9
Buffalo	3.2	-7.9	-4.3
Boston	7.9	0.8	5.0
Pittsburgh	-0.2	-5.2	-7.4
Midwest			
Chicago	12.1	2.0	1.6
Cleveland	8.1	-5.5	-2.6
St. Louis	12.4	-2.1	2.8
Detroit	12.3	-0.7	-1.8
Kansas City	14.9	4.4	9.3
Mid-Atlantic			
Baltimore	14.8	5.3	8.3
Washington	38.8	6.9	20.7
South			
Atlanta	36.5	27.0	32.5
Houston	39.8	43.0	19.7
Miami	35.6	40.0	20.8
Dallas	36.8	24.6	32.6
West			
Los Angeles	16.6	15.2	26.4
Phoenix	46.1	55.4	40.6
Denver	32.6	30.7	14.2
San Francisco	17.4	12.9	16.5
San Diego	31.4	37.1	34.2
Seattle	28.7	13.9	22.3

SOURCE: U.S. Department of Commerce, *Statistical Abstract of the United States.*

unfinished, for yet another shift has occurred in the years since 1978: a shift toward *no aid*.[17] Table 13.6 shows how dramatic the decline in federal aid to cities has been since 1978.

The Overall Effect

Any of these four factors—the tax-payer revolt, economic stagnation, shifting population, and cutbacks in federal aid—would have slowed the growth of service delivery in the city. But taken together, they resulted in an absolute

---

17. In December 1980, one of the last acts of the Carter administration was to publish a national urban agenda for the 1980s (*Urban America in the Eighties: Perspectives and Prospects*). It opened with the declaration, "A unified and coherent national urban policy designed to solve the problems of the nation's communities and those [who] live in them is not possible" (Ames et al. 1992).

reduction in the total revenue available to cities. In response to this crisis, cities were forced to respond in either of two ways: cut back services or find alternative sources of revenue. Most cities adopted a combination of these two strategies, and beginning about 1979, urban government entered an era of cutback management.

Creative Finance in the City

The handwriting on the wall foretold of municipal fiscal stress during the early 1970s; yet it was largely ignored until the end of the decade. Why the delay? The most convincing explanation is wishful thinking (Levine, 1980, has termed this the tooth fairy syndrome). We should not find it surprising, then, that administrators and politicians also resisted the notion that the good days had come to an end, and that instead of continuing to expand services they would be forced to cut them back.

The handwriting on the wall became hard to ignore in 1975, when New York City teetered on the brink of bankruptcy. But it was ignored, with municipal officials elsewhere arguing that, after all, the Big Apple was different. To point out these differences, a number of cities (including Wichita, Sacramento, Indianapolis, St. Paul, and Dallas) formed the National Alliance for Financially Responsible Local Government (Lineberry and Sharkansky 1978). The same kind of rationalization occurred after Cleveland defaulted in 1978 ("after all, what can you expect from a city whose major waterway catches fire?"). Even after Proposition 13 passed in California in 1978, people attributed it to "kookie California politics" (Clark and Ferguson 1983). But within a short time, it was clear that virtually all cities faced the challenge of cutting budgets without disrupting services. This challenge was met in various ways. These included cutting back services, coproduction and volunteerism, improving efficiency in service delivery, adopting user fees, and contracting out services to the private sector.

Cutting Back Services

The most obvious approach to saving money in the provision of municipal services is to cut them, and many cities adopted this strategy. Fifty-nine percent of all cities report having implemented hiring freezes at some point during the past decade, and 48 percent report having eliminated municipal programs as a way of saving money (Clark 1994). In a detailed study of the cutback strategies of Oakland, Cincinnati, and Baltimore, for example, Charles Levine and his colleagues (1981) found extensive curtailment of services. In Oakland, Proposition 13 left the city with a 4.6 percent decrease in operating capital. It attempted to meet this crisis by reducing library and museum hours, street sweeping details, street maintenance, and weed abatement, and by elim-

359

inating a city hall switchboard, some fire alarm boxes, and the film program at the public library. When further cuts were required the following year, the city closed a fire station and four branch libraries, reduced criminal investigation operations in the police department, and reduced park maintenance and after-school recreation programs in the recreation department. While these cuts reduced operational expenses, they also resulted in the loss of 170 municipal jobs. In Cincinnati, 893 full-time municipal positions were cut from the payroll in 1977 in the face of declining revenues. And in Baltimore, a decade-long economic crisis during the 1970s resulted in the reduction of 435 positions in the police department, nearly 100 firefighters, and 1,200 school district personnel; in addition, the library system suffered a 20 percent cut in professional staff and a 35 percent cut in maintenance personnel. These austerity measures continued through the 1980s: after his election in 1987, Mayor Kurt Schmoke implemented a municipal hiring freeze and shut down several neighborhood programs, including four fire stations (Imbroscio et al. 1995).

While reduction in services is an obvious solution, it carries with it two important political costs. First, each of the reduced services has a clientele that is likely to object to curtailments. For example, closing a branch library is likely to anger residents in the neighborhoods affected, as is closing a fire station. In most cases, cities opt to reduce low-visibility services with low demand (e.g., the library film program). But low demand is not the same as no demand, and even a small number of vehemently vocal citizens can be an embarrassment to the municipal administration. Second, municipal employees (and their unions) are unlikely to accept layoffs silently, or if they do, they extract a high price. For example, between 1974 and 1977 Detroit, Cleveland, and New York City all reduced their municipal work forces, but in the bargain, unions were able to extract higher wages for remaining employees (Clark and Ferguson 1983). If unions are able to achieve neither job security nor higher wages through negotiations, they may strike, resulting in political embarrassment for the city administration and potentially crippling its ability to govern effectively. Given these consequences, it is not surprising that cities have searched for alternative ways to save money in the provision of services.

Coproduction and Volunteerism

How can cities cut back services without actually reducing services citizens receive? While in an absolute sense this can be accomplished only with mirrors, many cities have adopted a reasonable approximation in the form of *coproduction*, an arrangement wherein the city and its citizens work together to provide services. For example, garbage collection in most cities is coproduced, with residents carrying their trash out to the curb, where it is picked up by municipal garbage trucks. So, too, police protection in many cities is coproduced, through programs such as the neighborhood crime watch.

A related concept is volunteerism, through which cities use unpaid volunteers to provide services that would otherwise be provided by municipal employees. The most obvious use of volunteerism is in fire departments. By 1994, 94.2 percent of American cities (serving 57.2 percent of the U.S. population) were using volunteer fire fighters either exclusively or to supplement paid fire fighters (Karter 1995). Although the trend is toward paid career fire fighters, the use of volunteers remains considerable.

Many cities have also initiated volunteer security patrols. For instance, during the 1990s, the 120-member East Midwood patrol was initiated to provide an all-night patrol service for a twenty-five-block area in Brooklyn; it asked residents in this area to donate a $10 annual fee to cover expenses. Around the same time, similar units provided service to approximately 25 percent of the neighborhoods in New York City. Other cities, such as Boston, Baltimore, St. Louis, Chicago, San Jose, Norfolk, Newark, Detroit, Washington, New Orleans, and Los Angeles, have also made use of volunteer citizen patrols (Poole 1980). And during the 1990s, in an effort to make many of its crime-ridden public housing neighborhoods safer, the Department of Housing and Urban Development encouraged local public housing authorities to establish tenant patrols.

A third area where volunteers are used broadly is public education. Many schools actively recruit parents to chaperon field trips (and in the upper grades, school dances), to help out in the classroom, and to grade papers and examinations.

Problems with coproduction and volunteerism. First and foremost, only some jobs appeal to volunteers. A city wanting to staff its garbage trucks with volunteers is in for a long wait; by the same token, volunteers are lacking for such activities as street repair, building and grounds maintenance, street and parking lot cleanup, and animal control. This is not to say that volunteers cannot be helpful in the jobs they seem to enjoy most (e.g., fire suppression, recreation services, and programs for the elderly). But cities cannot count on volunteers to staff all their departments. Second, paid employees may resist the use of volunteers in their department, particularly if they believe the department may someday replace them with these volunteers. Whatever is gained from the unpaid work of the volunteer may be negated by loss of productivity by the paid staff. Third, even though volunteers are not paid wages, they are not without cost to the organization. They must be recruited, usually by a paid volunteer coordinator. They must be trained. And they require supervision, even more so than do paid employees. Thus, volunteers probably should be viewed as supplementary or complementary to paid staff rather than as an alternative to paid staff; as such, use of volunteers should not be counted on to save money (Brudney 1989).

Beyond simple cost effectiveness, an obvious problem raised by the volunteerism and coproduction movements is the quality of services provided. As citizens rather than municipal employees, volunteers are largely unaccountable for their actions. The volunteer firefighter who does not respond to a fire alarm cannot be fired; nor can an unconscientious educational volunteer. Perhaps the greatest threat lies in the area of security patrols, however. Law enforcement officers receive considerable training, designed to (a) minimize the likelihood that they will be injured while performing their jobs; (b) minimize the threat to bystanders; and (c) preserve the rights of those they apprehend. While the purpose of security patrols is to observe and report crimes (and therefore never to get involved directly), they may nonetheless unavoidably be caught up in a crime. Yet, without the proper training, they may well pose a threat to themselves and to others.

Improving Efficiency

If asked, most people within the United States would probably say that their governments operate inefficiently; further, they would state that if governmental waste were stripped away, their taxes could be cut without sacrificing any crucial governmental functions. This logic contributed to the taxpayer revolts in California and other states, and to the federal tax cuts during the Reagan administration. Also at the federal level, it contributed to the formation of the Grace Commission. This commission consisted of people from the private sector, headed by businessman Peter Grace, who developed twenty-three thousand pages of suggestions that it projected would save the federal government over $420 billion. Several states and even some cities have adopted similar strategies.

Cities have used five strategies to improve efficiency in the delivery of municipal services. First, many cities have initiated practices designed to use municipal personnel more efficiently (Poole 1980), and 75 percent of all cities report implementing management practices designed to improve productivity (Clark 1994). For example, firefighters in many cities spend most of their working hours waiting for a fire alarm. Some cities have attempted to make more efficient use of this "down" time. While not actively fighting fires, firefighters in these cities give presentations on fire safety to community organizations, work with citizens to fireproof their homes, issue bicycle licenses, conduct municipal inspections, and repair city water meters. Police departments have also adopted management innovations during the past several years. For example, a number of cities (e.g., Scottsdale, Miami) have hired young adults to serve as community service officers (CSOs); these CSOs act as traffic control officers at accident locations, refer citizens to appropriate municipal agencies, write reports, perform first aid, and carry out crime prevention programs at about half the cost of sworn officers.

Second, cities have attempted to trim expenses through more efficient equipment acquisition strategies (Poole 1980). For example, some municipal fire departments (e.g., Syracuse, Des Moines) moved away from large pumpers to smaller mini-pumpers, which can be handled by two-person crews and cost only 20 percent as much as the larger pumper. In addition, many cities are purchasing compact or mid-sized police patrol cars rather than full-sized models. And, 46 percent of cities report having entered into joint purchasing agreements with other municipalities to achieve savings on equipment purchases.

Third, cities have begun using more aggressive maintenance procedures to sustain the life of their equipment. For example, the city manager in Olathe, Kansas, discovered that the park maintenance equipment experienced an inordinate number of flat tires, and crews were left idle while the tires were repaired. As a solution, he ordered that tires be filled with sand; this made for a less comfortable ride for recreation department employees, but it considerably reduced the down time for this equipment. In a similar vein, many cities have reduced the maintenance interval for their police patrol cars. While this creates a minor inconvenience every few weeks while the oil is changed and the engine is tuned, it reduces expensive repairs. Ironically, however, 37 percent of cities report that they have begun deferring maintenance on equipment as a cost-saving device (Clark 1994).

Fourth, most cities have purchased a mini-computer (or in some cases, a small mainframe computer) to serve a number of accounting functions, including budgeting, billing, and word processing. Some cities have computerized their traffic signals to achieve optimal traffic flow. Others use computers for law enforcement functions, for example, tracking suspected criminals and preparing court calendars.

Fifth, administrators in various cities have sought out inefficient work practices among municipal employees. In Pittsburgh, for example, Mayor Pete Flaherty took this task upon himself, arriving unannounced at worksites throughout the city in search of inefficiency. In San Diego, Mayor Pete Wilson hired a management consulting firm which conducted detailed time and motion studies to identify inefficiency. Changes growing out of these investigations resulted in approximately a 10 percent reduction in expenditures in each city (Clark and Ferguson 1983).[18]

What price efficiency? If we stop to consider exactly how much money can be saved by making urban government more efficient, however, we are

18. These results must be interpreted cautiously. A study conducted in 1927 at the Western Electric Company in Hawthorne, Illinois, showed that by changing the lights to a higher wattage, productivity among workers increased. However, this increase was short-lived. Then, in a follow-up study, wattage was decreased below the original level, and productivity once again increased (but again for a short period). In other words, almost any change in working conditions results in a short-term gain in productivity and efficiency. This is known as the *Hawthorne effect* (Roethlisberger and Dickson 1939). In the Pittsburgh and San Diego examples, a 10 percent reduction in the cost of producing services is impressive *only* to the extent that it represents a long-term effect.

bound to be disappointed. First, the major function of municipal government is the provision of services, and these services are labor intensive. For example, 74 percent of all municipal fire-fighting expenditures and 73 percent of all municipal law-enforcement expenditures are earmarked for employee salaries. Across all categories of the municipal budget, salaries account for approximately 48 percent of general expenditures.[19] The *only* way to cut this large segment of expenditures without also cutting services would be to reduce the number of administrators in each municipal department; for obvious reasons, this is a path that urban administrators are reluctant to pursue.

Second, the growth of technology is exacting a substantial toll on municipal governments. State-of-the-art fire-fighting equipment is costly, but most citizens would not want their city to settle for second-rate fire protection. State-of-the-art crime detection equipment is also expensive; and anyone who has purchased a new car recently knows that keeping the city's fleet of police cars up-to-date (even with compact models) is an expensive proposition. Municipal hospitals must purchase modern diagnostic and treatment equipment, none of which is inexpensive. Citizens demanding efficiency in the purchase of equipment ultimately face the tradeoff between expense and quality. Most, faced with the possibility that they may someday depend on that equipment, tend to opt for the more expensive but higher quality line.

Third, municipal governments now provide more services for more people than ever before, and many of these services are redistributive in nature. For example, many municipal budgets include funding for direct welfare payments to the needy.[20] Some include funding for health and social programs. For those who disagree with municipal fiscal policies, these are among the most criticized services. But criticism has little to do with improved efficiency, and, in turn, improving efficiency would have little impact on the cost of providing these services.

In the end, the introduction of efficient practices into the delivery of urban services will result in *little* long-term savings for taxpayers. While the exact savings is impossible to predict, it is unlikely to exceed even 5 percent

19. These estimates are derived from aggregate municipal statistics reported in the *Statistical Abstract of the United States*. Other estimates, derived from detailed analysis of expenditures in individual cities, are more revealing. For example, Miranda (1992) reports that nearly 80 percent of general fund expenditures in Chicago are for personnel and related items.

20. Different municipalities carry different responsibilities for funding various social and welfare programs. In some cases, the city bears no responsibility, with all funding provided by the federal government, the state, and/or the county. In other cases, however, the city's contribution is large. This helps explain why the fiscal crisis hit some cities harder than others. In the 1970s, for example, the state of New York mandated that New York City assume 25 percent of the cost of providing welfare and Medicaid to its residents, and the burgeoning cost of these programs occurred at a time when the city's financial resources were already stretched thin (see Stone et al. 1986).

of municipal general expenditures, with 1 percent to 2 percent a more realistic guess.[21] This, of course, is not to be scoffed at.

But the true benefit of efficiency in the delivery of urban services lies in the domain of public confidence. Citizens are more likely to support taxes if they believe that their tax dollars are being spent efficiently. And many of the management practices described above are public relations bonanzas. For example, computers epitomize efficiency, and it is no accident that the purchase of new computer equipment is accompanied by a front-page story in the local newspaper, complete with picture. By the same token, when the mayor goes on the road to root out inefficiency, publicity abounds. And by bringing in a management consulting team from the private sector, the city serves notice that it is serious about saving taxpayers' dollars. Finally, compact police cars are visible to motorists every day, and they serve as a constant reminder that the city is doing what it can to provide services for less money.

The end result, then, is that some money is saved (after all, even 1 percent of the general expenditures in Austin, Texas, amounts to $11.1 million, for example; and in New York City, a 1 percent savings amounts to over $425 million); but more important, the municipal administration is afforded some relief from the public pressure it faces on taxing and spending issues, and it is more likely to be successful next time it places a bond issue on the ballot.

User Fees

The previous chapter discussed user fees as a growing source of municipal revenue; indeed, 85 percent of cities report having implemented or increased user fees as a means of maintaining fiscal solvency (Clark 1994). Here, we consider how cities have applied the concept to their delivery of services, paying particular attention to the consequences of user fees particularly for the city's economically disadvantaged.

User fees are most commonly found in the area of municipal parks or recreation, where they might include parking and entrance fees, rental fees for equipment, and sales of souvenirs, food, and beverages. For example, a number of museums throughout the country aggressively pursue merchandising strategies, not just in museum gift shops but also through mail orders. The New York Metropolitan Museum of Art took in $88.2 million in retail sales in 1994, and the Museum of Modern Art took in $20.7 million through its auxiliary activities (including retail sales).[22] In addition, many art museums rent self-guiding

21. Ladd and Yinger (1991) conclude that *all* managerial improvements (including strategies such as tougher bargaining with unions, improvements in productivity, and contracting out certain services) would save no more than about 4 percent of a typical city's budget.

22. Expenses eat up most of this income; even so, the Metropolitan Museum netted nearly $2 million from its retail sales, and the Museum of Modern Art netted approximately $300,000 from its auxiliary activities.

cassette tours for a nominal fee, and many zoos rent devices that patrons can use to listen to recorded descriptions of exhibits. And in one of the most imaginative revenue-generating ventures to date, Cincinnati built a fountain in the Yeatman's Cove Municipal Park. Although water flows continually through the fountain, a quarter buys a spectacular three-minute display (Poole 1980).

Problems with user fees. One of the dangers in the aggressive use of fees as a means of generating municipal revenue is that people who cannot afford the fees are unable to use the service. Nationally, user fees accounted for approximately 17 percent of municipal general revenues in 1992, representing a flow of $30 billion into municipal coffers. The very size of these figures almost ensures that at least some of the people who cannot afford services are being systematically excluded from those services.[23] For example, when Oakland, California, removed admission charges to two municipal swimming pools serving low-income neighborhoods, attendance increased by 29 percent and 67 percent, respectively (Poole 1980). Presumably, if fees were introduced on free services, the number of economically disadvantaged people who use a service would decline dramatically. Yet, unlike the introduction of efficiency measures into municipal service delivery, user fees have become an important and integral part of municipal finance, one that most cities could ill afford to give up.

Privatization and Contracting-Out for Services

In the late 1970s, Visalia, California, like all other California cities, was contemplating life in the wake of Proposition 13. To survive, it developed a number of austerity programs, including privatizing and contracting out its services. In 1983, Visalia's city manager described the extent of these programs as follows:

> We gave the libraries to the county, the ambulances to private hospitals, day care centers to churches and the junior college, historic preservation to a private not-for-profit group, recycling to a private, not-for-profit group,

23. A number of cities have developed strategies to reduce the economic hardship of user fees (see Poole 1980). For example, many museums waive admission at least one day a month (and some as frequently as one day each week). Second, many cities (e.g., Dallas, Santa Barbara) have implemented higher fees for nonresidents to use recreational facilities. Thirds, some cities (e.g., Sacramento) have actively begun to encourage local businesses to provide "recreational scholarships" for low-income children. While these strategies no doubt improve access of low-income individuals to municipal services, their symbolic benefits may be greater than their real benefits. Municipal administrators may feel magnanimous about opening museum doors without charge on the third Thursday of every month; but this strategy may (a) lead to overcrowding and detract from enjoyment on those free days and (b) preclude people who must work at low-paying (and often inflexible) jobs during the week. Further, the city that encourages local businesses to provide recreational scholarships to economically disadvantaged youth may be providing a largely symbolic benefit to its low-income residents, especially since the number of disadvantaged likely exceeds the number of available scholarships.

public relations activities to the chamber of commerce (we pay them a fee), and animal control to the humane society. We sold the baseball franchise to the private sector, and gave a theater to the private sector. (Quoted in Belasich 1993, 105)

Like Visalia, many other cities around the country have opted to discontinue services (e.g., garbage collection) altogether, allowing market forces to dictate the private companies that will offer the service and the price they will charge. Other cities (Clark, 1994, reports 46 percent of all cities) have contracted with private companies to provide the services, awarding the contract on the basis of bids submitted by interested parties in the private sector. In either case, the city gets out of the service delivery business, and the private sector quite likely is able to provide the service more efficiently and at a lower cost. By contracting-out, the city still maintains ultimate responsibility for the service, while under privatization it relinquishes responsibility altogether.

Garbage collection is one service that many cities have turned over to the private sector, with 35 percent of cities contracting out their residential garbage service (Miranda 1992). For example, during the 1970s a number of cities (including Boston, Oklahoma City, Omaha, Dallas, Almagorda, New Mexico, and Utica, New York) all began to contract for garbage collection services at a substantial fiscal savings. In a comprehensive study of privatized garbage collection, Stevens (1977) found that 36 percent of all urban dwellers in the United States are served by private trash collection firms, with some rather sobering results. In cities with more than fifty thousand people, she found that costs of garbage collection by municipal agencies to be 68 percent higher than those of private firms. Several factors account for these savings: Private firms have lower absenteeism rates, use smaller crews, bigger trucks, and longer routes, and offer better labor incentives than municipal sanitation departments. An extreme example of the cost differential between public and private garbage collection occurs in a 1975 comparison between New York and San Francisco: The annual charge for municipal garbage collection in New York City was $297 per household, while the annual cost of private garbage collection in San Francisco was $40 per household (Poole 1980).

Fire protection is another area where privatization has become common. For example, in 1980 the Rural/Metro Fire Department, Inc. served thirty locations in five Arizona counties. Its fee structure of approximately $25 to $50 per year for most houses proved attractive, and it listed over fifty thousand subscribers (mostly homeowners) on its books. Rural/Metro responded to fires in the homes or businesses of nonsubscribers, but the cost was dear: The fee levied for this response was fourteen times the annual subscription fee, *plus* $50/hour per fire vehicle and $ 10/hour for each command vehicle used, *plus* $15/hour per firefighter responding to the fire (Poole 1980). Similar arrangements have been offered by private fire departments in Georgia, Oregon, Montana, and Tennessee.

In addition to complete privatization of fire-fighting services, some municipal governments contract with private fire companies to provide fire protection for their residents. For example, Scottsdale, Arizona, saved approximately 25 percent on the cost of fire service by contracting with Rural/Metro (Poole 1980).

A third area where private companies offer subscriptions is emergency ambulance service. For example, in 1980 the Acadia Ambulance Service served 480,000 rural residents in nine Louisiana parishes. Seventy-five thousand families in the area subscribed at a rate of $15 per year, with nonsubscribers charged directly for any services they required. Similar subscription services were adopted in Oklahoma City and Eugene, Oregon (Poole 1980).

A fourth area where private companies offer services is law enforcement. For example, Lexington, Kentucky, and St. Petersburg, Florida, both began contracting with private firms to patrol high-crime areas. Additionally, exclusive residential areas in many cities employ their own private security force, as do malls and other shopping centers. Estimates suggest that private security firms may employ as many uniformed guards and security officers as do municipal governments (Poole 1980).

Hidden costs of privatization and contracting-out. Across the board, privatization and contracting out for services may substantially decrease municipal expenditures. But those in favor of these strategies often lose sight of several hidden costs. First, private subscription services may not be affordable for people living near or below the poverty line. And given the increased costs of service for nonsubscribers, a nonsubscriber may perhaps not seek emergency ambulance service when it may save his or her life; or the nonsubscribing homeowner with a small fire may attempt to control it himself or herself, thus risking greater damage to the entire neighborhood; or he or she may attempt to defeat burglaries with deadly booby traps.

Second, private companies will provide services only so long as they are profitable. But once the profit has gone, the company has no legal obligation to continue the service, perhaps leaving the city and its residents in the lurch. Just as important, deregulation of private service providers may well result in differential fee structures for different neighborhoods: Those that generate the most demand will pay higher subscription rates than those with lower demand. Particularly in such areas as police and fire protection, those high-demand neighborhoods are likely to be low-income areas where residents are least able to pay subscription fees. The result may well be two levels of service: exemplary service for those who can pay for it and poor (or no) service for those who cannot.

Third, private security officers are not required to follow the same procedures as public law enforcement officers, with the result that many of the constitutional rights that we have come to take for granted are not necessarily protected. For example, private security officers employed by shopping centers can search people without provocation, and they can evict people from the premises because of the way they dress or their language. Further, they need not tell a person suspected of shoplifting of his or her right to remain silent or to have an attorney present; information gathered during these "interrogations" can be used in criminal prosecutions (Frieden and Sagalyn 1989).

Fourth, there exists some disagreement about exactly how much savings result from contracting out services. Some studies (e.g., Stevens 1977) show that contracting out services can result in savings as high as 42 percent (for garbage collection) to 96 percent (for asphalt overlay construction), reflecting the benefits of greater efficiency in the private sector and the use of economies of scale. However, other studies raise questions about whether economies of scale actually do produce desired cost savings *when quality is held constant* (see Hirsch, 1995, for a review).

Finally, there may be substantial political cost associated with contracting out services. A survey of Chicago residents, for example, showed that 51.6 percent opposed contracting out city services. Of those opposed, 21.7 percent worried that costs would actually increase, 35 percent worried that corruption or patronage would guide the choice of contractors, and 7 percent worried that the quality of service would decrease (Miranda 1992).

The Resurgence of Urban Service Delivery: 1983 to the Present

Figures 14.1 and 14.2, and table 14.3, suggest that the urban service delivery saga does not end on a negative note. Since 1982, municipal expenditures have once again been on the rise (figure 14.1), and cities seem once again willing to borrow the money they need to finance capital projects (table 14.3). Thus, the days of cutback management may be behind us, and cities may be—once again—foresquare in the service delivery business.

One explanation involves need. Richard Hill (1984, 309) describes an urban infrastructure literally falling apart.

> Two out of five of the nation's bridges must be replaced or repaired, at an estimated cost of $41 billion. $31 billion must be invested in sewer systems and waste water treatment plants over the next five years to meet pollution control standards. Cities must spend $110 billion over the next two decades to maintain their water systems.

In addition, the cost of repairing the nation's roads, many of which are in urban areas, stands at $600 billion (Feagin and Parker 1990). This state of affairs is not surprising, given long-term trends in spending: During the years between 1964 and 1987, total public spending to support the nation's infrastructure has declined from 2.3 percent of the gross national product to 1.7 percent (Bowman et al. 1992). Hill (1984) goes on to catalog what several older cities must do if they are to meet their needs:

- New York City will have to spend $40 billion to repair 6,000 miles of streets, 6,200 miles of sewers, 775 bridges, and a 1.5-billion-gallon-per-day water system;
- Chicago will have to spend $33 billion to repair or replace deteriorating streets, bridges, sewers, and transit lines;
- Dallas will have to spend over $700 million to repair a deteriorating water and sewer system.

Faced with these stark realities, many cities no doubt realize that increased expenditures are inevitable, particularly those involving capital improvements, and this realization helps fuel the growth in bonded indebtedness reflected in table 14.3.

Another explanation has similar origins. Faced with the need to cut back services, many cities laid off street-level bureaucrats, closed public facilities, or reduced service delivery schedules. To an electorate that had come to depend on these services, cutbacks pinched, and demands may have grown for services to be restored to their pre-1978 level (and beyond).

A third explanation holds that various strategies for financing municipal government during the 1979–1982 fiscal crisis were more successful than expected, bringing in sufficient municipal revenue to allow the expansion of services. For example, user fees and the sale of municipal property provided cities with over 17.9 percent of their general revenue in 1992, up from 11 percent in 1976. As cities developed additional revenue enhancements during the cutback years, they may have discovered that they had sufficient funds to provide more services without higher taxes.

A fourth explanation is tied to the economy. During the cutback years, the economy was sluggish, interest rates were high, and inflation was rampant. As a result, tax revenues were down, and cities were understandably reluctant to borrow money at prevailing interest rates. But since 1983, the economy has expanded, and both interest rates and inflation are down. And with economic recovery, tax receipts are up (see figure 14.10): Between 1982 and 1992, annual per capita taxes on urban residents have gone from $90.90 to $116.81 (in constant 1967 dollars) surpassing the 1977 high-water mark of $105.07. In times of economic well-being, with increased tax revenues and increased voter optimism in the future, politicians may be more willing to expand the scope of service delivery.

Whichever of these explanations holds—and it is likely that all have some merit—the delivery of urban services in the future is likely to follow an erratic path. The decaying infrastructure is not likely to improve at any time soon, and cities will continue to face the need for repairing, rebuilding, and modernizing their facilities. Yet, cities are unlikely to fund those projects without outside assistance: Recent history shows that taxpayers are unwilling to write the city a blank check. In an age-old dilemma faced by virtually all governments, citizens demand services, but they are unwilling to pay for those that do not benefit them personally. So we are likely to witness a growing demand, but a reluctance to pay for what is demanded. In addition, if the delivery of services continues to be tied to economic performance, city services are likely to rise and fall according to national trends completely beyond local control. Just as important, many of the largest cities, where infrastructures are in greatest need of repair and services are most in demand, continue to be on insecure financial footing. Evidence of a resurgent service delivery sector aside, these cities are struggling financially: Budget surpluses in the largest cities are down and tax burdens on their residents are up, suggesting that growing expenditures for municipal services cannot be sustained indefinitely (Ladd 1994). So if there is one certainty, it is that urban service delivery will be less certain than in the past, when the growth of services continued virtually unabated for three decades (1945–1978), unimpeded by economic fluctuations, voter sentiment, or need.

PART SEVEN

CHALLENGES FOR THE FUTURE

From the Window of 291, platinum print, 1915, 25.3 x 20.2 cm
Alfred Stieglitz Collection, 1949.709.
Photograph © 1996, The Art Institute of Chicago. All Rights Reserved.

CHAPTER 15

Poverty and the
Urban Underclass

As we discovered in the two previous chapters, financing urban services presents one of the greatest challenges that cities face. But an equally important challenge, and one that has enormous consequences for the character of cities and for the character of American society, has to do with the changing composition of inner cities and their residents.

In 1980, Ira Lowry described central cities in frightening terms:

> The quality of urban life has deteriorated. Interracial tensions periodically erupt in mob violence. Roving gangs of adolescents terrorize peaceable citizens. Muggings, burglaries, rape, and vandalism are commonplace. Drug abuse is widespread. Public schools are patrolled by guards, but classrooms are nonetheless vandalized, students robbed, and teachers beaten. . . . Unoccupied buildings are stripped and burned. Neighborhood retailers close their shops after a series of armed robberies or a night of looting. Public streets are littered and potholed. The sites of demolished buildings are piled high with rat-infested rubbish. (P. 161)

By most accounts, and in public perception, the situation has become even more desperate as we approach the new century. The risk of being mugged, caught in the middle of a drive-by shooting, or aggressively panhandled by the homeless and seeing homeless people urinate in an alley are sufficient for many of those living in suburbia to question the wisdom of venturing into downtown areas. And business owners, also aware of these risks and the difficulty of attracting shoppers, clients, and employees, have opted in record numbers to set up shop in less dangerous and offensive areas of town (Hill et al. 1995). Thus, suburbia is becoming more and more isolated from the central cities it surrounds, and edge cities and industrial parks have emerged in record numbers. But these changes have not occurred in isolation, and to understand them, we must explore another transformation that has occurred in America over the past quarter century.

Postindustrial Marginalization

The economic history of the large American city over the past twenty-five years is one of transition. Beginning in the mid 1970s, large manufacturing firms eliminated more than 900,000 jobs a year as they closed down domestic operations and moved their production overseas to take advantage of cheaper labor markets. Between 1978 and 1982, this resulted in the loss of between 3.5 million and 4 million jobs, or about 20 percent of the total manufacturing positions in this country (Harrison and Bluestone 1988). At about the same time, many of the remaining manufacturing plants moved to the suburbs (Kasarda 1989). Changing technology required companies to modernize their production processes if they were to remain competitive; and they found it less expensive simply to build new, modern plants on cheaper suburban land than to renovate existing plants in the central cities. In addition, many retail enterprises followed the great residential migration to the suburbs where they located in malls. In the wake of these desertions, downtown areas became office centers—places of administration, information exchange, finance, trade, and governmental services. But most inner-city residents, who tend to be undereducated and underskilled, were unqualified for the more sophisticated jobs that came with this transformation (Kelso 1994). Some tried to commute to the suburbs and the manufacturing jobs that had located there; but for the most part, they found that a variety of logistical barriers limited their access to these jobs (Holzer 1991), and they were largely unsuccessful (Ihlanfeldt and Sjoquist 1989).

The result, argue Harrison and Bluestone, was the emergence of a two-tiered urban labor market. The upper tier consists of the managers, lawyers, accountants, bankers, business consultants, and other technically trained people who are either employed in corporate offices or who provide business services for them.[1] The lower tier consists of unskilled urban workers who provide

1. Despite the dramatic migration of corporations to the suburbs during the past thirty years and the impact this has had on municipal finances, the bulk of corporate headquarters (68 percent) remain in large central cities (Ward 1994).

personal services to those in the upper tier.[2] "They are the ones who wait tables, cook meals, sell everything from office supplies to clothing, change beds and linens in the dozens of new downtown hotels, and find lower-level employment in the city's hospitals, health clinics, schools, and municipal governments" (Harrison and Bluestone 1988, 69).[3]

The result of this two-tier labor force is that more and more people are working at low-wage jobs, and the ranks of the urban poor are swelling. Whereas 13.1 percent of all full-time, year-round workers were in low-wage positions in 1973, 16.2 percent were in such positions in 1987. This shift was particularly noticeable for young workers (twenty to thirty-four years of age) and for those without high school diplomas. By 1987, 19.8 percent of young workers and 32.6 percent of those without degrees were working for low wages (Bluestone 1990). This situation is unlikely to improve any time soon. Six of the ten occupations where demand for new workers over the next decade is projected to be greatest are low wage positions, including cashiers, waiters and waitresses, nurse's aides and orderlies, and janitors (Harrison and Bluestone 1988).

Not only are more people being channeled into low-wage occupations, but the economic viability of these occupations has declined over time as well. Between 1973 and 1990, the inflation-adjusted wages of the bottom 20 percent of the workforce fell 25 percent (Juhn et al. 1991). Thus, the prospects that inner-city residents are able to obtain the economic resources to escape the inner city are dim. Employment, when it is available, is likely to be low-paying and without much job security, leading to low levels of connection to the formal labor force. In Boston, for example, 39 percent of the adults living in poverty in 1989 worked less than full time during the year; among those who did work, 48.8 percent held jobs paying $5.00 an hour or less (Osterman 1991). At a national level, by the late 1980s, fully one in eight full-time, year-round male workers earned too little to support a family of four above the poverty level (Devine and Wright 1993). Given these statistics, it is not surprising to find an increase in the absolute level of urban poverty: Between 1969 and 1992, the poverty rate in central cities rose from 12.7 percent to 20.5 percent. Nor should we necessarily expect that the burst of prosperity during the 1990s will have an impact on poverty in the inner city.

---

2. Some observers believe that service jobs are being lost in central cities as well (e.g., Mincy 1994). This is particularly devastating for the prospects of unskilled and undereducated workers, since these are often the first jobs available to young people; their loss would thus limit the long-term employment prospects of inner-city youths (Johnson and Oliver 1991).

3. Harrison and Bluestone go on to argue that the high cost of living in large cities requires that professional households include multiple wage earners if they wish to sustain a middle-class lifestyle. This, in turn, forces urban professionals to consume more and more of the services that workers in an earlier generation would have produced for themselves. The provision of personal services to these professionals becomes *the* major economic activity for the rest of the city.

377

Poverty in Urban America

In the following sections, we consider how poverty affects cities. But first we explore the demographics of poverty and how poverty affects the lives of the truly poor.

Demographics of Poverty

Two popular views of poverty in America are: (1) the vast majority of the nation's poor reside in cities and (2) most of the nation's poor are black or Hispanic. Neither statement holds up to scrutiny. In 1992, for example, over 5 million white families (24.5 million people) survived on incomes below the poverty level,[4] compared with approximately 2.5 million black families (10.6 million people) and 1.3 million Hispanic families (6.7 million people).[5] Further, while nearly 75 percent of the poor *do* reside in metropolitan areas (42.4 percent in central cities, 31.8 percent in the suburbs), over 25 percent live outside these areas.

However, when these two misconceptions are joined, they produce a different conclusion: *Urban* poverty and race are related. For example, 60 percent of poor blacks and Hispanics live in central cities, compared with 34 percent of poor whites. And, whereas 28.8 percent of the nation's poor are black, 40.6 percent of poor, central city dwellers are black. Similarly, 17.8 percent of the nation's poor are Hispanic, but 25.5 percent of the poor in the central cities are Hispanic.[6] Still, even in central cities, the vast majority of people live above the poverty line.[7] Tables 15.1a and 15.1b summarize these and other demographic characteristics of the poor.

The largest single age group living in poverty is children under six (25 percent of all children under six live in poverty), followed closely by older children aged six to seventeen (19 percent) and young adults aged eighteen to twenty-four (18 percent). The elderly, many of whom live on fixed pensions,

---

4. The definition of poverty is complicated, depending on family size and age of family members. In 1992, the cutoff levels for annual monetary income were as follows:

1 person			
under 65	$ 7,299	4 people	$14,355
65 or older	$ 6,799	5 people	$16,592
2 people		6 people	$19,137
householder under 65	$ 9,443	7 people	$21,594
householder 65 or older	$ 8,487	8 people	$24,053
3 people	$11,186	9+ people	$28,745

5. It is the case, however, that a larger *percentage* of blacks and Hispanics than whites live in poverty: In 1992, 8.9 percent of white families had incomes below the poverty line, compared with 30.9 percent of black and 26.2 percent of Hispanic families.

6. By way of comparison, 12.5 percent of the United States population is black, and ten percent is Hispanic.

7. Eighty-seven percent of white families, 67 percent of black families, and 69 percent of Hispanic families living in central cities have incomes above the poverty line.

Table 15.1a   The Demographics of Poverty in America, 1992

	Metropolitan Areas		Non-metropolitian Areas	Total
	Central Cities	Suburbs		
Families living in poverty (thousands)	3,387	2,520	2,053	7,960
Percent white	52.2%	74.4%	64.8%	69.0%
Percent black	42.6%	20.8%	30.6%	27.5%
Percent Hispanic[a]	25.4%	16.5%	17.5%	14.9%
Percent of all families living in poverty				
White	12.7%	6.3%	10.6%	8.9%
Black	32.9%	23.2%	37.6%	30.9%
Hispanic	31.2%	19.3%	29.4%	26.2%

SOURCE: Adapted from U.S. Department of Commerce (1992).
a. Hispanics may be of any race. Percentages therefore do not sum to 100.

Table 15.1b The Demographics of Poverty in America, 1992

	Nonpoverty	Poverty			
		All	White	Black	Hispanic[a]
Mean family size	3.11	3.51	3.44	3.64	4.07
Mean number of children	1.77	2.21	1.83	2.32	2.51
Percent of heads of households					
with a high school degree	83.6%	56.1%	57.0%	53.8%	32.6%
Percent of families headed					
by a female	15.3%	60.0%	50.4%	80.0%	45.9%
Percent of all persons living in poverty					
under 6		25.0%	19.3%	53.1%	42.6%
6–17		19.0%	14.2%	42.5%	36.5%
18–24		18.0%	15.3%	31.7%	30.0%
25–44		11.5%	9.3%	25.9%	23.6%
45–64		8.9%	7.4%	21.1%	19.3%
65 and older		12.9%	10.9%	33.3%	22.0%
Percent of heads of households not					
working during the previous year	9.6%	46.3%	41.2%	56.1%	41.0%
Percent of people living in					
households receiving:					
cash assistance		42.7%	36.0%	58.9%	39.7%
food stamps		51.3%	45.1%	66.6%	51.3%
Medicaid		56.4%	50.4%	70.3%	61.2%
subsidized housing		18.4%	12.9%	31.3%	15.0%
Percent of people not covered by					
health insurance	12.4%	28.5%	31.0%	22.6%	41.2%
Percent of people living in high poverty					
areas	11.3%	34.5%	24.7%	57.2%	43.0%
Ratio of males to females					
under 18	1.06	1.01	1.01	1.00	0.99
18–24	1.08	0.65	0.68	0.56	0.77
25–34	1.07	0.59	0.65	0.41	0.77

SOURCE: Adapted from U.S. Department of Commerce (1992).
a. Hispanics may be of any race.

constitute a fourth major poverty category (13 percent). Most families living in poverty are small. Fifty-six percent consist of three or fewer members, with a mean size of 3.51. Sixty percent of the families living in poverty are headed by mothers, although among blacks this figure reaches 80 percent. Over 50 percent of the heads of families living in poverty are high-school graduates (and 16 percent have completed at least one year of college); this figure is somewhat lower than the 84 percent high-school graduation rate for non-poverty families, although not as low as popular belief would lead us to expect. Of those families living in poverty in 1992, 54 percent were partially supported by the earnings of a family member who worked at least part time, usually in a low-paying job. Often this was the head of the household. Fifty percent worked at least part time, and 20 percent worked full time for forty or more weeks during the year.

Living and Dying in Poverty

Housing. For the most part, the poor do not live in decent housing. One rough and ready measure of housing inadequacy is related to overcrowding. On average, the majority of housing units within the United States are not overcrowded, although most of us wish for more space from time to time. For example, the 1990 census shows that only 4.9 percent of all renter-occupied living units housed an average of more than one person per room; however, this figure rises to 9.5 percent for families living in poverty (Grall 1994). These figures are subject to substantial city-to-city variation. Using this one-person-to-a-room criterion as a rough definition of overcrowding, 15 percent of the families renting units in New York City live in overcrowded conditions, compared with 28.8 percent in Los Angeles, 20.5 percent in El Paso, 15.1 percent in Newark, and 25.8 percent in Miami. Other cities have lesser degrees of overcrowding: For example, only 8 percent of families in Philadelphia live in overcrowded conditions, 5.9 percent in Seattle, 2.9 percent in Buffalo, and 5.9 percent in Minneapolis.

More troubling is the lack of indoor plumbing for 620,000 families in the United States. As might be expected, this is not a randomly distributed phenomenon: While only 0.8 percent of the housing units occupied by people living above the poverty threshold are without plumbing, 2.4 percent of those occupied by low-income residents are without plumbing. In another comparison, only 0.7 percent of those families renting uncrowded housing units in central cities (i.e., one or fewer people per room) are without indoor plumbing, compared with 2.4 percent of families renting overcrowded housing units (i.e., 1.01–1.5 persons per room) and 3.3 percent of those families renting severely overcrowded units (i.e., more than 1.5 people per room). Nearly 4 percent of residential units housing low-income families have exposed wiring, compared with only 2 percent of residences housing those living above the poverty line (Grall 1994). When these and other housing deficiencies are considered together, 22 percent of blacks live in inadequate housing units, compared with 7 percent of whites (Clay 1992).

Health. The lack of sufficient—or for the homeless, any—shelter is not the only health hazard faced by the poor. Robert Green (1977, 247) describes the reality of poverty this way:

> Poverty is protecting your baby from rodents, eating Argo laundry starch straight from the box, knowing chronic tuberculosis, accepting the neighborhood psychotic ("He's just crazy"), waiting and more waiting for health care in the clinic, tolerating painful tooth decay, feeling the clutches of death come early, filling out interminable forms, being denied medical treatment unless a magic insurance card or money is apparent, living in life-threatening housing, learning the virtues and limitations of home remedies, being jobless and without health insurance (or being unable to afford the deductible), feeling the lack of respect from professionals, praying that your children will somehow survive and face a better world.

A number of statistics attest to his conclusions. For example, blacks lose 13 percent more days to disabilities each year than whites, and people with low incomes lose over 170 percent more days than those with higher incomes.[8] As another example, blacks and whites see physicians at approximately equal rates, but whites visit dentists 80 percent more frequently than blacks. Even in the case of physician contact, different patterns emerge for blacks and whites. For whites, 59 percent of all contacts with physicians are through office visits, with another 14 percent through phone consultation. For blacks, less than 50 percent of all contact is through office visits, and only 8 percent is through phone consultation. Instead, 23.5 percent of all contact is in emergency rooms (compared to only 13 percent for whites), where individuals are treated either for accidents or for acute emergencies that might have been prevented through regular visits to physicians' offices.

These discrepancies are epitomized by morbidity and mortality rates. For example, asthma rates are twice as high among youths living in inner

8. This comparison between blacks and whites is not intended to emphasize a racial difference. Rather, it simply acknowledges that a larger percentage of blacks than whites live in poverty, particularly in urban areas. Thus, we should conclude that any differences are due to economic status rather than to race per se. Race serves as a proxy for economic status for two reasons. First, statistics are much more readily available by race than by income, making some comparisons possible and others easier. Second, income often confounds the comparison. For example, in comparing days lost to disability for different income classes, we face two problems. When days are lost to disability, income suffers, leading to the alternative conclusion that disability causes loss of income rather than that lack of income causes disability; and those employed in low-income jobs may face greater risk of disability than those in high-income jobs.

Challenges for the Future

Table 15.2   Health Status by Income, 1986–1992

Health Indicator	Family Income <$10,00	>$35,00	Risk Factor
Hypertension	24.8a	5.2a	4.77
Congenital heart failure	9.3	4.8	1.94
Asthma	57.2	40.6	1.41
Emphysema	20.2	3.9	5.18
Ulcer	27.4	13.4	2.04
Blindness or other visual impediment	47.1	29.0	1.62
Mental retardation	10.8	2.8	3.86
Arthritis	225.3	84.8	2.66
Anemia	26.5	11.5	2.30
Infant mortalityb	13.5	8.3	1.63

SOURCE: Infant mortality statistics are taken from Centers for Disease Control, *Morbidity and Mortality Weekly Reports*, Dec. 15, 1995; all other statistics are from the Collins (1993).

a. All statistics are rates per 1,000 people

b. Infant mortality rates are calculated for people below and above the poverty line rather than for people with incomes below $10,000 and above $35,000

cities than among those living outside inner-city locales; this may be due to the higher prevalence of cockroach infestations in inner-city dwellings (*Tuscaloosa News*, June 9, 1996). Prevalence of chronic and infectious diseases among blacks is considerably higher than among whites. For example, blacks are 5.8 times more likely to have HIV/AIDS and 8.1 times more likely to have tuberculosis than are whites (Plepys and Klein 1995), and blacks are 27 percent more likely to have hypertension than are whites.[9] Cancer survival rates (five years) are 37 percent higher for whites than for blacks. Low birthweight babies are 127 percent more common among blacks than among whites, and infant mortality rates are 143 percent higher. Diagnosis of schizophrenia is 4.2 times higher for blacks than for whites, and 4.3 times higher for those in the lowest quartile of SES than in the highest quartile. Chronic diseases of all types are higher for those living in poverty than for those with higher incomes (Collins 1993, Adler et al. 1993); table 15.2 shows prevalence rates for several chronic diseases. Overall life expectancy for white males is 8.3 years longer than for black males and 5.9 years longer for white females than for black females (U.S. Department of Health and Human Services 1990, 1991).

Disease is not the only threat to the health and well-being of those living in poverty. They are also especially vulnerable to human predators. For example, people with low family incomes (i.e., under $7,500 per year) are 2.3

9. Nancy Krieger and Stephen Sidney (1996) report evidence that elevated blood pressure among blacks may be tied to racial discrimination. Most at risk for hypertension are working-class minorities who experience racial discrimination but accept it as a fact of life.

382

times more likely to be victims of violent crimes than are people with high family incomes (greater than $75,000 per year); low-income people are also 2.8 times more likely to be robbed than are high-income people (Perkins et al. 1996). Crime in the United States tends to be committed by the poor (32.7 percent of prison inmates were unemployed at the time of their arrest; 41.8 percent had not completed high school). This, combined with the previous statistics, leads to the conclusion that crime in large cities tends to be committed by the poor against the poor.

The Concentration of Poverty and Growth of the Underclass

Just as important as the poverty rate in urban America is the intensity of poverty, which has increased dramatically over the past two decades. In 1977, 3.5 percent of the U.S. population lived below 50 percent of the poverty threshold (these are the poorest of the poor); by 1992, this had increased to 5.9 percent.[10] The growth of extreme poverty during this period was particularly pronounced among blacks, increasing from 9.3 percent in 1977 to 16.3 percent in 1992. Table 15.3 shows this growth in extreme poverty. But what is less obvious and more troubling for cities is that poverty has become concentrated in what have been called underclass or ghetto neighborhoods. The number of people living in extreme poverty areas (i.e., over 40 percent of residents live in poverty) grew from 3.8 million in 1970 to 5.6 million in 1980, an increase of 47 percent (Ricketts and Mincy 1988, cited in Mincy 1994). This growth was particularly pronounced in large cities, with increases of 256 percent in New York and 161 percent in Philadelphia (Jargowsky and Bane 1991). Between 1980 and 1990, this ghetto population increased by another 36 percent. During the period between 1980 and 1990, the number of ghetto census tracts increased by 54 percent (Jargowsky 1994).

Explanations for the Growth of Ghetto Poverty

The growth in ghetto poverty has occurred most rapidly among blacks, and it is at least partially the result of two factors: decreasing employability of

10. This is somewhat misleading, since the overall poverty rate was increasing during the same period (from 11.6 percent to 14.5 percent). But another comparison yields a similar conclusion: in 1977, 30.2 percent of the nation's poor lived below 50 percent of the poverty level, compared with 40.7 percent in 1992. Thus, not only was the poverty rate growing during that fifteen year period but the poor were becoming increasingly concentrated at the very lowest income levels. The concentration of poverty at the lowest income levels has been particularly striking for African Americans: whereas in 1977, 29.9 percent of the poor fell below 50 percent of the poverty level, in 1992, this figure had risen to 49.1 percent.

Table 15.3 Changing Rates of Extreme Poverty for Whites and Blacks, 1977–1992

	Whites		Blacks	
	1977	1992	1977	1992
Below 50% of poverty level	2.68%	4.29%	9.35%	16.32%
51%–100% of poverty level	6.18%	7.29%	21.92%	16.93%
Total below 100% of poverty level	8.86%	11.58%	31.27%	33.25%

SOURCE: U.S. Department of Commerce (1977, 1992).

unskilled blacks living in the inner city and the migration of skilled blacks out of the inner city.

Employment and employability. Harrison and Bluestone (1988) document the loss of good-paying manufacturing jobs in central cities across America and the emergence of an unskilled labor force whose members qualify for only low-paying jobs in the service sector of the economy. In many inner-city neighborhoods, the unemployment rate for young black males is as high as 15 percent (that is, 15 percent of those seeking employment are without jobs); but, in addition, a substantial number of young black males are no longer looking for employment,[11] bringing the effective unemployed rate to over 60 percent in some areas (Jargowsky and Bane 1990, Kasarda 1992, Wilson 1996).[12]

Outmigration of middle-income blacks. The declining employment opportunities for unskilled blacks living in inner-city neighborhoods has been accompanied by another significant development: the migration of middle-income blacks from those neighborhoods to the suburbs. Between 1960 and 1980, the percentage of blacks living in suburban areas surrounding the nations largest cities nearly doubled (Hirsch 1993, Farley 1987). But as the more skilled, bet-

11. There are several reasons why a young man may not be seeking employment. He may have become demoralized after searching for a job and not finding one, or a criminal record may effectively prevent him from being hired. He may be physically disabled, mentally ill, or addicted to alcohol or drugs. He may be employed in the underground economy, for instance, selling drugs or driving a gypsy cab. Or he may never have learned the importance of work or the work habits necessary to keep a job.

12. Ironically, affirmative action has done little to remedy this situation; in fact, it may have exacerbated the problem (Wilson 1987, Nathan 1987). It is true that affirmative action has helped skilled black workers obtain good jobs and promotions with greater ease and speed than would otherwise have been possible. But these workers are part of the upper tier of the urban labor force, and they are being hired or promoted into professional positions. (As we shall see shortly, they are also leaving the inner city for the suburbs.) On the other hand, affirmative action has done nothing to *create* new or better paying jobs for unskilled workers, and these jobs—where they exist—are seldom covered by affirmative action guidelines. Since affirmative action has traditionally been viewed as *the* means for righting past injustices, it diverts attention from the special employment needs of unskilled blacks. Thus, affirmative action helped those upwardly mobile African Americans who arguably would have gotten ahead even without it; but affirmative action has done little to help unskilled blacks who were in greatest need of help (Wilson 1987).

ter educated, and more affluent blacks have moved out of the inner city, they have left behind an increasingly concentrated black underclass that has no means of escape (Gramlich and Laren 1991, Jargowsky 1991, both cited in Mincy 1994).

Unfortunately, as poverty becomes increasingly concentrated, behaviors and attitudes that would have been seen as aberrant in economically mixed areas have become socially accepted and much more likely to be adopted (Wilson 1987). Just as important, the social support systems that had been available in economically mixed areas have weakened as inner-city residents increasingly have their own concerns to worry about. Finally, the sense of community that had so much characterized black inner-city neighborhoods and that was largely promoted by those most able to reach out to others has become undermined as these individuals moved away. They left behind a group of people whose main concern was survival rather than neighborliness.[13] All of these factors combine to exacerbate the effects of concentrated poverty and the entrenchment of underclass enclaves in inner cities.[14] These effects are strikingly apparent. Poor youths living in impoverished neighborhoods are more likely to drop out of school and/or get pregnant than poor youths living in nonpoverty neighborhoods (e.g., Crane 1991; Hogan et al. 1985; Corcoran et al. 1987, cited in Ellwood 1994). Other, even more troubling behaviors have also become part and parcel of life in underclass neighborhoods. These include drug use and drug dealing, violence, and welfare dependence. We will turn to these behaviors shortly, but first we must come to closure on a definition of what it means to be part of the underclass.

Definitions of the Underclass

Although concern about the underclass is at the heart of much of the current discussion about the future of cities, there is no single agreed-upon definition of what "underclass" means or of what those of the underclass do that prompts them to be labeled as such. Paul Peterson (1991, 3) discussed the origins and

13. During the Civil Rights era, "making it" meant rising to the top of the community, and as individuals progressed, so did the community. However, since the integration movement, "making it" has meant escaping from one's community (McGary 1992). As middle- and upper-class blacks moved from the inner city, they became less interested in self-help within the ghetto community and more interested in self-help within their professions in the larger society. In addition, they began to see the future more in terms of class instead of race (Thomas 1991).

14. Farley (1991) offers an alternative explanation for the growth of ghetto neighborhoods: the growth of poverty among blacks between 1970 and the mid 1980s. For example, poverty among blacks in Chicago increased from 24 percent to 36 percent, and in Cleveland, the rate increased from 25 percent to 40 percent. If the residential segregation of social classes remains about the same and the poverty rate increases, racially concentrated poverty must necessarily increase.

meanings of the term *underclass*[15] and why it invokes so much passion among those on both sides of the political spectrum.

> The term is powerful because it calls attention to the conjunction between the characters of individuals and the impersonal forces of the larger social and political order. "Class" is the least interesting half of the word. Although it implies a relationship between one social group and another, the terms of that relationship are left undefined until combined with the familiar word "under." This transformation of a preposition into an adjective has none of the sturdiness of "working," the banality of "middle," or the remoteness of "upper." Instead, "under" suggests the lowly, passive, and submissive, yet at the same time the disreputable, dangerous, disruptive, dark, evil, and even hellish. And apart from these personal attributes, it suggests subjection, subordination, and deprivation.

Apart from its emotional content, the definition of underclass has important implications for how big a problem it presents for cities. Definitions of the underclass range from inclusive to exclusive. At the inclusive end, some define the underclass as those living in poverty,[16] those living in high-poverty areas, or low-income people living in high-poverty areas (Littman 1991). At a somewhat less-inclusive level, Van Haitsma (1989) defines the underclass as those persons who are weakly connected to the formal labor force. At the other extreme are definitions based predominantly on behavioral or motivational considerations. For example, Ricketts and Sawhill (1988) define the underclass as able-bodied individuals whose behavior departs from mainstream norms such as attending school, delaying parenting until adulthood, working at a regular job, and obeying the law. And Murray (1990) views the underclass as a subset of the poor who chronically live off mainstream society (through welfare or crime) without participating in it. They take jobs only sporadically (if at all), do not share responsibility for the social or physical upkeep of the neighborhoods they live in, shirk the responsibilities of fatherhood and are indifferent (or incompetent) mothers.

Which definition we choose has important implications for the way we estimate the size of the underclass population living in the United States. If we consider those people living below the poverty level, the underclass population in the United States is very large—nearly 37 million. The number is also

15. Although the term *underclass* is relatively new, dating back only to the early 1960s (Myrdal 1963; see Ricketts 1992), its use recalls a number of equivalent notions from the past: the redundant population, the lumpenproletariat, and the social residuum, all defined in terms of a basic immorality manifest in sexual abandon, criminality, vagrancy, the abhorrence of labor, and an inclination to dependency. Even Marx, who saw poverty as an inevitable product of capitalism, identified a depraved and decadent "social scum" (Morris 1994).

16. Although that is the criterion we used in the first edition of this book, we now view it as too inclusive.

large if we consider those people who reside in low-income neighborhoods; using this criterion, the underclass consists of over 41 million people (Littman 1991). A more restrictive estimate, based on persons in families with persistently low incomes and headed by a person with limited education who worked less than three-quarters of the year, puts the underclass population at 8.1 million people (Reischauer 1987, cited in Mincy 1994). A definition that considers only *poor* people living in poverty areas puts the underclass population at between 1.6 million (Bane and Jargowsky 1988, cited in Mincy 1994) and 11.6 million (Littman 1991), depending on how strictly a poverty area is defined.[17] A still more restrictive definition, which considers all poor residents of neighborhoods with high levels of female-headed households, high school dropouts, welfare dependency, and men not regularly in the labor force puts the underclass population at 1.1 million (Ricketts and Sawhill 1988).

For our purposes, we will consider the underclass to consist of poor people who live in high poverty neighborhoods (sometimes referred to as ghetto neighborhoods).[18] Many of these people exhibit the characteristics included in other definitions (e.g., welfare dependence). But even if poor people living in ghetto neighborhoods do not themselves exhibit underclass attitudes and behaviors, they cannot help but be affected by their neighbors.

Race and Class

Earlier in this chapter, we noted that poverty and race overlap considerably, so it should not be surprising to find that class and race do as well. Not only do blacks and Hispanics tend to be economically impoverished, but they also tend to be least able to escape from the inner-city neighborhoods where crime, drug use, violence, and other underclass behaviors are rampant. In fact, the infrequency with which we find whites living in ghetto neighborhoods makes it tempting to conclude that there may be something about race beyond mere racism in the larger society that leads to the concentration of poor blacks and Hispanics in these areas. But this view can be dismissed based on data from recent studies of blacks and whites living in inner-city ghettos.

17. Poverty areas are almost always defined by census tracts. While almost nobody believes that a census tract is a neighborhood in any meaningful sense of the word, poverty rates for census tracts are determined every ten years and the results are easily accessible to researchers. Some studies (e.g., Littman 1991) consider a census tract in which at least 20 percent of the residents are living below the poverty level to be a poverty area; others (e.g., Bane and Jargowsky 1988) set the criterion at 40 percent.

18. Gans (1990, 1995) argues that the term *underclass* has been so hopelessly muddled that it should be dropped; given the plethora of definitions that have been advanced, it is easy to understand his conclusion. As an alternative, Wilson (1991) advocates use of the term *ghetto poor* and calls for a more concentrated focus on theoretical issues and less fixation on labels (see Morris 1994). We will continue to use the term *underclass*, and we will use the terms *underclass neighborhood* and *ghetto neighborhood* interchangeably.

One of the most important of these is an ethnographic analysis of Clarendon Heights, a public housing development located in an inner city (MacLeod 1987). But unlike most other urban public housing developments, approximately 65 percent of Clarendon Heights' residents are white, 25 percent are black, and 10 percent are other minorities. And like the racial distribution itself, the behaviors of blacks and whites living in Clarendon Heights defy racial stereotypes. The Hallway Hangers were a loosely organized gang of white boys who derived their name from their proclivity to "hang out" in the dark hallways of Clarendon Heights. While hanging in the halls, these boys regularly drank alcohol in large quantities and used drugs; most had dropped out of school, and several had spent time in jail. All were regularly involved in fights; in fact, status within the gang was determined largely by fighting ability. And all of the Hallway Hangers had a dim view of their future and were despondent about their prospects for social mobility. In contrast, the Brothers were a loosely affiliated gang of blacks who largely accommodated themselves to accepted standards of behavior. The Brothers attended high school on a regular basis. None of them smoked cigarettes, drank regularly, or used drugs. None had been arrested. And for the most part, they found it expedient to walk away from a street fight before it exploded into violence.

This study (and others)[19] suggest that race, per se, cannot account for underclass behaviors. The Hallway Hangers and the Brothers came from similar backgrounds and lived in similar circumstances; yet, one group adhered to social norms of behavior, while the other deviated from those norms. In this case, it was the white boys who deviated; in other cases, it may be blacks who do. But in most cases, when widescale social deviance occurs, those involved live in the midst of concentrated poverty; and this concentration of poverty is a far more consistent explanatory factor than is race. Just as important, a considerable majority of blacks in the inner city look upon those engaging in underclass behaviors with as much disfavor as suburban middle class whites do (Devine and Wright 1993).

Underclass Behaviors and Their Impact on City Life

Violence. Physical violence is a concern for people living in ghetto neighborhoods, with black males at highest risk. Nationally, one in every twenty-seven black males can expect to be murdered (Prothrow-Stith 1991). Within the nation's large cities, this figure may increase to one in twelve; and within some ghetto neighborhoods, it may increase to as high as one in

---

19. A study of two ghetto neighborhoods in Columbus, Ohio (Alex-Assensoh 1995) yields similar conclusions. One of these neighborhoods is predominantly white, the other predominantly black. Yet, behaviors among the residents of these two neighborhoods are strikingly similar.

nine.[20] In some public housing developments, virtually all children have had a first-hand encounter with a shooting by the age of five (Novello 1991), and in an inner-city Baltimore neighborhood, 24 percent of teens had witnessed a murder (Zinsmeister 1990). In some Chicago schools, 33 percent of all students report that they have carried a weapon, and in Baltimore, half of all high school males report having carried a gun to school (Holinger et al. 1994). Between 1980 and 1988, violent crime in Washington, D.C., ghetto neighborhoods increased at a rate that was almost five times higher than in other neighborhoods (Peterson and Harrell 1992).

The impact of inner-city violence on those living in its midst can be devastating (see Kotlowitz, 1991, and Canada, 1995, for particularly poignant discussions). Alex Kotlowitz chronicled the lives of members of the Rivers family, who lived in Chicago's Henry Horner Homes, a public housing development on the city's West Side.

> During the summer of 1987, when drugs and the accompanying violence swept through the neighborhood, [LaJoe Rivers] lived in daily fear that something might happen to her young ones. Though she would never say as much, she worried that they might not make it to their eighteenth birthday. Too many hadn't. Already that year, fifty-seven children had been killed in the city. Five had died in the Horner area, including two, aged eight and six, who died from smoke inhalation when firefighters had to climb the fourteen stories to their apartment. Both of the building's elevators were broken. Lafeyette and Pharoah [her sons, aged twelve and nine] knew of more funerals than weddings. So that summer, LaJoe wanted to prepare for the worst. She started paying $80 a month for burial insurance for Lafeyette and Pharoah and the four-year-old triplets. (P. 17)

While one type of inner city violence is random (as when two youths get into a fight and one has a gun), another is organized. This organized violence, perpetuated by street gangs, tends to be much more insidious and deadly. Anyone who reads the newspaper regularly, and particularly those who have watched the movie *Boyz 'n the Hood*, know about the Bloods and the Crips and how they have devastated neighborhoods in south central Los Angeles; but gangs are active in Chicago, St. Louis, Seattle, and most other large cities as well. During the 1970s, gang warfare was the leading cause of death for Chicano adolescents (Moore 1993), and since 1980 an average of sixty-five gang-related homicides were recorded by the Chicago Police Department each year (Hutchison and Kyle 1993).[21] Most

20. These estimates are based on extrapolations from homicide rates for black males reported in five cities (and within high-risk neighborhoods in those cities) by Rose and McClain (1990).

21. Actual violence is only one manifestation of gang activity; fear of violence is just as important. For example, 24 percent of the school dropouts in Chicago cited gang pressure and intimidation and gang violence as the primary reasons they dropped out (Hutchison and Kyle 1993).

gangs have a number of neighborhood "sets" in each large city; for example, by the early 1990s there were thirty-eight known Blood sets and fifty-seven Crip sets operating in Los Angeles (Bing 1991). Each set wanted to match or outdo other sets in standing up for the gang name. For many sets, this meant increasing the rate and intensity of violence, for example, with violence directed at bystanders during drive-by shootings in rival gang neighborhoods. After decades of escalation, lethal intergang violence in East Los Angeles began to decline in the 1980s—perhaps because gangs whose members are regularly killed have trouble recruiting new members, even among the most ambitiously rowdy youngsters (Moore 1993).

Drugs. Drugs are another concern of those living in ghetto neighborhoods; drug-related arrest rates in these neighborhoods are literally soaring. During the 1980s, drug-related arrests in Washington, D.C., ghetto neighborhoods increased at a rate six times faster than in the rest of the city, and in Cleveland's ghetto neighborhoods, the arrest rate increased twenty-two times faster than in other neighborhoods (Wiener and Mincy 1991, cited in Peterson and Harrel 1992). Although differential police enforcement policies, especially toward drug use, may explain part of these differences in the neighborhood arrest rates, there seems little doubt that drug use and drug-related crimes in most cities have grown at a faster rate in ghetto areas than in other areas (Peterson and Harrel 1992).

Drug dealers have become an increasingly prominent part of life in ghetto neighborhoods. Fagan (1992) found that nearly ten percent of male youths in three cities he studied had sold drugs in the previous year; among gang members, the rate was 25 percent. Case and Katz (1990, cited in Fagan 1992) found that 12 percent of the African-American males in Boston sold drugs during the previous year; the rate for white youths was 18 percent. Reuter and his associates (1990) estimated that in Washington, D.C., one in six African-American males between the ages of eighteen and twenty was arrested for dealing drugs; actual rates for dealing drugs were probably far greater.

Part of the reason for increasing drug use among the underclass is a general change in the availability of different types of drugs. In the 1950s and the 1960s, cocaine was known as an expensive upper-class drug, one used by avant-garde artists, poets, writers, and musicians, and by members of the medical profession. Around 1982, however, cocaine users began smoking freebase, cocaine with the hydrochloride removed to form a rock-like substance. More important, around this time crack cocaine began to dominate the illicit drug markets in most inner-city neighborhoods.[22] This occurred primarily because

---

22. Cocaine is converted to freebase or crack by boiling it in water ("cooking"). This produces a residue that, when cooled in cold water, forms an irregular hard mass. Pieces of this mass are chipped off to form "rocks," which can be packaged and sold in

coca leaf production in Latin American countries increased dramatically beginning in 1980, allowing both greater purity of the imported cocaine at a substantially lower price. Between 1979 and 1989, cocaine shipments smuggled into the United States increased from 50 tons a year to 200 tons a year (Williams 1992). An explosion of crack use began in 1984–85. What makes the crack epidemic so destructive for ghetto neighborhoods is crack's addictiveness. Crack addicts will go to almost any length to satisfy their craving (e.g., Vanderstaay 1992), with theft and prostitution the most common means for supporting a crack habit. In fact, crack has indirectly led to an increase in homelessness as parents are forced to put their teenage children out of the house for stealing and selling family possessions to buy the drug. Women are a prominent minority in the crack-using population, and they face a substantial risk of bearing crack babies; crack is also a factor in many child neglect cases (Inciardi et al. 1993).

Sexuality, pregnancy, and parenting. The statistics on sexual behavior and pregnancy among inner-city adolescents paint an alarming picture. Nationally, adolescents (particularly blacks) are becoming sexually active at an early age (Hofferth and Hayes 1987). However, poverty is an important predictor of early onset of sexual activity (Randolph and Gesche 1986); sexual activity is highest among adolescents (particularly blacks) living in ghetto neighborhoods. Zabin and her associates (1986) reported that by ninth grade, 92 percent of the boys and 54 percent of the girls in an inner-city Baltimore school were sexually active.

These high levels of sexual activity are alarming; but when combined with low rates of contraception, particularly among younger adolescents (Zelnik and Shah 1983), they produce an epidemic of early pregnancies. Among all girls who turned fourteen in 1990, 40 percent could expect to become pregnant during their teenage years (Winett et al. 1989). Among blacks living in inner cities, the trend is even more pronounced, with approximately 15 percent of these girls becoming pregnant *each year* (Kirby et al. 1991); as a result, 62 percent of African-American children are born to unmarried mothers (Jencks 1991), up from 23 percent in 1960.[23]

---

small quantities for as little as a couple of dollars. Crack differs from freebase in that it is mixed with other, cheaper chemicals (e.g., baking soda, lidocaine) as it is cooked, reducing the price even further. This allowed drug dealers to attract an inner-city clientele with very little income, although the price of maintaining a crack habit can become very expensive (Williams 1992).

23. The large number of female-headed low-income households, particularly among African Americans, may reflect a deficit in what Wilson (1987) called "the marriageable pool" of African-American men. For whatever reasons—and there are a number, including higher mortality rates and a high likelihood of incarceration for criminal activity—the number of African-American men of marriageable age (particularly those living

Indeed, marriage has largely disappeared as a meaningful option among poor blacks—a fact that Wilson (1987) cites for the growth of the underclass in recent years. Relationships within marriage are not important or reliable bases for family life and childbearing, and inner-city blacks are often suspicious of the intentions of the opposite sex (Massey and Denton 1993). As a result, childbearing for inner-city blacks has become increasingly disconnected from marriage. For girls, it signals a rite of passage to adulthood and validates their worth and standing among peers. In the absence of conventional avenues of work and family, young black men and women have increasingly turned for gratification to sex, the one commodity that reliably lies within their reach (Anderson 1990). Even when marriage does occur, divorce rates tend to be higher among those living in poverty (which is itself an important source of marital strain). Taken together, these factors result in high levels of female-headed households among the underclass. This potentially leads to a perpetuation of the underclass, with children raised in single-parent families more likely to engage in risk behaviors (e.g., dropping out of school, using drugs, becoming sexually active at an early age) and to live in poverty as adults than are children raised in two-parent families (see Kelso 1994 for a review).[24]

Welfare dependency. Given the political debate that has surrounded welfare reform during the mid 1990s, there is perhaps no other underclass behavior that is as emotionally charged as welfare dependency. At the heart of the debate are two important questions: (1) How many welfare recipients have passed the point of using welfare to get back on their feet and have become dependent on it? and (2) Does welfare, by its very nature, make people dependent on it? Each of these questions has generated substantial literature (although it is not our intention to suggest a definitive answer to them, it will be useful to summarize this literature).

The first question involves the meaning and extent of welfare dependency. By most accounts, someone who receives welfare for less than a year is not welfare dependent; just as certainly, however, someone who has been on welfare for more than ten years is dependent on welfare. The exact point where welfare ceases to be a safety net and becomes a way of life is difficult

---

in poverty) is far smaller than the number of low-income women at that age. For example, for every one hundred African-American women between the ages of eighteen and twenty-four living in poverty, there are only fifty-six African-American men; for every one hundred African-American women between the ages of twenty-five and thirty-four, the number of men decreases to forty-one (see table 15.1).

24. Some (e.g., Bane 1886) argue that these findings do not necessarily reflect the difficulties of raising children in single-parent households per se; rather, single-parent households are more prone to poverty, and the results may reflect the influence of poverty rather than single parenting. Thus, these findings should be interpreted cautiously.

to ascertain. Accordingly, it is difficult to assert how large a problem welfare dependency really is and whether it is growing over time.[25]

The second question asks whether welfare, by its very nature, makes people dependent on it. Several critics, epitomized by Charles Murray (1984), argue that the growth of the welfare state is the primary reason for the breakup of underclass families. When men receive minimal earnings, the lure of welfare benefits may encourage women to establish their own households; thus, welfare provides the opportunity for women to divorce their husbands. Murray supports this argument by showing that increases in family dissolution since the early 1970s parallel increases in welfare during that same period. However, further analyses (e.g., Wilson 1987) cast doubt on this conclusion.

An equally important aspect of this question is whether welfare keeps people out of the labor force. While it is certainly true that many welfare recipients are better off economically than they would be if they earned minimum wage,[26] there is less evidence of and agreement about whether welfare erodes their work ethic. On the one hand, Mead (1986) argues that "work is normative for the poor, but it is not something that they feel they must do, whatever the personal cost. . . . The work ethic for the disadvantaged appears to represent a morality of aspiration but not of duty." In contrast, however, Goodwin (1983) reports data showing that "acceptance or rejection of the

---

25. Even if a good measure of welfare dependence could be agreed upon (e.g., two years of continuous welfare receipt, ten years of continuous welfare receipt), different means of calculating rates of welfare receipt muddy the waters even further. For instance, Ellwood and Bane (1994) show that each of the following, seemingly contradictory statistics about welfare is true:

- Roughly 35 percent of all current recipients have been on welfare for two years (twenty-four consecutive months) or less; only about 20 percent have been on for ten years or more.
- Half of all spells of welfare last less than two years; only 14 percent last ten years or more.
- Less than 15 percent of all current recipients will be on welfare for two years or less; approximately 48 percent will be on welfare in ten or more years.

The reason that all three statements are true is too complicated to discuss here. However, suffice it to say that different people could use the same data to support very different conclusions about welfare dependency and to argue for different kinds of policies to address it.

26. Ellwood (1994) demonstrates the disincentive for work that faces a single female parent with two children living in Pennsylvania in 1991. If she did not work at all, her disposable income was $7,278 per year, with full Medicaid benefits. If she worked full time at minimum wage ($4.25 per hour), her disposable income was $8,047, again with full Medicaid coverage. If she worked full time earning $5.00 per hour, her disposable income would increase to $9,399, but she would lose her Medicaid benefits. Even if her salary increased to $7.00 per hour, her annual disposable income would only increase to $11,647, again with no Medicaid coverage. Ellwood concluded, "The nature of our welfare system is such that unless a single mother can find a full-time job that pays at least $5 or $6 or $7 an hour with full benefits, along with very inexpensive day care, she will be better off on welfare" (p. 148).

idea of welfare or work has no effect on the achievement of economic independence by welfare recipients judged able to work. There is virtually no evidence that welfare dependency is caused by preference for welfare."

Whether a family can actually survive on welfare benefits or on a minimum-wage job, let alone attain a meaningful quality of life, further clouds the issue. Most observers say no. Jencks and Edin (1990) reported that most welfare recipients supplemented their incomes, on average doubling them, through a combination of illegitimate income and legitimate earnings they did not report.[27] Other studies found that when high-paying employment is unavailable, young men "hustle" (e.g., Williams and Kornblum 1985, Fagan 1992, Mincy 1994): working "off the books" for an otherwise legal firm; selling books, jewelry, and other items on the street; or being involved in petty crime and drug selling. Participation in the underground economy may require no less work than holding down a legitimate job and often requires longer hours and hard work. If so, it calls into question the argument that low-income wage earners and welfare recipients lack a work ethic.

Even so, there is no denying the lure that street life holds for many people, and this life is made possible through a welfare system that does not require its recipients to work. Paul Peterson (1991, 12) describes the street culture of the underclass:

> Street life in the ghetto is exhilarating—at least in the short term. In a world where jobs are dull, arduous, or difficult to obtain and hold, it is more fun to hang out, make love, listen to and tell exaggerated stories of love and danger, plan parties and escapades, and exhibit one's latest purchases or conquests. Gangs provide young people thrills, protection, mutual support, friendship, prestige, and enough income to allow them to buy fashionable clothes, alcohol, and drugs. When men cannot earn enough to support their families, they avoid enduring relationships with female companions. Women respond by becoming self-reliant, domineering, and mutually supportive. But without an adult male figure in the household, they are unable to protect their children from the alluring street life that promises short-term excitement, if not much hope for a prosperous future. . . . [For blacks, personal disappointments and affronts can be seen] as the product of broad social forces—class dominance, racial prejudice and discrimination, cultural exclusiveness—over which they, as individuals, had little control; it was hopeless to fight the system; instead, one might as well rip off and enjoy as big a piece as one could.

27. Lein (1991, quoted in Bane 1994) reports considerable use of food pantries and soup kitchens among welfare recipients in the southwest United States; but these resources create an ethical dilemma for welfare recipients who use them, forcing them to lie about whether they received food stamps in order to be served. Lein (also see Bane 1994) argues that the system has lost moral legitimacy, forcing recipients to violate program rules in order to achieve the higher moral goal of feeding their families.

The situation easily becomes a self-fulfilling prophesy (cf. Ogbu 1988), with those more vested in the street life least able to willingly leave welfare for work.

Underclass Populations

As a way of further fleshing out the meanings that attach to the term *under-class*, we will consider in depth two underclass populations: the homeless and those living in public housing. Homeless people are part of the under-class by virtue of their weak attachment to social institutions—including work, family, and housing. People living in public housing are part of the underclass by virtue of the lack of individual resources and particularly their residence in neighborhoods where the poverty level reaches nearly 100 percent. Although the characteristics and circumstances of these two populations are described here, discussion of possible solutions to the prob-lems associated with homelessness and public housing will wait until chap-ter 17.

The Homeless

Former New York Governor Mario Cuomo, reporting for the 1983 Governors' Conference, described any attempt to enumerate the homeless as "counting the uncountable" (quoted in Rossi 1989, 47). The truth in this statement has been supported by numerous attempts to estimate the size of the homeless population. The late Mitch Snyder, a homeless advocate and founder of the CCNV shelter in Washington, D.C., placed the figure at a million in the late 1970s. However, he derived this estimate in a rather unscientific manner: "We got on the phone, we made a lot of calls, we talked to a lot of people" (interview with Ted Koppel, quoted in Jencks 1994, 2). Snyder went on to say that this estimate "has no meaning, no value." But it has considerable political value, and based on this estimate homelessness found its way onto the public agenda. Perhaps as a way of ensuring that it remained there, subsequent estimates by homeless advocates were even higher, reaching between 2 million and 3 million (Hombs and Snyder 1982). The Reagan administration, embarrassed by the magnitude of these estimates, asked the Department of Housing and Urban Development (HUD) to derive its own estimates. The HUD study (also based on a flawed methodology) concluded that there were only 250,000 to 350,000 homeless people in the United States (U.S. Department of Housing and Urban Development 1984).

Since then, some of the rhetoric has died down, and most current estimates of homelessness (see Burt 1992 for a review) hover between 500,000 and 750,000 on any given night.

Definitions of homelessness. Definitions of homelessness vary, and the magnitude of the problem depends on whether a broad or a narrow definition is adopted. Rossi (1989, 10–11) suggests the difficulty of reaching consensus on a definition:

> Homelessness, at its core, means not having customary and regular access to a conventional dwelling; it mainly applies to those who do not rent or own a residence. . . . The ambiguities of homelessness center on two critical components of the definition given above: What is a "conventional dwelling"? And what is "customary and regular access"? Conventional dwellings surely include apartments, houses, and mobile homes in a mobile home park, but does the concept include hotel rooms . . . , rented rooms in private dwellings, beds in dormitory-like accommodations, cars, trucks, vans, tents, or shacks made of scrap materials? Similarly, those who own or rent their own homes surely have "customary and regular access," as do current members of a household in which someone owns or rents a home. But what about someone who has been given temporary permission to share a conventional dwelling? What period constitutes "temporary"?

Virtually all studies of homelessness include people staying on the streets, in parks, in abandoned buildings, and in shelters; however, most exclude people staying doubled up with family or friends, in rooming houses, or in hotels (see Rossi, 1989, and Burt, 1992, for further discussions of definitional and methodological issues). These exclusions (particularly people living doubled up with family and friends) are based primarily on the difficulty of actually counting these individuals rather than on a philosophical or moral judgment that they are not homeless.

Beyond definitional problems, the causes and consequences of homelessness are not easily assessed. Contrary to what might be imagined, homeless people experience considerable transience in their living arrangements over the course of a year. One study of homelessness (Bolland and McCallum 1995a) showed that among males who spent the previous night sleeping on the street, 46 percent spent at least some time living with their family since becoming homeless; 57 percent stayed with friends; 63 percent stayed in motels; 88 percent stayed in missions or shelters; and 52 percent spent some time in jail. Thus, the overwhelming majority move onto and off of the streets, stopping in a shelter here or a motel there, spending the odd night (or week) with family or friends, perhaps even getting their own place for a while, and maybe doing some time in jail along the way. A person who sleeps on the streets today will probably not be there next week but may resurface next month. Thus, the number of people who are homeless on any given night is a far cry from the number who may be homeless over the course of a year or at some point during their lifetime.[28]

Characteristics of the homeless. Not all homeless people arrive at homelessness via the same path. Many women and their children have become homeless because of domestic violence; for most of them, time in a domestic violence shelter coupled with counseling and vocational training will allow them to move into a new home. Some people become homeless when they lose their jobs; but these casualties of economic displacement usually get back on their feet in short order with the help of shelters, vocational counseling, and sometimes vocational training.[29] A third group of people become homeless due to mental illness, substance abuse, adjustment problems, or lack of coping skills; these tend to be overwhelmingly men, and their homelessness is likely to last a considerable length of time. Just as we do not know how many people are homeless on any given night, we also do not know what percentage of the homeless population arrived at their homeless state due to domestic violence, economic displacement, or other causes. Most likely, however, the vast majority of homeless people are homeless for a short time before recovering. But even though they may be a small minority of the overall homeless population in the United States, the chronic homeless are those we typically think of when we consider homelessness, and they have come to personify the underclass and dominate the policy debate.

A study of homeless people in Mobile, Alabama, sheds some light on the characteristics of chronically homeless people (Bolland and McCallum 1995a). The typical chronically homeless person in Mobile is a male in his late thirties (see table 15.4) and African American. [30] Contrary to popular percep-

---

28. Based on a random sample of the U.S. adult population, Link et al. (1995) estimate that 7.4 percent of adults have been literally homeless at some point during their lives and that 3.1 percent had been homeless during the previous five years; these figures rise to 14 percent and 4.6 percent, respectively, if those who lived doubled up with someone else are counted. This produces estimates that 13.5 million adult residents of the United States have been homeless at some point during their lives, 5.7 million of them during the past five years.

29. A commonly held myth is that most Americans are only two paychecks away from homelessness. This is a reflection of the size of most people's bank accounts, however, rather than of their ability to find alternative employment were they to lose their job. To be sure, if an economic collapse of the magnitude of the Great Depression were to hit, and alternative jobs were simply not available, many people would find it difficult to maintain their traditional housing; however, as was demonstrated during the Great Depression, a substantial bank account was no gurarantee of economic survival. The very skills that allow people to find and keep jobs in the first place allow them to find new jobs as well.

30. Only a decade ago, the typical chronically homeless man was white. This change may reflect the growing poverty within the black inner-city underclass during the 1980s and the 1990s. This no doubt has made it much more difficult for families to provide homes for otherwise homeless relatives. But even more important, the growing use of crack cocaine among the impoverished inner-city underclass (which is predominantly black) may presage homelessness (e.g., Jencks 1994).

Table 15.4 Characteristics of Chronically Homeless Men Living in Mobile, Alabama[a]

Background and Demographics	
Median age	38.0 years
Percent African American	54.9
Percent born in Mobile	37.8
Percent who had family or friends in Mobile before becoming homeless	10.7
Median length of residence in Mobile	10.0 years
Percent high school graduates	41.3
Percent currently married	16.0
Percent ever married	61.3
Percent with children	61.3
Mental Health and Substance Abuse	
Percent with symptoms of mental illness	30.0
Percent with symptoms of clinical depression	61.4
Percent who have tried to kill themselves	17.3
Percent who have abused alcohol or drugs at some time	86.7
Percent who currently abuse alcohol or drugs	69.3
Physical Health	
Percent who are hypertensive	18.9
Percent who are epileptic or diabetic, or who have tuberculosis	17.3
Percent who suffer from upper respiratory distress	48.0
Percent who suffer from gastrointestinal distress	20.0
Other	
Percent who have eaten food during the past year that had been thrown away	57.3
Percent who have been a victim of a crime during the past year	52.0
Percent who have been physically assaulted during the past year	29.3

SOURCE: Bolland and McCallum (1995a).

a. Statistics are based on a sample of 75 chronically homeless men interviewed in 1994.

tions that the homeless are geographically transient, the typical chronically homeless person in Mobile has roots in the city; nearly 40 percent were born there, and many others have some connection to the city. Even more revealing, the chronically homeless person has been a resident of the city for ten years (much of that time living in a housed situation), longer than many of its housed residents.

The politics of homelessness lead many city leaders to argue that the city will, of course, take care of its own residents but that it should not have to take care of homeless people who flock there from afar to take advantage of its climate or services (and thus infringe on its hospitality). The implication is that most of the homeless who hang out in a city are transients from somewhere else. But the reality is that most of the homeless people in any city were born there, grew up there, lived there before becoming homeless, or have friends or relatives there; in short, they *do* belong there.

Most homeless people are only loosely connected to the social institutions of American society, but this disconnectedness largely predates their homelessness. Most dropped out of school before graduating. But although they lack a formal education, they do not necessarily lack intelligence: They could not survive on the streets if they were not smart. The vast majority are unmarried, but while many are divorced or separated, a large percentage have never married. Over 60 percent of Mobile's chronically homeless men have children; among these, nearly half have little or no contact with their children. Most of the chronically homeless men have had at least one good-paying job at some point in their lives; in fact, their incomes from these jobs were comparable to what the typical male resident of Mobile earns. Many homeless people have gone through a succession of these jobs; in almost all cases, they lost these jobs before becoming homeless.

As is often common with this type of disaffiliation, homeless people tend to have high rates of mental illness, depression, and alcohol and drug dependence. While a case could be made that homelessness would exacerbate these conditions for almost anyone (and cause them in some), the more likely scenario is that they predate episodes of homelessness. National estimates hold that a third of homeless people are mentally ill; results from Mobile are comparable. More important, however, over 60 percent of the chronically homeless showed symptoms of clinical depression, and nearly one-fifth report that they have attempted to kill themselves at some point in their lives. Substance abuse is rampant: nearly all have abused drugs or alcohol at some point in their lives, and nearly 70 percent were doing so at the time of the study. Sizeable minorities of the chronically homeless population suffer from hypertension, epilepsy, diabetes, tuberculosis, upper respiratory distress, and gastrointestinal distress. Over half occasionally eat food that has been thrown away ("dumpster diving," in the vernacular of the homeless); and over half have been the victim of some type of crime during the past year, with nearly one-third having been physically assaulted.

Causes of homelessness. If this is the reality of chronic homelessness, what are its causes? Explanations can be divided into two groups: macro explanations tied to societal trends and micro explanations tied to the circumstances of individual homeless people. At the macro level, four explanations have been advanced for the rise of homelessness during the 1970s and its continued growth into the 1990s: deinstitutionalization of the mentally ill, begun during the 1960s; postindustrial marginalization of the poor; dismantling the welfare state, particularly under the Reagan and Bush administrations; and destruction of low-cost housing during urban renewal. The deinstitutionalization explanation is perhaps the most popular, for it has a *prima facie* logic: As the patient census in state mental hospitals declined by over 400,000 people between 1955 and 1984, the number of mentally ill homeless people rose and may exceed 250,000 today. Yet, as obvious as this correlation may appear on its surface, it receives little empirical support. The National Institute for Mental

Health, in its 1990 report to Congress, concluded that deinstitutionalization played a relatively minor role in the growth of homelessness (Blau 1992). The numbers just do not add up. Whereas most of the deinstitutionalization occurred by 1975, the rapid growth of homelessness did not occur until a decade later, and it included mostly younger people who had never been in a mental hospital.[31]

The postindustrial marginalization explanation is more valid: As the number of good-paying jobs requiring unskilled labor decreases, more and more unskilled and undereducated people will find it hard to make ends meet. Most low-income people obviously survive in housed situations, but even for them, any financial crisis (a medical emergency, a car that breaks down) may make them unable to pay the rent and push them over the edge into temporary homelessness. For example, Link and his colleagues (1995) report that the lifetime prevalence of homelessness for people who did not graduate from high school (and who presumably have few technical job skills) is 16.2 percent, compared to 5.9 percent for high school graduates. Although this explanation accounts for the increase in overall homelessness, it does not account for the growth in rates of chronic homelessness.

The third explanation, centered around the contraction of the welfare state, is also partially valid; but it, too, leaves more unexplained than explained. During the Reagan presidency, eligibility standards for Aid to Families with Dependent Children (AFDC) were tightened, and the federal AFDC caseload declined by 442,000 people. At the same time, 491,000 people were removed from SSDI and 1 million low-income people were eliminated from the Food Stamp Program (Blau 1992). These cutbacks, coupled with declining wages for unskilled workers, would seem to place a substantial segment of the population at risk of becoming homeless, and it corresponded to the substantial increase in the homeless population during the 1980s. Yet, once again, temporal correspondence does not necessarily equate with causation. Most of these cuts affected women and children rather than men. And while some argue that women and children are the fastest growing segment of the homeless population, they account for only 17 percent (Jencks 1994) to 27 percent (Burt 1992) of the total homeless population.[32] Thus, even if changes in welfare policy affected each homeless woman and child, the overall impact would be modest. Other societal changes are arguably more important determinants of the growth of homelessness among women and children.

Perhaps chief among these is the growing awareness of domestic violence in the United States and the proliferation of shelters to house vic-

31. Only 16 percent of Mobile's chronically homeless men have ever been institutionalized for an emotional or mental problem.
32. This does not include people who are living doubled up; the preponderance of these are women and children.

tims of domestic violence (e.g., Loseke 1992). Evidence from the Mobile study suggests that approximately 40 percent of homeless women and children have become homeless due to domestic violence, further negating the conclusion that contractions in the welfare state caused the increase in homelessness.

The fourth explanation for the rise of homelessness centers around the loss of low-income housing. Historically, low- and middle-income city residents lived in downtown areas, staying in lodging houses (furnished in a spartan manner and rented by the day or the week) or rooming houses (furnished in a more homey manner and rented by the week or month). During the early years of the century, Chicago alone had over two hundred lodging houses (accommodating between 40,000 and 60,000 men *each night*) and 2,400 rooming houses. All of these provided guests with considerable independence to come and go as they pleased.[33] By 1960, an expanding post–World War II economy had dramatically reduced the demand for single room occupancy (SRO) housing. Chicago's Skid Row had a total of 9,011 single-room units; by 1970, this number declined to 4,037, and in 1980 it had further declined to 2,064 (Hoch and Slayton 1989). But this decline between 1960 and 1980 was much less a response to a changing economy than to shifting demands placed on Skid Row property. In some cities, such as San Francisco, owners of SRO hotels began to convert their property to offices, apartments, condominiums, and tourist hotels. Between 1970 and 1978, Portland, Oregon, lost 2,400 downtown housing units; downtown Denver lost twenty-eight of its forty-five inexpensive hotels, and San Francisco lost 6,085 units (Groth 1994; Ford 1994). Across the United States, various urban investment-disinvestment processes resulted in an average loss of 125,000 low-rent housing units each year between 1970 and 1980. Approximately half of the 2 million SRO units in existence in 1970 were razed, abandoned, or gentrified. Another million low-rent units were lost between 1980 and 1988 (Feagin and Parker 1990). Previous occupants of these rooms were left to fend for themselves, often on the streets; and many young people with low-paying jobs who might have stayed in SROs in times past joined the ranks of the homeless.

At the micro level, relatively little concrete information exists on causes of homelessness, due largely to the retrospective nature of most studies of homelessness. Bolland and McCallum (1995a, 88–89) speculate as follows:

33. For a wonderful depiction of life in New York's Bowery during this period, see Joseph Mitchell's book *McSorley's Wonderful Saloon* (reprinted with three other works as *Up in the Old Hotel* in 1992). In Mitchell's writings, SRO residents, panhandlers, and bums, some of whom were homeless all or most of the time, were viewed as eccentric rather than sinister and threatening. Perhaps it is a sign of the times that, as inner-city life has become more dangerous, those at the margins of society are viewed as taking on sinister qualities.

401

We believe that for many chronically homeless people, vulnerability to homelessness can be traced back to childhood experiences. Homeless people . . . in Mobile have an average of 4.84 brothers and sisters, indicating that they grew up in quite large families. Many indicated anecdotally that they grew up in poverty; and many also suggested that they were abused (physically, sexually, or psychologically) as children. Over 50 percent indicate that their childhood memories were either mixed or mostly unhappy. Thus, the situation in which many homeless people grew up was not one that led to their being nurtured; even a caring parent, raising a large family in the face of poverty, would not have had the time or the ability to provide a nurturing environment. Many of the homeless grew up in an era when they experienced pressure to experiment with drugs; and violence was beginning to become a fact of life for many at that time as well. Granted, many people grew up in environments that mirrored one or more aspects of this portrait, and they were able to avoid becoming homeless. It is just as true that some chronically homeless individuals had happy, safe, and nurturing childhoods. But we would argue that growing up in the presence of these factors increases a person's vulnerability to homelessness; and the fact that some people are able to overcome that vulnerability does not detract from its importance to others. . . . Many of the children who grew up in this type of environment never developed the personal resources to be able to cope with adversity. As a result, many ran away from home as they were growing up; and many dropped out of high school, not because they were not smart but because they were not able to handle the rules (and punishment for violating the rules). . . . Many went on to get good-paying jobs, despite their lack of education. . . . But those jobs did not last. Relationships often followed the same pattern as employment: so long as the relationship was happy, it lasted; but when fights occurred, it fell apart. For a large segment of the homeless population in Mobile . . . relationships never progressed far enough to result in marriage; and many others became homeless when a marriage fell apart.   [Many] of the literal homeless population in Mobile may be clinically depressed; and while much of that is situationally attributable to their homelessness, much of it may also have predated their homelessness and be tied to their lack of coping skills. Depression, coupled with lack of coping skills, may also be responsible for the relatively high rates of alcohol and drug abuse that predated their homelessness, or they may be exacerbated by substance abuse— or both. And finally, at some point these individuals lost the financial resources to pay the rent, and they ended up on the street.

Viewed from this perspective, chronic homelessness is not a simple problem.

Public Housing Residents

A second component of the underclass population consists of public housing residents, mainly by virtue of their individual poverty and their residence in the midst of concentrated poverty. HUD supports thirty-three hundred Public Housing Authorities in cities across the United States; they, in turn, provide subsidized housing for 10.5 million people. Most of these live in Section 8 or other forms of scattered-site housing; but 4.5 million live in public housing developments, known universally as "Projects." Overall, the vast majority of families living in public housing have incomes below the poverty line, with a 1995 median family income equal to $6,420.[34]

Popular conceptions of public housing: From good to bad to worse. Almost all public housing built during the 1950s and the early 1960s in large cities consisted of high-rise developments. The prevailing wisdom at the time held high-rise developments to be more economical to build than garden apartments—an assumption that later turned out to be wrong. In addition, proponents argued that public housing developments had to be large; otherwise they would be overwhelmed by the blight and disorder of their surrounding physical and social environment (Halpern 1995). This concern seems strange today, for in many cities large public housing developments have become the center of inner-city slums. But the early concept of public housing was to house the working poor; people with no jobs, people in ill health, single mothers and their children, and other dependent poor were ineligible for many early public housing programs. In this view, public housing would integrate insights and expertise from architects, urban planners, and sociologists to create healthy communities. But residence in these communities was intended to be temporary; small, spartan apartments served as a constant reminder that public housing was not intended as a long-term solution (Wright 1981).

In sharp contrast to this concept of housing for the working class, real estate interests wanted public housing to be used only for the poorest families. They were concerned about the effects of government competition within the private home-buyer and rental markets, and they used their considerable influence to steer public housing in this direction (Atlas and Dreier 1992). There was also considerable uneasiness within white working-class neighborhoods about where public housing developments would be located. These two factors led public housing developments in most cities to be sited in the heart of minority ghettos. Or if housing was constructed at the edge of these ghettos, it was bounded by a physical barrier such as a highway, railroad tracks,

---

34. While it is convenient to assume that all those in public housing live in poverty, this is not quite accurate: HUD's income eligibility guidelines fall above the poverty level. And while some people with moderate incomes do live in public housing, the figure is low; further, HUD mandates that rent be assessed at a rate of 30 percent of the resident's adjusted gross income. Thus, as income goes up, rent also goes up—sometimes exceeding what would be paid for comparable housing in the private sector. While such situations are unusual, they do sometimes occur.

or a river (Halpern 1995). Thus, what was originally intended as a reform in housing capable of improving the quality of life of both its own residents and those in surrounding neighborhoods quickly became a threat to the quality of life of its residents and those in surrounding neighborhoods. And the very size and density of the public housing population, originally seen as the only way to make the concept viable, became the biggest threat to the future of public housing.

The media portrayal of the projects emphasized the worst of public housing. For example, the 1972 decision of the St. Louis Housing Authority to demolish Pruitt-Igoe, a set of thirty-three eleven-story buildings containing twenty-seven hundred apartments that had in the space of twenty years become largely uninhabitable, was viewed as confirmation that public housing was a "failed experiment." Two years earlier, Lee Rainwater (1970) had documented some of the more troubling aspects of Pruitt-Igoe, including broken glass and trash on the grounds, dangerous elevators, rodents, people urinating in the hallways, children running wild, robbery, and assault. Even though Pruitt-Igoe commanded considerable public attention, the problems that hastened its demolition seem tame compared with what we have witnessed since then in other cities, most notably in Chicago.

- During the first two months in 1981, the Cabrini Green neighborhood in Chicago experienced eleven homicides and thirty-seven serious assaults, leading Mayor Jane Byrne to move in. Along with a contingent of police and bodyguards, she stayed for three weeks in a largely symbolic move to restore order.
- In 1994, after a truce between two rival gangs had broken down, the Chicago Police Department recorded more than three hundred shooting incidents in Robert Taylor Homes and Stateway Gardens in just four days; five people were wounded, and two were killed (*Newsweek*, April 18, 1994; *Time*, April 18, 1994).
- In a 1994 event that shocked the nation's conscience, five-year-old Eric Morse was lured to a vacant, fourteenth story apartment in Chicago's Ida B. Wells development and was dropped to his death from an open window by two older boys after he had refused to steal candy for them. (For a poignant investigation into this tragedy by two boys who grew up in the Ida B. Wells neighborhood, see Jones and Newman 1997.)

Perhaps the most graphic depiction of Chicago's public housing is provided by Alex Kotlowitz in his book *There Are No Children Here*. He chronicles the coming of age of two boys, Lafeyette and Pharoah Rivers, who lived in Henry Horner Homes, as well as the circumstances of their mother, LaJoe, their brothers and sisters, and their extended family. Kotlowitz (1991, 22) notes that, in general, Chicago's public housing developments were constructed on the cheap. There were no lobbies to speak of, only the open breezeways. There was no communication system from the breezeways to the tenants. During the city's harsh winters, elevator cables froze; in one year alone the housing authority in Chicago needed to make over fifteen hundred repairs. And that was in just one development. The trash chutes within each building were too narrow to handle the garbage of all its tenants. The boiler system continually broke down. There were insufficient overhead lighting installations and wall outlets in each unit. And the medicine cabinet in each apartment's bathroom was not only easily removed, but was connected to the medicine chest in the adjoining apartment. Over the years, residents had been robbed, assaulted, and even murdered by people crawling through their medicine cabinet. When a group of Soviet housing officials visited Henry Horner [Homes] in October of 1955, while it was still under construction, they were appalled that the walls in the apartments were of cinder block. Why not build plastered walls, they suggested. "We would be thrown off our jobs in Moscow if we left unfinished walls like this," I.K. Kozvilia, minister of city and urban construction in the Soviet Union, told local reporters.

Yet, during these early years, most people moved into public housing with great optimism. The apartments were theirs, something that had been built for them. And compared with the substandard housing they were used to, this was not bad at all; in fact, it almost seemed palatial. But by the 1970s, the Chicago Housing Authority had run out of money, and routine maintenance was often neglected.[35] The Rivers's apartment in Henry Horner Homes exemplifies the situation.

> The apartment itself defied cleanliness. In keeping with the developers' tight-fisted policies in building these high-rises, the Housing Authority continued its miserly regard for their upkeep. Maintenance was a bare minimum. The walls inside the home were . . . white cinder block. Along with the encrusted, brown linoleum-tiled floor, which was worn through in many places, and the exposed heating pipes, which snaked through the apartment, the home at night resembled a dark, dank cave. . . . The thirty-year-old kitchen cabinets, constructed of thin sheet metal, had rusted through. They were pock-marked with holes. LaJoe organized her dishes and cookware so as to avoid having them fall through these ragged openings. . . . The Housing Authority used to paint the apartments once every five years, but with the perennial shortage of money, in the 1970s it had

35. The problem of maintenance is not limited to Chicago or the past. In a 1992 HUD inspection of sixty-one randomly selected public housing units in Jacksonville, fifty-four failed to meet appropriate standards: Violations included sixty-six separate incidents of electrical hazard, thirty-four defective walls, thirteen defective ceilings, thirty-one inoperative or defective sinks, and thirty unsafe or defective hot water heaters. In a similar inspection of eighty-seven units in Philadelphia, eighty-six failed to meet appropriate standards (U.S. House of Representatives Subcommittee on Employment and Housing 1993).

stopped painting altogether. . . . But the apartment's two bathrooms were in the worst shape of all. Neither had a window, and the fans atop the building, which had provided much needed air circulation, had been stolen. In the first bathroom, a horrible stench, suggesting raw, spoiled meat, periodically rose from the toilet. On such days, LaJoe and the family simply avoided using that bathroom. Sometimes she would pour ammonia in the toilet to mitigate the smell. . . . The second bathroom housed the family's one bathtub. There was no shower, a luxury the children had never experienced. The tub doubled as a clothes washer, since the building's laundry was long ago abandoned and the closest one was one mile away. The tub's faucet couldn't be turned off. A steady stream of scalding hot water cascaded into the tub day and night. . . . In the winter, the building's heating system stormed out of control. The apartment could get like a furnace, considerably hotter and drier than in the warmest days of summer. (Kotlowitz 1991, 27–28)

In almost all of Chicago's public housing developments, what was created to enhance quality of life quickly became threats to quality of life. For example, in Robert Taylor Homes, a set of high-rise apartments that run for a two-mile stretch along South State Street, large grassy areas were left vacant to provide children with an opportunity to play in a park-like atmosphere. But with the growth of gangs and gang violence, these grassy areas became danger zones with nowhere to hide for those caught in the crossfire of gun battles.

The street culture of drugs and violence exists throughout inner cities, but it is often rampant in public housing neighborhoods. Kotlowitz describes the fear many parents have of losing their children to the streets:

It is not unusual for parents to lose out to the lure of the gangs and drug dealers. And the reasons aren't always clear. In one Horner family, a son has become a big drug dealer, a daughter a social worker. In another, one boy is in jail on a gang-related murder, another has set up a neighborhood youth program. Some parents simply won't let their children leave the apartment even to play in the playground. A common expression among the mothers at Horner is "He ain't my child no more." (Kotlowitz, 1991 86–87)

Given these realities, it is not surprising that Camilo Jose Vergara (1989) described public housing as "hell in a very tall place."

Not all public housing is as bad as Pruitt-Igoe or Henry Horner Homes or Robert Taylor Homes. In fact, since the late 1960s, no more high-rise public housing has been constructed (Halpern 1995), and today most public housing consists of garden apartments that are renovated periodically and maintained with some frequency. In many cities, public housing developments are, in appearance, indistinguishable from apartment complexes. Yet, life in public housing is different from non-public-housing neighborhoods due to the concentration of poverty and to the stigma of living in public housing. This stigma has come largely from negative portrayals of public housing in the media. "Ever since the 1950s, the press, radio, and television have not hesitated to remind Cabrini-Green residents that the place they call home is a slum. The mass media has shaped the image of the Cabrini-Green neighborhood as much as the residents themselves" (Marciniak 1986; see also Henderson, 1995, for a discussion of the portrayal of public housing in the print media). By the 1960s, public housing residents often belittled themselves, referring to their own communities as warehouses and reservations (Halpern 1995).

One study of public housing found that most residents are afraid to be out at night, and many are afraid to be out during the day. But fear also comes from feelings of isolation and alienation, with 28 percent of residents reporting that they have no close friends living in their neighborhood and 55 percent indicating that they never talk with a neighbor about a personal problem (Bolland and McCallum 1995b). This would not present a problem if there were other avenues of support for public housing residents; but most do not work, relatively few have cars, and many do not have telephones. Even though many public housing residents are deeply religious, their lack of transportation (coupled with many pastors' and other churchmembers' fears about venturing into public housing neighborhoods) leave them with little opportunity to use the church as a means of social support. Thus, most public housing residents feel alone as well as afraid, and this can be a particularly immobilizing set of forces. To the outside observer, this may appear to be an attitude problem: Public housing residents do not leave because they are content with their lives.[36] But this is not so; nearly 80 percent would move out of public housing if they could (Bolland and McCallum 1995b). Sister Souljah, a rap singer who grew up in public housing, put it this way: "I was surrounded all the time by fear and lack of understanding—fear of being victimized and a lack of understanding of how it came to pass that we all ended up there." Another public housing resident stated, "There is little point in sinking roots here. Nobody cares about anything" (both quoted in Halpern 1995).

Despite the stark realities of public housing, however, it is important to realize that for most of its residents, it is better than the alternative. Many public housing residents, particularly single women with small children, were homeless prior to moving into their apartments; in some cases, this meant staying on the streets, in cars, or in emergency shelters, while in other cases it

---

36. Others discuss these problems faced by residents of underclass neighborhoods (including public housing) as well and how they keep the underclass in poverty. Anderson (1992, 174) talks about the lack of "personal resources to negotiate the occupational structure." Kotlowitz (1996) talks about depression coupled with fear that can immobilize people living in poverty. And in an elaborate discussion, Mead (1996) suggests that people living in poverty lack the ability to commit themselves to relationships, work, and tasks; this, in turn, makes them unreliable workers who have a hard time holding jobs.

meant staying in welfare hotels or living doubled up with friends or family. Others faced imminent homelessness because of the loss of a job or the dissolution of a relationship. Thus, public housing represents stability in the face of an unstable and frightening situation. Some residents even have the courage to say, "This is my home, and I am proud to live here." Such a sentiment does not deflect from the harsh reality and the threats to daily existence that living there pose; rather, it reflects the fact that public housing is a tangible reality for many people who had nothing tangible before and who would have nothing tangible were they to leave. Thus, even though public housing may be hell in a very tall place, at least it is hell in *their* very tall place. And even Alex Kotlowitz's disturbing portrayal of life in Henry Horner Homes leaves the reader with a sense of hope—hope for the survival of the human spirit that he found in the people he talked with and came to know.

The Underclass and the Future of Cities

This chapter began with a statement about the deteriorating quality of American inner cities, and how that deterioration encourages the middle-class migration to the suburbs. Some of the deterioration is in the city's infrastructure: buildings decay, streets develop potholes, and sidewalks crack. Much of the deterioration has to do with the character of inner-city life, particularly the growth of inner-city poverty. Although poor people are an undeniable part of the urban landscape, however, poverty per se does not dominate the urban policy debate. Rather, it is the urban *underclass* that is the focus of this debate. Regardless of one's political ideology, the underclass is a central issue for cities and their future. On one side of the political spectrum are those who view the underclass as the primary reason for urban decline: the underclass and the social pathology that surrounds it keep others from investing in America's downtowns (and even from visiting America's downtowns).

On the other side of the political spectrum are those who view the underclass as victims of urban displacement. As jobs moved out of the cities and into the suburbs, often with the blessings and subsidies of federal and state governments, and as stable neighborhoods were torn down for urban renewal, those without resources were left behind to survive as best they could. The street culture of drugs, violence, and dependency is seen from a liberal perspective as the unintended legacy of this planned change.

Ultimately, both sides in this ideological debate are correct. The subsidized flight of the middle class to the suburbs may have been caused partially by their desire to escape the pathology of the city; but it also resulted from the newfound opportunity for architects, contractors, and others in the building industry to realize large profits by opening up the new American frontier. And whatever its cause, this migration to the suburbs did result in the increasing marginalization of those without resources to join in the suburban prosperity. But the growing and increasingly dangerous street culture that was left behind pushed additional people away from the inner city and reinforced the choice of those who had left; this, in turn, led to the increasing social and physical isolation of those who stayed behind, further reinforcing the inner-city pathology of the streets.

Whatever the true cause-effect relationship, two facts remain. First, the underclass is part of the inner city, and no attempt to wish them away will negate this reality. Second, the street culture associated with inner cities has taken fifty years to develop and has grown on the heels of one of the largest social movements ever to characterize the United States: suburbanization. Cities could not have created suburbs on their own; that required the outlay of billions upon billions of dollars by the federal government in the form of the federal highway program, the home mortgage deduction from federal income tax, and urban renewal. These factors combine to guarantee that (a) no solution to the "underclass problem" will occur overnight and (b) any attempt to change, in a fundamental way, the social pathology of ghetto neighborhoods will be very expensive, requiring far more than cities could ever afford to spend on their own. It took a vast, complex, and costly social movement to create a situation in which the pathological dimensions of the inner city could emerge; it will take no less of a social movement to create a situation in which this pathology can be effectively ameliorated.[37]

Poverty, Urban Services, and Public Policy

As the discussion thus far intends to suggest, federal, state, and local responses to poverty do not always have their intended consequences. Sometimes, they even make matters worse than those things they intend to remedy. The next chapter explores in further detail other unintended consequences of race and poverty policies.

37. Kaplan (1990) recognizes the inability of cities to solve the problems that have come to define them in so much of the contemporary literature; he concludes that the best urban policy is not limited to cities but, rather, is a "nonurban urban policy" (also see Lehman 1994).

From an American Place, chloride print, 1931(?), 18.8 x 23.8 cm
Alfred Stieglitz Collection, 1949.787.
Photograph © 1996, The Art Institute of Chicago. All Rights Reserved.

For the middle class, the police protect property, give directions, and help old
ladies. For the urban poor, the police are those who arrest you.
    Michael Harrington, *The Other America*

CHAPTER 16

Urban Services, Market Considerations, and the Underclass

Politics, as noted all through these pages, is the struggle for power, and an important aspect of power is the ability to set the political agenda, and through the agenda, to achieve one's desired ends. Policy is thus the embodiment of both politics and power. But politics and power are not limited to the single individual acting on his or her own behalf and seeking outcomes that are only personally rewarding. Politics and power are also group endeavors whose outcomes affect whole populations and large classes of people within those populations. These are the ideas that have guided our discussion thus far; and nowhere are these ideas more applicable than in an examination of the city's underclass and its prospects for the future.

But to prepare for the analysis that follows, it will be useful to extract from previous chapters other, equally important themes. Seven such themes provide the foundation for our exploration of how urban services and market considerations affect the lives of the urban underclass.

1. Most of the major urban problems are in the city but not of the city (their roots, however defined, are in the larger society and not in the city per se).
2. Major social problems are not readily or easily solved. Public policies usually carry unanticipated consequences. Moreover, most social prob-

lems have multiple causes, and attempted solutions usually involve heavy costs, both fiscal and social.

3. What is observed by social critics may be less a matter of "fact" than a matter of interpretation, with interpretation (in its turn) a consequence of deeply held personal values and beliefs.

4. American society is dominated by a long-standing commitment to a market economy. This translates into a commitment to the privileged place of private property, the idea that each of us is entitled to whatever share of life's goods and services we can pay for, and the belief that each of us bears a large measure of responsibility for the successes and failures in our lives.

5. American society also holds an equally strong commitment to the view that a reasonable share of life's goods and services ought to be the birthright of all. This commitment combines with that cited in 4 above to produce tension between social equity and market equity.

6. Concepts of lifestyles and territory create a metropolitan patchwork. This metropolitan patchwork, coupled with considerations of social and market equity, leads us to consider the (a) equity (or lack of it) in the disparity between central-city and suburban expenditures for urban services, and (b) strategies the affluent use to wall out the poor.

7. Public policy at the urban level is largely implemented by street-level bureaucrats. As a result, policy may be distorted, particularly in its application to the underclass, by uneven implementation practices.

With these considerations in mind, we turn to a further consideration of the urban underclass and how the delivery of urban services and considerations of the marketplace affect their lives.

The Ramifications of National Urban Policy

We now have had the experience of more than a half century of federal policies and programs that attempt to address the problems of poverty and discrimination in the city. All in all, these programs have done much to improve the lives of the poor and those who suffer the consequences of racial and ethnic discrimination. But as previously noted, these programs are not without their failures. Persistent and widespread problems do not easily give way to solutions. Their causes are manifold and deeply woven into the fabric of society. Accordingly, we can gain some better sense of the intractability of urban problems particularly as they relate to the underclass, by examining sources of inequality in housing, education, criminal justice, and other urban services. This examination may also assist in understanding how and why policies that seek major social change can never be undertaken without considerable social and political costs, and why policies seeking major social changes are never without disputation over fundamental values and beliefs.

412

Inequality in Education

Historically, the most important source of inequality in education has been segregated schools. Policies that created segregated schools were eliminated by a series of court decisions, beginning with *Brown v. Board of Education*, that first prohibited segregated schools and then ordered within-district busing of students to achieve integration when it cannot be achieved using neighborhood schools.

School Desegregation Revisited

The importance of desegregation became increasingly important with the publication of research by James Coleman and his colleagues (1966) showing that the quality of the school a child attended had little impact on his or her educational achievement; rather, achievement was most affected by (a) the parents' education background, (b) the family's standard of living, and (c) *the percentage of black students in the school*. Although originally questioned on methodological grounds (Cain and Watts 1972; Armor 1972), this latter finding provided part of the impetus for school busing, and it has been replicated since busing began. Achievement (particularly for young children) improves for black students who are bused without adversely affecting achievement of white children (Stephan 1978; Cook 1984; but see Armor, 1995, for a dissenting view). And some studies even show an improvement of racial attitudes as a result of busing, although others are equivocal (see Armor 1995, for a review).

Yet, no issue since fluoridation has generated as much local conflict as school busing. The integration of Boston's public schools was an exceptionally difficult and bitter case. It brought to play a long festering resentment of the predominantly Irish residents of South Boston against those whom they viewed as the old Protestant establishment. "Southies," as they call themselves, did not give in easily to the orders of the court. At several critical moments, they physically massed themselves against school buses to keep them from rolling, and the integration issue spilled into a subsequent mayoral election, with some candidates pledging themselves to stop integration. In the end, of course, the buses did roll, and integrated schools are now the norm in Boston.[1] (For an insightful account of the Boston school case and its effects on the lives of several families, see Lukas, 1985.)

In a number of cities, candidates for mayor, city council, and school board have also run on an antibusing platform. But, in no instance has local

---

1. For Southies, resentment against forced integration later found another target: defiance of the U.S. Department of Housing and Urban Development (HUD) order that the Boston Housing Authority admit black families to its 18,000 apartments. As of Spring 1988, a review by HUD found that the Boston Housing Authority had "systematically excluded" blacks from units in South Boston (*Time*, April 4, 1988).

protest against busing been successful, for ultimately it is the federal courts that decide when constitutional protection of equal opportunity is violated. However, actions by individual citizens, taken independently but having a great aggregate impact, have proved the greatest local threat to school integration. One such action involves enrolling students in private or parochial schools, most of which are not integrated and serve primarily whites. In 1993, approximately 16 percent of students in central cities were enrolled in such schools; while this is not a large figure, it noticeably constrains the overall effectiveness of integration efforts.

A much more important shift is the migration of white families to the suburbs. James Coleman and Sara Kelley (1976, 252) concluded that there is "sizeable acceleration of the general loss of whites from the central [city] school districts when substantial desegregation occurs within that system."[2] This led Coleman to reverse his earlier support for mandatory school desegregation. Others disagreed with this conclusion (e.g., Farley 1975, Rossell 1976), arguing that flight to the suburbs was occasioned by a host of other social and political factors; since their original dissent, however, both Farley and Rossell have modified their views and both now support voluntary desegregation solutions over mandatory solutions.

In the face of such criticism, Gary Orfield remains one of the strongest proponents of mandatory desegregation plans. His research shows that, while mandatory desegregation does result in some white flight from the central city, it produces no more flight than voluntary plans (Orfield and Monfort 1992). More important, he argues that "desegregating big city schools through busing is not an ideal or even a natural solution to segregation, but it is quite simply the only solution available if there is to be substantial integration in this generation" (Orfield 1978, 7); this is a conclusion he later supported with data, finding that mandatory plans are the only effective way to achieve effective desegregation within a school district (Orfield 1988).

But regardless of its immediate cause, white migration to the suburbs is a reality. And white flight, coupled with the Supreme Court's rejection of metropolitan-wide busing as a solution to school segregation, has largely defeated the utilitarian benefits of school desegregation. Harvard Sitkoff (1981) summarized the success of the first twenty-five years of school desegregation efforts with the following statistics: As of 1980, two-thirds of black students in the United States attended schools that were at least 90 percent

2. Denver provides a typical example of the impact of suburban migration and the problems of interpretation it presents. In 1995, about 28,000 Latinos and 13,000 blacks were enrolled in Denver's public schools together with 18,000 whites; white enrollment is down from around 63,000 whites in the year before busing began (*The Economist*, Sept. 30, 1995). But, as in other cities, it is difficult to ascertain how much of this white flight is due to school busing and how much is due to other social forces contributing to suburbanization.

black; and by 1980, more black students attended segregated schools than at the time of *Brown*. This trend is epitomized in New York City, where the white school population fell from 68 percent in 1957 to 17.5 percent in 1993. And Diane Ravich (1974) found minority students to outnumber whites in twenty-one of the twenty-nine largest cities. Schools, as she puts it, have not simply desegregated—they have *re*-segregated.[3]

Other Sources of Inequality in the Schools

School desegregation is not the only approach to improving educational opportunity for the economically disadvantaged and for minorities. In addition, the federal government has attempted to promote equality through compensatory education programs, largely designed to compensate for the lack of learning readiness among disadvantaged children. Head Start is the best known of these programs. It was initiated as part of the War on Poverty to provide preschool children from low-income families with a comprehensive program designed to meet their educational, social, health, nutritional, and psychological needs. In 1994, Head Start provided services to 740,000 children at a cost of $3.2 billion. Most school districts are delighted to accept federal money for this program, but their commitment to supplement these federal funds with local funds has been limited. In fact, Levy, Meltsner, and Wildavsky (1974) found a perverse form of equalization in the Oakland School District, which distributed local funds to those schools that did not qualify for federal compensatory education programs; this, of course, largely defeated the goal of the federal funds to equalize educational outcomes.

Oakland's experience (and other similar experiences) aside, how effective has compensatory education been at achieving its goals? The evidence is mixed. Some researchers (e.g., Smith 1975, Berrueta-Clement et al. 1984) have concluded that Head Start has been largely successful in meeting its stated goals; but even they report only modest gains. Others (e.g., Besharov 1987) have found the impact of Head Start to be limited and transitory, with any observed gains in intellectual skills or social-emotional development disappearing within two years. More generally, Eric Hanushek (1989), reviewing two decades of research, concludes that variation in educational expenditures seems to have no systematic impact on student performance.

---

3. Not only are schools resegregating due to demographic trends, they are also resegregating with the blessing of the Supreme Court. During the 1960s, Oklahoma City had implemented a court-ordered desegregation plan that involved redrawing school boundaries; in the 1970s, upon further review, the Court ordered busing to achieve desegregation. In 1991, the Court ruled in *Board of Education of Oklahoma City v. Dowell* (111 S. Ct. 630) that the city had achieved desegregation and allowed a return to neighborhood schools—and the inevitable resegregation that will be caused by the segregated housing patterns that exist there (Armor 1995).

Several factors may account for this. First, students spend relatively little time in school compared with the time they spend in their neighborhoods and their homes. It simply is not realistic to assume that a positive and supportive school environment (even were that the case) could counteract the negative effects of growing up in a ghetto neighborhood for the majority of underclass children. Even more than that, with the resegregation of the schools, the schools themselves become a reflection of the neighborhood. For children living in middle-class and affluent neighborhoods, school therefore reinforces what they learn in their homes and from their neighbors. But for children living in ghetto neighborhoods, school reinforces what they learn on the streets—and even several billion dollars spent on compensatory education cannot effectively overcome that.

Most indicators show that equality of educational outcomes is, if anything, getting worse. Consider, for example, the dropout rate: Whereas 24.6 percent of all high school students from lower socioeconomic strata drop out of school, only 10.1 percent of those from the middle socioeconomic strata and 2.3 percent of those from the upper strata drop out (U.S. Dept. of Education 1994); over time, the dropout rate is increasing for the lowest socioeconomic strata but decreasing for everyone else. Further, once they have dropped out, students of higher socioeconomic status (SES) are 2.5 times more likely to reenter school or attain a General Education Degree. In addition, children living in underclass neighborhoods (Crane 1991) and attending low SES schools (Mayer 1991) are more likely to drop out than those not living in underclass neighborhoods or attending low SES schools, regardless of their own poverty level.

Tracking and Ability Grouping

One reason that economically disadvantaged and minority students may do less well in school is the type of classroom education they receive there. For example, many schools use a tracking system, emphasizing college-preparatory courses for better students and a basic or vocational curriculum for less–able students; another, related approach is to place students in different classrooms on a subject-by-subject basis (e.g., science or English), based on their ability in these specific subjects. While these policies themselves may be without social or racial bias, their implementation is often biased in favor of upper- and middle-class white students.

For example, teaches often rely on stereotyped cues to identify those students who they think would benefit most from a college-preparatory curriculum or who are most able in a particular subject. Unfortunately, these cues may have a racial or class bias (Oakes et al. 1992, Oakes 1995).[4] As a result,

---

4. Often, these stereotypes are not motivated by overt racial or class considerations, but their implications for race and class are nonetheless important. For example, Oakes et al. (1992) cite one administrator who felt that students in "strong, two-parent families" would do better in academic classes; this, of course, is much more common in white and middle-class families than in black or underclass families.

students from low-income homes in general and blacks and Hispanics in particular are tracked disproportionately into the basic-skills and vocational curricula, with middle- and upper-class students in general and whites in particular guided into a college preparatory curriculum or other advanced classes (Goodlad 1984, Oakes et al. 1992, Oakes 1995).[5]

At first glance, this tracking bias would seem to be a rectifiable error. Even after being incorrectly categorized, students can demonstrate their ability, be reevaluated, and be reclassified into more advanced academic tracks. While this is possible in principle and has no doubt happened on many occasions, it is easier in principle than in practice. The underlying impediment to high student achievement in the face of negative teacher expectations is that teacher expectations, themselves, act as barriers to achievement. Teachers spend more time with, demand higher quality work from, and offer more encouragement to those students they expect to succeed; moreover, better teachers are typically assigned to classes with more advanced students. In contrast, students grouped in low-ability classes receive less exposure to instruction in essential knowledge and skills, and they receive less access to a whole range of educational opportunities and resources; this bias, however subtle, may keep minority and poor students from advancing as rapidly as white middle- and upper-class students.[6] Just as important, a student who is tracked into a basic skills or a vocational curriculum may grow to doubt his or her ability, and academic performance may suffer. So, for whatever reason, tracking negatively affects the achievement of students placed in the lower ability groups (e.g., Oakes et al. 1992, Wheelock 1992, Shell 1994, Oakes 1995).

5. Even when ability (as measured by standardized test scores) is held constant, differential assignments to vocational and academic classes occur. In one set of schools she studied, Oakes (1995) found that among students scoring above the ninetieth percentile, 56 percent of Hispanics, 93 percent of whites, and 97 percent of Asians were placed in accelerated classes. Data from the late 1980s (Wheelock 1992) show that overall, black, Hispanic, Native American, and low-income eighth graders are twice as likely as white or upper-income eighth graders to be in a remedial math class.

6. In their seminal study, which they published as *Pygmalion in the Classroom*, Robert Rosenthal and Lenore Jacobson (1968) examined the impact of teacher expectations on second grade students in San Francisco. They identified two groups of second grade students, ostensibly based on their first grade achievement test scores but in reality based on random assignment. Thus, while one group of students was identified as "academic spurters" and the other group as "ordinary students," the two groups were, in reality, no different in academic ability or achievement. Rosenthal and Jacobson shared these classifications with second grade teachers. At the end of the school year, student achievement levels were again measured, and the "academic spurters" outperformed the "ordinary students." Since at the beginning of the year these two groups were identical in academic ability, the only explanation for the change was differential teacher behavior toward the students.

Other Policies

Differential treatment of the poor and minorities is also manifest in the implementation of disciplinary policies within schools and school districts. For example, in 1977 the NAACP argued in a suit against the New York City Board of Education that black and Hispanic problem children were routinely assigned to problem schools, while white children with similar behavior problems were routinely helped in their own schools (Lipsky 1980; see Green, 1977, for other examples).

The point of this discussion is not that nothing can be done to scrub the educational process clean of class, racial, and ethnic discrimination. Rather, the discussion is intended to secure a basic idea: The causes of major social problems are manifold and that they are deeply woven into the fabric of our society. It is a point to be encountered again as we turn to issues and problems of residential segregation in urban America.

The Politics and Policies of Residential Segregation

Like segregation in the classroom, residential segregation has not ended. Until the middle years of this century, cities employed heavy-handed approaches to keeping minorities and the poor segregated. Two of the most egregious of these, the use of restrictive covenants and zoning regulations, were considered in chapter 12; restrictive covenants have been outlawed, and zoning has been at least partially regulated by court decisions. But several other practices remain in effect, even though they have been outlawed by federal legislation, most notably the Fair Housing Act of 1968 and the Community Reinvestment Act of 1977.

Real Estate Practices

Real estate owners and agents are forbidden by law to refuse to sell or rent housing because of race, religion, or national origin. That practice was ruled unconstitutional by the U.S. Supreme Court in 1968[7] and outlawed by the Fair Housing Act of 1968.[8] Yet, the practice continues informally and in most

7. *Jones v. Alfred Mayer Co.*, 392 US 409.
8. The Fair Housing Act made it unlawful to "refuse to sell or rent after the making of a bona fide offer, or to refuse to negotiate for the sale or rental of, or otherwise make unavailable or deny, a dwelling to any person because of race, color, religion, or national origin." However, the law offered an important loophole, by distinguishing between a strictly private act of discrimination (i.e., individuals selling private residences) and one relying on public resources *of any kind* (e.g., individuals selling residences through the use of real estate firms, the media, agents, mail, or posted notices). Under the law, the former acts are exempted, while the latter are prohibited. Note the similarity between this private-public distinction and the one used to define politics in chapter 5. One implication is that nonpolitical acts of discrimination are tolerated, while political acts of discrimination are not. For a useful discussion of the 1968 Fair Housing Act, see Arkes (1981).

418

instances seemingly beyond the reach of the law. For example, a telephone solicitor for a Wheaton, Maryland, real estate developer in 1969 (after passage of the Fair Housing Act) reported that if she contacted someone who she suspected was black, company policy dictated that she not follow up on that contact. Further, she reported, while solicitors were given a bonus when they arranged interviews between a salesperson and a prospective client, this bonus was not provided if the client turned out to be black (Arkes 1981). A housing audit conducted by HUD during the late 1980s produced similar findings. Pairs of potential home buyers (one white, one minority) were matched on a number of characteristics and sent to real estate agents who advertised houses or apartments. Approximately 20 percent fewer units were made available to the minority home buyer than to the white home buyer. Further, when a transaction was completed, minority home buyers were nearly 50 percent less likely than white home buyers to receive assistance from the real estate agent in obtaining financing for the home (Turner et al. 1991).

Several more subtle forms of discrimination also occur. One such practice is racial steering, where real estate agents show minority clients houses in black or Hispanic neighborhoods and white clients houses in white neighborhoods. Until 1950, the real estate industry's code of ethics encouraged racial steering (Metcalf 1988), assuming that its clients would feel more comfortable living among others of their own race.[9] However, Galster (1990a) has identified several other, less noble motives for racial steering. Some real estate agents may fear the loss of potential white clients if they sell homes in white neighborhoods to minority home buyers, and they therefore steer them toward minority or transition (e.g., racially mixed) neighborhoods. In addition, some real estate agents may believe that by selling homes in transition neighborhoods to minority home buyers, they create instability and raise fears among white home owners that housing values will decrease; this, in turn, speeds up outmigration among white home owners and increases the business the real estate agent can expect. Whatever the motive (and Galster

9. One commonly invoked explanation for residential segregation in the United States is that blacks prefer to live in segregated areas (e.g., Coleman 1979). However, several studies (summarized by Darden 1987; also see Yinger 1987) cast doubt on this conclusion; for example, a 1980 HUD survey found that 57 percent of blacks and 46 percent of Hispanics preferred a neighborhood that was half white and half minority. Darden (1983) explains the continuing popularity of the segregation-by-choice hypothesis by suggesting that it provides a rationale for maintaining the *status quo* and delaying or preventing residential integration. He suggests that its advocates, in drawing parallels to the white European immigrant groups who clustered together to enjoy a common linguistic, cultural, or religious tradition, fail to understand that blacks are drawn together not by choice but as an involuntary adaptation of white discrimination; and once together, they do not share a common culture so much as a common set of grievances. When it does occur, minorities' preference for segregated housing may reflect their concern about white reactions to them as neighbors—including physical violence and threats to themselves, their homes, and their families (Chandler 1992; see Krumholz, 1992, for a discussion of such violence in Cleveland and Chicago).

found support for both of these), considerable evidence suggests that racial steering still occurs. For example, a housing audit conducted in Memphis between 1985 and 1987 found that prosegregation steering occurred in 60 percent of the cases that were observed (Galster 1990b)—about the same level that was observed by Diana Pearce (1976) in her study of Detroit more than a decade earlier.

In addition to steering, William Tisdale (1983) outlines several procedures that real estate agents and apartment managers use to keep minority applicants away from rental housing. These include:

1. Requiring larger application fees (e.g., an entire month's rent and the security deposit) of minority applicants than of white applicants.
2. Requiring more stringent application criteria (e.g., higher income, longer time on the job, more references) of minority applicants than of white applicants.
3. Requiring that a prospective tenant be recommended by a present tenant.
4. Advertising available rental units only in publications with limited circulation (predominantly among nonminority readers), by word of mouth, or on bulletin boards of all-white churches or clubs.
5. Using a telephone answering machine to screen out applicants (i.e., calls from people suspected of being black are not returned).

Legal recourse. Although all of these practices are in violation of the Fair Housing Act of 1968, they require formal challenge by the harmed party before any action will be taken. But such action has seldom been initiated, for several reasons. First, many of the discriminatory real estate practices are subtle, and potential clients may not even be aware that they have been denied access to fair and equal housing (Galster 1990b). Second, even though the Fair Housing Act outlawed discriminatory practices, it lacked an enforcement mechanism, making it largely ineffective. Fewer than 30 percent of the complaints filed with HUD during the 1970s ever reached formal mediation, and nearly half of those remained in noncompliance after reconciliation efforts had terminated; only 10 percent of the cases HUD could not conciliate were referred to the attorney general for prosecution, and very few of those were pursued. The U.S. Supreme Court recognized the weakness of the law, stating that "HUD has no power of enforcement" (*Trafficante v. Metropolitan Life Insurance Company*, p. 210),[10] and that the Act's main enforcement mechanism "must be private suits in which . . . the complainants act not only on their own behalf but also as private attorneys-general in vindicating a policy that Congress considered to be of the highest prior-

10. 409 US 205 (1972); see also *Gladstone Realtors v. Village of Bellwood* (441 US 91, 1979).

ity" (p. 211). Not only was enforcement limited in these ways but plaintiffs could sue only for actual damages and up to $1,000 in punitive damages; further, they could not recover court costs or attorney fees unless the court judged them to be financially unable to cover these costs. Finally, suits had to be filed within 180 days of the alleged violation or 30 days of the date HUD mediation ended. Even if a realtor were found to be in violation of the law, the limit of $1,000 in punitive damages plus actual damages severely limited their liability (Massey and Denton 1993).

These limitations were partially remedied by the Fair Housing Amendments Act of 1989, which extended the time to file suit from 180 days to two years. In addition,

- it allowed attorney fees and court costs to be recovered;
- it created a streamlined process for trying cases before an administrative law judge and empowered administrative judges to order full compensation for damages plus a civil fine of up to $10,000 for the first offense (and up to $50,000 for the third offense and up to $100,000 for patterned offenses); and
- it required HUD to take a case before an administrative law judge if it found reasonable cause to believe discrimination occurred.

The first case prosecuted under this new system was settled in six months and resulted in a $75,000 fine, and damages as high as $624,000 have been awarded in other cases. In Chicago alone, complaints rose by 35 percent following implementation of the legislation (Massey and Denton 1993).

Banking Practices

In addition to real estate companies, banks have discriminated against home buyers seeking mortgages, both because of their race and the area of town where their property is located. Nationwide statistics show that blacks are turned down for home loans twice as often as whites and that high-income blacks are rejected at about the same rate as low-income whites (*Atlanta Journal-Constitution*, Jan. 22, 1989, 1). A more carefully controlled study conducted by the Federal Reserve Bank of Boston (Munnell et al. 1992, cited in Leven and Sykuta 1994) considered how several factors (e.g., ability to repay the loan, risk of default, potential fault loss amount, personal characteristics of the borrower) affected loan decisions for home mortgages; the study found that race matters, with minorities less successful in securing loans. Even so, evidence concerning racial discrimination against individual borrowers is inconclusive (Leven and Sykuta 1994).

Less inconclusive is the evidence for "redlining," or withholding loans based on the neighborhood where the applicant's property is

421

located.[11] Christine Klepper (1983) reports that lending institutions are much more likely to issue home loans to applicants buying houses in predominantly white areas of Chicago than to those in largely black areas. While several factors may account for this finding, she concludes that redlining and discrimination are critical.[12] After the *Atlanta Journal-Constitution* reported racial disparity in mortgage loan rejection rates in 1988, other studies dug deeper into the issue, documenting racial disparity in cities such as Milwaukee, Boston, Chicago, Baltimore, Washington, D.C., and Louisville (see Squires 1990 for a review).

The Community Reinvestment Act, passed by Congress in 1977 to allow families in low-income neighborhoods to obtain mortgages, has done little to alleviate these discriminatory practices; when mortgage money has gone to targeted neighborhoods, it seldom goes to the poorest or the most disadvantaged in those neighborhoods (*American Banker*, Dec. 29, 1988, 5). During the late 1980s, however, documented evidence of discrimination brought pressure on banks to reform these practices, and agreements have been negotiated in a number of cities to alleviate the disparity. The most common approach has been the creation of loan pools and community development funds to finance low-cost housing; for example, the Chase Manhattan Bank contributed $200 million to a community development fund in New York City. In one of the most sweeping attempts to rectify the problem, Wisconsin created a Fair Lending Action Committee to identify the reasons for racial disparity in Milwaukee and to explore ways to increase mortgage lending for blacks and other racial minorities. After six months of fact finding and contentious debate, the committee issued a report calling for Milwaukee area lenders to increase their loans to these groups (Squires 1990).

The major problem with these solutions is that they are strictly voluntary. Like the Fair Housing Act before it, the Community Reinvestment Act lacks any effective enforcement mechanism. Thus far, banks have complied, perhaps as a way of avoiding possible litigation. But such voluntary efforts cannot necessarily be counted on in the future.

11. The term "redlining" derives from the early practices of the Home Owners Loan Corporation (HOLC), a federal agency created in the 1930s to provide funds for refinancing urban mortgages in danger of default. HOLC developed a rating system to evaluate risks associated with loans made to specific urban neighborhoods. Four categories of neighborhood quality were established, and the lowest was coded with the color red (Massey and Denton 1993). Since then, bankers have used the practice of marking out an area on a map in red, thereby designating it as a high-risk investment area.

12. In addition to home loans, small business loans have sometimes been turned down on the basis of the applicant's race. In a study of small, established businesses asking for short-term loans, Ando (1988, cited in Bates 1993) found that black-owned businesses are more likely to be turned down than businesses owned by whites, even when their credit risks are equivalent. Whereas 61.7 percent of loans to black-owned businesses were approved, 89.9 percent of loans to white-owned businesses were approved. Part of the reason for the discrepancy was the location of the business, causing many newer black enterprises to avoid the inner cities and locate instead in central business districts or in outlying suburbs (see Bates 1993 for a discussion).

Siting Decisions

Low-cost housing. Previously we saw how zoning ordinances can enforce residential segregation within the private sector. But equally important are municipal decisions concerning the location of low-income public housing units within the city. In St. Louis, for example, public housing was constructed in dilapidated and run down areas, most of it surrounded by abandoned buildings (Meehan 1975). In Norfolk, Philadelphia, and Nashville, virtually all public housing was built in already black residential areas; in Norfolk, elementary schools were built adjacent to each public housing development, reinforcing patterns of segregated schools that still exist (Rabin 1987). Thus, by 1962, 80 percent of all public housing developments in the United States were occupied exclusively by one race (Lief and Goering 1987). Although HUD ordered an end to this practice in 1967, most public housing developments today still consist predominantly of one race.

Despite some claims to the contrary, public housing sites (as a rule) have not been selected to allow residents access to transportation, shopping, work, or efficient services. Rather (say many critics), they have been selected to keep the residents out of sight (Hartman 1975).[13] For example, in the late 1960s, approximately 96 percent of Cleveland's black population lived east of the Cuyahoga River. In an effort to break down residential segregation, the Cuyahoga Metropolitan Housing Authority proposed to construct public housing in West Cleveland, and it gained the necessary permits from the city council. However, in the 1971 municipal election, several council candidates proposed to revoke these permits in any area where the majority of residents opposed the project, and upon their election fulfilled their campaign commitment. The district court, however, overturned these revocations,[14] arguing that the city had not demonstrated good cause (Johnston 1984).

Urban administrators, politicians, and residents often justify these siting policies on the basis of fiscal considerations. After all, they argue, the cost of

13. In contrast, public housing for the elderly has been better located, more attractive, and more livable (Hartman 1975). This again suggests a class bias in urban public policy: the plight of the younger and middle-aged poor is of their own making (assumes the policy), and they should be held accountable while the plight of the elderly poor is due to the aging process, which they cannot control.

14. Another example of the politics of public housing and racial segregation occurred in Philadelphia (Rabin 1987). In 1959, the Whitman neighborhood in Southeast Philadelphia was cleared to provide space for a public housing site; the neighborhood had been predominantly black, and displaced residents moved into a nearby predominantly white neighborhood. Philadelphia then obtained federal approval to clear and rehabilitate about one hundred dwelling units in this neighborhood, every one of them occupied by a black household. Then, encouraged by Mayoral candidate Frank Rizzo, the neighborhood mounted a vociferous and often violent campaign to prevent the public housing units from being built, claiming that it would bring blacks into an all-white neighborhood. Construction was delayed for more than twenty years until a federal judge ordered that the public housing be built.

423

land is considerably lower in dilapidated areas of the central city, and to maintain low rent and an adequate number of units, the city must concentrate housing units in these areas. But the inadequacy of this explanation is pointed up by the fact that most of the cost is borne by the federal government and that some cities (e.g., New York) even forfeited federal funds rather than integrate low-income housing units into middle- and upper-class neighborhoods.[15]

Health and service facilities. A final means a city may use to promote residential segregation (or to exclude the underclass completely) involves siting policies for health and human service facilities. Many urban politicians and administrators have argued that it is more efficient to concentrate low-income families in one area because this allows them to take advantage of nonmobile municipal services housed nearby (e.g., sheltered workshops, community mental health centers, neighborhood health clinics, legal aid centers, drug treatment centers, day care facilities). A similar logic has been used to argue for the concentration of nonmobile municipal services around the poor (see Wolch, 1982, for a review; also see Dear and Wolch 1987). This circular logic creates a self-fulfilling prophecy, typically leading to segregated residential patterns: Those dependent on community-based health and human services are concentrated in one part of town, while the middle and upper classes are located in another. But, again, the public argument often masks a more important underlying logic: Residents of middle- and upper-class neighborhoods usually do not want to associate with service-dependent individuals, many of whom are recently deinstitutionalized mental patients, ex-convicts, former drug addicts or alcoholics, or juvenile wards of the courts (e.g., Rabkin 1974), and many residents fear a reduction in property values were the poor (or the service delivery facilities they use) to locate in their neighborhoods.[16] Similar

15. Palley and Palley (1981) report that during the late 1960s, the Department of Housing and Urban Development developed policies that encouraged cities to scatter low-income housing units throughout middle-income neighborhoods rather than concentrating them in poor neighborhoods. By the early 1970s, and in response to a specific HUD directive, New York City planned to locate 840 low-income housing units in Forest Hills, a white, middle-income section of Queens. However, this proposal generated considerable protest among Forest Hills residents, and the city scaled back its proposal to 432 units, 180 of which were designated for the elderly (who were more acceptable to community residents). As a result, the city was required to contribute a substantial portion of the construction costs of these housing units. Mario Cuomo (later to become governor of New York), who negotiated the compromise between city officials and community representatives, has set down a complete description of the project and its controversies (Cuomo 1975).

16. In fact, few of these concerns about property values are warranted. Numerous studies have failed to discover any significant effects of facility siting on either market activity or property values (see Wolch 1982 for a review).

arguments are advanced to keep health and human service facilities out of communities altogether.[17]

The Extent of Residential Segregation in American Cities

Just how pervasive are patterns of residential segregation? According to most statistics, very pervasive. In 1990, for example, central city populations in the United States averaged 22.1 percent black, compared to suburbs with an average of 6.9 percent black population. Studies of residential segregation within major U.S. metropolitan areas (summarized in table 16.1) show that between 1960 and 1970, little integration occurred (and in many cities, 1970 showed greater levels of segregation than 1960). By 1980, substantial movement toward integration had begun to occur in every city, and it continued through 1990; but even with this advance, many areas merely reattained their 1960 level of integration. Even by 1990, no metropolitan area even *approached* complete integration, and a number (e.g., New York, Chicago, Detroit, Newark, Cleveland, Milwaukee, Buffalo) remained substantially segregated (Clark 1986, Harrison and Weinberg 1992).

Even though there is a substantial migration of black families (particularly those with middle and upper incomes) to the suburbs, this has not produced any dramatic shifts in the level of residential segregation in most metropolitan areas. The reason is that most blacks who moved out of the central city went to suburbs that were predominantly black (Massey and Denton 1987, Hirsch 1993). Chicago is a case in point. During the past fifty years, Chicago has been one of the most segregated cities in the country. Fred Wirt and his colleagues (1972), for example, compared the 1970 racial composition of 147 Chicago suburbs (with over twenty-five hundred people). They reported nineteen (13 percent) of these to be exclusively white and another ninety-seven (66 percent) to contain fewer than 1 percent blacks; in only ten suburbs did they find greater than 11 percent blacks, and four of these were predominantly black (i.e., over 60 percent). By 1990, these figures had changed, but they still revealed substantial segregation. Sixty-two percent of the suburbs contained 2 percent or fewer blacks, compared with Chicago's central city black population of 39 percent. Also by 1990, fifty-four Chicago suburbs (18 percent) had black populations greater than 11 percent, but thirteen of these were *predominantly* black.

Although residential segregation by income is not nearly so pro-

17. People object not just to human service facilities in their neighborhoods, but to virtually all public facilities. Christopher Smith (1980) found that out of twenty-eight such facilities, urban residents wanted none located on their block, only one—a park—on the next block, and only two—an elementary school and a public library—within their neighborhood.

Table 16.1 Residential Segregation Indices for 38 Selected Metropolitan Areas, 1960–1990

	Dissimilarity Index[a]			
Metropolitan Area	1960[b]	1970[b]	1980[b]	1990[c]
New York	.744	.738	.728	.815
Low Angeles-Long Beach	.892	.885	.764	.728
Chicago	.912	.912	.863	.855
Philadelphia	.771	.780	.770	.771
Detroit	.871	.889	.871	.876
San Francisco-Oakland	.794	.773	.682	.638
Washington	.777	.811	.693	.659
Dallas	.812	.869	.762	.631
Houston	.850	.784	.719	.665
Boston	.808	.793	.758	.680
Nassau-Suffolk (NY)	—	—	.754	.761
St. Louis	.859	.865	.815	.769
Pittsburgh	.744	.745	.728	.710
Baltimore	.824	.810	.741	.713
Minneapolis	.833	.799	—	.618
Atlanta	.771	.817	.768	.677
Newark	.728	.788	.786	.822
Anaheim-Santa Ana	—	.723	.404	—
Cleveland	.896	.902	.875	.850
San Diego	.795	.762	.586	.579
Miami	.895	.857	.771	.699
Denver	.846	.847	.678	.640
Seattle	.833	.781	.656	.561
Tampa-St. Petersburg	.836	.845	.773	.693
Riverside-San Bernadino (CA)	—	—	.495	.439
Phoenix	.811	.754	.565	.502
Milwaukee	.904	.895	.834	.826
Cincinnati	.832	.818	.779	.757
Kansas City	.874	.833	.784	.725
San Jose	.656	.511	.403	.430
Buffalo	.868	.857	.796	.817
Portland	.813	.802	.680	.663
New Orleans	.650	.742	.704	.687
Indianapolis	.787	.838	.786	.742
Columbus	.761	.809	.727	.673
San Antonio	.768	.740	.545	.539
Ft. Lauderdale-Hollywood	—	.949	.833	.683
Sacramento	.721	.661	.525	.556
Median	.8115	.8095	.754	.687

a. The measure of racial segregation used here is the Racial Dissimilarity Index. It is calculated for geographical units (e.g., census tracts), and its specifies the percentage of blacks (or whites) that would have to move from their geographical location in order to achieve an equal distribution of that race across all subareas of the city. Thus, it ranges from 0.0 (indicating perfect integration to 1.0 (indicating complete segregation).
b. Reported in Clark (1986).
c. Reported in Harrison and Weinberg (1992).

nounced (Dimond 1978), wealthy suburbs in most metropolitan areas have nonetheless successfully prevented the poor from moving in. For example, median family income among Bostonians in 1990 was $34,377, compared with $50,000 for those living in Boston's suburbs. More striking is the distribution of low-income families in the area: Fifteen percent of those families living in Boston had an annual income under the poverty threshold, compared with only 4.1 percent of those families living in Boston's suburbs.[18] Similar trends hold for virtually all other cities in the Northeast and Midwest. Only in the sunbelt (e.g., Houston, Atlanta, Los Angeles) does the trend break down; and even there, suburban pockets of wealth exceed the general wealth of the central city.

Finally, we find that racial segregation is most pronounced when coupled with economic segregation. For example, Farley (1995) considers the probability of interracial exposure (i.e., blacks and whites living in the same neighborhood) for people of different incomes. For low-income whites living in St. Louis, the exposure rate is .15, compared to exposure rates of .07 for middle-income whites and .02 for high-income whites. Among blacks, a similar (albeit reversed) pattern holds. For low-income blacks, the exposure rate is

18. A geographical analysis of the distribution of income in Boston and its suburbs (first reported by Dimond 1978 and updated from the 1990 census) is even more revealing.

	Median Family Income	Percent of Families Below Poverty Level
Boston	$34,377	15.0
Inner Tier Suburbs		
Cambridge	39,990	7.2
Chelsea	29,039	22.9
Lynn	35,830	13.9
Malden	42,099	5.5
Medford	45,532	4.9
Somerville	38,532	7.6
Middle Tier Suburbs		
Arlington	52,749	3.3
Watertown	49,467	3.2
Belmont	61,046	2.1
Concord	80,184	2.1
Revere	37,213	8.6
Wellesley	70,030	1.3
Outer Tier Suburbs		
Burlington	60,323	2.8
Sudbury	84,036	0.8
Marshfield	55,524	2.6
Pembroke	51,033	3.5

In general, the further from the central city, the more affluent the suburbs become.

427

.17, compared to an exposure rate of .39 for middle-class blacks and .51 for high-income blacks. The implications are clear. Wealth allows blacks to attain residence in integrated neighborhoods, just as it allows whites to maintain residence in all-white neighborhoods. On the other hand, poverty forces whites to live in more integrated neighborhoods, and it prevents blacks from moving to these neighborhoods.

Inequality in the Criminal Justice System

The Police

An individual police officer is forced to make hundreds of decisions every day, ranging from the mundane (e.g., whether to cite a motorist going 32 mph in a 25 mph zone for speeding or simply issue a warning) to the critical (e.g., whether to shoot a suspect who *may* be reaching for a gun). While departmental guidelines suggest appropriate behaviors for the officer under these and most other circumstances, the officer is typically offered considerable discretion in implementing these guidelines. *[The theory of urban administration.]* Even in the case of the speeding motorist, the officer may take into consideration a number of factors in his or her decision to issue a citation or a warning: the weather conditions, traffic flow, evidence of alcohol consumption, and the demeanor of the driver. In deciding whether to pull the trigger in a life-threatening situation, the number of factors is much greater, and the officer must process and integrate all the available information in a very short time.

As a result, police officers tend to isolate a small number of specific cues (pieces of information) that they use to evaluate each type of situation they are likely to encounter, and they use these cues to make a decision (Swanson and Bolland 1983, Skolnick 1994). This reduces the complexity and stress of their jobs. Imagine if they had to treat each traffic citation as a completely unique event and evaluate a half dozen factors in their decision calculus. And relying on a limited number of cues may save lives in dangerous situations, for decisions based on one or two cues may be made more quickly and consistently than those based on twenty cues or more.

The tendency to stereotype is often inherent in these behavioral routines. For example, an officer's willingness to let a deferential motorist off with a warning while citing an argumentative and verbally abusive motorist may represent a belief that the former is a better, more governable citizen than the latter. The officer may believe that a verbally abusive motorist is likely to have committed other offenses for which he or she was not caught, and issuing a citation becomes a way of compensating for these other offenses. In more serious situations, the officer may view verbal abuse as an indicator of threat, and he or she may feel justified in taking more forceful action than might otherwise be warranted.

428

But this tendency to stereotype also creates a potential class bias in the delivery of police services, however, for members of the underclass may be less deferential in their dealings with police officers than members of the upper and middle classes, or even the working poor (cf. Charles 1986). Yet, this is perhaps the most important single cue in most police officers' decisions. Swanson and Bolland (1984) found that 69 percent of officers they studied relied primarily or exclusively on the deference of motorists suspected of drinking in deciding on what action to take. Even in domestic disturbances, where a number of cues (e.g., level of conflict, wife's condition, the presence of children, the husband's sobriety) may be critical in assessing the danger of the situation, 42 percent of officers ignored these objective indicators of threat and concentrated instead on the husband's deference toward them.

Another cue that officers use in determining their response, particularly in dangerous situations, is the suspect's race (Skolnick 1994). After all, the police may reason, blacks commit considerably more crimes per capita than whites, so a black suspect is more likely to be guilty than a white suspect (Ryan 1976). As a result, officers expect encounters with blacks to be more dangerous than those with whites, and their actions are likely to be more severe (e.g., arrest, physical restraint). In addition, their attitudes and actions toward blacks may be cautious and suspicious for the same reason. For example, the Massachusetts attorney general, investigating complaints of racial discrimination, found that Boston's police officers regularly stopped and questioned blacks without any basis for suspicion of wrongdoing. Several studies also show that police are more likely to arrest a black suspect than a white suspect in a crime, particularly when the evidence against the suspect is weak (for a review, see Walker et al. 1996). All of these practices exacerbate strained relationships between the black community and the police. For example, 44.8 percent of the complaints against New York City police officers were filed by blacks, even though blacks make up only 28.7 percent of the population (Walker et al. 1996). During the four-year period leading up to the Los Angeles riots in 1992, there were 8,274 complaints filed against the Los Angeles Police Department, 24 percent involving allegations of excessive force and many coming from neighborhoods with high concentrations of racial and ethnic minorities (Fukurai et al. 1994). It should not be surprising, then, that almost all of the urban riots of the past twenty years (and many before that) have been triggered by incidents involving police.

The Courts

By the same token, the courts invoke different sentencing criteria for the middle and upper classes than for the underclass. Among juveniles accused of offenses, blacks are likely to receive harsher treatment at all stages of the juvenile justice process than whites accused of similar offenses (Pope and

Feyerherm 1990, Bishop and Frazier 1988). Robert Emerson (1969) found that juvenile court judges determine sentencing severity largely on the basis of the apparent worthiness of the client; the implication of the previously cited studies is that race influences judgments of worthiness within the courts.

Among adults, similar patterns hold. Judges may stereotype blacks as less reliable and more prone to violence than whites (Walker et al. 1996); whether or not this is the causal factor, whites do receive more favorable bail decisions than blacks (Patterson and Lynch 1991) and are, therefore, less likely to be in prison at the time of their trial. This is important, since those in jail at the time of trial are more likely to be found guilty than those who are out on bail. Although studies of the effects of race on sentencing are mixed, they generally show that blacks receive longer sentences for certain types of crimes than do whites (see Walker et al., 1996, for a review).

Several studies also show that economic status predicts how those arrested for crimes are treated by the courts, with low-income and unemployed people more likely to be detained prior to trial than middle- or upper-class people; among those who are found guilty, the indigent are also more likely to serve prison sentences (Chiricos and Bales 1991, McCarthy 1990; see Reiman, 1996, for a review). Not surprisingly, when an arrested person is both black and indigent, these biases are even more pronounced (Chiricos and Bales 1991).

The War on Drugs

Over the past quarter century (but particularly during the past decade), drugs have ravaged inner-city neighborhoods. But the war on drugs has had no less devastating an impact on these neighborhoods. Between 30 percent and 60 percent of the black young-adult males living in large cities are in prison, on parole, or on probation (Mincy 1994, Miller 1996); and although they have been arrested and convicted for a variety of offenses, many are those caught in the expanding war on drugs.[19]

Nationally, blacks account for 39.3 percent of all drug arrests, but only 12.5 percent of the U.S. population. This, by itself, does not indicate bias in police practices. But other statistics indicate that blacks are only slightly more likely to use drugs than are whites (Walker et al. 1996) ; this, coupled with evidence of selective enforcement of the drug laws, suggests that blacks, and particularly blacks living in ghetto neighborhoods, are at particular risk of being arrested for drug-related offenses. Walker, Spohn, and DeLone (1996) describe several police operations notable for their infringement of minority rights. One of these was Operation Hammer, launched by the Los Angeles Police

---

19. Since the 1960s, the number of drug-related arrests has increased dramatically, from 162,000 in 1968 to 569,000 in 1977 and 1,150,000 in 1989. By 1992, 59 percent of inmates in federal prisons had drug offenses as their most serious crime (Reiman 1996).

Department in 1989. Up to one thousand officers each night went into inner-city neighborhoods to conduct street sweeps in a search for illegal activities, contraband, or drugs. Thousands of people, mostly gang members and all black or Hispanic, were arrested (most based on little or no evidence of wrongdoing).

Although such large operations are unusual, ghetto neighborhoods in virtually all cities are subject to frequent police patrols, and black males in these neighborhoods are often the target of intense surveillance and aggressive questioning (Miller 1996). Many, of course, are guilty of crimes (including possession of drugs, sometimes with an intent to sell them). But the police presence in the neighborhoods is viewed by many residents with contempt, and their pursuit of drugs is viewed as harassment.

This increased attention to drugs has had important implications for one type of underclass neighborhood: public housing. In 1996, President Clinton directed HUD to implement a policy which became known as "One Strike and You're Out." Under the One Strike policy, police and other law enforcement agencies are directed to inform local housing authorities of any criminal activity of its tenants (including use or possession of drugs); armed with this information, the local housing authority is required to evict anyone it has reasonable grounds to believe is using drugs. The "reasonable grounds" clause is much weaker than the "reasonable doubt" criterion required to convict a person in court of a crime. Thus, a tenant may be evicted even though the evidence of drug use is either weak or was obtained under an illegal search. In addition, HUD has interpreted the law to mean that each tenant is responsible for all that happens in his or her apartment; thus, even though the tenant may not have used drugs, he or she can be evicted if a family member or a visitor is caught doing so. The One Strike policy has been vigorously implemented by many local housing authorities, and in some neighborhoods, it has been used to evict a substantial proportion of tenants.

In addition to HUD's One Strike policy, a number of local housing authorities are working with police departments to establish and aggressively enforce a criminal trespass policy. In some cities, the local housing authority has authorized police to issue a verbal trespass warning to any nonresident who is loitering on housing authority property or who the police suspect of being involved in any drug-related activity. Once a warning has been issued, the warned person is prohibited from returning to the public housing neighborhood for a period of twelve months; if the person is apprehended on housing authority property during that period (for whatever reason), he or she is arrested.

All of these activities, which are part of the War on Drugs, have had a disruptive impact on underclass neighborhoods in general and public housing neighborhoods in particular. In their efforts to lead drug-free lives and to protect their children from drugs and drug dealers, many residents welcome the war on drugs. But many others resent what they feel is the menacing presence of increased police surveillance. They worry that they may get caught for doing something illegal; and because of the increased police surveillance in their neighborhood, their worry is well founded. In addition, public housing residents worry that they may be evicted if they, their children, or visiting friends are caught using drugs. Neighbors become potential informants, further breaking down a fragile web of relationships that makes the neighborhood a community.

Inequality in Health Care

Across the United States, approximately 30 million people are covered by Medicaid and another 40 million are uninsured.[20] As recently as 1991, their access to health services was quite limited, primarily because almost no private physicians would treat either group. Their health care options were therefore limited to "safety net" providers: city/county health departments, public hospitals, and federally funded community health centers. Unfortunately, not all urban residents have easy access to these facilities, and those using some types of public facilities receive inferior services; for example, the hallmarks of hospital-based primary care are excessive waiting times (three to four hours) and lack of continuity in care, with most patients never seeing the same physician twice (Ginzberg 1994).

Beginning in about 1994, however, many private physicians began serving Medicaid patients (and, in fact, actively competing for their business).[21] The result has been generally positive for those covered by Medicaid. A 1995 survey of health care consumers in fifteen cities (Knickman et al. 1996) showed that 58 percent of Medicaid patients believed that their ability to get care had increased during the previous three years and 57.6 percent believed that the quality of care they received had improved during that same period.

But the consequences of this shift for the medically indigent have been less happy. For example, most safety net providers use revenue from Medicaid and private insurance to underwrite the costs of providing care to the uninsured (Lipson and Naierman 1996). But with increased competition from the private sector, many public health providers have lost a substantial segment of

20. Overall, 14.7 percent of the population are without medical insurance, and 11.2 percent are covered by Medicaid. Among those living in poverty, the uninsured rate is 28.5 percent and the Medicaid rate is 47.2 percent; among adult males living in poverty, the uninsured rate is over 45 percent, while the Medicaid rate is 23.7 percent.

21. The reasons for this shift are primarily economic in nature and quite complex. Suffice it to say that they center around the uncertainty created by the health care reform legislation initiated by the Clinton administration and defeated by Congress in 1994 and by movement in the states toward a capitated managed-care system for Medicaid patients.

their Medicaid patients. This has led many city/county health departments to abandon their primary care programs altogether and return to their traditional public health mission (e.g., protecting environmental health, monitoring infectious disease, and health promotion). Public hospitals have also felt the pinch of declining Medicaid patients, and they have responded by buying established primary care clinics or by setting up Health Maintenance Organizations (Lipson and Naierman 1996). Both of these strategies are intended to attract insured (including Medicaid) patients, but both divert resources that had previously been used to serve the uninsured. Community health centers have also responded by reorganizing their services to make them more attractive to insured clients, but in doing so, they too have lost some of their capacity to serve the uninsured.

In addition to these changes, several factors threaten the future access of the uninsured to medical services. First, hospitals that had voluntarily admitted uninsured patients to their emergency rooms are finding that the cost of doing so is prohibitive. In Chicago alone, eleven voluntary hospitals located in the inner city have closed in recent years because of the financial burden imposed by uncompensated patient care (Ginzberg 1994). Second, fewer and fewer physicians are even practicing in low-income neighborhoods; physician-to-population ratios in inner-city neighborhoods are worse than 1:10,000, compared with ratios of 1:300 in the more affluent suburbs. To further complicate the situation, many of the physicians serving poor neighborhoods are graduates of foreign medical schools who have limited professional competence and who lack the language skills to enable them to communicate effectively with their patients (Ginzberg 1994).[22] Third, and perhaps most important, governmental support for safety net providers has declined over time. The most obvious source of concern is public hospitals, which are typically funded by municipal or county governments. Given the fiscal vulnerability of most large cities, public hospitals face a constant threat of budgetary cutbacks (and in some cases, closure). Less dramatic, but no less important, federal funding for community health centers has been steadily eroded by inflation. In both cases, sound financial management demands that non-revenue-producing services (including free care for the uninsured) be carefully considered for elimination. All of these factors are no doubt reflected in responses to the 1995 survey of health consumers cited earlier. Whereas 37 percent of uninsured respondents felt that their access to health services had increased during the previous three years, 43 percent felt that it had gotten worse.

---

22. The situation apparently has not changed much since the 1960s, when inner-city Chicago neighborhoods had only 10 percent of the physicians they needed and most of those lacked the credentials to admit patients to hospitals (De Vise 1973).

Geographical Disparities in the Distribution of Urban Services within Cities

The Shaw Decision

In 1971, the U.S. Fifth Circuit Court decided *Hawkins v. Town of Shaw*,[23] concluding that Shaw, Mississippi, was engaged in a racially motivated denial of equal rights in its provision of street, water, and sewer services to its residents. The statistics clearly demonstrate the disparity in service provision to whites and blacks (Merget and Wolff 1976). For example,

- 56 percent of the roads in black neighborhoods were unpaved, compared with 3 percent of the roads in white neighborhoods;
- 19 percent of black homes were not served by sanitary sewer lines, compared with 1 percent of white homes;
- 51 percent of white homes were located on roads served by storm sewers, compared with no black homes;
- 98 percent of the homes located on unpaved roads were occupied by blacks;
- most fire hydrants and traffic signals were located in white residential areas.

The *Shaw* decision was touted as a landmark case,[24] serving notice to municipal governments that the delivery of sharply different quantities or qualities of services to black and white neighborhoods would not be tolerated under the equal protection clause of the Fourteenth Amendment. However, it largely failed to live up to expectations (Lineberry 1984).

Tests of the Underclass Hypothesis

Lineberry (1984, 189) attributes this failure, in part, to the inherent lack of precedent in the *Shaw* case. The blatant inequality in Shaw was "more reminiscent of the Jim Crow era than representative of the intricate, subtle, and dif-

23. 437 F.2d 1286.
24. Several other cases, decided during the same time period, set similar precedents for the equal distribution of urban services (e.g., *Hadnott v. City of Pratville*, 309 FSupp 967, 1970; *Farmworkers of Florida Housing Project Inc. v. City of Delray Beach*, 493 F2d 799, 1974). However, some cities decided to discontinue the services rather than provide them on an equitable basis. For example, in 1962 Jackson, Mississippi, operated five swimming pools, four designated for whites and one for blacks. Rather than comply with a desegregation order, however, it chose to close four of the pools and revert the lease of the other to the YMCA, which operated it for whites only. The U.S. Supreme Court, in *Palmer v. Thompson* (403 US 217, 1971), upheld the constitutionality of that action. See Johnston (1984) for a discussion of these and related cases.

ficult-to-measure patterns of service delivery in a large, complex, urban system." In an effort to test the "underclass hypothesis,"[25] Lineberry (1977) explored these intricate, subtle, and difficult-to-measure patterns in the fire and library services offered by San Antonio. While he found clear variation in the quality and quantity of services received by various neighborhoods across the city, he found no consistent bias against any group or area across services. Lineberry terms this variation "unpatterned inequality." Further, he found that low-income and minority neighborhoods actually receive *better* fire and library services than higher-income and white neighborhoods. And while he urges caution in the interpretation of these results, he also suggests that they cast doubt on the generality of the conditions the court discovered in Shaw.

Like Lineberry, other researchers have studied the allocation of urban services among neighborhoods, with similar findings. Researchers studying the distribution of services relating to libraries (e.g., Martin 1969, Levy et al. 1974, Mladenka and Hill 1977), parks (e.g., Mladenka and Hill 1977), education (e.g., Baron 1971, Levy et al. 1974), police (e.g., Block 1974, Coulter 1980), streets (Boots et al. 1972), housing inspection (e.g., Nivola 1978), and fire (Coulter 1978) have found overwhelmingly that (a) resources are distributed in a manner that does not discriminate against poor and black neighborhoods; (b) variation in resources allocated to neighborhoods are inevitable, but tend to be unpatterned; and (c) these variations are just as likely (or more likely) to favor poor neighborhoods as rich neighborhoods. Urban administrators, it would seem, bend over backward to guarantee that the allocation of services within the city does not discriminate against low-income neighborhoods.[26]

The Underclass Hypothesis Reconsidered

With this accumulation of evidence, it might seem reasonable to lay the underclass hypothesis to rest and to conclude that Shaw, Mississippi was, indeed, an anomaly. Yet, several factors keep the underclass hypothesis alive. First, even in situations where allocation decisions are based on nondiscriminatory factors, the decisions may have unexpected consequences that bias the delivery of services in an inequitable direction. For example, Frank Levy and his colleagues (1974) found allocation decisions for streets and libraries in Oakland that, on the surface, seem equitable. They found highway funds to be allocated according to patterns of traffic volume, traffic flow, and accident rates, and library resources to be allocated according to circulation rates and other professional norms. But while these criteria may be legitimate guidelines, they may also affect the distri-

25. This hypothesis states that neighborhoods that are poorer, or have large shares of minority residents, or are politically unorganized receive less in services for their tax dollars than advantaged neighborhoods.
26. Several researchers, however, show results that contradict those reported above (e.g., Bolotin and Cingranelli 1983, Koehler and Wrightson 1987).

bution of resources in unintended ways. The criteria for allocating highway funds, coupled with legal requirements for the use of gasoline tax revenue, results in the allocation of funds primarily to freeways and cross-town arterials. These allocation guidelines primarily benefit upper- and middle-class residents of the city's outlying neighborhoods and suburbs. And while the criteria for allocating library resources primarily benefit the central library (which, in turn, benefits poor central-area neighborhoods as well as upper- and middle-class professionals employed in the downtown area), they also disproportionately benefit branch libraries located in more affluent neighborhoods.

This pattern of allocations raises an important equity question. Seldom should we expect to find a case where the delivery of services discriminates so clearly as in Shaw, Mississippi, and therefore we should not be surprised that the *Shaw* precedent has not controlled other cases. Yet, what would on the surface seem to be rational and equitable criteria for allocating resources may create subtle but important biases in the delivery of services. For example, would a municipal decision to concentrate books in branch libraries serving the better-educated (and more affluent) parts of town constitute discrimination? Or would a decision to locate the newest fire equipment in a station serving the most valuable houses (which would represent the greatest actuarial loss were they to burn) violate the equal protection clause of the Fourteenth Amendment? Or would a decision to locate golf courses on the outskirts of the city, where land values (and the cost of construction) are considerably lower, be inappropriate? Certainly, a strong case could be made for an affirmative answer to all three questions.

But consider Bryan Jones' (1980) study of services in Detroit: While he found little class bias in the *allocation of service resources* across neighborhoods, he found that *outcomes* of services tend to favor more affluent and white outlying neighborhoods over inner-city black neighborhoods. For instance, predominantly black, inner-city neighborhoods experience less satisfactory services related to environmental enforcement (e.g., control of litter, weeds, rodents, and so forth), garbage collection, and building inspection and code enforcement than more affluent neighborhoods on the city's periphery. Yet, in no case is this discrepancy due to an inequitable distribution of resources among these neighborhoods; in fact, the inner-city neighborhoods often received greater per-capita allocations than the outlying neighborhoods. Rather, discrepancies result from two other causes. First, inner-city neighborhoods have different and more complex needs than outer neighborhoods. For example, agencies enforcing building codes are less likely to obtain compliance with their citations in inner-city neighborhoods because absentee landlords, who own much of the housing, are more difficult to locate and more willing to abandon their buildings rather than pay for costly repairs.

Second, service providers often engage in discriminatory practices. For example, more uncollected garbage accumulates in inner-city neighborhoods than in outlying neighborhoods. The most likely explanation is that the supervision of garbage collection crews in black neighborhoods is more lax than in white neighborhoods. Thus, by asking a different question of his data, Jones draws different conclusions than his counterparts studying other cities. That question, for the most part, turns on the issue of need.

Distribution of Services on the Basis of Need

Richard Rich (1982) argues that the locational service-delivery question (i.e., *where* are services to be allocated?) should be preceded by a more important question: *Which* services are to be provided? By concentrating on the former rather than the latter question, researchers may bias their conclusions about equity, much in the way that Jones demonstrates in his study of Detroit. Rich argues that most urban expenditures are tied to distributional policies, directed at services that yield roughly equal benefits across all social classes, including public safety, education, roads, parks, and garbage collection. Yet, such expenditures, he concludes, serve to perpetuate the current distribution of wealth in the community. Only through redistributional policies, aimed at concentrating services in those areas where they are most needed, can the current distribution of wealth and opportunity—the cycle of poverty—be disrupted.[27]

If we examine the distribution of services according to this need-based standard of equity, we come to conclusions different from those reached by researchers employing an equal-distribution standard of equity. In a study of the distribution of four services (police protection, parks and recreation, public education, and garbage collection) relative to need in fifteen major cities, Doh Shin (1982) found strong evidence of inequity. His results show that in all fifteen cities, all-white and mostly white neighborhoods receive the most favorable police protection relative to need, while all-black and mostly black neighborhoods fare least well. He obtained similar results for other services. In a complementary finding, Terrence Jones (1982) shows that in St. Louis, transition neighborhoods whose populations are rapidly changing from white to black receive the least favorable services, while those that remain white (or that change slowly) receive the most favorable services.

Other Examples of Geographical Inequity

Other examples of inequity—relative to need—are readily identified, although we will consider them here in a cursory manner. The high crime rate and the high incidence of fires in inner-city neighborhoods, for instance, may suggest that the equal allocation of resources throughout the city is inadequate; to

27. This represents yet another manifestation of the different ideological perspectives that largely shape urban policy.

437

achieve equitable outcomes, *substantially* higher allocations of public safety resources may be required for the inner city. The lack of yards for most families living in the inner city suggests that more playgrounds would, at best, merely equalize the recreational opportunity for inner-city youths. And while enormous funds are spent to build and repair streets, equity in transportation can be achieved only by improving the city's public transit capability—since the poor have fewer cars than the middle class.

It is unlikely that cities will reverse these trends in the near future, for services that exclusively (or even disproportionately) benefit the poor are politically unpopular. After all, it was popular sentiment against public assistance programs that fueled support for Proposition 13 in California and similar tax revolts across the country. In short, services that provide equal benefits to all (even if the benefits they provide are "more equal" in richer neighborhoods) are popular with the middle and upper classes, while those aimed at redistributing wealth generate controversy.

With the notable exception of education, the courts have been concerned more with equity in the distribution of services than with equality in the achievement of outcomes. For example, in *Beal v. Lindsay*,[28] blacks and Puerto Ricans argued that parks in the Bronx were not maintained at a level commensurate with parks in predominantly white neighborhoods. While city officials did not dispute this point, they countered that the discrepancy was due to vandalism rather than neglect. The court sided with the city, finding that the city had met its obligations by providing equal levels of services, even though equal outcomes were not attained (Johnston 1984).

Intercity Disparities in the Delivery of Urban Services

Earlier in this chapter, we saw the potential impact school busing can have on white flight from the central cities. Whether this is cause and effect, or whether it is simply coincident with the great suburban migration can, for present purposes, be set aside. What is important is that central cities are losing a substantial portion of their tax base to the suburbs. This, in turn, puts fiscal pressure on cities to raise taxes, cut services, or both—which, in turn, can lead to even greater flight to the suburbs (Hill et al. 1995). Unfortunately, those who are least able to join the suburban migration (i.e., those residing in underclass neighborhoods) are also likely to be in greatest need of services and least able to pay for them. The potential for bias in the availability and cost of services is obvious.

We need not look far to find the first vestiges of bias in the differential taxation and expenditure rates among cities within the metropolitan patchwork. Over the past twenty years, suburban residents have fared better than

28. 468 F.2d 287, 1972.

their central city neighbors in the delivery of services and the price they pay for those services. Not surprisingly, income is higher in the suburbs. In 1987, the per capita income among residents in a typical large central city was only 85.9 percent of the per capita income among people living in its suburbs (Dearborn et al. 1992). This represents an absolute per capita discrepancy of nearly $2,000. Consider one example, shown in table 16.2. The city of Baltimore has a median family income equal to $28,217; however, three suburban counties around Baltimore have median family income equal to $44,505 (Baltimore County), $61,088 (Howard County), and $61,988 (Montgomery County). We should not find this discrepancy surprising, given the earlier discussion of the demography of poverty, but it does have important implications for the delivery of services.

First, the lower income in the central city is an indicator of greater need for services. For example, the greater prevalence of crime and fires in the central city suggests a greater need for public safety services, and the greater population density suggests a greater need for parks and recreation services. The greater prevalence of poverty suggests a greater need for health and human services, for publicly funded day-care facilities, and for public housing. And lower levels of educational achievement in the central cities, coupled with higher drop-out rates, suggests a greater need for compensatory and alternative educational services. These are all reflected in the statistics for Baltimore and its surrounding counties reported in table 16.2; substantial disparities exist between Baltimore and its suburbs in teen pregnancy, drop-out, educational attainment, unemployment, and crime rates.[29] Further, a number of central cities partially support municipal colleges and technical schools that service the entire metropolitan area. In addition, central cities are typically older than the suburbs, and hence their physical infrastructure (roads, bridges, sewers) is more likely to demand costly repair. Finally, as the hub of the metropolitan area, the central city often provides a repertoire of municipally supported cultural attractions (e.g., civic operas and symphonies; zoos; museums; repertory theaters) that service the entire metropolitan area.

Taken together, these factors place a substantially higher demand on the budgets of the central cities than on their suburban neighbors[30]; in the past,

29. These comparisons are possible because the city of Baltimore is not within any county jurisdiction; thus, all of Baltimore, Howard, and Montgomery Counties are truly suburban areas (although technically Montgomery County is not a suburb of Baltimore but rather of Washington, D.C.) Many of the statistics in table 16.2 were compiled by Imbroscio et al. (1995), who considered only these three counties. Other counties within the Baltimore MSA include Anne Arundel County, Carroll County, Harford County, and Queen Anne County. Per capita income in these counties ranges between $16,300 and $18,509, making them more similar to Baltimore County than to either Howard County or Montgomery County.

30. Neenan (1972) reports that during the late 1960s, Detroit residents subsidized their suburban neighbors at a rate of $80 per capita each year, with 6.5 percent of the entire city budget used to provide services to suburban "free riders."

Table 16.2 Disparity in Income, Expenditures, and Need in Metropolitan Baltimore

	Baltimore City	Balitmore County	Howard County	Montgomery County
Population	736,014	692,134	187,328	757,027
Median family income	$28,217	$44,502	$61,088	$61,988
Per capita income	$11,994	$18,658	$22,704	$25,591
Per capita taxes	902	$764	$904	$1,152
Tax burden	7.5%	4.1%	4.0%	4.5%
Per capita general expenditure	$1,751	$1,573	$1,813	$2,016
per capita expenditure for police protection	$209	$105	$94	$107
per capita expenditure for fire protection	$113	$66	$70	$80
per capita general expenditure for parks	$66	$25	$55	$106
per capita general expenditure for libraries	$20	$37	$33	$26
per capita general expenditure for education	$730	$889	$1,274	$1,155
per pupil educational expenditure	$4,947	$6,220	$6,695	$7,591
Instructional staff per 1,000 students	57.4	64.9	64	62.8
Families living in poverty	17.8%	3.8%	2.2%	2.7%
Children in poverty	31.3%	6.6%	3.5%	4.9%
Birthrate (girls under 15)	5.3	0.1	0.6	0.8
Birthrate (girls 15–17)	96.8	19.8	11.8	14.8
Crime rate (per 100,000 people)	11,371	6,650	4,757	4,517
Annual high school dropout rate	7.0%	3.1%	1.4%	1.8%
Adults with college degrees	15.5%	25.0%	46.9%	49.9%
Unemployment rate	9.4%	5.7%	4.1%	3.3%

SOURCE: Imbroscio et al. (1995); U.S. Department of Commerce, *County-City Data Book* (1994); U.S. Department of Commerce, *City Government Finances: 1991–92*; U.S. Department of Commerce, *County Government Finances: 1991–92*.

central cities spent more per capita than their suburbs on services (ACIR 1984). But over the past two decades, the tax base of many central cities has eroded, reducing their ability to fund needed services (Ladd 1994; see Dearborn et al., 1992, for a city-by-city analysis of fiscal strain). In contrast, the economic health of the suburbs is better than ever, and today their per capita expenditures generally exceed those of the central cities—despite the greater need for services in the central cities. Data from Baltimore and its surrounding counties (table 16.2) demonstrates the disparity in expenditures, particularly in education. Despite this disparity in expenditures, residents of central cities pay a higher percentage of the income in municipal taxes than their suburban counterparts. For example, the tax burden for residents of Baltimore stands at 7.5 percent, compared with around 4 percent in the surrounding counties (table 16.2).[31]

To restate the argument, residents of central cities must tax themselves at a higher rate than suburban residents simply to generate the same revenue level and at a *substantially higher rate* to generate sufficient revenue to address

31. In 1981, the national disparity in tax burden was lower, with central city residents paying 6.8 percent of their income in taxes and suburban residents paying 4.8 percent (ACIR 1984).

their special needs. Yet, given the discrepancy in income, even a comparable tax burden would be regressive, and the higher tax burden in the central city is severely regressive. This creates a paradox that is partially responsible for the white (and affluent) flight to the suburbs. The higher the tax burden within the central cities, the more likely the middle and upper classes are to vote with their feet, packing up and moving to the suburbs; but the more the tax base erodes through such flight, the greater the tax burden becomes on those who remain.

Except in cases of metropolitan consolidation, there have been few attempts to equalize spending patterns between central cities and suburbs. But there have been such attempts in education, and they have met with mixed success. Although the role of the federal government and the states in funding local education has increased since 1960,[32] the principal criterion in allocation decisions has not always been need; in fact, during the 1970s, suburban school districts actually received *more* aid per capita than did central city school districts. Not until 1981 did per capita aid to the central cities and the suburbs equalize. The issue of equalization has been contested in the courts with mixed results. One case grew out of the disparity between the Edgewood School District, located in San Antonio's inner city and the Alamo Heights School District, located in one of its suburbs. In 1971, Edgewood spent $356 per pupil ($26 from local taxes, $222 from state funds, and $108 from federal funds), compared with $594 per pupil in Alamo Heights ($333 from local taxes, $225 from state funds, and $36 from federal funds), even though Edgewood citizens were taxed at a much higher rate than their Alamo Heights counterparts. This disparity became the basis for a suit claiming that the Texas school system discriminates against the poor. However, the U.S. Supreme Court ruled that Texas policy did not violate the equal protection clause of the Fourteenth Amendment.[33] Although states are not allowed to provide fewer funds to poor school districts than to wealthy districts, they are not required to compensate for district wealth by providing more funds to the poorer districts (Johnston 1984). However, the California Supreme Court ruled that financing local education with local property taxes was inherently inequitable and that the state must develop a more equitable funding scheme.[34] State courts in ten other states (including Kentucky, Alabama, Tennessee, New Jersey, and Massachusetts) have issued similar rulings during the 1980s and the 1990s, requiring that state distribution of funds acknowledge the disparity in wealth among individual school districts (Underwood 1995; see also Morgan et al., 1995, for a detailed analysis of the Alabama case).

32. The federal share of local education budgets grew from 4.4 percent in 1960 to 5.9 percent in 1991, while the state share grew from 35.2 percent to 47.3 percent during this same period.
33. *San Antonio Independent School District v. Rodriguez* (411 US 1, 1973).
34. *Serrano v. Priest* (557 P2d 929, 1977).

But state courts in six other states (including Kansas, Wisconsin, Minnesota, and Virginia) have turned down equity finance cases.

Put differently, equalization through state aid means different things in different states, and accordingly, wide variation exists in the distribution of state educational funds to suburbs and central cities across metropolitan areas. As of 1981, educational aid to central cities in most northeastern and midwestern metropolitan areas exceeded that to suburbs, sometimes by a considerable amount. In the South and the West, however, the trend was reversed, with aid to the suburbs often exceeding that to the central cities. Although this regional variation can be explained at least partially by differences in central city need (i.e., central cities in the South and West are wealthier in comparison to their suburbs than those in the Northeast and Midwest), part of the explanation may also be attributed to regional differences in the perceived role of the central city in the metropolitan area. In the Northeast and Midwest, for example, central cities are held in high esteem as the cultural, professional, financial, and commercial center of the metropolis, with the suburbs serving largely as "bedroom communities." Money invested in the central city for education as well as other services represents a commitment to the quality of life for the entire metropolis. In the South and West, however, suburbs have largely taken over the professional and commercial functions of the metropolis, thus reducing the commitment to preserving the central city for its own sake.

Poverty and Urban Policies

Issues of equity and fairness in urban service delivery once again turn us back to a consideration of poverty in the cities. And from there, it is only a short step to the topic that awaits us next: What are cities doing to meet the challenges and problems that presently confront them?

From the Shelton, West, chloride print, 1931, 24.2 x 18.9 cm
Alfred Stieglitz Collection, 1949.784.
Photograph © 1996, The Art Institute of Chicago. All Rights Reserved.

If we would lay a new foundation for urban life, we must understand the historic nature of the city, and distinguish between its
original functions, those that have emerged from it, and those that
may still be called forth.

   Lewis Mumford, *The City in History*

CHAPTER 17

Reinventing the City: Policy and Reform as the Century Turns

At a fundamental level, cities are as they always have been—places where people live and work in proximity to one another. But more than this, cities constantly respond to crises and opportunities, partially changing their function and purpose as they do so. The pages of this book are full of examples. In response to corruption in municipal government during the late nineteenth century, many cities reformed themselves to remove politics from city life. In response to growing affluence and demands by their residents for a better life, cities turned to the delivery of services to make themselves better places to live. In response to suburbanization, central cities have attempted to become regional cultural and financial centers.

Today, a new crisis looms on the horizon—the crisis brought on by a changing economy and epitomized by a growing underclass trapped in the central city. For nearly two decades, cities have sensed the early stages of the crisis, hoping that through minor policy adjustments they could weather the storm (and that maybe some new opportunity would either draw attention from the crisis of the underclass or perhaps alleviate the problem altogether). But by the mid 1990s, it was clear that the problems created by a changing economy and a growing underclass were not going to vanish on their own.

Cities will not be undone by this newest crisis; there is too much history of resilience for that to happen. Even so, the city of the twenty-first century will be different from the city of the twentieth century.

In the final chapter, we will consider what the city of tomorrow may be. But before doing so, we explore in this chapter ways that cities have attempted to address the crisis of the underclass, for that will surely provide some hint of what the future may hold for America's urban places. In considering these responses to poverty, the underclass, and the changing American economy, we will do well to remember three things. First, no city has yet initiated the kind of major policy that will allow it to address these problems head-on. While not necessarily easy or painless or inexpensive, the solutions implemented thus far by cities have largely been ones of convenience, reflecting what can be done without too much disruption. But the crisis of the underclass may require the kind of transforming policy that *is* disruptive. Second, cities cannot undertake this kind of transforming policy on their own. The economic changes that have the greatest impact on cities are national (and even international) in scope. Thus, any response initiated by an individual city is unlikely to be effective. What cities can do must be done in conjunction with one another, their states, and the federal government. Third, all policies will have unanticipated consequences. In general, the more sweeping the intended transformation, the more extensive the unintended consequences will be. For example, the urban reform movement, by taking politics out of municipal government, made future change more difficult. And the expansion of municipal services created a municipal bureaucracy that threatens the fiscal well-being of virtually every city.

New Economic Bases for the City

During the late 1960s and the early 1970s, as city leaders realized that manufacturing jobs could not sustain the future employment needs of the urban workforce, they began to explore alternative economic futures for their cities. In most cases, this meant a physical change in the city's landscape, as developers built office towers, convention centers, and sports arenas with city funds. In large part, this massive construction boom was based on speculation and hope. City leaders reasoned that if they put funds into the redevelopment of downtown, business owners, shoppers, conventioneers, tourists, and sports fans would come to the city and use them. Most cities did build; sometimes business owners, shoppers, tourists, and conventioneers came, but sometimes they did not.

The Office Tower Boom

San Francisco's downtown growth is instructive. During the postwar period, growth in San Francisco's downtown area was slow; only 746,000 square feet of new office space was added between 1946 and 1954. By 1959, downtown development had begun to accelerate, with nearly a million and a half square feet added during that year alone. But it was not until 1965 when the thirty-three story Hartford Building was constructed that the skyline began to change. Between 1963 and 1977, approximately 23 million square feet of office space was constructed in the city's central business district (CBD). By 1983, thirty-six office towers had been constructed, more than in any other city during that period except New York City and Chicago (Ford 1994).

The growth in San Francisco was large but not atypical. By 1990, over 11 billion square feet of commercial office space was available in urban areas across the country, a large portion of it built between 1980 and 1990. Municipal leaders did much to encourage this development. Some of the encouragement was merely verbal but much of it was also financial. For example, New York City provided tax abatements to offset the cost of a number of skyscrapers during the 1970s and the 1980s, including $100 million to subsidize construction of Trump Tower and $42 million to AT&T for construction of its new corporate headquarters. Overall, during the period when New York City was in the midst of its fiscal crisis, municipal outlays intended to stimulate private development increased by 72 percent (Frieden and Sagalyn 1989). In another example, Minneapolis spent $334.2 million to assist downtown development projects between 1980 and 1990 (Schwartz 1995).

The trend toward downtown redevelopment that had started in the 1970s was given added impetus by a 1981 change in the federal tax code, which established a fifteen year accelerated depreciation schedule for buildings. This, coupled with relatively high interest rates, created a climate where buildings as tax shelters could be marketed aggressively to investors. The tax code was changed in 1987, however, putting a damper on the construction of new buildings in downtown areas (Feagin and Parker 1990).

Convention Centers, Hotels, and Downtown Shopping Centers

The construction of downtown office buildings was only one response to the void left by a declining industrial base. In addition, cities saw the potential for building a tourist economy, and they promoted the construction of convention centers, downtown hotels, and downtown shopping centers. This growth in tourist-related construction actually outpaced that of commercial office space. In 1970, convention centers in the United States offered a total of 6.7 million square feet of exhibition space, and only fifteen cities could handle a trade show for twenty thousand people. By 1990, convention centers boasted a total of 18 million square feet of exhibition space, and one hundred fifty cities were equipped to handle trade shows for twenty thousand people (Frieden and Sagalyn 1989, Sanders 1992). In almost all cases, construction of new convention centers has been paid for by the public, either through municipal governments or special purpose governments. For example, the $987 million expansion of McCormick Place in Chicago was financed through general obligation bonds, and debt service was paid with proceeds from the state cigarette tax; and New York's convention center was financed through a $375 million bond issue (Frieden and Sagalyn 1989).

Convention centers themselves seldom make a profit on the conventions and trade shows they host. Managers interested in attracting the largest number of conventions possible shave their rental fees to the bare minimum as they try to undercut one another for business. But it is not what the conventioneers do while *in* the convention center that makes them valuable to the city; it is what they do when they leave each evening. The World Congress Center (WCC) in Atlanta provides an example. The WCC, with 2.6 million square feet of exhibition space, attracted 1.3 million visitors in 1991 to sixty large trade shows and conventions (and a number of smaller ones). Overall, this generated $18 million in revenue for the WCC; the payroll for three hundred fifty employees and the enormous utility costs required to heat and cool a facility of that size ate up most of that revenue. But each out-of-town visitor to the WCC spends an average of $214 each day on food, lodging, transportation, and incidentals. This translated into $580 million (new dollars) pumped into the Atlanta economy in 1991 (Nelson 1995).

Conventioneers, as well as other visitors, need a place to stay when they are in town, and the construction of new downtown hotels largely kept pace with the construction of new convention centers. By 1982, hotel construction was adding an average of over fifty-four hundred rooms a year to the downtowns of the largest metropolitan areas, with New York City, Chicago, Washington, New Orleans, and Atlanta each adding more than seven thousand hotel rooms between 1960 and 1982. While these were partially funded through the private sector, cities contributed their share as well. Nearly one-third of the first fifty Urban Development Action Grants awarded in 1978 were for construction of hotels or hotel-convention center complexes, and cities also provided tax abatements to encourage new hotel construction (Frieden and Sagalyn 1989).

Conventioneers and other visitors have a lot of free time when they are not sleeping, attending meetings, and admiring exhibits. And one way they can usefully spend their free time is shopping. Cities have spent considerable time and money developing downtown shopping centers that will be convenient and attractive to visitors (and that may even attract out-of-towners in their own right). Between 1970 and 1988, more than one hundred new downtown retail centers opened; in three-quarters of these projects, cities were co-investors with private investors (the median public investment in these projects was about 33 percent of the total development cost). Approximately 30 percent of these shopping centers are festival or specialty malls, many of them constructed by James Rouse and his associates; the others are either regional shopping malls or mixed-use projects combining retailing with offices, hotels, a convention center, or housing (Frieden and Sagalyn 1989).

Professional Sports

A professional sports team may make a city more attractive as a convention site, or it may simply attract visitors to come to the city to see a ballgame. But neither of these is the primary incentive for investment of public funds to attract a professional sports franchise to a city (or to keep one there). Much more important is the "big league" status that it gives the city and the free advertising that comes with this status. The politics surrounding a city's image can be fierce, and sometimes sports gets enmeshed in these politics. For example, as Los Angeles was attempting to woo the Brooklyn Dodgers to the West Coast in the late 1950s, some of the city's leaders objected to the effort Mayor Norris Poulson was expending on the project; his response was to chide the naysayers for wanting to keep Los Angeles a "bush league city" (Baim 1994).

The cost of becoming, or remaining, a major league city can be substantial. Since 1988, Chicago, St. Petersburg, Baltimore, Arlington, Philadelphia, Atlanta, Cleveland, and Jacksonville have constructed or renovated sports facilities at a cost of over a billion dollars in public funds (Rosentraub et al. 1994). In some cases, these were intended to keep existing teams in the city; in other cases, they were built to attract a sports franchise to the city. For example, Chicago built its new Comiskey Park (at a cost of $185 million in public funds) to keep the White Sox from moving to Florida. And St. Petersburg built a domed stadium at a cost of $234 million in the hope that professional sports teams would choose to locate there (Watson 1995).

Professional sports teams are not the only drawing card for cities promoting tourism. Amateur sports have also become an important part of economic development for some cities. Between 1974 and 1992, for example, Indianapolis embarked on a $2.76 billion downtown construction program, with amateur sports as a central component. By 1989, seven national organizations and two international organizations had moved their governing offices to Indianapolis. Even though less than 10 percent of the total capital construction expenditure was dedicated to sports facilities, they have become an integral part of the downtown and its economy (Rosentraub et al. 1994).

Downtown Development: A Critical Assessment

To what extent have recent downtown development efforts changed the character of American cities, and how successful have they been in counteracting the negative effects of deindustrialization and the growth of the underclass? It will serve us best to consider these two questions together.

449

Building buildings is what cities have always done, and for the most part, done well. But in the past, city government has not often built these buildings; rather, it has been the private sector that has invested in the city and in itself through the construction of hotels and office buildings (although since World War II, construction of most stadiums and sports arenas has been underwritten by city government). Critics question the use of public funds to subsidize the profits of business at a time when municipal employees are being laid off, neighborhoods are crumbling, and services are being scaled back. Of course, the other side of the argument is that, without these subsidies, the businesses will simply go elsewhere (to other parts of the country, to suburbs and edge cities), leaving the city worse off than ever.[1] But we would do well to consider how publicly supported downtown development may affect the city and its residents.

For the most part, the types of recent downtown growth that cities have supported are aimed at visitors from out of town rather than at their own residents. Consider the construction of office towers, which provide employment primarily for skilled, white-collar workers. In many cities, however, these were the first migrants to the suburbs, and the suburbs continue to draw young urban professionals away from the central cities. Convention centers cater primarily to out-of-town visitors; in fact, they lose money on local residents who eat and sleep in their own homes. Hotels have little use for local residents. In other words, with the exception of sports arenas and stadiums, most of the publicly funded or subsidized downtown development is aimed not at the people who live in the central cities but at people who live on the urban fringe or who are visiting from somewhere else.

Downtown development often has encroached on and sometimes has destroyed underclass neighborhoods. In Atlanta, for example, WCC was constructed in Vine City, an historically black neighborhood, creating considerable disruption in the neighborhood and displacing many of its residents. We typically associate this type of dislocation with urban renewal

---

1. How is it that private businesses and corporations can extract such public subsidies merely by threatening to move? In the wake of the great economic restructuring of the 1970s, cities are literally fighting for their survival in the face of a declining tax base, and they are willing to pay a premium to keep current businesses in town and to attract new ones. Once this pattern is established, virtually no business is immune from the temptation of exploiting it and virtually no city is immune to its perverse impact. In the absence of a national urban policy, which might regulate intercity movement of business and industry through targeted tax policy, cities and states cannot avoid the bidding wars that they have been forced to participate in. An example of this powerlessness occurred at the National Governors Conference in 1993. Illinois Governor Jim Edgar sponsored a resolution to eliminate use of incentives by states to attract new businesses, but it failed to obtain sufficient support to pass. The best the conference was able to pass was a watered-down resolution stating, "States will always be in competition with each other for business investments. However, this competition should not be characterized by how much direct assistance a state can provide to individual companies" (Watson 1995, 59). A weak resolution lacking any binding enforcement is unlikely to stem the tide of competitive bidding.

from a bygone era, but it continues to occur in modern day downtown development.

In the best of situations, businesses and sports franchises will move to the city and fill the new office buildings and stadiums; tourists and other visitors will not be far behind, filling the hotels and convention centers, eating at restaurants, and spending money at retail shopping centers. For obvious reasons, this scenario will generate taxes for the city. It will also generate jobs. But how successful has downtown development actually been? Unfortunately, many downtowns were overbuilt, and there were not enough businesses to fill them. For example, Minneapolis had a 20 percent vacancy rate in its downtown commercial property in 1992 (although by 1994 it had declined to 12 percent), and the value of downtown commercial property has declined by 25 percent since its 1989 peak (Schwartz 1995). In 1992, vacancy rates for commercial property in the nation's fifty-six largest cities stood at 25 percent (Mohl 1993a). Even when jobs are created for the city's residents, they tend to be low-paying service sector jobs, for example, maids in hotels, wait persons in restaurants, janitors in office buildings, and sales persons in retail shopping centers. These jobs, for the most part, cannot lift people out of the underclass, so they do little to address the underclass problem.

Perhaps the biggest benefit, though, is symbolic. For at least thirty years (perhaps since the urban riots of the 1960s), cities have had a terrible image in the American consciousness. Recall Ira Lowry's glum assessment from 1970, quoted in chapter 15: interracial tension, street gangs, murder and other violence, drug abuse, burned-out buildings, littered streets, rat-infested rubbish. Even the areas where old slums had been cleared by urban renewal often remained in perpetual states of incompletion. For example, Buffalo's Ellicott Project was little more than a vacant lot littered with junked cars, piles of garbage, and rat nests thirteen years after it was initially cleared. St. Louis had its "Hiroshima Flats" and St. Paul its "Superhole" as symbols of unsuccessful urban renewal. Nationally, more than half of the urban renewal projects begun between 1960 and 1964 still had unsold lots a decade later (Frieden and Sagalyn 1989). The city of the 1970s simply was not a place where people wanted to live or even visit, and given the failure of urban renewal to solve the problems of the city, people were skeptical about prospects for turning around the city's misfortunes. So long as the American city was seen in this light, very few people would invest in its future. In short, the city was on a downward spiral toward abandonment. The only way to make a comeback was to change its negative image.

Seen from this perspective, municipal investment in new buildings, festival shopping centers in historic districts, sports stadiums, and convention centers was a public relations triumph that, in a number of cases, turned around negative public perceptions of cities. Cleveland, we hear, has made a comeback (only a quarter century ago, it was the only city in the country whose major waterway had caught fire). Boston is booming, part of the

Massachusetts "Miracle." During halftime of televised football games and between innings of televised baseball games, television viewers are treated to views of the host city from the Goodyear Blimp showing streets that literally have come back from the dead; cities could not buy that type of publicity at any price (although many did pay a substantial price, the price of a new sports stadium). In a sense, the middle class has come to feel new opportunities for "ownership" of the cities that they fled a decade earlier. Bernard Frieden and Lynne Sagalyn (1989, 239) describe this change:

> One of the guiding principles of rebuilding cities through downtown rede-velopment was to re-establish "middle-class control." In San Diego, this meant taking Horton Plaza back from the pornography merchants and the skid row bar keepers. In St. Paul, it meant replacing the rubble of the Superhole with a symbol of progress. Suburbanites who had avoided downtown for years were comfortable with the standard of behavior they found in shopping malls. . . . For middle-class people who were accustomed to suburban shopping, the downtown marketplaces were different enough to be exciting but familiar enough to make them feel comfortable.

Of course, this "transformation" is not so much of the city as it is of public opinion. The ghetto neighborhoods of the city have not gone away; in fact, they are getting bigger, and the drugs and violence in them is getting worse rather than better. Unless something is done to improve the city for the underclass, the problems endemic to the ghetto neighborhoods will continue to fester and will eventually overwhelm the revitalized downtowns of American cities. But cities have bought time, and with time they have bought a new opportunity, albeit at a substantial price. Now the question arises, Will the cities—and the nation—take advantage of this opportunity for true transformation?

Inner-City Economic Development

Enterprise and Empowerment Zones

The downtown development strategy seeks to address the problems of the inner city only indirectly, mostly by providing service jobs to unskilled inner-city residents. But another approach is more direct, using tax policy to stimu-late investment there and promote the economic viability of inner-city neigh-borhoods. Investment means jobs, and if the jobs pay moderate wages, they can allow underclass workers to escape from their poverty. In 1993, Congress passed legislation authorizing approximately $2.5 billion over five years to cre-ate six urban "empowerment zones" and sixty-six urban "enterprise commu-nities." Areas were to be selected by the Department of Housing and Urban Development (HUD) from nominations submitted by state and local governments. The eligibility of sites was determined by their size, poverty, unemployment, and other measures of economic distress and by the level of support committed by public and private sources to the project. Once an area is designated as an enterprise community or an empowerment zone, it receives flexible social service block grant funds, and businesses that conduct their operations there are eligible for a package of tax incentives if at least 35 percent of their employees are residents of the zone (Lehman 1994).

One city where this legislation was successfully implemented is Louisville, which received funding to create an enterprise zone on 2,400 acres of land containing twelve thousand residents, old industrial buildings suitable for rehabilitation, vacant lots, and existing businesses. The city committed $50 million to land clearance, construction, and infrastructure development to make the area more attractive to potential business investment. In addition, it worked with local banks to develop a pool of $30 million for loans to firms that choose to locate in the Enterprise Zone (Bates 1993).

Although the federal government did not pass empowerment zone legislation until 1993, several states had implemented the concept as much as a decade earlier. By the late 1980s, twenty-six states had created more than thirteen hundred free-enterprise zones in 615 cities. A case in point is Georgia's Urban Enterprise Zone Act (passed in 1983). To qualify as an enterprise zone, a census tract must have a median income of $14,800 or less; businesses that locate in enterprise zones receive tax abatements over a twenty-five year period. Five enterprise zones were developed in Atlanta between 1983 and 1985, but they were uneven in terms of the number of jobs they produced (e.g., Atlanta Industrial Park employed 1,913 people in 1991 but Southside Industrial Park employed only 398). Most states did not attempt to promote employment in poverty areas through their legislation. Very few states specify minimum poverty levels for their enterprise zones, and only nine zones meet such minimum poverty levels (Feagin and Parker 1990, Nelson 1995).

Enterprise and Empowerment Zones: A Critical Assessment

In principle, this should be one of the most effective strategies for cities to redevelop themselves, for inner city economic development brings the potential for jobs right into inner-city neighborhoods. And jobs give people the opportunity to escape poverty and their impoverished surroundings. But for the most part, empowerment and enterprise zones have not lived up to expectations (James 1991; see Lehman, 1994, for a review). An early experiment with inner-city development in Cleveland points out the difficulties. In the late 1970s, Cleveland spent more than $1.2 million to assist an inner-city industrial park that promised jobs for hundreds of people living in nearby public housing. Two new firms moved to the industrial park, and two existing plants expanded, all using city funds; but they hired only eight people from the public housing neighborhoods (Frieden and Sagalyn 1989). Other cities have had similar, albeit less dramatic, failures. One reason is that many inner-city residents, particularly those living in ghetto neighborhoods, are not prepared for work. Part of this is due to their lack of vocational skills; but just as big a problem involves job readiness and a sense of self. Chapter 15 described the factors that lead some individuals to homelessness: lack of coping skills, depression and mental illness, and drug or alcohol dependency. These factors are also in evidence in ghetto neighborhoods, and they limit the ability of many residents to obtain and keep jobs. For men living in ghetto neighborhoods the problem runs even deeper. Elijah Anderson (1992) argues that young people growing up in the inner city quickly become invested in the "oppositional culture" of the streets, providing them with a set of skills that are valuable in their day-to-day lives but of little value (indeed, a liability) in the world outside the inner city. Given the choice, it is rational for inner-city youths to develop these street skills, but it places them in poor position to compete for jobs and other resources in the larger society. All of these factors create a situation where there simply may not be a large enough labor force to sustain businesses locating in inner-city neighborhoods.

Second, many residents of ghetto neighborhoods may view businesses locating in their neighborhoods in "imperial" terms: in this view, businesses come in, with large tax subsidies supporting them, to exploit people living in the neighborhood through low-paying and dead-end jobs. While the reality is usually very different, and many companies locating in inner-city neighborhoods do so at least partially through a sense of civic responsibility, they often receive a rude reception when they arrive. It is hard for many businesses to maintain a positive attitude toward and employ the very people who are most critical of them.[2]

Third, empowerment zones are geographical in nature, usually defined by census tracts, but neighborhoods are social units determined by interaction patterns and sense of identity. This potentially creates a mismatch between problem and solution (Lehman 1994). All of this suggests that inner-city economic development efforts should occur within neighborhoods that are also socially viable communities whose residents are able to work together to address neighborhood problems and form partnerships with the businesses that locate there. The difficulty, of course, lies in the fact that most inner-city neighborhoods are not socially viable communities: The social pathologies that characterize ghetto neighborhoods prevent residents from establishing the relationships with and trust for their neighbors that are essential elements of

---

2. An example of this type of hostility appeared during the 1992 Los Angeles riot, when blacks directed much of their frustration at Korean merchants located in the city's South Central area. Resentment toward ethnic store owners in inner-city Detroit is also documented by Chafets (1990).

communities. No one knows exactly how to create a sense of community in ghetto neighborhoods, but several community development programs have been implemented in an effort to do exactly this, and we can learn from these.

Community Development Programs

Although most neighborhood development has attempted to establish the economic viability of inner cities, some has also been directed toward establishing the social viability of inner-city neighborhoods. David Chavis and J.R. Newbrough (1986, 337) define this *community development approach* as "a process that stimulates opportunities for membership, for mutual needs to be met, and for shared emotional ties and support." Robert Halpern (1995) describes one such program, the Dudley Street Neighborhood Initiative (DSNI). In the early 1980s, Boston's Dudley Street neighborhood had a population of twelve thousand people, 90 percent of whom were minorities. It had twenty churches, five parks, three elementary schools and a middle school, a library, and a homeless shelter; nearby was a multiservice center. But it had no major supermarkets, banks, community centers, or recreation facilities. More than 4 million square feet of the neighborhood was vacant property; in addition, many of the buildings and storefronts were abandoned, boarded up, or burned out. The neighborhood had become a dumping ground for illegal waste and abandoned cars. As an indicator of social dysfunction, fifteen hundred residents were on waiting lists for substance abuse programs.

In response to this situation, the Riley Foundation pulled together thirty community agencies to develop a neighborhood revitalization plan. But neighborhood residents rejected the plan, in part because they were not involved in its development. In 1984, the DSNI was formed to come up with a new revitalization plan; it consisted of neighborhood residents, human service agencies, churches, and businesses. In all, it had eighteen hundred members and a budget of $650,000. Between 1985 and 1987, DSNI organized neighborhood residents to tackle discrete problems in the neighborhood: cleaning up vacant lots, towing away abandoned cars, getting rid of illegal waste, getting new street lights and signs, and getting a rail stop to downtown Boston restored.

In 1987, DSNI initiated an inclusive planning process, resulting in a five-year strategic plan for developing the neighborhood. It included objectives for land use, housing, jobs, youth development, community services, safety, and environmental health—all the elements of a traditional community. One objective for the neighborhood was to gain control of vacant land, which was owned by 130 different individuals and corporations (including the City of Boston). In 1990, Boston granted DSNI the authority of eminent domain over thirty acres of privately owned vacant lots, which provided it with the ability to decide how to redevelop that land. In 1992, the Ford Foundation provided DSNI with a $2 million low-interest loan fund to buy vacant land for redevelopment, and construction has begun on a modest number of low-income housing units. In addition, a leadership academy was developed to teach leadership skills to local residents. However, with progress came the inevitable realization that building a socially viable neighborhood is a slow process, and that the initial five-year plan was too optimistic. A longer time frame for developing the neighborhood was therefore established. Peter Medoff, the first executive director of DSNI, stated, "Deep, grounded, real community building takes time. . . . You have to have patience and you have to have faith in the people who live in the neighborhood" (quoted in Halpern 1995, 205).

A second community development program designed to promote the social viability of an inner city is Community Building in Partnership (CBP), created within Baltimore's Sandtown-Winchester neighborhood (Halpern 1995; also see McDougall 1993). Sandtown-Winchester is a seventy-two square block area in west Baltimore with a population of ten thousand. In 1990, unemployment in the neighborhood ran close to 40 percent. Almost half of the adults lacked a high school diploma or a GED. Seventy-nine percent of the housing units were substandard, and 83 percent of all the children lived in poverty in single-parent families. The neighborhood had six hundred vacant structures (some owned by the city) and one hundred vacant lots. Drugs and drug dealing were pervasive, and violence was commonplace. In response to this situation, Kurt Schmoke (Baltimore's new mayor) and James Rouse (the developer and founder of the Enterprise Foundation) began meeting in 1990 to conceptualize ways of turning the neighborhood around. Largely through their initiative, CBP was created that same year. It involved the Enterprise Foundation, Sandtown-Winchester residents, Baltimore United in Leadership Development, the Sandtown-Winchester Improvement Association, and the City of Baltimore in a collaborative effort to develop the neighborhood. CBP's mission is to transform every dysfunctional system in the neighborhood, including housing, education, human services, health care, public safety, and employment. Through CBP, various strategic planning work groups were established; these identified well over one hundred discrete opportunities for action and made over fifty recommendations, including: condemn and acquire vacant housing for redevelopment; develop parks and play areas; improve programs conducted by the neighborhood recreation center; develop a comprehensive land use plan for Sandtown-Winchester to serve as a blueprint for community revitalization efforts; improve street lighting; develop a neighborhood-focused primary health care delivery system; monitor families with high truancy records; improve communication and cooperation between community residents and police; improve accessibility to competitively priced, clean, high quality retail goods and services; and improve residents' access to information about jobs located outside the Sandtown-Winchester area.

In 1992, professionally led task groups were established in four program areas: health and human services, education, physical and economic development, and community building. These groups worked to develop sustainable plans in each area; but in the process, they were committed to involving neighborhood residents in increasingly central roles and using existing resources to finance activities whenever possible. This process resulted in a recommendation to create a new local institution, Community Building in Partnership, Inc., to provide an organizational base for the Sandhill-Winchester initiative.

In addition to DSNI and CBP, several other important community development initiatives exist. Former President Jimmy Carter started the Atlanta Project, designed to promote both the social and the economic viability of inner-city neighborhoods in that city. And in the South Bronx, the Surdna Corporation (in conjunction with nine other major funders) put $5 million into six community development corporations, enabling them to develop strategic plans for addressing the social and economic issues in their neighborhoods (Peirce 1993). At least in physical terms, this strategy seems to be paying off, with eighteen thousand apartments in abandoned or vacant buildings rehabilitated (or in the process of rehabilitation) during the past decade (Halpern 1995). Jimmy Carter has had his hand in some of this development as well, personally wielding a hammer or a saw to help in the rehabilitation efforts. His well-publicized visit to the South Bronx early in his presidency produced few concrete results, but his largely unpublicized visits since 1980 have helped work wonders.

Community Development: A Critical Assessment

The programs to promote socially viable inner-city neighborhoods have several commonalities, and they allow several conclusions about this approach to community development. First, this is a long-term process. As the Dudley Street neighborhood discovered, five years was not nearly long enough to accomplish even some of its more modest objectives. Inner cities, and especially ghetto neighborhoods, evolved through decades of neglect; it is unlikely that solutions, particularly long-term solutions, will be achieved quickly. Second, the initial focus of all of these programs is on achieving social integration of the neighborhood through cleaning up vacant lots, rehabilitating vacant buildings, getting street lights, developing recreational programs for youths, developing parks and playgrounds, and establishing retail shopping. Jobs will come later. Sponsoring institutions realize that without social integration of the neighborhood, many residents will be unemployable even if there were jobs. Further, the best way to attract jobs is to transform the social structure of the neighborhood. Third, none of this was initiated by the neighborhood. For exactly the same reason that many residents of ghetto neighborhoods are unable to find or maintain jobs, they also lack the skills and resources to initiate a long-term project to change the character of their neighborhood. These social development projects are seldom initiated by business, which must be concerned about short-term profit and loss. A five-year or ten-year investment in the social viability of a neighborhood is usually beyond the capacity of most businesses. Rather, these programs are usually initiated by either government or a private foundation—or, as in the case of Baltimore, the two working together.[3] Finally, the cost of social development in a ghetto neighborhood is high. Just to achieve the goals of social integration of the neighborhood is likely to require over $1 million a year,[4] and the bricks and mortar projects will require substantially more than that.

Ultimately, efforts to develop neighborhoods as socially viable and economically viable entities must go hand in glove; just as surely, they must be sequenced. Without a social transformation of the neighborhood, residents are largely unable to support employers who might choose to locate there. But with appropriate social development efforts, these neighborhoods can turn themselves into communities, with residents feeling a sense of pride and providing mutual support for one another.

These socially viable communities are good environments for businesses. Jobs are a necessary component of community development. Without jobs, there can be no sense of a future; and without that, there can be no community. Thus, the creation of empowerment zones may be a step ahead of itself in that appropriate and necessary social development has not yet taken place in most neighborhoods designated as empowerment zones. Unfortunately, failures will be interpreted as black marks against inner cities, yet another indication that little can be done to turn them around.

Housing and Homelessness

The homeless have become a source of embarrassment for American cities attempting to change their image and attract tourists, shoppers, conventioneers, and business persons to their downtown areas. Virtually all downtown

3. Local governments have a hard time getting involved in community development projects for the same reason as businesses: the time it takes to transform a neighborhood is simply too long. Local elections usually run in four-year cycles, which means that a mayor who invests considerable public funds in community development of a ghetto neighborhood needs to demonstrate tangible results in a short time; a ten-year timetable for turning around an inner-city neighborhood (which perhaps is even too short) is unlikely to be countenanced by a mayor except under unusual circumstances.

4. For a neighborhood of ten thousand people, a staff of thirty may well be necessary to implement the labor intensive programs required for effective social development; these include, but are not limited to, recreation programs, parenting programs, health screening programs, drug and alcohol prevention programs, violence prevention programs, and compensatory educational programs to provide school-aged children with the life skills to keep the neighborhood from deteriorating during the coming years.

visitors are bombarded by requests for spare change from homeless people; for cities that promote new, revitalized downtowns as "fun places," these constant reminders that the city is also a place of poverty are unwelcome and annoying. Different cities have attempted to deal with the problem of homelessness in different ways; some have been effective, some have not.

Dealing with Homelessness

Regulating the homeless. Unlike other manifestations of poverty in the city, homelessness cannot be contained geographically. For that reason, it cannot be hidden from downtown visitors; it is there, in their faces. In the past, cities attempted to legislate against homelessness by passing vagrancy laws. These were found to be unconstitutional. In the 1980s, a number of cities routinely conducted street sweeps, rousting homeless people and sending them on their way—but to where? The most popular choices were to jail, to shelters, or to somewhere else (preferably far out of town). A federal court ruled on the unconstitutionality of these activities in 1992.[5] Despite this ruling, however, many cities continue to evict homeless people from public property (e.g., under bridges) when the political pressure from merchants and residents grows too strong, and some find ways to informally encourage homeless people to make their way to other cities (Stoner 1995).[6]

Services for the homeless. Most cities (including those that routinely roust homeless people from public areas) have struggled to develop programs that address the needs of a population that is difficult to serve (this difficulty derives from their dependence on alcohol and/or drugs and their inability to function well within a highly structured environment). Thus, programs that require homeless participants to be alcohol and drug free (e.g., most shelters) are likely to be unwelcome for and unwelcoming of many homeless people. Even those homeless who are drug and alcohol free may be unable to cope with the highly regimented rules invoked by most programs for homeless people (e.g., shelters require that everyone eat dinner at 7:00 P.M., lights off at 9:00 P.M., and so on). Of course, without rules, chaos would rule; but because of the highly structured rules most programs invoke, many homeless people simply do without service. They choose instead to sleep on the streets, dumpster dive or panhandle to get money for food (and sometimes alcohol or drugs), and do the best they can with what they have. Herein lies the inher-

5. *Pottinger v. City of Miami*, 810 F Supp. 1551, 1559, S.D. Fla 1992.
6. A recent example of this type of response occurred in Birmingham, Alabama, as it prepared to host the soccer competition of the 1996 Olympic Games. During April and May 1996, over fifty homeless people received free transportation and a cash incentive to move from Birmingham to Huntsville, where they were expected to stay until after the Olympics (*Huntsville Times*, May 8, 1996).

459

ent tension between most cities and many homeless people. On the one hand, cities (and charitable organizations within the cities) provide funding to shelters, soup kitchens, clothes closets, counseling centers, drug and alcohol programs, and other services—all developed to make the lives of homeless persons easier. When homeless people ignore these opportunities in favor of panhandling, sleeping on the streets, and conspicuously pawing through garbage to find food, the public tends to be outraged and demand punitive policies. On the other hand, many chronically homeless people view services as wholly misguided and aimed more to help relieve the guilt of the providers than to meet the needs of the recipients. Many are especially cynical about religious programs, where the price of a meal or a cot is attendance at worship service. Most are contemptuous of drug and alcohol treatment programs that provide housing during the program but then return the homeless person to the streets to fend for himself. For the typical homeless person, sobriety lasts only a short time. Finally, for long-term alcoholics, crack addicts, and some other people, detoxification is a painful and dangerous business, and it is not surprising that they do not jump at the chance to get clean. Thus, for many chronically homeless people, existing services simply do not meet their needs. Although they would probably not have chosen a life on the streets, staying there seems better than the alternatives. And they are offended by what they view as attempts to harass them into accepting services that they believe will not work for them.[7]

A solution advanced by some involves coexistence, either by providing "safe zones" where homeless people can stay without fear of harassment or by attempting to regulate aggressive panhandling and otherwise letting homeless people stay wherever they want. One almost universal thorn in the side of this strategy, however, is what to do about sanitation. Everyone—homeless people included—must answer nature's call; when there are no toilets readily available, homeless people have learned to make do with whatever facilities they can find (alleys, bushes). For obvious reasons, this is offensive to the public, and ultimately it poses a health hazard. But many find the alternative—public toilets that remain open all night—morally offensive. San Diego took the bold action of opening a public restroom in its downtown area, but at a substantial cost. A decade of controversy ensued, which "consumed some of that city's

---

7. One of the miscalculations of homeless advocates over the years has been to downplay the prevalence of alcohol and drug use and mental illness among homeless people. Their rationale was that if homelessness were portrayed strictly as an economic condition (e.g., the typical American is two paychecks away from the streets), homelessness would be viewed in a sympathetic light by the general public. However, this strategy has largely backfired, for the, public has come to view the chronic homeless—particularly those who use drugs and alcohol—as aberrant and personally responsible for their homelessness. In fact, many have come to believe that homelessness is simply a lifestyle choice for these people, but one that impinges on the rest of society. For a discussion, see Baum and Burnes (1993).

leading brains" (Coates 1990, 206). Other cities concluded that the fight was simply not worth the effort and abandoned campaigns to open public restrooms in areas where homeless people congregate. But that decision complicates the possibility of peaceful coexistence between the homeless, merchants, and the general public.

Peaceful coexistence with the homeless. One city that has been at least partially successful in fostering an atmosphere of peaceful coexistence is Seattle. Bill Speidel, a Seattle entrepreneur, stated: "We're not Newport, Rhode Island; we're an old gold rush town and the original skid row. If we didn't have the bums around, we would have to hire them from central casting" (quoted in Ford 1994, 79). This attitude is reflected in three of Seattle's most popular areas: the Pike Place Market, the Seattle Center, and Pioneer Square. The Pike Place Market has traditionally been a place where farmers sold their produce; over time, it has also become a major tourist attraction for the city, with more than 7 million people visiting each year. But despite the potential the market holds as a retail center, its managers have resisted the temptation to develop it as such; rather, they have attempted to attract low-income people, for example through their decision to sponsor three hundred subsidized apartments located within the market. In addition, they lease space to used clothing stores, pawnshops, and other economy retailers (Frieden and Sagalyn 1989). Thus, the Pike Place Market welcomes all residents of and visitors to Seattle, regardless of their social or economic status. The Seattle Center and Pioneer Square have developed similar reputations (Warren 1994, Frieden and Sagalyn 1989).

The acceptance of the homeless in places like the Pike Place Market, the Seattle Center, and Pioneer Square is perhaps most responsible for the national recognition that Seattle has received for its homeless programs. But even given this attitude of accommodation, the tension between the homeless, merchants, and the general public is strong. Several Pioneer Square merchants have proposed removing the benches that are scattered throughout the area; they believe that if the homeless do not have benches to sleep on, they will disappear (Stoner 1995). More severe, however, is a 1994 municipal ordinance that restricts panhandling in the city and limits the right of people to sit on sidewalks between the hours of 7:00 A.M. and 9:00 P.M. Thus, the pendulum of politics affects cities' responses to homelessness just as all other things. A city that has a reputation for oppression one year will respond in an innovative and supportive way the next, and a city that has a reputation for coexistence one year will enact policies designed to drive homeless people away the next.

Low-Cost Housing for the Homeless

As noted in chapter 15, the most convincing explanation for the rise in homelessness was the decline in low-cost housing brought about by urban renewal and other, more recent economic transformations of the city. It would seem, then, that one of the most effective ways to address the growth of homelessness would be through a large increase in the stock of inexpensive housing. Several cities have experimented with such programs.

Portland, Oregon, has been a pioneer in this area. In the 1970s a private group of investors remodeled Portland's Estate Hotel, making it available to people with few resources for long-term single room occupancy (SRO). In 1978, neighborhood leaders formed the nonprofit Burnside Consortium (now the Central City Concern) to coordinate services and preserve housing in Portland. In 1979, it began pushing the preservation of SRO quarters in the downtown area. In 1980, Congress passed legislation (promoted by Oregon Congressman Les AuCoin) making SROs eligible for federal low-interest rehabilitation loans and Section 8 housing funds (Groth 1994).

Other cities have invested in SROs as well. New York City offers a training course and internships in SRO management. In San Diego, the 207 room Baltic Inn opened in 1987; it was the first *new* SRO in the city and one of the first in the country to open in seventy years. In Berkeley, Studio Durant (an SRO) was planned for a large lot behind the city's downtown retail district and the University of California campus. In 1990, Los Angeles used Community Development Block Grant funds to renovate 520 SRO rooms on skid row, and it planned to build a new seventy-two room hotel. San Francisco bought and renovated six hotels (with a total of 460 rooms) and contracted with a nonprofit agency to manage them. Private developers in Quincey, Massachusetts, opened a sixteen unit rooming house in 1986; it was the first rooming house built in the Boston area in several decades (Groth 1994).

Responses to Homelessness: A Critical Assessment

Like inner-city development (both economic and social), programs to rehabilitate the homeless must take a long-term view of the problem and its solution. For most homeless people, homelessness took a long time to develop, and it will take a long time to ameliorate its underlying causes. Staying in emergency shelters cannot accomplish that; neither can other survival services that are intended to prevent morbidity (e.g., soup kitchens, emergency health services). Therapeutic services can achieve this goal but only if they are administered appropriately. Consider, for example, the effectiveness of a drug detoxification program that discharges its newly detoxed clients back onto the street, without arranging for stable housing for them. Not surprisingly, the benefits of the therapy are short-lived under those circumstances. To be effective, therapeutic services (e.g., drug and alcohol treatment, psychological counseling, supportive housing, vocational training) are best joined with one another to meet *all* of the developmental needs of the homeless person. But even with a complete menu of services, time will be needed to achieve the desired effect.

Few cities have the resources to put into such a comprehensive endeavor. The result is that the problem of homelessness is not likely to be solved soon.

SROs can help, even if they are unlikely to provide the support necessary for a homeless person to transition into mainstream society. They can at least get him or her off the street. But we need to consider two things about SROs. First, on any given night there may be as many as 750,000 homeless people in the United States, and over the course of a year, that number may balloon to several million. The SRO construction and renovation boom that has taken place during the past several years has added only a few thousand new rooms. If it is to be an effective palliative to homelessness, it must be expanded considerably beyond what has been achieved thus far. Second, the cost of a room must be reasonable if SROs are going to be used by homeless people. The newly renovated Los Angeles SROs cost $11 per night, too much for many homeless people to pay (and more than many others are willing to pay). If utilization rates are going to be high, nightly charges must be very low, perhaps no more than $2. Again, the cost of the subsidy may be more than most cities can afford.

Homelessness is the social problem that most defies solutions, for two reasons. First, its causes are so complex that a solution would likely be prohibitively costly. Second, the political costs of attempting a real solution are high, and few politicians are willing to countenance the risks that would be involved in overcoming those costs. Perhaps the most reasonable solution is peaceful coexistence, as Seattle has at least partially achieved. In the absence of a real solution, this may be the best that cities can hope for.

Public Housing as Solution or Public Housing as Problem

One of the most readily available forms of low-cost housing is public housing, although it is generally not available to single men (and therefore not directly relevant to a discussion of homelessness). Yet, it could be argued that without public housing there would be many more homeless women and children than we see today. So, in the 1990s public housing is part of the solution to the underclass problem that cities face. But it has also come to be one of the most difficult problems. Four different solutions have been advanced to address the most problematic aspects of public housing: decentralization, privatization, revitalization, and decreased tolerance of illegal behavior.

Decentralization of Public Housing

Most public housing consists of large, densely populated developments housing people living in poverty, and that represents its greatest problem. The inevitability of large public housing developments was challenged in August

1966 when Dorothy Gautreaux (a public housing resident in Chicago) initiated a class action suit charging the Chicago Housing Authority and HUD with discrimination in the location of federally assisted housing developments and in assignment of tenants to these developments. In 1969 the courts ruled in favor of the plaintiffs and ordered the Chicago Housing Authority to build its next seven thousand units in white neighborhoods. After a series of challenges and appeals, the Chicago Housing Authority finally agreed in 1981 to give rent subsidy vouchers to seventy-one hundred black families over the next decade, allowing them to find housing on a case-by-case basis in Chicago's white suburbs. Dorothy Gautreaux died before winning final victory in the courts, but the program that bears her name has placed more than thirty-nine hundred Chicago families in private-sector apartments, more than half of which are located in the suburbs. Some of these families have lived in their new communities for more than ten years (Massey and Denton 1993).

Two major strategies have been developed to achieve decentralization, not only in Chicago but elsewhere as well: construction of scattered-site public housing and use of Section 8 certificates. The use of scattered-site public housing has been sporadic to date, due largely to the unwillingness of residents living in established neighborhoods to allow rental property—particularly rental property designated for low-income renters—into their neighborhoods. Much more common is the use of Section 8 housing assistance payments, which allow very low income families to rent decent, safe, and sanitary units available through the private rental market. Currently, 2.5 million families are assisted under this program; the popularity of the program is also demonstrated by the size of its waiting list, with forty-eight thousand families waiting in line in Chicago alone (*Time*, Nov. 4, 1996).

Privatization of Public Housing

The use of Section 8 certificates to achieve decentralization is a form of privatization in that it provides the means for low-income families to secure housing in the private market. However, during the Bush administration, HUD Secretary Jack Kemp took the concept a step further and proposed selling public housing units to the tenants who lived there. In fact, limited privatization had been authorized by affordable housing legislation since the 1970s, and during the mid 1980s, several public housing authorities took advantage of this legislation (Section 5(h) of the United States Housing Act of 1937, amended in 1974) to sell public housing developments to nonprofit organizations for subsequent sale, lease, or direct conversion to condominiums. In 1987, the Housing Authority of Louisville, in partnership with Louisville Housing Service Corporation (a nonprofit housing development organization), used the terms of this legislation to convert College Court (one of its oldest public housing developments) into condominiums (U.S. Department of

Housing and Urban Development 1991). Residents of College Court were given first priority for purchase of these units, followed by other public housing residents in the city. The success of the College Court program led the Housing Authority of Louisville to initiate conversion of a second public housing development, LaSalle Place, into condominiums (U.S. Department of Housing and Urban Development 1995b). In these and other privatization programs, local housing authorities were required to replace each unit that was sold with a new housing unit that would be rented to low-income people who qualify for public housing; this requirement was abandoned during the early 1990s, however.[8]

Revitalization of Public Housing

Revitalization of public housing involves the planned demolition and rebuilding of decaying public housing developments in large cities, primarily those whose public housing authorities have been designated by HUD as "troubled."[9] As such, it also involves elements of both decentralization and privatization. Under HOPE VI (the most recent of the HOPE programs; see note 8), approximately seven thousand units of public housing had been slated for demolition by the end of 1995, and up to one hundred thousand public housing units are projected for demolition by 2000. Unlike earlier programs, HOPE VI does not mandate that replacement units be constructed on a one-for-one basis, although the program does contain substantial funds for replacement. Included among the housing slated for demolition are five of the eight high-rise towers that comprise Philadelphia's Raymond Rosen Apartments; 191 new units will be built to replace the 510 demolished units (U.S. Department of Housing and Urban Development 1995a). A number of other "notorious" public housing developments are slated for demolition (or have already been demolished) under HOPE VI. One is Chicago's Cabrini-Green development, comprising nearly forty-seven hundred units that at one time

8. Another privatization program, developed during the Bush administration, was Project HOPE (Home Ownership for People Everywhere). Whereas the 5(h) program allows individual public housing authorities to convert public housing units to owned homes, it does not provide funds to do so; thus, local housing authorities must either use part of their regular HUD allocation for this purpose, or they must find private sources to fund the conversion. However, under HOPE I, public housing authorities could apply to HUD for grant funds to facilitate this conversion. Between 1990 and 1995, HUD awarded 232 planning grants and 30 implementation grants to public housing authorities; by 1995 the program had been defunded, and there will no additional implementation grants awarded.

9. In 1995, sixteen large public housing authorities and seventy-six smaller public housing authorities (out of a total of thirty-four hundred public housing authorities located across the country) were designated as troubled. Although a small proportion of housing authorities, these account for account for nearly 20 percent of the total public housing units in the country.

housed thirteen thousand people. In Autumn 1995, the tallest building, a nineteen story high-rise with 660 units, was demolished and an additional 650 units are slated for demolition. The Chicago Housing Authority plans to build 642 replacement units, and more than twenty developers have submitted proposals to build mixed-income housing on the demolition site (U.S. Department of Housing and Urban Development 1995b; *New York Times*, Sept. 28, 1995). In Atlanta, Techwood Homes and Clark Howell Homes (built between 1936 and 1940 and consisting of 1,387 units) were demolished. These developments were located adjacent to housing constructed for the 1996 Olympic Games, and the land they occupied (nearly sixty acres) will be leased to private developers for housing and business construction (U.S. Department of Housing and Urban Development 1995a). In Newark, Christopher Columbus Homes, a set of high-rise buildings with 1,556 units, was demolished in 1995. The Newark Housing Authority plans to build 1,777 new units over the next several years, including seventy-four new homes already built across from the Christopher Columbus site (Kliment 1994, U.S. Department of Housing and Urban Development 1995a).

Restricted Tolerance

A final approach to improving public housing is to come down hard on the people who promote the social decay that has become so rampant in the projects: the drug dealers and users, gang members, and anyone else who disrupts the peace (Webster and Connors 1992). For example, in 1988, the Chicago Housing Authority initiated Operation Clean Sweep, which involved searching all apartments, storage areas, and common spaces for weapons and drugs (although after the sweeps were successfully challenged in court, they were modified to exclude occupied apartments). Other local housing authorities have initiated similar cooperative projects with police (e.g., strict enforcement of criminal trespass laws). And HUD's One Strike and You're Out policy has resulted in a large number of evictions that either would not have occurred or that could have required months of hearings under previous guidelines.

Public Housing Reforms: A Critical Assessment

Decentralization. All of these reforms have the potential for improving the quality of life for those who live in public housing—at least for those who remain in public housing after implementation of the "get tough" policies. For example, participants in the Gautreaux program who moved to suburban locations were more likely to find and hold jobs than those who remained behind. But like so many opportunities, this one was not without risk. Those who moved to suburban locations experienced barriers to child care and transportation, a sense of discrimination, and the lack of appropriate job skills for many of the employment opportunities located there (Rosenbaum and Popkin 1991). If public housing is to be decentralized, not only throughout the central city but also in the suburbs, these are challenges that must be addressed before potential benefits of decentralization can be realized.

Privatization. Privatization programs are based on the assumption that ownership instills pride in residents and benefits the community, and in some cases it has done so (Autry 1994). But more often, privatization programs have produced disappointing results. Grants issued during the first two years of the HOPE I program (see note 8) were designed to sell thirteen hundred units in seventeen relatively attractive public housing neighborhoods; but after two years, only a quarter of those units had been sold (Rohe and Stegman 1992, Halpern 1995). This may be an unfair indictment, however, for each of these neighborhoods, regardless of how attractive it has become, has baggage from a checkered past. Renovations and a new name cannot erase old memories, and people may be unwilling to buy property in a neighborhood that has, in the recent past, been home to violence, drugs, and decay. Moreover, many *impoverished* people are also unwilling to live in these neighborhoods. If the local housing authority assigns them residence in blighted public housing developments, they will opt to stay living doubled up with a friend or in a homeless shelter rather than move into the development. This reality is reflected in the vacancy rates of many troubled public housing developments, which approach 50 percent.[10] Thus, evaluation of privatization efforts should not be based on absolute occupancy rates in newly privatized neighborhoods; rather, it should reflect these occupancy rates relative to what occurred when the neighborhood was a public housing development. Given this comparison, privatization programs may not be overwhelmingly successful, but neither have they failed.

Revitalization. One concern raised by the revitalization efforts is that units that are razed are not always replaced. But, even though replacement units are not being constructed on a one-for-one basis, we should not conclude that a large segment of the public housing population will be left without shelter. The housing to be demolished is, for the most part, the worst of the worst, often not fit for human habitation. For example, all of the apartments in Christopher Columbus Homes in Newark and most of those in Raymond Rosen Apartments in Philadelphia had been vacant for some time prior to demolition. In addition, all were plagued by major infestations of drugs, gangs, violence, and crime; and all were showing substantial physical deterioration.

10. In Jacksonville, for example, Golfcreek Apartments had a vacancy rate of 49 percent during 1990 and 1991, and the Pottsburg development had a vacancy rate of 44 percent to 48 percent during the same period (U.S. House of Representatives Subcommittee on Employment and Housing 1992).

Another, larger concern is that many of the recently demolished developments (and some of those facing demolition) are located in areas of the city where property values had increased substantially (e.g., Cabrini-Green in Chicago and Techwood/Clark-Howell in Atlanta). Some might argue that public housing is a gross underutilization of valuable land. This argument has its roots in urban renewal, where the displacement of low-income residents was justified as a means for putting the land to a "higher and better use" (Feagin and Parker 1990). But it does raise questions about whether local housing authorities are allowing their property to deteriorate through neglect when its market value becomes sufficiently high. If this is so, public housing (and its residents) may be taking a "bum rap" for other ecological processes that are occurring within the city.

Regardless of whether the HOPE VI program is a new phase of urban renewal or an effort to revitalize public housing (and both interpretations are probably valid), it has resulted both in decentralization and in privatization of public housing. In Louisville, for example, 1,116 units demolished in Cotter and Lang Homes will be replaced on site by 599 units of public housing, 451 units of tax-credit rental housing, 175 units of market-value rental housing, and 350 homeownership units; in addition, 360 units of scattered-site public housing will be constructed elsewhere.

Restricted tolerance. Congress and the president mandated a "get tough" policy for public housing residents, to be accomplished nationally through the One Strike policy and locally through programs initiated by local housing authorities in conjunction with local police departments. All of these "get tough" measures no doubt diminish disruptive behavior within public housing neighborhoods, but they also come at a cost. Drug dealers are unlikely to quit dealing because they fear they will be evicted, and when they are evicted, they will continue selling drugs, either in the neighborhood or elsewhere. Drug users who are evicted—and more important, their families—will find housing elsewhere if they are evicted, but it will often be in run-down tenements that are less safe and in worse repair than the housing they were evicted from. Gang members will remain in their gangs whether or not they are in public housing. In other words, it may be possible to clean up public housing but that does not clean up the problems that are associated with public housing; they will simply move elsewhere in the city.

Ending Welfare as We Know It

1996 Welfare Reform Legislation

Given all that has been said about the urban underclass and the urban ghetto, few policy changes are likely to have as great an impact on our cities as changes in welfare policy. During the 1992 presidential campaign, candidate Bill Clinton promised "to put an end to welfare as we know it." It took nearly four years, but on July 31, 1996, the U.S. House of Representatives voted final approval for welfare reform legislation that had been hotly debated during the previous two years. A day later, the Senate also voted final approval for the legislation, and President Clinton signed it into law in mid-August. But rather than resolving the debate about welfare, this legislation intensified it.

The provisions of the welfare reform legislation are too numerous to detail here (for a complete description, see *Congressional Quarterly*, Aug. 3, 1996). The major provisions are as follow:

- A new block grant for Temporary Assistance for Needy Families replaces Aid to Families with Dependent Children. Funding levels are frozen at $16.4 billion per year through 2001, although several additional sources of funds are available to supplement the block grant. Financial incentives will be provided to states that reduce out-of-wedlock births, allowing them to receive up to a 10 percent increase in their funding.
- Adults receiving welfare benefits are required to begin work within two years of receiving aid. Welfare recipients who do not meet the work requirement will be denied food stamps. States are required to have at least 25 percent of their welfare case load engaged in work by 1997 and 50 percent by 2002. States that fail to meet this requirement will lose up to 21 percent of their block grant allocation.
- Adults cannot receive welfare for more than five years, and states can set shorter time limits if they wish to; each state is allowed to exempt up to 20 percent of its case load from this limitation, however. Individuals convicted of any felony involving illegal drugs will be denied welfare benefits and food stamps.
- States may opt to deny welfare assistance to children born to welfare recipients or to unwed parents under the age of eighteen.
- Legal immigrants generally are ineligible for Supplemental Security Income (SSI) and food stamps until they become citizens or have worked in the United States for at least ten years. States can opt to deny legal immigrants welfare and Medicaid benefits.
- Federal child-care programs are folded into the Child Care and Development block grant, which provides child-care services for low-income families. Initial funding of $1.1 billion per year will rise to $2.7 billion per year in 2002.
- Unemployed, able-bodied adults under fifty years of age and without any dependents are eligible for only short-term receipt of food stamps.
- Children with disabilities qualify for SSI only if the disability stems from a medically proven physical or mental disorder.

469

- States must continue to spend at least 75 percent of the state funds they previously spent on AFDC and related programs.
- States must continue to offer Medicaid coverage for one year to welfare recipients who lose their welfare benefits because of increased earnings.

Welfare Reform: A Critical Assessment

The complexity of the welfare reform legislation guarantees that it will require a considerable time to digest, but the outlines of the debate about welfare, which started during the 1980s, are clear. For critics of welfare the problem is not merely that it is costly and ineffective; rather, in their view, it is responsible for perpetuating the underclass. Going a step further, some critics view welfare reform as a way of shaping alternative lifestyles and behaviors for the underclass, providing them with an opportunity to escape from poverty. For example, Charles Murray (1996, 10) argues, "The problem facing America's low-income communities is not that too many women in those communities are on welfare but that too many children in those communities are being born to single mothers and absent fathers." For Lawrence Mead (1996), the problem is somewhat different: the underclass lack the discipline to find and keep jobs; and while this is not necessarily their fault, it prevents them from upward mobility. Welfare reform legislation addresses these concerns by invoking a critical assumption (supported by both Murray and Mead): underclass behavior is at least partially a lifestyle choice, and the calculus of that choice can be changed by making it very costly. Thus, by giving states the opportunity to deny benefits to children born to welfare recipients or to unwed teenagers, out-of-wedlock births can be reduced. And the legislation, by requiring that a female welfare recipient find work within a specified time, creates a powerful incentive for her to become disciplined and reliable in her quest for a job.

But many disagree with the validity of this assumption. The fundamental question they raise is whether female welfare recipients have the resources (both material and psychological) to get and keep jobs and to avoid bearing children out of wedlock. Certainly, the legislation will motivate some of these women to find jobs; but just as surely, it will not have this desired impact on others. Depending on how many barriers (e.g., lack of transportation, depression, fear of the future, lack of vocational skills, lack of coping skills, lack of communication skills) a woman has to overcome, the threat of being cut off welfare may be sufficient or insufficient to make her find and maintain employment.

The same logic holds for having babies. If this were a straightforward economic decision (i.e., the fewer babies, the larger the welfare payment), the legislation would likely be successful. But in most cases, this decision is much more complicated, and often it is not really a decision at all but something that just happens (e.g., Pearce 1993). The results of New Jersey's Family Development Program are instructive in this regard, since it limits welfare payments to only one child born to current welfare recipients. Evaluations of the program are still several years from completion; some preliminary findings suggest that the program has been successful in preventing illegitimate births, but other findings suggest that it has had little or no impact (Epstein 1996). As with the work requirement, some women will likely be more careful to prevent pregnancy in the wake of the welfare reform legislation; but just as likely, others will not. The critical question centers around whether the bulk of welfare recipients are in the former or the latter category.

The states are given some substantial leeway in exempting people from many of the requirements specified in the welfare reform legislation. For example, each state can exempt up to 25 percent of its case load from the work requirement; and states are given complete discretion about implementing policies pertaining to out-of-wedlock births. Even so, past experience suggests how difficult (and expensive) it may be for states to achieve the employment targets specified in the legislation (25 percent of welfare recipients working within eighteen months and 50 percent working by 2002). In this regard, it is instructive to examine the Family Support Act passed by Congress in 1988, which implemented the Job Opportunities and Basic Skills (JOBS) program. In contrast to earlier employment programs for welfare recipients, JOBS *required* participation for all women whose youngest child is older than two years of age. But as of 1992, only 7 percent of all adult AFDC recipients were participating in JOBS (Kane and Bane 1994). Another example is provided by the Massachusetts ET welfare-to-work program (Handler 1995). Overall, 22 percent of its participants were able to get jobs and stay off welfare, but to achieve this success rate, the state spent $68 million in 1988 and subsequent years, or an annual average of approximately $2,000 per participant.

Even states that have been successful in placing their welfare recipients in work situations face challenges. For example, Iowa shifted 35 percent of its welfare recipients to work between 1994 and 1996. However, most welfare spells tend to be short-term, with roughly 35 percent of current welfare recipients having been on welfare for two years or less (Ellwood and Bane 1994). So most of Iowa's 35 percent success rate would have been achieved *even without any governmental welfare-to-work intervention*. On the other hand, moving those who are long-term welfare recipients into work may be much more costly. For example, Alex Kotlowitz (1996) cites an inner-city Chicago jobs program whose director estimates that counselors must remain intimately involved with a client for two years before that client can become an independent and reliable worker. The law of diminishing returns, if applied to welfare reform, would hold that after placing those who are easy to place, it becomes more and more difficult and costly to place each additional person

471

into a work situation. States will be required to pick up the cost for this employment assistance, yet the welfare reform legislation cut state funds in this area. For example, Iowa's federal job training funds for welfare recipients and the working poor will be cut by 23 percent (*Business Week*, Aug. 19, 1996). Many states simply do not have the resources to accomplish what the welfare reform legislation requires of them. Faced with the prospect of losing up to 21 percent of their total block grant allocations for noncompliance, states may well choose the more expedient option of dropping people from their welfare rolls rather than spending large sums of money to find jobs for them that they may be unable to maintain.

Those who are cut from welfare rolls because they will not (and/or cannot) work will have no choice but to move in with friends or family or to find shelter in missions, abandoned buildings, or wherever else they can. Since these homeless people are hard to track and statistically invisible, they will not show up on official records as casualties of welfare reform; in fact, since they are no longer on the welfare rolls, they will be counted as successes. If the numbers are small, they will merely become part of a growing homeless population in the nation's cities, and few people will notice. But if the numbers are large, people will begin to notice. And at that point, the question will become one of public resources: Who is responsible for funding programs to get the homeless off the streets? In truth, we do not know how many people will be pushed by welfare reform into jobs and out of their ghetto neighborhoods and how many will be pushed into homelessness. But in the absence of such information, the risk for cities is great. For, as we previously discussed, the homeless more than any other group are constant reminders to urban visitors and residents that the city is home to some of the nation's most difficult social problems.

Looking toward the Future

As we consider what the future may hold for cities, we would do well to reconsider their recent past, how they have responded to it, and what new challenges these responses have created. In most cities, the recent past has been dominated by problems associated with the underclass: how to meet their needs, how to control them, how to build around them. It is this latter concern that is perhaps most critical for two reasons. First, by virtually any definition there are fewer than 10 million urban inhabitants who could be considered part of the underclass; some estimates place the number at closer to 1 million. Thus, underclass residents are a relatively small (but important) segment of the urban population. Second, although urban policies can change the quality of life for the underclass, and they can perhaps decrease the size of the underclass, they cannot eliminate it. Taken together, these suggest that cities should explore strategies for moving beyond the underclass debate or at least not becoming immobilized by the debate.

The presence of the underclass continues to dominate much of the urban policy debate. Transforming the city depends on investment, and investment depends on the ability to draw people *to* the city. The underclass, regardless of its size, has become the critical point around which issues of investment have turned: people are afraid of the inner city (including its downtown area), and they have been largely unwilling to support central city investments. From this perspective, we can see downtown economic development as an attempt to overcome the problem of the underclass by building a city around them; inner city development as an attempt to provide them with the jobs necessary to escape from poverty; homeless programs as an attempt to regulate them; housing programs as an attempt to change the decay that surrounds them; and welfare reform as an attempt to change their behavior. In all of this, there is the belief that once the underclass problem is brought under control the city can get back to the business of being a city. But somehow in the process, cities may have misplaced their vision of what it means to be a city, what makes urban life special. That was the question with which we began chapter 1, and it is the question to which we now return.

LOOKING TO THE FUTURE

Since changes are going on anyway, the great thing is to learn enough about them so that we will be able to lay hold of them and turn them in the direction of our desires. Conditions and events are neither to be fled from nor passively acquiesced in; they are to be utilized and directed.

John Dewey, *Reconstruction in Philosophy*

CHAPTER 18

The Shape of Things to Come

Themes and Counterthemes

We end this book as we began, invoking themes of urban life, economics, and politics. But as we have learned, the city is in large part a place of contradictions; for every set of themes, *counterthemes* can be invoked as well.

The Function of Cities

- Every city is a web of government and politics, of social relationships, of economic enterprises.
- With rare exceptions, every city is a collection of houses and apartments that shelter its residents. They are domiciles as well as commodities, bought and sold in the market.

BUT, a place where one lives is more than just a place to live. It represents status, social class, and a way of life. Thus, few things roil the politics of a city more than perceived threats to that way of life.

A City of Friends and Strangers

- Cities are place of people, both friends and strangers. In small towns, most encounters are among friends, while in large cities most encounters are among strangers.
- The essential purpose of a city's government is to make urban life practical and possible—with lives lived among friends and strangers, reasonably safe, comfortable, and free from violence.

BUT, to accomplish these purposes, every city is surrounded by and contained within a web of ordinances and statutes. Early in our country's history, each of the states assumed responsibility for its cities' well-being. During the Great Depression, the national government took on a large share of that responsibility, and in so doing unleashed a political debate that is still with us: does primary responsibility for the cities lie with the states or with the national government? Stated more realistically, if responsibility is to be shared, which level of government shall do what?

Governing Urban America

- The statutes and ordinances that affect and control urban life aim at achieving one or more policy purposes.

BUT, there is often a sizeable gap between intent and accomplishment. Of the many conclusions to be drawn about public policy, two surely stand out. First, policies have unintended consequences. Urban renewal, for example, destroyed more housing than it built. And public housing developments, intended to bring a good life to the poor, all too often have become unlivable places, lacking the maintenance to keep them in good repair and subject to the violence of warring street gangs and drug dealers. Second, most policies emerge from the ideologies of their sponsors. Thus, the most strenuously contested policies tend to be those that advance or diminish deeply held values (for example, policies intended to improve the lives of the poor by making taxes more progressive).

The Contested City

- Cities tend to be judged by the quality of life led by those who live in them. High on any list of things necessary for a good life are personal security and freedom from assault and violence.

BUT, as important as personal security is for evaluating the quality of urban life, it proves to be an elusive goal. The contested city has always been part of urban life. From their beginnings, American cities have been arenas of social, political, racial, and ethnic strife—Native Americans versus colonials, rich versus poor, old settlers versus new, speakers of English versus immigrants with no command of that language, reformers versus those who benefit from the status quo, whites versus blacks—and the list goes on. Usually, such conflicts are resolved within the political process, but more often than most would like to admit, the conflict has flared into group and personal violence.

The Culture of Cities

- Cities—especially big cities—are the creators and repositories of many of our cultural and artistic achievements.

BUT, the bigger the city, the more likely it is that its social, racial, and ethnic conflicts will be prolonged and difficult to manage. Two implications follow. First, the competition for funds is likely to be fierce, often pitting those who seek support for the city's cultural foundations against those who seek support for social services and neighborhood restoration. Second, as poverty and racial or ethnic conflict in a city become more overt and visible, they are likely to keep away the very people who may be attracted to the city by its cultural and artistic achievements.

The City in History

- As units of government, as networks of social roles and economic enterprises, and as carriers of our culture, cities are shaped by what has gone before, which is to say that the urban web is anchored to history.

BUT, that history is not exclusively urban. It is shared and shaped by larger social, economic, and political forces. For example, the victories of the Civil Rights movement were largely won in the rural parts of the Mississippi delta, in small-town lunch counters and bus stations, and in some middle-sized cities in the South. These victories brought with them a revolution of rising expectations that had profound repercussions in all American cities, even though there was nothing uniquely urban about Civil Rights.

As another example, the national economy has experienced a number of transformations since the founding of the republic, from small-scale manufacturing, to large-scale industry, to the postindustrial, computer-driven, and service-oriented society. Each transformation has brought new challenges and new opportunities to the cities and to the nation as a whole. In each of these examples, and a thousand more like them, the city is merely a reflection of the larger American society, which after all is increasingly urban. But as the United States has become more urbanized, national trends

479

take on a more magnified and immediate appearance in the cities (particularly the big cities), often creating the impression that cities are what is wrong with America.

If history has anything to teach us about American cities, it is that cities are constantly changing, constantly remaking themselves to meet the challenges and take advantage of the opportunities created by a changing nation and world. Accordingly, as epilogue, an important question confronts us here: What lies ahead for the American city?

The Physical Shape of Things to Come

History is a teacher, but hardly an infallible guide. Of the clues for the future that the past provides, the strongest is physical change, shaped and molded by changing technologies. Following the Civil War, America entered a steam-driven industrial age. The city center and the area beyond became factory sites. Employment opportunities beckoned, and immigrating Europeans swarmed to cities to find jobs and the promise of economic and social advancement.

As public transport improved, managers (and then workers) moved to ringlike settlements farther and farther from factory sites. By the 1920s, the automobile created a new urban frontier, the suburb. In the 1940s, wartime employment opportunities and the mechanization of southern agriculture sent millions of southern blacks streaming to northern cities, exacerbating racial tensions there. In the 1950s, a new system of federally funded roads (the interstate highways) made white-flight from cities to suburbs socially and economically feasible. Businesses and factories followed. By the 1960s, the present pattern of metropolitan sprawl was firmly fixed. Edge cities and megacounties are the newest forms of that sprawl.

Edge cities are primarily office centers, often high-rise buildings, usually sited in the unincorporated countryside. Those who work in edge cities can come and go only by means of the automobile. To save time and improve the quality of their lives, many of those who work in edge cities choose to make their homes in nearby, newly established incorporated suburbs. But others choose unincorporated clusters whose residents live under the rules and services of a private government (often called common interest developments; legally these are noncities). Both edge cities and new unincorporated suburbs increasingly rely on services provided by what has become an urbanized, densely populated county, a megacounty that takes responsibility for providing what in past times were exclusively *urban* services—police and fire protection, sewer and water lines, and sanitation.

Megacounties, of course, contain more than just office towers and residential suburbs. They also contain such urban amenities as restaurants, theaters, and shopping centers. As new settlers and newly recruited workers continue to move out from the central city and its immediate suburbs, problems and political challenges arise to trouble the future. High on any list of challenges to urban sprawl are the costs to society in commuting time, in highway construction and upkeep, and in the import of foreign oil.

It is estimated that 60 percent of every mile the motorist drives on the multi-billion-dollar suburban highway network is subsidized by taxes (gas taxes, property taxes) borne by the public at large. With so many other calls on the public purse, advocates for the poor have challenged any future expansion of America's highway network. In addition, environmentalists are increasingly concerned with the ways in which new roads pave over the countryside and traffic congestion spews pollutants into the atmosphere.

In addition to the concerns about the economic and environmental costs of highways, familiar tensions challenge suburban growth. For example, the tension between property as commodity and property as lifestyle lead some to applaud the rising property values that accompany suburban growth but lead others to lament the increased traffic, crime, and other "big city" problems that growth brings to their neighborhoods. Those already settled in the countryside, fearful for their own futures, often oppose low-cost housing and fight proposed new roads ("Not in my back yard!"). They enact no-growth legislation to control their own communities and they lobby state legislatures and county governments to do the same.[1] Thus, suburban growth creates tension between conflicting ideologies, pitting those who seek to use politics and government to regulate access to a good life (social equity) against those who wish to rely on the marketplace (market equity) for redress and change.

Urban sprawl will probably continue well into the coming century. Whatever the cost-benefit calculus, American dependence on the automobile is so ingrained in the public consciousness that it is unlikely to change any time soon. For many, all the costs of suburban sprawl seem trivial compared with the benefits of escaping from the rigors of life in the central city. Increasingly, in the popular press and in the public mind, central cities are perceived as unsafe, unhealthy places, with failing schools, high crime, and high taxes. Those who can afford it—white, black, Hispanic, and Asian—continue to seek the safety and security of suburban and *exurban* life. Moreover, commitment to a market economy is a cornerstone of American society. At the local level, market equity may be occasionally sacrificed to achieve social equity, but thus far such restrictions of the market have been rare.

---

1. For example, in Mequon, a Milwaukee suburb with low crime and low taxes, property developers were kept away by anti-growth ordinances that required every builder to provide cost-benefit environmental and traffic-impact analyses with their application for a building permit; to conform to zoning regulations requiring a significant percentage of green space on every lot; and to use expensive building materials in each new structure (*The Economist*, Aug. 13, 1994).

Population Shifts and Demographic Trends

Outward migrations from central cities to suburbs and beyond are not the only important migrations. Overall, the population of the entire country has been shifting southward and westward, to the so-called sunbelt. Some of this shift attaches to the "greying of America," with a longer living, older generation moving to the sunbelt to escape the rigors of northern winters. Some of this shift is for economic advantage and necessity. As the older industrial cities of the Northeast (the "rustbelt") have seen their heavy industries (steel, automobiles) close, many of their unemployed workers have looked south for replacement jobs.

Still another component of this shift can be traced to foreign-born immigrants—both legal and illegal. The United States, today as before, beckons those who seek a better life. New York City and Florida are now home to recently arrived Caribbean immigrants. California, Oregon, and Washington have become a settler's land for recently arrived southeast Asians and Koreans, who take their places (albeit in separate communities) alongside older Japanese and Chinese communities. And Texas and California are increasingly home to newly arrived Latinos, especially those from across the Mexican border.

Most, but not all, of the newly arrived immigrants have settled in cities. As was the case for the European immigrants of a century ago, cities provide immigrants with communities where their native languages are spoken and where their cultures can be preserved and cherished. But, as was the case a century ago, the new settlers arouse resentment and hostility. The state of California, for example, has sought to deny social services and public benefits to all but legal immigrants; and the 1996 welfare reform legislation exempts even legal immigrants (unless they have become citizens or worked in the United States for ten years or more) from welfare benefits. As another example, black communities in Los Angeles (and elsewhere) display resentment—and sometimes violence—toward recent immigrants (e.g., Koreans) in their midst.

The parallels between the past and present are instructive but far from complete. The cities of the nineteenth century were cities of heavy industry, with an expanding labor force and assembly-line production that could find ready places for immigrants with strong arms and limited education. Upward advancement was promised to all who would and could work hard. Today's immigrants confront a changed America, a postindustrial society. America's good-paying jobs are increasingly the preserve of an educated social class. Entry-level and service jobs are the only jobs available for the unskilled and uneducated, whether they are old settlers or new, and the competition is often fierce for any job paying more than minimum wage. Thus, the city is once again an arena of economic and social rivalries organized along ethnic and racial lines, and in an uncertain environment, these can easily turn violent.[2]

Urban Riots and the Two Societies

Thirty years ago, large-scale urban riots erupted across the nation. More than 257 cities were involved, including New York, Detroit, Washington, and Los Angeles. In 1967 alone, more than five hundred thousand persons were arrested for rioting, eight thousand were injured, and two hundred killed (see Feagin and Hahn, 1973, for more details).

Almost all the rioting took place in predominantly black urban areas. For many who attempted to analyze and explain the riots, their cause and meaning were clear: blacks were angry and frustrated over their relative poverty in a nation of affluence, their thwarted attempts to climb the ladders of economic opportunity, and their lack of full access to the political equality promised in the Constitution. A presidential commission agreed. The causes of the riots, it concluded, were rooted in the social and economic structure of our society. Our nation, said the commission,

> is rapidly moving toward two increasingly separate Americas . . . , a white society located principally in the suburbs . . . and in the peripheral parts of large central cities, and a Negro society largely concentrated within large central cities. (National Advisory Commission on Civil Disorders 1967, Introduction)

Since the commission's 1967 report, large-scale urban riots have continued to erupt. In 1980 and 1982, the Liberty City area of Miami exploded in riots. In the first instance, rioting was precipitated by the acquittal of white police officers who were charged with beating a young black businessman to death; in the second, it was triggered by a Hispanic police officer killing a black teenager. During the late 1980s, several highly publicized, racially motivated acts of violence in New York City triggered protests, none of which resulted in riots but all of which brought intensified scrutiny of the state of race relations in the United States. These violent acts include the attacks on Yusuf Hawkins in Bensonhurst and Michael Griffith in Howard Beach, the "wilding" attack on a white woman jogging in Central Park, and the subway shoot-

2. Several months before the 1992 Los Angeles riot, a Korean merchant in south-central Los Angeles shot and killed a black girl he accused of shoplifting. This and other events had heightened tensions between blacks and Koreans, and during the riot Korean merchants in Koreatown were targets of much of the destruction. Los Angeles is not the only city where these kinds of racial tensions exist. Chafets (1990) documents the tension between Arab storeowners in Detroit's inner city neighborhoods and the black residents of those neighborhoods. The topic was also the subject of Spike Lee's film *Do the Right Thing.*

ings by Bernhard Goetz. More recently, in Los Angeles in 1992, acquittal of a white police officer accused of beating black motorist Rodney King triggered the worst urban riot in U.S. history.

Given this background and the fact that the United States continues to separate into socially and economically disparate societies, black and white, few (if any) observers would predict a riot-free future for our large cities. But by the same token, the earlier worry (dating back to the 1960s) that the United States stands on the precipice of civil insurrection (Bienen 1968) now seems somewhat overblown. Perhaps we have grown used to rioting, or perhaps our experience thus far suggests that riots burn themselves out and do not escalate into a permanent state of siege. Or perhaps today's riots have come to be seen as no more than an extension of the everyday violence that has become so much a part of inner-city neighborhoods!

Urban Problems and Urban Policies

For the immediate and probably distant future, large and middle-size cities will continue to be beset by a long list of massive problems. To talk about these problems makes the future of the city seem bleak, but to ignore them is an even greater risk to the future of the city. These problems include homeless people living and sleeping in the streets, high crime, inner-city unemployment, housing decay, white flight, juvenile street gangs, drug dealing and drug abuse, school dropouts, the obsolescence and breakdown of the city's physical plant (water and sewage lines, bridges, and the like), the decline of public transportation, and for many cities, a sharply declining tax base, which limits their ability to deal with these and other problems.

When local problems appear insoluble, policy entrepreneurs (both in the past and today) seek the assistance of the national government. In the past, the national government has responded to many of these needs with programs such as public housing, urban renewal, and the Great Society (to name just a few). But for several reasons, few such national programs are likely to be launched in the near future.

One reason is the lack of money. The federal deficit and the ongoing attempts to achieve a balanced budget have left relatively few federal dollars for the cities, and the nation's priorities have shifted elsewhere. Second, when funds are scarce, policy proposals tend to be constrained by caution. Programs tend to gain support only after assurances are given that they will achieve intended results quickly, with minimal unintended consequences. Even in the best of policy times, such assurances are not easily given, and the history of past federal programs makes such assurances even more difficult to give. And major policy proposals (including costly proposals to aid the cities) will be forced to undergo close ideological scrutiny, and they may not survive the conflict that such scrutiny is bound to create. *[The theory of ideology.]*

On the one hand, economic conservatives take the view that city problems are closely linked to the operation of market societies. Capital flows to places of greatest profitability, they argue, and while dislocations (such as urban sprawl, joblessness, housing decay, and unemployment) are among the social costs of a market economy, the long-term benefits are greater than the costs. More important (they would probably argue) massive interventions to save the cities do no great good. Since 1965, the federal government has spent more than $2.5 trillion on programs of direct and indirect aid to cities (see Moore and Stansel 1992), yet the problems are, if anything, getting worse. Perhaps government ought to assist those who suffer economic dislocations as needed (they may say), but it should not engage in any more massive programs to save the cities.

On the other hand, liberals tend to argue the case for federal help to the cities, not so much to help the cities per se but to assist those who live there. They argue their case on grounds of compassion and social equity: public assistance to the poor, if directed toward job training and education, will constitute an investment in *human capital* that, in the long run, will ensure national prosperity and a rising standard of living for the entire nation (see Reich 1983 and Thurow 1980). What is more, liberals argue, the problems of the cities are not of their making but rather are embedded in larger social problems; as such, government at every level has an obligation to come to the aid of the cities and those who live there.

However forceful the liberal arguments may be, they are not likely to carry the day. In the immediate (and probably in the farther) future, existing social programs financed by the federal government are likely to be curtailed, and new ones are unlikely to be funded. As we approach a new century, the public mood seemingly has shifted from such programs and interventions.

Things to Do, Programs to Be Tried

While federal aid may be limited, states are not likely to neglect their cities, nor will cities cease their own attempts at creative problem solving. The situation in Camden, New Jersey, illustrates that state's continuing involvement with its cities. Camden, with a population of eighty-seven thousand, is a city in massive decay. In 1995, it recorded sixty murders, or one for every 1,450 residents. Street after street has "houses without windows, cars without doors." Those who are able to do so move the short distance to Philadelphia, for all its problems a better run and more prosperous city than Camden (*The Economist*, Aug. 10, 1996). By 1996, the state of New Jersey was forced to take control of the city's housing and parking authority and was considering the need to take control of federal funds earmarked for Camden. Much more directly, the state contributes about $50 million of the city's $96 million budget, and Governor Whitman announced that the state would appropriate $8.3

million to demolish a tract of slum housing and replace it with a new housing development (*New York Times,* May 19, 1996).

In addition to interventions by state governments, private initiatives (in Camden and elsewhere) play an important role in solving urban problems. One private initiative is *gentrification*, a term commonly used to describe the process whereby individual householders and small business firms buy up and transform an entire city neighborhood. Notable examples of gentrification include German Village in Columbus, Ohio; the Lincoln Park area of Chicago; Queens Village in Philadelphia; and Capitol Hill and Adams Morgan in Washington, D.C. As the term suggests, gentrification restores to former glory the physical character of a residential neighborhood, and brings to the area a gentry (i.e., middle class)—along with a rising tax base and up-scale stores and shops. In Seattle, for example, Capitol Hill had a seedy reputation and a high crime rate during the 1960s and into the early 1970s. But inexpensive land and an expensive housing market in many other parts of the city offered the opportunity to make a handsome profit on investments in the neighborhood, and a number of people did invest by buying both homes and businesses. Today, Capitol Hill is one of the fashionable shopping areas in Seattle, with a seemingly endless supply of ethnic restaurants, boutiques, and now an all-night, used-book store.

Urban restoration is the commercial counterpart of gentrification, where old commercial buildings are restored through private initiatives. Restoration projects usually receive some form of government assistance, and the restored projects are usually updated to house a variety of shops and boutiques. In 1966, Congress established a National Register of Historic Buildings, with buildings designated for inclusion in the register to be protected from the wrecker's ball. More important, registered buildings are eligible for several types of restoration grants and thus become attractive investments for mortgage lenders. Several cities now proudly display restored areas of Victorian and Romanesque architecture. These include Pioneer Square in Seattle, the former Tivoli Brewery in Denver, and the Old Post Office in Washington, D.C. (see Collins et al., 1991, for a discussion of downtown preservation projects).

Enterprise and empowerment zones, as their names suggest, are urban areas selected by federal and state agencies to receive funding and other forms of aid intended to attract private business investment to the inner city. With business investment in offices, warehouses, and factories, employment opportunities for inner-city residents may rise, potentially setting in motion a further set of changes. Neighborhood restoration may result; cities and their residents may achieve a sense of empowerment, enabling them to take control of their lives and futures; and indicators of neighborhood pathology (e.g., crime, drugs, teen pregnancy) may begin to decline. Of course, such far-reaching results are seldom, if ever, likely to be achieved in their entirety. But they can help make a difference in some neighborhoods, particularly if they are combined with another type of private initiative—*community development*. This is an effort, usually initiated by foundations (although sometimes in partnership with local government), to promote social integration within the neighborhoods. It encourages residents to establish connections with each other and with neighborhood institutions (e.g., churches, neighborhood associations, retail businesses, schools), and through these connections to develop a sense of direction and purpose in lives that are all-too-often buffeted by crisis and uncertainty (*empowerment* is a term that is used to describe this transformation). These community development initiatives encourage residents to work together to remove the physical symptoms of blight from their neighborhood, including vacant and deteriorating buildings, abandoned cars, and rubbish-filled empty lots. Examples of inner-city community development efforts include the Dudley Street Neighborhood Initiative in Boston and the Atlanta Project.

All of these forms of private initiative have produced some successes, even though they proceed slowly. But taken together, even small successes are encouraging, and they lead some urban analysts to assert the importance of revitalizing inner cities one block at a time—as one writer puts it, to "take big steps, modestly" (Gratz 1989).

The Urban Poor

Sooner or later, most attempts at improving, revitalizing, or saving our cities lead us to reconsider the urban poor. The millions of urban residents who are mired in poverty live their lives in and around a vast circle of attendant problems: street violence, hunger, inadequate medical attention, poor housing, woeful schools, indifferent education, joblessness, single-parent households, and teenage mothers (a world in which children beget children). The "two nations" of the Kerner Report still stand, separated and intact. Also intact (and perhaps growing worse) are the social and economic conditions that continue to erupt in riots.

Poverty, wherever found, is a matter of social conscience and concern, but it is the poverty of the urban ghetto that causes greatest concern. For it is a commonplace observation that the urban ghetto has nurtured a destructive culture—a culture, according to some views, where "sane, healthy adults refuse to follow norms of behavior that most of society endorses," and that "approves (or at least fails to disapprove) of idleness, single parenthood, theft, and violence" (Jencks 1988, 23).

Proposals to change the urban ghetto are easy to come by but exceedingly difficult to carry through. One proposal, discouraging in the extreme, is to leave the ghettos alone. Cities, wrote George Sternlieb (1971), no longer perform their historic functions. Formerly, with their deep pools of immigrant labor, they provided the work force that ran the American industrial system. But the need for strong backs and the fifteen hour workday

> has been reduced to almost nothing by the transportation revolution, which has the effect of homogenizing time and distance. Much of our labor-intensive work is now imported from abroad. Welfare legislation, minimum wages, maximum working hours, and the like have minimized the economic functions of the conglomerations of poor-but-willing people in our cities.

The city, said Sternlieb, has become a *sandbox,* a place where our society has parked those who are no longer productive, so that the rest of society "can get on with the serious things of life" (p. 17).

It is true, of course, that our contemporary, postindustrial economy has relatively little employment for the uneducated, even if willing, worker. Such jobs as are available tend to be low-paying service jobs. Moreover, many of the entry-level, unskilled jobs once found in the cities have moved out to suburbs and edge cities—where bus lines do not go and where the poor without cars cannot travel (e.g., Wilson 1996).

Even so, America is not likely to abandon its fight to improve the lives of the urban poor. For the foreseeable future, national aid to the cities (however much reduced in dollar amounts) is likely to come by way of block grants that will encourage the states to experiment with improving inner-city lives. The welfare reform legislation of 1996 is a portent. The act provides for block grants to the states and encourages each state to create its own version of a welfare program. More significantly, the act sets limits on the years of welfare payments, with the express purpose of ending long-term dependence on welfare (to end the welfare culture). Workfare, not welfare, is its purpose; but if this purpose is to be accomplished, bringing the poor into the workforce will also require such additional government programs as medical assistance, job training, incentives to the young to stay in school, financial incentives to employers to hire the unemployed, and perhaps government as the employer of last resort. If and when government becomes the employer of last resort, some of the job holders may be at work cleaning litter and possibly improving long neglected streets. But this scenario hardly begins to canvass the future of our cities. What, then, lies in store for our cities?

Cities and the Future: Through the Glass Brightly and Darkly Seen

The poverty and pathologies of the city will continue to challenge us. Governments at every level—and in varying degrees of effort—will attempt to ameliorate that poverty and (it will be hoped) curtail those pathologies. But as is the case for most all government programs, amelioration will be slow and uncertain. And while we wait for improvement, most of us will continue to fear inner-city violence and be greatly concerned about the city's racial and ethnic tensions. We will worry about urban crime and riots, and we will continue to watch middle-class flight from cities to suburbs. One scenario of the future, somber and pessimistic, is that some cities will implode, that they will collapse in on themselves as their residents move out, as houses and shops continue to be boarded up, as streets becomes increasingly unsafe.[3]

A Contravening Interpretation

But too much can be made of a dark future for our cities. Recall that American cities historically have been viewed with pessimistic suspicion. Given that history, we could reasonably ask, Are today's cities worse then the cities of, say, the 1890s? Many of the readily labeled urban crises of recent times have had an exceedingly short lifespan. For example, the 1970s were regarded as the decade of urban financial crisis, and New York City exemplified the city run aground on unsound fiscal practices, a declining tax base, and too many services. Today, a mere twenty years after its financial collapse, New York is on sound fiscal footing, held up as an example of how the modern American city should conduct its finances.

In a similar (albeit less dramatic) way, trends and fashions cast their shadows across our cities. A scant decade ago, Minneapolis was widely touted as one of the most liveable cities. Today, it has a disturbingly high homicide rate, and judgments concerning its liveability have changed. Perhaps, in a few years time, the homicide rate will decline, or perhaps public judgment concerning the qualities that make for liveability will shift. If so, those looking at Minneapolis's history may puzzle over today's critical account of life there.

Consonant with the foregoing ideas, it is useful to remember that the daily lives of most Americans are largely unaffected by today's urban crises. Even within Chicago, where the residents of Henry Horner Homes, Cabrini-Green, and Robert Taylor Homes face daily challenge and hardship created by their surroundings, most of the city's residents go on with their daily lives, not giving so much as a thought to the inner city and its problems. Nationally, no more than 10 million people live in ghetto neighborhoods, representing only about 5 percent of urban dwellers. Looking at numbers alone, we might conclude that the underclass and their struggle (some would say their lifestyle)

3. Devil's Night in Detroit is a real-life embodiment of this pessimistic scenario. For the past several years, on the night before Halloween the city explodes in flames. In an orgy of anger and frustration (and mindless entertainment), hundreds of fires are deliberately set in abandoned houses and factories—and sometimes in homes still occupied (Chafets 1990).

is but a minor issue for cities. But numbers tell only part of the story. For those who worry about the well-being of our society, the underclass problem is of grave concern, and it has become the dominant issue confronting most large cities (and many smaller cities). But even so, city councils meet, families attend PTA meetings, children go to school, and parents go to work, and a thousand and one other urban events occur unimpeded by the underclass (or even by thoughts of the underclass). In reality, the crisis of the cities is a crisis for the people who live in ghetto neighborhoods and for those who study and govern cities; it is no more than a passing concern for most other urban residents. *[The theory of multiple realities.]*

Again consonant with the foregoing ideas, the national society needs constant reminding that the horrifying events that frequently occur in cities are not always attributable to an urban pathology, that comparable events also occur in nonurban settings. Violence, though widely viewed as an urban problem, is also present in rural America—as exemplified in Truman Capote's *In Cold Blood* and in the shoot-out and conflagration outside Waco, Texas. Accordingly, and when considering our cities, it will be useful to keep in mind that most Americans live in urban areas, and as a consequence, violence is, perforce, more prevalent there than elsewhere. But violence is not, in and of itself, an urban problem.

Violence in cities (whatever its true state, whatever the statistics may tell us) is entangled in public perceptions, those who make municipal policy may be too readily tempted to seek policy remedies—especially in response to public outcry over acts of random violence—that promise quick and decisive results. But the problems of the city, and most especially the problems of the inner city, cannot be addressed either quickly or decisively. In attempting to fix today's problems, urban leaders risk being diverted from their larger task of identifying the functions the city should serve for its residents and developing policies to further those ends. Downtown revitalization is a step in the right direction. Revitalization builds on the city's strengths (its downtown, its people) and, at the same time, presents it in a new light to a doubting public. But, in the process of appealing to public perception, urban leaders ought not forget that the city is at its core a place of people, and that their long-term vision for its future must acknowledge the importance of all its inhabitants—including those who live in its ghetto neighborhoods.

Through the Glass Brightly: A Turn to the Future

In contrast to views of the cities as places of perennial crisis, an optimistic scenario reminds us that cities are more than the sum of their problems. They are social enterprises that symbolize what we and the rest of the world regard as the "American way of life." (After all, the modern skyscraper was invented in Chicago.) Cities are forever recreating and reinventing themselves, coping with adversity through change and adaptation. Examples include gentrification and restoration projects, bringing the equivalent of the suburban shopping mall downtown, rewriting zoning ordinances to encourage conversion of empty industrial buildings into apartments and studios, and offering tax inducements to industries willing to relocate to the inner city.

To the optimist's eye, big cities especially are seen and understood as the carriers of culture, places of industrial and business leadership, streets of dazzling architecture, places for chance and challenging encounters, creators of wealth, centers of creativity, vast shopping bazaars, and levers of social and political change. In short, and as the optimist would write a scenario of what lies ahead, cities will continue to be satisfying places to live and visit; true to their history, they will continue to change in ways that will blunt adversity and assure a reasonably successful future. As Jean Gottmann (1989, 168) says, "The modern metropolis is the largest and most complex artifact that humankind has ever produced."

References

Adams, Carolyn T. 1994. "Race and Class in Philadelphia Mayoral Elections." In George E. Peterson (ed.), *Big-City Politics, Governance, and Fiscal Constraints.* Washington, DC: Urban Institute.

Adler, Nancy E.; Boyce, W. Thomas; Chesney, Margaret A.; Folkman, Susan; and Syme, S. Leonard. 1993. "Socioeconomic Inequalities in Health: No Easy Solution." *Journal of the American Medical Association, 269,* 3140–3145.

Adrian, Charles R. and Press, Charles. 1977. *Governing Urban America.* 5th ed. New York: McGraw-Hill.

Advisory Commission on Intergovernmental Relations. 1973. *City Financial Emergencies: The Intergovernmental Dimension.* Washington, DC: U.S. Government Printing Office.

Advisory Commission on Intergovernmental Relations. 1980. *Citizen Participation in the American Federal System.* Washington, DC: U.S. Government Printing Office.

Advisory Commission on Intergovernmental Relations. 1984. *Fiscal Disparities: Central Cities and Suburbs, 1981.* Washington, DC: U.S. Government Printing Office.

Advisory Commission on Intergovernmental Relations. 1985. *Local Revenue Diversification: User Charges.* Washington, DC: U.S. Government Printing Office.

Alex-Assensoh, Yvette. 1995. "Myths about Race and the Underclass: Concentrated Poverty and 'Underclass' Behaviors." *Urban Affairs Review, 31,* 3–19.

Alford, Robert R. and Lee, Eugene C. 1968. "Voting Turnout in American Cities." *American Political Science Review, 62,* 796–813.

References

Alinsky, Saul D. 1946. *Reveille for Radicals*. Chicago: University of Chicago Press.

Alinsky, Saul D. 1971. *Rules for Radicals: A Practical Primer for Realistic Radicals*. New York: Random House.

Ambrose, P. and Colenutt, B. 1975. *The Property Machine*. Harmondsworth, England: Penguin.

Ames, David L.; Brown, Nevin C.; Callahan, Mary Helen; Cummings, Scott B.; Smock, Sue Marx; and Ziegler, Jerome M. 1992. "Rethinking American Urban Policy." *Journal of Urban Affairs, 14*, 197–216.

Anderson, Elijah. 1990. *Streetwise: Race, Class, and Change in an Urban Community*. Chicago: University of Chicago Press.

Anderson, Elijah. 1992. "The Story of John Turner." In Adele V. Harrell and George E. Peterson (eds.), *Drugs, Crime, and Social Isolation: Barriers to Urban Opportunity*. Washington, DC: Urban Institute.

Anderson, Martin. 1964. *The Federal Bulldozer: A Critical Analysis of Urban Renewal*. Cambridge, MA: MIT Press.

Ando, Faith. 1988. *An Analysis of Access to Bank Credit*. Los Angeles: UCLA Center for Afro-American Studies.

Andrews, Wayne. 1946. *Battle for Chicago*. New York: Harcourt, Brace.

Anglin, Roland. 1994. "Searching for Justice: Court-Inspired Housing Policy as a Mechanism for Social and Economic Mobility." *Urban Affairs Quarterly, 29*, 432–453.

Arkes, Hadley. 1981. *The Philosopher in the City: The Moral Dimensions of Urban Politics*. Princeton, NJ: Princeton University Press.

Armor, David J. 1972. "School and Family Effects on Black and White Achievement: A Reexamination of the USOE Data." In Frederick Mosteller and Daniel P. Moynihan (eds.), *On Equality of Educational Opportunity*. New York: Random House.

Armor, David J. 1995. *Forced Justice: School Desegregation and the Law*. New York: Oxford University Press.

Aronson, J. Richard and Hilley, John L. 1986. *Financing State and Local Governments*. Washington, DC: Brookings.

Atlas, John and Dreier, Peter. 1992. "From 'Projects' to Communities: How to Redeem Public Housing." *The American Prospect, 10*, 74–85.

Autry, C. J. 1994. "'HOPE' for Home Ownership." *Journal of Housing*, Sept./Oct., 36–43.

Bachman, Ronet. 1992. *Crime Victimization in City, Suburban, and Rural Areas*. Washington, DC: U.S. Dept. Of Justice.

Bachrach, Peter. 1967. *The Theory of Democratic Elitism: A Critique*. Boston: Little, Brown.

Bachrach, Peter and Baratz, Morton S. 1962. "Two Faces of Power." *American Political Science Review, 54*, 947–952.

Badger, Lee W.; Jones, L. Ralph; and Parlour, Richard R. 1981. "*Wyatt v. Stickney*: Context and Consequence." In L. Ralph Jones and Richard R. Parlour (eds.), *Wyatt v. Stickney: Retrospect and Prospect*. New York: Grune and Stratton.

Baim, Dean V. 1994. *The Sports Stadium as a Municipal Investment*. Westport, CT: Greenwood.

Bane, Mary Jo. 1986. "Household Composition and Poverty." In Sheldon H. Danziger and Daniel H. Weinberg (eds.), *Fighting Poverty: What Works and What Doesn't*. Cambridge, MA: Harvard University Press.

494

Bane, Mary Jo. 1994. "Increasing Self-Sufficiency by Reforming Welfare." In Mary Jo Bane and David T. Ellwood (eds.), *Welfare Realities: From Rhetoric to Reform.* Cambridge, MA: Harvard University Press.

Bane, Mary Jo and Jargowsky, Paul A. 1988. "Urban Poverty Areas: Basic Questions Concerning Prevalence, Growth, and Dynamics." Center for Health and Human Resources Policy Discussion Paper Series, Harvard University.

Banfield, Edward C. 1974. *The Unheavenly City Revisisted.* Boston: Little, Brown.

Banfield, Edward C. And Wilson, James Q. 1963. *City Politics.* Cambridge, MA: Harvard University Press.

Baron, Harold M. 1971. "Race and Status in School Spending: Chicago, 1961–1966." *Journal of Human Resources, 6,* 1–24.

Baskin, John. 1976. *New Burlington: The Life and Death of an American Village.* New York: Norton.

Bates, Timothy. 1993. *Banking on Black Enterprise: The Potential of Emerging Firms for Revitalizing Urban Economies.* Washington, DC: Joint Center for Political and Economic Studies.

Baum, Alice S. and Burnes, Donald W. 1993. *A Nation of Denial: The Truth about Homelessness.* Boulder, CO: Westview.

Bayor, Ronald H. 1988. "Roads to Racial Segregation: Atlanta in the Twentieth Century." *Journal of Urban History, 15,* 3–21.

Beer, Samuel H. 1993. *To Make a Nation: The Rediscovery of American Federalism.* Cambridge, MA: Harvard University Press.

Beer, Thomas. 1961. *The Mauve Decade: American Life at the End of the Nineteenth Century.* New York: Vintage.

Belasich, Deborah K. 1993. *Enterprise Zones: Policy Perspectives of Economic Development.* New York: Garland.

Bellah, Robert N.; Madsen, Richard; Sullivan, William M.; Swidler, Ann; and Tipton, Steven M. 1985. *Habits of the Heart: Individualism and Commitment in American Life.* New York: Harper and Row.

Bellman, Richard F. 1983. "Report on the Question of Zoning." In *A Sheltered Crisis: The State of Fair Housing in the Eighties.* Washington, DC: U.S. Commission on Civil Rights.

Bender, Leslie. 1983. "Home Rule Revisited." *Journal of Legislation, 10.*

Bennett, Larry. 1993. "Rethinking Neighborhoods, Neighborhood Research, and Neighborhood Policy: Lessons from Uptown." *Journal of Urban Affairs, 15,* 245–257.

Benton, J. Edwin. 1985. "American Federalism's First Principles and Reagan's New Federalism Policies." *Policy Studies Journal, 13,* 568–575.

Berkeley, George E. And Fox, Douglas M. 1978. *80,000 Governments: The Politics of Subnational America.* Boston: Allyn and Bacon.

Berman, David R. 1996. "State-Local Relations: Mandates, Money, Partnerships." *Municipal Yearbook.* Washington, DC: International City Management Association.

Berrueta-Clement, John; Schweinhart, Lawrence J.; Barnett, W. Steven; Epstein, Ann; and Weikart, David P. 1984. *Changed Lives: The Effects of the Perry Preschool Program on Youths Through Age 19.* Ypsilanti, MI: High/Scope Press.

Berry, Jeffrey M.; Portney, Kent E.; and Thomson, Ken. 1991. "The Political Behavior of Poor People." In Christopher Jencks and Paul E. Peterson (eds.), *The Urban Underclass.* Washington, DC: Brookings.

References

Besharov, Douglas J. 1987. "Giving the Juvenile Court a Preschool Education." In James Q. Wilson and Glenn C. Loury (eds.), *From Children to Citizens*, vol. 3, *Families, Schools, and Delinquency Prevention*. New York: Springer-Verlag.

Bienen, Henry. 1968. *Violence and Social Change: A Review of Current Literature*. Chicago: University of Chicago Press.

Bing, Léon. 1991. *Do or Die*. New York: HarperCollins.

Bingham, Richard D.; Hawkins, Brett W.; and Hebert, F. Ted. 1978. *The Politics of Raising State and Local Revenue*. New York: Praeger.

Bisgaier, Carl. 1977. "Notes on Implementation." In Jerome G. Rose and Robert E. Rothman (eds.), *After Mount Laurel: The New Suburban Zoning*. New Brunswick, NJ: Center for Urban Policy Research, Rutgers University.

Bisgaier, Carl. 1983. "Statement." In *A Sheltered Crisis: The State of Fair Housing in the Eighties*. Washington, DC: U.S. Commission on Civil Rights.

Bish, Robert L. 1971. *Public Economy of Metropolitan Areas*. Chicago: Markham.

Bishop, Donna M. and Frazier, Charles E. 1988. "The Influence of Race in Juvenile Justice Processing." *Journal of Research in Crime and Delinquency, 25*, 242–263.

Black, J. Thomas; Howland, Libby; and Rogel, Stuart L. 1983. *Downtown Retail Development: Conditions for Success and Project Profiles*. Washington, DC: Urban Land Institute.

Blau, Joel. 1992. *The Visible Poor: Homelessness in the United States*. New York: Oxford University Press.

Block, Peter B. 1974. *Equality of Distribution of Police Services: A Case Study of Washington, DC*. Washington, DC: Urban Institute.

Bluestone, Barry. 1990. "The Great U-Turn Revisited: Economic Restructuring, Jobs, and the Redistribution of Earnings." In John D. Kasarda (ed.), *Jobs, Earnings, and Employment Growth Policies in the United States*. Boston: Kluwer.

Bolland, John M. 1984. "The Limits to Pluralism: Power and Leadership in a Nonparticipatory Society." *Power and Elites, 1*, 69–88.

Bolland, John M. 1985a. "Perceived Leadership Stability and the Structure of Urban Agenda-Setting Networks." *Social Networks, 7*, 153–172.

Bolland, John M. 1985b. "Political Power and Public Policy: A Cognitive Interpretation." Paper presented at the annual meeting of the Midwest Political Science Association, Chicago.

Bolland, John M. and McCallum, Debra M. 1995a. "The Magnitude and Demographics of Homelessness in Mobile Alabama." Unpublished Report, Institute for Social Science Research, University of Alabama.

Bolland, John M. and McCallum, Debra M. 1995b. "Community Building as a Public Health Intervention." Paper presented at the annual meeting of the American Public Health Association, San Diego, CA.

Bolland, John M. and Redfield, Kent D. 1988. "The Limits of Citizen Participation in Local Education: A Cognitive Interpretation." *Journal of Politics, 50*, 1033–1046.

Bolland, John M. and Selby, John. 1988. "Race and Agenda-Setting Networks in the New South." Paper presented at the annual meeting of the American Political Science Association, Washington.

Bollens, John C. 1969. *American County Government*. Beverly Hills, CA: Sage.

Bollens, John C. and Schmandt, Henry J. 1982. *The Metropolis: Its People, Politics, and Economic Life*. 4th ed. New York: Harper and Row.

Bolotin, Fredric N. and Cingranelli, David L. 1983. "Equity and Urban Policy: The Underclass Hypothesis Revisited." *Journal of Politics, 45,* 209–219.

Boorstin, Daniel J. 1974. *The Americans: The Colonial Experience.* New York: Vintage.

Boots, Andrew J.; Dawson, Grace; Silverman, William; and Hatry, Harry P. 1972. *Inequality in Local Government Services: A Case Study of Neighborhood Roads.* Washington, DC: Urban Institute.

Bowman, John H.; MacManus, Susan A.; and Mikesell, John L. 1992. "Mobilizing Resources for Public Services: Financing Urban Governments." *Journal of Urban Affairs, 14,* 311–335.

Boyer, Richard and Savageau, David. 1993. *Places Rated Almanac: Your Guide to Finding the Best Places to Live in America.* New York: Prentice-Hall.

Boyte, Harry C. 1980. *The Backyard Revolution: Understanding the New Citizen Movement.* Philadelphia, PA: Temple University Press.

Brady, Henry E.; Verba, Sidney; and Schlozman, Kay L. 1995. "Beyond SES: A Resource Model of Political Participation." *American Political Science Review, 89,* 271–294.

Branch, Taylor. 1988. *Parting the Waters: America in the King Years 1954–1963.* New York: Simon and Schuster.

Bressner, Kurt. 1995. "An Opportunity to Learn, Part II." *Public Management, 77* (10), 17–26.

Brewer, Gary D. and deLeon, Peter. 1983. *The Foundations of Policy Analysis.* Chicago: Dorsey.

Bridenbaugh, Carl. 1938. *Cities in the Wilderness: the First Century of Urban Life in America (1625–1742).* New York: Ronald.

Bridenbaugh, Carl. 1955. *Cities in Revolt: Urban Life in America (1743–1776).* New York: Capricorn.

Bridges, Amy. 1984. *A City in the Republic: Antebellum New York and the Origins of Machine Politics.* New York: Cambridge University Press.

Brown, Lawrence, D.; Fossett, James W.; and Palmer, Kenneth T. 1984. *The Changing Politics of Federal Grants.* Washington, DC: Brookings.

Browning, Rufus P.; Marshall, Dale Rogers; and Tabb, David H. 1984. *Protest Is Not Enough: The Struggle of Blacks and Hispanics for Equality in Urban Politics.* Berkeley: University of California Press.

Brudney, Jeffrey L. 1989. "The Use of Volunteers by Local Governments as an Approach to Fiscal Stress." In Terry N. Clark, William Lyons, and Michael R. Fitzgerald (eds.), *Research in Urban Policy,* vol. 3. Greenwich, CT: JAI.

Bryan, John H. and Picard, Raymond (eds.). 1979. *Managing Fire Services.* Washington, DC: International City Management Association.

Bryce, James B. 1889. *The American Commonwealth.* 2nd ed. rev. London: Macmillan.

Buckwalter, Doyle W. 1982. "Dillon's Rule in the 1980's: Who's in Charge of Local Affairs?" *National Civic Review, 71,* 399–406.

Buenker, John D. 1973. *Urban Liberalism and Progressive Reform.* New York: Norton.

Burke, James. 1978. *Connections.* Boston: Little, Brown.

Burt, Martha R. 1992. *Over the Edge: The Growth of Homelessness in the 1980s.* New York: Russell Sage.

Bushman, Richard L. 1992. *The Refinement of America: Persons, Houses, Cities.* New York: Knopf.

497

References

Cain, Glen G. and Watts, Harold W. 1972. "Problems in Making Policy Inferences from the Coleman Report." In Peter H. Rossi and Walter Williams (eds.), *Evaluating Social Programs: Theory, Practice, and Politics,* New York: Academic.

Campbell, Angus and Schuman, Howard. 1968. "Racial Attitudes in Fifteen American Cities." In National Advisory Commission on Civil Disorders, *Supplemental Studies.* Washington, DC: U.S. Government Printing Office.

Canada, Geoffrey. 1995. *Fist, Stick, Knife, Gun: A Personal History of Violence in America.* Boston: Beacon.

Caro, Robert A. 1974. *The Power Broker: Robert Moses and the Fall of New York.* New York: Knopf.

Carver, Joan. 1973. "Responsiveness and Consolidation: A Case Study." *Urban Affairs Quarterly, 9,* 211–250.

Case, A. and Katz, L. F. 1990. The Company You Keep: The Effect of Family and Neighborhood on Disadvantaged Youths. Unpublished paper.

Castells, Manuel. 1977. *The Urban Question: A Marxist Approach.* Cambridge, MA: MIT Press.

Chafets, Ze'ev. 1990. *Devil's Night and Other True Tales of Detroit.* New York: Vintage.

Chandler, Mittie Olion. 1992. "Obstacles to Housing Integration Program Efforts." In George C. Galster and Edward W. Hill (eds.), *The Metropolis in Black and White: Place, Power, and Polarization.* New Brunswick, NJ: Rutgers University Press.

Charles, Michael T. 1986. *Policing the Streets.* Springfield, IL: Charles C. Thomas.

Chavis, David M. and Newbrough, J.R. 1986. "The Meaning of 'Community' in Community Psychology." *Journal of Community Psychology, 14,* 335–340.

Childs, Richard S. 1952. *Civic Victories: The Story of an Unfinished Revolution.* New York: Harper.

Chiricos, Theodore G. and Bales, William D. 1991. "Unemployment and Punishment: An Empirical Assessment." *Criminology, 29,* 701–724.

Chudacoff, Howard P. 1975. *The Evolution of American Urban Society.* Englewood Cliffs, NJ: Prentice-Hall.

Clark, Cal and Walter, Oliver. 1994. "Cuts, Cultures, and City Limits in Reagan's New Federalism." In Terry N. Clark (ed.), *Urban Innovation: Creative Strategies for Turbulent Times.* Thousand Oaks, CA: Sage.

Clark, Kenneth, 1956. *The Nude: A Study of Ideal Art.* Princeton, NJ: Princeton University Press.

Clark, Terry N. 1994. "Innovations That Work: A Menu of Strategies." In Terry N. Clark (ed.), *Urban Innovation: Creative Strategies for Turbulent Times.* Thousand Oaks, CA: Sage.

Clark, Terry N. and Ferguson, Lorna C. 1983. *City Money: Political Processes, Fiscal Strain, and Retrenchment.* New York: Columbia University Press.

Clark, W.A.V. 1986. "Residential Segregation in American Cities: A Review and Interpretation." *Population Research and Policy Review, 5,* 95–127.

Clay, Phillip. 1992. "The (Un)Housed City: Racial Patterns of Segregation, Housing Quality, and Affordability." In George C. Galster and Edward W. Hill (eds.), *The Metropolis in Black and White: Place, Power, and Polarization.* New Brunswick, NJ: Rutgers University Press.

Coates, Robert C. 1990. *A Street Is Not a Home: Solving America's Homeless Dilemma.* Buffalo, NY: Prometheus.

Cobb, Roger and Elder, Charles D. 1983. *Participation in American Politics: The Dynamics of Agenda-Building*. 2nd ed. Boston: Allyn and Bacon.

Coleman, James S. 1957. *Community Conflict*. Glencoe, IL: Free Press.

Coleman, James S. 1979. "Destructive Beliefs and Potential Policies in School Desegregation." In John W. Smith (ed.), *Detroit Metropolitan City-Suburban Relations*. Dearborn, MI: Henry Ford Community College Occasional Papers.

Coleman, James S.; Campbell, E.Q.; Hobson, C.F.; McPortland, J.; and Mood, A.M. 1966. *Equality of Educational Opportunity*. Washington, DC: Dept. of Health, Education, and Welfare.

Coleman, James S. and Kelly, Sara. 1976. "Education." In William Gorham and Nathan Glazer (eds.), *The Urban Predicament*. Washington, DC: Urban Institute.

Collins, John G. 1993. "Prevalence of Selected Chronic Conditions: United States, 1986–1988." National Center for Health Statistics. *Vital and Health Statistics 10* (182).

Collins, Richard C.; Waters, Elizabeth B.; and Dotson, A. Bruce. 1991. *America's Downtowns: Growth, Politics, and Preservation*. Washington, DC: Preservation Press.

Conlin, Joseph R. 1984. *The Morrow Book of Quotations in American History*. New York: Morrow.

Connery, Donald S. 1972. *One American Town: A Relic of the Past—A Model for the Future*. New York: Simon and Schuster.

Converse, Philip E. 1964. "The Nature of Belief Systems in Mass Publics." In David Apter (ed.), *Ideology and Discontent*. New York: Wiley.

Converse, Philip E.; Miller, Warren E.; Rusk, Jerrold G.; and Wolfe, Arthur C. 1969. "Continuity and Change in American Politics: Parties and Issues in the 1968 Election." *American Political Science Review, 63*, 1083–1105.

Cook, Stuart W. 1984. "The 1954 Social Science Statement and School Desegregation: A Reply to Gerard." *American Psychologist, 39*, 819–832.

Cook, Thomas D. and Campbell, Donald T. 1979. *Quasi-Experimentation: Design and Analysis Issues for Field Settings*. Boston: Houghton Mifflin.

Corcoran, Mary; Gordon, Roger H.; Laren, Deborah; and Solon, Gary. 1987. "Intergenerational Transmission of Education, Income, and Earnings." Unpublished paper, Institute of Public Policy Studies, University of Michigan.

Coulter, Philip B. 1978. "Equity and Efficiency in Fire Protection." Paper presented at the annual meeting of the American Society for Public Administration, Phoenix.

Coulter, Philip B. 1980. "Measuring the Inequality of Urban Public Services: A Methodological Discussion With Applications." *Policy Studies Journal, 8*, 683–698.

Coulter, Philip B. 1988. *Political Voice: Citizen Demand for Urban Public Services*. Tuscaloosa: University of Alabama Press.

Coulter, Philip B. 1992. "There's a Madness in the Method: Redefining Citizen Contacting of Government Officials." *Urban Affairs Quarterly, 28*, 297–316.

Cox, Kevin R. 1973. *Conflict, Power and Politics in the City: A Geographic View*. New York: McGraw-Hill.

Cox, Kevin R. 1978. *Urbanization and Conflict in Market Societies*. New York: Metheun.

Crain, Robert L.; Katz, Elihu; and Rosenthal, Donald. 1969. *The Politics of Community Conflict: The Fluoridation Decision*. Indianapolis, IN: Bobbs-Merrill.

Crane, Jonathan. 1991. "Effects of Neighborhoods on Dropping Out of School and

Teenage Childbearing." In Christopher Jencks and Paul E. Peterson (eds.), *The Urban Underclass*. Washington, DC: Brookings.

Crenson, Matthew. 1971. *The Unpolitics of Air Pollution: A Study of Non-Decision Making in the Cities*. Baltimore, MD: Johns Hopkins University Press.

Crewe, Ivor. 1981. "Electoral Participation." In David Butler, Howard Penniman, and Auston Ranney (eds.), *Democracy at the Polls: A Comparative Study of National Elections*. Washington, DC: American Enterprise Institute.

Croly, Herbert. 1909. *The Promise of American Life*. New York: Macmillan.

Cuomo, Mario. 1975. *Forest Hills Diary: The Crisis of Low Income Housing*. New York: Vintage.

Dahl, Robert A. 1961. *Who Governs? Democracy and Power in an American City*. New Haven, CT: Yale University Press.

Dahl, Robert A. and Lindblom, Charles E. 1953. *Politics, Economics, and Welfare: Planning and Politico-Economic Systems Resolved into Basic Social Processes*. New York: Harper and Row.

Danielson, Michael N. 1976. *The Politics of Exclusion*. New York: Columbia University Press.

Darden, Joe T. 1987. "Choosing Neighbors and Neighborhoods: The Role of Race in Housing Preference." In Gary A. Tobin (ed.), *Divided Neighborhoods: Changing Patterns of Racial Segregation*. Newbury Park, CA: Sage.

Davies, Don. 1980. "School Administrators and Advisory Councils: Partnership or Shotgun Marriage?" *NASSP Bulletin, 64*, 62–66.

Davis, Morris and Weinbaum, Marvin G. 1969. *Metropolitan Decision Processes: An Analysis of Case Studies*. Chicago: Rand McNally.

de Grazia, Alfred. 1965. *Political Behavior*. New York: Free Press.

De Vise, Pierre. 1973. *Misused and Misplaced Hospitals and Doctors: A Locational Analysis of the Urban Health Care Crisis*. Washington, DC: Association of American Geographers.

Dear, Michael J. and Wolch, Jennifer R. 1987. *Landscapes of Despair: From Deinstitutionalization to Homelessness*. Princeton, NJ: Princeton University Press.

Dearborn, Philip M.; Peterson, George E.; and Kirk, Richard H. 1992. *City Finances in the 1990s*. Washington, DC: Urban Institute.

DeHoog, Ruth Hoogland; Lowery, David; and Lyons, William E. 1991. "Metropolitan Fragmentation and Suburban Ghettos: Some Empirical Observations on Institutional Racism." *Journal of Urban Affairs, 13*, 479–493.

DeHoog, Ruth Hoogland and Whitaker, Gordon P. 1990. "Political Conflict or Professional Advancement: Alternative Explanations of City Manager Turnover." *Journal of Urban Affairs, 12*, 361–377.

DeLeon, Richard E. 1992. "The Urban Antiregime: Progressive Politics in San Francisco." *Urban Affairs Quarterly, 27*, 555–579.

DeSantis, Victor S. and Newell, Charldean. 1996. "Local Government Managers' Career Paths." In *The Municipal Yearbook*. Washington, DC: International City Management Association.

DeSena, Judith N. 1994. "Women: The Gatekeepers of Urban Neighborhoods." *Journal of Urban Affairs 16*, 271–283.

Devine, Joel A. and Wright, James D. 1993. *The Greatest of Evils: Urban Poverty and the American Underclass.* New York: Aldine de Gruyter.

Dillon, John. 1911. *Commentaries on the Law of Municipal Corporations.* 1872 ed. Boston: Little, Brown.

Dimond, Paul R. 1978. *A Dilemma of Local Government: Discrimination in the Provision of Public Services.* Lexington, MA: Lexington.

Dornbush, Sanford M. and Ritter, Philip L. 1988. "Parents of High School Students: A Neglected Resource." *Educational Horizons, 66,* 75–77.

Downes, Bryan T. 1970. "A Critical Reexamination of the Social and Political Characteristics of Riot Cities." *Social Science Quarterly, 51,* 349–360.

Downs, Anthony. 1973. *Opening up the Suburbs: An Urban Strategy for America.* New Haven, CT: Yale University Press.

Downs, Anthony. 1981. *Neighborhoods and Urban Development.* Washington, DC: Brookings.

Drennan, Matthew. 1991. "The Decline and Rise of the New York Economy." In John H. Mollenkopf and Manuel Castells (eds.), *Dual City: Restructuring New York.* New York: Russell Sage.

Dye, Thomas R. 1962. "Metropolitan Integration by Bargaining Among Sub-Areas." *American Behavioral Scientist, 5,* 11.

Dye, Thomas R. 1964. "Urban Political Integration: Conditions Associated with Annexation in American Cities." *Midwest Journal of Political Science, 8,* 430–446.

Dye, Thomas R. 1969. *Politics in States and Communities.* Englewood Cliffs, NJ: Prentice-Hall.

Dye, Thomas R. and Zeigler, L. Harmon. 1975. *The Irony of Democracy: An Uncommon Introduction to American Politics.* 3rd ed. North Scituate, MA: Duxbury.

Easton, David. 1953. *The Political System: An Inquiry into the State of Political Science.* New York: Knopf.

Edelman, Murray J. 1964. *The Symbolic Uses of Politics.* Urbana: University of Illinois Press.

Eisinger, Peter K. 1973. "The Conditions of Protest Behavior in American Cities." *American Political Science Review, 67,* 11–28.

Eisinger, Peter K. 1984. "Black Mayors and the Politics of Racial Economic Advancement." In Harlan Hahn and Charles H. Levine (eds.), *Urban Politics: Past, Present, and Future.* New York: Longman.

Elkin, Stephen L. 1987. *City and Regime in the American Republic.* Chicago: University of Chicago Press.

Ellwood, David T. 1994. "Understanding Dependency." In Mary Jo Bane and David T. Ellwood (eds.), *Welfare Realities: From Rhetoric to Reform.* Cambridge, MA: Harvard University Press.

Ellwood, David T. and Bane, Mary Jo. 1994. "Understanding Welfare Dynamics." In Mary Jo Bane and David T. Ellwood (eds.), *Welfare Realities: From Rhetoric to Reform.* Cambridge, MA: Harvard University Press.

Emerson, Robert M. 1969. *Judging Delinquents: Context and Process in Juvenile Courts.* New York: Aldine.

Epstein, William M. 1996. "Passing into Proverbs." *Society* (July/Aug.), 19–22.

References

Fagan, Jeffrey. 1992. "Drug Selling and Licit Income in Distressed Neighborhoods: The Economic Lives of Street-Level Drug Users and Dealers." In Adele V. Harrell and George E. Peterson (eds.), *Drugs, Crime, and Social Isolation: Barriers to Urban Opportunity*. Washington, DC: Urban Institute.

Fainstein, Susan and Fainstein, Norman. 1991. "The Changing Character of Community Politics in New York City: 1968–1988." In John H. Mollenkopf and Manuel Castells (eds.), *Dual City: Restructuring New York*. New York: Russell Sage.

Farley, John E. 1987. "Segregation in 1980: How Segregated are America's Metropolitan Areas?" In Gary A. Tobin (ed.), *Divided Neighborhoods: Changing Patterns of Racial Segregation*. Newbury Park, CA: Sage.

Farley, John E. 1995. "Race Still Matters: The Minimal Role of Income and Housing Cost as Causes of Housing Segregation in St. Louis, 1990." *Urban Affairs Review, 31,* 244–254.

Farley, Reynolds. 1975. "Racial Integration in the Public Schools, 1967 to 1972: Assessing the Effects of Governmental Policies." *Sociological Focus 8,* 3–26.

Farley, Reynolds. 1991. "Residential Segregation of Social and Economic Groups among Blacks, 1970–1980." In Christopher Jencks and Paul E. Peterson (eds.), *The Urban Underclass*. Washington, DC: Brookings.

Feagin, Joe R. and Hahn, Harlan. 1973. *Ghetto Revolts: The Politics of Violence in American Cities*. New York: Macmillan.

Feagin, Joe R. and Parker, Robert. 1990. *Building American Cities: The Urban Real Estate Game*. 2nd ed. Englewood Cliffs, NJ: Prentice-Hall.

Feiock, Richard C. 1986. "The Political Economy of Urban Service Distribution: A Test of the Underclass Hypothesis." *Journal of Urban Affairs, 8,* 31–42.

Finley, M.I. 1966. *The Ancient Greeks*. Harmondsworth, England: Penguin.

Fischer, Claude S.; Baldassare, M.; Gerson, K.; Jackson, R.M.; Jones, L.M.; and Steuve, C.A. 1977. *Networks and Places: Social Relations in the Urban Setting*. New York: Free Press.

Flickinger, Barbara and McManus, Katherine. 1996. "Have Public Finance Foundations Been Shaken?" *Public Management, 78* (1), 18–23.

Fogelson, Robert M. 1971. *Violence as Protest: A Study of Riots and Ghettos*. Garden City, NY: Doubleday.

Fogelson, Robert M. and Hill, Robert B. 1968. *Who Riots? A Study of Participation in the 1967 Riots*. National Advisory Commission on Civil Disorders, Supplemental Studies. Washington, DC: U.S. Government Printing Office.

Ford, Larry R. 1994. *Cities and Buildings: Skyscrapers, Skid Rows, and Suburbs*. Baltimore, MD: Johns Hopkins University Press.

Ford, Paul L. (ed.). 1914. *The Works of Thomas Jefferson*. New York: Putnam.

Frieden, Bernard J. and Sagalyn, Lynne B. 1989. *Downtown, Inc.: How America Rebuilds Cities*. Cambridge, MA: MIT Press.

Friedman, Milton and Friedman, Rose. 1981. *Freedom to Choose*. New York: Avon.

Frug, Gerald. 1984. "The City as a Legal Concept." In Lloyd Rodwin and Robert M. Hollister (eds.), *Cities of the Mind: Images and Themes of the City in the Social Sciences*. New York: Plenum.

Fuchs, Ester R. 1992. *Mayors and Money: Fiscal Policy in New York and Chicago*. Chicago: University of Chicago Press.

Fukurai, Hiroshi; Krooth, Richard; and Butler, Edgar W. 1994. "The Rodney King Beating Verdicts." In Mark Baldassre (ed.), *The Los Angeles Riots: Lessons for the Urban Future*. Boulder, CO: Westview.

Galaskiewicz, Joseph. 1979. *Exchange Networks and Community Politics*. Beverly Hills, CA: Sage.

Galster, George. 1990a. "Racial Steering by Real Esatae Agents: Mechanisms and Motives." *The Review of Black Political Economy, 19*, 39–63.

Galster, George. 1990b. "Racial Steering in Urban Housing Markets: A Review of the Audit Evidence." *The Review of Black Political Economy, 18*, 105–129.

Gans, Herbert J. 1990. "Deconstructing the Underclass: The Term's Dangers as a Planning Concept." *Journal of the American Planning Association, 56*, 271–277.

Gans, Herbert J. 1995. *The War Against the Poor: The Underclass and Antipoverty Policy*. New York: Basic Books.

Gardiner, John A. and Lyman, Theodore R. 1978. *Decisions for Sale*. New York: Praeger.

Gardiner, John A. and Olson David J. (eds.). 1974. *Theft of the City: Readings on Corruption in Urban America*. Bloomington: Indiana University Press.

Garreau, Joel. 1991. *Edge City: Life on the New Frontier*. New York: Doubleday.

Gelfand, Mark. 1975. *A Nation of Cities: The Federal Government and Urban America*. New York: Oxford University Press.

Gilbert, Claire W. 1968. "Community Power and Decision Making: A Quantitative Examination of Previous Research." In Terry N. Clark (ed.), *Community Structure and Decision Making: Comparative Analyses*. San Francisco: Chandler.

Ginzberg, Eli. 1994. "Improving Health Care for the Poor: Lessons from the 1980s." *Journal of the American Medical Association, 271*, 464–467.

Glaab, Charles N. and Brown, A. Theodore. 1976. *A History of Urban America*. 2nd ed. New York: Macmillan.

Glazer, Nathan. 1967. "Housing Problems and Housing Politics." *The Public Interest, 7*, 21–51.

Goldfield, David R. 1993. "Black Political Power and Public Policy in the Urban South." In Arnold R. Hirsch and Raymond A. Mohl (eds.), *Urban Policy in Twentieth-Century America*. New Brunswick, NJ: Rutgers University Press.

Goldman, Eric F. 1956. *Rendezvous with Destiny: A History of Modern American Reform*. New York: Vintage.

Goldman, Howard H. and Morrisey, Joseph P. 1985. "The Alchemy of Mental Health Policy: Homelessness and the Fourth Cycle of Reform." *American Journal of Public Health, 75*, 727–731.

Goodlad, John I. 1984. *A Place Called School: Prospects for the Future*. New York: McGraw-Hill.

Goodnow, Frank S. 1895. *Municipal Home Rule: A Study in Administration*. New York: Macmillan.

Goodwin, Leonard. 1983. *Causes and Cures of Welfare: New Evidence on the Social Psychology of the Poor*. Lexington, MA: Lexington.

Gottdiener, Mark. 1993. *The New Urban Sociology*. New York: McGraw-Hill.

Gottmann, Jean. 1989. "Past and Present of the Western City." In Richard Lawton (ed.), *The Rise and Fall of the Great Cities: Aspects of Urbanization in the Western World*. London: Belhaven.

References

Government of the District of Columbia. 1979. *Tax Burdens in Washington, D.C. Compared with Those in the Nation's Thirty Largest Cities, 1977.* Department of Finance and Revenue.

Government of the District of Columbia. 1988. *Tax Rates and Tax Burdens in the District of Columbia: A Nationwide Comparison.* Department of Finance and Revenue.

Grall, Timothy S. 1994. *Households at Risk: Their Housing Situation.* Washington, DC: U.S. Department of Commerce, Bureau of the Census.

Gramlich, Edward M. and Laren, Deborah. 1991. "Geographical Mobility and Persistent Poverty." Paper presented at the Conference on Labor Markets and Labor Mobility.

Grant, Madison. 1916. *The Passing of the Great Race: Or, the Racial Basis of European History.* New York: Scribner's.

Gratz, Roberta B. 1989. *The Living City: Thinking Big in a Small Way.* New York: Simon and Schuster.

Green, Constance M. 1957. *American Cities in the Growth of the Nation.* London: Athlene.

Green, Robert L. 1977. *The Urban Challenge—Poverty and Race.* Chicago: Follett.

Green, Roy E. and Reed, B.J. 1988. "Occupational Stress and Mobility among Professional Local Government Managers: A Decade of Change." In the *Municipal Yearbook.* Washington, DC: International City Management Assocaition.

Greer, Scott A. 1965. *Urban Renewal and American Cities: The Dilemma of Democratic Intervention.* Indianapolis, IN: Bobbs-Merrill.

Griswold, Alfred Whitney. 1948. *Farming and Democracy.* New York: Harcourt, Brace.

Groth, Paul. 1994. *Living Downtown: The History of Residential Hotels in the United States.* Berkeley: University of California Press.

Grumm, J.G. and Murphy, R.D. 1974. "Dillon's Rule Reconsidered." *Annals of the American Academy of Political and Social Science, 416,* 120.

Gunn, J.A.W. 1969. *Politics and the Public Interest in the 17th Century.* London: Routledge and Kegan Paul.

Haar, Charles M. 1975. *Between the Idea and the Reality: A Study in the Origin, Fate, and Legacy of the Model City Program.* Boston: Little, Brown.

Haar, Charles M. 1996. *Cities Under Siege: Race, Space, and Audacious Judges.* Princeton, NJ: Princeton University Press.

Halberstam, David. 1993. *The Fifties.* New York: Villard.

Hale, Dennis. 1985. "The Evolution of the Property Tax: A Study of the Relation between Public Finance and Political Theory." *Journal of Politics, 47,* 382–404.

Hale, George, E. and Palley, Marian Lief. 1981. *The Politics of Federal Grants.* Washington, DC: CQ Press.

Halpern, Robert. 1995. *Rebuilding the Inner City: A History of Neighborhood Initiatives to Address Poverty in the United States.* New York: Columbia University Press.

Hamilton, Alexander. 1961. "Federalist 9." In Alexander Hamilton, James Madison, and John Jay (eds.), *The Federalist Papers.* New York: Mentor.

Handler, Joel F. 1995. *The Poverty of Welfare Reform.* New Haven, CT: Yale University Press.

Handlin, Oscar. 1973. *The Uprooted: The Epic Story of the Great Migration That Made the American People.* Boston: Little, Brown.

Handlin, Oscar and Handlin, Mary F. 1975. *The Wealth of the American People: A History of American Affluence.* New York: McGraw-Hill.

Hanson, Norwood. 1958. *Patterns of Discovery: An Inquiry into the Conceptual Foundations of Science.* Cambridge, England: Cambridge University Press.

Hanson, Russell L. 1985. *The Democratic Imagination in America: Conversations with the Past.* Princeton, NJ: Princeton University Press.

Hanushek, Eric. 1989. "The Impact of Differential Expenditures on School Performance." *Educational Researcher, 18 (4),* 45–51.

Harrigan, John. 1985. *Political Change in the Metropolis.* 3rd ed. Boston: Little, Brown.

Harrigan, John. 1989. *Political Change in the Metropolis.* 4th ed. Boston: Little, Brown.

Harrington, Michael. 1962. *The Other America: Poverty in the United States.* New York: Macmillan.

Harrison, Bennett and Bluestone, Barry. 1988. *The Great U-Turn: Corporate Restructuring and the Polarizing of America.* New York: Basic Books.

Harrison, Roderick J. and Weinberg, Daniel H. 1992. "Racial and Ethnic Residential Segregation in 1990." Unpublished paper, U.S. Bureau of the Census.

Hartman, Chester W. 1975. *Housing and Social Policy.* Englewood Cliffs, NJ: Prentice-Hall.

Haskell, Thomas L. 1977. *The Emergence of Professional Social Science: The American Social Science Association and the Nineteenth Century Crisis of Authority.* Urbana: University of Illinois Press.

Hawkins, Brett W. 1966. *Nashville Metro: The Politics of City-County Consolidation.* Nashville, TN: Vanderbilt University Press.

Hays, Samuel P. 1964. "The Politics of Reform in Municipal Government in the Progressive Era." *Pacific Northwest Quarterly, 55,* 157–169.

Henderson, A. Scott. 1995. "Tarred with the Exceptional Image:" Public Housing and Popular Discourse, 1950–1990." *American Studies, 36,* 31–52.

Henderson, Anne T. 1988. "Parents Are a School's Best Friends." *Phi Delta Kappan, 70,* 148–153.

Henig, Jeffrey R. 1985. *Public Policy and Federalism: Issues in State and Local Politics.* New York: St. Martin's.

Hersey, John R. 1968. *The Algiers Motel Incident.* New York: Knopf.

Hershkowitz, Allen. 1987. "Burning Trash: How It Could Work." *Technology Review, 90* (July), 26–34.

Herson, Lawrence J.R. 1957. "The Lost World of Municipal Government." *American Political Science Review, 51,* 330–345.

Herson, Lawrence J.R. 1961. "In the Footsteps of Community Power." *American Political Science Review, 55,* 820–835.

Herson, Lawrence J.R. 1973. "Pilgrim's Progress: Reflections on the Road to Urban Reform." In *Political Science and State and Local Government.* Washington, DC: American Political Science Association.

Herson, Lawrence J.R. 1980. "The Liberal Arts Considered." *National Journal of Teacher Education, 31,* 3.

Herson, Lawrence J.R. 1984. *The Politics of Ideas: Political Theory and American Public Policy.* Homewood, IL: Dorsey.

Herson, Lawrence J.R. 1986. "Shooting the Messenger: Thoughts on Bureaucratic Reform." In Donald Calista (ed.), *Bureaucratic and Governmental Reform.* Greenwich, CT: JAI Press.

References

Herson, Lawrence J.R. 1990. *The Politics of Ideas: Political Theory and American Public Policy.* 2nd ed. Prospect Heights, IL: Waveland.

Herson, Lawrence J.R. and Bolland, John M.1990.*The Urban Web: Politics, Policy, and Theory.* Chicago: Nelson-Hall.

Herson, Lawrence J.R. and Hofstetter, Richard. 1975. "Tolerance, Consensus, and the Democratic Creed: A Contextual Comparison." *Journal of Politics, 37,* 1007–1032

Hill, Edward; Wolman, Harold L.; and Ford, Coit Cook. 1995. "Can Suburbs Survive Without Their Central Cities? Examining the Suburban Dependence Hypothesis." *Urban Affairs Review, 31,* 147–174.

Hill, Richard C. 1984. "Fiscal Crisis, Austerity Politics, and Alternative Urban Policies." In William K. Tabb and Larry Sawyers (eds.), *Marxism and the Metropolis: New Perspectives in Urban Political Economy.* New York: Oxford University Press.

Hirsch, Arnold R. 1993. "With or Without Jim Crow: Black Residential Segregation in the United States." In Arnold R. Hirsch and Raymond A. Mohl (eds.), *Urban Policy in Twentieth-Century America.* New Brunswick, NJ: Rutgers University Press.

Hirsch, Fred. 1976. *Social Limits to Growth.* Cambridge, MA: Harvard University Press.

Hirsch, Werner Z. 1995. "Factors Important in Local Governments' Privatization Decisions." *Urban Affairs Review, 31,* 226–243.

Hirschman, Albert O. 1970. *Exit, Voice, and Loyalty: Responses to Decline in Firms, Organizations, and States.* Cambridge, MA: Harvard University Press.

Hoch, Charles and Slayton, Robert A. 1989. *New Homeless and Old: Community and the Skid Row Hotel.* Philadelphia, PA: Temple University Press.

Hofferth, Sandra L. and Hayes, Cheryl D. (eds.). 1987. *Risking the Future: Adolescent Sexuality, Pregnancy, and Childbearing,* vol. 1. Washington, DC: National Academy.

Hofstadter, Richard. 1955a. *The Age of Reform: From Bryan to FDR.* New York: Knopf.

Hofstadter, Richard. 1955b. *Social Darwinism in American Thought.* Boston: Beacon.

Hofstadter, Richard. 1968. *The Progressive Historians: Turner, Beard, Parrington.* New York: Knopf.

Hogan, Dennis P.; Astone, Nan Marie; and Kitagawa, Evelyn M. 1985. "Social and Environmental Factors Influencing Contraceptive Use Among Black Adolescents." *Family Planning Perspectives, 17,* 165–169.

Holden, Matthew, Jr. 1964. "The Governance of the Metropolis as a Problem in Diplomacy." *Journal of Politics, 26,* 627–647.

Holinger, Paul C.; Offer, Daniel; Barter, James T.; and Bell, Carl C. 1994. *Suicide and Homicide among Adolescents.* New York: Guilford.

Holzer, Harry J. 1991. "The Spatial Mismatch Hypothesis: What Has the Evidence Shown?" *Urban Studies, 28,* 105–122.

Hombs, Mary Ellen and Snyder, Mitch. 1982. *Homelessness in America: A Forced March to Nowhere.* Washington, DC: Community for Creative Nonviolence.

Howe, Frederick. 1905. *The City: The Hope of Democracy.* New York: Scribner's.

Huckshorn, Robert J. and Young, C.E. 1960. "A Study of Voting Splits on City Councils in Los Angeles County." *Western Political Quarterly, 13,* 479–497.

Hunter, Floyd. 1953. *Community Power Structure: A Study of Decision Makers.* Chapel Hill: University of North Carolina Press.

Huntley, Robert J. and Macdonald, Robert J. 1975. "Urban Managers: Organizational

Preferences, Managerial Styles, and Social Policy Roles." In *The Municipal Year-book*. Washington, DC: International City Management Assocaition.

Hutchison, Ray and Kyle, Charles. 1993. "Hispanic Street Gangs in Chicago's Public Schools." In Scott Cummings and Daniel J. Monti (eds.), *Gangs: The Origins and Impact of Contemporary Youth Gangs in the United States*. Albany, NY: SUNY Press.

Hyneman, Charles S. 1956. *The Study of Politics: The Present State of American Political Science*. Urbana: University of Illinois Press.

Ihlanfeldt, Keith R. and Sjoquist, David L. 1989. "The Impact of Job Decentralization on the Economic Welfare of Central City Blacks." *Journal of Urban Economics, 26*, 110–130.

Imbroscio, David; Orr, Marion; Ross, Timothy; and Stone, Clarence. 1995. "Baltimore and the Human Investment Challenge." In Fritz W. Wagner, Timothy E. Joder, and Anthony J. Mumphrey (eds.), *Urban Revitalization: Policies and Programs*. Thousand Oaks, CA: Sage.

Inciardi, James A.; Lockwood, Dorothy; and Pottieger, Anne E. 1993. *Women and Crack-Cocaine*. New York: Macmillan.

Isaak, Alan C. 1984. *Scope and Methods of Political Science: An Introduction of the Methodology of Political Inquiry*. 4th ed. Homewood, IL: Dorsey.

Jackson, Bryan O. and Preston, Michael B. 1994. "Race and Ethnicity in Los Angeles Politics." In George E. Peterson (ed.), *Big-City Politics, Governance, and Fiscal Constraints*. Washington, DC: Urban Institute.

Jackson, Kenneth T. 1985. *Crabgrass Frontier: The Suburbanization of the United States*. New York: Oxford University Press.

Jacobs, Alan H. 1976. "Volunteer Firemen: Altruism in Action." In W. Arens and Susan P. Montague (eds.), *The American Dimension: Cultural Myths and Social Realities*. Port Washington, NY: Alfred.

Jacobs, Jane. 1961. *The Death and Life of Great American Cities*. New York: Random House.

Jacobs, Jane. 1970. *The Economy of Cities*. New York: Random House.

James, Franklin J. 1991. "The Evaluation of Enterprise Zone Programs." In Roy E. Green (ed.), *Enterprise Zones: New Directions in Economic Development*. Newbury Park, CA: Sage.

Janis, Irving L. 1982. *Groupthink*. 2nd ed. Boston: Houghton Mifflin.

Jaret, Charles. 1991. "Recent Structural Change and U.S. Urban Ethnic Minorities." *Journal of Urban Affairs, 13*, 307–336.

Jargowsky, Paul A. 1991. "Ghetto Poverty: Economic vs. Spatial Factors." Paper presented at the annual meeting of the Association for Public Policy Analysis and Management.

Jargowsky, Paul A. 1994. "Ghetto Poverty Among Blacks in the 1980s." *Journal of Policy Analysis and Management, 13*, 288–310.

Jargowsky, Paul A. and Bane, Mary Jo. 1990. "Ghetto Poverty: Basic Questions." In Laurence E. Lynn and Michael G.H. McGeary (eds.), *Inner-City Poverty in the United States*. Washington, DC: National Academy.

References

Jargowsky, Paul A. and Bane, Mary Jo. 1991. "Ghetto Poverty in the United States, 1970–1980." In Christopher Jencks and Paul E. Peterson (eds.), *The Urban Underclass*. Washington, DC: Brookings.

Jencks, Christopher. 1988. "Deadly Neighborhoods." *New Republic*, June 13, 23–32.

Jencks, Christopher. 1991. "Is the American Underclass Growing?" In Christopher Jencks and Paul E. Peterson (eds.), *The Urban Underclass*. Washington, DC: Brookings.

Jencks, Christopher. 1994. *The Homeless*. Cambridge, MA: Harvard University Press.

Jencks, Christopher and Edin, Kathryn. 1990. "The Real Welfare Program." *American Prospect, 1*, 31–50.

Johnson, James H. and Oliver, Melvin L. 1991. "Economic Restructuring and Black Male Joblessness in U.S. Metropolitan Areas." *Urban Geography, 12*, 542–562.

Johnston, R.J. 1984. *Residential Segregation, the State and Constitutional Conflict in American Urban Areas*. London: Academic.

Jones, Bryan D. 1980. *Service Delivery in the City: Citizen Demand and Bureaucratic Rules*. New York: Longman.

Jones, Bryan D. 1983. *Governing Urban America: A Policy Focus*. Boston: Little, Brown.

Jones, Charles O. 1983. *An Introduction to the Study of Public Policy*. 3rd ed. Monterey, CA: Brooks/Cole.

Jones, E. Terrence. 1982. "The Distribution of Urban Services in a Declining City." In Richard C. Rich (ed.), *The Politics of Urban Public Services*. Lexington, MA: Lexington.

Jones, LeAlan and Newman, Lloyd. 1997. *Our America: Life and Death on the South Side of Chicago*. New York: Scribner's.

Judd, Dennis R. 1984. *The Politics of American Cities: Private Power and Public Policy*. 2nd ed. Boston: Little, Brown.

Judd, Dennis R. 1988. *The Politics of American Cities: Private Power and Public Policy*. 3rd ed. Boston: Little, Brown.

Judge, David; Stoker, Gerry; and Wolman, Harold (eds.). 1995. *Theories of Urban Politics*. Thousand Oaks, CA: Sage.

Juhn, Chinhui; Murphy, Kevin M.; and Topel, Robert H. 1991. "Why Has the Natural Rate of Unemployment Increased Over Time?" *Brookings Papers on Economic Activity*, vol. 2, 75–142. Washington, DC: Brookings.

Kammerer, Gladys. 1961. *Florida City Managers, Profile in Tenure*. Gainesville: University of Florida Public Administration Clearing House.

Kane, Thomas J. and Bane, Mary Jo. 1994. "The Context for Welfare Reform." In Mary Jo Bane and David T. Ellwood (eds.), *Welfare Realities: From Rhetoric to Reform*. Cambridge, MA: Harvard University Press.

Kantor, Paul. 1988. *The Dependent City: The Changing Political Economy of American Urban Politics since 1789*. New York: Scott Foresman.

Kantor, Paul. 1993. "The Dual City as Political Choice." *Journal of Urban Affairs, 15*, 231–244.

Kantor, Paul, and Savitch, H.V. 1993. "Can Politicians Bargain with Business? A Theoretical and Comparative Perspective on Urban Development." *Urban Affairs Quarterly, 29*, 230–255.

Kaplan, Abraham. 1964. *The Conduct of Inquiry: Methodology for Behavioral Science.* Scraton, PA: Chandler.

Kaplan, Harold. 1963. *Urban Renewal Politics: Slum Clearance in Newark.* New York: Columbia University Press.

Kaplan, Marshall. 1990. "National Urban Policy: Where Are We Now? Where Are We Going?" In Marshall Kaplan and Franklin James (eds.), *The Future of National Urban Policy.* Durham, NC: Duke University Press.

Karter, Michael J. 1995. *U.S. Fire Department Profile Through 1994.* Quincy, MA: National Fire Protection Association.

Kasarda, John D. 1989. "Urban Industrial Transition and the Underclass." *Annals of the American Academy of Political and Social Science, 501,* 26–47.

Kasarda, John D. 1992. "The Severely Distressed in Economically Transforming Cities." In Adele V. Harrell and George E. Peterson (eds.), *Drugs, Crime, and Social Isolation: Barriers to Urban Opportunity.* Washington, DC: Urban Institute.

Katz, Daniel; Gutek, Barbara A.; Kahn Robert L.; and Barton, Eugenia. 1975. *Bureaucratic Encounters: A Pilot Study in the Evaluation of Government Service.* Ann Arbor: Institute for Social Research, University of Michigan.

Keating, Michael. 1995. "Size, Efficiency, and Democracy: Consolidation, Fragmentation, and Public Choice." In David Judge, Gerry Stoker, and Harold Wolman (eds.), *Theories of Urban Politics.* Thousand Oaks, CA: Sage.

Keech, William R. 1968. *The Impact of Negro Voting: The Role of the Vote in the Quest for Equality.* Chicago: Rand McNally.

Kelley, Robert. 1982. *The Shaping of the American Past.* 3rd ed. Englewood Cliffs, NJ: Prentice-Hall.

Kelly, Alfred H. and Harbison, Winfred A. 1955. *The American Constitution: Its Origins and Development.* Rev. ed. New York: Norton.

Kelso, William A. 1994. *Poverty and the Underclass: Changing Perceptions of the Poor in America.* New York: New York University Press.

Key, V.O., Jr. 1950. *Southern Politics.* New York: Knopf.

King, Martin Luther, Jr. 1964. "Letter from a Birmingham Jail." *Why We Can't Wait.* New York: Harper and Row.

Kingsbury, F. J. 1895. "The Tendency of Men to Live in Cities." *Journal of Social Science, 33,* 1–19.

Kirby, Douglas; Barth, Richard P.; Leland, Nancy; and Fetro, Joyce V. 1991. "Reducing the Risk: Impact of a New Curriculum on Sexual Risk-Taking." *Family Planning Perspectives, 23,* 253–263.

Kirby, Ronald F.; De Leeuw, Frank; and Silverman, William. 1972. *Residential Zoning and Equal Housing Opportunities: A Case Study in Black Jack, Missouri.* Washington, DC: Urban Institute.

Kitto, H.D.F. 1951. *The Greeks.* Harmondsworth, England: Penguin.

Klepper, Christine. 1983. "America's Blind Spot: The Devastating Impact of Residential Segregation." In *A Sheltered Crisis: The State of Fair Housing in the Eighties.* Washington, DC: U.S. Commission on Civil Rights.

Kliment, Stephen A. 1994. "Pruitt-Igoe, Act II." *Architectural Record,* May, p. 9.

Knickman, James R.; Hughes, Robert G.; Taylor, Humphrey; Binns, Katherine; and Lyons, Marie P. 1996. "Tracking Consumers' Reactions to the Changing Health Care System: Early Indicators." *Health Affairs, 15,* 21–32.

References

Knights, Peter R. 1971. *The Plain People of Boston 1830–1860: A Study in City Growth.* New York: Oxford University Press.

Koehler, David H. and Wrightson, Margaret T. 1987. "Inequality in the Delivery of Urban Services: A Reconsideration of the Chicago Parks." *Journal of Politics, 49,* 80–99.

Kotlowitz, Alex. 1991. *There Are No Children Here: The Story of Two Boys Growing Up in the Other America.* New York: Doubleday.

Kotlowitz, Alex. 1996. "Welfare: Hit and Myth." *New Republic,* Aug. 12, p. 19.

Kotter, John P. and Lawrence, Paul R. 1974. *Mayors in Action: Five Approaches to Urban Governance.* New York: Wiley.

Krieger, Nancy and Sidney, Stephen. 1996. "Racial Discrimination and Blood Pressure: The CARDIA Study of Young Black and White Adults." *American Journal of Public Health, 86,* 1370–1378.

Kristol, Irving. 1978. *Two Cheers for Capitalism.* New York: Basic Books.

Krumholz, Norman. 1992. "The Kerner Commission Twenty Years Later." In George C. Galster and Edward W. Hill (eds.), *The Metropolis in Black and White: Place, Power, and Polarization.* New Brunswick, NJ: Rutgers University Press.

Kuyper, Adrian, 1970. "Intergovernmental Cooperation: An Analysis of the Lakewood Plan." *Georgetown Law Journal,* 58, 777–798.

Ladd, Helen F. 1994. "Big-City Finances." In George E. Peterson (ed.), *Big-City Politics, Governance, and Fiscal Constraints.* Washington, DC: Urban Institute.

Ladd, Helen F. and Yinger, John. 1991. *America's Ailing Cities: Fiscal Health and the Design of Urban Policy.* Baltimore, MD: Johns Hopkins University Press.

Lake, Robert W. 1979. *Real Estate Tax Delinquency: Private Disinvestment and Public Response.* New Brunswick, NJ: Center for Urban Policy Research, Rutgers, University.

Lasswell, Harold D. 1936. *Politics: Who Gets What, When, and How.* New York: McGraw-Hill.

Laumann, Edward O. 1973. *Bonds of Pluralism: The Form and Substance of Urban Social Networks.* New York: Wiley.

Laumann, Edward O.; Marsden, Peter V.; and Galaskiewicz, Joseph. 1977. "Community-Elite Influence Structures: Extension of a Network Approach." *American Journal of Sociology, 83,* 594–631.

Laumann, Edward O. and Pappi, Franz U. 1976. *Networks of Collective Action: A Perspective on Community Influence Systems.* New York: Academic.

Leach, Richard H. 1970. *American Federalism.* New York: Norton.

Lee, Susan P. and Passell, Peter. 1979. *A New Economic View of American History.* New York: Norton.

Lehman, Jeffrey S. 1994. "Updating Urban Policy." In Sheldon H. Danziger, Gary D. Sandefur, and Daniel H. Weinberg (eds.), *Confronting Poverty: Prescriptions for Change.* New York: Russell Sage.

Leigland, James and Lamb, Robert. 1986. *WPP$$: Who Is to Blame for the WPPSS Disaster?* Cambridge, MA: Ballinger.

Lein, Laura. 1991. "The Formation of Community in Public Housing." Paper presented at the annual Conference on Ethnic Minorities and Gender.

Lemann, Nicholas. 1991. *The Promised Land: The Great Black Migration and How It Changed America*. New York: Vintage.

Leuchtenburg, William. 1963. *Franklin D. Roosevelt and the New Deal, 1932–1940*. New York: Harper and Row.

Leven, Charles L. and Sykuta, Michael E. 1994. "The Importance of Race in Home Mortgage Loan Approvals." *Urban Affairs Quarterly, 29*, 479–489.

Levine, Charles H. 1980. "More on Cutback Management: Hard Questions for Hard Times." In Charles H. Levine (ed.), *Managing Fiscal Stress: The Crisis in the Public Sector*. Chatham, NJ: Chatham House.

Levine, Charles H.; Rubin, Irene S.; and Wolohojian, George G. 1981. *The Politics of Retrenchment: How Local Governments Manage Fiscal Stress*. Beverly Hills, CA: Sage.

Levine, Erwin L. and Wexler, Elizabeth M. 1981. *PL 94–142: An Act of Congress*. New York: Macmillan.

Levy, Frank; Meltsner, Arnold J.; and Wildavsky, Aaron. 1974. *Urban Outcomes: Schools, Streets, and Libraries*. Berkeley: University of California Press.

Lewis, Oscar. 1959. *Five Families: Mexican Case Studies in the Culture of Poverty*. New York: Basic Books.

Lewis, Oscar. 1965. *La Vida: A Puerto Rican Family in the Culture of Poverty—San Juan and New York*. New York: Random House.

Lief, Beth J. and Goering, Susan. 1987. "The Implementation of the Federal Mandate for Fair Housing." In Gary A. Tobin (ed.), *Divided Neighborhoods: Changing Patterns of Racial Segregation*. Newbury Park, CA: Sage.

Lindblom, Charles E. 1977. *Political and Markets: The World's Political Economic Systems*. New York: Basic Books.

Lindblom, Charles E. and Cohen, David K. 1979. *Useable Knowledge: Social Science and Social Problem Solving*. New Haven, CT: Yale University Press.

Lineberry, Robert L. 1977. *Equality and Urban Policy*. Beverly Hills, CA: Sage.

Lineberry, Robert L. 1984. "Mandating Urban Equality: The Distribution of Municipal Public Services." In Harlan Hahn and Charles H. Levine (eds.), *Readings in Urban Politics: Past, Present, and Future*. 2nd ed. New York: Longman.

Lineberry, Robert L. and Fowler, Edmund P. 1967. "Reformism and Public Policies in American Cities." *American Political Science Review, 61*, 701–716.

Lineberry, Robert and Sharkansky, Ira. 1978. *Urban Politics and Public Policy*. 3rd ed. New York: Harper and Row.

Link, Bruce; Phelan, Jo; Bresnahan, Michaeline; Stueve, Ann; Moore, Robert; and Susser, Ezra. 1995. "Lifetime and Five-Year Prevalence of Homelessness in the United States: New Evidence on an Old Debate." *American Journal of Orthopsychiatry, 65*, 347–354.

Lipset, Seymore M. 1960. *Political Man: The Social Bases of Politics*. Garden City, NY: Doubleday.

Lipsky, Michael. 1980. *Street-Level Bureaucracy: Dilemmas of the Individual in Public Services*. New York: Russell Sage.

Lipson, Debra J. and Naierman, Naomi. 1996. "Effects of Health System Changes on Safety-Net Providers." *Health Affairs, 15*, 33–48.

Littman, Mark S. 1991. "Poverty Areas and the 'Underclass': Untangling the Web." *Monthly Labor Review, 114*, 19–32.

References

Lockard, Duane. 1963. *The Politics of State and Local Government*. New York: Macmillan.

Long, Norton. 1972. *The Unwalled City: Reconstituting the Urban Community*. New York: Basic Books.

Lorch, Robert S. 1995. *State and Local Politics*. 5th ed. Englewood Cliffs, NJ: Prentice-Hall.

Lord, J.D. 1977. "Spatial Perspectives on School Desegregation and Busing." Washington, DC: Commission on College Geography, American Association of Geographers.

Loseke, Donileen R. 1992. *The Battered Woman and Shelters: The Social Construction of Wife Abuse*. Albany: SUNY Press.

Lott, Tommy L. 1992. "Marooned in America: Black Youth Culture and Social Pathology." In Bill E. Lawson (ed.), *The Underclass Question*. Philadelphia, PA: Temple University Press.

Lotz, Aileen. 1973. "Metropolitan Dade County." In Advisory Commission on Intergovernmental Relations, *Substate Regionalism and the Federal System*, vol. 2, *Case Studies*. Washington, DC: U.S. Government Printing Office.

Lowery, David; DeHoog, Ruth Hoogland; and Lyons, Williams E. 1992. "Citizenship in the Empowered Locality: An Elaboration, a Critique, and a Partial Test." *Urban Affairs Quarterly, 28*, 69–103.

Lowi, Theodore J. 1969a. *The End of Liberalism: Ideology, Policy, and the Crisis of Public Authority*. New York: Norton.

Lowi, Theodore, J. 1969b. "Machine Politics—Old and New." *The Public Interest, 9*, 83–92.

Lowry, Ira S. 1980. "The Dismal Future of Central Cities." In Arthur P. Solomon (ed.), *The Prospective City: Economic, Population, Energy, and Environmental Developments*. Cambridge, MA: MIT Press.

Lubell, Samuel. 1956. *The Future of American Politics*. Rev. ed. New York: Harper.

Lubin, Roger. 1981. "How Should Managers Be Paid? Some Public and Private Sector Comparisons." *Public Management, 63*(10), 2–6.

Lucas, Charles Prestwood. 1917. *The Beginnings of English Overseas Enterprise: A Prelude to the Empire*. Oxford, England: Clarendon.

Lucie-Smith, Edward and Dars. C. 1976. *How the Rich Lived*. New York: Paddington.

Lucier, Richard L. 1980. "Gauging the Strength and Meaning of the 1978 Tax Revolt." In Charles H. Levine (ed.), *Managing Fiscal Stress: The Crisis in the Public Sector*. Chatham, NJ: Chatham House.

Lueck, Marjorie; Orr, Ann C.; and O'Connell, Martin. 1982. *Trends in Child Care Arrangements for Working Mothers*. Washington, DC: U.S. Government Printing Office.

Lukas, J. Anthony. 1985. *Common Ground*. New York: Knopf.

Lynch, Kevin 1960. *The Image of the City*. Cambridge, MA: MIT Press.

Lynd, Robert S. and Lynd, Helen M. 1929. *Middletown: A Study in American Culture*. New York: Harcourt, Brace.

McCarthy, Belinda R. 1990. "A Micro-Level Analysis of Social Structure and Social Control: Intrastate Use of Jail and Prison Confinement." *Justice Quarterly, 7*, 325–340.

McDougall, Harold A. 1993. *Black Baltimore: A New Theory of Community*. Philadelphia, PA: Temple University Press.

McFeeley, Neil D. 1978. "Special District Governments: The New Dark Continent Twenty Years Later." *Midwest Review of Public Administration, 12,* 211–245.

McGary, Howard. 1992. "The Black Underclass and the Question of Values." In Bill E. Lawson (ed.), *The Underclass Question.* Philadelphia, PA: Temple University Press.

MacIver, Robert M. 1942. *Social Causation.* New York: Ginn.

MacLeod, Jay. 1987. *Ain't No Makin' It: Leveled Aspirations in a Low-Income Neighborhood.* Boulder, CO: Westview.

MacManus, Susan A. 1981. "Special District Governments: A Note on Their Use as Property Tax Relief Mechanisms in the 1970's." *Journal of Politics, 43,* 1207–1214.

Macpherson, C.B. 1977. *The Life and Times of Liberal Democracy.* New York: Oxford University Press.

Madison, James. 1961a. "Federalist 10." In Alexander Hamilton, James Madison, and John Jay (eds.), *The Federalist Papers.* New York: Mentor.

Madison, James. 1961b. "Federalist 47." In Alexander Hamilton, James Madison, and John Jay (eds.), *The Federalist Papers.* New York: Mentor.

Madison, James. 1961c. "Federalist 51." In Alexander Hamilton, James Madison, and John Jay (eds.), *The Federalist Papers.* New York: Mentor.

Magleby, David. B. 1984. *Direct Legislation: Voting on Ballot Propositions in the United States.* Baltimore, MD: Johns Hopkins University Press.

Mandelker, D.R. 1977. "Racial Discrimination and Exclusionary Zoning: A Perspective on Arlington Heights." *Texas Law Review, 55,* 1217–1253.

Mansbridge, Jane J. 1980. *Beyond Adversary Democracy.* New York: Basic Books.

Marciniak, Ed. 1986. *Reclaiming the Inner City: Chicago's Near North Revitalization Confronts Cabrini-Green.* Washington, DC: National Center for Urban Ethnic Affairs.

Marris, Peter and Rein, Martin. 1973. *Dilemmas of Social Reform: Poverty and Community Action in the United States.* 2nd ed. Chicago: Aldine.

Martin, Lowell A. 1969. *Library Response to Urban Change: A Study of the Chicago Public Library.* Chicago: American Library Association.

Massey, Douglas S. and Denton, Nancy A. 1993. *American Apartheid: Segregation and the Making of the Underclass.* Cambridge, MA: Harvard University Press.

Mayer, Martin. 1978. *The Builders: Houses, People, Neighborhoods, Governments, Money.* New York: Norton.

Mayer, Susan E. 1991. "How Much Does a High School's Racial and Socioeconomic Mix Affect Graduation and Teenage Fertility Rates?" In Christopher Jencks and Paul E. Peterson (eds.), *The Urban Underclass.* Washington, DC: Brookings.

Mead, Lawrence M. 1986. *Beyond Entitlement: The Social Obligations of Citizenship.* New York: Free Press.

Mead, Lawrence M. 1996. "Welfare Reform at Work." *Society* (July/Aug.), 37–40.

Meehan, Eugene J. 1975. *Public Housing Policy: Convention versus Reality.* New Brunswick, NJ: Rutgers University Press.

Mencken, H.L. 1963. *The American Language: An Inquiry into the Development of English in the United States.* 1st abridged ed. New York: Knopf.

Merget, Astrid and Wolff, William. 1976. "The Law and Municipal Services: Implementing Equity." *Public Management, 58,* 2–8.

Merton, Robert K. 1957. *Social Theory and Social Structure.* Glencoe, IL: Free Press.

References

Metcalf, George R. 1988. *Fair Housing Comes of Age.* New York: Greenwood.

Meyer, John R. and Quigley, John M. 1977. *Local Public Finance and the Fiscal Squeeze: A Case Study.* Cambridge, MA: Ballinger.

Meyerson, Martin and Banfield, Edward C. 1955. *Politics, Planning and the Public Interest: The Case of Public Housing in Chicago.* Glencoe, IL: Free Press.

Miles, Rufus. 1976. *Awakening from the American Dream: The Social and Political Limits to Growth.* New York: Universe.

Mill, John Stuart. 1926. *On Liberty.* New York: Macmillan.

Miller, Jerome G. 1996. *Search and Destroy: African-American Males in the Criminal Justice System.* Cambridge, England: Cambridge University Press.

Mills, C. Wright. 1956. *The Power Elite.* New York: Oxford University Press.

Mincy, Ronald B. 1994. "The Underclass: Concept, Controversy, and Evidence." In Sheldon H. Danziger, Gary D. Sandefur, and Daniel H. Weinberg (eds.), *Confronting Poverty: Prescriptions for Change.* New York: Russell Sage.

Miranda, Rowan A. 1992. "Privatization in Chicago's City Government." In Kenneth K. Wong (ed.), *Research in Urban Policy,* vol. 4. Greenwich, CT: JAI.

Miranda, Rowan A. 1994. "Containing Cleavages: Parties and Other Hierarchies." In Terry N. Clark (ed.), *Urban Innovation: Creative Strategies for Turbulent Times.* Thousand Oaks, CA: Sage.

Miranda, Rowan A. and Tunyavong, Ittipone. 1994. "Patterned Inequality? Reexamining the Role of Distributive Politics in Urban Service Delivery." *Urban Affairs Quarterly, 29,* 509–534.

Mitchell, Joseph. 1992. *Up in the Old Hotel.* New York: Pantheon.

Mladenka, Kenneth. 1977. "Citizen Demand and Bureaucratic Response: Direct Dialing Democracy in a Major American City." *Urban Affairs Quarterly, 12,* 273–290.

Mladenka, Kenneth and Hill, Kim Quaile. 1977. "The Distribution of Benefits in an Urban Environment." *Urban Affairs Quarterly, 13,* 73–94.

Mohl, Raymond A. 1993a. "Shifting Patterns of American Urban Policy Since 1900." In Arnold R. Hirsch and Raymond A. Mohl (eds.), *Urban Policy in Twentieth-Century America.* New Brunswick, NJ: Rutgers University Press.

Mohl, Raymond A. 1993b. "Race and Space in the Modern City: Interstate-95 and the Black Community in Miami." In Arnold R. Hirsch and Raymond A. Mohl (eds.), *Urban Policy in Twentieth-Century America.* New Brunswick, NJ: Rutgers University Press.

Mollenkopf, John H. 1983. *The Contested City.* Princeton, NJ: Princeton University Press.

Mollenkopf, John H. 1986. "New York: The Great Anomaly." *PS, 19,* 591–597.

Mollenkopf, John H. 1991. "Political Inequality." In John H. Mollenkopf and Manuel Castells (eds.), *Dual City: Restructuring New York.* New York: Russell Sage.

Molotch, Harvey. 1976. "The City as a Growth Machine: Toward a Political Economy of Place." *American Journal of Sociology, 82,* 309–332.

Molotch, Harvey. 1993. "The Political Economy of Growth Machines." *Journal of Urban Affairs, 15,* 29–53.

Moore, Joan. 1993. "Gangs, Drugs, and Violence." In Scott Cummings and Daniel J. Monti (eds.), *Gangs: The Origins and Impact of Contemporary Youth Gangs in the United States.* Albany: SUNY Press.

Moore, Stephen and Stansel, Dean. 1992. "Cities Are to Blame for Their Own Decline." In Charles P. Cozic (ed.), *America's Cities: Opposing Viewpoints*. San Diego, CA: Greenhaven.

Morgan, Martha I.; Cohen, Adam S.; and Hershkoff, Helen. 1995. "Establishing Education Program Inadequacy: The Alabama Example." *University of Michigan Journal of Law Reform, 28*, 559–598.

Morris, Charles R. 1980. *The Cost of Good Intentions: New York and the Liberal Experiment 1960–1965*. New York: Norton.

Morris, Lydia. 1994. *Dangerous Classes: The Underclass and Social Citizenship*. London, Routledge.

Moss, Mitchell and Ludwig, Sarah. 1991. "The Structure of the Media." In John H. Mollenkopf and Manuel Castells (eds.), *Dual City: Restructuring New York*. New York: Russell Sage.

Moynihan, Daniel Patrick. 1969. *Maximum Feasible Misunderstanding: Community Action in the War on Poverty*. New York: Free Press.

Moynihan, Daniel Patrick. 1970. "Policy vs. Program in the '70's." *The Public Interest, 20*, 90–100.

Muir, William Ker. 1977. *Police: Streetcorner Politicians*. Chicago: University of Chicago Press.

Mumford, Lewis. 1938. *The Culture of Cities*. New York: Harcourt, Brace.

Mumford, Lewis. 1961. *The City in History: Its Origins, Its Transformations, and Its Prospects*. New York: Harcourt, Brace, World.

Munnell, A.H.; Browne, L.E.; McEneaney, J.; and Tootel, G.M.B. 1992. "Mortgage Lending in Boston: Interpreting HMDA Data." Working paper, Federal Reserve Bank of Boston.

Muñoz, Carlos, Jr. 1994. "Mexican Americans and the Promise of Democracy: San Antonio Mayoral Elections." In George E. Peterson (ed.), *Big-City Politics, Governance, and Fiscal Constraints*. Washington, DC: Urban Institute.

Muñoz, Carlos, Jr. and Henry, Charles. 1986. "Rainbow Coalitions in Four Big Cities: San Antonio, Denver, Chicago, and Philadelphia." *PS, 19*, 598–609.

Munro, William B. 1920. *The Government of American Cities*. 3rd ed. New York: Macmillan.

Murray, Charles A. 1984. *Losing Ground: American Social Policy 1950–1980*. New York: Basic Books.

Murray, Charles A. 1990. "The British Underclass." *The Public Interest, 99*, 4–28.

Murray, Charles A. 1996. "Keeping Priorities Straight on Welfare Reform." *Society* (July/Aug.), 10–12.

Mushkin, Selma J. and Vehorn, Charles L. 1980. "User Fees and Charges." In Charles H. Levine (ed.), *Managing Fiscal Stress: The Crisis in the Public Sector*. Chatham, NJ: Chatham House.

Myrdal, Gunnar. 1963. *The Challenge to Affluence*. New York: Pantheon.

Naipaul, Shiva. 1979. *North of South: An African Journey*. New York: Simon and Schuster.

Nathan, Richard. 1987. "Will the Underclass Always Be With Us?" *Society, 24* (March/April), 57–62.

References

National Advisory Commission on Civil Disorders. 1968. *Report.* New York: Bantam.

National Municipal League. 1964. *A Model City Charter, With Home Rule Provisions Recommended for State Constitutions.* 6th ed. New York: National Municipal League.

Neenen, William B. 1972. *Political Economy of Urban Areas.* Chicago: Markham.

Nelson, Arthur C. 1995. "Regional Growth Management and Central-City Vitality: Comparing Development Patterns in Atlanta, Georgia, and Portland, Oregon." In Fritz W. Wagner, Timothy E. Joder, and Anthony J. Mumphrey (eds.), *Urban Revitalization: Policies and Programs.* Thousand Oaks, CA: Sage.

Nelson, Dale C. 1979. "Ethnicity and Socioeconomic Status as Sources of Participation: The Case for Ethnic Political Culture." *American Political Science Review, 73,* 1024–1038.

Nelson, Richard R. 1974. "Intellectualizing about the Moon-Ghetto Metaphor: A Study of the Current Malaise of Rational Analysis of Social Problems." *Policy Sciences, 5,* 378–414.

Nelson, William E., Jr. 1987. "Cleveland: The Evolution of Black Political Power." In Michael B. Preston, Lenneal J. Henderson, and Paul L. Puryear (eds.), *The New Black Politics: The Search for Political Power.* 2nd ed. New York: Longman.

New York City Department of Finance. 1996. "Comptroller's Report for Fiscal 1995." Office of Tax Policy, Department of Finance, City of New York.

Newby, Robert G. 1989. "Problems of Pragmatism in Public Policy: Critique of William Wilson's *The Truly Disadvantaged.*" *Journal of Sociology and Social Welfare, 16 (4),* 123–132.

Nivola, Pietro S. 1978. "Distributing a Municipal Service: A Case Study of Housing Inspection." *Journal of Politics, 40,* 59–81.

Novello, Antonia C. 1991. "Violence Is a Greater Killer of Children than Disease." *Public Health Reports, 106,* 231–233.

O'Neill, Thomas P. 1987. *Man of the House: The Life and Political Memoirs of Speaker Tip O'Neill.* New York: Random House.

O'Sullivan, Arthur; Sexton, Terri A.; and Sheffrin, Steven M. 1995. *Property Taxes and Tax Revolts: The Legacy of Proposition 13.* Cambridge, England: Cambridge University Press.

Oakes, Jeannie. 1995. "Two Cities' Tracking and Within-school Segregation." *Teachers College Record, 96,* 681–690.

Oakes, Jeannie; Selvin, Mollie; Karoly, Lynn; and Guiton, Gretchen. 1992. *Educational Matchmaking: Academic and Vocational Tracking in Comprehensive High Schools.* Santa Monica, CA: Rand.

Ogbu, John U. 1988. "Diversity and Equity in Public Education: Community Forces and Minority School Adjustment and Performance." In Ron Haskins and Duncan MacRae (eds.), *Policies for America's Public Schools: Teachers, Equity, and Indicators.* Norwood, NJ: Ablex.

Oldenquist, Andrew. 1986. *The Non-Suicidal Society.* Bloomington: Indiana University Press.

Oliver, Melvin L.; Johnson, James H.; and Farrell, Walter C. 1993. "Anatomy of a Rebellion: A Political-Economic Analysis." In Robert Gooding-Williams (ed.), *Reading Rodney King, Reading Urban Uprising.* New York: Routledge.

Orfield, Gary. 1978. *Must We Bus? Segregated Schools and National Policy.* Washington, DC: Brookings.

Orfield, Gary. 1988. "School Desegregation in the 1980s." *Equity and Choice.* Special Issue, 25–28.

Orfield, Gary and Monfort, Franklin. 1992. *Status of School Desegregation: The Next Generation.* Washington, DC: National School Boards Association.

Orum, Anthony M. 1995. *City-Building in America.* Boulder, CO: Westview.

Osterman, Paul. 1991. "Gains from Growth? The Impact of Full Employment on Poverty in Boston." In Christopher Jencks and Paul E. Peterson (eds.), *The Urban Underclass.* Washington, DC: Brookings.

Ostrom, Elinor. 1973. "On the Meaning and Measurement of Output and Efficiency in the Provision of Urban Police Services." *Journal of Criminal Justice, 1,* 93–112.

Ostrom, Vincent; Bish, Robert L.; and Ostrom, Elinor. 1988. *Local Government in the United States.* San Francisco: Institute for Contemporary Studies.

Palley, Marian Lief and Palley, Howard A. 1981. *Urban America and Public Policies.* Lexington, MA: Heath.

Park, Robert E.; Burgess, Ernest W.; and Makenzie, Roderick D. 1967. *The City.* Reprint of the 1925 ed. Chicago: University of Chicago Press.

Parker, R. Andrew. 1995. "Patterns of Federal Urban Spending: Central Cities and Their Suburbs, 1983–1992." *Urban Affairs Review, 31,* 184–205.

Parkes, Henry Bamford. 1959. *The United States of America: A History.* New York: Knopf.

Patterson, E. Britt and Lynch, Michael J. 1991. "Bias in Formalized Bail Procedures." In Michael J. Lynch and E. Britt Patterson (eds.), *Race and Criminal Justice.* New York: Harrow and Heston.

Pearce, Diana. 1976. "Black, White, and Many Shades of Gray: Real Estate Brokers and Their Racial Practices." Ph.D. diss., University of Michigan.

Pearce, Diana M. 1993. "Children Having Children: Teenage Pregnancy and Public Policy from the Woman's Perspective." In Annette Lawson and Deborah L. Rhode (eds.), *The Politics of Pregnancy: Adolescent Sexuality and Public Policy.* New Haven, CT: Yale University Press.

Peirce, Neal R. 1993. "An Urban Agenda for the President." *Journal of Urban Affairs, 15,* 457–467.

Pelissero, John P.; Henschen, Beth M.; and Sidlow, Edward I. 1992. "The New Politics of Sports Policy Innovation in Chicago." In Kenneth K. Wong (ed.), *Research in Urban Policy,* vol. 4. Greenwich, CT: JAI.

Perkins, Craig A.; Klaus, Patsy A.; Bastian, Lisa D.; and Cohen, Robyn L. 1996. *Criminal Victimization in the United States, 1993.* Washington, DC: U.S. Department of Justice.

Perkins, Douglas D.; Florin, Paul; Rich, Richard C.; Wandersman, Abraham; and Chavis, David M. 1990. "Participation and the Social and Physical Environment of Residential Blocks: Crime and Community Context." *American Journal of Community Psychology, 18,* 83–115.

Perry, David C. and Watkins, Alfred J. (eds.). 1977. *The Rise of the Sunbelt Cities.* Beverly Hills, CA: Sage.

Perry, Huey L. and Stokes, Alfred. 1987. "Politics and Power in the Sunbelt: Mayor Morial of New Orleans." In Michael B. Preston, Lenneal J. Henderson, and Paul

L. Puryear (eds.), *The New Black Politics: The Search for Political Power.* 2nd ed. New York: Longman.

Persons, Georgia A. 1991. "Politics and Changing Political Processes in Urban America." In Marvel Lang (ed.), *Contemporary Urban America: Problems, Issues, and Alternatives.* Lanham, MD: University Press of America.

Persons, Georgia A. 1992. "Racial Politics and Black Power in the Cities." In George C. Galster and Edward W. Hill (eds.), *The Metropolis in Black & White: Place, Power, and Polarization.* New Brunswick, NJ: Rutgers University Press.

Peterson, George E. 1991. "Historical Perspectives on Infrastructure Investment: How Did We Get Where We Are?" Paper presented at the AEI-House Wednesday Group Infrastructure Conference.

Peterson, George E. and Harrell, Adele V. 1992. "Introduction: Inner-City Isolation and Opportunity." In Adele V. Harrell and George E. Peterson (eds.), *Drugs, Crime, and Social Isolation: Barriers to Urban Opportunity.* Washington, DC: Urban Institute.

Peterson, John E. 1981. "Big City Borrowing Costs and Credit Quality." In Robert W. Burchell and David Listokin (eds.), *Cities Under Stress: The Fiscal Crisis of Urban America.* New Brunswick, NJ: Rutgers University Press.

Peterson, Paul E. 1981. *City Limits.* Chicago: University of Chicago Press.

Peterson, Paul E. 1991. "The Urban Underclass and the Poverty Paradox." In Christopher Jencks and Paul E. Peterson (eds.), *The Urban Underclass.* Washington, DC: Brookings.

Pfiffner, James P. 1983. "Inflexible Budgets, Fiscal Stress, and the Tax Revolt." In Alberta M. Sbragia (ed.), *The Municipal Money Chase: The Politics of Local Government Finance.* Boulder, CO: Westview.

Pinderhughes, Dianne M. 1994. "Racial and Ethnic Politics in Chicago Mayoral Elections." In George E. Peterson (ed.), *Big-City Politics, Governance, and Fiscal Constraints.* Washington, DC: Urban Institute.

Pinderhughes, Howard. 1993. "'Down With the Program': Racial Attitudes and Group Violence Among Youth in Bensonhurst and Gravesend." In Scott Cummings and Daniel J. Monti (eds.), *Gangs: The Origins and Impact of Contemporary Youth Gangs in the United States.* Albany: SUNY Press.

Pirenne, Henri. 1925. *Medieval Cities: Their Origins and the Revival of Trade.* Translated by Frank D. Halsey. Princeton, NJ: Princeton University Press.

Piven, Frances Fox and Cloward, Richard. 1971. *Regulating the Poor: The Functions of Public Welfare.* New York: Pantheon.

Plepys, Christine and Klein, Richard. 1995. *Health Status Indicators: Differentials by Race and Hispanic Origin.* Washington, DC: U.S. Department of Health and Human Services.

Polsby, Nelson W. 1980. *Community Power and Political Theory: A Further Look at Problems of Evidence and Inference.* 2nd ed. New Haven, CT: Yale University Press.

Poole, Robert W. 1980. *Cutting Back City Hall.* New York: Universe.

Pope, Carl E. and Feyerherm, William H. 1990. "Minority Status and Juvenile Justice Processing: An Assessment of the Research Literature (Part I)." *Criminal Justice Abstracts, 22,* 327–335.

Popper, Karl R. 1959. *The Logic of Scientific Discovery.* New York: Basic Books.

Popper, Karl R. 1963. *The Open Society and Its Enemies.* 2nd ed. Princeton, NJ: Princeton University Press.

Powledge, Fred. 1970. *Model City: A Test of American Liberalism.* New York: Simon and Schuster.

Pressman, Jeffrey L. 1972. "Preconditions of Mayoral Leadership." *American Political Science Review, 66,* 511–524.

Preston, Michael B. 1987. "The Election of Harold Washington: An Examination of the SES Model in the 1983 Chicago Mayoral Election." In Michael B. Preston, Lenneal J. Henderson, and Paul L. Puryear (eds.), *The New Black Politics: The Search for Political Power.* 2nd ed. New York: Longman.

Prewitt, Kenneth and Nowlin, William. 1969. "Political Ambitions and the Behavior of Incumbent Politicians." *Western Political Quarterly, 22,* 298–308.

Prothrow-Stith, Deborah. 1991. *Deadly Consequences: How Violence Is Destroying Our Teenage Population and a Plan to Begin Solving the Problem.* New York: Harper.

Quante, Wolfgang. 1976. *The Exodus of Corporate Headquarters from New York City.* New York: Praeger.

Rabin, Yale. 1987. "The Roots of Segregation in the Eighties: The Role of Local Government Actions." In Gary A. Tobin (ed.), *Divided Neighborhoods: Changing Patterns of Racial Segregation.* Newbury Park, CA: Sage.

Rabinowitz, Francine. 1969. *City Politics and Planning.* New York: Atherton.

Rabkin, Judith G. 1974. "Public Attitudes Toward Mental Illness: A Review of the Literature." *Schizophrenia Bulletin, 10,* 9–33.

Rainwater, Lee. 1970. *Behind Ghetto Walls: Black Families in a Federal Slum.* Chicago: Aldine.

Rakove, Milton. 1975. *Don't Make No Waves—Don't Back No Losers.* Bloomington: Indiana University Press.

Randolph, Linda A. and Gesche, Melita. 1986. "Black Adolescent Pregnancy: Prevention and Management." *Journal of Community Health, 11,* 10–18.

Ransom, Bruce. 1987. "Black Independent Electoral Politics in Philadelphia: The Election of Mayor W. Wilson Goode." In Michael B. Preston, Lenneal J. Henderson, and Paul L. Puryear (eds.), *The New Black Politics: The Search for Political Power.* 2nd ed. New York: Longman.

Ravitch, Diane. 1974. *The Great School Wars, New York City, 1805–1973: A History for the Public Schools as a Battlefield of Social Change.* New York: Basic Books.

Rawls, John. 1971. *A Theory of Justice.* Cambridge, MA: Harvard University Press.

Reagan, Michael D. 1972. *The New Federalism.* New York: Oxford University Press.

Redick, Richard W.; Witkin, Michael J.; Atay, Joanne E.; and Manderscheid, Ronald W. 1994. "Highlights of Organized Mental Health Services in 1990 and Major National and State Trends." In Ronald W. Manderscheid and Mary Anne Sonnenschein (eds.), *Mental Health, United States, 1994.* Washington, DC: U.S. Department of Health and Human Services.

Reich, Robert B. 1983. *The Next American Frontier.* New York: New York Times Books.

Reiman, Jeffrey. 1996. *... And the Poor Get Prison: Economic Bias in American Criminal Justice.* Boston: Allyn and Bacon.

Rein, Martin. 1976. *Social Science and Public Policy.* New York: Penguin.

Reischauer, Robert D. 1987. "The Size and Characteristics of the Underclass." Paper presented at the annual meeting of the Association for Public Policy Analysis and Management.

Renner, Tari. 1988. "Municipal Election Processes: The Impact on Minority Representation." In *The Municipal Yearbook*. Washington, DC: International City Management Association.

Renner, Tari. 1990. "Appointed Local Government Managers: Stability and Change." *Municipal Yearbook*. Washington, DC: International City Management Association.

Reuter, Peter; MacCoun, Robert; and Murphy, Patrick. 1990. *Money From Crime: A Study of the Economics of Drug Dealings in Washington, D.C.* Santa Monica, CA: Rand.

Rice, Mitchell F. 1993. "State and Local Government Set-Aside Programs, Disparity Studies, and Minority Business Development in the Post-*Croson* Era." *Journal of Urban Affairs, 15*, 539–553.

Rice, Roger L. 1968. "Residential Segregation by Law, 1910–1917." *Journal of Southern History, 34*, 179–199.

Rich, Richard C. 1982. "The Political Economy of Urban-Service Distribution." In Richard C. Rich (ed.), *The Politics of Urban Public Services*. Lexington, MA: Lexington Books.

Rich, Wilbur C. 1987. "Coleman Young and Detroit Politics: 1973–1986." In Michael B. Preston, Lenneal J. Henderson, and Paul L. Puryear (eds.), *The New Black Politics: The Search for Political Power*. 2nd ed. New York: Longman.

Rich, Wilbur C. 1996. *Black Mayors and School Politics: The Failure of Reform in Detroit, Gary, and Newark*. New York: Garland.

Ricketts, Erol R. 1992. "The Nature and Dimensions of the Underclass." In George C. Galster and Edward W. Hill (eds.), *The Metropolis in Black & White: Place, Power, and Polarization*. New Brunswick, NJ: Rutgers University Press.

Ricketts, Erol R. and Mincy, Ronald B. 1988. "Growth of the Underclass, 1970–1980." Working Paper, Urban Institute, Washington, DC.

Ricketts, Erol R. and Sawhill, Isabel V. 1988. "Defining and Measuring the Underclass." *Journal of Policy Analysis and Management, 7*, 316–325.

Riedel, John. 1964. "Boss and Faction." *Annals of the American Academy of Political and Social Science, 353*, 14–26.

Rifkind, Carole. 1977. *Main Street: The Face of Urban America*. New York: Harper and Row.

Riis, Jacob A. 1957. *How the Other Half Lives: Studies among the Tenements of New York*. New York: Hill and Wang.

Riker, William. 1964. *Federalism: Origin, Operation, Significance*. Boston: Little, Brown.

Riordan, William. 1963. *Plunkitt of Tammany Hall: A Series of Very Plain Talks on Very Practical Politics*. New York: Dutton.

Ripley, Randall B. and Franklin, Grace. 1987. *Congress, the Bureaucracy, and Public Policy*. 4th ed. Homewood, IL: Dorsey.

Rivlin, Alice M. 1971. *Systematic Thinking for Social Action*. Washington, DC: Brookings.

Roethlisberger, F.J. and Dickson, William J. 1939. *Management and the Worker: An Account of a Research Program Conducted by the Western Electric Company, Hawthorne Works, Chicago*. Cambridge, MA: Harvard University Press.

Rogowsky, Edward T. and Berkman, Ronald. 1995. "New York City's Outer Borough Development Strategy: Case Studies in Urban Revitalization." In Fritz W. Wagner, Timothy E. Joder, and Anthony J. Mumphrey (eds.), *Urban Revitalization: Policies and Programs.* Thousand Oaks, CA: Sage.

Rohe, William M. and Stegman, Michael A. 1992. "Public Housing Home Ownership: Will It Work and for Whom?" *Journal of the American Planning Association, 58,* 144–157.

Rose, Harold M. and McClain, Paula. 1990. *Race, Place, and Risk: Black Homicide in Urban America.* Albany, NY: SUNY Press.

Rose, Richard. 1980. "The Making of a Do-It-Yourself Tax Revolt." *Public Opinion, 3,* 13–18.

Rosenbaum, James E. and Popkin, Susan J. 1991. "Employment and Earnings of Low-Income Blacks Who Move to Middle-Class Suburbs." In Christopher Jencks and Paul E. Peterson (eds.), *The Urban Underclass.* Washington, DC: Brookings.

Rosenberg, Mark L. and Mercy, James A. 1991. "Assaultive Violence." In Mark L. Rosenberg and Mary Ann Fenley (eds.), *Violence in America: A Public Health Approach.* New York: Oxford University Press.

Rosenthal, Robert and Jacobson, Lenore. 1968. *Pygmalion in the Classroom: Teacher Expectation and Pupils' Intellectual Development.* New York: Holt, Rinehart, and Winston.

Rosentraub, Mark S.; Swindell, David; Przybylski, Michael; and Mullins, Daniel R. 1994. "Sports and Downtown Development Strategy: If You Build It, Will Jobs Come?" *Journal of Urban Affairs, 16,* 221–239.

Ross, Bernard H. and Stedman, Murray S., Jr. 1985. *Urban Politics.* 3rd ed. Itasca, IL: Peacock.

Rossell, Christine H. 1976. "School Desegregation and White Flight." *Political Science Quarterly, 90,* 675–695.

Rossi, Peter H. 1989. *Down and Out in America: The Origins of Homelessness.* Chicago: University of Chicago Press.

Royko, Mike. 1971. *Boss: Richard J. Daley of Chicago.* New York: Dutton.

Rusk, David. 1993. *Cities Without Suburbs.* Washington, DC: Woodrow Wilson Center.

Ryan, William. 1976. *Blaming the Victim.* Rev. ed. New York: Vintage.

Rybczynski, Witold. 1995. *City Life: Urban Expectations in a New World.* New York: Scribner's.

Sale, Kirkpatrick. 1975. *Power Shift: The Rise of the Southern Rim and Its Challenge to the Eastern Establishment.* New York: Random House.

Salisbury, Robert. H. 1964. "Urban Politics: The New Convergence of Power." *Journal of Politics, 26,* 775–797.

Sanders. Heywood T. 1980. "Urban Renewal and the Revitalized City: A Reconsideration of Recent History." In Donald Rosenthal (ed.), *Urban Revitalization.* Beverly Hills, CA: Sage.

Sanders, Heywood T. 1992. "Building the Convention City: Politics, Finance, and Public Investment in Urban America." *Journal of Urban Affairs, 14,* 135–159.

Sbragia, Alberta M. 1983. "Politics, Local Government, and the Municipal Bond Market." In Alberta M. Sbragia (ed.), *The Municipal Money Chase: The Politics of Local Government Finance.* Boulder, CO: Westview.

Scarborough, George. 1982. "A Council of Governments Approach." *National Civic Review, 71,* 358–361.

References

Schlesinger, Arthur M., Jr. 1945. *The Age of Jackson*. Boston: Little, Brown.

Schlesinger, Arthur M., Jr. 1957. *The Crisis of the Old Order*. Boston: Little, Brown.

Schlesinger, Arthur M., Jr. 1959. *The Coming of the New Deal*. Boston: Little, Brown.

Schlesinger, Arthur M., Sr. 1933. *The Rise of the City 1878–1898*. New York: Macmillan.

Schoenberg, Sandra P. and Rosenbaum, Patricia L. 1980. *Neighborhoods that Work: Sources for Vitality in the Inner City*. New Brunswick, NJ: Rutgers University Press.

Schumaker, Paul D. 1975. "Policy Responsiveness to Protest Group Demands." *Journal of Politics, 37*, 488–521.

Schumaker, Paul D. 1978. "The Scope of Political Conflict and the Effectiveness of Constraints in Contemporary Urban Protest." *The Sociological Quarterly, 19*, 168–184.

Schumaker, Paul D. 1990. *Critical Pluralism, Democratic Performance, and Community Power*. Lawrence: University of Kansas Press.

Schuman, Howard; Steeh, Charlotte G.; and Bobo, Lawrence. 1988. *Racial Attitudes in America: Trends and Interpretations*. Cambridge, MA: Harvard University Press.

Schumpeter, Joseph. 1947. *Capitalism, Socialism, and Democracy*. New York: Harper.

Schwartz, Alex. 1995. "Rebuilding Downtown: A Case Study of Minneapolis." In Fritz W. Wagner, Timothy E. Joder, and Anthony J. Mumphrey (eds.), *Urban Revitalization: Policies and Programs*. Thousand Oaks, CA: Sage.

Scott. W.R. 1910–1912. *The Constitution and Finance of English, Scottish, and Irish Joint Stock Companies to 1720*. Oxford, England: Oxford University Press.

Sears, Bill. 1976. "How the Dome Miracle Became Reality." *Kingdome Magazine*, March, p.8.

Sears, David O. and Citrin, Jack. 1982. *Tax Revolt: Something for Nothing in California*. Cambridge, MA: Harvard University Press.

Sennett, Richard and Cobb, Jonathan. 1972. *The Hidden Injuries of Class*. New York: Knopf.

Shafritz, Jay M. 1988. *The Dorsey Dictionary of American Politics*. Chicago: Dorsey.

Sharp, Elaine B. 1982. "Citizen-Initiated Contacting of Government Officials and Socioeconomic Status: Determining the Relationship and Accounting for It." *American Political Science Review, 76*, 109–115.

Shefter, Martin. 1980. "National-Local Interaction and the New York City Fiscal Crisis." In Douglas E. Ashford (ed.), *National Resources and Urban Policy*. New York: Methuen.

Shefter, Martin. 1984. "Images of the City in Political Science: Communities, Administrative Entities, Competitive Markets, and Seats of Chaos." In Lloyd Rodwin and Robert M. Hollister (eds.), *Cities of the Mind: Images and Themes of the City in the Social Sciences*. New York: Plenum.

Shell, Ellen Ruppel. 1994. "Off the Track." *Technology Review*, Oct. 6, pp. 62–64.

Shin, Doh C. 1982. "Subjective Indicators and Distributional Research on the Quality of Public Services." In Richard C. Rich (ed.), *Analyzing Urban-Service Distributions*. Lexington, MA: Lexington Books.

Silberman, Charles E. 1978. *Criminal Violence, Criminal Justice*. New York: Random House.

Sisk, Dorothy A. 1987. *Creative Teaching of the Gifted*. New York: McGraw-Hill.

Sitkoff, Harvard. 1981. *The Struggle for Black Equality 1954–1980*. New York: Hill and Wang.

Skogan, Wesley G. 1990. *Disorder and Decline: Crime and the Spiral of Decay in American Neighborhoods*. Berkeley: University of California Press.

Skolnick, Jerome H. 1994. *Justice Without Trial: Law Enforcement in Democratic Society*. 2nd ed. New York: Macmillan.

Smith, Christopher J. 1980. "Neighborhood Effects on Mental Health." In D.T. Herbert and R.J. Johnston (eds.), *Geography and the Urban Environment: Research in Progress and Applications*, vol. 5. New York: Wiley.

Smith, Marshall S. 1975. "Evaluation Findings in Head Start Planned Variation." In Alice M. Rivlin and P. Michael Timpane (eds.), *Planned Variation in Education: Should We Give Up or Try Harder?* Washington, DC: Brookings.

Smith, Michael P. 1979. *The City and Social Theory*. New York: St. Martin's.

Smith, Richard A. 1993. "Creating Stable Racially Integrated Communities: A Review." *Journal of Urban Affairs, 15*, 115–140.

Snyder, Richard C.; Bruck, H.W.; and Sapin, Burton. 1962. "Decision-Making as an Approach to the Study of International Politics." In Richard C. Snyder, H.W. Bruck, and Burton Sapin (eds.), *Foreign Policy Decision-Making: An Approach to the Study of International Politics*. New York: Free Press.

Sofen, Edward. 1963. *The Miami Metropolitan Experiment*. Bloomington: Indiana University Press.

Sonenshein, Raphe. 1986. "Biracial Coalition Politics in Los Angeles." *PS, 19*, 582–590.

Squires, Gregory D. 1990. "Biased Lending." *Journal of Housing, 47*, 182–185.

Staley, Sam. 1992. *Drug Policy and the Decline of American Cities*. New Brunswick, NJ: Transaction.

Stauber, R.L. and Kline, Mary. 1965. "A Profile of City Commissioners in Kansas." *Your Government,* April 15.

Stave, Sondra Astor. 1995. *Achieving Racial Balance: Case Studies of Contemporary School Desegregation*. Westport, CT: Greenwood.

Steffens, Lincoln. 1931. *The Autobiography of Lincoln Steffens*. New York: Harcourt Brace.

Stein, Maurice R. 1960. *The Eclipse of Community: An Interpretation of American Studies*. Princeton, NJ: Princeton University Press.

Stephan, W.G. 1978. "School Desegregation: An Evaluation of Predictions Made in *Brown v. Board of Education*." *Psychological Bulletin, 85*, 217–238.

Sternlieb, George. 1971. "The City as Sandbox." *The Public Interest, 25*, 14–21.

Stevens, Barbara J. 1977. "Service Arrangement and the Cost of Refuse Collection." In E.S. Savas (ed.), *The Organization and Efficiency of Solid Waste Collection*. Lexington, MA: Lexington Books.

Stevenson, Charles L. 1963. *Facts and Values: Studies in Ethical Analysis*. New Haven, CT: Yale University Press.

Steward, Frank M. 1950. *A Half Century of Municipal Reform: The History of the National Municipal League*. Berkeley: University of California Press.

Stinchcombe, J.L. 1968. *Reform and Reaction: City Politics in Toledo*. Belmont, CA: Wadsworth.

Stone, Clarence N. 1980. "Systemic Power in Community Decision Making: A Restatement of Stratification Theory." *American Political Science Review, 74*, 978–990.

References

Stone, Clarence N. 1989. *Regime Politics: Governing Atlanta, 1946–1988.* Lawrence: University of Kansas Press.

Stone, Clarence N.; Whelen, Robert K.; and Murin, William J. 1979. *Urban Policy and Politics in a Bureaucratic Age.* Englewood Cliffs, NJ: Prentice-Hall.

Stone, Clarence N.; Whelen, Robert K.; and Murin, William J. 1986. *Urban Policy and Politics in a Bureaucratic Age.* 2nd ed. Englewood Cliffs, NJ: Prentice-Hall.

Stoner, Madeleine R. 1995. *The Civil Rights of Homeless People: Law, Social Policy, and Social Work Practice.* New York: Aldine de Gruyter.

Sundquist, James L. 1969. *Making Federalism Work: A Cast Study of Program Coordination at the Community Level.* Washington, DC: Brookings.

Swanson, Cheryl and Bolland, John M. 1983. "Judgment Policy and the Exercise of Police Discretion." In Stuart Nagel, Erika Fairchild, and Anthony Champagne (eds.), *The Political Science of Criminal Justice.* Springfield, IL: Charles C. Thomas.

Swisher, Carl B. 1954. *American Constitutional Development.* Edited by Edward M. Sait. 2nd ed. Boston: Houghton Mifflin.

Tabb, William K. 1984. "The New York City Fiscal Crisis." In William K. Tabb and Larry Sawers (eds.), *Marxism and the Metropolis: New Perspectives in Urban Political Economy.* 2nd ed. New York: Oxford University Press.

Thernstrom, Stephen. 1964. *Poverty and Progress: Social Mobility in a Nineteenth Century City.* Cambridge, MA: Harvard University Press.

Thomas, Lewis. 1983. *The Youngest Science: Notes of a Medicine Watcher.* New York: Viking.

Thomas, Richard W. 1991. "The Historical Role of Contemporary Urban Black Self-Help in the United States." In Marvel Lang (ed.), *Contemporary Urban America: Problems, Issues, and Alternatives.* Lanham, MD: University Press of America.

Thompson, Wilbur R. 1968. *Preface to Urban Economics.* Baltimore, MD: Johns Hopkins University Press.

Thurow, Lester C. 1980. *The Zero Sum Society: Distribution and the Possibilities for Economic Change.* New York: Basic Books.

Tiebout, Charles M. 1956. "A Pure Theory of Urban Expenditures." *Journal of Political Economy, 64,* 416–424.

Tisdale, William R. 1983. "Housing Discrimination: A New Technology." In *A Sheltered Crisis: The State of Fair Housing in the Eighties.* Washington, DC: U.S. Commission on Civil Rights.

Toqueville, Alexis de. 1945. *Democracy in America.* Henry Reeve text, edited by Phillips Bradley. New York: Knopf.

Trounstine, Philip J. and Christensen, Terry. 1982. *Movers and Shakers: The Study of Community Power.* New York: St. Martin's.

Truman David B. 1951. *The Governmental Process: Political Interests and Public Opinion.* New York: Knopf.

Tucker, Harvey and Zeigler, L. Harmon. 1980. *Professionals Versus the Public.* New York: Longman.

Turner, Margery A.; Struyk, Raymond J.; and Yinger, John. 1991. *Housing Discrimination Study: Synthesis.* Washington, DC: U.S. Dept. of Housing and Urban Development.

Underwood, Julie K. 1995. "School Finance Adequacy as Vertical Equity." *University of Michigan Journal of Law Reform, 28*, 493–519.

U.S. Department of Commerce. 1987. *1987 Census of Governments*, vol. 2, *Taxable Property Values*. Washington, DC: U.S. Dept. of Commerce.

U.S. Department of Commerce. 1994. *1994 Census of Governments: Government Organization,* vol. 1, no. 1. Washington, DC: Dept. of Commerce

U.S. Department of Commerce, Bureau of the Census. 1977. *Poverty in the United States.* Washington, DC: U.S. Government Printing Office.

U.S. Department of Commerce, Bureau of the Census. 1984. *Geographical Mobility: March 1982–March 1983.* Washington, DC: U.S. Government Printing Office.

U.S. Department of Commerce, Bureau of the Census. 1992. *Poverty in the United States.* Washington, DC: U.S. Government Printing Office.

U.S. Department of Education. 1994. *The Condition of Education, 1994.* Washington, DC: National Center for Educational Statistics.

U.S. Department of Health and Human Services. 1990. *Health Status of the Disadvantaged: Chartbook 1990.* Rockville, MD: USDHHS.

U.S. Department of Health and Human Services. 1991. *Health Status of Minorities and Low-Income Groups.* Hyattsville, MD: USDHHS.

U.S. Department. of Housing and Urban Development. 1984. *A Report to the Secretary on the Homeless and Emergency Shelters.* Washington, DC: USDHUD.

U.S. Department. of Housing and Urban Development. 1991. *Home Ownership and Affordable Housing: The Opportunities.* Washington, DC: USDHUD.

U.S. Department of Housing and Urban Development. 1995a. *Office of Community Relations and Involvement Reference Manual.* Washington, DC: USDHUD.

U.S. Department of Housing and Urban Development. 1995b. *Transforming Public Housing: Building Community Pride.* Washington, DC: USDHUD.

U.S. House of Representatives, Subcommittee on Employment and Housing. 1993. *Public Housing, Public Disgrace.* Hearings, May 28 and July 21, 1992. Washington, DC: U.S. Government Printing Office.

Van Dyke, Vernon. 1960. *Political Science: A Philosophical Analysis.* Stanford, CA: Stanford University Press.

Van Haitsma, Martha 1989. "A Contextual Definition of the Underclass." *Focus, 12*, 27–31.

Vanderstaay, Steven. 1992. *Street Lives: An Oral History of Homeless Americans.* Philadelphia, PA: New Society.

Verba, Sidney and Nie, Norman H. 1972. *Participation in America: Political Democracy and Social Equity.* New York: Harper and Row.

Verba, Sidney; Schlozman, Kay L.; and Brady, Henry E. 1995. *Voice and Equality: Civic Voluntarism in American Politics.* Cambridge, MA: Harvard University Press.

Vergara, Camilo José. 1989. "Hell in a Very Tall Place." *Atlantic Monthly*, Sept., pp. 72–78.

Vergara, Camilo José. 1995. *The New American Ghetto.* New Brunswick, NJ: Rutgers University Press.

Vidich, Arthur J. and Bensman, Joseph. 1958. *Small Town in Mass Society: Class, Power, and Religion in a Rural Community.* Princeton, NJ: Princeton University Press.

Vose, Clement E. 1959. *Caucasians Only: the Supreme Court, the NAACP, and the Restrictive Covenant Cases.* Berkeley: University of California Press.

References

Wagner-Pacifici, Robin. 1994. *Discourse and Destruction: The City of Philadelphia versus MOVE.* Chicago: University of Chicago Press.

Waldo, Dwight. 1948. *The Administrative State: A Study of the Political Theory of American Public Administration.* New York: Ronald Press.

Walker, David B. 1981. *Toward a Functioning Federalism.* Cambridge, MA: Winthrop.

Walker, Samuel; Spohn, Cassia; and DeLone, Miriam. 1996. *The Color of Justice: Race, Ethnicity, and Crime in America.* Belmont, CA: Wadsworth.

Wallach, Michael; Kogan, Nathan; and Bem, Daryl J. 1962. "Group Influence on Individual Risk-Taking." *Journal of Abnormal and Social Psychology, 65,* 75–86.

Walton, John. 1966. "Substance and Artifact: The Current Status of Research on Community Power Structure." *American Journal of Sociology, 71,* 430–438.

Walzer, Michael. 1965. *The Revolution of the Saints: A Study in the Origins of Radical Politics.* Cambridge, MA: Harvard University Press.

Walzer, Michael. 1983. *Spheres of Justice: A Defense of Pluralism and Equality.* New York: Basic Books.

Ward, Sally K. 1994. "Trends in the Location of Corporate Headquarters, 1969–1989." *Urban Affairs Quarterly, 29,* 468–478.

Warner, Sam Bass, Jr. 1972. *The Urban Wilderness: A History of the American City.* New York: Harper and Row.

Warren, Stacy. 1994. "Disneyfication of the Metropolis: Popular Resistance in Seattle." *Journal of Urban Affairs, 16,* 89–107.

Watson, Douglas J. 1995. *The New Civil War: Government Competition for Economic Development.* Westport, CT: Praeger.

Watts, T.D. 1982. "Three Traditions in Social Thought on Alcoholism." *International Journal of the Addictions, 17,* 1231–1239.

Weber, Max. 1946. *From Max Weber: Essays in Sociology.* Translated by H.H. Gerth and C. Wright Mills. New York: Oxford University Press.

Weber, Max. 1947. *The Theory of Social and Economic Organization.* Translated and edited by A.M. Henderson and Talcott Parsons. New York: Free Press.

Webster, Barbara and Connors, Edward F. 1992. "The Police, Drugs, and Public Housing." Washington, DC: U.S. Dept. of Justice.

Welch, Susan 1975. "The Impact of Urban Riots on Urban Expenditures." *American Journal of Political Science, 19,* 741–760.

Welch, Susan and Bledsoe, Timothy. 1988. *Urban Reform and Its Consequences: A Study in Representation.* Chicago: University of Chicago Press.

Wellman, Barry. 1979. "The Community Question: The Intimate Networks of East Yorkers." *American Journal of Sociology, 84,* 1201–1231.

Wheelock, Anne. 1992. *Crossing the Tracks: How "Untracking" Can Save America's Schools.* New York: New Press.

White, Morton and White, Lucia. 1977. *The Intellectual versus the City: From Thomas Jefferson to Frank Lloyd Wright.* Oxford, England: Oxford University Press.

White, Sheila C. 1972. "Work Stoppages of Government Employees." In J. Joseph Loewenberg and Michael H. Moskow (eds.), *Collective Bargaining in Government: Readings and Cases.* Englewood Cliffs, NJ: Prentice-Hall.

Whitlock, Brand. 1914. *Forty Years of It.* New York: Appleton.

Whyte, William H. 1988. *City: Rediscovering the Center.* New York: Doubleday.

Wicker, Tom. 1987. "Clouds Loom for Economy." *Tuscalossa News,* Aug. 8.

Wiener, Susan J. and Mincy, Ronald B. 1991. "Social Distress in Urban Areas: Variations in Crime, Drugs, and Teen Births During the 1980s." Paper presented at the Urban Opportunity Conference on Drugs, Crime, and Social Distress, Urban Institute.

Wikstrom, Nelson. 1985. *Councils of Governments: A Study of Political Incrementalism.* Chicago: Nelson-Hall.

Wilburn, York. 1973. "Unigov: Local Government Reorganization in Indianapolis." In Advisory Commission on Intergovernmental Relations, *Substate Regionalism and the Federal System*, vol. 2, *Case Studies.* Washington, DC: U.S. Government Printing Office.

Wildavsky, Aaron. 1979a. *Speaking Truth to Power.* Boston: Little, Brown.

Wildavsky, Aaron. 1979b. *The Politics of the Budgetary Process.* 3rd ed. Boston: Little, Brown.

Williams, Linda. 1987. "Black Political Progress in the 1980s: The Electoral Arena." In Michael B. Preston, Lenneal J. Henderson, and Paul L. Puryear (eds.), *The New Black Politics: The Search for Political Power.* 2nd ed. New York: Longman.

Williams, Oliver P. 1971. *Metropolitan Political Analysis: A Social Access Approach.* New York: Free Press.

Williams, Terry M. 1992. *Crackhouse: Notes from the End of the Line.* New York: Penguin.

Williams, Terry M. and Kornblum, William. 1985. *Growing Up Poor.* Lexington, MA: Lexington Books.

Wilson, Edmund. 1958. *The American Earthquake: A Documentary of the Twenties and Thirties.* Garden City, NY: Doubleday.

Wilson, James Q. 1962. *The Amateur Democrat: Club Politics in Three Cities.* Chicago: University of Chicago Press.

Wilson, James. Q. 1972. *Varieties of Police Behavior: The Management of Law and Order in Eight Communities.* Garden City, NY: Doubleday.

Wilson, James Q. 1975. *Thinking About Crime.* New York: Basic Books.

Wilson, William J. 1987. *The Truly Disadvantaged: The Inner City, the Underclass, and Public Policy.* Chicago: University of Chicago Press.

Wilson, William J. 1991. "Studying Inner-City Social Dislocations: The Challenge of Public Agenda Research." *American Sociological Review, 56*, 1–14.

Wilson, William J. 1996. *When Work Disappears: The World of the New Urban Poor.* New York: Knopf.

Winett, Richard A.; King, Abby C.; and Altman, David G. 1989. *Health Psychology and Public Health: An Integrative Approach.* New York: Peragamon.

Wirt, Frederick; Walter, Benjamin; Rabinowitz, Francine; and Hensler, Deborah R. 1972. *On the City's Rim: Politics and Policy in Suburbia.* Lexington, MA: D.C. Heath.

Wirth, Louis. 1938. "Urbanism as a Way of Life." *American Journal of Sociology, 44*, 1–24.

Wirth, Louis. 1964. *Louis Wirth on Cities and Social Life: Selected Papers.* Edited by Albert J. Reiss, Jr. Chicago: University of Chicago Press.

Wolch, Jennifer R. 1982. "Spacial Consequences of Social Policy: The Role of Service-Facility Location in Urban Development Patterns." In Richard C. Rich (ed.), *The Politics of Urban Public Services.* Lexington, MA: Lexington.

Wolfinger, Raymond E. 1972. "Why Political Machines Have Not Withered Away and Other Revisionist Thoughts." *Journal of Politics, 34*, 365–398.

References

Wolfinger, Raymond E. 1974. *The Politics of Progress.* Englewood Cliffs, NJ: Prentice-Hall.

Wood, Robert C. 1959. *Suburbia: Its People and Their Politics.* Boston: Houghton Mifflin.

Wood, Robert C. 1964. *1400 Governments: The Political Economy of the New York Metropolitan Region.* Garden City, NY: Doubleday.

Wright, Deil S. 1968. *Federal Grants in Aid: Perspectives and Alternatives.* Washington, DC: American Enterprise Institute.

Wright, Gwendolyn. 1981. *Building the Dream A Social History of Housing in America.* New York: Pantheon.

Wright, Quincy. 1950. "Political Science and World Stabilization." *American Political Science Review, 44,* 1–13.

Yates, Douglas. 1974. "Service Delivery and the Urban Political Order." In Willis D. Hawley and David Rogers (eds.), *Improving the Quality of Urban Management.* Beverly Hills, CA: Sage.

Yates, Douglas. 1977. *The Ungovernable City: The Politics of Urban Problems and Policy Making.* Cambridge, MA: MIT Press.

Yergin, Daniel. 1991. *The Prize: The Epic Quest for Oil, Money, and Power.* New York: Simon and Schuster.

Yinger, John 1987. "The Racial Dimension of Urban Housing Markets in the 1980s." In Gary A. Tobin (ed.), *Divided Neighborhoods: Changing Patterns of Racial Segregation.* Newbury Park, CA: Sage.

Zabin, Laurie S.; Hirsch, Marilyn B.; Smith, Edward A.; Streett, Rosalie; and Hardy, Janet B. 1986. "Evaluation of a Pregnancy Prevention Program for Urban Teenagers." *Family Planning Perspectives, 18,* 119–126.

Zeigler, L. Harmon and Jennings, M. Kent. 1974. *Governing American Schools: Political Interaction in Local School Districts.* North Scituate, MA: Duxbury.

Zelnik, Melvin and Shah, Farida K. 1983. "First Intercourse among Young Americans." *Family Planning Perspectives, 15,* 64–70.

Zimmerman, Joseph F. 1984. "The New England Town Meeting: Pure Democracy in Action?" In *The Municipal Yearbook.* Washington, DC: International City Management Association.

Zink, Harold. 1930. *City Bosses in the United States: A Study of Twenty Municipal Bosses.* Durham, NC: Duke University Press.

Zinsmeister, Karl. 1990. "Growing Up Scared." *Atlantic Monthly,* June, pp. 49–66.

Zisk, Betty H. 1973. *Local Interest Politics: A One-Way Street.* Indianapolis, IN: Bobbs-Merrill.

Author Index

Author Index

Author Index

White, Lucia, 42, 66
White, Morton, 42, 66
White, Sheila C., 125
Whitlock, Brand, 61n
Whyte, William H., 22, 88, 148, 161, 195
Wicker, Tom, 356
Wiener, Susan J., 390
Wikstrom, Nelson, 23
Wilburn, York, 251
Wildavsky, Aaron, 178, 205, 415
Williams, Linda, 118
Williams, Oliver P., 246
Williams, Terry M., 391, 394
Wilson, Edmund, 64
Wilson, James Q., 59, 80, 104n, 121, 173, 226, 250
Wilson, William Julius., 36, 171, 384, 385, 387n, 391n
Winett, Richard A., 391
Wirt, Frederick, 425
Wirth, Louis, 6n
Witkin, Michael J., 347
Wolch, Jennifer R., 424
Wolfe, Arthur C., 169
Wolff, William, 434

Wolfinger, Raymond E., 63, 218
Wolman, Harold L., 35, 376, 438
Wolohojian, George G., 349
Wood, Robert C., 19, 241
Wright, Deil S., 270
Wright, Gwendolyn, 403
Wright, James D., 11, 224, 377, 388
Wright, Quincy, 70
Wrightson, Margaret T., 435n

Yates, Douglas, 35, 79, 108, 117, 125, 154, 157, 172, 197, 208, 306n
Yergin, Daniel, 203n
Yinger, John, 365n, 419, 419n
Young, C.E., 111

Zabin, Laurie S., 391
Zeigler, L. Harmon, 73, 107, 189
Zelnik, Melvin, 391
Ziegler, Jerome M., 269, 287, 292, 358n
Zimmerman, Joseph F., 105n
Zink, Harold, 57
Zinsmeister, Karl, 389
Zisk, Betty H., 161, 162

Subject Index

Lakewood Plan, 249
Land developers, as policy entrepreneurs,
216-17
Law enforcement. *See also* Crime
inequities in, 428-32
as municipal service, 335-36
privatization of, 368
Lawrence, KS
political participation in, 146-47
political power in, 180-81, 183n
League of Women Voters, 149, 150
Lee, Richard C., 116-17, 217-18
Life-style and territory, theory of, 33-34
Lobbyist, city as, 263-64
Local Community Action Agencies
(LCAAs), 283-85
Los Angeles. *See also* Bradley, Thomas
mass transit in, 64
political incorporation of minorities in, 164
riots in, 166-67, 454n, 483n

Machine politics, 52-59
and businessmen, 55-56
as cause of urban reform, 59-63
demise of, 62-63
and immigrants, 57-58
Majority rule, as democratic norm, 73
adherence to, by municipal government,
106-7
Mandates, 262-63, 293
unfunded mandates, 293
Market externalities, theory of, 31-32
Mass transit systems, finance of, 342-44
Mayor, 114-18
ceremonial, 117
in council-manager plan of city government, 100
entrepreneurial, 117
as policy entrepreneur, 216
in political networks, 116-17
political power of, 188-89
political roles of, 114-18
resources needed to be effective, 115-16
in strong-mayor plan of city government, 97
style of, 116-17
in weak-mayor plan of city government, 94
McCulloch v. Maryland, 311n
McLaurin v. Oklahoma State Regents, 305
Mental illness
as cause of homelessness, 399-400
and services for the needy, 346-47

Metropolitan area
and annexation, 247-49
and city-county consolidation, 250-51
and Councils of Government (COGs), 253
and service delivery contracts, 249-50
as system, 246
and two-tier government, 251-52
Metropolitan Statistical Area (MSA), 14-15
Miami, FL
riots in, 483
two-tier government in, 252
Miller v. Johnson, 113n
Milliken v. Bradley, 296n
Minneapolis, downtown development in,
447, 451
Minority rights as democratic norm, 74
adherence to, by municipal government,
107-8
Model Cities program, 284-87
Moses, Robert, 242-43, 340
MOVE (Philadelphia), 164
Multiple realities, theory of, 37-38
Municipal administrators, 118-26
minorities as, 123
as policymakers, 121-22
political power of, 189-90
women as, 123
Municipal bonds, 326-29
Municipal bureaucracy
hierarchy in, 123-24
impersonality in, 124-26
as policymakers, 225-27
specialization in, 124
Municipal finance
bonded indebtedness, 326-29
fines and forfeitures, 326
growth and retrenchment in, 306-7
health of, 369-71
interest payments, 326
intergovernmental revenues, 322-25
sale of municipal property, 325
taxes, 307-17
user fees, 317-22, 365-66
utility charges, 325
Municipal property, sale of, 325
Municipal services
cutbacks in, 348-59
decline of, 348-59
distribution of, 434-38
efficiency in, 362-65
inequality in, 434-38

and community commitment, 182-83
as a democratic norm, 75
in low-income neighborhoods, 131-35
and political power, 180-84
proactive versus reactive, 108-9
social trends affecting urban, 80-81
Political parties, citizen participation in, 142-43
Political power
of advisory boards, 191-92
of business owners and managers, 193-95
and city size and heterogeneity, 183
and community commitment, 182-83
of the governing body, 187-88
and governmental structure, 183
of homeowners, 193-95
idiosyncratic factors affecting, 195-96
implications for public policy, 196-97
of the mayor, 188-89
of municipal administrators, 189-90
of municipal bureaucrats, 190
of neighborhood groups, 193-95
and nonpolitical participation, 181-82
and political participation, 180-84
of protestors, 192-93
social stratification in, 178
types of, 184-87
of voters, 192
Politics. *See also* Urban politics
as conflict, 70-71
definitions of, 69-73
as the exercise of power, 71
human quality of, 70
Population shifts, 482-83
Port Authority of New York and New Jersey, 239-41
Poverty
culture of, 224
demographics of, 378-80
and health, 381-83
and housing conditions, 380-81
and race, 378-80
Poverty and the underclass, theory of, 36-37
Prescriptive theories, of social justice, 243-44
President's Task Force on Urban Problems, 284
Private action versus public action, 71-73
Private power versus public power, 84-87
Private space versus public space, 87-88
streets and sidewalks as, 87-88
malls and shopping centers as, 88
Privatization of municipal services, 366-69

Privatization of public housing, 464-65, 467
in Louisville, 465
Proactive political participation, 108-9
Progressivism, 59-62
Property rights in colonial towns, 45
Property tax, 308-13
assessment of, 309
problems with, 310-13
rationale for, 308
Proposition 13, 352-55
Proposition 2½, 355
Protest, citizen participation through, 161-71
Pruitt-Igoe (St. Louis), 277, 404
Public action versus private action, 71-73
Public good
definition of, 8n
municipal funding for, 321, 343-44
Public housing
in Chicago, 404-8
decentralization of, 463-64
disrepair of, 405n
Home Ownership for People Everywhere (HOPE) program, 465-66, 467-68
life in, 402-7
in Louisville, 465
One Strike and You're Out policy, 431-32, 466
in Philadelphia, 405, 423, 467
popular conceptions of, 403-8
revitalizing, 465-66
in St. Louis, 277, 404
Section 8 and, 402-3, 464-65
vacancy rates in, 467n
Public policy
class bias in development of, 196
constraints imposed by limited knowledge, 202-3
definition of, 8
development, 211-12
distributive, 209-10
implications of political power for, 196-97
incremental, 205-6
as rational enterprise, 201-3
reconstructive, 205-6
redistributive, 210-11
regulatory, 208-9
stages of, 222-27
substantive, 206-7
symbolic, 206-7
time constraints in, 207-8
unintended consequences of, 202-3

547

Subject Index

Public power versus private power, 84-87
Public space versus private space
  streets and sidewalks as, 87-88
  malls and shopping centers as, 88

Quality of life issues in urban politics, 77-78

Race, and poverty, 378
Racial discrimination
  in banking practices, 421-22
  in courts, 429-30
  and growth of the underclass, 384-85
  and housing patterns, 425-28
  legal recourse for, 420-21
  by police, 428-29
  in real estate practices, 418-21
  in school classrooms, 416-18
  and school desegregation, 294-96
  and zoning, 297-300
Reagan, Ronald, 292
Real estate practices
  legal recourse for discriminatory, 420-21
  and racial discrimination, 418-21
  and residential segregation, 418-21
Reconstructive policy, 205-6
Recreational programs, as municipal services, 339
Redistributive policy, 210-11
Redlining, 421-22
Regulatory policy, 208-9
Renaissance Center (Detroit), 219-20
Residential segregation
  banking practices and, 421-22
  de facto, 295
  de jure, 295
  and health care facilities, 424-25
  legal recourse for, 420-21
  and low-cost housing, 423-24
  real estate practices and, 418-21
  and zoning, 297-300
Restrictive covenants, 296-97
Revenue sharing, 291-92
Richmond, VA, minority set asides in, 301-2
Riots, 166-68, 482-84
Roosevelt, Franklin D., 272-79
Rotary Club, 148-49
Rouse, James, 196n, 220-21, 448
Rural communities
  characteristics of, 6
  conflict with urban areas, 259-60

St. Louis
  public housing in, 277, 404
  residential segregation in, 427-28
St. Petersburg, riot in, 167
Sales tax
  problems with, 313-15
  rationale for, 313
San Antonio
  Good Government League in, 146
  underclass hypothesis tested in, 434-35
San Antonio Independent School District v. Rodriguez, 441n
San Diego. *See also* Wilson, Pete
  homelessness in, 460-61
  improving efficiency in, 363
  sale of municipal property in, 325
San Francisco
  downtown development in, 446-47
  freeway construction in, 159
  hotel demolition in, 401
  no-growth movement in, 147-48
San Jose
  growth versus no-growth in, 192
  political participation in, 147
  political power in, 192
San Telmo Associates v. City of Seattle, 263n
Schmoke, Kurt, 164-65, 360
School busing, 295-96, 413
School segregation, 294-96, 413-15. *See also* Residential segregation
Seattle
  historical preservation in, 160-61
  homelessness in, 461
  no-growth movement in, 148
Segregation. *See* Residential segregation; School segregation
Self-rule, in colonial towns, 44
Serrano v. Priest, 441n
Service delivery. *See* Municipal services
Shaffer v. Valtierra, 297n, 298n
Shaw, MS, 434
Shaw v. Hunt, 113n
Shelley v. Kraemer, 296-97
Shopping malls
  implications of, 203
  private versus public space in, 88
Single Room Occupancy Hotels (SROs)
  destruction of, 401
  and homelessness, 462, 463
Social justice
  in metropolitan area, 244-46
  prescriptive theories of, 243-44

548